Livingstone

Salisbury

R H O D E S I A

Bulawayo   Fort Victoria

W A N A

N A L A N D)

Serowe

Messina

Louis Trichardt

Pietersburg

Gaberones   Nylstroom   Phalaborwa

Steelpoort

Mafeking   Graskop

Pretoria   Nelspruit

Johannesburg   Lourenço Marques

Potchefstroom   Vereeniging   Mbabane

Sasolburg   **SWAZILAND**

Harrismith

Kimberley   Ladysmith

Bloemfontein   Eshowe

Tugela R.

LESOTHO   Pietermaritzburg
(BASUTOLAND)

Durban

Colesberg   Kokstad

Aliwal North

TRANSKEI

Queenstown   Port St. Johns

Umtata

Umtata R.

Graaf-Reinet   King William's Town

Great Kei R.

Grahamstown   East London

Port Elizabeth

M O Z A M B I Q U E

K R U G E R   P A R K

I N D I A N   O C E A N

International Boundaries

Democratic Provincial Boundaries

Bantu Homelands

"A VERY STRANGE SOCIETY"

By Allen Drury

Fiction

ADVISE AND CONSENT
A SHADE OF DIFFERENCE
THAT SUMMER
CAPABLE OF HONOR

Non-Fiction

A SENATE JOURNAL
THREE KIDS IN A CART

SOUTH AFRICAN GOTHIC:

The Board of Governors of the South African Broadcasting Company, 1965–66

Sitting, left to right: Mr. H. J. de Villiers, Dr. P. J. Meyer (Chairman), Mr. J. C. McIntyre (Vice-Chairman), and Mr. E. V. Williams. These four members constitute the Executive Committee.   *Standing:* Mr. J. T. Elliot, Prof. B. Bradshaw, Mr. P. H. van der Linde, Prof. S. Pauw, and Prof. J. P. A. Yeats.

"A VERY STRANGE SOCIETY"

A Journey to the Heart of South Africa

Allen Drury

TRIDENT PRESS · NEW YORK · 1967

"Once a year I can entertain Them
in my office," said the young professor
in Pretoria. "I can serve Them tea, I can even
shake hands with Them. We can at least
try to talk to one another like human beings
—once a year. The Government knows
about it and doesn't object. But
I certainly can't do any of these things
any other time, or anywhere else."
He shook his head with a curiously wistful,
quizzical smile, "We have," he said,
"a very strange society."

Contents

Dedication

I think I should dedicate this book to you, indomitable, indispensable Helen, and to Div and Anton and Harry and Piet Cillié; to Neil Malan and his delightful family, to the Flemings and Jan and Peggy Marais and to shrewd, keen-eyed Tom Muller; to the earnestly cooperative, eternally hopeful older Indian and his hard-eyed, hard-nosed, graspingly ambitious younger compatriot; to the Lion and the Student and the little black lawyer drinking himself to death, and to all their lonely lost company of the Banned; to Bob and Mildred and Athol and Brian, to Louis and Willem and Alan and Van; to sadly worried Larry Gandar and deeply unhappy Alan Paton, to tragic "Dr. V." and tough John Vorster; to Dick Dickerson and Dick van der Ross, to wry Alan de Kock and my comfortably disinterested fellow-Americans in Port Elizabeth; to amiable, invaluable Bill and Odette Toomey, and to Ambassador Bill Rountree; to gallant Moira Henderson and all her gallant ladies; to Eschel and Desmond and dear, delightful Paula; to gracious Linnéa, showing a stranger through Zululand, to Tertius and Bob welcoming him generously to the Press Gallery, to kindly Theo guiding him through the fascinations of Kruger National Park and the haunted lowveld; and to all the many other good friends, of all races and all political persuasions, who made me feel so much at home and helped me so many times along my journey through a lovely, troubled land. But most of all, perhaps, I think I should dedicate it

TO

VAN DER MERWE

who, after half a century of grimly determined striving, has arrived at last in absolute control of his beloved country; and who seeks for her, and for himself and all his tribe, a future composed of safety and decency and justice—as he sees them; and who may—or may not—make it. . . .

Note

In mid-1966, after a year of reading and research on the nature and the problems of the Republic of South Africa, it came time to put the people with the statistics and try to make of them some reality and some sense; and so I embarked upon a journey that was to take me to many fascinating places and bring me into contact with many valiant people.

Some were White or "European" (and I shall use throughout their customary capitalizations, terminology, and spellings), some were Black, some were brown, some were in-between. Within the White or European group, some were Dutch-, German-, and Huguenot-descended—"the Afrikaners" or "the Afrikaans" (as one would say interchangeably "the Frenchmen" or "the French"); some were English-descended—"the English-speakers." Of the rest, some were Indian, some were Coloured (whom we would call mulatto), some were "Bantu," meaning simply "The People"—meaning, in official parlance, the Black People, the Africans, the Natives.

Almost without exception all were friendly, cooperative, hospitable, helpful. Almost without exception all possessed qualities of perseverance, endurance, generosity and goodwill which might—could they but be fused together somehow into a truly national fabric—take the Republic to heights of leadership on the raddled, chaotic continent of Africa that even her most optimistic dreamers cannot envisage.

But it is not, of course, that simple. It is not as simple as dreamers in the Transvaal or the Cape would have it, nor is it as simple as smug, all-knowing gentlemen snug-abed in Washington and London and elsewhere around the watching globe would have it.

It is not, in fact, simple at all.

Two weeks after I arrived, arguing late at a party in Johannesburg—as one always argues late, about South Africa, in South Africa—I said, "I am beginning to conclude already that South Africa is a puzzle without a solution, and that all you can do is live it out and hope for the best." With varying degrees of unhappiness or dogged optimism, my fellow-arguers agreed.

There are herein some suggestions for an ultimate solution of the puzzle; but you will not find any certainties about it. If you want certainties, I refer you to the writings and pronouncements of those who have not been there; or who, having been there for a day, or two, or possibly three or four, have come away with the same preconceptions with which they arrived.

No one, I think, possessed of an ounce of understanding or compassion, can fail to be deeply moved by South Africa, or can fail to fall in love with it, or can fail to wish it, most desperately, well. No one of such mind can say flatly what is right or what is wrong for it.

Only the pieces of the puzzle can be presented. Those who live within the country must somehow find the certainties with which to put the puzzle together and make it work from day to day. Those who live without, if they would truly serve the cause of human advancement, can only offer understanding, patience, encouragement, and a hope for improvement that can never be too direct, too forceful, or too outspoken—for if it is, it will simply turn South Africans of all colors in upon themselves, huddled together in terror of what they always refer to as "the outside world," and so defeat all the purposes of all the decent in all the races.

I was made to feel at home in the Republic from the moment I arrived, was allowed for the most part to go where I pleased and see whom I pleased; under surveillance a good deal of the time, I am quite sure, but able now and then to break away and see those I was not officially supposed to see, pry into areas officialdom perhaps wished that I not pry into. Many people talked to me freely, many expressed themselves with a most generous confidence to a stranger who might, for all they knew, go away and publish their most candid thoughts to the world, together with their names. Their trust imposes an obligation to protect them, and so I have tried to do, for two reasons: there is decent discretion, and there is the Government. The Government is filled with charming people, but the Government is the Government. Whether they are in it or out of it, your friends are all subject to the Government.

So, quite frequently, you do not name them when you quote or paraphrase what they say. You resort to subterfuges and concealments that will help to preserve the integrity of their thoughts and their persons, integrities which in South Africa are becoming increasingly hedged about with fear each day. You protect your sources, in other words, because in the Republic they may need protection. Such is another aspect of the beloved country.

From several hundred interviews large and small I have culled for direct quotation those which seem most pertinent in illuminating the life, the mood, and the atmosphere of South Africa. I shall always be indebted to those who talked to me, as I am to all of those who assisted me before, during, and after the journey. I could name a great many, but to do so would be to appear to select some above others, and this I should not like to do, for all were invaluable to my purpose. Also, I expect that some of my conclusions are not going to be popular with the Government, and I don't want good friends embarrassed by being associated with them. None of them of course is responsible in any way for my personal views or my manner of presenting what I saw. Many disagreed with me, but that never diminished their kindness nor curtailed their willingness to help. The Government might not understand this objectivity of which many of its citizens are still capable; for in many areas of discussion, it is no longer objective.

In presenting material, I have followed as simple a typographical pattern as possible: the direct interviews and personal commentary printed in regular type, with a large initial first letter; pertinent newspaper items and editorials in italics; basic statistical matter about the country's development and economic condition, with which even the Republic's severest critics can have little quarrel, in smaller type, designated "Official Sources."

So here is the journey, the country, and the puzzle: important to our times and, in its broader implications on the African continent and through the world, important to each of us individually as we strive to manage our own countries, secure our own futures, and assist if we can in the safe and sensible conduct of the world.

ALLEN DRURY

I
JOURNEY'S START

In Pretoria the Old Man stands in the square, the Monument stands on the hill. All around stretch the gentle hills and soft blue distances of the rolling Transvaal, land of lost dreams recaptured and lost wars won. This is where the journey begins.

COMING DOWN FROM London, overwhelmed and made mellow by the industrious hospitality pressed upon one by the charming stewardesses of the BOAC—snacks, drinks, meals, more snacks, more drinks, more meals, in seemingly endless chain as the miles purr away and continents disappear—I fell presently into conversation with my seatmate, a worried-looking English engineer from Tanzania. He was perhaps fifty-five, thin, tanned, eyes nervous, voice low as of one accustomed to expressing thoughts that once were stated freely but now are contraband.

He asked my destination, I told him. His eyes lighted with a rather grim approval.

"They know how to handle things down there," he said, in that hushed, conspiratorial tone. "No nonsense in South Africa. I travel all over the continent, and I see what's going on. They're the only ones with the right idea."

"They're about the only ones who are white nowadays," I said. "Maybe that's what gives them the conviction that they have the right idea."

"Oh, they have," he said. "No mistake about it. I've seen the others, and it's a mess. An absolute mess."

"In what way?" I asked, still fresh from many briefings in Washington and London, still filled with the reluctance of many of my briefers to acknowledge that there might be a white side to any issue in which Whites contended with Blacks. For how could there be, after all? The world was moving on, we were in an untidy century given to the creation of slogans and their employment to place the incompetent in power: Nothing sanctified chaos like color, providing it was the right one. I was curious.

"You take Tanzania," he said, and his voice dropped so that I had to lean toward him across the empty seat between us. "I can't say very much"—and it was obvious he felt he really couldn't, though Tanzania was still five thousand miles away—"but things there are going very fast —very fast. We don't know what's going to happen from one moment to the next. Everything's going to pot, everything may be expropriated at any minute, the Whites may be kicked out altogether—we don't know."

"Why don't you leave?"

His eyes darkened with the look of the hunted, forever and always akin, whatever their race or origin, in their eternal hegira down the centuries.

"It isn't so easy. I have a home, my family's there, I've been there forty years. How do you throw away all that? And anyway, I can't afford just to let everything go. I'm not all that well off. I can't leave unless I can sell at a reasonable price." He gave a grim little smile. "If the Government will let me, that is. They may just take it. It's the same all over Africa. And if you will forgive me, I think your country has had more to do with creating a mess here than almost any other power."

"Well, we have certain beliefs: we try to stand by them. Not always very astutely, perhaps—"

"Stupidly, I'd say, if you'll forgive me."

"Oh, I'll forgive you. But that doesn't change our policies much."

"You people don't understand Africa." He shrugged with a sudden sad expression. "Who does?"

"I thought you felt that the South Africans do."

"They do, as I see it," he said, "but how long will the world let them last? Everybody's after them."

"Maybe the world thinks what they're doing is wrong."

"You wait until you get there," he said as the stewardess came by to interrupt with one more offer of refreshments. "You may find it isn't as simple as the world thinks."

Two hours later, waking from a fitful doze, no sound now but the gentle drone of the VC-10, the continent rushing away in the velvet night, there gleamed far below a tiny circle of campfires. It looked infinitely lonely, outward-defying, inward-turning. No other sign of life or light showed anywhere. *Who are you down there, and how goes it with you, and of what are* you *afraid?* Immense and silent, Africa slept.

The great red glow of African dawn crept slowly up the east, the "white highlands" of Kenya, no longer quite so white, appeared below. Many farms still looked to be in fair condition, but some were gone back to jungle, the skeletons of cultivation showing faintly through the bush. We landed in Nairobi, my seatmate and many others got off to stop in Kenya or fan out across the lower continent as their destinies took them. Black maintenance crews rushed on, quick, impatient, sullen, shouting angrily at one another in Kikuyu. The stewards and stewardesses of BOAC, and all of us, stood quietly out of their way and were very, very polite.

Soon after leaving Nairobi, the captain said, "There on your left, seventy miles away, is Mount Kilimanjaro," and sure enough there it was, clear and massive above the clouds that now covered the land, the famous snows looking beautiful and forbiddingly cold, the mountain itself curiously impersonal as if to say, like all the African earth, "Keep your distance, humankind. I am not impressed."

"We are now passing over Salisbury, Rhodesia," the captain said. Clouds hugged Salisbury, too, which used to be a port of call, but now, under defiant Ian Smith, is called upon no more.

The cloud belt scattered, bare brown plains and hills began to appear. We had traded summer for winter, the land lay cold and fallow. "The river you see is the Limpopo," the captain said. We were over the northern Transvaal, in South African air at last.

Scattered farms, scattered towns, a frontier look about it still, a bigger town or two, more emptiness rolling to the horizons. Then a substantial city began to appear. "Pretoria," the young South African next to me said with a lilt of excitement. We completed our landing cards, checked

"White." Out a way from the pleasantly sprawling capital in its fold of hills we saw row upon row of small brick houses, as neatly laid out, as practical and economical, as alike, as lifeless and without inspiration as any low-rental housing development in America. "The native township," the young South African said. The clouds had burned away into a clear thin sunshine. The seat belt sign went on, we passed over Pretoria, began our descent. Farther south in the distance we could just see the start of another city. "Johannesburg," the South African said. We glided down, touched land at Jan Smuts International Airport. Good friends from the South African Department of Information, one Afrikaans, the other English, speeded arrival through the relative-welcoming crowds to customs and the waiting car. The brown land stretched away into gentle hills and rolling plains.

"It looks like Lawrence, Kansas," said the Afrikaner, accurately.

"Things go better with big, BIG Coke," said the first billboard we came to.

We sped down the narrow two-lane road toward Pretoria. "The Government is going to widen this soon, it's an absolute disgrace," the English-speaker said. "We have one of the world's highest traffic death rates," the Afrikaner agreed. "You can see why." On our right, a field filled with impala, South Africa's most prevalent type of antelope. For a second it seemed they might be wild, then the fence appeared, the hope of lost innocence died. "More and more farmers are establishing their own private game reserves," the Englishman observed. "That," said the Afrikaner, pointing to a drive-in movie on the left, "is one of the twenty-four reasons why the Government isn't letting us have television."

"Are movies popular?"

"Frightfully," the Englishman said. "They're a great social event here. When a good film comes, people get up dinner parties and book weeks in advance."

"The opiate of the people," the Afrikaner said with a chuckle. "One of the twenty-four reasons," he repeated thoughtfully, "why we aren't allowed to have television."

The thought prompted him to tell the first of the hundreds of Van der Merwe jokes that I was to hear during my sojourn. Van der Merwe ("Fonder-*mair*-vuh") is South Africa's "Smith," probably the most common Afrikaner name in the Republic. Poor Van der Merwe is the key figure in a constant stream of jokes, and it can be said for his countrymen that he is the butt of the majority of them. (The Bantu come next, then the English, and, trailing, the Coloureds and Indians.) Van der Merwe is usually engaged in some impossible situation, in this first instance his unsuccessful attempts to find out why the Government wouldn't let him have television. The punch line is lost now, but the purport was his own vast gullibility, as it usually is. Van der Merwe's countrymen, among the shrewdest and most determined in the world, like to think of him, and themselves, as being simple, easily hoodwinked folk.

There is one most interesting aspect of the Van der Merwe jokes, I found: he almost never gets involved in, or expresses concern about, or pokes fun at, politics. He almost never has an irreverent or disrespectful thought about his Government, its leaders, or the political situation in which he and they find themselves. He is not a release for national tensions, as the man-in-the-street is in the jokes of other cultures. For Van der Merwe, politics is too grim. This makes Van der Merwe, perhaps, sadder than he knows.

We laughed at his troubles with television, and sped on.

Pretoria began to take shape. In the left distance a dun-colored structure, squat, chunky, massive, sat atop a hill.

"That's the Voortrekker Monument," the Afrikaner said with a touch of pride.

The city came nearer, we entered suburbs that looked much like those of any American municipality save for the jacaranda trees in every street, dulled now by winter, gorgeously purple in spring. We entered the downtown area, buildings and traffic increased, the signposts of a modern civilization appeared:

WIMPY BURGERS . . . HELENA RUBINSTEIN . . . DISCOUNT HARDWARE . . . GENERAL ELECTRIC . . . CHEMISTS . . . PEPSI-COLA . . . LADIES' AND MEN'S HAIRDRESSERS . . . BILL AND WALLY'S HAMBURGERS . . . CUT-RATE GOODS . . . CALTEX . . . KENTS . . . EATS . . . KODAK . . . FORD . . . GENERAL MOTORS . . .

We came to a big, open, grassy square surrounded by old-fashioned brownstone Government buildings and a modern glass-front or two.

On a pedestal stood the statue of an old man dressed in a stovepipe hat, a rusty black suit and frock coat, an enormous ornamental sash across his chest: dumpy, stolid, expressionless, impassive. Looking north.

"Oom Paul Kruger," said the Afrikaner, again with pride. "President of the Transvaal Republic and leader of the Boers in the Anglo-Boer War."

Later, before a long and needed nap at the plain but comfortable hotel, a quick look through the English-language newspapers, a rapid realization that this was no half-formed nation in the bush. "But they're *big cities!*" well-educated friends at home had exclaimed when, in the months of research, I had shown them pictures of Johannesburg, Preto-

ria, Durban, Cape Town. "Yes, they are," I had said, perhaps not quite
believing it myself. The efforts of the advertising agencies in the pages
before me, like the busy streets of Pretoria I had just come through,
brought it home once and for all:

"A man's best friends are his HUSH PUPPIES . . . Mamma-mia!
F & M spaghetti has the true Italian touch—a skill brought all the way
from Italy! . . . BRYLCREEM the perfect hairdressing . . . Found
the world over: GRANT'S SCOTCH WHISKY . . . AFTER YOUR
LAST COLD are you *still* 'chesty'? Then treat the 'chestiness' *not* the
cold! DO-DO tablets are so very good and effective that they are regularly used by Asthma sufferers who find them remarkably relieving . . .
Only ARWA stockings are gifted with soft-as-mink ARWALON . . .
The soft feminine look is *in* again. Delicious curves that follow your
natural shape but make it even more so—in a breathing, stretchy bra
that you'll never top for comfort or sheer seductiveness. Warner's by
Symington . . . Paint the PLASCON way—and see your walls come
smiling back at you! . . . Nerves can cause CONSTIPATION! Fruit-
ros tablets—more than a LAXATIVE—a RE-LAXATIVE! . . . Why
is Valiant South Africa's fastest selling six? Come on down and let
one loose—you'll soon know! . . . With free beauty tips from America
—with a host of brand-new ideas on skin care and fashion makeup—
Julie Wakeham from New York will help you discover an entirely new
individual beauty. CHARLES OF THE RITZ . . . We are demon-
strating the new YES/NO POLAROID SWINGER every day! . . .
CLEAR THAT STUFFY HEAD fast with easy to use, convenient to
carry GRANEODIN nasal spray . . . VIDOR, the only metal-cased,
leakproof batteries that give you GUARANTEED PERFORMANCE!
. . . For clear, sparkling eyes, morning, noon, and night, keep eyes
bright with EYE-GENE. Famous in the eyes of the world . . . Vasoline
LIP-ICE balm soothes! Heals! Protects! *Quickly* . . . Just fluff it on—
and suddenly, softly, you're blushing! 'BLUSH-ON' by Revlon . . .
Become Viceroy-conscious—a name that ensures good taste . . .
DISCOUNT RIOT! We buy for less—sell for *much* less! New Furniture and Appliances all guaranteed at DISCOUNT CUT PRICES. Up to
40 per cent off! . . . GOLD CREST—the lager with more flavour per
glass . . . Jeeps are stronger/Jeeps last longer . . . A fella could go
steady/With a girl who has ready/A cup of Joko Tea . . ."

I put the papers aside: South Africa was not so different after all. It
should be easy to understand this modern, booming country. Apparently
it was just like ours.

That evening they called for me again, the charming Afrikaner joined
now by his charming wife, the English-speaker alone, all of them anxious
for gossip of Washington where they had served their Government off and

on in recent years. We ate an excellent meal at an excellent restaurant as good as any anywhere; a three-piece orchestra played "Happy Birthday" to someone, a cake with one candle was brought. "We are still a poor country," the English-speaker remarked, but it was not apparent there nor at many another fine restaurant I visited in the course of my journey. Then they took me back to get a good night's sleep before the round of official interviews beginning at eight next morning.

In the lobby of the hotel I asked about an enormous display of pro-teas, that beautiful and fantastic national flower of the Republic that grows in thirty or forty dramatically differing varieties.

"Named for the god Proteus," one of my hosts explained, "because it can take so many different forms."

"Just like——," said the other, mentioning a recent prominent visitor from overseas.

"Shame on you!" his wife said with a comfortable chuckle and they said goodnight, their knowing laughter still ringing, as I turned away, upon the clear, cold air.

It was only as I turned in for a real sleep at last that I had time to remember the "Whites Only" and "Non-Whites Only" signs at the air-port and elsewhere; to reflect that, while I had seen many black faces on the streets and in the stores, the places they were permitted to enter, and the amount of money they could earn with which to purchase, were both tightly controlled by law; to realize that while I had been welcomed with the most cordial of greetings, it was only because the Government thought I was friendly and would be kind to it; and even more basic, to realize that I could now move about freely and be relatively at ease in my travels only because of a fact for which the Lord, not I, was responsible: my skin was white.

The comforting thought of the afternoon was not so comforting at night.

Perhaps this kindly, welcoming, hospitable nation was not so familiar after all. Perhaps it wasn't just like ours.

Perhaps the harsh lessons of its past had more bearing on its present than a hurried trip to Pretoria from Jan Smuts Airport and a whirl of first impressions could inform one. Perhaps it would be well not to forget those lessons as one went along: perhaps the journey needed an open mind but a cautious heart, lest one get swept too easily into the euphoria of the beautiful, cordial country whose rulers and people never let them-selves forget the long trail of hardships and reversal that brought them where they are.

FOR THE STUDENT who wishes to study South African history in depth there are many sources such as these I have drawn upon principally here: Eric A. Walker's standard and exhaustive *A History of Southern Africa,* and the pioneering and invaluable works of Professor F. A. van Jaarseveld of the University of South Africa, *The Afrikaner's Interpretation of South African History* and *The Awakening of Afrikaner Nationalism.* But for the immediate purpose of the journey, a quick survey of three hundred years should suffice to indicate the well-springs of those attitudes which I was to find sometimes strengthening, sometimes weakening, often disturbing and making difficult the serenity and onward progress of the Republic.

The European powers had flirted with Southern Africa since 1487 when the Portuguese Bartholomew Díaz named the beautiful peninsula at the continent's tip the "Cabo de Boa Esperanca" because it furnished the "good hope of discovering the Indies." But it was not until the late 1500's that the great thrust of trade which was to bring Europe to the Cape and establish a continuing dichotomy between contending Whites, and a perhaps insoluble problem with ever-proliferating Blacks, resulted in the first stirrings of permanent settlement.

These came following the annexation of Portugal by Spain in 1574 and the end of Portuguese venturing in those waters. The Dutch and the English, both of whom felt they had good reasons, set out to "singe the King of Spain's beard." The English were more interested in doing so in European and Atlantic waters, the Dutch moved south and toward the Indies. Presently the voyagers of the Dutch East India Company, founded on ambition, adventure and avarice in Amsterdam in 1602, were sailing regularly past the Cape. In 1641 "Jan Compagnie" established a refreshment station there. In 1652 Jan van Riebeeck arrived with three ships and orders to make the station permanent. The Cape Colony had begun.

For 150 years the Cape was subject to Amsterdam as point of last resort and more directly to the Company's Governor-General at Batavia in Java. But Amsterdam and Batavia were far away. In practice the Cape was largely left to its own devices as long as it continued to perform the task set for van Riebeeck when he first came out; to garrison the Fort (today the Castle) of Good Hope which he built; to plant gardens and raise herds to provide fresh fruit, vegetables and meat for the Company's ships; and to maintain good relations with the natives so that all could go forward peaceably and in good order.

From this beginning a somewhat erratic but nonetheless vigorous colonization developed; and rapidly also developed the first stages of South African racial problems. Van Riebeeck and his men found at the

Cape a scattered three or four thousand primeval Bushmen and aboriginal Hottentots, and instinctively—probably inevitably, since the natives were lazy, thieving and constantly covetous of the cattle the Dutch were trying to raise—resorted in short order to the four alternatives of colonizers dealing with a difficult indigenous population: push back, contain, absorb or eradicate.

To this day there exists at the Cape a remnant of van Riebeeck's bitter-almond hedge, the first attempt at apartheid. The careful commander ordered it planted after he and his men had defeated the Hottentots in a small war brought on by the expanding colony's need for more land and the Hottentots' stubborn insistence that the land belonged to them. Van Riebeeck decided that the way to settle all this was to defeat the Hottentots, plant a hedge, draw a line and let each of the parties live in its own place.

This small conflict, and similar skirmishes down through the years, was with the Hottentots and the Bushmen. There was no quarrel with the Bantu, because they were not there. They were no more native to South Africa than the Whites. And the flood of their immigration came almost a hundred years later, long after the Whites, by virtue of colonization, diligence, lifesblood and the creation of a viable society, had come to think of South Africa as theirs.

Still, Jannie van Riebeeck's hedge perhaps has more ironic significance today than many of his heirs would like to admit. There is something about its logical, determined, stubborn inadequacy that raises modern echoes. There it stands. It should have solved the problem. Any sensible man can see that. But somehow it did not.

The Hottentots refused to be contained beyond its prickly boundaries, the expanding Europeans soon had to go across to find new land and more cattle. Further, van Riebeeck was called upon to mediate intertribal disputes. And the need for labor quickly brought into the growing colony a few detribalized Hottentots, a few Bantu slaves from far north above the Zambesi, and a few Moslem criminals sent from the Indies to work out their sentences. Inevitably the tiny size of the settlement and the lack of marriageable women brought about the solution generally accepted in the Indies: intermarriage with the heterogeneous non-white population was officially approved. The Cape Coloureds were born.

When van Riebeeck sailed away in 1662 to do the Company's bidding farther east, scarcely five hundred Whites were in the Cape. But the infant town of De Kaap at the foot of Table Mountain was an unmistakable and growing outpost of European civilization. Already its races were in inextricable and often uneasy mixture. Already its burghers were showing increasing signs of independence and a noticeable inclination to go their own way.

Given the restless nature of the Europeans and their enterprise and determination, there could thereafter be only one impulse, growth, and only one direction, out and away from the Cape. Although there were periods of stagnation, particularly during the seventeen years between van Riebeeck's departure and the arrival of "the second founder," Governor Simon van der Stel, the next hundred years saw a generally steady progression. The Hottentots and the Cape Dutch eventually formed a reasonably amicable alliance against the Bushmen, and these tiny unfortunates were either absorbed into the general population or were driven upcountry. (Occasionally today on Adderley Street in Cape Town some squat little face will startle the eye, looking straight out of three hundred years. But only a handful of pure Bushmen, mostly in South-West Africa, are still to be found.) The Hottentots themselves were steadily pushed back or absorbed by intermarriage. The Whites were strengthened, particularly in the last two decades of the seventeenth century and the first two of the eighteenth, by a wave of Dutch and German immigration which brought the ancestors of most of the present Afrikaans population. A small but fruitful complement of French Huguenots, assisted by the Company, fled their own land and settled in the Cape to become an industrious and valued part of the population and sire the Marais, the du Toits and the du Plessis that one meets in Jo'burg or Cape Town today. Commerce, despite occasional periods of depression, steadily increased. The machinery of administration became steadily more complex, more sophisticated, more responsible. Council, church, courts and school began to form that quartet which is so characteristic of the modern Republic. A government was in being and it had a constantly rising population to care for.

Care for, but not always please; for the farmers, the *boers,* who had from the first been a vitally necessary but always stubbornly independent element, were now in process of moving out, and still farther out. They had always been frontiersmen, and now, as they became increasingly restive under what they regarded as the unnecessarily restrictive orders of the tiny central government at Cape Town, they were rapidly becoming *trekboers:* far-ranging men, usually young, who pushed on north through the empty veld and the misty mountains in search of new lands to settle and cultivate, new places where the nearest neighbor, as in the pioneer American West, was too close if you could reach him in a day's riding.

Inevitably the Company's governors felt their administrative fabric unraveling at the hands of these devil-may-cares, and inevitably they tended to respond by becoming anxious and overarbitrary. At the same time the burghers who remained at the Cape were giving trouble: they resented the fact that Simon van der Stel's son and successor, Willem, was giving his friends exclusive contracts for the handling of wine and meat in the colony. They forwarded charges to the Company, the Company established a commission of inquiry that found Willem guilty, and that was the end of Willem. It was also the end of a long period of assisted immigration, which the Company's directors, the all-powerful "Seventeen Gentlemen" in Amsterdam, seemed to feel had caused a good deal of the colony's recent troubles. Not until the English 1820 Settlers did another large group of assisted immigrants come to South Africa. During almost the entire eighteenth century the colony grew only through the natural increase of the 1,700 free white souls who were in the Cape when Willem van der Stel was recalled in 1702. The population was divided into the burghers of Cape Town, the wine and grain farmers of the Berg River Valley beyond the sandy Cape Flats, and the trek-boers already far out on the highveld. To distinguish themselves from the mostly Dutch-born officials at the Castle of Good Hope, those born in the colony were already beginning to call themselves Afrikaners.

Trekboers, disgruntled burghers, Afrikaners; and one other important feature, destined to play a great part in South African history, and still just a hint away should the need ever arise again: the commando, organized along the near frontiers of the Cape to drive off cattle-marauding Bushmen. Small in number, mounted, carrying rifles, living off the country or the most sparing of supplies, the first commandos took the field to start a long line of riders down through history.

And yet one more thing of permanent consequence: in the eighteenth century the trickle of slave labor begun in the earliest days became a full-fledged river with the growing needs of the community. The Cape Colony before long became a society and an economy based upon black labor: not native, for most of it came from East Africa, the Indies and India and there were no native Blacks aside from the rapidly disappearing Hottentots and Bushmen, but black nonetheless. The habit and necessity of depending upon black labor also entered the history of South Africa and there, though the black labor is no longer slave but now gets its rand or two per day, it remains.

On the frontier a new society was developing. An increasing number of Boers now owned one and often two enormous farms of 3,000 morgen and more, originally granted on a loan basis by the Company but soon regarded as a legal right to be handed down from father to son. The ties to Cape Town became increasingly tenuous, society more casual and open, language simpler and more direct (the change from High Dutch to Afrikaans already beginning), life hard but also expansive and outgoing, a new civilization clinging to the Bible as perhaps its only real unifying force. In faraway Europe the fortunes of the Netherlands and with them the fortunes of Jan Compagnie steadily declined in the revolutionary fore-rumbles of the Napoleonic era.

Inevitably the revolutionary impulses reached the Cape, four hundred of the three thousand free men in the colony signed a petition to the

Company seeking more self-government (not a single frontier Boer signed and it is doubtful how many even knew about it) and the Company responded with halfhearted attempts at reform. Then abruptly in 1791, realizing that the colony was costing more than all its other East Indies stations combined, the Company recalled its governor, closed down its fortifications and military posts and virtually abandoned a community now numbering nearly 14,000 burghers, 17,000 slaves and some 1,500 officials. Two commissioners came out for one last, futile attempt to save the situation, but Holland was now allied with Britain against the new French Republic and Jan Compagnie was dying. In 1794 it declared itself bankrupt and the Cape Colony was virtually cut adrift, its European anchor lost, its seaborne trade drastically reduced as world war grew, its currency falling, its economy in shambles, its government close to collapse. And in the Eastern Cape the Boers were in near-revolt because they were finally faced with the problem that is still the problem: the Bantu were arriving in force at last.

They had gradually been coming down, in scattered tribes and wandering bands, into what is now the Transvaal and Orange Free State, into Northern Natal and into the Eastern Cape as far south as the Fish River. In 1778 Governor van Plattenberg made the second experiment in apartheid by declaring the Fish River the dividing line. It proved as ineffective as van Riebeeck's hedge, although, as in the case of the hedge, the violations for a while were generally peaceable on both sides. Then came the full flow of both populations and with it a continuing contention between two groups of agriculturalists, equally hardy, equally tricky, equally certain they had a right to whatever they could conquer. The first Kaffir war broke out in 1779 and the story of modern South Africa began to develop.

There were many reasons for conflict but essentially they all came down to the age-old frontier battle for land and water. The Whites were expanding north: they needed land and water to live. The Bantu were expanding south: they needed land and water to live. Something had to give. Eventually it was the Bantu, though it took almost a century to do it. One Kaffir war followed another, culminating in the bloody nineteenth-century battles with the great Zulu warrior chiefs Shaka, Dingaan and Cetewayo. Parallel with the early stages of this running conflict came another problem that still bothers the heirs of Jan van Riebeeck: the British arrived.

They took the Cape Colony in 1795 to prevent it falling into the hands of the French; returned it to the Batavian Republic, successor to the United Provinces of Holland, in 1803; found themselves at war with the Batavian Republic when it went over to Napoleon, took the Cape again in 1806; acquired formal suzerainty under the general peace settlement of 1814; financed nearly five thousand "1820 Settlers" with a 50,000 pound grant from Parliament in an attempt to strengthen the English element in the population; and found themselves increasingly embroiled with burghers and Boers, whose independent spirit and desire to cling to slavery in the face of a growing British humanitarianism that was soon to abolish it throughout the Empire, spelled trouble.

By 1823 things had reached a point at which burghers, Boers and British were so obviously unhappy with one another, with the ineffectual government of the colony, with the slavery issue and with a postwar economic depression, that Parliament voted to include the Cape in a list of colonies to be examined by a special commission of inquiry. The commission came and the Boers opted out, in the event that now supplies the rationale, the emotional ideal and the basic mystique of Afrikanerdom— the Great Trek.

It was a while coming, though, for first the commission had to report, recommend its reforms, and the British had to try to enforce them. A fiscal reorganization was launched, a stronger legislative council was established, more representation was granted the citizens of the colony. Then came the reform that finally sent the Boers trekking: slavery was abolished.

The Hottentots, still around, still lazy, still amiable, were granted civil liberty by the British in 1828 along with the few remaining Bushmen and "other free persons of colour." The rights of the Cape Coloured were thus established and were so to remain until the Nationalist Government took power 128 years later and began building its own van Riebeeck's hedges among the races. Next came abolition of slavery, in 1834. Owners were paid only partial compensation, vagrancy laws were inadequate to curb the released flow of wanderers, the economy was thrown still further out of balance. At the same time the Bantu were pressing along the frontiers, a great burst of warfare among all the tribes broke out (still referred to as "Mfecane," the crushing) and devastated much of Natal and the southeastern areas of what are now the Transvaal and Free State. Shaka was beginning to murder and consolidate out of Zululand, and the government at the Cape found itself unable to work out a consistent or effective program for dealing with all this. Policy vacillated, the frontier was uncertain and largely undefended, the British were felt to be generally critical and antagonistic toward the undisciplinable Boers whose understanding of freedom seemed to be: leave us alone to do exactly as we please. Finally came the most desperate insult of all. British reformers, in the words of Anna Steenkamp, sister of the Trek's first great leader, Piet Retief, were attempting to give to the ex-slaves an "ungodly equality" with the white man. The Boers' racial pride, not for the last time, was being affronted by demands that people of darker skin be considered equally human. Suddenly a great frustration boiled over.

More or less spontaneously, the women seeming "more bent upon it than the men," the Trek groups formed and started north and east in 1836. By the time Victoria ascended the throne in 1837, some two thousand trekkers, Voortrekkers as their descendants would call them when they came to build them their suitable monument on a hill in Pretoria, were into Natal, across the Orange River, and pushing toward the Vaal.

In the heavy, ponderous Voortrekker Monument, with its great echoing central room set about with stone bas-reliefs, a museum of artifacts and portraits in the basement below, the major leaders and events of the Trek are heroically set forth. Afrikaner families move reverently through; the English-speaker feels that he is not only intruding in some private place but, rather embarrassingly, observing some private emotional ceremony. The achievement, as with the westward pioneers of America, is impressive and moving enough in its own right, filled with great determination, heroism and bravery. But it has been raised through official emphasis into a shrine and a mystique that make the non-Afrikaner somewhat uneasy. It is not the sort of monument that leaves the visitor alone: it demands. It is not up to you to decide whether what it honors is heroic, as of course you would if left to your own devices: it tells you so, with all the massive, humorless weight of which a generally good-natured and humorous people is capable in its more graceless and self-conscious moments.

But the achievement is probably not diminished. Fighting from horseback or firing their heavy elephant guns from within the "laager"—ox-wagons formed in a great circle, wheels locked together by chains, spaces between wheels filled with thornbushes, women and children at the center, men firing outward from around the ring—they pushed on against hostile Bantu east into Natal, north beyond the Orange. Two embryo Boer republics were established, a first claim was made to genuine independence. Some parties were lost (Piet Retief and his men, thinking they had the pledge of Dingaan, Shaka's successor, that they could occupy Natal, were lured unarmed into his kraal and mercilessly murdered), but others got through. Two English expeditions, despite official disapproval of the Trek, were organized and sent out when the trekkers asked for help. But by the spring of 1838 it seemed the whole enterprise must collapse, for the Zulus had killed 361 trekkers, some 200 Coloured servants, 13 English and many Bantu of other tribes who were friendly to the Trek.

Then sympathy and fellow Boers came to the rescue. Andries Pretorius, for whom the capital is named, led an expedition into Natal and on December 16, 1838, overthrew Dingaan's impis at Blood River in one of the historic events of Afrikanerdom; his cost was three slightly injured Boers to three thousand dead Zulus, a tribute to guns against spears. The Natal trekkers promptly established a capital at Pietermaritzburg and elected a Volksraad, or legislature. Pretorius negotiated with a much-chastened Dingaan a treaty that this time began to work, giving the Boers much of Natal. The Colonial Secretary in London ordered the withdrawal of English troops that had been sent to Port Natal (now Durban) in a halfhearted attempt to head off the trekkers. For the moment it seemed the Trek had carried all before it, at least in Natal.

Pretorius formed the three embryo Boer republics into a federation and prepared to send a deputation to Cape Town to treat for independence under the British Crown. The project died rapidly as renewed Bantu depredations led to Boer reprisals and a growing feeling in Cape Town and London that Britain must step in and pacify Natal. Internal jealousies also plagued the Boers and presently the Natal republic fell apart, many trekkers pulling out and going north to join the Orange-Vaal groups. But there were also internal squabbles; Bantu pressures and Cape Town's determination to assume control of all Southern Africa brought collapse. In 1848 the British High Commissioner asserted the sovereignty of the Queen over all races resident between the Orange, the Vaal and the Drakensberg massif to the east.

There followed a period of Balkanization, attempts to establish various semi-independent Boer states under the Queen's umbrella. All failed. In 1852 in the Sand River Convention the British recognized the right of "the emigrant farmers beyond the Vaal" to manage their own affairs in a Transvaal republic, subject only to a guarantee that neither side of the Vaal would encroach upon the other. Two years later the British finally gave up attempts to run the jimcrack "Orange River Sovereignty" they had tried to establish between the Orange and the Vaal, and the Orange Free State came into being. And two years later, because it was essentially English, because it controlled the eastern seacoast and because, perhaps, its greenness appealed to memories of home, Britain annexed Natal and established it as a Crown Colony independent of the Cape.

And so, though there would be other titles, volksraads, laws and constitutions as the decades passed, the land fell into the essential pattern it was to have until the Anglo-Boer War of 1899–1902: two uneasily independent Boer groupings, one between the Orange and the Vaal, the other across, or trans-Vaal; Natal, then as now predominantly English; and the old Cape Colony, part Cape Dutch, part British, with the latter influence dominant since it was the seat of the Queen's government in Southern Africa. History does not show, though it is now one of the basic tenets of Afrikanerdom, any great voracious English desire to conquer the whole of the land: that would come later, with the discovery of gold and diamonds. For much of the nineteenth century the English attitude was one of genuinely charitable interest, a rather befuddled willingness to carry the burdens of a troublesome colony as long as its inhabitants could not, a patient sense of obligation about spending lives and treasure to hold back marauding Bantu from ungrateful Boers, and a rather wistful desire to sluff off the whole business as soon as it could gracefully be done.

Significantly during these immediate forerunning days of the present Republic, different policies toward race became established in the four different areas. The Transvaal and Free State Boers, accustomed from life on the frontier to regard the Bantu as either laborers or enemies, and in any case completely inferior to the white man, clung to Piet Retief's original mandate to "maintain such regulations as will suppress crime and preserve proper relations between master and servant." The Cape, backed by two hundred years of easy commerce with the Coloureds, permitted much more freedom of association and development to all races; Natal, confronted with a growing problem involving the Indians brought over in mid-century to work the sugarcane, and still stinging from many bruising encounters with the Zulus and the Xhosa, was somewhere in between.

In 1867 both gold and diamonds were discovered. Within a year both rushes were on, and South Africa changed forever.

With this came, suddenly, prosperity; and with it also came the great adventurers and empire builders such as Cecil Rhodes, Starr Jameson and Barney Barnato. And with them came, inevitably, a lively renewed British interest in South Africa and a determined drive to reannex and confederate once more with the prickly Boers who were now, by a decision of nature and God that they were ever after to regard as a personal commendation, sitting atop a wealth far greater than the Indies', found finally, in one of history's great and fateful ironies, at the Indies' way station.

It was upon the period prior to the Great Trek and down through the second British attempt to confederate the country that Afrikanerdom was subsequently to erect those legends that form the basis of the Afrikaner mystique today. Someday under the pressures of the outside world there may come a time for the unity the Afrikaners talk about to move from talk to reality, and when that day comes these events may be appraised with fairness and justice in the histories, educational texts and political speeches of the Republic. But the time is not now, nor was it in the days when the legend was being created. To build themselves into a nation, to give themselves the will to survive and the determination to succeed, the Afrikaners had to have a villain. If the villain at times erred through simple bumbling British inadvertence, this human justification had to be erased from the story. Only Big Vicious England, the Unrelenting Enemy, could suit the psychic and emotional needs of the embryo Afrikaans nation; and to this day it is Big Vicious England who provides the emotional goad, even though Big Vicious England is now just Poor Little Worried England huddled away in a tiny far-off island, and her descendants in the Republic are no longer responsible, if they ever were, for her past misdeeds, alleged and actual, against the heirs of Jan van Riebeeck.

So the legend was created, and so it dominates South Africa today: the poor, downtrodden Afrikaners, hunted and harassed and harried by an insatiable imperial power, until finally in sheer desperation, deeply loving freedom (for those with skins of the right color), dedicated to democratic independence (for those with skins of the right color), bravely and courageously seeking new homelands (for those with skins of the right color), inspired, selfless, supreme, ennobled (in the cause of those with skins of the right color), they struck forth into the wilderness like the people of Israel fleeing Pharaoh, an analogy that still echoes daily from the pulpits of the Dutch Reformed Church and the political platforms of the Nationalist Party.

Here entered that religious aspect of Afrikanerdom that is so striking in the Republic today. The scattered impulses of discontented, unruly, disorganized Boers who frequently could not stomach one another, let alone the British, were redrawn into one single, noble purpose blessed by Providence. They were sent forth to do the work of God by ruling the dark-skinned children of Ham, whose ordained and eternal relegation to the position of hewers of wood and drawers of water had been revealed to the Boers by their Bibles and confirmed by the Kaffir wars. The Afrikaners were "the chosen people . . . sent to do God's mission . . . protected and directed by Divine Providence." God called them, God guided them, God raised them up and showed them the path: God is Afrikaans to this very day.

So in the wilderness they sent down new roots and created new nations, and there, still hounded and harried (with a little more merit to the argument, now), they found themselves in the Orange Free State deprived of their diamond fields, and in the Transvaal faced with a gold-inspired attempt to federate and reannex which they met with the First Transvaal War of Independence in 1880. When that war ended, largely because the Gladstone Ministry in London had other problems and was embarrassed before the world by the spectacle of Big Vicious England attacking Poor Little Transvaal (a spectacle that did not deter another ministry nineteen years later when the true extent of the gold and diamonds was more clearly revealed), the Transvaal was recognized as having "complete self-government subject to the suzerainty of Her Majesty."

It was at the end of that war, when the South African peoples of Dutch-German-Huguenot descent in the Cape, in Natal, in the Orange Free State were united in a fervor of sympathy and brotherhood with their compatriots in the Transvaal, that there came the moment of mutual recognition in which the Afrikaner nation was truly and forever born. And it was then that its leaders, writers, predicants, teachers and historians united in a systematic recasting of history that would create a firm foundation of legend and belief to support the ethos of the race.

Again it was one of history's ironies that both South African-born Afrikaans and English had the same goal of a single, united, powerful country, for all of them loved it, as all of them do today. Left to themselves, ordinary folk might have worked peaceably toward that end, for there is much in the earlier writings and statements on both sides to indicate a desire for true unity. But governments, businessmen, politicians, empire-builders and adventurers intervened, as they always do in the generous impulses of ordinary folk; and so presently the big war came, the one in which the newly found, newly united Afrikaner race formed its commandos and took up arms against its overwhelmingly powerful imperial enemy. And in due course, after three years of sporadic and inconclusive fighting that brought England universal opprobrium and raised the Afrikaners to a peak of international popularity they would never know again, the Transvaal and the Orange Free State and all their secret and not-so-secret Afrikaans sympathizers in the Cape and Natal were brought to their knees and the dream of independence was over.

Or so it seemed, for a little while. Actually they never considered themselves beaten, began immediately to plan for a return to power through political means, and, aided by that strange element of history with which so many states and races have been able to gain their own ends over the years—The Conscience of England—they managed it very well.

They were beaten, but very shortly London was handing them back their independence—within the framework of a new Union of South Africa, it is true, but with title and form retained in the four provinces, and with the road to political power now wide open on a national basis with no barriers in the way of any group that could secure a majority of the votes.

So from the slough of despond, where their stubbornness never really permitted them to believe they were, the Afrikaners came doggedly and determinedly back; and although they suffered depression and hard times and struggles and setbacks, the years from the Act of Union in 1910 to the triumph of the Nationalist Party in 1948 have about them in retrospect some of the same inevitability the Afrikaners themselves profess to see in everything since the Great Trek—indeed, everything since Jan van Riebeeck. Two world wars threatened to rip the fabric and cancel forever their surge to recovery and ultimate, complete control, but fortunately for them—although some of them bitterly resented it and the present Prime Minister, John Vorster, was interned by the Smuts Government for his anti-British activities in World War II—their Afrikaans-led governments of the day had the sense to stand by England and hold the Union together. If they had not, South Africa would have fallen apart again, and the Afrikaans nation might well be back wandering irretrievably now in a Black wilderness at the tip of the continent.

Thus in a hasty glance at three hundred years, the story from van Riebeeck to Vorster: a story that in the legends of Afrikanerdom is now portrayed as one single, inevitable, God-blessed and God-guided onrush of destiny from 1652 to 1967; but which, like all histories of all races, is really compounded of the erratic and uncertain activities of men, which only in after-times can be made to appear to have had a pattern.

But in the Republic, as everywhere, the pattern is important; and to it the heirs of Jannie van Riebeeck cling with a fierce and determined emotionalism that brooks precious little opposition and forgives precious little criticism.

II
JOURNEY'S COURSE

1.
Pretoria

THE MORNING WAS cold but clear, promising a warm day. Coal smoke filled Pretoria's valley as it does every winter morning.

"We have so much cheap coal," my guide said, "seventy-five billion tons, they tell us, enough to supply this country and all of Africa, if need be, for hundreds of years, that everybody burns it. We don't have central heating as you do. Actually," he explained, coughing and sneezing like most South Africans in wintertime, "our winter is so short that we don't really need it. It's—*kerchoo!*—over before we know it."

We went first to the Department of Information, housed temporarily in an office building downtown. As in Washington, the Government's functions are scattered, ultimately to be consolidated but existing for the time being in an administrative sprawl over half of Pretoria. The type of architecture varies from the old buff stone of Oom Paul's day to the same blank steel-and-glass impersonals that disfigure most of the world's capitals now.

We took an automatic elevator, moved down long aseptic corridors. From time to time as we walked along we would come to a native, mopping the floor or engaged in some other janitorial task. Instantly he would stiffen, jump back against the wall, stand rigid and silent, eyes down, until we had passed. My hosts almost literally, I think, did not see the Bantu, proceeding as though they were not there, calling out cheerful good-mornings to one another in Afrikaans or an almost Cockney-accented English, slipping easily from one language to the other as do many Afrikaners (though fewer English, for, as an Afrikaans friend was to tell me, "The Afrikaans language does not lie easy on the English tongue").

It very soon became apparent that of all the busy little civil servants scurrying officiously about, of all the higher functionaries meeting jovially on the way to work, perhaps no more than one in ten was of English origin. There is a very cozy Afrikaner in-group feeling about the Government; not hostile, at least to me—though I was to find that there are many attitudes toward the home-grown English-speakers, ranging from acceptance to contempt—but just—comfortable. "We are governed by the lions of the north," I was told, sourly, much later, at the Cape. "The Transvaal-Orange Free State axis has us at its mercy." Here on my first morning in Pretoria I could already sense as much.

We came to a closed door, a nameplate, a title. My guide knocked, made introductions, left. My interviewee was the first of that short, stocky, round-headed, ruddy-faced, neat-mustachioed Afrikaner type that was to become so familiar. It is a type coming directly from the Dutch, frequently given a darker shading of skin, a rounder skull, a curlier hair, by some ancestral wandering that seems to have occurred, in many old Transvaal and Cape families, somewhere back before the days of apartheid and separate development.

Deliberately in this first week I had placed myself in the hands of the Government, partly because it was the most disarming thing to do, but also because it seemed desirable to first get the Government's views and report them fully and fairly before I went on through the Republic to match words against reality. My host of this hour was primed for me, and after brief cordial greetings, launched at once into his statement.

"The greatest confusion in the outside world," he began, employing that locution which, significantly, is used by all South Africans, of whatever race, "comes in referring to the Blacks as Africans. There are no Africans. Among the 12,500,000 now estimated to be resident in this country, there is only one common factor—pigmentation. There is no unity of interest, no singleness of concept or purpose, not even, in most cases, minimal friendship. They hate each other. They would kill each other if we didn't stand between them, just as they do all over Africa today where the white man's restraining influence has been removed. They are as different from one another as night from day.

"Now, you take this map—" and he turned to the map on the wall behind him, the map which is standard in most Government offices, the map which shows the great Black horseshoe enclosing the Republic, starting thinly across the western and northern Transvaal, running to the east coast, thickening down through Zululand, Natal, the Transkei, thinning out again toward the Cape.

"Here you see what our problem is. We are approximately three and a half million Whites, composed of about two million Afrikaners and a million and a half English-speakers. Against that we have perhaps a million and a half Coloureds, descended from Whites, Bushmen, Hottentots and Malays in the Cape; more than 500,000 Asiatics, mostly Indians centered in Natal; and the estimated 12,500,000 Blacks or Bantu." He turned back with a small smile.

"Perhaps one of our errors was to coin the term 'Bantu,' because it has given the outside world, particularly your country, the idea that we have a single unified black race to deal with, as you do. But as I have explained, we do not."

"How are they broken down?" I asked, and he turned again to the map to illustrate as he went along.

"We classify them roughly into seven major ethnic groups. There are the Zulu"—and he pointed to lush Natal, at that moment still just a name on the map—"some three and a half million of them there, our major warrior tribe, as you know. South of them, in what is now the semi-independent Transkei, north of the Kei River, and the still-tribal Ciskei, south of the Kei River—are about three million Xhosa (and he gave that click so characteristic of certain tribal languages, so that it came out something like: 'TsiCosa,' run rapidly together). There are about three million Sotho (pronounced 'Sootoo'), the northern, central and western, spreading out from Basutoland (now the nation of Lesotho) into the central Transvaal, the southern Free State and the western Cape. The Tswana are to the north. Then there are the Bapedi and the Shangaan. And then the more minor tribes, the Pondo, Tembu, Venda, Fingo, Lebedu, Ndebele, and so on, offshoots of other tribes.

"I like to think of the major tribes as the fingers of a hand reaching down into the Republic. The Government has said that it might someday be willing to entertain the idea of these groups rejoining the former High Commission Territories that are now becoming independent, Basutoland, Bechuanaland, Swaziland.

"We might," he said thoughtfully, expressing that rather terrifying Afrikaner passion for logic, neatness and order which sometimes produces such fine results and sometimes such frightful ones, "like to round off their boundaries so that everything would be tied together in its proper place."

"You don't think, then, that the answer lies in more freedom for them within the Republic's white-controlled society—" I began. For a moment he looked quite stern.

"We must work out something suitable in our own circumstances," he said flatly, "and not what someone from overseas tells us we should. There can be a lot of talk in international circles about what we are doing, but our African neighbors know what we are doing, and what happens? They come down into the Republic illegally all the time, to find work and a place to live. We estimate we have about one million here illegally right now. Why do they come, if our conditions are so bad? Why don't they stay away?

"And also, there are the Bantu themselves. You can't force them to do what isn't in their cultural pattern and habit; they have to be convinced, themselves, of the need for changes. There's a very interesting parallel" —and he chuckled comfortably, as all Afrikaans- and English-speaking South Africans do, united in at least one thing, their delight in catching the United States in what they consider an embarrassing position—"between our situation and yours in the Southwest with your Mexican farm immigrants. I remember when I was in the States a couple of years ago I was shown some Mexican labor camps in Texas. Some of them, you know, are not very good. But in one I saw, they had done it up right. The farmers were ordered by the Government to provide the Mexicans with fresh peaches, but peaches weren't in season, so they gave the Mexicans canned peaches. The Mexicans wouldn't touch them. Our Bantu are the same way, you can't force them to do what isn't in their cultural pattern and habit.

"But, mind you, one thing is certain: our whole future is so tied up with Africa and the other African states that we would really be stupid if we didn't show our neighbors that we were acting in good faith."

His tone changed, the amiable smile disappeared, the eyes became sharp.

"We shall do everything we can to survive in Africa," he said. He hit the desk impatiently with his open hand.

"Why, damn it all, look at Basutoland. Britain makes her into independent Lesotho. Why are we criticized for creating Bantustans when Britain creates them out of areas that have nothing? Lesotho isn't viable in any sense of the word. It's a difference in method. We create African states when they are viable, have trained personnel and are able to exist on their own. There is a tremendous difference between a premature birth and one that is on time. . . .

"When will the next Bantustan be created, now that we've established the Transkei? I would say the Tswana are leading by a neck. The Zulus have been lagging behind, lately—they have an inbuilt inability to come straight out with decisions. The greatest military nation of all these tribes, but they have a monolithic tribal structure that makes it difficult for them to reach decisions.

"You see, we say to them: here is a pattern for your development. It is for you to say when you are ready. None as yet has come forward like the Transkei and said they were ready to negotiate a new Bantustan."

"Are they informed of the possibility?"

"Radio-wise, reading-wise and picture-wise," he said firmly, "our Bantu are well informed. When the Transkei had its first election three years ago, 78.8 per cent of the people voted, mainly because we showed them a series of very simple films—'How an Old Man Votes,' and we showed an old man voting; 'How a Woman Votes,' and we showed a woman; 'How a Young Man Votes,' and we showed a young man—the same thing, but a different person, a different age doing it each time. That's how they are, absolutely literal-minded: you have to show them exactly how it is, then they understand and know what to do. It's the same way with their own independence. We're showing them how, but they aren't hurrying, and we don't want to hurry them. We want them to be ready.

"We would be stupid not to recognize the differences that exist between us and the Bantu, but we do not believe that the mere fact of difference should be an automatic guarantee of rights when they are not capable of handling them."

He looked thoughtful and sighed.

"We are trying our damnedest to train them in social sciences, in technology, in scientific pursuits, but very few take to it. Now, when it comes to politics"—he smiled, a rather grim little smile—"you can find any number you want to go into politics, you don't have any trouble there. . . .

"Our friends up north are constantly saying in the United Nations that the Bantu areas don't have good soil. They were given 10,729,435 morgen of land by inalienable right under the Land Act of 1913, and that was increased by an arrangement for purchase or expropriation of an additional 7,250,000 morgen in certain 'released areas' consisting principally of white farmlands. Over two-thirds of this additional amount has already been purchased at a cost of 23,000,000 rand. It is true, as they say, that only about 13 per cent of the Republic's territory has been reserved for Bantu homelands, but you mustn't forget that we don't have all that good an amount of land to play with. Approximately 70 per cent of our territory consists of mountainous land or semidesert areas in which neither Bantu nor anybody else could make a living. On that basis, we say that about 45 per cent of our most fertile land is actually located in the Bantu homelands.

"Anyway," he said impatiently, "the problem isn't the Bantu land. They have some of the best soil in the Republic, but the basic problem is not the potential of the soil, it's the human factor. If we had Bantu entrepreneurs on the equivalent basis as we have them in the white society, we wouldn't worry. But to find Bantu entrepreneurs capable of starting viable businesses, to create something like a Ford or a General Motors, or even a modest business capable of making a reasonable go of it, will take a hell of a long time.

"Up to now, you see, though we've invited them to come forward and have offered them Government financing, we've only been able to start things of a relatively junior nature, a couple of furniture factories, a few bus companies, a rug factory or two. If we could get more to come forward, we would thank God on our knees. It is not because we are denying anybody a chance that South Africa isn't crawling with black millionaires, it is because these people simply haven't had the experience. . . .

"If the African people," he said slowly, "had the ability to do the ordinary everyday things such as keeping ledgers and accounts and decent records, the things that European people do every day in their ordinary lives, we wouldn't have all this shouting at the UN. They would be too busy, right here and up north, in building their own enterprises.

"Some people in your State Department," he remarked dryly, "fly with their ears. They shouldn't listen so hard to what our enemies say about us. They should find out for themselves."

He turned once more to the frustrating map, studied it silently for a moment, sighed, turned back.

"They can say a lot of things outside, but as long as we are doing our best to make things go well in our own backyard, the attackers are not going to find much real grist for their mill."

He smiled suddenly, the charming Afrikaner at his best.

"Or so I and my Government believe."

PASSPORTS FOR 12 NON-WHITES REFUSED (Star, *Johannesburg, English*) . . . *A member of the Zulu royal house, an assistant bishop and the leader of the Opposition Democratic Party in the Transkei are among 12 non-Whites who have recently been refused passports to travel abroad on American or British study grants.*

Several priests and teachers have had to abandon plans to study at overseas universities or to join study tours for the same reason.

The Government has given no reasons for turning down their passport applications. . . .

MORE ARE BANNED (Cape Times, *English*) . . . *The name of Eric Gordon Flegg, of Rathfelder Avenue, Constantia, has been added to the list of people prohibited from attending gatherings for five years in terms of the Suppression of Communism Act, according to a notice in the Gov-*ernment Gazette *yesterday by the Minister of Justice.*

The names of seven other people have been added to the list of people prohibited from attending gatherings for a period of two years in terms of the same Act. All are Africans.

DEFINITION

The law of the Republic states that a White person is "a person who (a) in appearance obviously is a White person and who is not generally accepted as a Coloured person, or (b) is generally accepted as a White person and is not in appearance obviously not a White person, but does not include any person who freely and voluntarily admits that he is by descent an African or a Coloured person, unless it is proved that the admission is not based on fact."

—Official Sources

"OUR COURT," said the Afrikaner Justice of the Supreme Court, small, neat, tidy, possessed of a pleasant voice, a quick wit, a friendly and hospitable manner, "applies the law as it finds it. We regard it to be our duty to interpret the law as Parliament has put it on the statute books, not to frustrate the will of Parliament by wide-ranging interpretations of things that Parliament never intended.

"We see," he said, and a dry little smile turned the corners of his lips and briefly touched his eyes, "what mischief can be created when courts attempt to rewrite legislation. That is not our system. . . .

"Do federal laws protect the rights of the citizen? You must remember that we do have a subversive element of frankly and openly Communistic leanings. We believe we cannot allow freedom to be used to destroy freedom.

"What we have done must be judged against that background, it cannot be separated, it does not stand alone. You express some question about the ninety-day detention law, which permitted the Minister of Justice to hold a suspect for that period of time without bringing charges or permitting him a trial. The Minister has now suspended that, you know, though of course the 180-day provision which permits substantially the same thing is still in effect and a part of permanent law. That is designed basically to protect a witness from being intimidated while he is awaiting trial.

"I will grant you," he said gently, though with a little frown as he considered it, "that some provisions of our laws may seem a little harsh to the outside world. But the Government has considered it necessary to have the power to meet subversion and overcome it. Nobody has been able to point to a case in which these provisions were employed unfairly. The detained *have been* Communists.

"What about third-degree methods in the prisons, you ask?" He smiled.

"I think you have been reading our English-language press too assiduously. You will learn to put it in proper perspective as you come to know South Africa better.

"No third-degree methods," he said firmly, "have been proved. It is true that if a witness takes the stand and refuses to speak, he can be imprisoned for it. Recently the courts have been empowered to impose up to a year for refusal to testify. But no one has proved third-degree methods in a court of law. . . .

"The banning laws? I will admit that there has been some concern expressed in the country about the banning of the young student, Ian Robertson, who, as president of one of our student groups, extended the invitation to one of your famous countrymen to visit us recently. But we all assume," he said, "that in due time the Minister of Justice will make clear that he had good reasons for this banning.

"Yes, I grant you banning imposes great hardships, a person can be restricted entirely to his own home, he can be prohibited from meeting anyone outside his immediate family, he is denied any access to the press or radio, they are not allowed to disseminate his views. But you must remember, as I say, that so far, all of these cases have ultimately been proved to be Communists.

"It is this fact, I think, which has removed the apprehensions that were first voiced by the Bar when the laws were passed. There was fear expressed that the Government's powers were too great, that the individual citizen would be endangered. But as the extent of the danger has become apparent, the measures have been accepted as justified. . . ."

"Many American lawyers who have studied our system have become somewhat confused by the fact that our courts, which claim to do justice to all, are daily enforcing discriminatory legislation. But the answer is that South African constitutional law acknowledges the sovereignty of Parliament and rejects the concept of a fundamental law. From the very beginnings of our history our law has taken the position that Whites and non-Whites could not and would not merge into a common society. Therefore legislation founded on that principle is recognized as valid and is accordingly upheld by the judiciary.

"To take care of our enormous Bantu population, there has gradually been created a system of specialized tribunals meant exclusively for them and largely applying native law and custom. The State President is empowered to confer jurisdiction upon what we call 'courts of chiefs and headmen,' which are usually rather rough and ready affairs, sometimes held under a tree or in a kraal, dispensing immediate justice in the same way it has always been dispensed under tribal custom. Appeals may be made to the local Bantu commissioners, but in practice there aren't very many of these, which would seem to indicate that in the natives' eyes the chief's courts do a pretty good job.

"Now," he said with a smile, "Americans always want to know about the type of punishment we use here, and they are also very concerned to find out about our jury system. We are dealing for the most part with a primitive population, and so we do frequently use corporal punishment for crimes of violence. Ten strokes is the maximum permitted by law, and in practice it usually doesn't exceed six. If the offender is fifty years or over, the lash is not permitted. Imprisonment rarely exceeds twenty years, but an indeterminate sentence with a minimum of nine years is often imposed.

"As for the jury system—and this will probably shock you, as it does most of your countrymen—it is practically extinct in South Africa. Trial by jury was abolished in civil cases in 1918, on what we consider the practical reasoning that it is absurd to expect complete laymen to decide complicated issues of fact. In criminal trials in the Supreme Court—which, incidentally, isn't like yours, but consists of some sixty or seventy judges from the whole structure of higher courts—juries are still recognized in the statute books, but it's a slim thread. In most cases, except political ones covered by the summary powers of the Minister of Justice, an accused has the right to demand trial by jury. But in practice nearly all choose to be tried by a judge sitting alone.

"This is a tribute to the fairness of the judiciary—and also, perhaps" —he smiled gently—"to the suspicion on the part of native accused persons that all-white juries might not give them a fair trial. You see, probably 95 per cent of the accused in superior courts are natives, while juries by law are all white and all male. You are not the only country"— the smile broadened—"where there have been blatant cases of race prejudice in jury trials, and so in 1935 the Minister of Justice was given the power to deny a jury trial in cases involving alleged injury by a White on a Black or a Black on a White.

"Aside from a few of our English-speaking friends," he said, "no tears have been shed in South Africa over the demise of the jury system. We think its abolition makes the administration of justice quicker, more dignified and more accurate." He smiled. "You're probably horrified, but don't be. We like it that way."

He smiled and placed his hands outspread upon the desk. A little twinkle of amusement crossed his face.

"With regard to that famous countryman of yours," he said gently, "it does sometimes seem to us that there are other problems in the world than our small country, and I do wonder, really, if the American Negro is actually so concerned about the problems in Africa. I wonder whether he is not more interested in his own pay-packet and his own conditions.

"It does seem that possibly there are more votes to be garnered by staying home and helping to solve one's own problems than there are to be gained by coming here and lecturing us on ours."

The smile became a grin.

"Or does that seem farfetched?"

REBUKE FOR LOWER COURTS BY JUDGE (Rand Daily Mail, *English*) . . . *Cape Town—A sentence of six cuts imposed by a Beaufort West magistrate on a 10-year-old Coloured boy for the theft of 10 empty soft-drink bottles valued at 25¢ was set aside by a full bench of the Supreme Court in Cape Town yesterday.*

The boy received the cuts.

The matter came to the attention of the Supreme Court on review of the conviction and sentence to a reform school of a 15-year-old boy who was accused with the boy.

Mr. Justice J. H. Steyn said that corporal punishment was too frequently used by magistrates as a "wonder remedy" to correct criminal tendencies.

"Corporal punishment is a weapon in the hands of the courts. It is also a weapon that ought not to be used indiscriminately.

"Magistrates are as aware as this court is that the imposition of strokes, even juvenile strokes applied by an official of the police, cannot be compared in severity with the chastisement administered by a father or teacher.

"Even a father realises that corporal punishment must be administered moderately and only when necessary.

"This court, therefore, appeals to the lower courts not to impose corporal punishment on juvenile first-offenders, particularly in view of the fact that such sentences are not subject to automatic review."

The judge said that magistrates should consider the placing of such offenders under the care of probation officers, as provided for in law.

GEOGRAPHY

The greater part of South Africa has an average elevation of over four thousand feet, both the weather and the climate being profoundly affected by the elevation of its land surface. In general appearance South Africa has been likened to an inverted saucer, with high escarpments rising steeply on the east and southeast and sloping gradually to the semidesert plains of the west coast. In other words, South Africa is composed of a vast interior plateau system, the great escarpments surrounding the system comprising such well-known ranges as the Drakensberg, Stormberg, Nieuwveld, Komsberg, Roggeveld, Bokkeveld, and Kamiesberg. Based upon elevation, there are four well-defined areas:

(a) The Coastal Belt which varies in width from three to thirty miles with an average elevation of five hundred to six hundred feet above sea level.

(b) The Little Karoo, also known as the Southern Karoo, a tableland about fifteen miles in width, separated from the Coastal Belt by the Langeberg and Outeniqua ranges, with an average elevation of fifteen hundred feet.

(c) The Great Karoo, separated from the Little Karoo by the Swartberg and Suurberg ranges, with an average elevation of two thousand to three thousand feet.

(d) The Highveld of the Free State and Transvaal, ranging from four thousand to six thousand feet in elevation. Parts of Johannesburg, the "Golden City" of the Transvaal and the largest city in the Republic, are six thousand feet above sea level.

—Official Sources

"I EXPECT you thought you would find us a very backward little country," said the Attorney-General of the Transvaal, an English-speaker grown old in the civil service, white-haired, ruddy-cheeked, enormously mustachioed. "But I can tell you we're not. Ha! We had our first kidnapping last week. We're getting as modern as the best of you!

"Yes, I decide who will be prosecuted in these native cases, I have a good bit of authority. My job is to see that the law applies equally to all, and that's what I try to do. The state pays for a lawyer if a man doesn't have one, and I see to that, particularly in a case where there's likely to be a death sentence.

"We haven't had any real sabotage since the Rivonia trial, when they caught a number of Communist conspirators in a Johannesburg suburb, but we keep busy on lots of other things. Ho, ho, ho, yes! We keep busy. . . .

"The native is a problem, because he is so easily inflamed by drink. To insult his mother is a deadly affront and cause for battle. To trample on his foot, or knock over his beer—that is particularly serious, no matter how innocently it may be done.

"His emotions are right on the surface, you know, he never stops to think. He strikes out instinctively with whatever he has at hand. Frequently it's a knife, and then there's trouble.

"But as a matter of fact, if you train them well and keep an eye on them, you can get quite a bit of work done, actually.

"You have to know when to be lenient, when to be strict. After all, you can't be lenient all the time, can you?"

SOME ACCUSED REJECT LEGAL AID SCHEME (Cape Times, *English*) . . . *The Government's new scheme to provide legal defence for persons accused of political offences is being met with suspicion by some accused.*

As a result a number of political accused, particularly in regional courts, have preferred to do without legal representation rather than accept lawyers appointed on their behalf.

Mr. N. C. Masters, Attorney-General of the Eastern Cape, where most political trials have been held and where the new scheme is already in operation, said yesterday that not all political accused who could not afford their own defence made use of the opportunity now provided by the State.

"The suspicion which apparently exists [against White lawyers] *is totally unwarranted," Mr. Masters said. . . .*

"WE ARE DOING our best to help them," said the tall, rangy old Afrikaner, permanent civil service undersecretary for Bantu Administration. "We're trying to decentralize industry to the areas where the normal labor force lives, just as you are doing, as Britain and Italy are doing, in fact as all industrial states are doing presently. We admit it has its difficulties, but we are trying to place industries where the labor is. . . .

"Our policy when it is necessary to remove Bantu from a given area, for reasons of a separate development, or under the Group Areas Act that permits the Government to move and consolidate racial units?

"Whenever we take land from them," he said firmly, in his heavily accented English, "we give them compensating land. We pay them in cash and allow them to purchase equally good land in other areas."

(*"Ask them why they won't allow Africans to have freehold of land,"* the exiled black Communist had said in London. *"Why do they make us lease it for thirty years instead of allowing us to purchase? What sort of stability can a man feel, what sort of business can he create, when he knows his land may be arbitrarily taken away from him at any moment on somebody else's whim?"*)

"In the process of negotiating this exchange," the weathered Afrikaner said, "the Bantu are always consulted. It is never forced upon them. The individual doesn't get title in the reserves because it is tribal custom for the chief to hold all the land and he in turn distributes it to them. So the chief makes the allotments, it is their tribal custom. . . . If they wish to farm, we state that they need a minimum of so many acres. . . .

"We are doing everything we can to build them up. In the Transkei, the first native state we've set up, they have six government departments. Yes, you will say white civil servants are working with them and are really administering the country, but it is our policy to build a black staff, to replace the Whites as soon as possible. We work with them very closely, we guide them as closely as we can, we give them constant advice.

"We have agricultural colleges, universities, trade schools. In Durban there's a medical school for Bantu and Indians." A note of pride came into his voice. "There are over one hundred Bantu medical practitioners in the Republic. There are over four hundred trained Bantu in agriculture in the Transkei alone. We have special schools for the sons of chiefs and headmen, we give them special training in agriculture, in administration. . . .

"When we set up a plan for an area, it is not put into effect unless the people themselves approve. We grant money on a rand-for-rand basis. If they come to us with a plan and say, It's going to cost ten thousand rand, we say we will match it, rand-for-rand.

"The Bantu is always attended to and looked after. That is our policy. We are doing it every day."

AREA

In size the Republic is 472,359 square miles or 5¼ times the size of Great Britain, and larger than Germany, France, Italy and Portugal put together.

The Republic consists of four provinces of which the Cape Province covers an area of 278,465 square miles, the Transvaal 110,450 square miles, Orange Free State 49,866 square miles and Natal 33,578 square miles.

South-West Africa, which is administered by the Republic of South Africa, has an area of 317,725 square miles.

Because of the configuration of the country, South Africa has no

navigable rivers. The two most important rivers are the Orange River
with its tributary, the Vaal, and the Limpopo which both drain the interior plateau. The Orange River, with a catchment area of some 261,-
000 square miles, is South Africa's longest river, discharging its waters
into the Atlantic Ocean on the west coast. The Limpopo drains the
bushveld area of Transvaal and discharges into the Indian Ocean
through Portuguese East Africa. Some 300 miles from its mouth, the
Orange River goes over a fall of some 400 feet at Aughrabies and there
is a series of rapids in the river lower down.

A number of rivers rise on the escarpment or watershed and mainly
flow into the Indian Ocean. None are navigable for more than a few
miles, and they are frequently shut off by sandbars where they enter the
sea.

—Official Sources

"THE AFRIKANERS are a very serious people," the American diplomat said, "very little sense of humor, very defensive. They
mounted a really impressive military display at their recent Republic Festival, on the fifth anniversary of their leaving the Commonwealth." He
shook his head in a rather puzzled fashion, thoughtfully scanning the
Johannesburg *Star*'s headlines on the latest State Department condemnation of apartheid. "They seem to be quite touchy."

"The Indians are a very strange people," the Afrikaner said, glancing
at the *Cape Times'* headlines on the latest Government drive to resettle
Indians outside the city limits of Durban. "Very odd, very exclusive,
very separate. They have no sense of humor. Very sensitive. They are an
odd people."

DISTANCES BETWEEN PRINCIPAL TOWNS

From Johannesburg to Cape Town 906, Port Elizabeth 693, East
London 636, Durban 411, Kimberley 295, Bloemfontein 265, Pretoria
36, Lourenço Marques [Mozambique] 384, Belt Bridge 344, Bulawayo
[Rhodesia] 551, Salisbury [Rhodesia] 714, Windhoek [South-West
Africa] 1,263.

From Cape Town to Bloemfontein 641, Durban 1,074, East London
695, Kimberley 625, Port Elizabeth 497, Windhoek 979.

From Durban to Bloemfontein 433, East London 371, Port Elizabeth
639, Kimberley 509, Lourenço Marques 453, Windhoek 1,505.

—Official Sources

Two favorite Bantu crop up frequently in South African conversation with the visitor.

The first is "an old farmer named George"—or Jim or John—"in the Eastern Transvaal"—or the Orange Free State, or Natal, or the Cape. "He lives on the farm of a friend of mine, and after a while my friend said to him, 'George, you've been a hard worker and loyal to me, so I'm going to give you some land of your own.' So he gave him about two morgen a year for several years until George had quite a good-sized farm, for a Bantu. I was out there visiting my friend recently, and seeing old George (or Jim or John), I asked him, 'George, what's your biggest problem now that you're farming on your own?' He answered me without a moment's hesitation, 'My biggest problem, Baas, are these no-good lazy Bantu I have to hire as farm labor.' " (Laughter.)

The other favorite Bantu is also named George—or Joe or Henry— and he too works on a farm in the Transvaal/O.F.S./Cape or Natal. This old George—or Henry or Joe—also works for "a friend of mine." "After he had worked for him for a couple of years, my friend said, 'George, I'm going to give you two more rand a week for doing such a good job.' George promptly became very indignant and quit. 'But what's the matter?' my friend asked. 'If I'm that good,' George said, 'why didn't you pay me that much money to begin with?' " (Laughter.)

I met these two everywhere.

CAPITALS

According to Section 23 of the new Constitution, Pretoria is the seat of the Government of the Republic and according to Section 27, Cape Town is the seat of the Legislature of the Republic.

—Official Sources

I was taken through another crisp smoke-filled morning to the headquarters of the Republic's military command. The big brick buildings are out a little from the center of Pretoria, set back in neatly kept grounds.

Strapping young Afrikaners ushered me down halls ringing with the crack of boots and the rattle of rifles. There was an air of quiet efficiency, not afraid.

My host was not afraid either. A small, compact, solid Afrikaner with intelligent eyes, a cautious manner, a brief but pleasant smile, he bade me sit down beside him at a big, round, oaken table and went immediately into his argument:

"I think I can honestly say that for the first time since the end of the Anglo-Boer War, the Afrikaans nation feels threatened. We think this threat comes from our fellow-states in Africa, and we feel that it comes from the United States, which is the only power strong enough to support a UN action against us.

"Our neighbor states we think we can handle, but we know we could not withstand a determined assault by the United States. For the first time since 1902, we feel threatened."

He paused and then resumed in a thoughtful tone, his eyes far away.

"I think, however," he said softly, "that we have established a reasonable deterrent. We have our regular nine months of training for our young men, with a refresher period of two weeks each year over a three-year period. We have our active civilian reserve force. We have a professional force of about 16,000. We have in the defense forces at present about 17,412 Europeans, 6,060 Bantu, 2,648 Coloureds and one Asiatic.

"We are spending very substantial sums, for us. As compared with almost 46,000,000 rand—about $64,000,000—spent in the fiscal year 1960–61 on defense, in the fiscal year 1964–65 we spent 232,000,000 rand, or almost $325,000,000. [The rand is valued at $1.40, U.S.]

"Our professional force, as I say, is now about 16,000, compared with 9,109 in 1960. Our civilian citizen force, which consisted of about 2,000 men annually receiving two months' training in 1960, is up to almost 17,000 annually receiving nine months' training. Our entire commando organization increased from 48,281 officers and men during 1960 to 51,847 officers and men at present. We are also developing air commandos making use of light private aircraft to provide air support, principally in scouting and spotting activities. We are adding new craft to our navy and both buying and building new airplanes, items which are classified but which I can assure you"—and he smiled again—"are not being neglected in our planning.

"In addition to new jet-fighters and naval craft that we are either now manufacturing ourselves or will soon be manufacturing, we will also shortly be making about 140 different types of ammunition and bombs. We are now capable of manufacturing the whole range of infantry weapons and armor plate equal to the best quality produced anywhere in the world.

"The outside world has pushed us," he said dryly, "and we have responded. The outside world should not be surprised."

The smile faded and he spoke without bluster or guile, absolutely matter-of-fact, obviously meaning every word of it:

"Of course in the event of serious attack, we would arm everyone,

young men, old men, women. Boys of twelve could fire a rifle, and we
would give them rifles. The whole nation would rise, and I think I can
say with certainty that our English-speaking brethren would fight with
us.

"All of us in South Africa," he said quietly, "will fight to the death in
defense of our white way of life."

There was a knock on the door, his aide entered with the inevitable tea
which Britain has left behind her around the world, and which in South
Africa is as unvarying and pleasant a custom as it is in London.

When he resumed speaking it was in a more relaxed tone.

"We think, in relation to our neighbor African states, that we have
established a sufficient deterrent to stop any adventuring. Our problem
might rather lie in the realm of infiltration over the border. The isolated
farmer and his family might get chopped, we would have to be prepared
for that. But no other African nation has a military establishment re-
motely comparable to ours. We could go through them like a knife
through butter from the Cape to Cairo and they know it. They do not
worry us.

"The United States," he said soberly, "is another matter. You will find
many of our people deeply disturbed about your country. But here, too,
we think we have a deterrent, for we do not think the task would be easy
for you. We would fight until no one was left. It would be drawn out, it
would be frightful, it would waste much of your substance as well as
ours. It would not be easy.

"We hope these things will not come, will not be necessary. We have
no designs on any other country—obviously if we did, now having the
strength, we would be about it. We just want to be left alone but we are
fearful we will not be. For the first time in half a century we feel threatened and that is why we are building up."

REPUBLIC BECOMING A MARITIME NATION (Cape Times,
English) . . . *In a world rumbling with angry threats of trade sanctions
against South Africa—even though they are more emotional wishful-
thinking than serious threats—it is very understandable that recently
South Africa has quietly and purposefully been enlarging her maritime
fleet.*

*The recent crippling strike of British seamen was, almost certainly, an
added inducement for South Africa to acquire, build and sail more of her
own vessels.*

*We may not be thought of as a nation of sea-goers, but, for many
years, efficient coastal and fishing fleets have plied the home waters. Now
the steps the Republic's shipping industry is taking to expand its fleet and*

to train and attract men to build, maintain and run them are quite impressive.

In the yards of Cape Town and Durban, shipbuilding and ship-repairing, which are long-established industries, gather momentum with the accelerated construction of tugs, tankers and coasters and with far-sighted plans for the building of larger ocean-going vessels.

In Durban, one old-established firm of shipbuilders is at work on a huge 28-acre site, on which will rise foundries, machine shops and slipways, capable of building and launching ocean-going vessels of up to 15,000 tons. It is estimated that in two to three years' time this project will employ over 2,000 people.

Close by, at the head of Durban Bay, the huge sheds and skeletal structures of yet another mammoth shipbuilding project grow rapidly against the skyline. Work goes on apace at a 100-foot slipway which will accommodate ships of up to 30,000 tons.

In the Cape, in addition to existing shipyards already working to capacity on small vessels and repairs to craft of all types and sizes, plans for yet another vast shipbuilding enterprise have been carefully explored and may well come to fruition later this year. . . .

MERCHANT SHIPPING

The South African merchant fleet has expanded significantly during the last few years. This expansion has been due almost entirely to the growth of one company in particular, the South African Marine Corporation Ltd. New vessels added to this company's fleet are specializing in specific cargoes, particularly fruit, pig iron and sugar.

In 1939, South Africa's whole mercantile fleet, ocean-going as well as coasters, measured only 22,000 tons. The fleet consisted of 16 coasters, operated by seven companies, with a total tonnage of approximately 7,000 tons and three deep-sea ships owned by the South African Railways and Harbours Administration. During World War II, this small fleet suffered heavy losses.

South Africa now has 57 registered ships of more than 100 tons in the merchant marine service. Total tonnage is 201,386. The combined gross tonnage of the foreign-going vessels represents 82 per cent of the total.

—Official Sources

"A ND DO YOU not have a similar problem with your Indians?" they
asked politely at the lovely Afrikaner home with its Franz Hals
originals, expensive furniture and beautiful drapes. "Do you not keep
them on reservations, and are they not ignorant and difficult to train?"

I said that, yes, many were on reservations, but they were given education, many voted, and many of the younger ones went away to college
and didn't come back but went on to make their way in the general
society. The smiles were polite but skeptical.

"How is your integration program coming?"

I said that it was working fairly well, that in many areas school integration was coming along with reasonable smoothness.

"And what do you do when standards are lowered because black children are studying with white children?"

I said that the hope was that the standards for all could gradually be
raised rather than lowered, and that in some places it was not the problem many white parents at first had feared.

"But do not some of your loudest supporters of integration take their
children out of integrated schools and put them in private white
schools?"

I said, yes, they did.

"Well."

There was a silence and the talk turned presently to other things. But
inevitably it came back, and our host related some incident he had heard
involving a Bantu who didn't have his pass-book and the problems he
had in getting home that night and how worried his wife was before it
was all straightened out; and everybody laughed in a comfortable what-
can-you-expect-of-them way.

And our host, feeling expansive and warm after the coffee and brandy,
chuckled suddenly and remarked,

"Wouldn't it be hell to be black?"

And everybody smiled and chuckled and nodded agreement; and presently, remembering things in their country and mine, fell still.

THE ANGER OF BEKKERSDAL . . . by STANLEY MOTJUWADI
*(Bantu Reporter, Rand Daily Mail, English) . . . For a typical South
African like me to sit up and think seriously, something most unusual has
to happen, like an eminently respectable gentleman roaring marine epi-
thets, and a prim, matronly minister's wife prancing about, wiggling her
bottom, ululating and chanting war cries.*

And when such things happen in a drowsy little dorp like Bekkersdal, on the far West Rand, it's as certain as I haven't a vote that this is material for reflection.

Normally the people of Bekkersdal, a township outside Westonaria, go about their unexciting little lives unexcitedly. But they had a meeting last weekend which was the stormiest affair I've witnessed since the A.N.C. [African National Congress] *and P.A.C.* [Pan African Congress] *were banned.*

The common—and unrehearsed—cry of the people at that meeting was that they had not been consulted when the local bus company increased its fares by 1 cent a single journey.

Tactful pleading, coaxing, cajoling and smooth talk in other categories by the Advisory Board men could not stop the roars and the war cries. Nor could threats; and the meeting ended in confusion with the most unlikely people shouting bus-boycott slogans.

Outside the hall I picked out a bent and wrinkled old woman, obviously a political novice, and asked her what it was all about.

"They should have talked to us first," she snapped. "Who do they think they are? If they want to change something to do with us, then they must discuss it with us."

I was stunned at such big talk from what looked like a meek old girl.

I was tempted to ask her if she was ever consulted before some piece of legislation meant for her safety and advancement was introduced in Parliament. But the atmosphere was so tense I had to be discreet and let my curiosity go unquenched.

Still, I couldn't help wondering what on earth had shaken these easy-going people out of their lethargy. Money, I know, means a lot to people who go through life without much of it. But I wasn't convinced that this mob's anger arose from any high regard for a cent. Because many of those who had been trudging four miles to work every day for four weeks were too tired at the end of a day to put in any overtime, so financially they were losing much more. And those who went by taxi paid double the bus fare without a murmur.

I braced myself and confronted a burly fellow.

"Look, chum," he bellowed, pounding his barrel chest, "if you're doing business with someone, wouldn't you have a word with him before putting your price up, even to soften him up?"

Then he pounded his chest again and shook his fist at me. With the little dignity I could muster I scuttled for the safety of my Press car.

I made up my mind to forget the burly man. But I couldn't forget that bent old woman who insisted she had every reason to be piqued for not having been consulted.

And it occurred to me that some day I, too, might demand that I be consulted.

Come to think of it, why shouldn't I be?

"**I** HAVE TRAVELED to the States and then spent some time in London on the way back," the professor said. "I returned to this country and this people, and I wondered:

"Here is this Afrikaner nation, defeated in war—ground down to nothing—revived despite great adversity—filled with courage and with spirit—possessed of a great tradition. But how does it feel to be constantly criticized by the rest of the world, to feel that the outside world is constantly against us? What is it doing to us inside? I wonder. I wonder how long we can stand it psychologically, the feeling of isolation and criticism. We have been alone before, as a people, but then it was only the British we had to contend with. Now it is all of you. What will it do to us as time passes? How will we stand it?"

Remember the day you discovered champagne . . . that's SOUTH AFRICA.

Suddenly, you've found the good life your taste commands. A little bit heady at first—but your senses adjust quickly to the bouquet of jacarandas; the brilliance of stark sunlight and more stars than astronomers can count. Then the feeling of sheer, unadulterated comfort in company with people who speak your language and enjoy the prosperity of the most Western republic east of Greenwich. . . .

—South Africa Tourist Corporation

CONSTITUTION AND GOVERNMENT

On May 31, 1961, the Republic of South Africa came into being. On the same date, the Republic of South Africa ceased to be a member of the British Commonwealth, but remained a member of the sterling area.

The head of the Republic is the State President, who discharges the ceremonial functions formerly discharged by the British Governor-General. He exercises legal powers, including the power to declare war and make peace, on the advice of the Government.

The legislative power of the Republic is vested in the Parliament, which consists of the State President, the Senate and the House of Assembly. There shall be a session of Parliament once at least in every year.

Parliament is the sovereign legislative authority in and over the Republic, and has full power to make laws for peace, order and good government of the Republic. The party having a majority of seats in the House of Assembly elects the Prime Minister from its ranks.

Since the Union of South Africa in 1910, there have been only seven
Prime Ministers: General Louis Botha (1910–1919), General J. C.
Smuts (1919–1924 and 1939–1948), General J. B. M. Hertzog (1924–
1939); Dr. D. F. Malan (1948–1954), Advocate J. G. Strijdom (1954–
1958), Dr. H. F. Verwoerd (1958–1966), Advocate B. J. Vorster
(1966–   ).

—Official Sources

B IG, TALL, loose-limbed, rangy, an open, professionally candid face,
glasses, an amiable smile, a manner smooth as butter behind the
facade of relaxed, unworried friendliness: General Van Den Burgh, interned as pro-German by the Smuts Government in World War Two,
head of the Special Branch in the Nationalist Government today.

"Perhaps I should just review this whole situation for you," he said,
lolling back comfortably, "so that you can understand our problem from
its origins.

"Around 1920–21, Communism in this country had a membership
composed of Whites only. Then they found they could make no headway
with the Whites, so they switched to the Blacks.

"Presently they formed the African National Congress. It was originally a fine organization, formed primarily to improve the conditions of
the Africans. But before long it became infiltrated by the Communists, so
that presently the secretary-general of the A.N.C. was trained in Moscow, though the rank-and-file were not aware of this, or of how deeply it
was infiltrated.

"So, in the same fashion"—and he paused to shift position a little,
swing one leg loosely over the other—"the Springbok Legion was formed
after the Second World War to look after the returned soldier. But here,
too, the Communists took over. Presently the 'Torch Commando' was
formed. Most people believed it was not Communist, but it never seemed
to see anything wrong with Communism.

"Then in 1948 the Nationalist Government came to power, as you
know, and in 1950 the Communist Party was declared illegal. By that
time the Communists had taken over the African National Congress, the
Indian Congress, the Coloured Congress.

"Supported by certain newspapers"—and he did not name them, but
from that certain tone the Afrikaner gets when he considers the opposition, it was obvious they must have been English-language—"a 'Congress of Democrats' was formed. On its executive were eleven listed
Communists—which means, with us, that we list them officially as Communists when we have final proof; two known Communists, known by
associations and actions; and two suspected Communists.

"So you can see"—he smiled—"that all was not as it should have been with the so-called Congress of Democrats.

"In 1960, therefore, the 'Congress of Democrats' was declared illegal. But there were a few acts of sabotage as time went on, the Sharpville incident, which was Communist-inspired and which the Communists still use against us in the outside world, the Rivonia ring which was smashed. The 'Pan-African Congress' was formed, the 'Umkhonto we Sizwe,' or 'Spear of the Nation'—100 per cent Communist, the aim to rid South Africa of the white man. Its members were, and are, taught all about sabotage. Many have been trained in Peking, Algiers, Russia, Ethiopia.

"However," he said, with a comfortable pride, "the Security Branch was able to penetrate the Communist network and picked up most of the people involved. It is charged against us that we have a network of informers, but what kind of charge is that? Of course we do: we would not be able to do our work without a large and loyal body of Bantu in this country. This is life and death for us, it is not a game. We use informers as any security agency anywhere uses informers, to find out what we have to know to protect our country. So let them talk about 'informers.' It does not disturb us!

"In any event," he said, calmly again, "April 8, 1963, was the date they had chosen for so-called liberation from the white man. They intended to murder at least a thousand white leaders over the entire country. But then we moved in on them and it collapsed. Most of the Whites fled to England, as did some of the Blacks. Others went to the other African states. Perhaps you have talked to some of them?"

"In London, and Washington, yes. Some have come to us."

"They are interesting people," he said thoughtfully. "They actually thought they could overturn this Afrikaner nation. How little they know us."

"Or you them, perhaps."

"They are very different," he said, still thoughtfully. "Very. . . . Well, some escaped, as I said, others we took and now have imprisoned, principally on Robben Island off Cape Town. A large section of course was not militant and they have come over to us and given up all activity.

"With the life sentencing of the attorney Bram Fischer—Abram Fischer, who was a senior advocate in Johannesburg, became a Communist, worked with the A.N.C. and Umkhonto we Sizwe, jumped bail last year and was picked up ten months later—I think militant Communism in South Africa has come to a stop. Quite a number of nonmilitant, nonsubversive Communists remain, but we know who they are and they do not worry us. They are not sophisticated saboteurs."

His tone became patronizing and a little amused as he ticked them off:

"Members of the Liberal Party, the National Union of South African

Students which represents the students in our English-speaking universities—some of the faculty members, some of those who work for the English-language newspapers—they are annoying, but"—he smiled—"we
don't really have to worry about them.

"In other words, while militant action is licked, Communism as such
in South Africa is not licked. But as long as they are not militant and do
not commit sabotage, no police action will be taken.

"Anyhow, there is really no basis on which militant Communism can
operate, now. Basically, the native is a capitalist, he isn't a Communist.
He doesn't want to share with anyone, he wants his own land and his
own life. In South Africa at the moment the remnant of the African
National Congress is very small, no more than 2 to 5 per cent of our
native population.

"The African, after all," he said as he stood up and held out a confident hand, "appreciates what is being done for him by the Government,
and what the Government wants to do for him in the future."

SOUTH AFRICAN WAY OF LIFE

Biltong and *braaivleis* are reminders of the pioneering days when
meat, and preferably the meat of wild game, was dried out so that it
could be carried as *biltong* in the ox-wagons which served as the pioneers' homes. At outspan fresh meat was grilled on an open fire, known
as *braaivleis;* but this word is now used for festive occasions and even
for official functions held out of doors when meat is grilled over the
open fire.

—Official Sources

For a man in the rather interesting position of an Afrikaner opposing separate development, Dr. N. J. Rhoodie of the University of
Pretoria seemed very chipper this particular day. He is very chipper anyway, small, bright-eyed, quick-spoken, outspoken.

"This concept of separate units without geophysical states is nonsense," he said flatly. "Our problem can only be settled on a radical basis
of geopolitical separation. This mutual division of interests can only be
decided by actual separation—by partition.

"The trouble with the Whites in this country," he said in some disgust,
"is that we never had it so good. We have never been confronted with the
problem in its naked sense, we have managed to push it aside or argue
around it. But it is becoming more than an academic matter.

"Oh, the Government is doing a wonderful job of trying to get the influx of Bantu into reverse gear—we have approximately 600,000 in the mines and industries now. The $64,000 question, though, is whether the economic mechanism in the proposed Bantu territories can be synchronized and made to work.

"Twenty years ago, I grant you, it was possible for a White minority to keep the Bantu majority down, but now the whole idea of a minority dominating a majority is antiquated and completely out of date. It's an unhealthy situation to have your people sharing a country with a group which is numerically superior. The only solution is to separate them entirely, to partition the country so that each group will have its own entirely distinct area."

"Would the Whites actually stand for breaking up the country that way?"

"Will they stand for the Bantustans, if they're actually put into effect elsewhere than the Transkei?"

"I have my doubts there, too," I said. "In any event, supposing you did try partition, who would select the areas the Bantu would have, and how would you, how could you, be sure they would have a fair share?"

"We would have to negotiate with the Bantu nations. It would be very difficult, I grant you. But geophysical partition is the only long-term solution, and I think it could be done because I think the Afrikaner people would welcome it, once they were convinced of its practical necessity.

"The Afrikaner also wants his own exclusive area, you know," he said with a quick birdlike smile. "He doesn't like to have to share anything with anyone else. The Afrikaner is a peculiar person. You in the outside world tend to forget the depth of Afrikaner nationalism."

"I don't think I'll ever forget it. How are you getting along with the English section these days?"

The smile increased.

"I am not advocating partition for them, though I am sure some of my fellow Afrikaners might like to see it. Seriously, bilingualism is increasing apace. The Afrikaner knows English is his bridge to the outside world. Without English, we would be white barbarians. . . .

"What I am saying in advocating partition for the Bantu is simply this: if you really believe in separate development, you should have the courage of your convictions. You can't sit on two chairs at once. If it can't work, then have the guts to discard it and go to some form of integration. If it can work, then go all the way—to partition."

"Do you find much support for that in Government circles?"

"It's being talked about," he said. "There's some thinking being done."

"But no sign of official endorsement."

"Not yet," he said cheerfully. "But the imperatives of the geophysical facts will help in due time."

SYMPOSIUM ON PARTITION (Sunday Times, *Johannesburg, English*) . . . *The move by a group of younger English-speaking South Africans to accelerate South Africa towards a form of partition is to be carried a stage further* (*they aim at "incorporating positive aspects of Government policy while eliminating the worst aspects, in a pattern which will recognise liberal values"*).

An all-day symposium on "Partition: an English-speaking point of view" will be held at the University of Natal, Durban, on August 27. . . .

A statement issued by the organisers says: "By formulating a fresh point of view on partition as a positive course in race relations, and in insisting on the recognition of liberal values in its implementation, the group looks forward to joining forces with those Afrikaners of similar mind, to acting as a catalyst on Afrikaner intellectuals and to engaging English-speaking South Africans more positively in our national life."

REFERENDUM TO ESTABLISH A REPUBLIC

The result of the [white] referendum held on October 5, 1960, was as follows:

	FOR A REPUBLIC	AGAINST A REPUBLIC
Cape	271,418	269,784
Transvaal	406,632	325,041
Natal	42,299	135,598
Free State	110,171	33,438
South-West Africa	19,938	12,017
Totals	850,458	775,878

Majority in favour of a Republic: 74,580. Total votes cast: 1,633,572. Number of voters who did not vote: 167,376.

—Official Sources

TRIM, QUICK, white hair, handsome dark eyes, distinguished head, upright carriage—the high officer of the Dutch Reformed Church welcomed me to his modest, pleasant home and told me how liberal South Africa's dominant and virtually all-powerful religion is toward its black children.

"Ever since the Dutch Reformed Church started doing missionary work with the Hottentots in 1652," he said in his swift English, somewhat less accented than that of many of his fellow Afrikaners, "we have felt a special solemn responsibility to bring the gospel to the savages. Originally, all converts were added to the white congregation, but from the beginning of course there was always a fixed caste system as between master and servant, so naturally that began immediately to affect the church.

"Servants usually just by habit sat in the back rows. There was never any special fuss made about it, it was just the way things were done. It really was not until the mid-nineteenth century that the problem was discussed at the synod level."

He paused and gave me a candid, level glance.

"I don't want to belabor this," he said with a smile, "I just want you to understand that it was nothing new, that it developed naturally out of the history of Afrikanerdom."

"I think I understand your point."

"Good. Well, it was discussed, as I say, in the mid-nineteenth century and it was decided to simply give formal stature to the practice that history itself had created. In 1857 the synod decided to allow separate congregations and let Coloured and Bantu members worship in separate groups. But it was no deep-seated racial feeling—the church acknowledges there can be no separation in the Body of Christ—but for practical reasons—and because some members did object to combined congregations—it was thought best to have separate congregations.

"This, as you realize, was long, long before the concept of apartheid, of separate development, was born."

"I understand."

"When the white settlers met the Bantu as the Bantu pushed down from Central Africa and the Whites pushed east and north from the Cape, there was no question of any black problem at all. It was simply a matter of raiding cattle and farms on the black side, and of self-preservation on the white side. Then in time, as peace came and the frontier was pacified, the Bantu were accepted as the responsibility of the Whites in a master-servant relationship. The Bantu came into the family circle at prayer-time, and they still do on many farms in the Transvaal and the Orange Free State. The father reads the Bible, they all sing, then the Bantu return to complete their work. But in formal congregations, it was, as I say, decided by the synod in 1857 that there should be separate congregations—not because of any apartheid, but simply as history dictated—"

"Yes, I do understand."

"—and in the early 1900's the principle was reaffirmed when the Coloured members asked that they be allowed to have a separate service at 3 P.M., simply because it was not convenient for them, with their working schedules, to meet at the same hours the Whites did, at 10:30 A.M. or 7 P.M. Thus again, it was simply a natural historical development—"

"Yes, you do make it clear."

"—which has gradually determined the form of our church, our congregations and our services. Today we have a number of independent Bantu and Coloured churches, still served by European missionaries under European leadership. But we are all one family, all one church with separate governing bodies, the Mother Church and the daughter churches, one in the Body of Christ, together.

"Now," he said, and his tone became more businesslike and also more amused, "there is one other matter you may hear about from some of our English friends, and perhaps even from some of our own people when in a critical mood, and that is that the Dutch Reformed Church is all the time involved in politics and is simply an arm of the Government. Some people like to refer to us sometimes as the 'agter-ryer' of the Government—'the after-rider,' the servant who came behind with his master's belongings on commando in the Anglo-Boer War, where the term originated. They say that is why we have developed separate congregations, ignoring all this historical development I have just explained to you.

"As you now know, that charge is not true. And furthermore, there is not such a big difference between us and the other churches in South Africa. The Anglican Church and the Catholic Church and the others may say, 'All races, all services, all times,' but in practice it doesn't work out very well, and you find them forced more and more into separation. We in the D.R.C. accept the principle that separate congregations are better, simply because people's needs are different.

"You see," he said, and he leaned forward earnestly as his charming wife brought tea, "you've got to adapt your approach in the ministry to the level of understanding of the people you are serving. You can't be expected to preach in hundreds of tribal dialects to a mixed congregation of Whites and Blacks. And in any event, one doesn't know what they are thinking. A European can't bring the message of Christ to non-Europeans in a way they will understand. Only their own people can do that.

"We have to take cognizance of overall practical considerations. It is just not practical to try to bring them into our white congregations. We say they are our wards. We have a very serious responsibility—we are their guardians."

He stopped to drink his tea and as he did so his wife spoke with a gently sad smile.

"And yet I wonder," she said, "whether we do enough. I wonder whether we open our hearts enough, and whether theirs are not becoming hardened against us. I wonder whether we really do all that Christians should do to make them brothers in the service of Christ. I wonder, and it worries me."

RC BISHOPS HIT AT RACIALISM (Cape Times, *English*) . . . *The Roman Catholic bishops of South Africa, in a joint pastoral letter released yesterday, have declared that the Christian conscience required a re-examination of the whole question of race relationships in the Republic.*

The letter was approved at a plenary session of the Southern African Catholic bishops' conference in Pretoria, under the chairmanship of Cardinal McCann, of Cape Town.

The conference was attended by 31 Roman Catholic bishops from the Republic, South-West Africa, Basutoland, Bechuanaland and Swaziland and included Archbishop Garner, of Pretoria, and Archbishop Hurly, of Durban. . . .

The letter says that the decrees of the Vatican Council "will be our norm of action for many years to come."

It states also that:

—The natural right of free association among men cannot be taken away on racial grounds, on the pretext that such association will damage the common good;

—Racial discrimination is vigorously condemned and must be eradicated as contrary to God's intent.

—It is a grave violation of the dignity of the human person to prevent anyone, on grounds of race or nationality, from choosing his own mode of living, to restrict his choice of employment, the right of free movement, his place of residence, his free establishment of a family.

—Any system of migratory labour involving the enforced separation of husband and father from wife and children over a long period is not only unjust, but must result in grave injury to the community as a whole.

The letter, calling for a reexamination of racial relationships in the light of Christian conscience, urges a just solution to the problem through the cooperation of all Christian communities and persons.

And it says its message is offered "in a spirit of humility and service, of solidarity and compassion," to the people of South Africa.

33 ANGLICAN CLERGY BACK RC BISHOPS (Cape Times, *English*) *. . . Thirty-three Anglican clergymen have signed a letter to the* Cape Times *giving their support to the 31 Roman Catholic bishops who earlier this week, in a pastoral letter, condemned apartheid.*

The Anglicans' letter appears today on page 8. Its signatories include the new Bishop-Suffragan of Cape Town, the Rt. Rev. Philip Russell, the Dean of Cape Town, the Very Rev. Edward L. King, and six canons.

The clergymen "rejoice" in the bishop's pastoral letter, and affirm that too little is being done by churches in South Africa to counteract racial discrimination.

TOTALITARIAN TENDENCY IS DEPLORED (Cape Argus, *English*) . . . *The Synod of the Cape District of the Methodist Church, meeting at Woodstock this afternoon, unanimously reaffirmed a resolution taken at the Church's last annual conference deploring a growing tendency to totalitarianism in South Africa.*

The chairman of the Synod (the Rev. D. W. Timm) said: "This is what we believe and we must shout it from the rooftops."

He said a resolution before the Synod calling on the annual conference to make representations to the Minister of Justice requesting that banned persons be given the reason for their banning or charged without delay was not strong enough.

"We want to say this as strongly as we can," he said. "We carry about a deep ache in our hearts because of it. . . ."

ARCHBISHOP HITS AT BANNINGS (Star, *Johannesburg, English*) . . . *The safety and security of the State was the first responsibility of the Government, but it was difficult to believe that when a country was not at war it was ever justifiable to use such drastic powers, said the* [Anglican] *Archbishop of Cape Town, the Most Rev. R. Selby, in his diocesan news letter for July, published in* Good Hope.

The Archbishop, who recently returned from a visit to the Holy Land and Greece, added: "During my absence from South Africa a number of persons were banned and placed under appalling restrictions which this sentence involves. A banning order ought to lead us to believe that the person banned had committed or was planning to commit some crime against the State.

"If this is in fact so, then the banned person ought to be charged and be given an opportunity of defending himself by being brought before a court of law. When no charge is laid, we are compelled to conclude that the person's only crime is that he holds views which differ from those of the Government.

"Everyone has the right to their own opinions, even when these differ from those of the Government, and it is only when these opinions can be

*shown to interfere with the security of the State that the Government has
the right to interfere."*

"KERKBODE" ON NEWS VALUES (Cape Times, *English*) . . .
*Christian South Africans must not be misled into believing that race ten-
sion, fear and distrust formed the true climate in the Republic's inter-
racial relationship, says an editorial in the latest issue of the* Kerkbode,
the official journal of the Dutch Reformed Church.

*Referring to a Press report about an African who had given his life
while trying to rescue a White man during a mine disaster, the editorial
says: "Reports such as these have no value for export to overseas countries. Some of our neo-liberal countrymen are too fond of broadcasting
stories of fear, tension, mistrust and hate on wavelengths to which the outside world listens.*

*"We do not say that we have nothing to fear in South Africa, but we
are more afraid of outside interference which is encouraged by unjust
reports. . . ."*

"WHEN ARE YOU planning to create another Bantustan?" our host
asked the Minister of Bantu Administration, his tone friendly
yet betraying a little of that uneasiness that a good many Afrikaner intellectuals feel as they contemplate the apparent disinterest of their Government in speeding up the policy of separate development to which the
intellectuals have somewhat doubtfully given their support because the
Government says it is the right thing to do.

The Minister smiled.

"In time," he said. "In time, but probably not too soon. Not too soon.
We want to give them more experience, first—give them more to do, put
more responsibility on them and see if they can handle it. It will come in
time, but not too soon, I expect.

"After all"—and he stretched comfortably in the comfortable chair, in
the comfortable home snug against the black tide always lapping, lapping, lapping just outside the stout front door—"we're going to be here
forever—and they're going to be here forever—and so we can take a
while to work out our problems together. . . . It won't be too soon."

TOP BANTU POST FOR AFRICAN (Star, *Johannesburg, English*)
*. . . An African was today appointed to one of the most senior posts in
the field of Bantu administration by the Minister, Mr. M. C. Botha.*

He is Mr. N. K. Nkademeng, who was appointed Assistant Bantu Af-
fairs Commissioner for the Hammanskraal area at a ceremony attended
by four foreign ambassadors, two Deputy Ministers and senior officials
of the Department of Bantu Administration and Development.

He is the first African to be appointed to this post in the Tswana Re-
serve. There are two other Africans who hold similar posts—in Zululand
and in the Ciskei.

An Assistant Commissioner has far-reaching powers in the area he ad-
ministers. He can try civil and criminal cases in court, allocate land, con-
sider pension applications and is in general control of administration in
his area.

Mr. Botha said: "This is the beginning of many others who will follow
as soon as trained Bantu personnel are available."

BANTU AUTHORITIES

A Bantu Tribal Authority consists of a chief or headman and a group
of councillors. The Minister of Bantu Administration may at any time
in his absolute discretion depose any chief or headman and cancel the
appointment of any councillor. The local Bantu Affairs Commissioner
may veto the proposed appointment of any councillor appointed by a
chief or headman. The Minister, the local commissioner, or their depu-
ties may at any time attend any meeting of any Bantu Tribal Authority
and intervene in its deliberations.

The Minister may also, by giving notice in the official Government
gazette, prohibit a gathering in a private home at which an African is
present if he considers the gathering undesirable from the standpoint of
the racial area in which the home is located. Any African attending
such a prohibited gathering is guilty of an offence and liable to a fine
not exceeding five rand, imprisonment not exceeding two months, or
both.

—Official Sources

"I EXPECT YOU WILL be seeing my brother-in-law," the churchman
had said, and see him I did, in the shining new offices in Pretoria
from which he seeks to protect and strengthen the cultural development
of Afrikanerdom. He is short, stocky, square-faced, dark-haired, has a
downturning mouth and frequently a rather pained, almost uncertain look
when his face is in repose. He is in his forties, deadly serious and grimly
determined to protect his people from the insidious onslaughts of everything from folk music to mini-skirts.

I asked him about his recent brush with some of the more liberal Afrikaans authors—"liberal" in the South African context being anyone who deviates in the slightest from the rigidly Calvinistic traditions of what Afrikaans politicians and press like to refer to as "Die Volk," the folk.

He smiled a small, deprecating smile and nodded his head.

"Oh, yes, there is a little controversy going on right now. There is a certain group of writers here who call themselves 'The Sixties,' very intelligent, very smart, you know. They feel they have to be very liberal, very far-out. They have tried to bring in what you might call the French influence into our literature—they're trying to promote a moral revolution, they try to be 'sexy,' if you want to use that term. They are dangerous to our ideas, in my belief and that of many others of the Afrikaner people. There is also a group of musicians and singers who are attempting to use so-called folk songs and pop music to spread their un-South African ideas."

He leaned forward earnestly.

"Now, I don't want to deny anybody the right to his point of view— but we have a right to express our point of view, too. Most of our younger people are well balanced, but a number are very leftist, and it is some of those who have joined together to form these movements. They have a right to differ, but at the same time"—his small, rather uncomfortable, almost shy laugh—"other people have a right to differ, too.

"You take apartheid," he said, somewhat abruptly. "The outside world—the West—is always calling it an ideology. We don't consider it an ideology, but a policy. We regard an ideology as something that influences a whole people's life. But we don't regard apartheid as that, at all. It is not monolithic. It is changing as we develop and as our ideas change.

"As for Bantustans, these people are not developed to the point where they can take over. The Whites still have to guide these people—help them to help themselves. You shouldn't force them too fast or hold back too much. The Transkei, for instance, has a tremendous potential, but we have to help them or they will go down the drain like the Congo."

"But how long can you help these people, that is the question. . . ."

"You know," he said, "tribal rivalries will crop out. We sometimes have to keep them from killing each other. They have yet to find a common ground; it will probably be generations before they can grow together into a unified racial group of people capable of really governing themselves. You see it all over Africa—the proof is there, in spite of all the UN's talk."

He looked thoughtful as the inevitable tea was brought in.

"They are such different people, really. A Bantu minister said to me once, 'We don't understand you Whites. If you're riding along the road and your horse stumbles and hurts his foot, you'll treat the foot. We treat the hole in the road that made him stumble.'

"That's about the sum of it, I'd say. They want to treat the hole in the road!"

NEW GROUP TO STOP RED INFILTRATION (Star, *Johannesburg, English*) . . . *A new group formed in Pretoria to stop "Communist and liberal infiltration" into Afrikaans literature will be helped in its task by a Security Branch policeman who will make a study of ideological tendencies.*

The group is the Afrikaans-Christian Culture Action. The chairman is Prof. P. F. D. Weiss, the ex-chairman of the Suid-Afrikaanse Akademie vir Wetenskap en Kuns.

Culture Action has formed nine committees to study aspects of Afrikaans cultural life and how it is being threatened. The Security man serves on its committee on ideological tendencies.

Other aspects to be studied by different committees are music and ballet, literature, films and theatre. There is also a committee for the Press and radio.

The vice-chairman, Prof. A. B. du Preez, told a recent meeting of the Afrikaanse Kulturraad in Pretoria that the biggest threat to the Afrikaaner at present was not Communism, but the attitude of aplomb and self-satisfaction which was blind to the dangers in national life. . . .

RUBBISHY RECORDS OUR RUIN—DE KLERK (Rand Daily Mail, *English*) *South Africans, because of a lack of good musical taste, fell prey to "the biggest rubbish on records," from England and America, the Minister of Education Arts and Science, Senator De Klerk, said in Pretoria on Saturday night.*

He said at the granting of official recognition to the examinations and teaching diplomas of the Pretoria Conservatoire of Music: "Trashy music from overseas is without a vestige of cultural value, totally foreign to the national character and is often even dangerous to morals and national traditions. . . ."

FOLK-SONG FANS FIGHT BACK: ALLEGATION UPSETS COFFEE-BAR SET (Sunday Times, *Johannesburg, English*) . . . *Many of Johannesburg's folk-singers and coffee-bar patrons are seriously per-*

turbed by the University of Pretoria Students' Representatives Council's attack this week that they are "subversive, Communistic and threaten the future of the Afrikaner."

Some fear that the banning of a folk-singing group on the Pretoria University campus may lead to other and more drastic steps being taken against modern folk-singers.

Die Pederby, *the university's weekly newspaper and mouthpiece of the S.R.C., says the reason for the S.R.C.'s stand is that folk-singing is a propaganda evil which is making South Africa the target of "protesting youth—the folk-singers."*

It says that folk-singing is a "monster" posing as art and is being used to further the aims of Communism. . . .

A group of Stellenbosch University students has established a "folk-singing workshop" in an old barn in the centre of Stellenbosch where they meet regularly to sing well-known South African and foreign folk-songs, including so-called protest songs.

The folk-singing workshop is well patronised by students at weekends.

The Stellenbosch folk-singers do not fear a ban such as has been imposed on singers at the University of Pretoria . . .

Mr. "Boy" Geldenhuis, chairman of the Stellenbosch University S.R.C., told me today that folk-singing was not a "problem" on the campus.

He said: "There are no folk-singing groups actually on the Stellenbosch University campus.

"If a few individuals sing this kind of objectionable song, it is not the S.R.C.'s concern or that of the university authorities."

A spokesman for the Council to Combat Communism on the Rand has condemned folk-singing, stating that in some of these songs attacks are made on the Security Police and on the 90- and 180-day laws.

The folk-sings were opposed to the traditions of the Afrikaner people, he said . . .

T HE FACE, the voice, the manner, were the face, the voice, the manner which have seen an Empire rise, an Empire fall, a Commonwealth form, a Commonwealth begin to crumble: bland, intelligent, interested, intrigued by the passing show because nowadays, old boy, that's about all a British Embassy can do, isn't it, be intrigued?

"It's all very hidden, you know? They've suppressed any possible rebellion so successfully that one doesn't know who leads it, or where they are, or indeed if there is one. Some say they're sitting on a volcano that may explode at any moment, others that there is no volcano and there won't be any explosion. I must say I agree with the latter conclusion myself . . . although one doesn't know, really, does one?"

CONSERVATIVE OUTLOOK

To illustrate the conservative outlook of the Republic in matters of finance, it may be mentioned that even inter-governmental debts to the United Kingdom, arising from World War I, were paid by the Republic when due, although Great Britain defaulted on her obligations and the moratorium provisions of 1931 would have permitted the Republic to postpone such payments.

South Africa has never requested nor received any grants from the United States Government under any of the post-war aid programmes. South Africa assisted Great Britain in 1948 with a gold loan of R160-million.

South Africa settled the whole of its Lend-Lease debt in cash—the only country in the world which has done so.

Total receipts for year ended March 31 (R million): 1961, 779.7; 1962, 787.2; 1963, 863.2; 1964, 1,000.3; 1965, 1,129.2.

—Official Sources

A TINY LITTLE DARK face, keenly intelligent, a small, stooped figure, a precise, pedantic voice—another guardian of the flame of Afrikanerdom, Dr. Pauw, president of the University of South Africa, in his office in Pretoria:

"The University," he said with an air of always choosing his words very carefully, "started in 1873, when the leaders of the Afrikaner nation determined that it was time to provide an adequate form of higher education for their children. It is presently a correspondence school, about to move to new quarters on what we consider"—he permitted himself a very small smile—"the most spectacular site in Pretoria—with an enrollment of 19,700 students, of which fifteen hundred are Bantu, eight hundred are Asiatics and five hundred are Coloured, representing all parts of the Republic and including, additionally, more than one thousand outside the country, of which twenty-eight are in the United States of America.

"Although we do not encourage foreigners to enroll in the University, we are nonetheless flattered and willing to teach them when they do, particularly when they come from such a great and erudite nation as your own."

"Yes."

"Our students," he went on serenely, "support the Government almost, I should say, 100 per cent, in its policies both domestic and foreign. You see, we are an Afrikaans university: we feel that the English section has their universities, and therefore we regard the traditional role of the University of South Africa as that of the guardian of the standards of the country."

"Does the University find itself directly involved in politics?"

"Politics?" he repeated gently, the little head swiveling around, the keen eyes peering sideways. "It is the policy that the University is an academic body. As a university it has to make provision for all sections of the people, and must stringently avoid falling into the controversies of society. The University respects each individual student but it also respects the laws and customs of society. . . .

"The staff?"—again that peering, as-from-a-cave look. "I expect it probably leans toward conservatism, but in the country as a whole, I would say we are a liberalizing influence. It is true that our staff is over 90 per cent Afrikaans-speaking, but that is simply because Afrikaans-speaking teachers seem to be more interested in academic matters than the English-speaking.

"Race is not a standard for selection of staff. In fact, I can remember only one case in which race was a deciding factor, and that was when there were two applicants for a certain position, one Afrikaans-speaking and the other English-speaking. I cast my vote for the English-speaking applicant because we wanted an English-speaking member to counter the charge that we were opposed to letting the English on our faculty.

"He has since," he said with a gentle slowness, "left us and gone to another university, where I am confident he will . . . presently . . . become . . . a professor. . . ."

NOT ENOUGH AFRIKANERS MATRICULATED (Star, *Johannesburg, English*) . . . *Because the basic subjects were being neglected at school certain important careers remained "closed" to Afrikaners when they went to university, Dr. S. M. Naude, chairman of the Council for Scientific and Industrial Research, said today.*

He was reading a paper on the task of the Suid-Afrikaanse Akademie vir Wetenskap en Kuns in the field of Natural Science at the general meeting of the Akademie at the University of Stellenbosch.

Dr. Naude said there were 442,774 children in Afrikaans schools in South Africa in 1963 of whom 14,120 were in Matric [high school]. In the same year there were 267,052 children in English schools and 10,179 of them were in Matric. A much higher percentage of the English-speaking children therefore stayed in school.

"Because the basic subjects at school are neglected certain important careers are closed to the Afrikaners when they go to the university. For instance, in 1963 only 27.4 per cent of the medical students were Afrikaans-speaking, 33.6 in engineering and 42.5 per cent of the law students.

"Other statistics also show that the position among the Afrikaners is not healthy . . ."

"**I** HAVE BEEN HERE too long in this God-damned country," the American diplomat said with a bitter smile. "I'm not objective anymore; I'm too emotionally involved with what's going on. When I see these bloody bastards with their apartheid it's all I can do to keep from screaming out loud. They're telling you all about how perfect everything is, are they? Well, I can tell you a different story and so can everybody who's got an ounce of objectivity. They're such bloody hypocrites, I despise the lot of them. I'm leaving, and by God, it can't be too soon for me."

"You've simply got to see X in Pretoria," they told me in Washington. "He can really tell you what's going on."

So I saw X, and while he didn't tell me much, in an hour's diatribe, about what was going on, he did convince me that it was, indeed, time for X to go.

ORANGE FREE STATE BAN ON PUBLIC CUDDLING (Rand Daily Mail, *English*) . . . *Bloemfontein has banned public cuddling at its swimming baths.*

In future, new regulations decree, couples will not be allowed to get nearer to each other than one foot. Nor will they be allowed to put their arms around each other.

Necking and petting are banned, too—under regulations that forbid all forms of fraternisation and horseplay at the municipal baths.

Explaining the new regulations, gazetted yesterday in the Free State Gazette, *the baths superintendent, Mr. S. A. Enslin, said many complaints had been received from people offended by public love-making at municipal baths.*

Parents had complained that their young children got so interested in watching that they completely forgot to swim.

Also banned at the baths are naked people, gambling, liquor-drinking, "ducking" of others, and dogs.

Superintendents may order away anybody whose conduct is not in conformity with public morals.

No bathing is allowed during Sunday morning and evening church services.

N OTHING DELIGHTS the South African quite as much as the troubles of the United States—an attitude for which he cannot be blamed, since the United States is frequently to be found joining his enemies and supporting the pack of tribal hypocrites who yap at his heels from above the Zambesi. Even so, his childlike pleasure in turning the knife in America's hide is so obvious as to be virtually a national characteristic of both Afrikaans and English.

It was a rare day in the Republic on which I was not greeted, usually with a polite, concerned regret that did not quite conceal the glee, with the latest news of riots here, demonstrations there, psychopaths amok.

And to this day in correspondence with South African friends, and I suppose as long as I am fortunate enough to have them, I receive clippings on South African events which somehow always seem to have on the reverse side RACE RIOTS ROCK SAN FRANCISCO or GUARDS CALLED OUT IN DETROIT or MODEL STUDENT SHOOTS FIFTEEN IN KILL SPREE. And somewhere along the line, in even the chattiest family letters, I will be told how "we went to the farm and sat in the sun, watched an American tractor, ate American peanuts and smoked American cigarettes, but we didn't hear any rifle shots or see any demonstrations—too quiet and peaceful down here in this backward unenlightened land, I guess."

ROADS

South Africa is well served by roads. There are approximately 5,170 miles of national and 462 miles of special roads, 14,000 miles of major provincial roads, 38,000 miles of primary and 33,000 miles of secondary provincial roads. Provincial subsidiary roads are estimated at 130,-000 miles.

Licensed motor vehicles in the country exceed 1,000,000 in number and the Council for Industrial and Scientific Research estimates that the investment in new motor vehicles at present increases at an average compound rate of 8 per cent per annum. In the light of the foregoing it must be anticipated that the number of motor vehicles will grow to 2,000,000 in 1975 and will exceed the 4-million mark by 1990.

—Official Sources

AGAIN, THE ACADEMIC: small, precise, a plain but pleasant face, a kindly smile, the great personal warmth and charm of the Afrikaner at his best—Professor Rautenbach, head of the University of Pretoria, an institution more deeply devoted to the cause of Afrikanerdom, if possible, than the University of South Africa on the other side of town.

"We have presently in this University," he said in his rather gentle but firm voice, "an enrollment close to eleven thousand students of both sexes, in an academic complex which was formally designated the University of Pretoria in 1908. It grew out of the School of Mines and Technology established at Kimberley in 1894, and was so created as a university because General Louis Botha, the first Prime Minister of the Union of South Africa, and General Jan Smuts, his closest associate and subsequently Prime Minister, desired that there be formed a college of arts and sciences for Die Volk, as we call them—the Afrikaner people.

"Up to the early 1930's, we were a bilingual university. Then there occurred"—he smiled a wry little smile—"an event famed in song and story at the University of Pretoria.

"We had at that time a lecturer in French whose name was Lamont. For some reason unknown to history, Mr. Lamont felt that he must publish, under a pseudonym, a book about the Anglo-Boer War. He chose to entitle it *War, Wine and Women,* and in the course of it he said such things as that the Boers took a bath only once a year, and other comments on their personal habits—personal habits," he smiled again, "which might perhaps have had some connection with the fact that they were engaged in a war for survival against a vastly superior enemy, but which, when baldly stated in peacetime, after that war but while its emotions were still high among the Afrikaner people, perhaps understandably aroused some hostility against the author.

"Therefore Mr. Lamont, our lecturer in French, found himself one night in the unfortunate position of being tarred and feathered. He chose to sue for damages. In the course of the trial it came out that he was, indeed, the pseudonymous author of *War, Wine and Women.* He was asked to leave and did so. The consequences of his deed, however, were not long delayed.

"At that time 80 per cent of the students at the University were Afrikaans in origin and speech. They petitioned that the University be declared an exclusively Afrikaans-language institution. The move was attacked by the English-language newspapers, but the government of the day decided to accede to the request and the University was thereupon declared to be exclusively Afrikaans in language, though it remained open to students of both races who might wish to attend and could qualify.

"Now, ironically enough"—and he again was amused, the amusement of a practical man confronted by practical realities—"we teach in Afrikaans, but the great majority of our textbooks are in English. We find it impossible to persuade the students to use Afrikaans textbooks, and indeed the reasons are simple: we do not yet have a great scientific or technical literature in Afrikaans, and English is really the scientific and technical language of the world. So we are Afrikaans, but we are English, too; which in a way," he said gently, "is as it should be.

"As a matter of fact, you know, it was a lecturer at Columbia University in New York, whose writings I have read, who first drew my attention to the fact that the Afrikaners really have more in common with the English in South Africa, and resemble them more, than they do their ancestors back in Holland. By an accident of history, which has sometimes been tragic for South Africa, sometimes good, but I think in the long run will prove to be more good than bad, the two races have the same climate and environment in which to grow, have more or less the same ancestral stock, have histories that in general coincide and are parallel where they are not intermingled.

"I don't hold," he said quietly, "with the theory of blood differences between peoples. What divides two peoples is an accident of history. There is actually a close affinity between us, though there has been sometimes a conflict. That conflict is now in its final stages. With the English we have a common sense of humor, a common attitude toward sports, we are bound by a common lot and a common destiny. The mystique of a country has its effect upon us all, you know—and now we face together a common danger from the outside world which has brought the English-speaking people into a linkage with the Afrikaans-speaking. I have never found a greater cohesion between us in my sixty-four years than there is now. . . ."

(A young American friend, visiting the University of Pretoria about the same time I did, selling English-language textbooks, found the professors cold, uncooperative, hostile to his product and himself. Many of them refused to speak English though they knew he could not speak Afrikaans. His sales pitch had to be translated and he did not sell very many English textbooks for official use in the University.)

"Separate development, apartheid, the Bantustan program? Let us say we hope—we hope. It is a politician's idea to be positive, but we do not take so positive a stand in academic circles. If we are honest with the Blacks—and we have to do somewhat more than we have done, I think —then our policy has a chance. I think America has done rather better than we have, on the whole, though you have many problems still. But you are a vast white majority dealing with a relatively small black minority. We are a very small white minority dealing with a very vast black majority. It will take compassion—it will take time. And so we hope—we hope. . . ."

"THE THING YOU must realize, Mr. Drury," cried the renegade English-speaker, savage critic of every race save that of his employers of the South African Broadcasting Company, his wild eyes flaring out of his dark face with a savage intensity, his frantic admonitory finger jabbing my knee, "is that we are cursed in this country by one of the most damnable and inexcusable creations of man, the English-language press.

"Oh, Mr. Drury, if you only understood what the English-language press has done to this country, what it has been responsible for! If you only knew the evils to which it has exposed South Africa, the evils it has brought about in this unhappy land!

"I am English, Mr. Drury, my family has been in this country for a hundred years and more, but I say to you, I am ashamed of the English! I am ashamed of the English-language press! I am ashamed of what my own people have done and are doing to South Africa!

"Why, Mr. Drury, they will tell you that the Afrikaans people hate the Bantu, that those of us who support the Nationalist Government's policy hate the Bantu! Nothing could be further from the truth, Mr. Drury. *We love them. We absolutely love them.* I myself grew up with them, Mr. Drury, we rolled in the dust and played together as little children on the farm, Mr. Drury! How could one help but love such simple, dependent creatures?

"Yet read what the English-language press has to say about the Government's sympathetic and enlightened treatment of them, read what it has to say about all the vast majority in this country who support the Government!

"It is vicious, Mr. Drury, it is inexcusable! There is no more vicious or unfair element, no more violent or hysterical voice in this country, Mr. Drury, than the English and the English-language press, and I say it to you who am English born and bred!"

JEUGBOND WANT NIGHT CURFEW ON ALL AFRICANS (Star, *Johannesburg, English*) . . . *A motion proposing that the Minister of Bantu Administration and Development be asked to introduce legislation prohibiting all Africans—including domestic servants—from being in*

*White areas at night, will be discussed at the annual Natal Congress of
the Jeugbond (junior wing of the Nationalist Party) in Zululand early
next month.*

*The motion is one of a number to be placed on the congress agenda by
the "Dagbestuur" of the Jeugbond.*

*Another congress motion, approved at the latest meeting of the "Dag-
bestuur," will propose that "the authorities" (Parliament, or the Provincial Councils) introduce legislation making it compulsory for all public
representatives—including M.P.s, M.P.C.s and town councillors—to be
bilingual. . . .*

*Mr. Matie Barnard, Natal leader of the Jeugbond, said this week that
the Jeugbond had accepted a "Young Progressives" invitation to take part
in a debate in Durban on August 30 on two conditions—that there be
"no mixed audience" and that two of the four Progressive speakers speak
in Afrikaans, while two of the four Jeugbond speakers would speak in
English.*

D RIVING OUT from Pretoria over the narrow macadamized road that
leads to the northern Transvaal, one sees presently, off to the left
on a bluff commanding a view of tumbled valleys and low-lying purple
hills, the strange futuristic structures of Pelindaba, principal experimental
site of the South African Atomic Energy Board. The installation is set in
beautifully landscaped grounds, surrounded by green lawns interrupted
gracefully here and there by rock gardens containing orange aloes and
other succulents of the semiarid countryside. An air of quiet efficiency
covers all, particularly in bright sun, crystal-clear air and temperature in
the mid-sixties.

On this day an occasional car drove through, native laborers passed
chattering to one another, a few white staff members walked by in quietly talking twos and threes. The air of serene, deceptive peace that rests
upon such places as Oak Ridge rested upon this. Things were going on
underground, behind closed doors, and in the clever minds of men, that
could spell doom if let loose, but outwardly all was country-calm and
beautiful in the placid winter's day.

I was greeted first by one of those absolutely efficient, absolutely humorless young Afrikaans females who act as secretaries to so many of
the Republic's important men. If they ever smile, the visitor concludes, it
is accidental; if they ever see the funny side of things, it is strictly inadvertent. But they are unsurpassed for getting you to an interview exactly
on time, for arranging your schedule with impeccable precision, for making sure that you see exactly what you are supposed to see when you are
supposed to see it. They are quite invaluable, though an outsider might

find it a little wearing to work with them for any length of time. Those who do work with them, being of the same race and often of the same temperament, must find them ideal.

The one who greeted me at Pelindaba—"Place of Meeting"—explained with great precision just what the schedule of the visit would be. As she concluded, a slight, sandy-haired, sandy-complexioned gentleman came toward us. An expression of distaste, faint but unmistakable, appeared upon the face of Miss X. This was Mr. Y., and whatever else Mr. Y. may have been, he was indubitably of English extraction and it was quite obvious that Miss X. did not like him for that reason. There may have been others, but there was no doubt that was paramount.

It was obvious as we went along through the morning that the same applied to Mr. Y.'s fellow officials at Pelindaba. Mr. Y. was in the unfortunate position, apparently, of being the only English-speaker of any particular rank in the whole administrative structure of Pelindaba. How he had made it, I never found out, but how long he would remain so, I had a pretty good idea. I got the distinct impression that within the upper echelons, where all but he belonged to Die Volk, Mr. Y. was virtually regarded as a spy. Not only outside enemies of the Government might discover dangerous things at Pelindaba, it appeared, but so might Mr. Y.; and while he was inescapably part of the operation, still his Afrikaans colleagues were uneasy about him. Who knows what the English-speakers might do with the knowledge of Afrikaner atomic experiments? Mr. Y. must always be watched.

It was obvious that Mr. Y. felt this, to some degree, for behind the bland manner and politely efficient smile there could be sensed a certain tension, heightened by the very apparent way in which his colleagues were cool to him but perfectly cordial and relaxed toward the foreigner. Mr. Y. and the Afrikaner reaction to him did not loom terribly large in the scheme of things, but they said a good deal about South Africa. The relationship between the two white sections may be better than ever, as my Afrikaans friends kept earnestly assuring me, but every so often the curtain lifts and it becomes apparent that genuine liking still has quite a way to go.

My principal host was Dr. Schumann, Deputy Minister for Atomic Development, a tall, craggy old Boer in his seventies, with a heavily broken accent, a very kindly smile and a weatherbeaten face covered with a thousand wrinkles and stamped with the map of the Transvaal. He was not too long a South African, he explained—his parents had come from Holland a hundred years ago—but no one could have been more typically Boer than he. ("Were you born here?" he demanded suddenly of Mr. Y., later on when we were having the lunch to which Mr. Y., undaunted, had more or less invited himself. "Doctor!" Mr. Y. exclaimed in genuine dismay, "you know better than that! My family has been here since the 1870's." Dr. Schumann did not look entirely convinced.)

I received the usual tour the visitor receives at an atomic installation, the scientific offices and laboratories, the models of machinery and future expansion, the blank, unrevealing physical structures. We came in due course to the reactor, thoughtfully and silently contemplated the Monster, asleep for the moment but needing only the proper touch to be called to ominous life. South Africa's atomic program, they told me, was designed to develop peaceful uses of nuclear power; but isn't everybody's? Pelindaba was the same Place of Meeting for the idealism and the savagery of man that exist in an increasing number of countries around the globe. No one could say which element would predominate, but my hosts of the Republic, in this as in so many other things, were obviously making sure that they would have the ability to make a choice, should events force them to it.

Then came tea and a casual talk about television ("I really think we should have it," Dr. Schumann said. "Think what could be done educationally with the Bantu."), the old days in the Transvaal, the hardships following the Anglo-Boer War (for which Mr. Y. was in some indefinable but definite way given to understand that he was personally responsible), and then the pleasant drive along a dirt road through brown hills to the old converted farm that now is a comfortable inn and restaurant.

We sat for a while on the terrace in the sun, Dr. Schumann, a young Afrikaans assistant, myself and Mr. Y. "Why is he coming?" Dr. Schumann muttered to his assistant when we started out, as Mr. Y. moved toward us with a bright determination. "Why are you coming?" he demanded sharply of Mr. Y. Mr. Y. explained smoothly that he was coming along to drive Mr. Drury back. "Nobody said that you should come," Dr. Schumann said bluntly, but Mr. Y., who had evidently decided that this time he was not going to be intimidated, put a slightly glazed look of determined courtesy on his face and came along anyhow. Dr. Schumann, outmaneuvered, shrugged and relaxed, and in due time, over the excellent meal, aided by the excellent South African wine, the talk turned amicably to race and its problems, to the hectoring by the Republic's enemies to the north, and to the grimly satisfied conclusion by all three of them that South Africa was far out in front of the rest of the continent in atomic development and would remain so.

The ride back to the entrance to Pelindaba, where my driver was waiting, was relatively silent until we were almost there. Then Dr. Schumann sighed.

"You know," he said heavily, "I once thought, when I was younger, that I would write a book called 'The Black Problem.' Now I think it should be called 'The White Problem'—how we can survive as a White

society in a sea of Blacks. This"—and he gestured in the direction of
Pelindaba's hill—"isn't any solution, even if we thought of it in that way,
which we don't. We only think of it for peaceful purposes, and for our
protection in case of attack, not as a means of making anybody do anything.

"The problem goes a lot deeper than that: how we can survive peaceably in a sea of Blacks."

He sighed again. The car stopped and with a conscious effort the
kindly smile returned to the wrinkled face. He stepped out and extended
a gnarled, enormous hand in farewell.

"Come back and see us," he said. "We will survive, you can be sure of
that. I don't know exactly how we will do it, but we will survive."

He raised his arm and waved, the craggy old indomitable Boer, and so
did his Afrikaner assistant and so did Mr. Y.: agreed absolutely on that,
however wary they might be of one another on other things.

FEWER WHITE BABIES BORN (Star, *Johannesburg, English*) . . .
*Fewer South African White babies are being born now per head of popu-
lation than at any other time in the country's history.*

*In just over 50 years the White population has trebled, but the birth-
rate in the same period has dropped by almost a third.*

*Government calls for Whites to have more children appear to have
gone unheeded.*

*The latest plea came in a radio broadcast at the weekend by Dr. P. J.
Riekert, economic adviser to the Prime Minister and chairman of the
Economic Advisory Council. Dr. Riekert stressed that one of the main
solutions to South Africa's manpower shortage was to increase the birth
rate of Whites who had traditionally supplied the skilled labour.*

*Despite a massive influx of over 150,000 immigrants in the past few
years, South Africa's White birth graph has continued to curve down-
ward.*

*In 1910, with a population of only 1.4 million, White South Africans
produced nearly 41,000 children—a rate of 32.5 per thousand. Last year,
with a population of nearly 3.5 million, only 77,000 babies were born—
a rate of 22.8 per thousand.*

*The drop in the birth rate has had an equally serious impact on the
natural increase in population—that is the number of births over the
number of deaths. In the six years from 1959 to 1965 the natural increase of the White population has slumped from 16.4 to an all-time low
of 13.6.*

"❝ **I** N A WAY," said my young Afrikaner guide, "it has been good for **us** to have the world imposing boycotts and threatening sanctions. It has forced us to get busy and develop things for ourselves. Here you see one of the results."

His gesture encompassed a complex of some twenty-five major modern buildings scattered over 347 acres of spaciously landscaped grounds on the edge of Pretoria—"Scientia," home of the South African Council for Scientific and Industrial Research.

"The C.S.I.R. was established by Parliament in 1945," he said as we walked across the broad lawns (our first objective a ten-foot wind-tunnel they were using for a Defence Department project on velocity). "It is similar to your National Research Institutes in Washington, though of course our effort is on a much smaller scale, since we are so much smaller and poorer. But," he said with a justifiable pride, "we're coming along."

And so they are. There are thirteen national laboratories and institutes on the grounds and additional research projects are carried out under C.S.I.R. supervision in Pretoria, Johannesburg, and a number of university and private research centers throughout the Republic.

"More than 14,500,000 rand (approximately $20,000,000) have been invested in buildings and equipment since 1945," he said. "More than 70 per cent of our income is derived from Parliamentary grants and from fees for special research projects undertaken for Government departments. Overseas funds, mainly from America for operation of the Hartbeestehoek Radio Space Research Station north of Pretoria, total about 17 per cent. Industries contribute the balance. Our expenditures, totaling about 8,500,000 rand (about $12,000,000) in 1964–65, broke down into research and services for industries; fundamental research for the Government, defense projects and that sort of thing; research in what we think of as 'community problems,' such as water— which you know is a very troublesome thing right now, with the drouth we've been having in the past five years—housing, roads, transport; and grants for medical research and various university research projects."

"Do other countries in Africa make use of your research and assistance?"

He smiled that peculiar smile, composed about equally of tolerance, amusement, pity and contempt, with which the South African contemplates his neighbors, always denouncing him but always running to him for the help they haven't the competence to provide for themselves.

"Oh, yes. You'd never guess it from all the shouting, but we get a lot of requests for help. And we give a lot, too. . . .

"Basically, though, our work is designed primarily to help South

Africa. We support university and private medical research. We have on
the grounds here our National Building Research Institute, which is
constantly conducting experiments on how to provide economical but
suitable housing for the Bantu. We also do something else for them that
may amuse you—we make their beer.

"Bantu beer, you know, is their great drink. Nutritionally, it *is* a great
drink, because it's based on mealies—what you call corn—and it provides practically all the basic ingredients of a good diet. It's a meal in
itself. Bantu beer production increased 300 per cent between 1953 and
1963, and it's still increasing. Therefore the C.S.I.R. established a special Bantu Beer Unit with a view to improving brewery production and
hygienic practices. The municipality of Pretoria, working closely with us,
built the Waltloo brewery near Mamelodi Bantu township a few miles
out from town. If you had time you could go out there and see stainless-
steel fermenters, each with a 2,500-gallon capacity, in a scientifically
managed brewery that has a total output of approximately 37,000 gal-
lons every twenty-four hours. That comes under our National Chemical
Research Laboratory, which of course has a lot more to do than improve
Bantu beer. Nonetheless," and he looked wry, "that's something this
hard-hearted Government does for its black people. That and many
other things, in housing, medical assistance, and so on. . . .

"Then we have the National Research Institute for Mathematical Sciences; the National Mechanical Engineering Research Institute; the National Nutrition Research Institute; the National Institute for Personnel Research, which makes constant experiments on how to improve
work conditions and increase worker productivity; the National Physical
Research Laboratory, which carries on research in such things as smog.

"Did you know," he said, "that in this town alone on a winter morning
we have found that there is an average of 14.2 tons of fallout of solid
matter per square mile in the central area? The same smog conditions
apply to most of our major cities. As a result of research under our
direction, the Government passed an Atmospheric Pollution Prevention
Act in 1965." He looked toward Pretoria, still shrouded in its morning
pall, and shook his head. "Can't say as it's done much good yet, but I
suppose that helps support our claim to being a modern civilization—
smog. . . .

"The Republic Observatory is also here; the National Institute for
Road Research; which"—again wryly—"is certainly needed, as you can
see when you drive some of our roads; the National Institute for Tele-
communications Research, the National Institute for Water Research,
the South African Wool Textile Research Institute; the Information and
Research Services, which includes such things as our library, public relations, scientific liaison work with other countries, and so on; our Technical Services Department, which designs and produces scientific equip-

ment for the whole complex and gives us invaluable experience as we move toward self-sufficiency in many of these fields; and finally the Industrial Research Institutes through which we aid those industries that seek our assistance.

"Like you, we love initials, so under this last group we have FIRI—Fishing Industry Research Institute, at the University of Cape Town; LIRI—Leather Industries Research Institute, at Rhodes University in Grahamstown down on the east coast below Durban; SAPRI—the South African Pain Research Institute at the University of Natal; SMRI—the Sugar Milling Research Institute, also at the University of Natal."

"You're really humming right along, aren't you?"

He smiled.

"Oh, yes. And every time your country or somebody in Africa threatens to cut us off, we hum a little more. That's our nature, you know. This isn't a country to sit around and whine. We pitch in and get to work. Others in Africa might profit from our example, but"—he shrugged—"as long as they'd rather keep harassing us instead of building up their own economies, we'll go right ahead and build up ours, thank you very much. . . . Here's the wind-tunnel."

We entered, examined, watched an experiment in Mach II velocities. As we left I commented on the personnel.

"Weren't most of those technicians Japanese?"

"Yes, we bought the equipment from Japan and they're here to service it and help us get started with it. We had an American journalist through last week who asked why we didn't buy it from you. I said, because how do we know you won't do to us what you did to Rhodesia?"

He laughed amicably, and so, perforce, did I.

"But the Japanese themselves intrigue me. I thought with the Government's racial policies—"

"Oh, they're officially classified as White."

"But—"

"It may be due to some shade of skin coloration not apparent to you and me," he said dryly. Then he grinned. "Or it might be due to the fact we have a big trade deal with Japan. Anyway, don't make the mistake of considering them non-European. Why, they're as White as you or I."

BIG SIX ASKED TO BUILD MORE TANKS (Sunday Times, *Johannesburg, English*) . . . *Dr. Verwoerd, on the advice of Mr. Jan Haak, the Minister of Planning and Mines, wants the six big oil companies trading in South Africa to double the capacity of their storage depots and tanks. . . .*

This is only one of seven phases of the Verwoerd-Haak Planning

Council-Board of Trade plan to measure up to the threat of possible
sanctions against South Africa by the world's oil producers and carriers.

One oil field in South Africa, Dr. Verwoerd believes, would make the
country invulnerable against any military or economic attacks. . . .

SEARCH FOR OIL UNDER THE SEA (Rand Daily Mail, *English*)
. . . Carrying specially imported equipment, the South African Navy's
survey ship Natal *sailed for the Agulhas Bank yesterday to begin the first*
intensive—but preliminary—soundings for oil beneath the sea.

The Natal *is to work in the next four months in an area stretching west*
of Mossel Bay to Duiwelshock River, 60 miles away near Cape Infanta.
Her first voyage will last for about three weeks. . . .

The results of the preliminary seismic work are to go to Soekor, the
government-sponsored oil exploration company which is about to begin
drilling for oil at Murraysburg, Cape.

From the results, geologists will be able to tell if there are pockets of
oil. If there are, a much more intensive survey of the area will have to be
made.

CAUTIOUSLY OPTIMISTIC ABOUT OIL FIND

Great excitement prevailed following the reported discovery of a
vast underground oil field near Riversdale in the southwestern Cape,
where drilling for oil has been in operation for some time.

The official attitude, however, is one of cautious optimism. According to the Johannesburg *Star,* the Minister of Planning, Mr. Jan Haak,
said in an interview that he could not express any opinion or optimism
until the technical analysis had been completed.

—Official Sources

TALL, THIN, stooped, serious, yet with an occasional unexpected gleam
of sardonic humor, the Deputy Minister of Commerce sighed somewhat impatiently when my opening question reflected the newspapers'
lively concern about a possible slump in the economy.

"We are not in a slump," he said in his emphatic, somewhat mechanical accent. "Certainly 5 per cent growth per annum is not a slump. Our
problem is too fast and uncontrolled expansion. Our economy is growing
in all directions at a rate in excess of our available resources—in all
directions, financial, material, basic services, everything. High public expenditure and high consumer income have generated a demand for goods

and services beyond our present capacity to satisfy. That is the problem.

"Therefore in the third quarter of 1965 the Government decided that, in order to slow down the growth, it would impose restrictions, mainly fiscal, on credit, investment, dividends, etc. Despite our hopes that this would have the needed deterrent effect, these measures apparently did not go far enough. After a short dip in the growth rate, a new spurt of growth occurred in the fourth quarter. There was a new wave of interest in industrial expansion, a new rush of foreign investment capital. I expect the Government may take further measures in coming months to control it, but it is difficult when an economy is booming as ours is. . . .

"One of our main problems, as you know, is manpower to keep up with the growth. The pressure is mainly on the technical side, engineering, science, the upper brackets of the building trades, the artisan class. We hope to draw immigrants from Europe who have technical skills, but we are not the only ones who want them, you know. Even the United States wants skilled technicians to come in. We are a small, relatively poor country and we are not in a very good position to compete, particularly with a country like yours. We get some skilled people, of course, our immigration rate is rising and we are making a real effort to entice the trained types, but there still is a great shortage. . . .

"Why don't we train the Bantu? That"—a dry smile—"is one of the pet panaceas of the English-language press, of course. Also some of our more vociferous foreign critics. Well, I will tell you, since we know nothing about it, we only live with them: the Bantu is not the easiest person in the world to train in the habits of an industrial society. The problem isn't money or the educational system, the Government is giving direct support to training the Bantu in those types of skills for which there is an evident need in our society. The problem is the Bantu himself.

"You have to get non-white people to become accustomed to a regular labor performance on a daily, weekly, monthly, yearly basis. Oh, I know," he said, raising a hand to forestall a question, "I know that our critics charge that we won't train them beyond a certain level of minimal skills because of our policy of separate development. But supposing we did, could we count on them to get a job, stay with it, be on time day after day, do what they were supposed to do? Experience has not made us greatly optimistic.

"A good many of them are simply not regular workers, it seems to be a racial characteristic. They don't, as a rule, want to undertake steady employment. They want to take on four or five months' work and then return to their domestic pursuits for the remainder of the year. It isn't very easy for an employer to replace a man who wants to work for a week, earn enough in that time to support himself for perhaps a month, and then go home until he runs out of money and feels he must find work again.

"In a few areas, some of the so-called border industries we are trying to establish in the vicinity of the native reserves, we have been quite successful in getting some of them to accept the Western concept of steady work. But the border industries take time to establish, it is a task to persuade business firms to build their plants away from the natural commercial and industrial centers, even though the labor supply is there. And we find more Bantu who do not want to work steadily than we do those willing to accept the European concept. . . .

"But," he said abruptly, "these are dry economic problems—"

"But important to an understanding of your country."

"Oh, yes, but dry, very dry. You won't get any readers unless you write something sensational about South Africa. That's the only way to write about South Africa, be sensational. Then you'll have all the readers you want."

"Sometimes rather dry things can be illuminating when put in perspective."

"Oh, but not like blood, thunder, murders, unrest. We are much too peaceful here."

"Perhaps that can be illuminating, too."

For just a second his eyes looked sharp and shrewd. Then he shrugged.

"You'll see. Write something sensational. It's the only way."

AIR TRAVEL

South Africa's international airport is Jan Smuts Airport, midway between Johannesburg and Pretoria.

The following are the State-owned national airports: Louis Botha National Airport, Durban, D. F. Malan National Airport, Cape Town, J. B. M. Hertzog National Airport, Bloemfontein, East London Airport.

Intermediate airports (municipal-owned) are at Port Elizabeth, Windhoek, Kimberley, Beaufort West, Victoria West, etc.

The number of Civic Aerodromes is 337, of which 182 are private aerodromes and 155 public aerodromes.

The number of aircraft on the South African Civil Aircraft Register in 1964 (July) exceeded 1,000. Of these 778 are single-engined aircraft, 85 twin-engined aircraft and 28 multi-engined aircraft. The register includes 58 sailplanes, 44 ultra-light aircraft and 10 helicopters.

The number of passengers flown is as follows:

	1951	1959	1961	1962	1963	1964
Total All Services	167,866	334,880	402,950	446,082	513,642	605,387

—Official Sources

"THE PROBLEM OF Africa is skill," the head of the Bantu Investment Corporation said. "To find competent people is the headache of the continent. In South Africa we have plans and money; we don't have enough capable Bantu, as yet, to make them fully feasible."

He was in his early forties, businesslike, decisive: the typical small Afrikaner moustache emphasizing a typical square face.

"In 1904 we had an estimated 3,500,000 Bantu in this country. Now it's up to about 12,500,000, and by the year 2001 the official estimate is that we will have 23,000,000; although, as you know"—he smiled—"official estimates on things like population always seem to lag behind. Let's say we hope it won't be any more than that.

"In 1965 our present Bantu population commanded slightly less than a quarter of the net purchasing power of the Republic, or close to 1,500,000 rand—about $210,000,000. The urbanized Bantu, working in the mines, factories, shops and homes of major urban centers such as Johannesburg and Pretoria, has about 50 per cent of the total native purchasing power, with the remaining 50 per cent divided fairly equally between Bantu resident in the homelands and those living on European-owned farms.

"We are embarked on a four-phased program whose first aim is to develop agriculture, primary industry and towns within the Bantu areas. Secondly we are trying to encourage development of commerce and industry by the Bantu inside their homelands with the guidance of this organization, the Bantu Investment Corporation. Third is the so-called border industries program, to encourage white industrialists to establish their plants on the edges of the Bantu homelands where the labor supply resides; and fourthly, a concentrated effort to educate the Bantu technically and academically to take on the responsibilities of developing their own areas and businesses."

He paused and took a drink of tea.

"It has its problems," he confessed with a humorous air, "but we are determined people. We are operating at present under a five-year plan for Bantu development drawn up in 1961 and providing for an estimated expenditure of 114,000,000 rand, or about $160,000,000. The major stress is on agriculture, because that has been the traditional pursuit of the various tribes when they haven't been killing one another; it is the basic type of existence they have always followed, and know best.

"We have simply introduced two new principles which are quite revolutionary to them: we are insisting that the available land must be used effectively by full-time farmers, and we are insisting that if a Bantu farmer is to devote his full time to farming, he must work an economic holding.

"In many cases, present land allotments granted by tribal authorities are too small to be economically self-sustaining, and in a great many other cases the Bantu wants to get a crop off his land this season and go somewhere else next season after exhausting his land. Traditionally, he doesn't want to use land conservation practices or stop erosion or do any of those things white farmers learned to do long ago to preserve their land and increase its value.

"It's strange, you know," he said abruptly. "It's the same land of Africa, and in many areas the black man has had the same chance at it as the white man. Yet it has never occurred to him to husband his land and make it productive. One wonders why. . . .

"In any event, we have the problem of trying to help them now. This means planning, and in a good many cases, this means what seems to them, and to some of our critics of the outside world, to be hardship for the Bantu. If you are to build farms of a size that are sufficient to be productive, however, it means consolidation and an end to small, uneconomic units, and that means a gradual resettlement of Bantu who own very little land to towns in the Bantu areas. The hope is that in the towns these consolidated Bantu will offer their services in areas other than agriculture and will be able to find economically productive work there and so be able to have full family lives right there instead of having to be away at the mines or factories for long periods.

"So far, we have classified about 40 per cent of the Bantu land into residential areas, arable land and common grazing ground, in the hope we can thus stop overgrazing and the practice of piratical farming, which are very widespread among them. They own 40 per cent of the cattle in the Republic, and we are trying to introduce sound methods of care, of breeding and of culling herds to develop healthy strains. This meets with a lot of resistance, because in their society cattle represent wealth and they'd rather have fifty sickly ones than twenty-five healthy, but we are trying to educate them, and are beginning to have some reasonable success.

"We are also trying to increase grain production on their land, are trying to get them started planting sugar cane, sisal and other fibrous plants in areas, particularly in Natal, which are suitable for them. We are also engaged in an afforestation program and have planted some 130,-000 acres of an estimated future forestry estate of 687,000 acres. Here again, they don't like to use their land for trees, which take some years to show results, but we are trying to show them that the economic return is worth it. The development of tree plantations has already resulted in establishment of some sawmills and furniture factories where some of them are finding jobs.

"In connection with the five-year program we have planted approximately 14,000 miles of conservation grass strips; put some 6,000 acres under cultivation; built 250 conservation dams, sunk 400 boreholes and built some 500 miles of country roads.

"We are also studying future expansion of the mining industry in the hope that it also can be used to benefit the Bantu areas.

"So you see," he said with a smile, the smile of the South African who occasionally becomes a little ironic under the constant pressure of his critics who say he isn't doing anything for the Bantu, "we are rather busy.

"Housing for those who have to move to towns? Oh, yes, we have housing, too, a five-year program for the Bantu who become landless under the agricultural program, and for those who will work in the border industries. Our original plan called for the establishment of 35 towns with a total of more than 90,000 houses at a cost of R76 million. Because of the acceleration of the land rehabilitation program and the interest shown in development of border areas, this goal was revised upward to 105 towns for present and future development. These towns will even have self-contained shopping centers, and they will be erected by Bantu artisans, thus providing an enormous amount of income.

"With the towns, we hope, will come eventual concentrations of purchasing power that will in time lead to bigger and stronger commercial concerns and the gradual establishment of light industries. Then in time, hopefully, will come heavy industry.

"Bantu participation in commerce is growing. At the end of the Second World War there were 891 Bantu retail traders. By 1951 there were 3,871 and today there are more than 12,000 licensed Bantu traders, of whom slightly less than half are residing in the homelands. More than 250 small grain mills, bakeries and other small industries are conducted by Bantu.

"To help in this area, the Bantu Investment Corporation was established in 1959. Since then we have made 596 loans, amounting to R2,476,000, for the establishment or extension of commercial concerns, service industries and manufacturing industries. A lot of Bantu have the desire to get into business, but to us it seems foolish to grant a license or extend financial aid unless a man is capable. So only about 15 per cent of the applications we receive have been granted. Typical loans have assisted in the erection of a cane furniture factory, transport and bus services, brickyards, bakeries, garages, funeral parlors, retail shops and the like.

"We have also started a program of building business premises for them in the homelands, and have spent about R600,000 on it so far. The traders and businessmen who occupy these premises are free to purchase if they wish, and several are doing so. We are planning to build another 90 business premises in the immediate future at an estimated cost of R400,000.

"We don't expect consumer goods factories to be economically feasible for quite some time because the purchasing power of the Bantu in the homelands is low. Also, the market is adequately supplied by white firms. Therefore, we are encouraging service industries and those closely associated with primary production in the homelands, such as pulp and paper factories, furniture factories and sawmills, abattoirs, spinning and weaving plants, grain mills, building industries, and the like. . . .

"Do we check up on them after loans have been granted? I should say we do. Trained officials of the Corporation visit them regularly to give advice and guidance. We offer this service free of charge and we also encourage those who don't borrow from us to make use of it. Quite often our people will give lectures, and usually we concentrate on basic, elementary training such as how to keep stock records, how to keep books, how to handle inventory.

"It is not our theory," he said with a trace of dryness, "that the way to help the black man is to dump dollars in his hands and run away and leave him. We think he needs a little training in ordinary, common-sense management.

"As far as white border-industry development is concerned, it's been slow. We haven't persuaded as many white entrepreneurs as we would like to establish factories on the edge of the homelands, but the number is growing and we hope it will continue to grow. We are doing everything we can to encourage it. . . .

"One thing I try to emphasize to the Whites who deal commercially with the Bantu," he said thoughtfully, "is that they should meet the black customer in a manner which will be respected and understood. I've told our people repeatedly that they should let the Bantu feel he is getting what he wants, they should allow him to ask questions about the merchandise. There's been too much take-it-or-leave-it in the past, and they remember it and resent it.

"Many of our modern selling programs in the white world are geared to the highly sophisticated world audience and they simply don't reach the Bantu customer, who depends heavily on visual understanding, understanding by example. We have to show him and we have to be very patient, because he thinks and reasons in terms of visual images. Abstract advertising concepts don't succeed with him. The patience that is required to bring all our races into harmony with one another is monumental"—he smiled—"but we haven't any choice in the matter. We have to try."

GETTING TO THE HEART OF THE RACE PROBLEM (*Editorial, Star, Johannesburg, English*) . . . *An unofficial assessment this week predicted an "extremely bright future" for the African worker in industry.*

There are already half a million employed on the manufacturing side—with an annual wage packet of R220,000,000, incidentally—and "with the growing shortage of trained industrial labour and the increasing orientation of Bantu workers to modern industrial methods," said the report, "this surely presages a much larger, more skilled and higher-paid Bantu labour force in South African industry."

All this is to the good—the good of the country and the good of the African people. It increases their contribution to the wealth of us all. It deepens their commitment and their sense of belonging and reverses the tendency towards abdication which is probably the greatest long-term threat to this country's security.

But it would be a grave error to suppose that this is enough or that it solves everything. The material progress of the Africans will help to take the crueler edge off apartheid. But as long as apartheid remains a denial of the humanity of the non-White, as long as it makes him a stranger in his own land, a cipher to be "allowed in" or "endorsed out" without his consent—no statistics about housing and wages rates and job opportunities can make it right for Black or White either.

Two simple current examples will suffice to show again the approach that apartheid produces in Nationalists as well as non-Nationalists. Two African women university graduates from Johannesburg were given the opportunity of going on a study course to the United States. Up to the day they were to leave they had not heard a word about their passports. Nobody has bothered to tell them even now: they might as well not exist.

A few days later a respected African from the Eastern Cape, Bishop Zulu, had to tell the World Council of Churches that he would not be able to attend their conference in Geneva because he could not get a passport. The only intimation he had from the South African Government was the return of some bank statements he had submitted with his passport application.

These are not isolated examples; and it is precisely because such an attitude prevails among Whites that opponents of apartheid say that no matter how benevolently it is implemented, it remains wrong and in the long run a peril to South Africa and all its peoples.

Because of this, a good many of those who oppose apartheid in principle believe they can or ought to do nothing constructive within its framework. Better no education than Bantu education, they say. Better no development in the rural areas than that of the Bantustan kind. Better keep slums than have group areas. Better have sanctions than relative prosperity under apartheid. They think that by taking up this stance they will kill apartheid quicker.

This is a failure to distinguish between the service of an ideology and the service of purely human needs which must go on irrespective of what ideology is to triumph here in the longer run.

But if human needs are to be honestly served then the most important of them all—the recognition and respect of human dignity—must be sedulously practised: by State officials, employers and indeed by everybody. . . .

L OST BACK IN the stark hills beyond Pelindaba is the missile-tracking station operated for the United States by the South African Government. It too is filled with futuristic machines, busy men ostensibly impatient of political matters; yet here, too, the world intrudes.

"Why is the Government so upset at the idea that America might send a Negro technician here?" I asked my English-speaking guide. "Couldn't housing be found for him, wouldn't he get along all right with the rest of the staff?"

"Oh, yes," he said, "there is no doubt of that. But the Government feels—and we agree with it—that to send such a man would simply be an open and obvious provocation. It would simply be an invitation to trouble. We think, perhaps unjustly, that this would be your government's purpose in sending him here, and therefore it seems best to avoid such possible unpleasantness by keeping him out."

PROVINCIAL SYSTEM

ADMINISTRATOR. The chief executive officer of each province, known as the administrator, is appointed by the State President for a period of five years.

PROVINCIAL COUNCILS. Each of the four provinces of the Republic has a unicameral Legislature elected on the same franchise as the House of Assembly. The provincial Legislatures are known as Provincial Councils and their legislation as Ordinances. . . . As under the South Africa Act, the powers of the provinces are also limited by the Republican Constitution and a provincial ordinance requires the assent of the State President before it has the force of law. Ordinances may be made mainly in respect of the following matters: direct taxation to raise revenue for provincial purposes; the borrowing of money on the sole credit of the province; education other than higher education and Bantu education; the establishment and maintenance of hospitals and charitable institutions, municipal institutions, divisional councils and other local institutions, roads, ponts, bridges, markets and pounds, fish and game preservation, etc.

—Official Sources

TALL, BALD, self-effacing, soft-voiced, a curiously strained smile, a curiously shy and hesitant manner—General Steyn, Director of Prisons, occupant of perhaps the most sumptuous office in Pretoria, an enormous room with thick carpeting, massive furniture, pictures of the Prime Minister and the Minister of Justice staring down beningly upon this, their servant in the Republic's ceaseless drive to rid itself of the slightest taint of subversive or anti-Government thought.

At the moment, he was under heavy fire from the English-language press because of a current case involving charges of prison brutality, and his approach was more defensive than it might otherwise have been.

"I have traveled," he began immediately. "I am not so provincial here that I am not familiar with other prison systems throughout the world. Taking into account the social and cultural backgrounds of the prisoners we have to deal with, I believe my prison system compares favorably with any to be found elsewhere.

"We are working in close cooperation with United Nations' standards here. . . .

"Now, as far as punishment is concerned, our emphasis is constantly on trying to rehabilitate our prisoners. We try to form and mold the criminal into a good citizen, so that when he is released he can find some useful place in society. We have found that the only way to get a contented person in prison is to give him good food, clothing, bedding, nice surroundings, plus good medical treatment when he is sick. We have tried to get these factors together."

He gave me that pained, strained smile, a quick side glance, shy and defensive.

"We find that the most important thing of all is the influence of our officers upon the prisoners. You lead prisoners not only by lectures and discipline, but by good example. We are constantly seeking good officer material, and you know, it isn't always easy to find. This isn't an easy life, in the police. Many men prefer other pursuits. We must constantly seek better material. Our White force now is about 87 per cent Afrikaans, 13 per cent English-speaking. . . .

"In our rehabilitation programs we stress such things as the construction trades, woodworking, farming and other types of manual labor for which the Bantu is best suited. The Government allows us to build our own buildings, the actual prisons themselves, also the houses for staff, the farm buildings and so on. These are all built by prisoners who are thereby trained in these building techniques and are thus assisted to find work outside when they leave.

"Some of them," he said, with an air of pride, and he got up and went to a table on which was displayed a most intricate and elaborate wooden chess set, "become very skilled. This chess set, for instance, was carved for the Prime Minister by one of our best workers, a Bantu who is in for murder but who will eventually be rehabilitated out if he continues along the lines of improvement he is showing. . . .

"On our prison farms," he said, resuming his seat, "we raise all the food that we use, mealies, beans, cattle, pigs, sheep, vegetables, and so on. There, too, we are training the Bantu for a productive place in society. We have eleven large prison farms and several small ones in the Republic.

"We are steadily improving the training of our wardens, and of our officers. After all," he said, again with the shy side glance, "you have a great many types of people on your staff, just as you have a great many types of prisoners. Our officers can't, of course, be friendly with the prisoners when they are on duty. But on the other hand, no warden can lift a hand against a prisoner—it means discharge, if proved. A prisoner must be disciplined under regulations, and these provide for several stages of appeal. . . .

"Now, the English press is criticizing us all the time, as you know." The smile, if anything, became shyer, more hesitant, more pained. "These things they say—why, they are ridiculous on the face of it. Why, no sensible man would brush his teeth with urine. You wouldn't, I wouldn't. Now, what reasonable man would do a thing like that? It's ridiculous for them to say any prisoner would do that.

"It is absolutely against the policy of our department to permit any brutalizing of prisoners.

"After all," he said, and he gave me an appealing glance, wistful and bothered by the world, "even in an ordinary home, things don't go perfectly every day, now, do they?

"Why expect it in a prison?"

POLICE CALL MORE RECRUITS (Rand Daily Mail, *English*) . . . *Although the South African Police Force was better staffed than at any time since the war, it was still not getting enough recruits, Brigadier G. J. van Wyk, recruiting officer of the S.A.P., said in Pretoria yesterday. . . .*

Brigadier Van Wyk revealed that 1,480 recruits would graduate from the Police College at the end of the year. He added that 100 matric recruits would start their six-month training course at the beginning of next month.

About one-sixth of the recruits at the Police College were matriculants who underwent a six-month training course. Recruits with less than matric qualifications were given a year's training.

Brigadier Van Wyk said the present White strength of the police force exceeded 15,000 men. Because of the continually increasing field of duty of the police force more and more men were required.

Since the Police College was enlarged to take up to 2,000 recruits, the police force was being strengthened continually.

"We never turn away recruits," he said. "When they apply during the year we send them to police stations for practical training while they wait for a course to begin."

CALL ON ENGLISH TO JOIN POLICE (Star, Johannesburg, English) . . . An appeal for more young English-speaking men to join the police force was made by the Commissioner of Police, General J. M. Keevy, at a passing-out parade of 514 recruits at the Police College yesterday.

He said the police force had been drawing more and more men from the English-speaking community, but many more should be encouraged to make the police their career. . . .

2.
Johannesburg

I WAS DRIVEN THE forty-odd miles from Pretoria to Johannesburg late on a soft winter's evening, when the plains and ridges spread out misty and darkening to horizon's edge and both lanes of traffic on the two-lane road scheduled soon to be a freeway raced almost bumper-to-bumper between the twin cities of the Transvaal.

We passed Jan Smuts Airport, already a long way back in time and knowledge, and presently my host said, gesturing off to the left, "Over there is the farm where General Smuts used to live." The ghost of "Slim Jannie," too clever and too pro-British by far for his fellow Afrikaners, came briefly to mind and whirled away again, blotted out by the rushing autos.

Presently we began to enter the bedraggled outskirts of any modern city, the sleazy hamburger joints, the run-down dry-goods stores, the small dirty groceries, the occasional garish second-run movie house, the liquor stores. In due course these began to improve: we were entering the second level, the inner urban ring. The stores were a little smarter, the streets more brightly lighted and somewhat cleaner. Then abruptly sky-scrapers appeared, tall apartment buildings, smart shops and stores: we were into the city known to Black Africa as "Egoli," the City of Gold, South Africa's Manhattan. Somewhere even at that twilight hour the sound of construction rose. Coal smoke in the morning will always be Pretoria's symbol in memory; the sound of the jackhammer and the crash of the wrecking crew will always belong to Jo'burg.

Here it sits surrounded by its yellow mine-dumps, the capital of the Big Deal and the Fast Buck, the perfect flowering of the fantastic min-eral wealth of the Witwatersrand, unique in its own land as New York is in America: both representing the best and the worst in modern indus-trial society, both offering the best and the worst of their respective lands, both wielding the decisive economic power of a country and a continent.

Many South Africans do not like Johannesburg, but it is where the ambitious and the greedy come if they would make a million. "They say in Jo'burg," they told me in Cape Town, "that it takes us all day to make a decision. We say it takes them until 10 A.M., but then they spend the rest of the day undoing the damage."

Yet you have to hand it to Johannesburg, big, vigorous, crude and brawling, filled with the insistent pulse of life that will not be denied. In eighty years it has come from open veld to modernity as vital as any city's anywhere—except that thousands of Blacks wander its streets rest-lessly day and night, its crime rate is the highest in the country, and here as in no other place in the Republic the racial problem is always with you. In most other places you can occasionally forget it for a little while.

You never do in Jo'burg.

1,158 NATIVES ARRESTED IN RAND SWEEP (Cape Argus, Eng-lish) . . . *More than 1,000 police, moving through the Jeppe area of Johannesburg in a massive six-hour "Operation Clean-up" last night, arrested 1,158 Natives.*

Brigadier Louis Steyn, chief of police for the Witwatersrand, said this morning that a "very large number" of Natives would be charged with offences ranging from the possession of firearms, weapons and stolen goods, to trespass.

The raid was one of a series of police sweeps through areas of Johan-nesburg and Soweto [the largest Bantu township] *aimed at rooting out the criminals responsible for big crime in Johannesburg and on the Reef.*

THE BIG white house was in Houghton ("Howton"), the wealthy suburb of Johannesburg represented in Parliament by Helen Suzman,
South Africa's only office-holding member of the Progressive Party. The
furnishings were pleasantly expensive, the company pleasantly well-to-do
—well-to-do and worried, for this was a Jewish household and in South
Africa, Jews are uneasy. There is no overt reason why they should be,
the Afrikaners are so obsessed with the English that the Jews are rather
far down the list of racial groups to be concerned about, but they are
uneasy as wealthy Jews are uneasy everywhere: they are automatic targets when the world tires of toying with someone else. In time, they feel,
the Afrikaner is going to get around to them.

This gives to their life, which in the main centers in Johannesburg, is
supported by the wealth of Johannesburg which they have done so much
to develop, and gives to Johannesburg an aspect foreign to the rest of the
Transvaal and indeed the rest of South Africa, a certain tension. The
tension is increased because inevitably a great many of them are opposed
to the Government's racial policies: opposed because of a natural sympathy for the underdog, opposed because of a fellow-compassion for
those who suffer at the hands of authority, opposed because the Government's policies are now beginning to interfere with the flow of black
labor into the Witwatersrand, the black labor upon which mines and
factories and great commercial enterprises, in the last analysis, depend.

So far, it is true, the Government has done nothing officially to bother
the Jews. And aside from the occasional wisecrack or Jewish-slanted Van
der Merwe joke, neither has the average Afrikaner, who is basically a
pretty tolerant and decent fellow providing everybody stays in his proper
place. The place of the Jew is to make money in Johannesburg, and
while there is occasionally some resentment of his success at it, there is
little of the open hostility that can often be found in America and elsewhere in the West. There is only one area where there is open annoyance
expressed, and this the Jews themselves will ruefully acknowledge—
most of the proved Communists who have been caught plotting to overthrow the Government have been Jewish, their feeling for the underdog
apparently carried, as it has been in so many places, to the extreme of
complete identification with the one philosophy most implacably destructive of underdog and topdog alike. But even this is regarded more with
an impatient annoyance than a real resentment by other white South
Africans.

Now and again the ugly snarl of anti-Semitism purely for its own sake
will flare across the floor of Parliament at Helen Suzman, coming from
some bull-necked Nationalist back-bencher whose skull is as thick as his
brain is small; sometimes a Government minister's wife will turn the

knife delicately as she tells the visitor, "We don't have anywhere else to go, you see, if we lose South Africa. Even Mrs. Suzman doesn't have anywhere else to go—unless perhaps it's Israel. . . ." But on the whole, the Jews are not actively resented, being so firmly involved in the economy of the Republic that it would collapse without them.

Nonetheless, they worry; and the worry was present this night, under the expansive hospitality, the martinis and the casual, comfortable joviality of the big house in the exclusive suburb. Someone had just come back from London, someone else from Rhodesia, yet another had recently been to the United States. South Africans of a certain class travel far these days, and for a time we talked of their journeyings and mine. Inevitably by dinnertime, of course, we were discussing South Africa.

"You see, what is lacking here," the most vocal of the gathering told me earnestly, "is a dialogue. Now as I see it, the ideal components of a democracy are to have an executive, a legislature and an electorate, and then a dialogue in which the executive consults the wishes of the whole community and is modified in its actions by the community's wishes.

"But that," he said with a sort of gentle, blank disbelief, "is where our system breaks down. The dialogue is not maintained. The National Government does not consult the wishes of the electorate, particularly of the minorities who should be protected in an ideal democratic system."

"I am beginning to get the idea that possibly this is not ideal. In any event, I thought the Nationalists consulted the electorate last March and won the biggest mandate any South African Government has ever won?"

"Oh, that is true," he acknowledged gently while a black butler and two black maids moved silently about the table, ignored, almost unseen, by the party. "That is true. But still in an ideal system, the Government should still take into consideration the feelings of the minorities —or even, in our case, the majority, the black majority. Don't you think so?"

"Oh, I do," I said, "I do. But it seems to me the Government can argue logically that it has just gone to the country and received an overwhelming endorsement for its policies."

"But it should consult, in an ideal system," he said with a dogged insistence.

"Do you think it ever will?"

"There is hope," he said, his eyes lighting up with it. "You see, there is an argument going on among the Nats about the proposed monument to one of our past Prime Ministers, Johannes Strijdom—you know him in the outside world as the one who tried to establish 'baaskap' in South Africa—"

"Which you don't have now."

His eyes widened in surprise.

"Oh, no. We have apartheid, or 'separate development.' It isn't the same. Baaskap was absolute domination of White over Black. Apartheid or separate development contemplates just what it says, the separate development of the Blacks in their own areas inside the geographic boundaries of the White South African state. At any rate, there is an argument going on among the Nats over the design for the Strijdom monument, and that indicates, to me at least, some split in Nationalist ranks, some sign of a divided opinion—"

"Surely you don't mean that an argument over design of a monument can indicate a genuine split in Nationalist policy?"

"You never know," he said with a gently stubborn insistence. "In our peculiar country sometimes you just see the top of the iceberg—there may be a great deal more beneath the surface."

"The Afrikaners are so secretive," the lady next to me said in an annoyed tone, "how can you tell?"

"Well, perhaps it is because the night here is so dark," he said with an apologetic little smile. "We see the faintest gleam of light, we seize upon it and try to make it into something far larger than it is. But it does seem to me there is some restlessness in Nationalist ranks right now—that perhaps this is the start of a shift—that perhaps we may yet arrive at a dialogue in which influential Nationalists will say to the Government, 'Look, you've got to take into account the feelings of these other people, you can't just ride roughshod over them—' "

"I think you're completely at their mercy," I said. "I think they will go ahead and do exactly as they please."

"Of course they will," the lady said. "Of course they will."

"No, I'm not so pessimistic," he said. "I think they may not—I think they may not." Then he gave a characteristic little shrug, a characteristic motion of the hands. "But perhaps," he said ruefully, "we are so used to grasping at straws that we grasp at anything, no matter how small."

"Forgive me for being blunt—I haven't been here very long—but so far I haven't seen any signs at all of any possibility that they will change in the slightest anything that they are doing."

"Well," he said, the ruefulness deepening, "perhaps you're right. Perhaps you're right."

"Of course you're right," snapped the lady, after which a glum, thinking silence fell.

S.A.—KEY PRODUCER OF PLATINUM

In a further expansion program Rustenburg Platinum Mines is to spend $30.8 million before 1970. Production is to be nearly quadrupled from the 200,000 ounces of refined platinum marketed in 1964 to 750,-000 ounces by the end of 1970.

The new expansion will bring Rustenburg far into the lead among world platinum producers and will make South Africa the key producer in world markets for the metal.

In a preliminary statement for the year to August 31, 1966, Rustenburg says that its reduction works, smelter plants, mining facilities, plant and equipment are to be extended to meet the swift surge in world demand for platinum.

The directors report that the 40 per cent increase in production capacity announced in 1964 was completed on schedule in March 1966, and that refined platinum from the expanded plants is now coming on to the market.

Demand for producer-priced metal showed no sign of abating and had in fact continued to exceed supply, the statement said.

—Official Sources

"ENDORSED OUT"

If a Native is ordered to leave an area—is "endorsed out"—and refuses to comply with the order, the State President has absolute discretion to order that he be summarily arrested, detained and removed from the area without court trial or further investigation.

—Official Sources

THE LIQUID DARK eyes looked with an apparent candor into mine—the same dark eyes, the same apparent candor, that I had seen in the exiled Communists now teaching in Washington, the exiled Communists now running around in tight little circles in London, that I would see on several more occasions here in the Republic and would see again in London on my way home. The approach was so reasonable, the intelligence so apparent—what a waste that they should be banished and not at home working for a better future for their country.

What a waste that they should have compounded the error of their former white masters by giving their former white masters such a good excuse to boot them out.

For they were, and of course are, Communists, devoted to the destruction not only of the Government of South Africa but to the destruction of all stable governments everywhere in the world, and therefore, of course, enemies of all decent people and of everyone who believes in the democratic process and the imperative need for orderly change if a disorderly century is to be rescued from its own excesses.

But you forget this, for a while, talking to them. They are so earnest, so intelligent, so persuasive, so reasonable.

This particular one, to whom I had come through the back alleys and side streets of Johannesburg in the company of two friends who had promised to take me to "someone who can really tell you what's going on," was in his early thirties, born in the Transkei, wanted by the Government, one jump ahead of Robben Island or the blandly named "exit permit" (the South African Government being as good at word-games as the American), which means you are permitted to exit on the condition you never return.

"I expect you have already met here," he said in the clipped, guttural English which is the mark of the educated African, "men who are absolutely convinced that they are going to maintain forever—not just for a little while, but *forever*—their domination over the Bantu."

"I got that impression," I said. A scornful expression came into his eyes.

"They are insane."

"They seem to be doing pretty well so far. What have you got to offer as an alternative?"

"Well," he said. "Well, their days are numbered."

"I know you like to think so, but seriously: what, actually, can you do? What actual chance does any underground movement have here? It seems to me they've checkmated you so scientifically that there really isn't much—"

"We have our methods."

"With outside help, maybe, but where is it going to come from?"

"It will come."

"And how can it be effective? Really, I'm not being hostile, I'd like to know. It seems to me that the Government has pretty well thought of everything. And with the network of informers I'm told it has—"

The dark eyes widened in anger, an expression of bitter contempt flashed for a second across the black face.

"Oh, yes, they have informers, all right. Africans won't stick together, that's our trouble. We'll sell each other out for a couple of rand."

"Then how can you hope to organize anything that will be effective?"

"Because we've got to hope," he said fiercely. "Because—we—have —got—to—hope. We can't let this go on forever—"

"Aren't the natives getting better pay all the time? Aren't many of them housed better, even in the townships, than they ever were in the shantytowns or back in the locations?"

"You should see their houses!"

"I intend to, but from what I've already seen, even from a distance, they appear fairly adequate. Not mansions, but adequate."

"Why shouldn't we have mansions?"

"I'm not saying you shouldn't, if you earn them. That's what the white people do."

"On our backs."

"True enough, in some cases. I'm not arguing that with you. I'm just wondering how you're going to go about it. Most of your leaders have been driven underground, there aren't very many of you left, you're in hiding yourself, they may catch you any minute. How can you hope to accomplish anything?"

"We'll get help. Perhaps America will help us."

"I wouldn't count on it. But even if we did, do you actually think you have enough trained people to run this whole country? It seems to me this is a highly developed, organized society that takes a lot of sophisticated running. Have the Bantu got leaders who have the skills to do it?"

"How do we get the skills unless we have the chance?" he demanded fiercely. "How do we learn anything unless we have the opportunity to educate ourselves? How do we ever achieve anything as long as we're kept down all the time?"

"That's my point. It isn't your fault, but you have been kept down. So you don't have the leaders. So you don't have the skills."

"We'd learn them soon enough if we had the chance. We'd have to learn them."

"You see nothing of any value to you in the Bantustan program—"

"Bantustans! That will take forever."

"But if they're established—"

"They won't be. If they were established and the policy of eventually creating some sort of mixed commonwealth of South African states were followed, then we'd have them where we want them, because we'd be organized into political states and functioning governments and we'd be in the majority. But they know that, so it's all a game. They'll never establish any more, you wait and see. They wanted the Transkei established so they would have something to point to when the outside world wants a look, but that's as far as it will go. You'll see."

"What would you do if you were in control of the country but were three and a half million Blacks to twelve and a half million Whites?"

He smiled with a certain cold bleakness.

"Exactly what they're doing: keep them down. But you see, that's not my problem. We're not in the minority and we're not in control of the country. We're in the majority, and we're not in control of it. And we should be and we will be."

"They'll die first."

"So will we. More millions of us to die than there are of them."

"And you're all one unified people who will stand together and fight them—the Zulu won't turn on the Xhosa and the Tembu won't slaughter the Pondo the minute the Whites' backs are turned—and if outside pressure is put on the country, you'll all fight united against the Afrikaners and the English—"

"Some of us will."

"For what? So outside tribes from up north who want to take this great rich country away from all you South Africans, White and Black, can do it?"

"Some of us will," he repeated stubbornly. "Look, you take this message back: there is an underground here, we will have a revolution, we will take the country, we will end all this injustice."

"How soon?"

"When the time comes."

"So far I haven't seen many signs of it."

"You wouldn't, coming from outside."

"Maybe not, but you don't convince me much."

"Keep on moving around. You'll find out."

"I'm not sure I will."

And although I traveled far from that secret interview and saw many people of many shades, and though there are injustices that might under less tightly controlled conditions bring it about, I neither saw nor heard anything to convince me of its imminence or even of its possibility. Nor have I yet.

LIAISON BETWEEN RACES ESSENTIAL (Star, *Johannesburg, English*) . . . *Liaison between non-Whites and Whites is essential in South African sport. "The South African Amateur Boxing Association is sending a team to Italy this year," said Mr. Frank Braun, the Chairman of the S.A. Olympic Games Association at a Council meeting last night. "We must learn from this effort."*

After the meeting Mr. Braun emphasised how important it was that South Africa should show the rest of the world that non-Whites were being given a chance to "run their own sports."

He said: "This is what the Olympic Council has asked for and we are trying to meet their requests."

Mr. Braun however has not yet given a report on the last Olympic Council meeting. He said his committee would be referring the matter to the new Ministry of Sport before making any recommendation.

WHITE SOCCER CHIEF PLANS NON-WHITE N.F.L. (Sunday Express, *Johannesburg, English*) . . . *South Africa's soccer chief, Mr. Dave Marais, M.P. for Johannesburg North, plans the introduction of a non-White National Football League in South Africa next season.*

He was drawing up a memorandum for submission to the Minister of Sport, Mr. Waring, within the next few weeks, he told me yesterday.

He would also submit the memorandum to local authorities.

"With goodwill on all sides the league could be introduced next season," he said.

"Non-White football is going backwards instead of forward, and I feel it is my job as president of the Football Association of Southern Africa to improve it. . . ."

The non-Whites were keen on professional soccer and he would like to see their matches organised on a national basis similar to the White National Football League.

THE VISITOR IS told in the descriptive pamphlet handed out at the gate that frequently the performers at the weekly mine dances dedicate their act to some one of the mine managers, or use it to make some comment—humorous, the pamphlet tells you—on conditions in the mines.

We had come out ten miles from Johannesburg on a Sunday morning through the yellow dumps that define the arc of the fabulous gold-bearing Reef, and as we arrived and took our seats some such sally must have just been offered, for the Whites seated on one side were chuckling and nodding graciously and the Blacks seated on the other were laughing uproariously.

In the center of the small informal stadium, which must have seated about a thousand all told, ten or twelve natives from Zambia, dressed in their tribal regalia, were stomping and shouting in rhythmical unison, pausing now and again while their leader tossed some further comment to the white stands. There was an air of dutiful, slightly uneasy jollity about it all. The mine dances are one of the few remaining public events the Government permits both Whites and Blacks to attend together, and across the dusty arena there flowed one of the few remaining currents of shared experience left in the Republic.

Strangers stared at one another across the circle, and the forced nature of their laughter was tribute enough to the success of the Government's policies. Strangers they were, and getting stranger. Applause for some particularly well-executed leap or step, laughter at some permissibly impudent sally, were all that linked them now.

So We sat in the shade while They sat in the sun—They actually had the better of it this day, for it was a nippy winter's forenoon and the shade was a little uncomfortable for Us—while eight or ten other tribal groups, drawn from the African states to the north that send so many thousands to work in the Republic's mines, displayed their colorful talents.

Then We had tea, and so, presumably, did They, or Their equivalent of it. Then everyone returned to the arena and another five or six groups performed, after which it ended and We and They straggled out together to make our separate ways back to Jo'burg, or the mine barracks, or the townships.

It was colorful, it was fascinating, it was enjoyable, it was unique. It said a lot about Them and Us; more, perhaps, than the Government realizes when it decrees that dutiful, allowable jests and patronizing, uneasy laughter are all that We and They can experience together, these days.

HEAD IN THE SAND (Editorial, World, Johannesburg, Bantu) . . . Latest population figures released by the Non-European Affairs Department of the Johannesburg City Council make interesting reading. In fact, we would suggest they are highly significant to anyone lacking the ostrich mentality.

They show that Johannesburg's African population now numbers 733,-339, while Soweto alone can boast a population of 505,950 Africans. Meanwhile the Department puts the city's White population at 867,652.

As a measure of the growth of South Africa's premier city these figures are indeed impressive. Its citizens—both Black and White—can be justly proud of the fact that—Egoli—today is no mean city.

Together they have contributed to its growth. Together they have watched it grow. We have no reason to doubt that the process will continue.

Yet the Government would have us believe otherwise. Apartheid, separate development, call it what you will, is their cry. They are adamant that there can be no real place for our people in the White cities.

Yonder lies your homelands, they declare, pointing to the Bantustans. One strains one's eyes. One would be forgiven, we suggest, for blinking in sheer disbelief. Can they really be serious?

The ostrich when frightened sticks its head in the sand but it at least takes it out again. We can't help wondering when the Government will do the same.

AGAIN A RENEGADE English-speaker, this time a young one, swarthy, keen-eyed, wavy-haired, a voice and manner suggestive of a younger and somewhat immature Richard Burton; very smooth, very intelligent, very ambitious. In the last election, he had left the United Party, broken bitterly with family and friends, moved his wife and children to another area, contested and lost a seat for the Nationalists.

I would come to understand the attitude of the Afrikaners toward such English, whom they regard with amusement and use with contempt. I never did come to understand the attitude of the English who let themselves be so regarded and so used.

However, he had obviously worked it out in his own mind to his own satisfaction, and now as we sat in his comfortable home—many homes in South Africa are comfortable, a greater percentage perhaps than anywhere else, for construction is cheap, rents are cheap, fuel and electricity are cheap, and domestic labor is so cheap that you can have a dozen faceless Blacks swarming the place to do your bidding, if you please, at very little cost—it was obvious that he felt well pleased with himself. He had not won his election, his relations with the Government were tenuous, he really was still outside, standing on tiptoe and anxiously trying to peer in the windows—but he was still pitching.

And he was also right in there with his facts and figures on the United States, not the first and certainly not the last of that long string of both Afrikaans and English South Africans I met who are prepared at the remotest hint of criticism to cover their country's shortcomings with a defensive smog of American errors.

First, however, he and his other guests—a shrewd young Afrikaner and his charming wife—had to make clear to me what they thought of "the bloody British" and the way they had treated the Boers in the Anglo-Boer War and, apparently, forever after. My host was positively virulent in his condemnation, so much so that even the Afrikaner seemed to blink a little now and then. But he wanted to make clear to me—and perhaps to the Afrikaner as well, for one never knows in South Africa how things get back to important places, so one is always well-advised to be on guard—how really, deeply, passionately, irrevocably committed he was to the Nationalist cause. And he gave me once more the standard "slating," as they call it in the Republic, of the English-language press.

Then we turned to America.

After I had listened for a while to the usual contrasts—you with your enormous White majority and your homogeneous Negro mass, we with our small White minority, our enormous hodgepodge of sharply differing tribes—all of which is entirely true—I ventured to mention the subject which it seemed to me that most Americans, and indeed most really free people (as distinct from free-talking but dictatorial-acting, as in other African areas up north) find most repellent in the Republic. I too was not sure but what it would go right straight back to the Security Police the moment I left the house, but there comes a point in a visit to South Africa at which one decides for the sake of self-respect that from then on one will be polite but will take no more guff on the things one really believes in as an American.

"I think most of us can understand that you have a terrific racial problem, and to some extent we can sympathize with you whatever we may think of how you're trying to handle it, because we have one too. But I think where most of us balk is at things like the 90-day detention law and the 180-day detention law and bannings and exilings and so on—"

"But didn't your President Roosevelt ban 100,000 Japanese in the Second World War?" my host demanded triumphantly. "Didn't he send them into exile away from their homes—"

"In wartime, in wartime. And that was an emergency power, not a condition of regular law on the permanent statute books. Be fair, now."

"We believe *we* are in a war. We believe our very existence is threatened. Therefore, do we not have a right to safeguard ourselves?"

"And furthermore," the young Afrikaner broke in, "it has been proved, you know, that these people *were* Communists. The ones who have been picked up and held under these laws, or driven out of the country, *were* trying to overthrow the Government. That's been proved, you know."

"I know, I'm not arguing that. I'm just saying that if there were some safeguards on the use of these powers, if the Minister of Justice were required to bring charges and make his case in open court, then perhaps the rest of the world wouldn't be quite so critical because then you would have some democratic procedures to point to."

"All I can say," my host repeated, "is that this is a war, for us. We don't feel we have time to stop and indulge in niceties. We feel we would be destroyed if we didn't act, and quickly."

"We act—"

"Yes, and how slowly! How long does it take you to bring a Communist to justice when he wants to overthrow your government!"

"Sometimes years, but it hasn't been overthrown yet."

"We don't feel we are big enough—or rich enough—or powerful enough—to afford that luxury. We are a small, threatened power—threatened by you, among others. Who knows what encouragement you people are giving to subversive elements—"

"Oh, come on, now. Come on."

"Well," he said. "All right. But even so, to have you opposing us at all of course encourages them. And we haven't got time to sit around and debate about it. We've got to stamp them out quickly and completely or suffer for it."

"But if you could only do it with some protections for the individual and his rights. That is where a good many of us part company from you, I think. Our whole history has been a battle for individual rights."

"Mr. Drury," the young Afrikaner said solemnly, by now a little more solemnly than before, for we were through dinner and into some wonderful K.W.V. brandy, South Africa's, and possibly the world's, best, "all I can say to you is this: this is an honest people. These men in government are honest men. They will not use these powers unless a man is actually a Communist."

"But how do you know that? How can you be sure? There's nothing in the law that says they won't be knocking on this door to take you away, ten minutes from now, if they decide they don't like you or disapprove of your views."

"But I'm not a Communist," he said simply, "so I don't have to worry. Nor does any honest man in this country. Mr. Drury, I can just repeat to you—the Afrikaners are an honest people. We trust our government. This is an honest country. We don't persecute innocent people. We trust our leaders and we know they will not misuse these powers."

And of course they didn't, at this house, and of course there was no knocking on the door. At least, that door.

Later the young Afrikaner drove me back to the hotel.

"The last thing I want to say to you, Mr. Drury," he said solemnly as we shook hands, "is this: we will never weaken." And meant it, as do they all.

ENGLISH-SPEAKING RIGHTS: DESCENDANTS OF PIONEERS SUPINE (Letter to the Editor of the Star, *Johannesburg, English)*
. . . SIR:—With reference to Mr. G. A. W. Baird's letter in The Star *of June 14, in which he calls for more aggressiveness in insisting on equal rights for the English-speaking section, I could not agree with him more. Not since Colonel Stallard, that grand old leader of the Dominion Party, left the scene of political battle has any leader had the temerity to stand up publicly for the rights of this section.*

Clever Nationalist propaganda soon silenced any such attempts with a new swear-word, "English Jingo," which implied that one was not only un-South African but downright unpatriotic even to suggest that this large minority of the population had any rights.

The outcome has been that, with a pathological fear of "offending" anybody, this section has all but ceased to exist as an entity, and long since gave up the unequal struggle of fighting for anything that it held dear.

Nevertheless, it is unbelievable that the descendants of hardy British pioneer stock should, in one short generation, have become so utterly supine as to accept everything that the Nationalist Government decrees, as "inevitable."

To their eternal glory let it be said that the Afrikaners fought every inch of the way to get where they are today, but to their discredit let it also be said that in the process they have not hesitated to trample underfoot all the feelings and sentiments of fellow South Africans.

If your home language was English, you automatically became "the enemy" and what was precious to you no longer counted for anything.

It is fashionable today to be an Afrikaner Jingo and the word no longer has a sinister meaning, whereas, in fact, it denotes narrow sectionalism of the most selfish kind, seeking, not a square deal for all South Africans, but privilege for its own at any cost.

The latest example of the way it operates is the proposal to destroy a 60-year-old club [the Johannesburg Country Club] *of over 6,000, mostly English-speaking members to make way for an Afrikaans university for which there is no need at all, except insofar as it will introduce a few more thousand Nationalist votes to boost the number of city councillors —no longer even a secret objective of the Nationalist Party.*

An interesting "statistic" at this point is that the English-speaking population of Johannesburg is more than double that of the Afrikaans-speaking and the Witwatersrand University can accommodate only 598 students in residence. If any more university accommodation is needed it is obvious where it is most urgently required.

                                        (MRS.) MAISIE OWLES
                                        VAN RIEBEECK STREET,
                                        POTCHEFSTROOM.

POLITICAL INDIFFERENCE: SCHOOLS SHOULD PLAY A BIGGER PART (*Letter to the* Star, *Johannesburg, English*): *Sir,—Mr. G. A. W. Baird* (The Star, *June 14*) *is right when he calls for the English-speaking people to be more aggressive. We have become increasingly indifferent and apathetic towards the Government. All its measures are accepted in this docile fashion.*

We will protest for a short while to our friends and associates but beyond that we go very phlegmatically if we ever bother to voice dissenting views.

We need an outspoken strong leader. Of this there is no question. It is incredible to think that we have not had a great English leader in the past 50 years or so. Even General Smuts was an Afrikaner. . . .

"THE MORAL ISSUE of apartheid is pretty well settled now among the whole community," said my luncheon host at the Johannesburg Country Club, where we had just met one of my countrymen, a famous general who was touring the country as an official guest and being suitably appreciative in numerous press interviews.

"The moral issue did bother a good many people for a long time, you know, but the last election gave the Nats such an overwhelming majority that it pretty well quieted the talk and convinced most people that it really wasn't a moral matter, anymore.

"The issue now is whether separate development will be implemented fast enough to take care of the problem before the outside world interferes. We feel we are constantly being betrayed by our friends. Someone like Clarence Randall, for instance, whom we have always regarded as friendly to South Africa, will say something like, 'In the event of a UN decision to intervene, the U.S. fleet will be off Plettenburg Bay tomorrow morning,' and while many of us know it's just politics or thoughtlessness that makes him say it, still people remember it. It disturbs and alarms them. Many of our people are genuinely afraid of American intervention.

"But there is no chance whatsoever of anything like that succeeding unless every last white South African were to be put to death. We would all stand together. And by the same reasoning, there is no chance of toppling the Nationalist Government by ordinary political means for a long time to come. In time it will go, but right now it is perfectly adapted to the nation. It is perfectly suited to a people who feel themselves threatened. As long as the threat remains. the Nats will remain. It is a very simple, direct equation."

TOP U.P. MAN SHOCKS PARTY BY RESIGNING (Rand Daily Mail, *English*) . . . *United Party leaders in Johannesburg were surprised yesterday by the public resignation of one of their leading members on the Reef, Dr. J. A. Ellis.*

Dr. Ellis, chairman of the Springs division of the United Party until a few months ago, said:

"I think most of the members in Springs know I have been unhappy about things for a number of years, and I certainly indicated in my report to the annual meeting that I was pessimistic.

"I said then—and this is one of my main reasons for resigning—that the United Party had failed in the election and had always failed because it had no concrete alternative to the present policy of separate development.

"I'm not saying that separate development is the answer—but at least the Nationalists are making a sincere effort to solve our race problems while we just bark at their heels like a little puppy dog.

"What is needed is not for us to be constantly told what they're doing wrong, but what we can do. The race federation policy of the United Party is too complicated and involved—a dream.

"I have the greatest respect for Sir de Villiers Graaff—and I think he is a wonderful leader—but the United Party has to be able to offer some better, more concrete policy."

SOUTH AFRICA IS CLOSING TRADE GAP

South Africa's adverse trade gap closed by $367.64 million during the first ten months of the year [1966], compared with the same period last year, according to statistics released in Pretoria by the Department of Customs and Excise.

Total imports for the first ten months of this year were $1.9 billion while total exports amounted to $1.4 billion for the same period. South Africa's total exports for the January–October period rose by $156.38 million and total imports fell by $211.26 million.

Imports during October amounted to $210.28 million, compared with $198.24 million during the previous month. Exports during October amounted to $159.72 million compared with $133 million during the previous month.

—Official Sources

I N THE HOTEL corridor two pairs of dark eyes stared at me with a desperate earnestness as I stood at the door of my room:

"Oh, yes, master. We afraid before, we did not know you want to stay in room and work. We just afraid to knock on door till you leave, master. Yes, master, we fix room, master, thank you, master, yes, master. Oh, *yes,* master, we fix right away, master, yes."

And all I had said was, politely, "Do you think you could clean the room sometime soon, please?"

WHITES MUST START RESPECT (Rand Daily Mail, *English*) . . . *It was essential for all South Africa's racial groups to respect each other, Dr. I. S. Kloppers, Commissioner-General of the Botswana, said in Johannesburg yesterday.*

Speaking at a meeting of the Maria van Riebeeck-klub, he said there was far too much racialism in the country. The Whites, as the most developed sector of the population, should set the example by creating better understanding.

"It is essential to teach our children these things through the home and through schools," Dr. Kloppers said.

In his area there were 1¼ million Botswana—nearly half the White population of South Africa—and although he had close contact with Africans all his life and worked with them for many years, they were still not entirely predictable.

There were great problems, therefore, in administering these territories but every effort was being made to meet these problems.

The absence of recent uprisings among the seven African ethnic groups showed that there was not dissatisfaction at the moment.

V ERY TRIM, very brisk, very smiling, very smooth, the young-looking managing director of the Industrial Development Corporation explained how his quasi-governmental agency, like so many things controlled by the Government, was not really socialistic—just practical, in the way hardheaded, forward-looking, pragmatic Afrikaners who seek the advancement of Afrikanerdom are practical.

"We have just one basic rule for investing in a business that comes to us for help, and that is, *is it economically feasible and can it make a profit?*

"We are very conscious of the profit motive here"—he flashed his quick, automatic smile—"because the law says we must be. The Investment Development Corporation was established by Parliament on May 14, 1940, and its basic purpose, by law, is to assist in the financing of new and existing industrial projects so that the country's economic requirements may be met and her industrial development can be speeded up, and at the same time be conducted on sound business lines.

"In addition to giving financial assistance to private business, we are also empowered to establish and conduct financial undertakings if the private sector is unable or unwilling to do it. We are not confined to the geographical limits of the country but can undertake anything, as the law says, 'whether within the Republic or elsewhere which may be necessary for, or incidental or conducive to, the attainment' of any of our objectives." He smiled again. "You can see we have a rather broad charter."

"Isn't that rather socialistic—or even"—with a smile of my own, for in the Republic one must be carefully jocular in the way one uses these words—"Communistic? It seems to me the Government—"

"Oh, no," he said quickly, at first with complete seriousness, then with a sudden grin—"certainly not! It is true that the Government exercises a good deal of control, but you must remember our basic rule: *will it make a profit?* Now, you don't find socialistic or Communistic enterprises operating that way! They don't care whether they make a profit or not. We do.

"The Government's control is really designed to be sure of this, I would say. When the I.D.C. was established, Parliament authorized two series of shares, an A series of 500,000 shares representing operating capital, and a B series of 4,500,000. The Government was required to subscribe to all of both series but was given the right to dispose of all or a portion of the B shares if it was considered appropriate. Now, the A shares can only be disposed of by an act of Parliament, and the law says that the Government must always retain enough A shares so that its number of voting shares will always exceed by one the total number of votes to which all other shareholders of the Corporation, in the aggregate, may be entitled. The corporation's authorized share capital as of June 30, 1965, amounted to 175,000,000 rand, of which R156,184,000 had been issued for cash to the Government."

"And you're managed by an independent board of directors?"

"We have an autonomous board," he said promptly, "consisting of not less than five or more than nine members. The State President appoints five—"

"Whom the Government recommends—"

"—with the Government's advice—and the holders of the B shares elect the other four."

"So, for all practical purposes, you are a Government agency, then."

"In the interests of sound business management and the profit motivation," he said cheerfully, "the Government maintains a rather tight control. Now, what do we do?

"First of all, as I said, we help private business and we establish and run enterprises that private business is unable to initiate or maintain. There is no limit on the size of business, large or small, that we can assist, and while we are not established to assist the distressed borrower or be a lender of last resort if a borrower can't find help elsewhere, still we do have authority to help, providing the basic economic condition is sound. Remember, that is always our guideline.

"We also give assistance in setting up better business methods, we give advice and we do planning for industries that need it." He gave his quick, efficient smile. "You might say that basically we do anything that will advance South Africa economically."

"Do you insist on being represented on the boards of companies you give loans to?"

"We don't necessarily insist, no, though in practice we do have representation on the majority of the companies we assist. That is a matter for negotiation. Of course, everything is treated with the strictest confidence. So, then, one of our major activities is the attempt—not 'the attempt,' that sounds as though we might be failing"—he chuckled heartily —"and we don't intend to fail—to establish our so-called border industries near the native homelands. As of our last accounting report in June, 1965, we had invested a total of 216,635,400 rand in 202 industrial undertakings, of which 18,665,061 rand has been invested in border industries. We have eight major regions scheduled for border area development, Central Natal, the Natal Coast, the lowveld of the Eastern Transvaal, the Pretoria-Northwestern area, the Northern Transvaal, the Transkei, the Ciskei and the Western Transvaal.

"As a matter of fact," he said, giving me a sudden gleam of teeth, "the South African Government really does do a great deal to encourage and develop the country. You might, in other countries, call it socialistic, I suppose, but here we feel it is different. We don't think of it that way. We think of it as helping us to become stronger, more self-sufficient, more able to withstand the onslaughts of the outside world. As a matter of fact"—he gleamed again—"even if critics were to call it socialistic, I imagine we wouldn't mind, as long as it strengthens South Africa."

AFRIKANER'S STAKE IN BUSINESS SOARING (Natal Mercury, *Durban, English) . . . The Afrikaner's share in the entrepreneurial function in South African finance rose from five per cent in 1939 to 21 per cent in 1964.*

This was one of the points made in Durban last night by Professor J. L. Sadie, Professor of Economics at the University of Stellenbosch, who addressed the first annual conference of the South African Society of Commerce and Economics Students. . .

Professor Sadie said Volkskas was responsible for 21 per cent of commercial banking business while the Trust Bank ranked first among hire-purchase banks.

The most spectacular rise was in mining, where the Afrikaner's share shot up from less than 1 per cent before the establishment of Federale Mynbou Beperk to 10 per cent in 1965.

He said the Afrikaner had gained control over 10, 28 and 18 per cent, respectively, of gold, uranium and coal output.

The Afrikaner's share in the private sector of the economy (excluding agriculture) had increased from 9.6 per cent in 1948–49 to 18.6 per cent in 1963–64.

He said the activity of the Afrikaner in the newspaper world was of interest. Three big concerns, Nasionale Pers, Afrikaanse Pers and Voortrekkerpers, had pushed up the circulation of Afrikaans daily and weekly newspapers from 15.3 per cent of all Afrikaans and English medium papers of that type in 1950 to 20.8 per cent in 1965. . . .

INCREASED OUTPUT OF MANUFACTURED GOODS

The latest figures from the Bureau of Statistics show that manufacturing output in the first six months of 1966 was 5.9 per cent higher, by physical volume, than for the same period last year.

Of various individual sectors, tobacco recorded the biggest rise in June, with an index of 185.9 compared with 114.6 last June. Textiles improved from 253.5 to 300.1.

Other good increases were in food (140.9 to 172.1), gas and coal products (279.1 to 305.2), non-metallic minerals, electrical machinery (207.3 to 224.2), transport equipment (281.2 to 318.7), and miscellaneous (224.5 to 276.2).

A decline occurred in beverages, leather and leather products, rubber products, basic metals and metal products.

—Official Sources

THE YOUNG LIBERAL Afrikaner stared out the window at the striving skyscrapers of raucous Johannesburg stretching toward the golden mine-dumps of the Reef. His eyes narrowed and with an explosive, indignant, yet curiously self-satisfied emphasis he exclaimed,

"I wouldn't be Black for ten thousand rand a year, thank you very much. What could I spend it on? I couldn't go to the theater I wanted to go to, I couldn't own a decent home, I couldn't start a decent business, I couldn't buy my children a decent education, to say nothing of all the other indignities I'd have to take. No, thank you, I'll be White, thank you very much."

IMPORTANT LEGISLATION OF RECENT YEARS

THE SUPPRESSION OF COMMUNISM ACT, passed in June, 1950, prohibits Communists from holding positions in any public service or trade union. The Communist Party dissolved itself before the Act was finally passed.

THE GROUP AREAS ACT, of July, 1950, makes provision for the gradual introduction of residential segregation of Whites, Indians, Coloureds and Bantu. Persons of one group will not be allowed to own or occupy property in the controlled area of another group, except under permit.

THE POPULATION REGISTRATION ACT, passed in July, 1950, introduces a system of registration for all persons resident in the Republic. The Identity Card that is issued includes the photograph of the holder and details of the national racial unit to which he belongs.

THE IMMORALITY AMENDMENT ACT, passed in July, 1950, prohibits sex relations between Whites and non-Whites. Previously the Act applied to Whites and Bantu only, but it has now been extended to the Coloured group as well. The Mixed Marriages Act, passed in July, 1949, prohibits marriages between Whites and non-Whites.

THE BANTU AUTHORITIES ACTS (URBAN AND RURAL), 1952, extended self-rule to Bantu communities.

THE PUBLIC SAFETY ACT, passed in March, 1953, empowers the Governor-General to declare a state of emergency in any specified area where public safety or the maintenance of public order is threatened.

THE NATIVE LABOUR (SETTLEMENT OF DISPUTES) ACT, of 1953, gives Bantu industrial workers representation in matters concerning their conditions of work.

THE CRIMINAL LAW AMENDMENT ACT, passed in March, 1953, provides penalties for resistance campaign offences and for offering and receiving financial support of such resistance.

THE BANTU EDUCATION ACT, of 1953, authorizes the transfer of the control of Bantu education from the Provinces to the Native Affairs Department of the central Government, and makes provision for the creation of Bantu school boards and committees as well as for the registration of private schools.

THE SOUTH AFRICA ACT AMENDMENT ACT, of 1956, establishes the sovereignty of Parliament. It takes away the testing rights of the Courts, except for clause 137 of the South Africa Act which provides for equality of English and Afrikaans as official languages; and it validates the SEPARATE REPRESENTATION OF VOTERS ACT of 1951, which was declared invalid by the Appeal Courts. The 1951 Act envisaged the creation of separate voters' rolls for White and Coloured voters in the Cape, in place of the existing common roll. The Coloureds presently elect four Whites to represent their interests in the House of Parliament.

THE BANTU EDUCATION AMENDMENT ACT, No. 36 of 1956, makes the registration of Bantu Schools subject to such conditions as the Minister of Native Affairs may determine. A school shall not be registered if the Minister is satisfied that the establishment thereof is not in the interest of the Bantu people.

THE NATIVES (URBAN AREAS) AMENDMENT ACT, No. 69 of 1956, authorizes local authorities to order Natives whose presence in a certain area is detrimental to the maintenance of peace and order to leave such area.

THE HOUSING ACT, No. 10 of 1957, provides for the construction of dwellings and the carrying out of housing schemes and to that end the establishment of a National Housing Commission, a Bantu Housing Board and a National Housing Office. Certain powers are conferred upon local authorities in connection with the construction of dwellings and the carrying out of housing schemes.

THE GROUP AREAS ACT, No. 77 of 1957, consolidates the law relating to the establishment of group areas, the control of the acquisition of immovable property and the occupation of land and premises.

THE GENERAL LAW AMENDMENT ACT, 1962 ("ANTI-SABOTAGE ACT"). The General Law Amendment Act is designed to close certain loopholes which enabled Communists to evade the provisions of the Suppression of Communism Act, 1950. It also amends the Public Safety Act, 1953, the Criminal Procedure Act, 1955, the

Riotous Assemblies Act, 1956, and the Unlawful Organizations Act, 1960.

The Minister is authorized to prohibit persons engaged in Communistic activities from attending certain meetings, belonging to certain organizations or publishing certain classes of newspapers.

If the Minister has reason to believe that a newspaper will spread Communist propaganda he may require it to deposit up to R20,000 with the Minister of the Interior, which sum or part thereof may be forfeited if the paper does in fact make itself guilty of Communist activities.

The publication or dissemination of statements by persons restricted under the Suppression of Communism Act is also prohibited unless it takes place with the consent of the Minister. Lists will be published in the *Government Gazette* so as to acquaint the public with the names of the persons whose speeches may not be published, broadcast or printed. The Act also enables the Minister to remove from the list the names of persons who have ceased their Communist activities.

The Act empowers the Minister to confine persons restricted under the Suppression of Communism Act to a definite place and he may prohibit such persons from receiving any visitors except their legal advisors.

Section 23 of the Act, which deals with sabotage, defines it as any wrongful and wilful act whereby any person damages, destroys, or endangers the health or safety of the public; the maintenance of law and order; water supplies, the supply or distribution of light, power, fuel, foodstuffs or water, or of sanitary, medical or fire extinguishing services; any postal, telephone or telegraph services or installations, or radio transmitting, broadcasting or receiving services or installations; the free movement of any traffic on land, at sea or in the air; and any property, whether movable or immovable, of any other person or of the State.

It also includes attempting, inciting, instigating, commanding, aiding in, advising or encouraging any of these acts.

From the definition of sabotage as a "wrongful and wilful act" it follows that the State has to prove, first and foremost, that an accused person has committed certain offences and that he has committed them wrongfully and wilfully.

Only after this has been proved to the satisfaction of a judge of the Supreme Court, is the accused called upon to show that his act did not have sabotage as its purpose.

THE BANTU LAWS AMENDMENT ACTS, No. 76 of 1963, and No. 38 of 1964, established labour bureaus, controlled the entry of foreign Bantu into South Africa, and generally circumscribed the conditions under which Bantu may live and work in White areas.

THE COLOURED PERSONS EDUCATION ACT, No. 47 of 1963, placed the education of Coloured persons under the control of the Department of Coloured Affairs.

THE GENERAL LAW AMENDMENT ACT, No. 37 of 1963, permitted the Attorney-General to direct that summary trials should be held in a Supreme Court without a preliminary examination in a magistrate's court. Its most important provision (suspended at discretion of the Minister of Justice on January 11, 1965) in clause 17, enabled a police officer to detain for interrogation for periods of up to 90 days, any person he suspects upon reasonable grounds of having committed or intending or having intended to commit any offence under the Suppression of Communism Act, or the offence of sabotage, or who in his opinion is in possession of any information relating to any such offence. Courts do not have jurisdiction over any detainee, and the detainee may be kept in solitary confinement. Another provision, permanently in effect, empowers the Minister of Justice to detain for 180 days, on the same conditions, any person he suspects.

—Official Sources

TRUE TO HIS promise in Pretoria the week before, the director of prisons arranged for two of his bright young officers to pick me up on a cold, clear Johannesburg morning and take me to Leeuwkop, the model prison farm some twenty miles out from town (already threatened by advancing suburbs, destined soon to be shoved still farther out as the city sweeps on across the highveld). My hosts were most cordial, most courteous, most friendly, as the Afrikaners at their best can be, and to the visitor usually are. And Leeuwkop seemed a model prison farm.

We had tea on arrival. The Native who served it, twenty-four or twenty-five with an ugly scar down one cheek, was in for murder, would soon be released to take up employment as a domestic in a private home.

"We place many of them that way after we train them here," one of my hosts said casually.

"There's practically never any trouble with them," the other said. "Murder is a crime of passion, once it's over they settle down. Murderers do all right when they get out. Their employers find them most reliable."

Following tea we spent the morning going from the machine shop to the vegetable gardens to the greenhouse to the house-building project to the piggery to the minimum and maximum security areas. The farm even has its own small private game reserve, begun, like the vegetable garden and greenhouse, by and for the permanent White staff members.

Everywhere the emphasis, just as the director had told me, appeared to be on rehabilitation. Everywhere, save the maximum security area, prisoners were being trained as domestics, gardeners, construction workers, farmhands. Discipline was firm but relaxed, the officers in charge having that peculiar combination of formality, informality, official reserve yet intimately personalized humor that is the mark of the experienced hand at managing the Natives. There is a certain instinctive ease that such men acquire when they spend their lives dealing with a level of mentality which, despite its vehement defenders elsewhere, is still extremely primitive over vast areas of the continent. The laughter they evoked from the prisoners I was shown appeared to be quite genuine, the response they were able to get in human terms seemed perfectly sincere: they liked their charges and their charges appeared to like them. In other prisons less sunny and less open to the visitor other things might be going on, but there was no evidence that day at Leeuwkop that anything other than a model experiment was being conducted in a model way.

There were just a couple of things that lingered after. When we inspected the maximum security barracks (having been joined now by four or five more uniformed officers and a couple of most terribly earnest, most frightfully at-attention young Afrikaans enlisted men), we entered one of the standard sleeping-rooms inhabited by some thirty or forty prisoners—murderers, rapists, cutthroats all, products of the townships and the jungle world of the urbanized Bantu. The room gave onto a large courtyard containing an exercise area, latrines, a shower room, all spotlessly clean (as were the kitchens we visited later, and indeed all of Leeuwkop that I was permitted to see). The room itself was spotlessly clean, bare walls, bare concrete floor, sleeping pallets neatly laid out along three walls.

As we entered, the prison commandant barked a sharp call for attention in Afrikaans, a company of black bodies in plain cotton tunics jumped to their feet and stood rigid against the walls. Enormous dark eyes stared at us with a dumb uncertainty. Held up beneath each pair of eyes, at about chin level, was the inevitable accompaniment of the native, his pass-book. They were in prison, stripped of all belongings, naked but for their tunics, held in maximum security—but here were their pass-books. And because they were required to—and also, obviously, because it was an absolute instinct with them—they presented them instantly to authority.

That remains.

And one other thing, in the same maximum security area: the prison choir, in another warm, sunny courtyard surrounded by high walls, with the officers and their guest drawn up in solid phalanx at one end, the choir at the other. And the beautiful voices and the instinctive rhythm which, again despite the indignant protests of a certain school of thought elsewhere, really is a distinct and definable racial characteristic: "What A Friend I Have In Jesus"—and "Rock of Ages"—and finally, after it was ascertained that the visitor had no requests and really did not wish to command them to stay and entertain him longer, "God Be With You 'Til We Meet Again."

COMPUTER INDUSTRY BOOMING

The computer industry in South Africa is having a great boom. New systems totaling several million dollars have been installed in the past few months and computers worth $15.4 million are expected to be installed within the next 18 months.

Included in the new orders are some of the largest computers in the southern hemisphere. A spokesman for a computer firm said: "Big business and public bodies are beginning to turn to computers as never before. Many smaller firms are also ordering them, while orders for scientific systems are also increasing. The computers will help a lot to ease the manpower shortage."

—Official Sources

"AT WHAT POINT did you part company with the Nationalists?" I asked another liberal young Afrikaner, this one a newspaperman who lays his liberalism—and very likely, one of these days, his livelihood if not his life—on the line in the public prints.

"When they removed the Coloureds from the general voting list," he said promptly. "They had always been on there, in the Cape, it was part of the Cape tradition, part of the agreement everybody made when the Union was formed in 1910. It seemed to me a betrayal of a lot of things. Of course I had become uneasy about a good deal before that, but I think that was what finally drove me out.

"My only problem now," he said with a wry smile, "is that I don't know where to go. I can't stomach the United Party—Div Graaf is just too charming and too ineffectual for words, and all the U.P. tries to do is outpromise the Nats. They're really the reactionaries on race and the Nats are the liberals, in our terms. And as for Helen Suzman's Progressive Party—they're so mixed up about their graduated franchise that I don't think they know what they want. And Alan Paton's Liberals who want one man, one vote—that's insane in the context of present-day South Africas, as it's been proven to be insane in the context of most of the rest of Africa. So I have quite a little problem. In a sense I've left my own people—because we're very clannish, we Afrikaners, you know, and the Nats have pretty well taken over the tribe—but where will I go now? I'm damned if I know. . . .

"Do I think geographic partition such as Dr. Rhoodie proposes is the answer to our race problem?" He gave a sudden grin. "Sure, I'd be for partition. Let 'em have Natal—that's where all the bloody English live!"

NO COLOUR BARS IN EMERGENCY (Star, *Johannesburg, English*)
. . . Emergencies know no race barriers in Johannesburg—and the city's ambulances consequently have no race barriers. The Westonaria Town Council has decided to support representations from the South African Indian Council that any ambulance arriving at the scene of an accident be permitted to render assistance, regardless of race.

Such special representations would not have to be made by Johannesburg, said Mr. George Cain, Johannesburg's fire and ambulance chief today.

"We have separate White and non-White ambulance services for medical cases," said Mr. Cain. "But should an emergency ambulance be called out to an accident our first-aid and removal service would be the same no matter the race of the victim.

"The principle of operation of an emergency ambulance service is that an ambulance must respond to an emergency case with as little delay as possible and give whatever help it can to whoever it can."

Every ambulance is cleaned and disinfected after every time it has been used, no matter the race of the patient who was moved. The emergency ambulances also carry special blankets for non-Whites. . . .

O N THE SCHEDULE arranged for me by the Department of Information in Johannesburg, there appeared, along with various other prominent Afrikaners, the editors of the three most powerful pro-Government Afrikaans newspapers.

There are also present in Johannesburg the editors of the Johannesburg *Star,* the *Rand Daily Mail,* the *Sunday Times* and the *Sunday Express.*

Neither they nor any other English-speakers appeared on the list of official contacts arranged by the Government. Yet as I told someone later at the Cape when I had come to understand the country better, it could have been deliberate but it is entirely possible that it simply did not occur to the Department of Information that it was being one-sided. It is entirely possible that in its collective Afrikaans thinking the English-language papers simply do not exist as serious subjects for interview.

Of the twenty-one daily newspapers printed in the Republic, sixteen are printed in English, five in Afrikaans. There are seven Sunday newspapers, all of national circulation, six published in Johannesburg, one in Durban. Of the Sunday papers, three are printed in Afrikaans, four in English. One of the English papers is for non-white readership only.

There are approximately 130 weekly or semiweekly papers, the majority containing sections printed in both the official languages. There are also several fortnightly and monthly publications. Estimated circulation of English-language newspapers and periodicals is about 2,200,000; of Afrikaans publications, about 1,700,000.

Yet not one of the English papers, nor all the English circulation, has one-tenth the impact on national policy of the three small papers I was to visit this day.

"English-speakers will try to tell you that we Afrikaans are still fighting the Anglo-Boer War," said the editor of *Dagbreek,* the Sunday paper published by the printing combine chairmanned by the Prime Minister. "But that's nonsense. We've won that battle hands down, now, we don't have to worry about it anymore. There are more important things in the world for South Africans to worry about now."

"Our most pressing concern," said the editor of *Die Transvaaler,* daily newspaper published by the Prime Minister's combine, "is the outside pressures against South Africa that are trying to bring down our traditional and necessary way of life. That is creating more unity than we have ever had."

"As long as the Republic is under fire from abroad," said the editor of *Die Vaderland,* spokesman for the powerful old-line Afrikaners of the Transvaal and the Orange Free State, "we have but one task, and that is to preserve and build up our national strength for whatever may face us."

"It is true the Prime Minister is the chairman of our publishing company," said the editor of *Die Transvaaler,* "but we pursue a vigorous, independent line of thought. If our editorials and news stories in general reflect the Government's position, that is because we happen to agree with it."

"The Prime Minister's chairmanship does not affect us," said the editor of *Dagbreek.* "The positions we take, we take because we believe in them. Naturally you would not expect us to attack the Government when it is doing its best to lead the country through such difficult times, would you?"

"We feel our basic mission is to strengthen the cause of Afrikanerdom," said the editor of *Die Vaderland.* "We feel we exercise independent judgment in the highest traditions of a free press. Possibly those critics of the English-language press who charge us with being spokesmen for the Government overlook the fact that we sincerely happen to agree with what the Government is doing. We do not feel that this detracts from our stature as independent journalists. Do you?"

S.A. LOSES MORE ON ROADS THAN U.S. IN WAR (Rand Daily Mail, *English*) . . . *In the past year, South Africa lost more people through road accidents than the United States did in the Vietnam war, Dr. C. J. S. Strydom, chairman of the Cape Peninsula Road Safety Association, said yesterday.*

The death toll on roads in South Africa topped the 5,000 mark last year for the first time, and it appeared that it would continue to go higher, he told the annual meeting of the association in Cape Town.

But, as soon as anything drastic was proposed, "there is a storm of protest.

"It can be proved that liquor plays a large role in road accidents but the public is not prepared to allow any curtailment of its freedom. It can also be proved that speed is a tremendous factor in accidents, but if there is a proposal to introduce a speed limit of 70 m.p.h. on open roads, we hear again that the freedom of the individual is being curtailed.

"It is difficult to combat a danger if you are not allowed to use all the powers at your disposal, but it is even more difficult if you are forced to tackle it with kid-glove methods."

WORLD GOLD PRODUCTION (TOP SIX, EXCLUDING USSR)
(In '000 fine oz.)

	1962	1963	1964
South Africa	25,492	27,432	29,111
Canada	4,158	4,000*	3,760*
USA	1,556	1,500*	1,450*
Australia	1,073	1,050*	950*
Ghana	888	921	870*
Rhodesia	555	566	575

—Official Sources

* Estimated.

THERE WERE TWELVE of us at the party, young professional men and their wives for the most part; two couples English-speaking, the rest Afrikaans, two couples from Pretoria, the rest from Johannesburg. The drinks were good, the food was good, in due course there came the inevitable question: "What do you think of us?" After that, the inevitable discussion.

(Later on, midway in my journey, I would have a charming host and hostess who sharply challenged my comment that South Africans talk about South Africa all the time—after they had spent forty-eight hours of incessant argument trying to convince me that all was for the best in their best of all possible countries.)

This night the conversation was liberal in tone, these were for the most part members of the United Party or Progressives. There was much uneasiness expressed about the Nats—until I recounted my conversation earlier in the week concerning the 180-day law, and the implicit faith my companions had shown in the honesty of the Government. Immediately the conversation turned around 180 degrees and went straight in the direction of 180 days.

"But you must realize," said my host, an English-speaker who only a moment before had been bitterly denouncing many aspects of apartheid, "that the people who have been taken under this authority have been Communists. They have been trying to destroy us. It seems to me these facts justify the law."

"Well, I'm sorry, but I react to things on the basis of my upbringing and tradition, just as you do, and mine says that unlimited arbitrary power in the hands of anybody is a desperate danger to everyone. Now, obviously yours doesn't, but doesn't it concern any of you that the Government could move in here right now if it didn't like what we were saying and take you off for 180 days?"

"But, you see, it won't," he said simply. "We know it won't. We are not the ones the law is designed to catch."

"You don't feel there is a gradual closing-in under way, a narrowing of the areas where the individual can speak and act freely? You don't feel threatened at all by the Government?"

"I do," said one of the Afrikaners from Pretoria abruptly, and they all looked at him with a genuine surprise. "But I don't feel that it stems from the 180-day law. I feel it stems from the Government's increasing unwillingness to accept criticism made in good faith, or to regard even the mildest opposition as being anything but hostile in intent. I feel that, all right."

"You do?" said his fellow Afrikaner from Pretoria in a tone of complete skepticism, while at his side his small dark wife got a curiously thoughtful, closed-off expression on her pretty little face.

"Oh, yes," the first said. "Definitely, in Pretoria. Maybe I'm oversensitive, but I'm Afrikaans myself and I must say in my work I meet a lot of Government people and a lot of educators; and the climate is changing, or at least it seems that way to me."

"How is it changing?" persisted his fellow Pretorian.

A certain defensive stubbornness came into his voice.

"I get the distinct feeling that if I say anything—anything at all—against the Government, or not even necessarily 'against' it, just even mildly critical, then they become hostile and try to close me out. I definitely do feel that. It is getting so that I am becoming almost afraid to say what I think when I am in Pretoria."

"Really?" our English-speaking host said with the same disbelief with which they were all reacting. "I don't think we've run into that here, do you?"

"Of course the Nats are very strong politically," his fellow English-speaker said, "but possibly the atmosphere here is freer, anyway. People probably talk more freely in a big city like Jo'burg than they do in a small-town political center like Pretoria. But, I would have to say that I haven't felt it."

"Well, I have," the first Afrikaner said with a stubborn set to his mouth. "I feel it everywhere I go over there in those Government offices. They make you feel that you're almost a traitor, you might say, if you say anything contrary to Government policy. I think that's bad for the country. It disturbs me."

"I found that too, when I was over there," I said, and across the room the wife of the other Afrikaner from Pretoria gave me a sudden sharp glance.

"I sometimes get the feeling that everything I say goes right to the Security Police," the first Afrikaner said with a rueful, not entirely joking laugh.

"I, too," I said. "Not that we're going to stop."

"No," he agreed, still ruefully amused, "though I may regret it. You're all right, you can always get out. I live here."

Then everybody laughed and assured us that it was all nonsense and there was nothing to be concerned about. The talk went on to something else. But the small, dark wife of the other Afrikaner did not laugh as much as the rest, nor did she enter the conversation, and from time to time thereafter she gave us both her swiftly calculating glance.

WATER CONSERVATION

Water has been defined as the most essential raw material which the Republic must develop for its future growth.

Nearly 60 per cent of the Republic has less than 20 inches of rain per annum and can be considered barren.

For nearly 90 per cent of the area of the Republic water additional to the rainfall is either essential to any agriculture at all or necessary for full production. . . .

The vast R450-million Orange River Project, which will take more than 20 years to complete, is under way. The scheme was announced in March 1962 and preliminary work on the first of the six stages has started. The purpose of the scheme is to irrigate 1,000 miles of South

Africa's most arid land, to provide water to major cities and to supply hydroelectric power to industrial areas.

A region extending for about 1,000 miles from Port Elizabeth on the Indian Ocean to Port Nolloth on the Atlantic will receive direct benefit from the project. The water supplies to cities such as Bloemfontein, Kimberley and Port Elizabeth will be ensured. . . .

—Official Sources

I WENT TWICE TO Broadcast House on Commissioner Street in Johannesburg, home of one of the most bitterly controversial institutions in the country, the South African Broadcasting Corporation. My first visit was to Radio Bantu—or, to give it the triumphant pronunciation of one of its native announcers on the Tswana and Northern Sotho Service, "Rrrrrrrradio *Ban*—tu!"

"Show Mr. Drury your programming schedule," the Afrikaner told the African, and the African, small, wiry, wearing big horn-rimmed glasses and an air of desperate earnestness that almost made him sweat, did so with a dogged attention to detail that finally prompted the Afrikaner to say, "Just the highlights, now, just the highlights. Hurry it along, now."

But the African, though he obediently speeded his delivery to the point where his words were almost unintelligible, was obviously genuinely unable to skip a word once he had started. So I got it all, broadcast by broadcast, quarter-hour by quarter-hour, for an eleven-and-a-half-hour day. At the end the African uttered an instinctive, unconscious sigh of relief, and over his head the Afrikaner, who is the director of Radio Bantu, gave me a smile and a wink and said, "That was very fine. Thank you very much. Now, Mr. Drury, if you'd like to come this way and see the physical plant—"

But there is of course much more to Radio Bantu than either programming or physical plant. It is one of the most obvious, and most expensive, features of apartheid. It does an undeniable amount of good and, in the minds of its critics, an undeniable amount of bad, in that it of course gives the Government an ideal medium for political propaganda and persuasion.

"You ought to hear what they tell them all the time about what a wonderful place the Transkei is, and how great the housing developments are, and what a wonderful education they're giving the Bantu, and how perfect the Nats are and how much they've done for the natives," I was to be told bitterly elsewhere on a later day. "Then you'd know why they spend so much money on Radio Bantu!"

But, as with most things in South Africa, there are several aspects, all equally valid and all leaving the lover of absolutes on shaky ground. Radio Bantu does provide musical programs, it does provide educational services, it does put on the air such things as a program on Freud for the Zulu Service which even in that beautiful language—or perhaps because of it—comes through to the listener as a most impressive production. To think of broadcasting a program on Freud to the Natives out in the kraals takes, in itself, quite an imagination and quite a concept of responsibility. It is not all Government propaganda, though that naturally enough has its major place.

In Broadcast House, however, there is obvious among the Natives actually working on the programs no feeling of resentment or questioning about what they are doing. There is instead a definite air of satisfied achievement. They have it made, and it is quite apparent that they feel that way. One avenue to prestige and self-expression almost comparable to that of the white world has been graciously opened by their masters, and they have been lucky enough to become part of it. It is clear enough indication how their fellow-Bantu feel when the records show that since the inauguration of day-long programs two years ago, more than thirty thousand Natives have applied for positions with Radio Bantu.

"We estimate," the Afrikaner said when we were back in his comfortable office drinking tea, "that we have more than two million adult listeners throughout the country to our six separate program services. We received a total of 1,635,627 letters from listeners in 1965 [They had shown me one from a Xhosa in Umtata: "If you had a quarrel with your wife and you switch on your FM radio, she flashes a smile at you after a short while and that is the end of the quarrel."] and we think that is quite a respectable showing.

"Our six channels include the Zulu Service, from Durban and Johannesburg, which is on the air from 5 A.M. to 11 P.M.; the Southern Sotho, from Johannesburg, also from 5 A.M. to 11 P.M.; the Tswana and Northern Sotho, originating from Pretoria, both on the air for eleven and a half hours a day; the Xhosa, from Grahamstown in the Ciskei, Eastern Cape Province, also for eleven and a half; and the Venda-Tsonga Services, originating here in Johannesburg for two hours daily. That makes seventy-two and a half hours a day total, in seven languages and six services; That is quite an advancement over 1940 when we began with fifteen minutes a day, and that was all.

"Our present program staff numbers more than two hundred, of whom forty-five, mostly in administrative or advisory capacities, are White. All of our seventy-two announcers are Bantu, and many other Bantu are employed as program compilers, record librarians, typists, clerks and record players. We also employ a great many Bantu in addition on a part-time basis as actors, musicians and entertainers.

"You heard our Zulu program on Freud, which we're submitting this year as our entry in an international competition in Tokyo, and you'll also be interested in the fact that we have also translated and produced such things as *Hamlet* and Homer's *Iliad*. Frequently these things are done for the Zulu service"—he smiled—"the Zulus seem to like heroic things, being an heroic people themselves. . . .

"Also, we put on such things as original Christmas plays, serials and stories. We offer a real outlet for native talent, and they appreciate it. We had one short-story competition, for instance, for which we got nine hundred submissions, and of these, two hundred were usable. It speaks well for them, you know?" he said thoughtfully. "They seem to have quite a bit of talent, when it has a proper outlet. Quite a bit. . . .

"One thing would amuse you, and that is that many of our announcers rapidly become national personalities, to the point where some have had hit tunes composed in their honor by well-known Bantu composers."

He chuckled.

"I think radio was made for the natives, they love to talk so, they're such natural orators. You never find many of them freezing at a microphone! . . .

"News programs? Oh, yes, we have many of them—a total of thirty-six daily bulletins on the six services. They cover both international and national events, with regional items contributed by more than six hundred Bantu correspondents all over the country. Some of these correspondents would really put a white man to—some of them really work hard. We have one in Vendaland who actually sent in sixty-six items consisting of almost 20,000 words, in the course of one week. How is that for enterprise?

"Then we have music, which covers the whole range from traditional tribal songs to the latest jazz from overseas. We hold weekly auditions to find new talent for recordings that we make of modern stuff here in Broadcast House, and in the traditional field we have a Radio Bantu mobile recording unit that travels constantly around the country to record indigenous music.

"We want to preserve and strengthen their own culture, you know," he said seriously. "It is part of the Government's separate development policy, true, but also we feel there is something unique that the Bantu have that we should help them keep. Africa has many heritages, and theirs is one of them: we are trying to preserve it for them.

"In addition to our contests for written and musical material, we also have riddle competitions—they draw the most entries. The two Zulu programs—'Iziphicophicwano' and 'Imfumbe'—get many thousands of letters each month, and the Northern Sotho riddle program for young people, 'Thaka etshesane,' was responsible for more than fourteen thousand letters in one month. We also have daily religious broadcasts and weekend sports commentaries, both of which are very popular, particularly with older listeners. . . .

"We try to attune our programs to the ways and moods of the people," he said. "For instance, we have an opening musical program in the morning for the Zulus and an evening program of the same type. They have such a wonderful language, anyway, you know, so we call the morning program by the term for 'dawn,' which is 'mpondo zanko mo' [and he gave it the lingering, loving pronunciation of the Zulus, mmmm—*pone*—do zaaaan—*ko*—mo] which means the time when the horns of the cattle become visible. And we call the last program of the day 'umutsha wendoda' [ooom—*oot*—sha wennnn—*do*—da], which means sunset, the time when a man can relax after his work is done."

STATE BAN ON COLOURED SOLOIST AT CONCERT (Cape Argus, *English*) . . . *Growing Government rigidity on cultural apartheid is likely to kill Coloured cultural and recreational movements and intensify frustrations among Coloured youth, a social worker said today.*

The latest example is the Government's refusal to allow the South African Broadcasting Corporation to have a Coloured soloist with the S.A.B.C. Symphony Orchestra at a performance in the Coloured residential area of Coronationville, Johannesburg.

This was confirmed today by the Minister of Community Development (Mr. W. A. Maree), who said the decision was taken by an official of the department under delegated authority.

Recently the Government refused permission for White adjudicators to judge the final ballet competitions of a Coloured youth club in the Cape Town area. Coloured community centres have also been refused the use of halls previously available to them for their gymnastic and physical culture competitions. . . .

Explaining the refusal of the permit to the S.A.B.C., the Minister said a principle was involved. It was accepted that a White orchestra or concert group could perform before a non-White audience and that a non-White group could perform before a White audience.

But this was subject to the condition that the performing group must consist entirely of members of one race only.

No exception could be made for the Coloured singer. If this were done there would certainly be requests from others for the inclusion of, say, instrumentalists or choir members of a different race from the rest of the group, Mr. Maree said. . . .

THE YOUNG AMERICAN scientists at the University of the Witwatersrand were very circumspect on that warm, sunny, almost autumnal day when we had lunch. They were very careful in what they said about the Government, their references to current events were indirect and jocular when uttered at all. A countryman could tell how they felt, but as long as they had a while yet to serve on their various experiments, it was obvious that no Afrikaans eavesdropper was going to be able to carry back any tales to the Government upon whose sometimes rather erratic mercies their stay in the country depended.

DIAMONDS

According to *Minerals,* journal of the Department of Mines, sales of South African diamonds were as follows:

	1964 METRIC CARATS
MINE STONES	
Transvaal	2,224,413
Cape	1,538,005
O.F.S.	108,870
Total	3,871,288
ALLUVIAL STONES	
Transvaal	163,427
Cape	414,329
O.F.S.	2,021
Total	579,777
Grand Total	4,451,065

VALUE OF SALES:

	1964 R
MINE STONES	
Transvaal	8,438,597
Cape	18,157,868
O.F.S.	2,655,139
Total	29,251,604
ALLUVIAL STONES	
Transvaal	1,209,902
Cape	13,686,366
O.F.S.	55,598
Total	14,951,866
Grand Total	44,203,470

—Official Sources

"**M**Y BROTHER-IN-LAW says you would like to see me," said the clear, light voice that has the constant undertone of wry amusement in it.

"Yes, I would. I think you're one of the main duty-stops on the road of every American visitor, aren't you?"

She laughed.

"Apparently. I'm delighted about it. Could you come to dinner tomorrow night and then go on to the African show at Wits University with us?"

I said I could, and so found myself meeting Helen Suzman a little earlier than I had planned. I would be in Cape Town a month later when Parliament opened, and had intended to see her there.

I had heard a good deal about her, for as the sole member of the Progressive Party remaining in office after the last election, she had received some attention abroad, particularly from those who see in her the symbol of a great rebellion against the Government. She is a symbol, true enough, but only of a charming, courageous and gallant lady. The effect she has upon Government policies of which she disapproves, she is the first to say with a cheerfulness that conceals the constant hurt of it, is nil.

Yet in this, as I would come to find out, she is perhaps a little harsh on herself, because she does perform one vitally important function: she asks questions in the one place the Government can't dodge them—the floor of Parliament. And the answers—or deliberate lack of them, which is often more revealing—go into *Hansard,* the record of debates, for all the world to read.

Many and many a fact about the Republic sees the light of day for no other reason than that Helen has thought of it and had the guts to stand up and ask. Few of her male colleagues of the United Party, who might be expected to have a duty to do the same, perform it or if they do, it is usually with a delicate forebearance that stays the sting. Treated with open scorn by Nationalist back-benchers—barely spoken to, with a cold courtesy, by the Prime Minister and the Cabinet—coolly snubbed by the U.P. from which she defected a decade ago—she goes indomitably on, year in, year out, getting the facts on the record. Though she constantly deprecates her contribution to South Africa, it is far greater than her countrymen perhaps realize. Certainly it is greater than any of them outside her own party will admit.

The door at the big rambling home in the Johannesburg suburb of Houghton, which she represents, was opened by a small, vivacious woman in her late forties, with brown hair, keenly intelligent eyes, a pretty face, a quick, droll smile. It was a cold night, she explained, so she had a coal-fire burning. An older woman friend and the Netherlands Ambassador were already there; her husband, a doctor, would be home soon. She fixed drinks and immediately plunged into what I was coming to think of as The Question:

"Well, what do you think of South Africa?"

For the time being I gave one of The Answers, I don't remember now which one: "It's certainly beautiful"—or "It's fantastic"—or "It's quite a country"—one of those remarks akin to Sir Winston Churchill's, "That *is* a baby!" that the visitor to South Africa soon adopts in self-defense.

She laughed merrily.

"I don't think you're being honest with us. But, never mind. We'll read it all when it's published."

"If they allow it in down here, which I rather doubt, since inevitably it isn't going to be 100 per cent in favor of the Government."

"If you're not 100 per cent for this Government," she said crisply, "you're OUT. Don't you agree, Mr. Ambassador?"

The Netherlands Ambassador, a very diplomatic gentleman, murmured his equivalent of "That *is* a baby!" and took a discreet sip of his drink. Helen dissolved in laughter again.

"I can't get *anybody* to commit himself tonight. I see I'm not making the drinks strong enough."

"Oh, quite, quite," the Ambassador murmured hastily, whereupon we all laughed.

I asked about Parliament, and what she thought the Nats would do, now that they had been returned with such a huge majority. She sniffed.

"Exactly what they've been doing up to now—exactly as they please."

"Will there be more repressive laws passed?"

"*More* repressive? How could they be *more* repressive? Yes, they'll do what they can to tighten the screws. Why shouldn't they?" She gave a mocking little laugh. "Certainly they're not going to stop because *I* say they should."

"How about the United Party?"

She sniffed with a wry expression.

"You wait until you get down to Parliament and then tell *me* about the United Party. I think I'd better make *my* drink stronger, on that one! And drink to Div Graaff. Are you going to see him?"

I said yes, that Sir deVilliers Graaff, leader of the United Party, had responded cordially to the letter I had written.

"Then you can judge for yourself."

"Why did you leave the United Party to help form the Progressives?"

"Partly because of his lack of leadership. Partly because the U.P. was becoming more reactionary than the Nats. They are, about race, you know. They don't even want separate development. They don't know what they want, as a matter of fact. So I got out."

"And the Progressives? I hear you're a little vague, too."

"We want a graduated franchise for the Bantu, the Coloureds and the Indians, based upon educational and economic qualifications."

"Not one man, one vote?"

"No," she said. "That isn't quite South Africa's wicket, I think, at least, not at her present stage of development. One man, one vote needs a sophisticated electorate to make it work. I think you'll find as you go around the country that we certainly haven't got that now among our native population. Not that it's their fault, of course, it just isn't there."

"How soon will it be?"

"Poof!" She shrugged. "Never, if the Nats have their way. And," she added, suddenly serious, "the Nats will, I suspect. Well, shall we go in?"

After another of the many beautifully cooked, beautifully served meals that I was to consume in South Africa (native cooks being good, native house-help being easily available for modest incomes and lavishly available for middle and upper incomes), we went off to Wits ("Vhits") —the University of the Witwatersrand ("Vhit-*vhahters*-rahndt"), established by Cecil Rhodes and other far-seeing Englishmen in the pioneer days of the Reef, and now ranking with the University of Cape Town as one of the two leading English-language universities in the country.

Wits sits on a pleasant hill above Johannesburg, crowded now by industries and apartment developments so that its original view has been lost, but still a gracious, open campus filled with the old-fashioned, comfortable buildings and the new steel-and-glass intruders that distinguish most prosperous campuses these days. Its enrollment is pushing seven thousand, its relations with the Government are touch-and-go, and from time to time already it has felt the sting, in appropriations withheld and grants refused, of the Nationalists reacting to severe liberal criticism from members of the faculty. Like all English-speaking institutions in the Republic, it feels the steady wind of Afrikaans advance. An uneasiness fills its atmosphere, and it does not take long for the visitor to sense it as he talks to faculty and students.

Tonight the atmosphere was uneasy, too, for this was a performance of a musical play by Bantu composers, writers, directors and actors from the townships, principally Soweto ("Soh-*wett*-oh" from "South West Townships"), the 600,000-black population complex that sprawls on the edge of Jo'burg.

It had been necessary first to obtain an official permit to allow the Bantu to present it. Second, it had been necessary to obtain a permit to allow it to be shown to a White audience. The audience was not mixed, otherwise that would have required a permit, too, and it very likely would not have been granted. And it was only because the purpose was to raise funds for charities assisting the Bantu that it had been permitted at all. And it was only because Wits was English-speaking, available and willing, that it was given there. Had the white sponsors of the Bantu charities had the temerity to request permission to present the show at the University of Pretoria, for instance, the official No would almost certainly have been inevitable.

At any rate, here it was at Wits and it was not, as Helen and everyone else remarked ruefully, very good. Occasionally these annual affairs strike a real spark, real talent emerges, a tightly knit show has a big success and even goes overseas: *King Kong* is the example everyone talks about nostalgically. But tonight, though it had an occasional bright spot in the choral numbers ("They always sing so well," the tuxedo-clad, cream-of-Johannesburg-society-and-finance audience told one another comfortably at intermission, just as audiences do back home. "They have such a natural sense of rhythm."), it failed to get off the ground.

Yet in certain ways it proved very illuminating. There was a Bantu storekeeper: he was murdered by some Bantu thugs. The young Bantu hero was repeatedly waylaid by Bantu gangs: his attempts at honesty were constantly thwarted by his own people. His parents and their friends were good-hearted, decent, well-meaning souls: they were held in thrall by a vicious little group of murderous Bantu criminals.

A real and palpable fear of one another came innocently but quite clearly through the Bantu-written, Bantu-produced script. This was not a white man's view of the townships. This was a Bantu glass we were looking through.

It could not in fairness be said—though it has been said in unfairness by many overseas—that this was the Government's fault for having moved them to townships in the first place. The histories of the old tin-shack huddles such as Sophiatown are authenticated and are even worse. The situation for the urbanized Bantu really is better, now. But, as we saw through Bantu eyes this night, not much.

After the curtain the chairman of the evening arose, in his plump, well-fed Johannesburg way, to express the thanks of the audience to the co-authors, who came forward in a bowing, humble, we-know-our-place-and-you-can-rest-assured-we're-not-getting-out-of-it fashion, to take a bow.

"One of the wonderful things about this great production," he said, "is that these two Bantu"—he hesitated on the verge of "boys" but caught himself at the last instant—"these two Bantu—men—wrote this show and put it on completely by themselves, without White"—and Johannesburger, English-speaker, good South African that he was, he gave the capital "W" its full emphasis—"without White Supervision or Control. That is just wonderful, that these Bantu could do this fine, marvelous job, and I know we're all proud of them. I think we should give them a hearty round of applause."

And his audience did so dutifully, but not without reaction, for many, including my hostess, looked openly annoyed. And as they went away into the chilly night to get their cars in the parking lots, there was audible indignation on every side: "Did you hear the way he patronized those Bantu? Did you *hear* that pompous ass? My dear, I am so ashamed for the Whites. I only hope They don't hold it against us!"

So it was illuminating on several accounts, my evening with Helen at the native musical. After the party had returned to her house for a night-cap, we shared our regrets that the show, since it was such an opportunity for the Bantu—They trying so hard to please Us, We so wanting to be pleased—had not somehow managed to be just a little better. And we got indignant all over again about the chairman, and how patronizing he had been, and how unfortunate it was.

"Be sure to look me up when you come down to Parliament," she said as we said goodnight, and I said I certainly would.

She sighed and for a moment looked openly tired and discouraged.

"You see what we are up against, on every side. It makes it all so difficult."

"Everyone expects her to be there, you know," the Afrikaner M. P. said complacently in Cape Town. "She's recognized and accepted—an acceptable Opposition. We'd rather miss Helen. We hope she stays in for a long time. We're used to her." He chuckled. "She doesn't really bother us, you know. We like to have her around, now." His chuckle bubbled. "You might almost say she's part of us. We can always count on Helen!"

WALKING IN FEAR (Editorial, World, Johannesburg, Bantu) . . . Everyone living in Soweto is aware of the serious crime rate in the township. As we pointed out in our leader yesterday, violent crime is taking over Soweto.

What we ask now is: What do the authorities intend doing to meet the critical menace in Soweto? What measures are being undertaken to direct youth away from crime?

Let there be no mistake about this. The White is in no position to view the situation in Soweto with equanimity.

If the present trend continues, the waves of crime in our townships will inevitably spill over into Johannesburg's White areas.

Today the Black walks in fear. At the rate things are going, it won't be long before the White will have good reason to do so.

THE BANTU

"The all-embracing traditional unit in the social organisation is tribe, based upon a central group or nucleus of families descended from a common ancestor or ancestors. . . . The central group provides the men of authority in the tribe in accordance with the principle of inherited status, and other elements are assimilated to this group. The binding factor, upon which the survival of the tribe as a unit depends, is the chief.

"Another strong element holding the social fabric together is family relationship, based on the patrilineal system. . . . Of great importance also is the fact that every individual, in accordance with a system of classification of relationships can have several 'fathers,' 'mothers,' 'brothers' and 'sisters.' This fosters the formation of a large group of mutually dependent people, with mutual privileges and responsibilities.

"By following definite marriage rules, based on the system of family relationships, or consanguinity, families come into being which, through their various marital relationships, act as a network holding the whole tribe together. . . . These social ties are further strengthened by the handing over of goods, mainly cattle, by the family of the husband to the family of the wife. The goods are generally known and described as 'lobolo.' The marriage system and handing over of 'lobolo' have the effect of placing the whole tribal community in each other's debt, a chain reaction that ultimately returns to its starting point and there initiates a new cycle.

"Although monogamous marriage is quite common, Bantu society is definitely oriented toward polygamy. The propagation of children is a fundamental requirement placed upon marriage, and childless marriages or birth-control, in the Western sense, are unthinkable under the Bantu system.

"Among all the Bantu tribes there is a definite order of rank under which the wives of a polygamist are classified according to seniority or status. Such classification is an outward symbol of the position of the children of each wife, in regard to their inheritance. . . .

"The personal and legal standing of individual members of a family are mainly governed by three principles:

"(i) the hierarchy deriving from differences in age;
(ii) differentiation between male and female sex groups; and
(iii) differences deriving from the rank of the various wives in a polygamous household. . . .

"Within the social structure as a whole, each individual has his permanent and special position, rights, duties and responsibilities. Each phase of life is entered upon after passing through ritual processes and ceremonies. . . .

"The economic system of the Bantu consists mainly of the keeping of stock, the cultivation of crops, the collection of wild fruits and spinach, etc., in the veld, the hunting of game and the practice of home industries. Within this pattern which betokens a simple existence, provision is made for food requirements, clothing and ornaments, utensils and weapons, housing and other needs of life. . . .

"Land for cultivation is allowed by the chief to members of the tribe, each allotment measuring, as a rule, a few acres. Cultivation of the soil is mainly the duty of the woman. On the other hand, the man is solely concerned with the care of animals, cattle, sheep and goats. Cattle exercise such a powerful influence throughout their lives, quite apart from economic considerations, that especially among the Nguni, a formidable cattle complex has developed. Numbers and not quality give special status to the owner. Cattle are the key to marriage, to political and social advancement, and play a leading part in religious life.

"Generally the economic system is characterised by the absence of currency in the form of cash or other exchange tokens, by a high degree of uniformity in the standard of living of all members of a tribe, and by the rarity of professional or other specialised activities.

"The Bantu believe in the existence of a Supreme Being, far removed from man and only approachable by a hierarchy or the ancestral spirits who serve as mediators between Him and human beings. The Bantu is, however, essentially a man who prays to his ancestors, a form of prayer arising from the belief that the dead live in another world just like our own whence, as abiding members of the organic tribal life, they are still able to influence earthly affairs. . . .

"Faith in magic, the belief that man can manipulate supernatural forces in his own interest, plays a most important role in Bantu life.

"Training of the young and education are integrated with the whole cultural system. In the main the young learn their place and their task in life from the older members of their own generation. In the tribal or initiation schools, training of a more formal kind is given separately to the two sexes. . . . The principal subjects dealt with are the position and duties of the pupil in the social hierarchy (citizenship), sex instruction and the acquisition of the necessary skills such as hunting and warfare for boys, and hoe-cultivation for girls.

"In the Bantu community there are no special institutions for caring for those in need. People in need are in the direct care of their relations, as in any other simple society. In the home, the wider family circle and in the tribal sphere, the Bantu have a strong sense of mutual responsibility, so that those in want are helped, in accordance with custom, by those in better circumstances.

"The Bantu system of government derives its authority from the chief in council, while the tribe and the tribal land are subdivided into larger or smaller administrative units as the case may be. The whole tribe is like a pyramid directed towards the chief who is at the apex of the political structure, the law, defence, economic development, and, last but not least, the religious life of the community."

—From "The Tomlinson Report" on the future of the Bantu, issued by the Tomlinson Commission appointed by the Governor-General of the Union of South Africa in 1954, and still the basic reference-point for South Africa in considering the Bantu problem.

"WHY, MR. DRURY," said the roly-poly little white-haired Afri-kaner with the neat little moustache, host on my second visit to the S.A.B.C., "the English-speakers are always charging that we use our broadcasts for Government propaganda. They are always saying that we give the preponderance of our broadcasts in Afrikaans. But, Mr. Drury, that is ridiculous. We wouldn't do such a thing. Why would we do such a thing? It is ridiculous.

"Statistics will show you," he said, getting up from his desk and pac-ing excitedly up and down his handsome office, "statistics will show you that we maintain a balance, a balance, Mr. Drury, between the two official languages. In fact, they will show you that we actually broadcast more hours of English, if anything. Why, what would it serve us to an-tagonize deliberately our English-speaking brethren? We take the great-est care to insure that absolute equality—*absolute equality*, Mr. Drury! —is maintained between the two official languages.

"Now, of course"—and he paused suddenly to stare at me with great seriousness—"you will no doubt, no doubt you will, hear from certain English-speaking critics that our Afrikaans broadcasts stress the heritage of the Afrikaans people and uphold the history of Afrikanerdom, and that perhaps these programs go rather more into detail about the history of Afrikanerdom than comparable programs do in English about the his-tory of our English settlers. But, Mr. Drury, the Afrikaner founded this country. The English only came later, long after the country was estab-lished, they only came when it paid them, to expand their empire and later to get gold and diamonds. South Africa was more or less an inci-dental to them"—he gave his snuffling, excited little laugh—"a very rich incidental, as it turned out, but really only an incidental, whereas it was, and is, everything to us.

"The Englishman, Mr. Drury, doesn't really care too much about his history here, as we see it. It is really only since we became a republic five years ago that the Englishman has ceased to look to England and has shown much interest in his history in this country. We try to give our listeners what we think they will like, and our Afrikaner listeners are always anxious to learn how our ancestors founded and developed our beautiful fatherland. We don't feel that our English listeners have so much interest.

"And of course they will tell you about our program 'Current Events,' which no doubt you have heard for yourself?—yes, I was sure you had— and in which we try to present to our Afrikaans- and English-speaking listeners a balanced picture of events. It is true that this is an editorial program, Mr. Drury, you yourself can detect that, it may possibly reflect something of the position of South Africa, the official position, but what is wrong with that? We feel that the S.A.B.C. has an absolute right, Mr. Drury, to present its side of things, an absolute right. Are we not always under attack by the English-language press? Aren't they always charging us with all sorts of things? Then why are we not perfectly justified in having an editorial voice, too, and in responding to criticism? They say we are a public service depending on Government funds and charging our listeners for annual licenses, and so we should be objective. But who is objective in this country, Mr. Drury? It is perfectly true that we get loans and assistance from the Government, though we are fully autonomous and the Government respects this. But, Mr. Drury, who is the true representative of South Africa, if it is not the Government which has just won the greatest majority in South African history!"

He bounced back to his desk and began fiddling impatiently with the papers on it, his nervous little smile flashing back and forth across his face, his quick, wheezing little laugh punctuating his words.

"When it comes to national and international affairs of vital interest to the Republic, Mr. Drury, I assure you this corporation does its best to proceed with circumspection and preserve objectivity, balance and responsibility. Let me read you these words from our annual report for 1965, which sum it up:

" 'To a neutrality urge which could jeopardize the security and well-considered interests of the country and the people, the Board of Governors conceded nothing more than might be expected from a South African institution occupying the strategic position of the S.A.B.C. It is firmly convinced that the Corporation is obliged to serve this country and its population groups in spite of limited but vociferous movements serving aims that undermine and ultimately destroy the happiness, prosperity and future of our country.'

"That says it, Mr. Drury, that says it. This 'neutrality urge,' Mr. Drury, on certain policies of vital importance to the country—we have to fight it. We have to oppose what the report calls 'limited but vociferous elements' that would undermine us. We have to respond to the English-language press and the attacks of the outside world. We could not serve our people otherwise, Mr. Drury, we really could not!

"No, Mr. Drury"—and he leaped to his feet again and began his pacing—"they cannot make the charge stick, they cannot make it stick, Mr. Drury. We are fair in our presentation of what is best for South Africa, best for the English, best for Afrikanerdom. Why, how could we be otherwise? We would be false to our public duty if we were otherwise.

"I think you will find the S.A.B.C.," he said, suddenly solemn, "one of the most interesting facets of what I suspect you find a rather interesting country. We are a humble country, Mr. Drury, our history has made us that, but what an arrogant country, too! What a strange mixture we are!

We are filled with uncertainties on the one hand, but on the other we have the greatest this, the most that, the best the other. Our mountains are higher, our seas are bluer, our natural wealth is greater, our future is brighter—well, it is if we can just attain it, Mr. Drury! It is.

"I understand you visited Radio Bantu the other day. You saw what a job we do for our Bantu population there. I think we do equally well for our European population. Just let me read you some statistics—" and he hopped back to his desk, dropped into his seat, searched his papers, found what he wanted:

"We have a staff of approximately 2,200, of whom about 1,500 are White, the rest non-White. Total number of radio sets in use at the end of this year was estimated at 2,500,000, with a total estimated audience of 7,000,000. Our news broadcasts, in all services exclusive of Radio Bantu, number 98 per weekday for a total of 627 per week. We receive material for our broadcasts from five international news agencies, namely Reuters, Associated Press, United Press International, Agence France-Presse and Deutsche Presse-Agentur. We get about 400,000 words daily from these sources and the South African Press Association. We have full-time S.A.B.C. reporters in Johannesburg, Pretoria, Durban, Pietermaritzburg, East London, Port Elizabeth, Bloemfontein, Cape Town and Windhoek, South-West Africa. We also have about 1,200 part-time correspondents throughout the Republic and South-West. We have a full-time European correspondent headquartered in London, and part-time correspondents in New York, Paris, Hilversum and Salisbury.

"So, you see, Mr. Drury," he said with a triumphant chuckle, "we are quite well-covered in news matters, indeed we are. We are especially proud of our regular week-night feature which is broadcast on the English service as 'The News at Nine,' and on the Afrikaans service as 'Die Nuus om Nege.' In addition to factual reports, these programs carry recordings of the voices of figures prominent in the day's news, eyewitness reports, commentaries, and so on.

"We try hard, Mr. Drury, we really try hard, to make the English and Afrikaans services quite comparable to one another in every way. There may be a little more stress on religious broadcasts on the Afrikaans service, but then, as you know, we have the three branches of the Dutch Reformed Church and our people, particularly out on what we call the 'platteland'—the prairies, I guess you would say, the countryside of the Transvaal and the Orange Free State, in particular—are very religious still in their approach. All these small country towns, these 'dorps,' as we would say, close up tight on Sundays. Religious observance and a big meal are the main activities of the day. We take cognizance of this.

"But basically we try to make the two services quite parallel, in spite of what our critics no doubt may tell you. Both provide drama, frequently by South African authors. We have features on such things as 'The

Houses of Parliament,' 'The Lost City of the Kalahari,' and so on. We have talks on such things as the birds of South Africa. And we have our historical programs, which we have already discussed. The English, Mr. Drury, have their historical programs, too—'It Seems Like Yesterday,' was one, for instance, covering the years from 1915 to 1939.

"Then we have our 'University of the Air' programs, our youth and children's programs, and, above all, we have sports.

"Sports, Mr. Drury," he said, and his quick little snuffling laugh burst out again, "might be said to be, if one wished to be facetious, the 'opiate of the people' of South Africa. We are so sports-conscious, my goodness! It is possibly one thing the English have contributed, this intense love of sports we have. You will already have noticed for yourself the space the newspapers devote to sports events, and the S.A.B.C. does its share, Mr. Drury, I can assure you we do our share! Last year was a banner year for us aside from international rugby, in which our Springboks had a disappointing time, but in most other areas the Republic did handsomely. Handsomely! You can be sure the S.A.B.C. was there, Mr. Drury"—he chuckled, bobbing behind his desk—"in both official languages!

"In addition to our two European-language services on AM radio, we have in recent years built a great many FM towers around the country and have inaugurated special FM services, the two principal ones being Radio Highveld and Radio Good Hope. These are basically musical, though with news bulletins on the hour, and talks by famous personages from time to time. And then there are our external services, which we are steadily improving and expanding. We have to, Mr. Drury! South Africa must speak up for herself"—he got up and began pacing again—"no one else is!

"The first phase of our external services, which eventually will broadcast from four powerful shortwave transmitters, thirty and a half hours a day in nine languages in all directions excepting south, was inaugurated just a month or two ago. At the moment we broadcast in English, which is really our bridge to the outside world, Mr. Drury; without it we could not communicate, which is why it is so silly to say we don't want to preserve the English language here; we also broadcast in French and Portuguese, and in Zulu. The Zulu program, like the French and Portuguese, lasts forty-five minutes and is broadcast five days a week to all those areas in Africa where Zulu is understood, and that is quite an area. All our external programs are aimed at presenting a positive and factual picture of South Africa and the way of life of all its inhabitants in all racial groups. Possibly the Zulu program"—he laughed and plumped into his chair again—"is accountable in part for our flood of illegal Bantu immigrants who come down from the north. They must think we have something good here. Our factual broadcasts evidently convince them!

"You can be sure," he added, quite serious for a moment, "that if the broadcasts weren't factual, they wouldn't come. No radio network can improve upon the word-of-mouth network of the Native, Mr. Drury. If South Africa weren't the contented land we say it is, they would know soon enough, Mr. Drury, you can be sure of that!

"We also send transcriptions overseas as part of our effort. In 1965 we sent a total of 5,420 disks overseas; 605 stations in 98 countries are regularly broadcasting S.A.B.C. material to their local audiences, which we estimate gives us an overseas listenership of approximately 450,000,-000. Not bad, for our little corner of the world!

"So you see, Mr. Drury, the S.A.B.C. performs its function. It serves the interests of the Republic, which we conceive to be its duty, while at the same time furnishing entertainment and instruction for all of its peoples. It is only a few English-speaking critics who complain, Mr. Drury. And the English"—he uttered his wheezing little laugh—"well, the English! We just have to be patient, for we know they will not change."

SOME THOUGHTS (ENGLISH) ON THE S.A.B.C.

"[It has] *unashamedly become the propaganda arm of the party in power . . . dutifully echoing its master's views . . ."* (*Johannesburg* Star)

"*This farrago of isolated quotations and innuendo . . ."* (Cape Times)

"*The tendentious and partisan attitude of the S.A.B.C. . . . The Government's propaganda machine . . . disgraceful smear tactics . . . an abuse of monopolistic power . . ."* (Rand Daily Mail)

"*Tendentious, slanted comments . . . mastery of the smear technique . . . sly innuendo . . . a national scandal . . . Broederbond propaganda . . ."* (*Johannesburg* Sunday Times)

"*Anonymous propaganda . . . brainwash broadcasts . . . Broederbond-controlled S.A.B.C. [which] continues to follow the example of Dr. Goebbels . . ."* (*East London* Daily Dispatch)

"**I** REALLY THINK," the English-speaker said with a chuckle, "that they'd like to let the Immorality Act just quietly fade away and be forgotten. After all, they're the ones it hurts the most, you know—the great majority of European males who are arrested for cohabiting with Bantu women are Afrikaners. It all makes it rather hypocritical, doesn't it?"

"We have a joke about the Immorality Act," the Afrikaner said with a chuckle. "It seems this old Afrikaner from the platteland was visiting in

London and somebody asked him if he was in favor of abolishing the
Act. He blinked for a minute—'Yes, I am.' 'But how is that; aren't you
afraid it would lead to the degradation of the native population?' 'Not at
all,' he said. 'No sensible Bantu woman is going to go to bed with a
bloody Englishman!'

"I guess," the Afrikaner remarked wryly after his laughter ended,
"that one rather cuts everybody both ways, doesn't it?"

THE AFRICAN YOU WORK WITH (Daily News, *Durban, English*)
*. . . African tribal life is based on its own moral code, strictly adhered
to. In industry and the city home the worker, now away from his tribal
life, needs the structure of a moral code. But this will only impress him
if it is practiced as explicitly as it is told him. "Practice what you preach,"
and obey the rules you give him.*

"I THOUGHT HE WAS very shrewd, very tough," said the far-right Afrikaans student who had met him in Johannesburg. "But," he said
slowly, "he seems very immature. Somehow I just couldn't conceive of
him as President of the United States."

"I found him very intelligent—very hard, underneath," said the far-
left English-speaking student who had met him in Durban. "But," he
said, and a speculative look came into his eyes, "he is too young. He
doesn't seem responsible enough. I really find it impossible to think of
him as President of the United States."

BANTU BUYING POWER WILL RISE TO $6.3 BILLION

The purchasing power of the Republic's Bantu population, which is
already responsible for 17.6 per cent of consumption expenditure, is
expected to rise to more than $6.3 billion a year by the end of the cen-
tury, according to the documented report of a National Development
and Management Foundation of South Africa conference held in Durban last year. The conference was attended by experts in the various
fields relating to the Bantu population groups.

The National Development and Management Foundation states that
the marketing prospects among the Bantu are so promising that the
British Board of Trade drew up a special report on it for British ex-
porters who are likely to become keen competitors for South African
industrialists and their wares.

—Official Sources

"**O**H, MY GOD," cried the slightly drunken lady at the home of the liberal author. "Oh, my God, why doesn't somebody do something about them? Why doesn't somebody *do* something? They are such *horrible* people!"

We were discussing, as is customary in South African liberal households, the Nats, and had reached that impasse which always comes, in liberal households, at the contemplation of their overwhelming and unshakable strength. The obvious fact that nobody could do anything about them did not deter the lady from voicing her plaint dramatically once more into the discouraged silence:

"Oh, my God, my God! Why doesn't somebody *do* something?"

"The result it all has," said the author crisply, ignoring the uproar, "is to discourage one from doing anything, really. You try and try, you make protest after protest—and they simply ignore it. It is just as though you weren't there. It's like shouting into the wind, or shouting down a well—no"—a wry little smile—"at least, shouting down a well, you sometimes get an echo, and with the Nats you don't even get an echo. They are utterly impervious.

"And after a while, it begins to affect you, you know? You think: well, what's the use? Nobody's listening, nobody's going to reply—why should I keep trying? Why bother? You know you shouldn't feel that way, but it's only human. You tell yourself you're betraying your friends and the causes you believe in, but—you just get tired, you know? You just get tired. And so, after a while, you begin to stop. You begin to find reasons why you shouldn't bother, because it isn't going to do you any good to fight anymore. It isn't going to accomplish anything.

"And at that point"—very quietly—"you know the Nats have won. Because that's exactly how they want you to feel. And knowing this, and despising yourself but knowing you can't keep up the effort much longer —you stop."

"Oh, my God," cried the drunken lady to the sad little group. "Isn't anybody going to do *anything?*"

BOTHA HITS AT "HUMAN RIGHTS" PHRASES (Rand Daily Mail, *English*) . . . *True unity and cooperation would never be achieved in South Africa by destroying traditions and stifling the conscience of the nation with "hollow-sounding phrases such as human rights and the brotherhood of men," the Minister of Defence, Mr. P. O. Botha, said in Stellenbosch last night.*

Mr. Botha, who was opening the annual congress of the Afrikaanse

*Studentbond, was the first Cabinet Minister to address students at Stellen-
bosch since Senator Robert Kennedy spoke there last month.*

*He said South Africa's policy of separation was the only way in which
Whites could free themselves from the future grip of a Black proletariat.*

*The time had come for South Africa's Whites to make the "final"
choice between having a White nation with dangers, or throwing in the
towel and having no hope of a future of their own.*

*Acceptance of a policy of separation meant that White South Africans
must not have doubts when they contemplated the future with Black
states as their country's neighbours.*

*In the past decade in South Africa, there had been a struggle between
forces that wanted to create a "dead uniformity" and those who thought
that South Africa's "beauty and power" lay in the development of the
concept of separation.*

*He questioned whether South Africa would have reached its high level
of development if its White people had not preserved their rights within
their own group.*

*Mr. Botha said that liberalism had not proved anywhere in the world
that it guaranteed better human relationships and good order. . . .*

DANGER

If a policeman has reasonable grounds for believing that a meeting
is taking place which may endanger the internal security of the Republic, he may enter the premises without a warrant if he believes that
securing a warrant would cause undue delay.

—Official Sources

"I DO NOT THINK," said the Johannesburg businessman complacently,
"that any Government can control South Africa which is not firmly
based on the Witwatersrand."

*RAND WARNED: STOP LABOUR FLOW (Star, Johannesburg, Eng-
lish) . . . The Deputy Minister of Bantu Administration issued a stern
warning to Rand businessmen today:*

*"The flow of Bantu labour to the Witwatersrand must be reduced, then
it must be stopped, and then it must be turned back."*

*Opening a symposium of the National Development and Management
Foundation in Benoni, the Deputy Minister, Mr. Blaar Coetzee, added:*

"This is the policy of my Government . . . and please make no mistake about it—the Government is in deadly earnest and is absolutely determined that it will succeed."

He did not know anywhere in the developed world where there was a greater wastage of labour than on the Rand, he said.

"The time has come that all employers should realize that there is no such thing as cheap Bantu labour in the European areas and that the policy of employing large numbers of Bantu workers in that belief is neither in their own interests nor in the interests of the Bantu," Mr. Coetzee said.

He outlined five ways by which the number of Africans on the Rand could be reduced:

Influx control.

Effective employment.

The industrial, commercial, agricultural and mining development of the African homelands.

Decentralization of industries to the border areas.

Utilization of mechanization.

Mr. Coetzee said that the African population of the Rand exceeded the White population by more than 500,000. . . .

REEF FACTORIES HURT BY INFLUX CONTROL (Rand Daily Mail, *English*) *. . . Some Reef factories have been forced to cut production after an official influx control drive which left a number of concerns without a full complement of trained staff . . .*

According to the Garment Workers' Union of South Africa, a large clothing factory near Germiston reported it was recently "invaded" by a team of "peace officers" who sent 95 of its [Bantu] women workers for questioning.

Of these, 58 were given permission to stay and the rest had to be given 30 days' notice.

The works manager of the factory said it would be impossible to replace the lost workers—many of them highly trained—within 30 days. The production of the factory would certainly be affected.

The union added that several other clothing manufacturers were served with warnings or summonses because they were employing staff which were not officially allowed in their respective areas.

Commenting on the situation yesterday, the union said that the unabated tempo of influx control had caused upheaval in industrial circles and disturbed the daily lives of many workers.

"Influx control has had a marked effect on the economy of the industries in the metropolitan area and the pattern for the year 2000 is shaping according to design," the union said.

(*The Prime Minister, Dr. Verwoerd, wants the number of Africans in the White areas at this date to be the same as the number in 1950.*)

SOUTHERN TRANSVAAL MOVE TO BOOST AFRICAN EARN-INGS (Sunday Times, *Johannesburg, English*) . . . *A rate-for-the-job African pay structure, where the earnings of the worker "will not depend on the individual but the value of the job he does," and a scheme for training Africans to specialise in their work, will soon be implemented in industries in the Southern Transvaal complex, said the regional manager of the National Development and Management Foundation, Mr. F. W. Stegman, in Benoni.*

"*Effective training of the African will give rise to bigger production. It will also mean a substantial increase in the salaries of Africans," said Mr. Stegman.*

Mr. Stegman attributed the introduction of this new African pay structure to the warning that the Minister of Bantu Administration and Development, Mr. M. C. Botha, gave to industrialists in May—that industrial land in the Southern Transvaal complex may be controlled if industrialists insist on establishing new factories on the Reef and employing large numbers of Africans instead of moving out to the border areas . . . [Mr. Botha] said that the great freedom existing for the establishment of factories must not be abused. Industries employing large numbers of African workers must not put them in the ["wrong"] *jobs.*

Industrialists interpreted this as a warning that restriction of African labour could be a Government instrument to inhibit further industrial development in the Southern Transvaal complex. . . .

USE OF SKILLED LABOUR—WARNING (Cape Argus, *English*) . . . *The Deputy Minister of Bantu Administration and Development, Mr. Blaar Coetzee, today issued another stern warning to industrialists "who may be and are toying with the idea of using Natives in skilled and semiskilled capacities in White industries."*

He said: "They are toying with a most dangerous idea and will be set for a head-on clash with the Government."

SPEAKING PLAINLY (Editorial, World, *Johannesburg, Bantu*) . . . *"It is not necessary to allow a single additional Bantu into the urban areas; the increase through births is more than sufficient."*

This statement was made by the Minister of Bantu Administration and Education, Mr. M. C. Botha, in Parliament. . . .

Anybody who had any doubt about the Government's determination to make the existing industrial areas and cities a preserve of the Whites now knows the truth. Mr. Botha made it quite clear for all the country to know where they stand.

Influx control goes to the root of the question of ensuring the existence of the Whites in the predominantly White areas. The aim is to reduce the proportion of non-White workers in the metropolitan areas to one White to less than one African, according to the Minister.

The present situation is that there are 2.2 non-Whites for every one White. This means that the Government aims to reduce the number of Africans in these areas by more than half.

The Minister says that the rate of reducing Africans by 5 per cent every year, which is being enforced in the Western Cape, could be applied to the whole country. . . . At the rate of a 5 per cent reduction it means that literally hundreds of thousands must be removed from the urban areas every year. Where will they go to find work?

A revolutionary situation is taking place in the country beneath our noses.

The least that we can now ask is for the Government to demonstrate the equally revolutionary arrangements they are making for the many thousands of Africans who are being sent to the Bantustans.

What industries in the Bantustans are ready to absorb annually over a hundred thousand Africans? Are these thousands merely to swell the numbers of Africans who are living in poverty in the congested rural areas? Once again the Government has stated the position very clearly on the negative side. We would like more evidence of the contribution they propose making towards a positive solution to the problem of the non-White in the country of his birth.

"YOU KNOW," the English-speaking doctor said with a whimsical air, "our Black friends up north do a lot of talking in the UN about how awful we are to our natives down here—that is, the Black politicians do a lot of talking. The ordinary Blacks know differently, or they wouldn't keep coming down here in such thousands, legally and illegally. They know that in the area of welfare and medical services alone we are so far ahead of the rest of the continent that it isn't even funny. And furthermore, they know the Whites here do more for them than their own black countrymen would, even if they did have the facilities we have.

"Now, mind you," he said, "I'm not an apologist for the Nationalists. There's nobody more insufferable than an arrogant Afrikaner, and some of these boys in the Government are bloody arrogant. God, are they arrogant! Especially to somebody like me"—he smiled wryly—"whose family came here with the 1820 Settlers, and so has a claim to being just as good a South African as some of them whose forebears got here later.

"But, whatever you think of them—and I married an Afrikaans wife, and many of my best friends are Afrikaners, so it's no problem for me, really—you do have to give credit where it's due. And it is due in welfare and medicine.

"Of course we have this funny pretense here that we're not a socialist state, you know. You've run into that. Great emphasis is put upon private charitable organizations, big-business people like Harry Oppenheimer and John Schlesinger and the rest make enormous contributions, the mines and other industries do a vast amount. The churches of both races are always busy with bazaars and cake-sales and suppers. Students of all the major universities put on shows for charity once a year. Every Wednesday and Saturday morning, as you've noticed, the women are out with their collection-boxes for the blind, or the maimed, or the children, or something or other. The great majority of all this goes to the Bantu."

He paused and an amused expression touched his face for a second.

"There are those," he said thoughtfully, "who claim that this is all part of a guilty conscience—Afrikaners do have a fearful conscience, you know, it's part of the strict religious background that is still so predominant in so many areas, and many of them do feel guilty, inside, about what they conceive to be the necessary restrictions they so often place on the Bantu. The restrictions *are* necessary, in their minds—and, frankly, I don't mind telling you, in the minds of a majority of white South Africans, too: for most of us, it works out as a simple matter of surviving in a black sea. But anyway, along with the necessity goes a lot of conscience about it. What the Afrikaner feels he must do to survive doesn't always sit easy with him. One way to forget it, I suppose, is to concentrate on doing all kinds of things for the Bantu.

"As one of my friends remarked recently"—his expression turned wry —"we have a society filled with charity but devoid of compassion. . . .

"And for those who benefit from the charity," he said after a moment, "perhaps it doesn't really matter. Maybe they don't really mind the lack of compassion, as long as they can be sure of getting the charity. Their standards are different from ours, their way of thinking isn't the same— compassion is one thing they conspicuously don't always have in *their* society, out in some of the bloody tribes who only understand the law of blood. So perhaps it doesn't matter that there isn't much heart in it—that for the Afrikaners, and I suppose for most of the English-speakers, it's duty instead of heart. . . .

"Well, I didn't mean to get off into philosophy, which does nobody any good, in South Africa. We were talking about our non-socialistic socialistic state, weren't we?

"So, business and private efforts contribute. But the bulk of it comes from the state. The state gives all old people a pension. It considers medical care a primary responsibility. It considers housing a primary responsibility—I know you'll talk to others about that, or have already, so I'll concentrate on the medical part of it. The Government provides most of the hospitals and most of the medical services in remoter areas where there aren't many hospitals. Every community also has a district surgeon who is a Government employee, and he gives free care to all who can't afford a private doctor.

"The average charge per day for a Bantu out-patient at a clinic in the Republic is twenty-five cents, and patients who can't afford that are treated free. Hospital patients pay fifty cents on admission, and that's all. Medicines and specialized treatment are given free. This makes a trifle tiresome some of the wild talk we get from the outside world about how cruel we are to the Bantu. My God, who else does as much?

"But, of course," he remarked with a tired impatience, "they know this, elsewhere in Africa. Their politicians can fool your country, where most of our critics don't know anything about us and deliberately won't let themselves find out, but they know themselves what the truth of it is. God, they are hypocrites! They are such bloody hypocrites. . . .

"But there I go again. Back to statistics and leave out the emotion, there's the ticket. Welfare services, privately organized—more than 2,130 unofficial organizations are registered with the Department of Social Welfare and Pensions. Most work with both white and non-white sections of the population, but of course it's the non-Whites who get by far the major share, for the simple reason there are so many more of them. Most of these organizations are subsidized in some degree, some very heavily, by the Government.

"For instance," he said, reading from a list on his desk, "we have the National Council for Child Welfare, the National Council for Mental Health, the National Council for Cripple Care, for Alcoholism—a major problem, with us, as with you—the National Council for the Blind, for the Deaf, for the Aged, and so on. All non-White men may apply at age sixty-five, all non-White women at sixty, for old-age pensions which in 1964 totaled 13,800,000 rand. We have special grants for disability, special maintenance grants for children who are disabled or homeless. Another R7,000,000 went for those in 1964; '65 figures aren't available yet, but it's certain all categories increased with the growth of population.

"The Government also subsidizes a great many special institutions, usually run under licence by private organizations. We have more than fifty children's homes, caring for more than six thousand children. There are more than one hundred fifty Government-subsidized crèches where working mothers can leave their children up to five years of age, for the day. There are workshops for the blind and the deaf. We have five old-age homes for Coloureds, two for Indians. In the Bantu homelands we have four Government settlements for aged Bantu, with five more under construction and two more planned. In urban areas there are several Bantu old-age homes, three subsidized by the Government.

"Then there are other services, such as about thirty domestic-science classes throughout the country, the Government paying about 50 per cent of the operating costs, including materials used. Distress relief is given families where the father dies suddenly, or something else takes away the livelihood or causes disaster. There are a number of specialized rehabilitation centers for various types of illness or disability throughout the country, also largely Government-subsidized.

"Wages and salaries of welfare workers, and their training also, are usually Government-subsidized. Of course here damned apartheid raises its head again, because they emphasize special training centers for non-Whites and they try to restrict non-White welfare workers to working with non-White cases. Lord knows how much ability and talent we lose by refusing to let people work across the line. But, that's another story.

"Anyway, that's the welfare side. On the hospital side, there were 87,-000 beds available for non-Whites in seventy-seven hospitals throughout the Republic in 1965. That works out to an average of 5.78 beds for every thousand members of the community, as against the accepted world standard of 5 beds per one thousand members of the community. Leprosy, tuberculosis and mental health are continuing problems here, and they are regarded as a special responsibility of the Government, which provides 3,109 beds for non-Whites in eleven state tuberculosis hospitals; 1,688 beds are available for non-White lepers—although in 1964 we had only 526 cases of leprosy and fortunately the disease seems to be on the decline.

"There are 8,847 beds for non-White mental patients in fifteen state institutions, and private hospitals provide a further 361 beds for the non-Whites.

"The result of all this," he said with some irony, "is that we are simply making our enormous problem even more enormous, because the better we care for them and the healthier they become, the more they breed and the worse the population pressure becomes on us. You can't get them to take the pill, you know, or accept any kind of practical birth control, because it's against their tribal tradition. The women would like to have it, many of them tell us so, but it's a sign of a man's virility to have a lot of children, and the men aren't about to permit the women to stop. So on they go, healthier and healthier, thanks to us, defended from illness and kept alive longer, and outbreeding us faster and faster. It's really funny, in a weird and awful sort of way. . . .

"Missions do a great work in this country—as long"—and he smiled dryly—"as their ministers or their parent churches don't criticize apartheid too much, in which case they are likely to find themselves requested to leave and turn their work over to less disputatious organizations. But many are very active, many from America, from Britain and Europe. They have an uneasy sort of marriage with the Government, but on the whole, it works out fairly well. And the Bantu profit.

"The pride of it all, of course, is here outside Johannesburg, at Baragwanath, which is the largest hospital on the continent and where they do wonderful work on research and preventive measures as well as on routine hospital care. Baragwanath is exclusively for the 600,000 urbanized Bantu on the Rand. It has 2,300 beds, ten operating theaters and has an annual budget of around R4,000,000, provided by the provincial administration of the Transvaal. There are 220 doctors, of whom I am proud to be one, about half of us specialists. Twenty-four of us are non-White, and that is a great gain for everybody.

"So there you have it," he said. "Not quite the evil picture painted in the outside world. Of course evil is here, but, obviously, so is good. Makes us rather a complicated country, doesn't it?"

He smiled, not without irony.

"I hope you understand us. I don't."

EQUALS OF ANY MAN (*Editorial,* World, *Johannesburg, Bantu*)
. . . The praise given to our nurses at Baragwanath Hospital by the Chief Matron, Miss Agnes Simpson, is indeed merited, for an African nurse at the hospital is now ranked as a world expert in the care of paraplegics.

Miss Simpson, from practical experience, says that the Africans can accept responsibility if it is given them, and they are also allowed the necessary authority.

This is a view we have always held. We congratulate Baragwanath Hospital for the faith they have shown in the African.

We also congratulate the African nurse concerned and her colleagues who, in doing their work faithfully and efficiently, have earned recognition for our people.

The challenge goes to all of us in other professions to strive for similar excellence in the performance of our duties, whatever they may be.

Given a chance, we are equals of any man.

"HAS THE GOVERNMENT ever thought of moving Parliament to Pretoria from Cape Town?"

A sudden, knowing smile crossed the shrewd Afrikaner face of the Johannesburg editor.

"It could only be done by a Prime Minister who timed it exactly right

and then got it through Parliament in ten minutes. It couldn't be done by
making it a matter of policy and letting a lot of debate develop. He
would have to time it just right and then"—he made a slashing gesture
with his hand, chopping off English heads from Durban to Jo'burg—
"zip!"

"They'll never do it," said the English-speaking politician in Cape
Town. "The Transvalers love the Cape too much. After all"—he sniffed
—"it's pretty nice to leave that desert up there and come down here to
God's country."

AGRICULTURE

The producers' price index increased from 100 in the basic period of
1947–48 to 1950, to over 180 during 1950–51. It declined till the
1958–59 season and gradually recovered to 140 for 1962–63, and to
155 for 1963–64.

Prices of capital goods such as tractors and lorries, and of current
means of production such as fuel and fertilizers, increased sharply during the early fifties but the overall increase in the prices of farm requisites remained reasonably stable and in proportion to the increase in
the general price level.

The gross value of agricultural production of European farmers increased by 71 per cent since 1951–52, total expenditure by 93 per cent
and net income by 55 per cent.

For 1963–64 the gross value of agricultural production is estimated
at R792 million. Expenditure on farming requisites was estimated at
R244.9 million, cash wages for Bantu labourers at R82.0 million, and
depreciation at R72.8 million, giving an estimated net income for the
1963–64 season of R392.5 million.

—Official Sources

"Now, YOU UNDERSTAND, Albert, that you are to go through the
line with the others and we will be waiting for you in the court.
Do you understand?"

The round dark eyes were trying hard to follow, a trace of cautious
smile was on the round black face, there was a struggle going on inside
somewhere, unreachable by us—that struggle for comprehension, wary
and wild, that I was to see on so many native faces: not really understanding the strange ways of the white man but willing to go along with
them for the moment because there was, in truth, nothing else to do.

"Yes, madam," he said, his breath, like hers, showing white and misty
in the cold Johannesburg morning. "Yes, madam, I understand."

"Good," she said. "Then you go along, now, and go through the line
and we will be waiting for you in the court. All right, Albert?"

"All right, madam."

"All right: go now, then."

"I go, madam," he said, and turned away to rejoin his fellow-prisoners, a short, stumpy figure in faded brown coveralls.

"Look at them!" she said with a deep disgust as we stood in the
crowded yard of the Bantu Administrator's Court. "Herded in like cattle.
And nobody," she added with an equal disgust when an enormous Bantu
guard shoved Albert roughly into the line shuffling slowly toward the
court door, "treats them worse than their fellow-Bantu. I tell you—!"

There must have been three hundred prisoners, divided about equally
between men and women; the men crowded together in a big wire pen,
the women standing outside in the open earthen courtyard, many with
babies on their hips or slung in blankets on their backs.

The offense of nearly all of these involved their pass-books. Either they
came from the neighboring townships and had been in the city without
their passes when challenged by the police; or they had outstayed the
seventy-two-hour limit during which a Bantu with a pass may remain in
the city; or they were from some country area and did not have the
special permits which provide the only legal way in which a Bantu from
some other area can enter.

These are the most common native offenses in the Republic; and day
after day, week after week, month after month, year after year, these
slowly shuffling lines move up to the doors of the Bantu Courts in Johannesburg, Pretoria, Durban, Cape Town, Bloemfontein, Pietermaritzburg,
Port Elizabeth, East London, any other place you care to name from the
Limpopo to the Cape . . . an endless chain of innocent forgetfulness or
willful disobedience on the part of the Natives, of sometimes routine,
sometimes punitive checking by the police, of bored, automatic, three-
minute justice by civil service "judges" who with a flick of the hand or a
terse sentence or two can fine a man, send him to jail, or set him free.

I do not think I attended a single dinner in the Republic at any home,
Afrikaans or English, at which sooner or later someone did not relate her
own experience, or that of a friend, in having to "go down to court tomorrow and go bail for Mary [or John or Deborah or Susan or Henry].
She forgot her pass-book yesterday and got picked up downtown. My
dear, what a headache!"

And a headache for the Native, too, who often, true enough, knows
better and is deliberately chancing arrest; but who often, also, forgets
quite innocently, or for some genuine emergency reason is compelled to
stay beyond the seventy-two-hour limit; or comes down from the country
and doesn't realize a permit is required; or in some other way quite un-

wittingly violates the law and so comes to the endlessly emptying, end-lessly filling prison-pens of the Republic.

Albert's home was some seventy miles up-country. His offense began when he received the offer of a job helping to paint a house, and was instructed by his prospective employer that he must get a work-permit from the Johannesburg authorities. He had accordingly done so, through the Bantu Administrator in the dorp where he lived. But his request had apparently gone astray—another frequent experience for the Native—because almost three months had passed without word.

Albert needed the job, he needed the money, he was a good boy, as they say in the Republic, and he really wanted to work. And being a Native, he did not understand that his request might have been lost in the white man's red tape—or that quite possibly the white man, in line with the Government's policy of trying to discourage the black influx into the Witwatersrand, had deliberately filed and forgotten his request.

So, being a Native and being from the white man's view tricky and difficult and from his own view direct and uncomplicated, he had hopped on his bicycle, unencumbered by either a work-permit or a pass to be in Jo'burg at all, had pedaled the seventy miles in to town and had gone to his prospective employer, ready to go to work.

But it so happened that his prospective employer, who lived next door to my hostess and guide of this morning, had gone to Durban for the July holidays. So my hostess, who was also having some painting done, had given Albert a temporary job helping at her place. At the end of the first day Albert went walking downtown, was challenged for his pass by the police, and so had been brought to where we saw him now.

All of this, from Albert's point of view, was obviously ridiculous and unnecessary, because of course he had done what the white man had told him to do: applied for a work-permit; waited three months, far beyond the time that events, even in the normally slow-moving Native world, might reasonably be expected to develop; and had then come to Johannesburg and found an honorable job on his own. Now he was being punished for his enterprise. It was perhaps understandable if he did not quite comprehend.

It would have been understandable also if he had been deeply offended and outraged; yet this is the point at which all my English and Afrikaans friends throw up their hands and confess themselves baffled. "Who knows what They really think? You can never tell how They really feel about things. It's like a blank wall."

Yet behind the wall, it seems safe to say in purely human terms, a vast resentment must be building. It is far from being at the point of explosion, and indeed the Government with its tight controls has made explosion virtually impossible. Yet looking, as we were now on this cold morning, at the hundreds of black faces staring impassively back at us, hearing the high, clicking chatter of many native languages saying things we could not understand, it was possible to feel that a collective judgment upon the white man must be in process of formulation.

It was also possible to feel that the pass system and the constant challenges by police are designed to counteract this judgment: that somebody somewhere in officialdom has decided that the best way to keep the Bantu off-balance is to keep them so busy worrying about passes that they haven't got time to think about much else. This is a psychological gamble that only a Government with nerves of steel would take. The Nats take it as a matter of course, day after day, time without end.

Time without end—so far.

Anyway, we watched Albert being pushed and shoved by his giant fellow-Bantu ("Zulu, I think," my companion murmured); we watched for a while as the line moved slowly toward the court; we heard the high, clicking voices; we watched the crowded pens and we saw the sullen, uncommunicative faces; and then we went in to do what we could for Albert.

The judge was a bored old English-speaking civil servant who had obviously done this sort of thing for twenty years and obviously would never do anything else. His courtroom was bare of everything but the essentials, a high bench for him, a bare wooden dock for Albert, bare wooden seats for us. The door opened, Albert was pushed in by his fellow-Bantu, officious in his dirty uniform and obviously enjoying his work. Albert gave us a fleeting, uncertain look and was shoved down in his chair.

"Do you speak Afrikaans or English?" the judge asked, and Albert, feeling safer in his native Sotho, said no. Another Bantu seated at a small table below the judge began immediately to question him in short, sharp sentences, obviously the bare facts of age, residence, offense.

"Is there anyone here to speak for this boy?" the judge asked automatically. My hostess rose, gave her name and address, explained the facts of Albert's transgression; doing it earnestly and politely, humbling herself in tone and manner before this tired old civil servant who had such power to flick a man into jail or back to freedom, as he pleased. (With appeal, of course, to the Minister of Bantu Administration or his deputy. But who ever heard of a Native with the time or money to appeal?)

"Will you go bail and be responsible for seeing that this boy goes back to his home and remains there until his work-permit is issued?"

"Yes, your Honor."

"Come in my office in five minutes and sign the bond. Case dismissed."

And Albert was escorted out by his fellow-Bantu, who again took occasion to give him a shove or two, just for the fun of it.

Afterward we stood in the chilly street, sniffed the winter coal-smoke from the snug homes of Johannesburg, and tried once more to get through to Albert.

"Now, Albert," my hostess said, "you may stay at my place tonight, and then tomorrow morning you must go back to your home and wait for the work-permit. And you must not go out on the streets today or tonight, Albert, or you may get arrested again. Do you understand me, Albert?"

"Yes, madam. I understand, madam."

"You must go right straight back to my house right this minute, Albert, and you must not go out on the street again today or tonight, and tomorrow morning early you must take your bicycle and ride back to your home. All right, Albert?"

"Yes, madam."

"And you must not stop on the way, Albert, because the police will be watching for you now, and if they arrest you again you will probably have to go to jail. You must go straight to your home and stay there until the work-permit comes, Albert. You do understand, do you?"

"Yes, madam."

"All right, Albert. Now you get your bicycle and come right along to my house. I will be waiting for you. All right, Albert?"

"All right, madam. I go."

"To my house, Albert."

"Yes, madam."

"Will he?" I asked as he trotted off.

She sighed.

"God knows."

"And will he ever get the work-permit?"

She smiled without humor.

"I wouldn't waste many rand on a wager."

"Does the average White have any idea that this is going on all the time?" I asked as we drove back downtown. She shook her head.

"Only if their own help is involved. Many people either just don't realize it, or—more accurately, I think—just don't let themselves realize it. There are an awful lot of decent Afrikaans and English, including some of my good liberal friends, who would rather not think about it. So they don't."

"I should think the knowledge of all the human discomfort and misery involved would drive people like you, who do worry about it, crazy."

"The only way you can keep sane," she said, skillfully negotiating the morning rush-hour traffic of the central city, a grim set to her lips, "is by doing what you can in each little instance that comes your way. It isn't much, but at least it keeps you busy. And sometimes you can feel that maybe you've accomplished a little something.

"The important thing is to keep busy. . . ."

COAL

Coal may prove South Africa's most valuable mineral asset. The known deposits have been conservatively estimated at 75,000,000,000 tons.

Vast coalfields which have not yet been systematically prospected are known to exist in various parts of the country, such as the Springbok Flats, the Komatipoort area and the Waterberg and Zoutpansberg districts. A considerable proportion of the reserves may consist of low-grade coal, which, however, will be suitable for the generation of electric power and for conversion into petrol and oil.

Of the estimated reserves of 75,000,000,000 tons, Transvaal possesses approximately 70,000,000,000 tons, Natal 2,700,000,000 tons and the Orange Free State 3,400,000,000 tons. Coal reserves will be ample for many hundreds of years, even at a largely increased scale of exploitation. South Africa produces 91 per cent of all coal mined in Africa, and South Africa's coal reserves represent 80 per cent of the estimated reserves in Africa.

As a result of these factors, the Republic has the cheapest coal in the world and the cheapest steam-generated electricity. The average pit-head per ton is as follows: United Kingdom R8.00; United States R3.46; South Africa (Transvaal) R1.57.

—Official Sources

"YOU HAVE TO understand the historical background," said my youthful Afrikaans guide as we drove through the morning rush toward the outskirts of Johannesburg. "A place like Soweto and the others the Government has built just didn't come about overnight. There was an evil, and the Government corrected it."

This was said with a precise and definitive satisfaction, for he was one of those humorless young Afrikaners one finds in the Government service: imbued with the mystique of Afrikanerdom, as rigid and unyielding as any old farmer out on the platteland, unable to relax for a moment from the mission of Die Volk. They are rather disturbing portents, particularly when placed against the many relaxed and charming Afrikaners who love nothing better than a good meal, a good joke, a good laugh, and warm hospitality.

Unfortunately it is not the relaxed ones who are running the Government. Nor is it the relaxed ones who are the Government's heirs. The Government is choosing its heirs, and they are exactly the type I was with this morning.

But he did know his facts, of course, and despite the constant misrepresentations of the outside world, the facts are impressive and represent a quite remarkable achievement, unmatched in Africa and perhaps any-where else. Contrary to the flat statement I saw in a major American picture-magazine when I returned home—"the majority of the Natives live in tin shantytowns like this"—the majority of the Natives do not live in tin shantytowns like this. They either live out in the kraals on the open hills as they have always lived, and where the majority of them prefer to live, or they live in very modest but relatively snug brick houses in vast, sprawling housing developments that the Whites have built for them, at enormous cost to themselves, over the past forty years.

The Government that magazine hates has spent many millions of rand, local and provincial authorities have spent many millions more, to eliminate "tin shantytowns like this." And they have succeeded remark-ably well, for there aren't many left, and before another decade has passed there won't be any.

"South Africa's first housing law was enacted in 1920," said my guide. "Under its provisions the Government was permitted to give local authorities money to start their own housing schemes, and also to lend to private builders. Although many authorities availed themselves of these schemes, there was still a great need for housing at the time of the begin-ning of the Second World War."

"Were you born then?"

"Just," he said, with the first flicker of a smile since our meeting at the hotel. But it passed.

"During the war," he resumed with complete seriousness, "there was of course a great demand upon South African industry. Even though many people were not convinced of the wisdom of South Africa's entry into the war, nonetheless once the Jan Smuts Government had com-mitted us, our industries responded. This resulted in a great demand for labor, and that in turn brought an enormous number of Bantu into our urban areas, creating enormous problems. As I believe it did," he added with that polite air of we-know-all-about-you-you-have-problems-too-you-can't-fool-us with which virtually all South Africans, even the most charming, sooner or later challenge the American visitor, "in the United States.

"So, then, there were many thousands of Bantu who had come in from the tribal locations to work in the war effort. Since the Jan Smuts Gov-ernment was then aiding the British and unable to devote much money to the concerns of South Africa, they were simply allowed to build for themselves shantytowns such as Sophiatown and others of which you have no doubt heard.

"These," he said rather severely, "were natural developments and in-evitable, since the Smuts Government was then aiding the British war. Nonetheless, they were very serious problems. The houses, if one could

call them that, were constructed of tin or wood, whatever scraps the
Natives could find. Many were illegally built on vacant land owned by
Whites. None of these slums had running water or proper sanitation.
Disease, crime and immorality were everywhere."

"I'm told there is still a lot of crime and immorality, though everybody
seems agreed the disease rate has gone down drastically."

"Mr. Drury," he said soberly, "there is only so much the Whites can
do for the Natives. We do our best to eradicate crime and immorality,
but we are only human."

"Is it partly, perhaps, the breakdown of tribal disciplines when they
come to the townships—"

"Weren't tribal disciplines broken down in the shantytowns? It was
greatly worse, there."

"Are the townships patrolled at night by police?"

"There are a few native policemen," he said. He smiled rather grimly.
"Whites rarely go in at night."

"I notice on our pass here, as a matter of fact, that it says we are
entering Soweto at our own risk right now. Apparently it isn't so safe in
the daytime, either."

"Oh, it is quite safe. They would not dare to attack Whites in broad
daylight. Or any other time," he added quickly.

"What would happen if they did?"

He shook his head impatiently.

"They know it would not be wise. So: that was the situation in 1951,
when the Government ordered a national survey which showed that there
was an immediate shortage of 167,000 houses for the urban Bantu, and
that an additional 186,000 houses would be needed during the following
ten years. In line with its program of orderly development in all spheres,
the Government then asked the National Building Research Institute—I
understand you have visited the National Center for Industrial and
Scientific Research in Pretoria? Yes—to provide recommendations on
building methods for housing as economical yet comfortable as possible.
As a result, the Building Research Institute produced plans for a decent
family dwelling for as little as 600 rand. In Daveytown, for instance,
near Benoni, the Government was able to build a three-room brick house
with kitchen and bathroom with shower for only 418 rand."

"These are decent homes by whose st—"

"By the standards of what they had in the shantytowns," he said
promptly as we passed the city's outskirts and headed into open country.
"By the standards of what they have in the kraals. By the standards
of—you will see. They are not what you or I would want to live in, but
you must remember what they had. It is a matter of comparison."

"How far is Soweto from the city?"

"About fifteen miles."

("I will say for the Government," said an English-speaking lawyer in Cape Town later, "that they've been bloody clever with these townships. They put them quite far out, you know, quite far, and they place them in exposed areas that could be quickly surrounded by troops in case of trouble, completely open places that could easily be bombed if anything happened. Then they make sure that all the water and electric power lines come through a central control point so that they could be shut down at once. The bloody Natives would be absolutely helpless if they tried to start anything. The Government isn't leaving anything to chance.")

"Are there regular trains for them?" I asked.

"Oh, yes," he said. "In fact, there's one now"—and he pointed to a chain of eight or ten streetcar-type units zipping along on a track some distance off, paralleling the road. "Very frequently in the mornings and evenings, when they're coming in to work or going home, less regularly during the day. But"—a little defensively—"they still can get in and out almost any time they want to."

"And they have to return in the evenings, they aren't allowed in the city?"

"Only house servants and a few workers who are on night jobs."

"I've been struck at the number of Natives I've seen on the streets, even as late as midnight."

"The Government has been trying to reduce the number," he said, "and it did issue a regulation that only one house servant could stay overnight. But"—he shrugged, and for the second time a small smile appeared—"you can always appeal and it's very easy to get exceptions. A lot of people in Johannesburg couldn't live without three or four servants."

"Do you have any?"

"We did," he said gravely, "but when the Government asked that people help to reduce the number of Natives in the city by giving up their servants, my wife and I decided it was the patriotic thing to do, so we complied."

"She's Afrikaans too?"

"Oh, yes," he said with some surprise, as we swung off the main road and the thousands and thousands of brick houses of Soweto began to appear ahead.

We drove after that for perhaps an hour through Soweto, neighboring Meadowlands, Dube where the wealthier Bantu live, and Orlando. There was no formal gate, no fence, no check-in point where anyone scanned our pass; simply a sign saying "Soweto," a turnoff, and at once into row upon curving row of small brick houses.

Much has been made of these. Famous visitors come and deplore, politicians north of the Zambesi make their moan, the UN rocks and roils. But when all the fuss is allowed for, the houses are actually not so bad. They are not mansions, neither are they hovels. They are the practical answer of a practical Government faced with a virtually insoluble problem, and as such they are plain, unadorned, strictly utilitarian, cheap but sturdily constructed. What they become after that is up to the occupants, and as with any housing development anywhere, some are neatly kept with clean-swept paths, small gardens and vines, others are run-down, slovenly, unkempt, unattractive. Riding slowly through the endless rows, it appeared that pride outweighed irresponsibility, the proportion of well-kept homes was substantially larger than the slovenly. The overall impression, while generally uniform and drab, was not as heartless as outside criticism would lead one to believe. At least the Government has done its best to meet the problem, not with great imagination or variety, perhaps, but as efficiently as economic limitations and sheer numbers will permit. Six hundred thousand Natives live in Soweto and the number grows every day. What, as South Africans always say, would you do?

So we rode on through the interminable streets, which in mid-morning were populated mainly by women and children, an occasional grouping of men around a beer-hall or store, very occasionally a policeman walking slowly along. We were very conscious we were White, or at least I was, but it was as my guide had said: nothing happened in broad daylight.

"Is it possible for the occupants to buy these houses?"

"Oh, yes."

"Can they secure freehold?"

He shook his head.

"No, that's not permitted, except in the tribal locations or the Transkei."

"Then they can't actually own—"

"They can own the houses," he said, a trifle severely. "The land is leased for a period of time, sometimes up to thirty years. They can build their own houses, too"—we were now swinging into Dube, where some of the Department of Information's pet Bantu, the millionaire storekeeper, the wealthy auto dealer, the rich doctor and lawyer, have their residences—"and some of them are not bad. That one there, for instance"—it was two-story, brick below, frame above, with a flower-filled garden and big windows that looked out upon the poorer rows that marched the bare brown hills—"and that one. . . .

"If they have the money," he said, "they can design and build their own. The Government wants them to. If they can't afford to do that, they can rent."

"Oh, this isn't free housing, then?"

"Oh, no, except in hardship cases, in which case it is. Most of these

Natives rent. Rents range from 4 to 8 rand ($5.60 to $11.20) a month, depending on the size of the house. The majority are one or two-bedroom, but there are some threes as well."

We came presently to Oppenheimer Tower, the small stone platform that Harry Oppenheimer has dedicated to the peoples of the townships, from which their sprawling honeycomb can be viewed stretching in every direction, literally as far as the eye can see: broken here and there by the schools the Government has erected, interrupted now and again by the embryo sports areas where hopefully the jungle life portrayed in the stage production at Wits University will be somewhat alleviated, the embryo shopping-centers where Bantu traders and shopkeepers are already forming the nucleus of what the Government hopes will someday be a self-supporting economy.

The view is endless, overwhelming, and depressing—not because of its drabness, which a few years, some trees and more plantings will tend to soften, but for two reasons, one Native, one White.

For the Natives, that they should have to live there at all.

And for the Whites, because of Soweto's size and because of the problem its size represents.

There, and later among the unending native huts dotting the hills and valleys of the Transkei, there comes to the visitor a sudden vision of the Government, like Sisyphus, striving forever to push uphill a stone that is forever toppling back upon it.

There is no end to such a process, and no permanent solution save surrender—and that is something the Whites will never do. So the heart is saddened and the mind, ultimately, retreats: the problem is too big.

"Has the Government ever thought of disseminating birth-control information to the Natives, to try to induce them to hold down the population to some extent?"

My guide gave me a blank look, sharp and sudden.

"Oh, no, it couldn't do that," he said quickly. "The Natives would think we were afraid of them."

POLICE MOVE INTO SOWETO (Star, *Johannesburg, English*) . . . *Brig. Louis Steyn's campaign to clear Johannesburg of crime moved into Soweto today. Contingents of uniformed police were stationed at several points in the township this afternoon and began combing the area.*

"THE THING THAT is so repugnant to so many of us," said the liberal English-speaker as we walked along busy Jeppie Street in the warm, sunny day, seeing on every side the strolling crowds of Whites and Natives going freely in and out of the stores together, "is this minor discrimination—these elements we call 'petty apartheid'—the separate entrances, the separate conveyances, the separate beaches and sports areas and benches in the parks, the refusal to permit mixed attendance at cultural events, the harassment over passes—all these deliberate little niggling slaps in the face of the Native. That's what we can't stomach."

"And that's what you call 'petty.' Is there something bigger?"

"Yes," he said, looking puzzled. "Apartheid per se—or 'separate development,' to use the Government's term—that's major apartheid. It's these petty little things that I'm talking about."

"I should think those would be exactly the things that would offend the human dignity of the Native and hurt and demean him most. But here you call them petty."

"In the sense of little in size," he said somewhat impatiently. "Small. Minor. Really just pinpricks, you know. . . . Actually," he added comfortably as we passed the "Non-Whites Only" entrance of the General Post Office and observed its chattering, busy traffic, "they take it quite well, on the whole. Sometimes I think some of us sentimentalize too much about petty apartheid."

A LAND GROWN STALE IN ITS THINKING (Star, *Johannesburg, English*) . . . (*A Reef African, who has been working for several years in Central Africa, finds coming home a confusing experience: a mixture of warmth and futility.*)—*The plane glides down into Jan Smuts Airport. All along I have been called "Sir." Now, as I lean back, fastening my seat belt, I know I shall be a "Bantu," a "Native," even a "Kaffir" again.*

I am cleared through the Customs by a burly immigration officer who asks me: "You back home?" I nod. Then he says: "How's it out there? Things mixed up with Communists working themselves in?" I laugh and he says: "Don't you worry, you are one of us."

I thank him for his courtesy and move over to wait for my luggage. I am suddenly overwhelmed by the warmth of the Afrikaner. They are always like that. You meet them outside South Africa and you realize how nice they are. It is only that you become mad at South Africa's iniquitous laws.

After collecting my baggage, I saw two African sweepers looking at me furtively. Perhaps they thought I was a Negro or West African. Then

*one of them spoke in Sotho: "Is he South African?" I nodded and said
in Sotho: "I'm one of you."*

*What saddened me was that they thought I was from Mars, out of
dreamland, for to them the possibility of ever being out of South Africa
is as remote as a journey to the Moon.*

*My friends and relatives came forward, all beaming and yet slightly
shy. From the onset, my brother warned: "This way, please—that door
is for Whites only."*

*I was still not sure whether this was the old South Africa that I loved,
and suddenly I became sad. I had been wrenched out of a world where
human beings were human beings, irrespective of their colour. The reality
that faced me left me depressed.*

*When I boarded a train from Naledi in Soweto the washerwomen—
burly and noisy—pressed me into the coach until I was left gasping. And
as I landed against the seats, laundry parcels towering over me, I felt
terrified. But all treated it as a joke. I ended up by joining in the laughter.*

*The women's ruggedness frightened me. One asked me why I was such
a sissy and I merely shrugged. "Sure you come from the country, the
platteland. You're a moogie—a fool."*

*One said: "Look at his trousers. He's so out of place." Another said:
"Gee, he looks Continental, doesn't he, with all the well-fitting suit?"
There was laughter.*

*I wanted to bark at them all and tell them that the world I had been
to was not so alien. But I had to admit I WAS out of touch. Life in places
like Johannesburg—especially in the African townships, moves so fast
that a day is like a year anywhere else. The vocabulary of residents
changes almost daily and dances change almost weekly.*

*Johannesburg fascinated me, but the fascination soon wore off at five
P.M. when the mad rush started. Long trains whined out of the city, carrying away the Black masses to their separate residential places. Their desire to be back in the townships bewildered me. I wondered how long this
desire would last.*

*While at home I had a lot to talk about with my old friends and school-
mates. They were hesitant to say exactly what they felt about the situation in South Africa.*

*I met some Afrikaner youths too, and English-speaking ones. Every
time the conversation ended with my heart bleeding for South Africa's
youth—both Black and White. They were entangled in a situation that
had reached a point of no return, and so was I too, though I wanted to
run away from the fact.*

*I felt terrified by their silence. Whereas throughout the civilized world,
youth is the hope of tomorrow, in South Africa youth has been doomed
to frozen silence.*

Among the Africans I found a vague but slightly unrealistic hope that one day, when Black rule came to just across the Limpopo, things would change.

I had an interesting talk with an Afrikaner university student whose sincerity touched me. He was convinced South Africa was heading in the right direction.

"Where else in independent Africa do you hear of Africans running their own hospitals, schools and even universities? In most cases they still depend on expatriates," said the student. He was a hundred per cent for separate development.

The next man I interviewed was an Afrikaner dominee. He had that same shining quality of sincerity. "I don't sleep," he told me. "I can't sleep, because of the evil that's in our society. I pray day and night that God show us the pathway—and brother, have patience, the Afrikaner will soon change his heart and will accept you wholeheartedly."

I had an interesting talk with an African who spent a year in one of the independent states. "Man, I'm all right here in self-imprisonment. I'm all right with separate development. Up north there is so much pretence. I've seen the most horrifying hypocrisy there and it made me sick."

Once more I had been cleared through Jan Smuts Airport, and outside the airport buildings a jet airliner was getting ready to pick us up.

"This way, please," said one of the hostesses, "and take a seat anywhere you like, sir."

Once more as the plane roared into the skies, I looked down at the beautiful country that had become stale in its thinking.

"WELL, you've now been in the country two weeks," my Afrikaner host said, giving me a quizzical look. "Do you find all this tension here that we read about in the overseas press?"

"I find a lot."

"You do?" he said with a blank and perfectly genuine surprise. "I wouldn't have said we had so much. Where do you see it? Are there riots in the streets, like you're having in Chicago? Do you see bloody revolution breaking out? Is anybody being killed? Are there great protest marches and disturbances?"

"Maybe that's it: there aren't any."

"Well, doesn't that suggest to you that this is a peaceful and happy country—aside from this God-damned Government and all its fool laws suppressing the Natives, with which I don't happen to agree?"

"It suggests to me that it is a very well-controlled country. I don't know how happy it is, or how peaceful it would be if the controls were relaxed."

"You mean," he asked, and he gestured at the black faces peering quickly in and away again as they hurried past the windows of the crowded hotel lounge, filled with Whites snug and warm against the winter wind that had risen with the dying of the sun, "that those chappies out there are getting ready to rise up and overwhelm us?"

"Do you go out for a casual stroll in the streets of Jo'burg at night?"

"Well, no."

"Would you go out to Soweto alone, any time?"

"No again, but that doesn't mean we're on the verge of revolution, man. Where do you get all this tension stuff?"

"I'm sorry, you asked and I told you: yes, I do find it. The Natives aren't rising up and obviously they aren't going to, they're too antagonistic to one another and their leadership has been scientifically removed by the Government—"

"And basically the great majority of them are still out in the tribal locations and perfectly happy."

"And basically, the great majority of them are still out in the tribal locations and perfectly happy. Granted, I believe that; it's perfectly obvious. But that doesn't take care of your urban ones, or of the many Whites who are becoming increasingly afraid to say what they think."

He gave a skeptical sniff.

"Who's that, Helen Suzman and her Progs?"

"The Progs and a lot of other people. Why should any of them have to feel afraid?"

"Nobody in America is afraid?"

"Most people in America speak out if they have a gripe. Anyway, you South Africans always want to change the subject to America. I'm here to find out about your country, now."

He grinned.

"Well, maybe we have a little tension. You'd think so to read the English-language press, right enough, and I suppose if you've been talking to some of the professors at Wits—"

"It isn't just professors at Wits. It's the whole atmosphere."

"Man, man!" he exclaimed, as Afrikaners do. "I really think you've been talking to too many liberals. Now, I'll grant you"—and the joviality faded, his expression became annoyed and grim—"I do think this Government has the God-damnedest policy toward the Natives. It's the human side of it that worries me. Why do they humiliate them so? Why" —and he pounded a fist into a palm—"do they do such mean, nasty, unfriendly things? Why do they treat them like animals? I'm Afrikaans too, but by God I can't stand it, and neither can a lot of other Afrikaners. Maybe that's another thing you think, that all of us Afrikaners are 100 per cent behind the Government. I can tell you we're bloody well not. There are a lot of us who aren't, a lot of us. And the thing that does it is that they just aren't decent; they just aren't kind. Afrikaners are a kind people, you know, we really are—most of us. The ones who aren't go to Pretoria, I guess."

"But there isn't any tension."

He grinned again and relaxed.

"Have another drink, man, and tell me about those riots in Chicago."

PULP AND PAPER INDUSTRY

South Africa's pulp, paper and board industry has grown substantially, especially since 1938, to become a significant part of the country's economic structure. The industry has faced and surmounted many difficulties in reaching its present development.

Since the end of World War II, the annual consumption of paper and board in the Republic has risen from less than 150,000 tons (in 1946) to its present level of more than 500,000 tons. During the same period, local production has increased from 28,000 tons to 330,000 tons, of which 16,000 tons were exported. Thus, the country's need for imports has dropped from more than 80 per cent of consumption in 1946 to about 35 per cent at the present time.

As the expansion projects of the industry, which are at present under construction, come to fruition over the next few years, the tonnage of paper and board produced will increase substantially and the need for imports will be confined mainly to specialties and items which cannot be economically made in the country. The export tonnage of certain grades is also expected to grow.

—Official Sources

"AND NOW," the old Afrikaans professor said with a satisfied smile, "we are going to build a monument to Die Taal and it will be suitably honored as it should be."

"A monument? That's very nice."

"It is," he said. "Do you know of any other language that has a monument erected to it? I am unaware of one. Yet Die Taal—'The Language' —Afrikaans—is about to achieve this distinction. Does that tell you something about us?"

"Yes, it does."

"We are a proud people, you see."

"Yes."

"And one with a heavy history. That, perhaps, is why our language has meant so much to us—does mean so much to us. It has seen us through thick and thin, Mr. Drury. Now we are going to honor it."

"Tell me how it developed. I've met Dutch people here, Dutch from Holland, who tell me it seems to them like a very simplified form of their language."

"The Dutch from Holland!" he said with a sudden asperity. "They are everywhere in South Africa these days, Mr. Drury, trying to get into our industry and finance—and succeeding quite well, I may say. They have decided they will try to reclaim their lost colony through the banker's door. We weren't good enough for them for a long time, but now they are back again." He smiled with a better humor. "Eh, well, I daresay we can defeat the Dutch, too, as we have the English. The Afrikaner is a tough bird, Mr. Drury. And so is his language.

"Die Taal, you see, developed, really, out on the platteland, the isolated farms, the frontier. Our people were driven out from the Cape, as you know, they embarked upon the Great Trek, they settled far from the old High Dutch centers. In the eighteenth century they had already begun to develop their own language, and these events that occurred early in the last century gave it new impetus. It was a very simple language, very direct—a frontiersman's language, stripped to its essentials yet borrowing from other languages too, so that in time it began to emerge as a distinct tongue in its own right. When the republics of the Transvaal and the Orange Free State were established, the Boers retained Dutch as their official written language, but the language of everyday, the language of the country, was really Afrikaans.

"Funnily enough, however, the first move to transform Afrikaans into a written language to replace Dutch originated in the Cape with its strong English influences and not in the Boer republics. And some of the leaders in what became known as the First Afrikaans Language Movement of 1875 were actually Dutch from Holland who recognized Afrikaans as a unique and special language."

He chuckled.

"The church was very much opposed, you know. My father was a dominee—a reverend, as you might say—and I can remember his tales about that. You see, the Gospel was rendered in High Dutch and the church was very upset that Afrikaans—what it called 'the kitchen language'—might replace Dutch. But in due time, the kitchen came into the church and now it rules the oven.

"The turning point really came," he said soberly, "with the Anglo-Boer War. It was then, in the midst of defeat at the hands of the British Empire, that our people suddenly perceived their language as something special and unique—something which represented this defeated people with all its sorrow, its tragedies, but its indomitable, tenacious strength.

"Poets rose, Mr. Drury, to sing of war's agonies and the triumph of the spirit which rises above wars and sometimes brings a people back to nationhood and to new glories to replace the old. A sense of common destiny filled the Afrikaans people, and Die Taal was seen to be the instrument of that destiny. Suddenly Afrikaans became respectable in the eyes of everyone, a precious thing for Afrikanerdom to have. A literature began to appear, at first about the war but then soon about other things, about nature and the beauties of our country and all the many aspects of human life.

"In 1914 Afrikaans was made a medium of instruction in schools beside English. In 1916, it replaced Dutch in the churches. In 1925 it became an official language of South Africa coequal with English. In 1934 the Afrikaans Bible was published, and now the language is triumphant everywhere in the Republic."

"I understand it is a very descriptive language."

"It is almost a made-up language, day-to-day; almost a shorthand of living. Some new need for expression arises, Afrikaans finds how to say it. Do you know of any language, Mr. Drury, which has a word meaning 'someone who drives with one hand outside on the roof'? We say he is a 'dakvink.'

"A backseat driver is known to us as a 'bekdrywer.' A tongue twister is a 'snelseer.' Someone who spends the night on your premises without permission is a 'sluipslaper.' "

"Does that happen often?"

He looked startled for a second, then smiled.

"Enough so we need a word for it, evidently. Let me show you the picture—I have it here somewhere—of the monument. Yes, here it is"—a modernistic, swooping form of concrete and stone starting on the slope of a hill, soaring sharply to a pinnacle.

"At that point," he said, indicating it with his pencil, "the monument is to be 185 feet high. It will cost an estimated $420,000 and will be erected in the near future on the slopes of Paarl Mountain, a few miles north of Cape Town in the Cape Province."

"Why there? Why not in the Transvaal or the Orange Free State?"

"Because South Africa began in the Cape, Mr. Drury. And Die Taal did too."

"Not because it might annoy the English-speakers to have it in the Cape?"

He gave a mischievous little smile.

"Mr. Drury, Mr. Drury! What do you think of us Afrikaners, anyhow?"

"But I suppose they needn't worry, because of course the Government is going to put up a monument to the other official language too?"

He slapped his knee, his shrewd old face quite pink with laughter.

"Afrikaans will have to develop a new word, I can see. It will mean 'the visitor who understands and makes fun.' Give us a moment, Mr. Drury, and Die Taal will do it."

IMMIGRANTS SHOULD LEARN AFRIKAANS, URGES BODY,
(Daily Dispatch, *East London, English*) . . . *The Federasie van Afrikaanse Kultuurvereniginge (F.A.K.) Congress adopted a resolution here yesterday that the Government should be asked to ensure that all immigrants to South Africa were informed about the demand for bilingualism in the country before they settled here.*

It was decided to drop two parts of the resolution asking that immigrants be compelled to know Afrikaans within 12 months and that they should know Afrikaans when they became citizens.

The Afrikaner must accept that immigration had come to stay and it was therefore necessary to adopt a positive attitude towards immigrants, Dr. P. Koornhof, M.P. for Primrose and chairman of the South African Cultural Academy, said.

He said that the stream of immigrants to South Africa would increase in the future.

The Afrikaner could not try to find a solution to the problem of the preponderance of Africans and at the same time become involved in a struggle with other Whites who basically agreed with them.

South Africa needed 10,000 new economically active White men annually. This meant that, in all, 30,000 men, women and children should come to South Africa each year.

In 1965 the figure was 38,326.

People who thought that immigration constituted a threat to the Afrikaner did not take into account that, partly through immigration, the number of English-speaking South Africans had only increased by 11,500 in the period 1946 to 1961, compared with an increase of 30,000 in the case of Afrikaans-speaking people.

There was some concern among Protestants about the number of Catholics coming to South Africa. This position was, however, under control. In the period from May, 1963, to February, 1964, 66.7 per cent of immigrants were Protestants and 23.6 per cent Catholics.

The most important task would be in connection with the children of immigrants. In 1964, only 19.1 per cent of immigrant children in the Transvaal were in Afrikaans-medium schools compared with 63.6 per cent in English-speaking schools.

The immigrant children should be brought from the start into contact with Afrikaans.

Afrikaners should not knowingly allow immigrants to use English as their language. Careful pressure should be brought to bear on immigrants to learn Afrikaans.

WARNING ON THE FUTURE OF ENGLISH (*To the editor of the* Star, *Johannesburg, English*)

SIR:—*The leading article, "Bush English," in* The Star *on June 14, is a serious warning to all sections of the English-speaking community of South Africa to consider the future of its language. It is a warning which cannot be allowed to pass unheeded.*

All sections must band together to save the situation.

Part of the problem lies in the serious shortage of English-speaking teachers—teachers who should be highly qualified and well trained.

The spate of letters, published recently, shows very clearly the deep concern parents have about the future of their children. . . .

3 ENGLISH POCKETS? (Cape Argus, *English*) . . . *Closing the conference on English as communication in Johannesburg yesterday, Prof. Guy Butler, president of the academy, said that in a generation or two there would be three English pockets in South Africa—Johannesburg, Durban and Cape Town.*

It was important to realize that in South Africa, the number of native-born English-speakers was shrinking.

The academy was well aware of the vast areas of English literature that were sadly neglected. The universities must play a greater part in the teaching of English as a second language.

Professor Butler welcomed the suggestion from the Afrikaans Akademie vir Wetenskap en Kuns that they and the English Academy should get together to exchange all the knowledge they had.

FEWER BOYS TRAINING AS TEACHERS IN TRANSVAAL (Rand Daily Mail, *English*) . . . *The Johannesburg College of Education—the only English-medium teachers' training college in the Transvaal—is seriously perturbed by the lack of interest among male matriculants in training as primary school teachers.*

A college spokesman said yesterday that the ratio of men to women student teachers for the courses for primary school teachers was about one to nine and appeared to be dropping.

"This is a very poor ratio. We are worried about it," he said.

Interest among parents in encouraging their children to become teachers appeared to have increased after recent publicity. "But the response is still far below what it should be.

"In fact it is estimated that we must step up our enrollment to 2,000 from the present 1,600 to meet the demand for English-medium teachers."

APPEAL FOR SPREAD OF AFRIKAANS (Cape Argus, *English*)
. . . An Afrikaans author warned yesterday that it was necessary to spread the Afrikaans language to non-Whites in South Africa.

Speaking at the congress of the Federasie van Afrikaanse Kultuur-vereniginge (F.A.K.), Prof. W. J. du P. Erlank (the writer "Eitemal") said he was perturbed by the fact that many Indians and Zulus were not taking Afrikaans as a school subject.

It had become necessary to spread Afrikaans to the non-Whites. The Coloured people had already made an important contribution to the "suppleness" of Afrikaans, and other groups could also contribute.

Professor Erlank said it was important to spread Afrikaans to the non-Whites to explain to them that apartheid really meant separate freedoms. . . .

THIS TIME AN Afrikaans civil servant with a real sense of dedication; the short, stocky, dark-skinned, small-mustachioed type, his round dark eyes sparkling with enthusiasm; one of those who genuinely believe in their responsibility to the Bantu and who find a genuine satisfaction in doing it.

There are many of these, some at the highest levels, some further down. There is an odd admixture of the practical, the cynical and the idealistic in the ranks of the Government. Quite frequently, far more often than the Republic's critics acknowledge or perhaps even realize, one comes upon the idealistic, doing their best in good faith to make apartheid work in a way that will advance rather than hinder the Natives. Here was such a one.

"Bantu education? I must tell you what we are doing for Bantu education, because we are proud of it. No one else in Africa is doing as much. No one else is even hardly beginning. Mind you, I don't say we are perfect yet, or maybe ever will be, but we are making a gigantic effort. I think you will agree, a gigantic effort.

"Our estimates are not absolute, of course, because it is virtually impossible for us to run an accurate census on the tribes, for many reasons —time, money, remoteness of some areas, scattering of peoples, inability or unwillingness of tribal leaders to assist us in getting accurate figures— and so on. But according to our latest estimates based on reports from schools throughout the country, we now have over 2,000,000 Bantu children in school. This includes both the Republic and the Transkei. There are some 33,000 schools in the Republic and close to 2,000 in the Transkei."

"These are Bantu schools strictly?"

"Oh, yes," he said. "Naturally so. It is our policy, you know, that the Bantu peoples should have full development within their own areas and their own society. These figures I give you represent an estimated 85 per cent of all Bantu children in the age group seven to fourteen for the Republic as a whole, including the Transkei. The percentage is somewhat higher in the Transkei alone, and also in the urban areas of the Republic.

"This 2,000,000-plus figure is nearly three times the number of Bantu pupils in 1948 and more than double the number in 1954. It is obvious we are making progress."

"Are the teachers for these children mostly Bantu also?"

"We have about 35,000 Bantu teachers in the country at present. The great majority of the more than 7,200 Bantu community schools—which are attended by more than 1,500,000 pupils—have Bantu principals, though most of the 140 Government Bantu schools and the 513 private Bantu schools have white principals."

"Do the Bantu have any control over the education of their children?"

His sunny face clouded for a second.

"They do in the Transkei," he said thoughtfully. "And of course, elsewhere there are many Bantu advisory committees. But, you must understand that one perhaps should not make too much of these, since the system does not seem to be very popular with either Bantu parents or Bantu teachers. The Government has tried to persuade them to support it, but there is a steady falling-away. The Transkei Government under Chief Kaiser Matanzima has already abolished the advisory system altogether and placed all education under the Transkei Department of Education."

"I hear that Matanzima has also decreed that all education in the Transkei should be in English. Is that in line with Government policy?"

Again his cheery aspect dimmed.

"No, it is not. In fact, it is counter to the policy followed in the Republic, which is to give education in their tribal languages."

"The Government, then, is making a deliberate attempt to cut them off from English?"

"No, Mr. Drury," he said, quite indignantly. "You state it entirely too harshly and the wrong way 'round. The Government's aim is not to deprive the Natives of anything—it is to preserve and strengthen their *own* traditions, make them strong in their *own* society. Now, surely, you will admit that language is the guardian of both traditions and society. There-

fore the Government feels that the way to increase the dignity of the
Native is to make him proficient in his own traditional language."

"But surely that also has a tendency to further fragment the tribes,
doesn't it, to remove any cohesive bridge—which English of course is—
between them, to separate them still further and render them impotent as
to any unified action?"

"What do you mean by 'unified action'? Something hostile to the White
races of South Africa? Surely you do not propose seriously that we encourage that!"

"No, sir, I wouldn't expect you to. I'm just curious as to the real
reason why the Government wants to keep the Natives from learning a
common language, English, and why Matanzima in the Transkei has deliberately thwarted this policy by providing that all instruction there shall
be in English."

"Matanzima," he said with a frown, "is another matter. One does not
know with much certainty about Matanzima. As for the Government, I
have explained the reason. Now, you must not think that there is *no*
opportunity for the Native to learn English. Heavens, Mr. Drury, when
he comes to the urban areas himself, or when his relatives go and come
back, he picks it up very quickly. When he goes to work in the mines,
coming together from many tribes, he is taught at once by the mine operators a common lingua franca which includes many words and phrases
from English, so that he can communicate with his fellow-workers and
with his employers. No, English is readily available to the Native. It is on
every side."

"But not in his schools, evidently."

"Not in his schools."

"How high can he progress in the educational system?"

"Through senior matriculation, which would correspond to your high
school, I think."

"What about technical and vocational training? I should imagine the
Government comes down strong on that."

"It does indeed, and for the soundest of reasons: because as we create
more and more Bantu homelands—"

"When will the next one be established?"

"That," he said seriously, "is a subject upon which I am not qualified
to speak. I will say, however, that I do not believe it will be too long
delayed. No, I do not believe so. It is a matter the Government must
handle very carefully, but I do not honestly believe it will be much delayed. With new homelands of course will come a greatly increased need
for technically trained Bantu."

"There is no thought of permitting technically trained Bantu to find
jobs at the skilled and semiskilled levels in White society? There seems to
be such a shortage of skilled workers in the country—"

"Oh, no. That, too, would be counter to policy. No, there will be plenty for them to do in their own areas, believe me!"

"But aren't you arbitrarily denying yourselves valuable assistance in industry and the professions when you deny them the right to participate?"

"We will manage, Mr. Drury," he said firmly. "We have immigrants coming at a steady pace, as you know; we are seeing to it that many of them are selected very carefully for the technical skills they can contribute to the country, we are encouraging our own young people to enter skilled trades—we will manage."

"But it won't be easy."

"When was South Africa afraid of challenges?" he demanded with a confident little laugh. "This is a country of challenges, that's what makes it so exciting to live in. No, don't worry about us in the White society. And don't be concerned that we will slight our Bantu charges in the technical area. For instance, we now have vocational training for Bantu at some forty-six vocational schools and facilities. Approximately five thousand pupils are enrolled, two-thirds of them males. These facilities are available to all ages in the Bantu population.

"Our major progress with Bantu training has come, of course, in the building trades. In 1951 Parliament passed a Bantu Building Workers Act which made it legal to employ Bantu artisans in building housing for Bantu, and in consequence many of our municipalities now employ thousands of carpenters, plumbers, painters, electricians, joiners, brickmakers, bricklayers, and so on for their local Bantu housing projects.

"In addition the Government is offering such vocational courses as a two-year course in homecraft and basketry; a four-year course in building, woodwork, plumbing, leatherwork and tailoring; a three-year course in domestic science, homecrafts, dressmaking, needlework; a two-year course for electricians; training as motor mechanics; a course to train Bantu instructors for vocational schools; and training in textile spinning, weaving and winding.

"All in all, the Government is providing facilities for training in some twenty-six vocations. Our policy is to provide each major Bantu ethnic unit with at least one vocational school and one technical school."

"And the results of all this you are denying yourselves just because—"
He laughed.

"The results are not monumental yet, and one will have to wait and see whether they are. The Government is not forcing the Natives to take advantage of these facilities, you know, it is just offering them. In some fields, the building trades particularly, response is quite good—there is a clear relation between work accomplished and financial reward given. The Native is very visual, you know; he thinks in terms of what he can see, and like others, he tends to work where he sees the rewards are greatest. Other fields, the response is slow so far. But we are hoping it will spread."

"But in any event, you are denying yourselves the use of black technical labor which could be of real help to you in your industries."

"We are not denying it to ourselves, we are trying to provide it for them, in their own areas, by their own people."

"Yes. Well. I think I neglected to ask earlier about university education for Bantu. Is there any?"

"There are a few Bantu students still studying at White universities, but under the Government's policy these are being, as I think you would say in the States, 'phased out.' In time there will be a number of Bantu universities established to take care of them."

"But for the time being, for all practical purposes, university education is denied the overwhelming majority."

He smiled.

"Unavailable, Mr. Drury, *unavailable*. Not 'denied.' You must get away from these liberal clichés about us."

"How many past Bantu university graduates would you say there are?"

"Well, of course, again the figures are somewhat uncertain, but our best estimate is that there are about three thousand in the country. Or," he said dryly, "in exile in London or Washington. With some, a little knowledge has proved a dangerous thing, from our point of view. About 125 a year are still coming from the White institutions such as the University of South Africa and the University of Cape Town which still have a few enrolled."

"And that's the last 'generation' of Bantu university students, for a while?"

"Only for a while," he said cheerfully. "The Government has its plans and they will be implemented in due course."

"You sincerely believe that."

He looked calm and confident and his reply was uttered with an obviously genuine and unshakable conviction.

"I sincerely do. This is not a Government which goes back on its word or shirks its obligations. The Natives are our responsibility, and they must be educated if they are to carry on their traditions and their society and contribute to the future good of South Africa."

BANTU SERVICES LEVY ACT, 1962

This Act is administered by the Department of Bantu Administration and Development. Contributions of 25¢ per week per adult Bantu employee must be made by employers towards a Fund from which the

provision of certain essential services to Bantu townships is being
financed. The contributions are payable monthly direct to the urban
authority concerned. In certain areas the contribution may be increased
to 35¢ per week.

—Official Sources

3.
Durban

IT WAS COLD in Johannesburg the morning we left to drive down to Durban; when we got out of the city and headed south over the open plains toward the Orange Free State there was frost on the mealie stalks still standing from the summer's crop and we were glad of coats, closed windows and the heater in the car. Off in the distances we could see the typical low rolling hills and kopjes of the great central plateau that forms so much of the Transvaal and the Free State. Here and there were dotted the comfortable farmhouses and extensive agricultural workings of the thrifty descendants of the trekking Boers. We were leaving the heart of Afrikanerdom and heading for lovely, tropical, English-dominated, resented Natal.

There was little traffic on the road, another of the two-lane arteries destined soon to be replaced by freeway. Most of it had gone yesterday, or much earlier this morning, for we were traveling down on the day of "the Durban July"—that great horse race that annually absorbs the Republic's attention. This year the excitement was even greater than usual because the favorite had been shot from ambush a couple of weeks before; not enough to take him out of the race but enough to cast the outcome into doubt. Many a thoughtful citizen to whom I had spoken in recent days had taken occasion to refer to this event with an "Absolutely shocking!" or "Perfectly frightful!"—displaying a vehemence considerably greater than most of the vehemence expressed over other South African problems, such as race.

"You might think this was America!" I was told, not always in jest, on several occasions. A certain South African smugness was rocked by it, and while no one wants a horse to be shot, it still was not altogether possible to suppress a small satisfaction that they had been made to realize that even in that trim, tight, well-ordered society, the ugly and the unbalanced could appear. For a brief moment it humanized the country to some degree: smoothly ordered, accustomed things could suddenly fly out of pattern on someone's insane impulse, even here.

So the great rush south to Durban was mostly over as we drove along, and so our journey went swiftly. Before long we saw ahead a little bridge, an almost-dry riverbed meandering through the plain.

"The Vaal River."

"So that's the famous Vaal. It looks as dry as some of ours in the West."

"We're having a terrible drouth, as you know—have had for five years. Nobody knows when it will break, but we certainly hope soon." [It did.]

We crossed the bridge. "Oranje Vrystaat," a sign said. We were in the second of the old Boer republics.

The platteland continued, the gentle hills, the kopjes, the bare brown fields resting from one year's harvest, not yet ready for the next. Quietly the land began to change, valleys deeper, hills more pronounced. Far off to the right a high range of mountains appeared.

"Basutoland—soon to be the Kingdom of Lesotho." A wry snort. "One million Blacks, some beautiful mountains, an absolutely unviable economy, and absolutely nothing else. That's a nation? One vote in the UN, coming up!"

We stopped for tea high on the border of the Province of Natal. Now the land was becoming sharper and more dramatic, there were trees, the aspect was much greener. A softness was in the air, the temperature was climbing steadily. "The Garden Province," where the Transvaal and the Orange Free State go for their winter holidays, and where Durban is often known as "Jo'burg-by-the-Sea," was beginning to justify its name.

We hurried on, came to the edge of the great plateau, dropped sharply down three thousand feet to the coastal plain. Someone passed us. I HATE HAROLD, the bumper-sign said. Someone came toward us. CHARGE OR RELEASE, the bumper-sign said.

A chuckle: "Somebody doesn't like the way Mr. Wilson's treating Rhodesia." A more thoughtful note: "Somebody thinks Minister of Justice Vorster isn't doing the right thing by Ian Robertson."

"Robertson?"

"He was president of NUSAS—the National Union of South African Students, which is the organization of English-speaking students. He's the one who invited Bobby Kennedy. Vorster banned him shortly after."

"Was that why?"

A dry smile.

"The Minister isn't in the habit of divulging his reasons."

We stopped for lunch at a pleasant inn, ate a pleasant meal, moved on. We went through little towns, bustling and busy now with Saturday shoppers, pregnant once with great events: Harrismith—Ladysmith—Colenso. The savage battles and bitter sieges of the hated war came to mind.

"They won, but we made them pay for it." He was twenty-five or twenty-six and spoke as though he had been there.

An increasing number of Natives began to appear, wandering along the sides of the road, riding bicycles or just standing, gossiping, in the gentle sun. The day was passing into afternoon. Low, round, mud-and-thatch huts became visible here and there.

"Zulus. This is historic country, too. All this land was fought over in the days of Dingaan and Chaka."

"Ulundi Battlefield," a sign said, pointing to somewhere behind the jumbled hills; "Rorke's Drift."

We met a sudden black apparition, a woman dressed in colorful rags, daubed head to toe in white clay.

"That's an ngoma," he said, giving it the loving touch of the South African who grew up among the Zulu—"nnnn-go—mah. A witchdoctor. They are still very powerful here."

The sun began to drop more rapidly, shadows lengthened, the vegetation now was lush and tropical everywhere. We came to the "Valley of the Thousand Hills," just before we reached Durban, stood on a high point for a moment and surveyed its tumbled, tree-clad ridges. Then we moved on, down into the suburbs, down into the great seaport city. Indians, suddenly: Indians everywhere. Big modern office buildings in the heart of town. Along the curving edge of the Indian Ocean, miles of modern hotels, motels, apartment houses.

"Our Miami Beach," he said dryly. "The home of the English and the playground of the Afrikaans."

We came to my hotel, on City Hall Square. From their pedestals of stone, General Smuts, George V, Victoria, stared impassively into far, historic distances.

"Durban," he said as he stopped the car, four hundred miles and eight hours almost to the minute from Jo'burg. "Tea, anyone?"

"I WILL SAY FOR the Government," the gray old English-speaker said, "that when it decides to approach the outside world, it does occasionally call on all of us who can help, not just on the Afrikaners. Even I"—he smiled wryly—"have been permitted to write articles for dissemination overseas. Even I have been allowed by the S.A.B.C. to speak to Britain and America. Even I am consulted, from time to time.

"And so," he said, more seriously, "with a lot of us. And we are glad to help, because you must always remember that South Africa is our country, too. When you threaten South Africa, you threaten us as well as Afrikanerdom. We all help to form the laager when that happens. It is something the outside world tends to forget.

"I doubt that any other country on the continent, or many in the world, has as efficient and active a publicity organization as we do. Nobody likes to think of what he does as propaganda, but of course that is what it is, and quite legitimately so. After all, your government is bombarding the world with pro-American propaganda around the clock, and so is practically everybody. We feel we have the same right as all, and perhaps a greater necessity than most, since we are being attacked around the clock.

"We began our first serious information effort under General Hertzog in 1937. It was called an Information Bureau, then, and when we went to war at England's side in 1940 it became a war propaganda office. After the war it rather poked along—the world had other things to think about, South Africa wasn't the universal whipping boy she has since become—until the Nats took over in 1948. And then—*then*"—he spoke with an ironic exaggeration—"things began to move. The Afrikaner attention to detail—that rather terrible logic of theirs which is so humorless and so determined—and so effective—took over. And of course it wasn't only the Afrikaners who realized we had to speak up and defend ourselves, we all did. We realized we were in a fight for our existence, along about then. We have been at it ever since.

"The Nats found that we then had three information offices overseas, one in London established in 1939, one in New York established in 1942, one in Nairobi established in 1943. They reorganized the information setup, created the Department of Information, raised the number of information assistants and attachés overseas to sixteen in 1949 and started a real drive. The budget went up and up after that, and the qual-

ity, I think one can honestly say, did likewise. The Government greatly
increased the number of information staff people both at home and overseas. The New York office in particular, since it has such direct and easy
access to the UN, became a key outlet. Washington and San Francisco
also receive a great deal of money and assistance."

"In addition to the S.A.B.C., as you say, and to the South Africa
Foundation and the South African Tourist Corporation—"

He smiled.

"Both the Foundation and Satour will tell you they don't engage in
propaganda, but they make a point of helping foreign visitors who come
here. They're helping you, aren't they?"

"The Foundation is giving me leads to a few people and helping to set
up some interviews. Satour is going to take me to Kruger Park later on to
see the wild animals. My expenses aren't being paid—except for four
days at Kruger. I'm not an official guest, and I don't feel corrupted.
Should I?"

"Watch out for the lions and the elephants and the giraffes," he said
with a twinkle. "They are powerful propagandists for South Africa. So,
then: the Nats took over, organized, got things humming, and they're
humming today, as you know. I imagine you've found it hard to get away
from the Department of Information people these past couple of weeks,
haven't you?"

"They couldn't have been nicer or more helpful."

"But a little sticky, at times? You haven't felt overwhelmed?"

"They couldn't have been nicer or more helpful."

"But you've managed to break away enough to get what you wanted, I
expect. Determined visitors usually can."

"They couldn't have been nicer or more—"

He laughed.

"All right, all right. And of course you have seen the printed material,
as well—things like *Panorama* and *Scope.*"

"Very effectively done, I think."

"Oh, admirably. There are six regular periodicals, you know—*Panorama,* which in typography and general style and richness is similar to
Life, I would say; *South African Digest,* a weekly compendium of official
statements and recent economic developments; *Bantu,* which is distributed principally inside the Republic, but also goes to some outside as
well; *South African Summary,* which presents in brief form material ca-
bled daily from Pretoria to the New York office; *Business Report,* whose
title is self-explanatory; and *Scope,* which is an illustrated monthly on
current developments in the Republic.

"And in addition to that, of course, there are innumerable factual
books and pamphlets, excerpts or complete texts of official speeches and
statements, reprints of articles on policy written by people like me. Plus

the audiovisual section of the Department of Information, which produces films in English, Afrikaans, French, Dutch, Spanish, Italian, Portuguese—and wins awards with them, too, the latest being in October, 1965, when the film entitled 'White South Africans' won first place over 224 other government films from around the world at the San Francisco film festival. Quite a rumpus that was, too, but the film was excellent, and deserved it.

"Now great stress is being put on television films, though it's sometimes rather hard to get favorable South African material on television programs, particularly in America and England. They're always quick to play up any crisis, but anything constructive is apt to be left out."

"And of course your diplomatic officials and information people make a lot of speeches and appear on a lot of programs—"

"Oh, yes, all the time. Hundreds, every year."

"I would say the Government has pretty well thought of everything."

"In this I think you will find that most of us support it."

"On the theory that you are fighting for your lives."

"On the fact that we are fighting for our lives."

NAT. ATTACK ON EDITOR—SUSPICION SOWN, SAYS "DAWIE"
(Cape Times, *English*) . . . *Two Cape Nationalist-controlled newspapers, the* Burger *and* Beeld, *this weekend accused the editor of the South African Observer, Mr. S. E. D. Brown, and "a group of Afrikaners who should know better" of sowing dissension among the Afrikaans people. . . .*

On Saturday, Dawie, the Burger's *political columnist, referred to a group of northern Afrikaners who allowed themselves to be led by an English-speaking South African who is connected with "such strange oversea organizations" as the League of Empire Loyalists, the Candour League and certain* baasskap *groups in the United States.*

Dawie said the S. A. Observer was sowing suspicion among Afrikaners about certain prominent Afrikaners.

Among these were Dr. Donges [Minister of Finance]; Prof. H. B. Thom, Rector of the University of Stellenbosch; the Rev. J. S. Gericke, Moderator of the Cape NG Kerk; and leading businessmen like Dr. Anton Rupert, Dr. M. S. Louw, Dr. H. J. van Eck and Dr. P. E. Rousseau.

Dawie also says that four or five Afrikaans newspaper editors have been brought under suspicion.

Dawie also disclosed that the S. A. Observer received the support of the Nationalist Party in all four provinces up to a year or two ago. But now it was following the methods of the late American Senator McCarthy of "guilt by association."

"If you sit with a real or supposed liberal on a body like the South Africa Foundation, the South African-American Exchange Programme and company directorates, then you are a liberal and an enemy of the people."

The Beeld *said yesterday that the* S. A. Observer *is still distributed free and "in inner circles there is certainty about which Afrikaners in Pretoria pay for the costs of the paper."*

What shocks both the Beeld *and the* Burger *is that the recent Afrikaanse Studentebond congress at Stellenbosch praised the work of Mr. Brown and the* S. A. Observer.

O N THE BEAUTIFUL manicured lawns and terraces of the official residence of the American Consul-General, just south of Durban on the lush, green hills that slope down to the placid Indian Ocean, we gathered, black and white and mahogany brown, to celebrate the 190th anniversary of the independence of a land as puzzled, and perhaps as troubled, as this. The Bantu were there, ministers and chiefs and teachers from Zululand and the Transkei; the Coloureds, the Indians, the Americans, the Canadians, a smattering of other diplomatic representatives. No one represented the Government—"They often telephone their private regrets, but no one dares to come."

Three police stood outside on the road, watching the arrivals and making notes but otherwise offering no interference. "Now we can relax, we're on American soil," a native minister remarked as he walked past them, his brightly garbed lady on his arm. One of the young Afrikaners gave him a cold and ironic smile.

At first we stood about in little groups of determinedly mixed color, everybody being very Friendly and Congenial and Enlightened. But quite soon, under the persuasions of the beautiful warm day (in the mid-eighties, far now from the sparkling chilliness of the winter-wrapped Transvaal), the good food, the punch and soft drinks (illegal to serve liquor at a mixed gathering, illegal to have a mixed gathering at all, but the Americans persist every year in acting like Americans and so far have got away with it), a more relaxed and genuine easiness began to enter the gathering. Only then, with a sudden surprise, was it possible to realize actually how much tension did exist, just beyond the hedges. Some indefinable but ever-present weight seemed suddenly, if only temporarily, lifted: it was indeed good to stand again on American soil, torn with her own tensions though America is. At least one could be proud of the goal, however difficult it might be to achieve. Here the goal was more elusive, obscured by many things. The ugly necessities of survival robbed the goals of grace:

"I believe they've slipped over into Swaziland, haven't they? I'm sure the Security Police know about it, but apparently they're content to leave them there for the moment. . . . Tommy? Oh, I think he's in Basutoland right now, but I'm told he gets in again from time to time. Terribly dangerous. . . . Yes, I talked to her in Jo'burg last week: she seems quite undaunted about her latest book being banned; doesn't like it, of course, but she isn't letting it get her down. . . . We're planning to sail for the States next week, but we don't know at this point whether the Minister of Justice is going to let us back in. We want to return, there's so much to be done at the Mission they can't handle it alone, but you know how it is: we may just have to take our chances, though it will be damned inconvenient getting everything home if we find he's decided to keep us out. . . . I did see him in Cape Town, yes; he thinks they're closing in on him, he feels he may be banned any day now. It's a pity. . . . That case is going to the Appeals Court, I think, but she hasn't a prayer, really. . . . Yes, their son's been taken up under 180-days. All part of this general attack on student liberals, apparently. . . . He said he wanted to write a really strong editorial about that situation we were discussing the other day, but he doesn't really dare. The police have already raided his office twice, and he thinks about once more and he will have had it. We don't have censorship here, you see, we just gradually eliminate the people who write against the Government, and then the publishers find somebody more agreeable to the Government to take their place. . . . We want to go down on the South Coast for our holiday but our houseboy got in a fight with some Xhosas and killed one of them, and we may have to stay until that's straightened out. . . . Of course the Nats are making big inroads here in Natal, but what are we in the United Party expected to do? As long as the outside world is threatening South Africa, we're going to keep losing and the Nats are going to keep gaining. . . . Yes, I saw them when I went down to Grahamstown last week. They want to put the children in an English-language school but the Government is going to insist that they put them in an Afrikaans school instead. . . . I understand he's in London working for the International Defense and Aid. He left right after it was banned down here—one jump ahead of Vorster, so I hear. . . . Her mail is being opened and everyone who comes to the house is being photographed. They have a special officer staked out in the house across the street. It's getting so he waves to her when she goes in and out. It won't be long before she's banned. They've already lifted her passport. . . . He's in Robben Island. His wife tells me he's having a rough time of it. They questioned him for five hours last week—nailed his penis to a table and made him stand up all the time. She says he fainted twice. . . ."

Later, the last rich hors d'oeuvre eaten, the final glass of Coke consumed, the guests departed and the Security Police went back to headquarters to write up their annual report on the difficult, uncooperative Americans and their mixed, illegal party. The musing speculation began again, as always:

"And so what do you make of this beautiful, unhappy country whose people are so charming and so hospitable and where such terrible tensions exist?"

"I can see how things developed as they have—"

"Yes, anyone who is willing to approach the country with a little patience and understanding can see that."

"And I can see why they feel threatened—"

"Yes, that too. And how it makes them do some of the things they do."

"But I don't see the answer to it, do you?"

"Does anybody? It's such a wonderful country in so many ways, its people, of all races, have such fine qualities—and yet here they are, trapped in this awful dilemma. You can see why the Whites feel as they do, it's their country, they were here first, it isn't any question of colonialism, they started it and built it up, they are the original South Africans —and yet here are all these millions of Blacks, who came in late, true, but nonetheless here they are. What do you do about them?

"So you watch the Whites getting more and more defensive and militaristic, the Republic Day Festival, the big armed-forces display, the little kids organized and marching like something out of the Hitler Youth. Yet your average Afrikaner is one of the nicest people on earth, decent and friendly and kind, and the English here are like the English everywhere, obeying some standard of reserved behavior that sets them a little apart from everybody else, but also decent and friendly. And the enormous wealth and enormous potential of it all. Here, you feel, is one country on earth that was born to succeed. Then you come up bang against the race question, and at once everything is thrown under its shadow, the whole picture changes, all of society is wrenched and twisted out of shape in response to its demands—or to what the Government conceives to be its demands. Our problems are bad enough, but, God, I'm glad we don't have these."

"You can't help but feel sorry for the country—you can't help but like it—you can't help but get involved with it. It has so much—and yet—"

"And yet."

TRIBESMEN CLASH (Rand Daily Mail, *English*) . . . *An African was shot dead and another injured when more than 50 tribesmen clashed in the Mambula Location in the Kranskop district at the weekend. Three groups were involved in the fight in which sticks and firearms were used.*

THE HOUSE WAS huge and old, high on a Durban hill, filled with antiques, ancestry and the rich, comfortable, characteristic wealth of the English settlers who made good—very good. There is some corner of almost every foreign land that is forever England, and usually it consists of just this type of house, just this type of atmosphere, just this type of attitude. A sort of well-fed security; a calm, self-confident optimism; a bland assumption that everything will work out for the best because it always has (whatever history may say); a graciously genuine interest in the welfare of the natives (small *n*); and a lively concern for one's own skin.

It made for an interesting discussion.

These were traditional United Party supporters, English of the most English, backbone of Natal for generations, directors of this bank, presidents of that corporation, lawyers, financiers, the English-speaking money-men who still control 80 per cent of the Republic's economy—though the Afrikaner, like a favorite in the "Durban July," is coming up fast on the turn. And the world threatens. And around the high-ceilinged citadel with its gorgeous furnishings, its complement of Bantu servants and its sedate, innate, unconscious but unshakable conviction of superiority, the winds of change are blowing.

Blowing politically, too. These were traditional United Party supporters, but now most of them were for the Nationalists, some openly and with a frank conviction, others quietly and privately, anxious to maintain the symbol of an opposition party, however much their secret ballots and their secret financial contributions to the Nats may be eroding it away.

"I think," said one of the ladies, her long diamond earrings glittering when she turned her aristocratic head, the ruby ring on her right hand flaring in the candlelight as she spooned soufflé from the giant silver bowl held by the silent black presence at her elbow, "that the Government is going too fast. I don't think we should give Them so much. They don't appreciate it. Give Them a finger and they will take the hand, as the Afrikaans say. I agree."

"My dear girl," her husband said from down the table, gold studs gleaming on white shirt-front, "you're three hundred years behind the times. You may be entirely right—"

"Of course she's right," the lady on his left, emerald necklace glowing, remarked tartly as the black presence, silent, unobtrusive, almost not there, moved to her side and held out the bowl of soufflé, "and we all know it. But as you say, she's behind the times. You can't stop it, darling, the outside world is after us. We've got to do something for Them, whether it's safe or not. I think the Government's policy is as safe as can be, under the circumstances. That's why I voted for the Nats."

"You did?" A feminine voice across the table sounded startled and somewhat dismayed. The masculine voice that responded was hearty and jovially amused.

"Come, come, don't sound so shocked. Of course she did. Most of us did. Didn't you?"

"I did not!"

"Well," said the lady of the ruby ring, "I did."

"But I thought you were just complaining that the Government is doing too much for Them. How do you justify—"

"Because," she said, as the silent black presence passed unobtrusively along the other side of the table, bending down, holding the bowl, straightening up, moving on, bending down, holding the bowl, "the Government is tough. And we need tough leadership. The Americans and the UN may be here tomorrow morning. I'd rather have this Government in power to meet them. Though I still don't like their giving so much to the Natives. It isn't appreciated, and it will only lead to trouble when they get the idea that they should have more independence."

"Janet obviously doesn't believe in separate development," her husband said with a smile as the silent black presence, task completed, took the bowl silently out the door.

"No, I don't. I think it will only encourage Them to make trouble later. Mark my word, we'll live to regret it."

"I can't agree," said the owner of the hearty voice, red-faced, cherubimic, lively. "By Jove, I can't. I think it's the only way—the only way. Give 'em all they want but keep 'em in their own areas. Let 'em develop there to their heart's content."

"And when They ultimately want membership in this so-called South African Commonwealth the Government talks about?" the lady of the ruby ring demanded. "And we've helped to educate Them and raise Them up to political sophistication? What then? We'll still be a minority, only then we'll be a minority amongst a lot of educated and politically active Natives. John Vorster won't be able to put Them all in Robben Island, then. What will happen to our 'Commonwealth'? We'll be voted or swamped out of existence."

"Too gloomy," the hearty-voiced one said, "entirely too gloomy. First of all, it will be a long, long process—"

"How long will the world allow us?"

"A long, slow process, and what makes you think the Government is going to allow subversive elements to come to the top in the Bantustans? These chappies are shrewd fellows, you know—they're as tough as you say they are. You don't really think they're going to permit anyone to get in there who will upset the apple-cart—"

"They've let Mantanzima in the Transkei, and that's a nice kettle of fish."

"Yes," the hearty one agreed thoughtfully. "Matanzima may be something else again. But let Matanzima start really getting out of hand and don't you think the Government will remove him? Not openly, perhaps, but there are ways. The same thing will happen in other native homelands. They won't take any chances, don't you be fooled."

"Of course I rather think," said the lady of the emerald necklace with a deprecatory but nonetheless rather nervous little laugh, "that what the Transvaalers really want to do is turn all of Natal into one big Bantustan and consolidate Them all here. They would just love to do that to us, wouldn't they?"

"The Nats aren't going to do anything to antagonize the English-speakers if they can help it," the hearty-voiced one said confidently. "They need us too much. As long as the Republic's threatened the way it is, they're going to do everything they can to create national unity."

"On their terms," said the lady of the ruby ring.

"Oh, of course I don't really think they would ever do that to Natal," the lady of the emeralds said, "but you know deep in their hearts a lot of them would probably like to. Still, we voted for them, Janet, so I suppose we would only have ourselves to blame."

"I would do it again tomorrow," Janet said, "things being what they are in the outside world."

"So would most of us," said the hearty-voiced one as the silent black presence came in again, this time with cheese and crackers on an enormous silver tray; and all down the gleaming table in the gentle candlelight in the beautiful old house there were nods and murmurs of agreement.

SHOULD NOT SAY TOO MUCH DONE FOR NON-WHITE (Cape Argus, *English*) . . . *It was a pity that some people accused the Government of doing too much for the non-Whites, the Moderator of the Ned. Geref. Kerk* [Dutch Reformed Church], *the Rev. J. S. Gericke, said here yesterday.*

Addressing 100 students attending a leadership conference arranged by the Afrikaanse Studentebond, Mr. Gericke outlined certain steps to be taken if South Africa wanted to change the attitude of the world.

Firstly, South Africans should be prepared to make the sacrifices which a just solution of their problems demanded. This would require not only finance but patience, perseverance and love.

It was to be hoped that those who thought the Government was doing too much for the non-Whites would always be in the minority.

Secondly, a bigger loyalty to South Africa was needed. Everybody had a democratic right to criticise, but South Africans should not "wash dirty linen overseas." That was doing a lot of damage.

Lastly, no expense and effort should be spared to keep South Africa happy for all its inhabitants.

THIN, WIRY, EARNEST, with a curious diffident gentleness underlying his outward confidence, the young Bantu editor looked across his cluttered desk in the ramshackle office on the edge of Durban's Indian quarter and described solemnly how it is to run a black man's paper in a white man's world.

He had been introduced by the paper's editorial director, an English-speaker, young, tough, glib. That is part of how it is: the real operative power rests safely in White hands, as it does in all the Native publications in the Republic. And one works constantly under the eye of the Government, and that is another part of how it is.

Nonetheless, he maintained, his paper was not a spokesman for the Government, nor was he, as some Bantu charged, a Government stooge. His paper is sixty-two years old, white-owned, conservative "because it is printed in Zulu principally for a Zululand audience, and we Zulus are a very conservative nation"; costs five cents twice a week "which is a lot, for them," and has a total press-run of about 315,000 copies each week, reaching a readership estimated to be well over one million "because it passes from hand to hand in the kraals."

"In general," he said slowly, thinking about it as he spoke and framing his words with care, "we could be said to follow an anti-Government line, though of course there are limits"—and he smiled a patient little smile—"on what we can print in that direction. Yet we are reasonably free." He paused and looked at the stack of material on his desk. "Yes," he said precisely, "reasonably free. . . .

"After all, it is the news which concerns the Zulus, rather than agitation for the gaining of power. Therefore, there would not be much interest in agitation anyway, were we to engage in it. A very considerable number of our readers are 'below the breadline,' you might say, and so their main concern is simply to make a living, to have enough cattle, enough wives, raise enough mealies and play their part in the tribal life they have always known.

"But, as I say, in general we are anti-Government, criticizing where we feel criticism is warranted but giving credit where credit is due. After all"—again that patient, rather wistfully ironic little smile—"look at the history of Radio Bantu. It takes a violently pro-Government line, and it is an enormous success with the Bantu. So possibly that is another indication that more violent opposition and criticism from us would be rather pointless. Our relationship with the Government," he said seriously, "is very, very good. . . ."

He had, he said, thirteen African journalists on his staff. Several of them came to him for advice as we talked, youthful like himself for the most part, intelligent, neat, soft-spoken.

"Our managerial staff is White, and so is our advertising staff. The reason for this being that most White business firms won't deal with Africans"—he said it quite simply and without any show of anger, that's just how life was in the land of Jan van Riebeeck's heirs—"and also, Africans as a rule don't have the skills necessary for managerial and advertising work. Our Linotype operators and our stereo man are African."

How had he come into journalism? Was he a university graduate?

No, he said, he was not, though he had gone through most of the lower grades.

"I began working as a factory hand, but I always, as long as I can remember, wanted to write and reach people with my ideas that way. So I found that factory work was not giving me satisfaction and fulfillment. I went to the library and began reading and studying everything I could find, newspapers, magazines, books, everything. After a time I applied to be a correspondent in the native areas for this paper, and for other papers. This was successful, so presently I was able to become a staff member here, and then four years ago I became editor."

"What editorial position do you take on the Bantustans?"

He looked thoughtful and solemn.

"At first the Zulus were much opposed to the whole idea. Right now, they are not saying much one way or the other, because the climate of the country is such that people are afraid to talk, especially if they oppose the Government.

"However, I do not think the Zulus do oppose the Government on this—or at least, what the Government says it intends to do. At first there was opposition because they felt that it would deprive them of their lands, that families would be moved from areas where they have lived for scores of years. Now, however, when they see the Transkei, when they see that many are not forced to move, when they see some independence being granted, they think differently. The Transkei has produced many private talks in Zululand hoping for a Bantustan for the Zulus. The Transkei, from what I can gather, is appearing to have quite a bit of success. The Government people are doing their best to make the whole venture a success.

"The Zulus can't understand why the Government is not giving them a Bantustan." ("The Zulus seem unable to make up their minds," I had been told on my first day in Pretoria.) "They think the Government is stalling.

"The Zulus are only too willing, now, to have a Bantustan, but they think the Government is afraid because Matanzima's speeches have given them quite a few anxious moments, I think. The Government's delay is interpreted by the Zulus as fear."

Did he find that white journalists made him welcome, was he able to cover stories on the same basis? A pleased smile came to his face, he relaxed a little.

"Oh, yes, they are very kind to me. I was permitted by the Government to go to London last year, and I went to Parliament. I found it rather drab physically, you know, the chamber rather small, not much decoration, but I liked the informality of it, the members attacking each other, the free debate. The white journalists made me welcome and I had no trouble."

And in Cape Town?

He did not seem in the least upset, stating it all as he did everything else, just part of the white man's world.

"There, also, the white reporters are very good to me, very friendly and helpful, but of course the Government doesn't let me sit in the Press Gallery with them. I have to have my own little bay on the ground floor where I sit by myself. But I am able to use all the facilities, the telephones and typewriters that I need, and so on. Are you going to be in Cape Town for the next session?"

I said I was.

"I will look for you there. Someday," he said, "I hope I can write a book about our country. It is very different and very interesting, I think."

"You would have a different point of view."

"Yes," he agreed with that gentle, serious diffidence. "I believe the South African point of view is somewhat different."

ANOTHER STEP IN THE WRONG DIRECTION (*Editorial*, The Leader, *Durban, Indian*)

The Government aims to tighten up on the question of separation in the provision of amenities for the different groups in the Republic. It is said banks, building societies and business houses may be called upon to provide separate entrances and facilities for White and Black.

This means that, for the first time, private institutions may be called upon to enforce, by law, rigid racial separation.

We believe this to be a move in the wrong direction. The authorities should leave well enough alone, and leave it to the good sense of the people concerned to decide how they should deal with their customers, be they White or Black.

We believe this to be a move in the wrong direction because what we

*require is not more and more rigid racial separation, but the removal of
the bar sinister slowly but surely.*

*We believe that, in the long run, South Africa can develop into a great
nation only on the basis of unity, not only unity between the various
white sections of the community but between all the race groups that go
to make up this country of ours.*

*How can we achieve the ideal of unity of the races if we go on divid-
ing them more and more into rigid racial compartments, and if the non-
Whites are to be reduced to the status of "untouchables?"*

*By adopting policies which are quite out of step with the rest of the
world our country is fast relegating itself to an untouchable among the
Family of Nations.*

*In a world which is shrinking daily and in which no nation or people
can afford to "go it alone," all our efforts and endeavors should be aimed
at achieving greater unity not only internally but internationally.*

*That is why we view with profound regret the latest move on the part
of the authorities.*

$15.4 MILLION AMMONIA PLANT TO OPEN IN NATAL

The largest ammonia factory in the southern hemisphere, costing
$15.4 million and now under construction at Umbogintwini, Natal, will
be ready for operation in March next year. The factory will function
as a "parent" plant which will feed a giant complex of ancillary industries expected to grow up around it.

The major part of the plant's daily output of 600 tons of ammonia
will be used in the manufacture of fertilizer, a valuable South African
export.

—Official Sources

THE DURBAN CAMPUS of the University of Natal (there is another at
Pietermaritzburg, forty miles north) occupies one of the most commanding sites in the country. Resting on a couple of the city's highest
hills, it dominates the skyline with a gracious tree-filled campus that
speaks of England and tradition and the quiet, diligent pursuit of knowledge.

Except that these days, in South Africa, knowledge is not pursued
quietly and diligently, for all the campuses are aflame with unrest and
agitation for and against the Government. Things more insistent than
the pursuit of knowledge have captured the loyalties and efforts of the

more vocal portions of the young: if they are English young, here and at Cape Town, Wits and Rhodes University at Grahamstown, a constant protest against bannings and apartheid; if they are Afrikaans young, at Stellenbosch, and Bloemfontein, Potchefstroom, Pretoria and Port Elizabeth, a steady drumfire of resolutions, statements and mass meetings in support of Afrikanerdom.

As with all campuses everywhere, these movements in both sections of the White student population are conducted by minorities, and the great majority of students really are pursuing knowledge and the goal of a career without fanfare, excitement or agitation. Yet the minorities, as always, make the headlines and catch the attention; and since in the Republic the issues are considerably more fundamental than the use of dirty words by dirty people, the protests are worthy of serious attention.

Certainly the Government thinks so, for through the Minister of Justice it spends a great deal of time in the attempt to thwart and detain the leaders of the English-speaking students' organization, the National Union of South African Students. And it is constantly sending top officials, including Cabinet members, to address and inspire the meetings of NUSAS' opposite number in Afrikanerdom, the Afrikaanse Studentebond. Their elders war on one another through NUSAS and the ASB; and the students themselves are always eager to advance the battle.

This was the opening night of NUSAS' annual convention. Its recent president, Ian Robertson, had just been banned by Minister of Justice Vorster, following Robertson's invitation to Senator Robert Kennedy to visit the country as NUSAS' guest. The organization itself was under severe attack by the ASB, the Afrikaans press, the Government and Nationalist members of Parliament. Its delegates literally did not know whether they might not all be taken off to jail by the Security Police at any moment, particularly since their convention, quite illegally, included representatives of all the races. It was true that their bravery was undoubtedly compounded of many things, including the thrill of defying authority, the thrill of mingling with black and brown skins and weren't supposed to mingle with, the thrill of headlines. Yet underlying was an obvious deep devotion to a cause that was becoming increasingly dangerous. I was to hear many savagely sarcastic attacks on NUSAS as I pursued my journey, from Afrikaners and from English-speaking Nationalists; but it was impossible not to admire the organization, misguided and extreme though some of its positions are. The basic devotion to a decent standard of humanity is worthy of much respect, for in this period of the Republic's life it takes more than excitement and the thrill of headlines to make one stand up to John Vorster and the majority of one's countrymen. It takes guts and NUSAS has them.

The opening meeting was held in the evening in a university auditorium that was new, steep-pitched and tiny, built to seat three hundred people ("They say they ran out of money, but it's the law that no assembly may consist of more than three hundred people, so that was a convenient point at which to stop"), accommodating on this occasion probably 250. The majority were White; the next most numerous group, by far, were Bantu, with here and there an occasional Indian or Coloured. With a few blue-jeaned, long-haired, bearded exceptions, most of the students were clean, neatly dressed, earnest, intelligent. Here and there a professor and his wife sat among them. There was a good deal of ostentatious White-sitting-with-Bantu, a lot of loudly bright jesting back and forth; but even here, defiant and determined though the participants were, there was an indefinable but inescapable sense of separation, a certain uneasiness of contact that not even the most desperate fraternization could quite overcome. The jests were a little too loud, the laughter a little too forced, the sitting together just a trifle too deliberate and organized.

Even here, try as they would, they could not escape their country's heavy burden. Perhaps the Government did not need to worry too much, when all was said and done.

But the speeches, of course, were staunch and admirable of purpose. There were many calls upon Mr. Vorster to either release Ian Robertson from ban or bring him to trial and present the evidence for his banning; many condemnations of apartheid. A white-haired little man with an upthrust jaw, a bulldog manner, a bitter face, author of perhaps the most beautiful and moving book ever written about the strange society, was ushered to the podium amid great applause to deliver the keynote address: Alan Paton, author of *Cry, the Beloved Country*. His speech was as bitter as his face, the utterance of a deeply frustrated and unhappy man hurling his scorn against a John Vorster far away and obviously utterly impervious.

"I defy the Minister!" he cried. "Why does the Minister not tell us . . . It is the Minister's responsibility . . . I say to the Minister . . . The Minister has . . . The Minister should. . . The Minister must . . . I defy the Minister . . ."

But the Minister, and the Government he represented, said no word. It was not that they did not care, for their informers were at the convention, their spies were keeping them advised, their police were taking notes. It was just that they did not answer; and their silence was more crushing, perhaps, than anything they might have said.

Later, after the speeches were concluded, after the resolution of support for Ian Robertson had been passed, we adjourned to another building for cocktails. Here again, with a self-conscious and almost grimly convivial defiance, White mixed with Black, illegally, and drank liquor together, illegally, and many an ironic toast was drunk to the Minister and his Government before the party ended.

It was a curiously moving yet curiously pathetic scene; and the visitors from another land who had spent the evening with them went back down into Durban, convinced of their courage but saddened by the realization that this small, ineffective organization, battered and beleaguered and possibly not to be allowed to live much longer, is one of the major voices still left opposing the Government.

THREAT TO S. A. CULTURAL WELL-BEING (Daily News, *Durban, English*) . . . *The Government was responsible for threatening the cultural well-being of South Africa and for increasing racial tension.*

This was part of a motion condemning apartheid in cultural matters which was passed by an overwhelming majority at the NUSAS congress in Durban yesterday.

The motion also called on local councils of NUSAS to organize as many nonracial functions as possible.

In another motion, the Bantu Laws Amendment Act was described as "harsh and cruel." The act had deprived the majority of the South African people of their few remaining rights.

The Assembly noted that the Minister of Justice planned to introduce amendments to the Suppression of Communism Act which would destroy the independence of the legal profession.

This might force many law students to withdraw from legitimate opposition organisations.

NUSAS was totally opposed to this extension of autocratic rule in South Africa, and called on the minister to withdraw this proposed legislation.

Other resolutions last night stated: That NUSAS condemned the policy of church schools of admitting White pupils only. It regarded this as hypocritical and noted that the St. George's Grammar school in Cape Town had again rejected the application of the son of Mr. J. S. Thomas.

That the Department of Social Welfare has asked welfare organisations to introduce racial segregation. This encroachment of political ideologies into the field of welfare organisations was deplored.

There were severe practical impediments to the working of racially separate welfare organisations, and NUSAS deplored the segregation of the National Council for the Blind in spite of there being no legislation to enforce this.

That the refusal of passports and visas on numerous occasions was condemned as a restriction on freedom of movement.

That NUSAS was opposed to all totalitarian and authoritarian ideologies.

THE TRUTH ABOUT NUSAS (Cape Times, *English*) . . . *Margaret Marshall, 21-year-old Witwatersrand University student, is the new president of the National Union of South African Students, NUSAS. She takes over from Ian Robertson, banned by the Minister of Justice earlier this year. Here Miss Marshall answers a series of questions about the controversial organisation.*

The Government says NUSAS is unpatriotic. What do you say to this?

MISS MARSHALL: The accusation is nonsense. For 42 years we have been serving the interests of South Africa and its students. What the Government really means is that NUSAS objects to some National Party policies.

The Government also says that NUSAS besmirches South Africa overseas . . .

Throughout the world, national student organisations exchange information about their countries, especially on education. We do this also, and we believe we present a fair and honest picture of our country. Whatever information we send overseas is also freely circulated within South Africa so that anyone can see what we say.

I know that the Government claims that we have lobbied for international sanctions against South Africa. This is just not true. In fact, at a recent international students' conference, we were the only body which voted against a boycott-South Africa motion.

At the same time, when our president is banned, we openly appreciate the support which students in other countries give us, just as we support them in their difficulties.

Is NUSAS a political organisation or are you concerned about helping students with their everyday needs?

The question implies that the two aspects are mutually exclusive. This is not so.

Firstly, NUSAS is a students' organisation and its primary aim is student welfare. Most of our work—what we call our "trade union" activity—is taken up with providing scholarships and interest-free loans for students, arranging for discounts on a range of goods and running our large travel department which organises tours overseas at cheap rates.

We arrange lectures on a wide variety of subjects at our member universities and training colleges as well as intensive seminars on topics which students want to study deeply.

But, in addition to all this, we are a union of all South African students, including non-Whites. We represent and fight for the interests of non-White students as much as we do for our White members. If this makes us political, then we accept it.

But the reports of your congress earlier this month seemed to show that NUSAS spent much time passing resolutions on political issues.

Resolutions dealing with student loans and welfare are not of much general news value, I suppose, and are not reported by the Press. Most of our time, in fact, was taken up with bread-and-butter problems.

I would, however, agree that we do spend quite a lot of time talking about education in South Africa because it is of direct importance to us. In any other country this would be straightforward enough. In South Africa, however, the policy of apartheid underlies the educational system, so that when we debate education we necessarily enter the political field.

It would surely be absurd for us to refrain from discussing as basic a matter as education simply because others have made it political.

But didn't you also discuss things like the 180-day detention law, bannings and so on at your congress?

Yes, we did. We are over the age of 18, these laws affect us as they do every citizen, and we are fulfilling our responsibilities as citizens by expressing an opinion on them.

NUSAS claims to speak for South Africa's students. How true is this claim in fact?

It is most certainly true. Students of all viewpoints are represented in the organisation—and this is as it should be. It would be a sad day if NUSAS consisted of people with a uniform outlook. Some students may, and do, disagree with some aspects of NUSAS policy. The organisation is not static and its policy fluctuates from year to year as students come and go.

NUSAS isn't a tightly controlled organisation. It is a federation and its policies are reviewed and formulated anew at the annual congresses attended by delegates sent by students at all our affiliated centres.

But hasn't your rival organisation—the Afrikaanse Studentebond, ASB—got considerably more members? And doesn't this make the ASB more representative?

The ASB claims to have 28,000 students as against our 21,000. But this does not make the ASB representative of South Africa's students. The ASB is a "closed shop" organisation, representing sectional interests. It restricts itself to Afrikaans-speaking Christians, and it refuses to admit any non-White students.

To participate in NUSAS, the only qualification required is that you are a student at an institution of higher learning. Our largest centres are the English-language universities and training colleges, while we have

members too at non-White colleges and branches at Afrikaans universi-
ties.

The essential difference between NUSAS and the ASB can best be seen at international level, where the ASB is rejected because it has a discriminatory membership. This is a universal practice: you simply cannot have an organisation representing people if it represents only some of them.

NUSAS NOT NEWSWORTHY, SAYS S.A.B.C. (Daily News, *Durban,* English) . . . *Two student bodies opened their annual conferences last night. The S.A.B.C. news at 7* A.M. *today covered the Afrikaanse Stu-dentebond conference at Stellenbosch, but not the NUSAS conference at Durban.*

Asked why the Corporation had ignored the NUSAS conference, the head of news, Mr. J. van Zyl, said: "We did not regard it as newsworthy enough."

THE MORNING WAS sunny, warm and gentle, so I decided to walk to my interview with the two leaders of the Indian community, passing first along the bustling arcades of West Street, the principal European shopping area, with its camera shops, jewelry stores, chemists and stationers, clothiers and department stores. Most of the names on the windows were English, interrupted now and then by an Afrikaans name as startling as an English name on the stores of Pretoria or Bloemfontein. Eight blocks from the hotel I turned right and in-stantly was in India, swarming with life in the shops and bazaars lin-ing the arcades of Grey Street.

Now the names were Pradjit, Prather, Singh, Hansa. Now the skin was very dark, almost as black as the Bantu in many cases, the eyes large and liquid, the features often aquiline, the glance quick, shrewd, appraising. Children of one of the earth's most intelligent races were open for business, making the best of what is permitted them in the odd world they have inherited from the sugarcane laborers of the past century.

This was the area where in 1949 dreadful riots broke out between the Bantu and the Indians, the Bantu charging that the Indian shopkeepers were consistently shortchanging and cheating them. One hundred and forty-two were killed, 187 were injured, a permanent hatred was engen-dered between the two races who now exist in an uneasy relationship based upon commerce and suspicion. The Government stepped in, stopped the riots, and restored order. Another argument was added to the many the Government offers that the races—all races—must develop separately in South Africa.

My hosts this morning were of the older generation. I was to see the younger generation, and also less compliant members of the older, later on. Today I heard the story of those who resent but comply because they have no choice, and out of their compliance fashion a desperately hopeful, wistful rationale.

The office in which we talked was plain but substantial. Outside a Jaguar and a Cadillac were parked. One of my hosts was in his fifties, plump, earnest, struggling hard to put the best light on things. The other was in his seventies, white-haired, dignified, soft-spoken but frequently acerbic. Both used the term "Europeans" for Whites, which is the usage preferred by the Government.

"About 250,000 of the Republic's half-million Indians live in Durban or its near vicinity," the younger said. "For some reason, I don't know why, Durban and Natal have always been the spearhead of agitation against the Indians, so much so that in the 1920's the Government of India actually sent a deputation here to try to help the Indians of South Africa. Some concessions were secured and to some extent pressures were alleviated a little. Even so, despite harassments, Indians in Natal up to the 1940's could buy anywhere, rent anywhere, trade anywhere."

"Could they in the other provinces?"

"To some extent in the Cape," the older said. "Much more restricted in the Transvaal, where President Kruger set aside certain streets for Indians. Not allowed at all in the Free State."

"Even so," the younger repeated, "in Natal the situation was quite liberal, quite liberal. Then came the Second World War. Like many people in South Africa, the Indians began to make money, they began to buy homes and businesses in the European areas."

"The Europeans didn't like that," his senior interjected dryly.

"No," he said, with a worried little smile, "for in 1943 property was pegged. In other words, any transfer from a European to an Indian required an official permit—"

"Practically never granted," his senior said in the same dry tone.

"Yes, that is correct, practically never granted. Then in 1946 the Government issued a schedule of areas that would be transferred to Europeans and areas that would be Indian—"

"Actually," the old man interrupted again, "there has been a constant and steady erosion of our rights, our political rights, educational rights, property rights. The Group Areas Act has been used to strengthen and secure the property rights of Europeans. Many areas that we had built up with our own toil have now gone to Europeans. A board passes on it, but it always judges on the basis of European interests. Europeans need not appear before the board at all, but the Indians always have to go in person. We have spent thousands and thousands of pounds, but nothing helps. This area right here on Grey Street—our people have sunk probably ten million pounds into developing it, and though it is still a controlled area for Indians, there are indications the Government is going to transform it into a European area and we must move out."

"But, Mr. Drury," his junior said hastily, the worried little smile coming and going, an earnest frown on his face, "you must not think that the picture is all black. No, with all respects, it is not all black. The amazing thing is that our people are still interested in building, we are still interested in investing in South Africa. We have an implicit faith in the country—after all, it is *our* country, we have been here for a hundred years, we know nothing of India or other places. South Africa is *our* country; the Indian makes money and he puts it back into South Africa. Within the confines of separate development one must admit, yes, one must admit, Mr. Drury, that the Government has done a great deal for the Indians. Through the Indian Development Corporation we have been encouraged to go into big industry, some of our people have built textile mills, rice mills and so on, and we will build more. Then there are new Indian housing developments, such as Chatsworth—"

"Do you gentlemen live there?"

"No," the older said with a gentle irony. "We have managed to get the area where we live declared Indian. We are of an economic status that perhaps permits a more direct discussion with the Government than those who are being moved out to Chatsworth."

"Oh, but you must not downgrade Chatsworth," his junior said with an almost desperate insistence. "They are planning a whole city parallel in many ways to Durban, with its own local council, the equivalent of a mayor, town clerk, town treasurer. It will set its own rates. The Government is sincerely trying to upgrade Indian education, for instance. Oh, yes, the Government is doing a great deal. . . . Except for denying us the vote and uprooting thousands of our people," he said earnestly, "the Government is doing very well for the Indian."

"That strikes me as quite an exception," I remarked. He shot me a wan smile and his elder shook his classical white head impatiently.

"They want the Indians to have nothing to do with the Europeans," he said, "yet they want to draw on Indian labor wherever they need it. They are building freeways, now, so that the Indians won't even be permitted to cross European areas when they go to and from work. They are restricting us here on the beaches of Durban, so that areas we once enjoyed freely with the Europeans are now for Europeans only, and we are being pushed off to small and less desirable areas. The European attitude seems to be that the Indian is inferior, he is all right to do the work, but he is not acceptable socially. We believe the educated Indian has a right to be judged on his own merits. The attitude of color is very childish in the twentieth century, when we accept the idea of man as man, not on the basis of his skin color. World events are moving too fast for this sort of thing. South Africa might have to change her pattern."

"We moderates," the younger said, and something in his elder's remarks had apparently finally released him, too—to some extent, "believe that the best policy is to accept whatever benefits we can get from the Government, though of course we cannot agree with many things. Now, I am a graduate of the University of Natal, but no longer is it possible for an Indian to go there, no, no longer possible. They are forcing us to use the Indian University. But, Mr. Drury, a university is a place to exchange ideas, not to separate people. We feel this is wrong, but they have determined to do it. They are spending ten million rand to establish our university and we feel it would be pointless to boycott it. We are gaining all the time, and our children would only suffer. We are very determined that the standards of education not be lowered, and they have given us assurances that they will have exactly the same standards as the European universities. Actually, there is already a change for the better since they took over Indian education from the provinces. They are centralizing all education, as you know, in the Government, and for the Indians it will mean an improvement. They will give us more money for education—of 288 Indian schools in Natal now, 258 were built with Indian money matched rand-for-rand by the Government—and there will be many more."

"There is of course," his senior said gently, "the wage differential."

"Oh, yes, yes," he agreed, "and there is no denying it. We have some four thousand Indian teachers: their salary is only 65 per cent of the European scale. Our doctors and dentists get only 65 per cent of the European scale, our clerks and waiters and professional help also get sometimes as little as 45 or 50 per cent of the European scale. But we are working to get it up to 80 or 90 per cent, we are working all the time, you must not think we are standing still in the Indian community."

"Then in general you go along with Government policies."

"Our attitude toward our friends in the United Party," he said with some asperity, "is that they want to kill us, but we feel the Government wants to help us. We will go along until such time as we find they are not honest about it. After all, Mr. Drury, Indians are no longer a general target of attack, as was the case originally. We are a decent and thriving and law-abiding community, Mr. Drury. We realize Indians must be law-abiding, and we are. We treasure what was said at the recent Republic Day Festival, we treasure it when one of the principal speakers said, referring to the Indians, 'We are proud of our fellow South Africans, who have done so well,' meaning the Indians. We can fill the gap in skilled labor that they want us to fill. They want us to help them, in the process we are being helped."

"We as a group," his elder said with a certain irony, "are possibly more conscious of the need to preserve civilization than perhaps even the Europeans—we have been civilized much longer than the Europeans and the Bantu have."

"And you are making no attempts at all to better your condition through political channels."

"There was a period," the younger said, rather nervously, "when we tried that. Some Indian leaders joined with the African National Congress for a time, but that is all over now. The A.N.C. is banned, and our group was banned, and it is all over now. We as a community are no longer concerned politically, Mr. Drury, we have given that all up."

"The minute you stand up against the Government now, you are banned," his elder said dryly. "So we have given it up."

"We are going to concentrate now on bettering ourselves," the younger said earnestly, "making a model community of ourselves, rearing our children to be decent and productive and law-abiding South Africans. We are making progress. Five years ago Indians were admitted to the Durban Chamber of Commerce, we have a couple of Indian directors. We are making real progress—"

"Tell what happened when Harold MacMillan came here," his elder suggested gently. The younger hesitated, then gave his nervous little smile.

"You must understand," he said, "that this was the English who were involved this time, not the Afrikaners. They gave Prime Minister MacMillan a big bash at the Durban Country Club—"

"And they needed a proper limousine," his elder prompted, "and none of the members had one sufficiently grand, and so—"

"So I lent them mine."

"But you couldn't enter the Durban Country Club to participate in the festivities unless you went dressed as a waiter and waited on table, is it not so?" his elder inquired.

"Yes," he said, "yes, that is so. And I did it, for it was an historic occasion and I did not wish to miss it. But, Mr. Drury, you must not

think that we are not making progress. This is our country, and we
are satisfied that if there is no interference from outside with South
African policies, and if separate development is allowed time, South
Africa will work out all its problems."

"Certainly we would fight beside the European if any attempt were
made to interfere from outside," his elder remarked, for a moment no
longer ironic but quietly serious. "We would help to defend South Africa, the world need make no mistake of that."

"Right now," the younger said earnestly, "the Indian is regarded,
you might say, as the little brother of the European. Big Brother is
driving the car, we can't get in right now, but someday we think, if we
are decent and productive and law-abiding, Big Brother will say,
'Little Brother, you can ride in back.' Maybe someday he will even
say—'You can drive a little.' "

Again he gave his quick, worried smile.

"So we are going along, and we are happy, Mr. Drury. We are
happy with our Government!"

SECURITY POLICE ARREST BOY, 16 (Star, *Johannesburg, English*)
*. . . Security Police paid a pre-dawn visit to the home of a prominent
Indian businessman in the Asiatic bazaar today and took the man's 16-
year-old son away for questioning.*

*The youth, whose name is believed to be Sooboo, is the sixth to be
detained by the Security Police in connection with incidents at the Indian
High School during the Republic Festival celebrations, when sweets were
thrown away by scholars and many children refused to sing the National
Anthem.*

LACK OF AMENITIES FOR INDIANS (Editorial, The Leader, *Durban, Indian*) *. . . The Durban City Council is notorious for its neglect
of Indian areas. In many parts of Durban, where Indians own property
and reside, there are no proper roads or footpaths. The road verges are
overgrown with weed and bush and cleared about once a year.*

*There is inadequate lighting in the streets. There are no playing fields
for the children, let alone the grown-ups. Parks and gardens are a luxury
unheard of. Only now, there is some talk in municipal circles of a few
swimming baths being built in the future in some Indian areas of Durban.*

*There is but one reason for this neglect on the part of the City
Fathers. The Indian areas are populated by the City's stepchildren, the
Indians.*

It is of no consequence that Indians, too, contribute handsomely in rates to the City Council. And there is no one in the City Council to speak up for the voiceless citizens of Durban. . . .

Down a small side street half a block long, standing where it has stood for a hundred years and more, as full of history, tradition and tacky old furniture as any of its similars along Pall Mall, is the Durban Club, than which, in Durban, there is no whicher.

Like the house on the hill, this too is England. Portraits of the city's bearded founders and important men since the early days cover the dark-stained walls; ancient wicker chairs on the veranda overlooking the Indian Ocean carry the sagging imprints of many prominent bottoms; faintly on the soft wind from the water seem to come the strains of "Pomp and Circumstance" and "God Save the Queen"— and the Queen is not Elizabeth. From this club Durban has been ruled for a century, and to a great extent still is, though even in Durban the financial and political power is beginning to shift toward the Afrikaners, and the world of the English-speakers is not quite as inevitable as it used to be.

At the bar the faces were round, red, rich and self-satisfied; around the luncheon table the bellies were as vast, overwhelming and almost as full of personality as their owners. They jiggled and bounced and quivered and got fuller and fuller of good food and good wine as the talk raged back and forth on one of the most absolutely agonizing issues in the Republic—the Durban July.

The shooting of the favorite, the conviction of the bookmaker who had been taken in on the charge, the pros and cons of bookmaking itself, the stories of great races of the past, the predictions of great champions to come, the muted but fiercely competitive boasting of how much money had been bet, how much won—these were subjects so hotly argued and vehemently discussed that it was almost possible to believe, for a little while, that there were no other problems in all of South Africa.

Certainly it was almost impossible to believe that a few minutes before I had been talking to two unhappy Indians, or that shortly I would be talking to one of the most famous unhappy Bantu; or that just down the street fantastic poverty and squalor, desperation and the frantic scrambling for the bare bones of living existed virtually side by side with all this opulence; or that the complete denial of all those human dignities that make life halfway endurable was at this very instant torturing hundreds of thousands of the city's dark-skinned children.

Nor was it easy to believe that all these fine, courtly, distinguished and decent gentlemen could actually endorse, support and be ready to defend with their lives the preservation of all these things. Yet it was the fact, of course, and it lent to the luncheon and to the club itself that air of unreality that touches so many facets of life in South Africa. It is sometimes almost as though it were a charade, a shadow-game, so many fantastic things existing side by side, so many conflicting elements living one with the other, so vast a gap between what decent men know to be right and what they feel the necessities of their own survival must compel them to do to the necessities of others.

So the talk went on, and only once, and that was privately, did it leave the Durban July. This occurred when a fellow-guest, an Afrikaner from the Cape whose embonpoint bumped the table every bit as nobly as those of his English-speaking hosts, made some loud, emphatic pronouncement and capped it with the triumphant observation, "They aren't so dumb anymore, these chappies from the platteland, you know! They're getting smart, these Afrikaner chappies!"

"Fifteen years ago he wouldn't have been allowed in here," an English voice murmured quietly in my ear.

FOR WHITES ONLY? (Editorial, The Leader, *Durban, Indian)* . . . *The Minister of Community Development, Mr. W. A. Maree, has rejected an application by the Coloured members of the Union Whaling Social Club for permission to hold a dance in the Durban City Hall.*

The City Hall belongs to the City and should be open to all the citizens irrespective of colour.

We may point out that it has proved a popular venue for many a non-white function over the years and no one has had any cause for complaint—yes, even when multi-racial functions were held.

We must assume, then, that the sole reason for the refusal is the skin colour of the citizens, in this case the Coloureds.

It is a bad sign for the Indian community, too, which, although it is now endowed with some splendid school halls for such functions as weddings and receptions, still chooses the City Hall for important occasions.

The writing is on the wall for us too, and we do not like the look of it.

"I've just come back from America for home leave," the charming blonde English girl said, "and I find one has to adjust all over again to certain things. My home is in Zululand and my parents have a maid who cleans the bedrooms in the morning. My things were lying about and having been in your country where one is used to doing for oneself, I said without thinking, 'Don't bother, Letta, I'll do that.' She looked quite stricken and said, 'Don't you consider me worthy to clean your room?' I had to apologize quite profusely to make her realize that I was not insulting her. I think she still isn't sure."

Two friends from the Fourth of July reception had volunteered to take me to the man I wanted to interview (the Government having been polite but firmly uncooperative), and presently we came, through endless acres of sugarcane that marched the rolling hills, to the appointed place.

For a few minutes we stood in the sunshine talking to the people who lived there, casually but nonetheless frequently scanning the several roads we could see from our vantage point. An occasional passenger car went by, now and again a cane truck or a farmer's pickup. Nothing official appeared to be in the vicinity, although, as my hosts remarked, the Security Police were clever enough to use camouflage too.

But gradually we relaxed and began to think that perhaps we had not been followed and were not being observed. (There was never any indication later that we had been—literally half an hour after I got back to the hotel one of those lilting little female Afrikaner voices had phoned and said, "Mr. Drrroooorree: Preetooreeah is verree sorree, but it will be eempossible for you to see Mr.——. We are verree sorree, Mr. Drrroooorree." As far as I ever knew, the interview passed unnoticed, though such is the psychological image the police have created that one can never be sure.)

Presently a battered Chevrolet came chugging into sight over a nearby hill and someone said, "There he is." The car drew up, a dignified, white-haired old Bantu in faded but clean khaki pants and a worn brown coat got out. We shook hands and went inside. He sat down in a rocking chair, we grouped ourselves around him, committing the second illegality under the banning order—illegal for him to leave his home, illegal for him to see more than one person at a time. (Illegal to write about it, too, or to publish what he said, if one expects to have one's book allowed into the Republic. But no picture of

South Africa is complete without him, though he is no longer a force but a symbol—and to many of his own people, thanks to the Government's diligence, already a fading one.)

What was the situation among the Bantu now? Was there any real resistance to the Government? Was there any hope of bringing about a change in Government policies?

He looked quizzical for a moment, then smiled.

"There is a lion over there. It is roaring loudly and threatening to kill us if we do not behave. Our voices are not strong enough to drown out the lion, and the lion is standing on our spears so that we are helpless to kill the lion. . . . No, I don't see much hope of a change right now, or perhaps for a long time—a long time. There was resistance to the Government, but you know, the Government stamped it out. Now there may be a scattering here and there—I am rather out of touch, now, they tell me a few things but it is difficult for them to communicate with me, and many now are afraid to do so. Yes, I have the impression there are a few things going on, but fragmented, you know. Not unified."

Was that one of the Bantus' problems, that there is very little unity? Again he smiled, a quick, shrewd glance.

"We are many peoples. Some exist amicably together, many do not. Historically, you know, we have warred much upon one another, my own tribe perhaps more than any other. No one need exclaim"—an ironic expression—"if many of the others regard us still with suspicion. But of course it applies to all. There are many differences, many jealousies, hatreds, ambitions, desires. It is only human. So it will be for my lifetime, and for yours and possibly far beyond."

What did he think of the Bantustan policy? Again the shrewd, ironic look, the slow smile.

"I think the Government does not know what to do with it now that it has been formulated. I think they would be happy to forget about it if they could, but the Bantu will not let them. Nor will the world let them. It is what they have to show the world when the world demands proof of good intentions."

"You think the intentions are good, then?"

He shrugged.

"Who can say? With some yes, with others no. I think probably— yes. I think they would like to find a solution that would be fair to all."

"Is this it?"

He shrugged.

"If Bantustans are to succeed, the land must be good. It is not good in many areas they say they wish to give the Bantu."

"Not in the Transkei?"

"Some parts of the Transkei, yes. More than other places in South Africa."

"Do you think the Transkei experiment will succeed?"

"Time knows that, not you or I or the Government."

"Will there be a change in South Africa without some form of outside pressure?"

"Who will apply it? I do not know. In time, possibly . . . in time."

"What do you think—" But the question died unfinished, we all stood up suddenly: there was the sound of an engine, we could see through the window along the dusty road a car with two white men in it approaching the house. The old man moved swiftly down the hall, stepped into a closet, closed the door. We sat down again, poured ourselves more of the tea we had been drinking, chatted brightly and perhaps a little too loudly about the beauties of Natal.

"What would happen if it turns out to be the police and we get caught?" I murmured.

"He'd probably be jailed for violating his ban, and you and we"—a cheerful grin—"would be thrown out of the country."

But nothing so dramatic occurred. There was a murmur of voices in another room, the sound of laughter; after a few moments, waving cordially, the white men drove off. We never did know who they were, but in that sudden flurry of trepidation the Government was with us.

In a minute or two, smiling broadly, the old man returned. We poured him some more tea, asked a final question or two on a personal level: how did they treat him, was he comfortable, what did he need?

"Comfortable, yes, reasonably so—reasonably so. Of course they restrict those I can see and talk to. Some come officially, some"—he chuckled—"come unofficially, and then we have excitement sometimes. I have enough, I live comfortably, but I need books. Send me books."

"Will the Government allow them to reach you?"

"Most things, if they are not unsuitable to the Government. If they are, our friends here will know how to get them to me. I do need books, I am quite out of touch."

Outside in the sunlight we shook hands once more. He stood there smiling and waving to us as we drove off, his handsome head erect and commanding.

He was a lion once, too, but the lion over there has silenced him.

GO WITH AIDA PARKER: IT'S SLAVERY, I SAY (Sunday Tribune, *Durban, English*) . . . *With joy and wonderment I see that the gentlemen are at it again.*

202 JOURNEY'S COURSE

*A Cape magistrate has gone on public record as saying: " . . . the
suggestion that a young woman could not look after four children in a
three-bedroomed house without the aid of a servant fills me with horror.
I wonder how many women look after more children in much larger
houses without any help at all?"*

This sort of talk really makes me wild, wild, wild.

*I wonder if any man has ever had the privilege of spending a day in a
house with four small children? I wonder if he has any conception of
what it is like, cooking and washing and ironing and scrubbing and beating the carpets and cleaning windows and running after four small
squalling kids?*

*To suggest that a woman, in these circumstances, does not need hu-
man help, if her husband can afford it, is so much eyewash.*

*This, my dear friends, although men may not understand it, represents
real work. Work, did I say? Slavery, more like it. . . .*

FOR LUNCH WE drove out a little way from the center of town, into an
Indian area: dry, dusty, treeless, a straight, flat neighborhood with
straight, flat streets and straight, flat houses—solidly middle class,
with eyes on something better.

Our host was small, dark, stocky, intense. His favorite expression,
spoken very rapidly, was, "Let-us-be-honest-about-it." He too had his
eyes on something better. He is one Indian the Government does not
need to worry about.

Not so, three fellow-guests, the saturnine Brothers D. D/1 was fat-
saturnine, D/2 and D/3 were skinny-saturnine. They upset our host
dreadfully, because after he had burbled along for half an hour
through the elaborate meal describing the marvelous progress the Indians were making, D/1 fixed him with an implacable gaze and said,
"Hell."

"What?" said our host rapidly. "What, what, D.? Surely, D., let-us-
be-honest-about-it, let-us-be-honest-about-it, the Indians today are better
off than we have ever been before—"

"Better off how?" D/1 demanded bluntly. "I can't vote, I can't go
into certain places and certain clubs, I can't meet White business people
on an equal basis, I can't take my kid to the most convenient beach
nearest my home, I have to take him to some other God-damned place
—how the hell are we better off?"

"Well, now, D.," our host said, "now, D., let-us-be-honest-about-it,
under the Government's policies—"

"Who decides the Government's policies?" asked D/2 sharply.

"Do we have anything to say about it?" demanded D/3.

"We do," our host began, but all three D's stared at him ironically. "Let-us-be-honest-about-it," he said, looking flustered, "the Government is consulting us through the Indian Council—"

"Damned stooges," said D/1, obviously enjoying himself. Our host positively quivered.

"Now, D.," he said, "you must remember that I—"

"You're not on it yet," D/1 interrupted. "We know you'd like to be."

"I do not know whether I will be or not," our host said with dignity, "but in any event, let-us-be-honest-about-it, the Council is going to make great strides forward, it will give us a voice the Government will listen to—" His voice became a little uncertain as D/1's expression said, "———." D/1 didn't actually say "———," but he didn't have to. "A voice the Government will listen to, and then we will be able to—to—"

"To what?" inquired D/3. "Wait on table? Sweep the streets? Dust off the front steps of the Durban Club? What is it the Indians will be able to do then? What does your Government tell you we will be able to do then?"

"It isn't my Government!" our host said vehemently. "Or, rather, it is, D., now let-us-be-honest-about-it, it is the only government we have, and we have to work with it. What could we do if we refused to cooperate with the Government? Nothing, I tell you, why, nothing, D., let-us-be-honest-about-it, absolutely nothing!"

"I don't like to be just a lackey," D/1 said dourly. "Some people may like to wait for crumbs from the Government's table, but not I. I prefer to be treated like a human being."

"Well, be that as it may, D., let-us-be-honest-about-it, the Indians are not in any position to demand things, D., they are not and you know it. Let-us-be-honest-about-it. The only way, the *only way,* is through cooperation with the Government. No, we all know that. Nothing else would produce any results at all. Anything else would be self-defeating. It is only by cooperating with the white man—"

"I wouldn't give one rand for any white man in this country," D/1 said flatly. Our host gasped and glanced nervously at his two white guests. But we were enjoying D/1's performance as much as he was.

"No," D/1 repeated. "Not one rand. Not one *cent.*"

"But, now, D., let-us-be-honest-about-it," our host said nervously, "without the white man, where would we be? Why, the Bantu—"

"Or for them, either," D/1 said with relish.

"What would They do to us if the white man were not here, let-us-be-honest-about-it. We couldn't survive without the white man, D., you know it. All this talk is so much nonsense, let-us-be-honest-about-it. Now, we are steadily improving our position—"

"I repeat, in what way?" D/2 interrupted.

"Very well," our host said quickly. "Very well, then, D., in what way, in what way! You have built a big plant nearby, we all know that, D., and you built it with funds from the Indian Investment Corporation, now, we all know that. Where would your plant be without the Government, D., answer me that and let-us-be-honest-about-it."

"We may have received some Government money," D/1 said, "but it took our brains and our ability to work with other Indians to get it built. It's taking our brains and ability to keep it running. The Government doesn't know how to work with Indians, let us be honest about it yourself, and that's why we get assistance from the Government. It isn't any kind, charitable impulse from Pretoria, don't kid anybody about that. Why, hell! If they didn't want something out of us, if they didn't feel they were threatened by the outside world, they wouldn't lift one finger for the Indians, not one. Let us be honest about that, too!"

"Nonetheless, D.," our host said doggedly, "nonetheless, it is the fact, let-us-be-honest-about-it, the Indians are steadily improving their position and will continue to do so—"

"I went to the University of Natal," D/3 said dryly. "I have three sons. Are they going to go to the University of Natal? No, they are not going to go to the University of Natal."

"All right!" our host said excitedly. "All right, then! I went to the University of Natal, too, and I have sons, too, but do you hear me crying because now it is no longer possible for an Indian to go to the University of Natal? No, you do not hear me crying. I am going to send my sons to the Indian University, to the Indian University, I shall be proud to have them educated as Indians by Indians. Let-us-be-honest-about-it, I shall be proud that we are Indian!"

"I'm proud to be Indian, too," said D/1 with a grim humor, "but I'm not going to pretend it makes me Maharajah of Durban. More like Street-Sweeper of Durban. God damn it," he said with a sudden explosive fury, "I can't associate socially with Whites in Durban that I do business with, I can't vote for my Government, I can't do anything that an ordinary, normal, decent human being ought to be able to do. Because I'm an Indian! Why, ——" And again he almost said it, but didn't.

"Just one question, if I may. Do you really think the average Indian is as concerned as you are about going to a convenient beach or being able to join the Durban Club? Do you really think he's even concerned about the vote? Does it really mean that much to the crowds on Grey Street?"

"Well," D/1 said more calmly, with a rueful smile, "there, of course, you have me. I must confess that this is probably true. I imagine that of all our half-million, maybe not more than a handful are really concerned about the vote, really concerned about the universities, really concerned about being accepted as equals. After all, we have to admit the economy is booming, and we have to admit that the Indian share of it, small though it is, is steadily becoming larger. The average Indian is making more than he ever did, he has a roof over his head and more food than he ever had, he is infinitely better off than the Indians in India . . ."

His expression became ironic.

"Economics is the answer for all South African protests, you will find. Indian, White, Coloured, Bantu, everybody is doing better. When you are doing better, you don't go into the streets. You enjoy it, you work, and you hope to do better still. That is the story of South Africa today. We will all go along as long as the economy is booming. Let it collapse" —his eyes widened thoughtfully—"other things might happen. But not now. My brothers and I are rather unusual, I expect. It is our friend here who is the perfect Indian of today. He is not only satisfied, he is *actively* satisfied." He gave our host a friendly clap on the shoulder as we pushed back our chairs. "You will be on the Council yet, my friend. I shall recommend you to the Prime Minister."

"Let-us-be-honest-about-it," our host said as we stood on his doorstep and watched the Brothers D. roar away, D/1 in a Lincoln Continental, D/2 in a Buick and D/3 in a Cadillac. "Under our laws, an automobile must have at least 40 per cent South African-manufactured parts if one is to purchase it at stated price. If you buy a foreign car like those you must pay 100 per cent duty, *100 per cent duty*. Now, where would they be without the Government, those three? I ask you now, let-us-be-honest-about-it, where would they be?"

INDIANS LOSE OUT AT CATO MANOR (Natal Mercury, *Durban, English*) . . . *Hundreds of anxious Indian property owners in the controversial Cato Manor area are fighting a losing battle in their bid to save their homes from being expropriated under the Group Areas Act for future occupation by Whites.*

This was indicated by Mr. P. Seebran, the chairman of the Cato Manor Indian Ratepayers' Co-Ordinating Council, at its meeting recently when he urged the council to drop the appeal to the Supreme Court that it planned for last-minute protection.

He said that the Co-Ordinating Council's lawyers were unable to give assurances that the Court would upset a Group Areas proclamation setting aside Cato Manor for Europeans, or interfere with expropriation notices being served on the property owners by the Department of Community Development.

The position of the property owners was becoming desperate, as the department was not only expropriating properties but also demanding the payment of high rent in some cases where the owners were still occupying the properties.

No useful purpose would be served by instituting a Court action, as the Government was certain to amend the Group Areas legislation to achieve the purpose for which the Group Areas Act was passed, even if by some chance the Court should decide in favour of the Indians affected.

Mr. Sooboo Rajah, the Co-Ordinating Council's general secretary, pressed the council to go ahead, however, with its plans to appeal to the Court as a last resort. His move was defeated.

The council will hold a mass gathering on Sunday, July 31, to inform the property owners and residents of Cato Manor of the latest development and to seek a fresh mandate.

INDIANS DRIVEN FROM CITY! (Editorial, The Leader, *Durban, Indian*) . . . *The Durban City Council, in collaboration with the State Department of Housing, is planning another housing scheme for Indians in the Phoenix, Mount Edgecombe, Newlands area.*

It is all there on paper just now, and may take a decade before it comes to fruition with a population of some 250,000 Indians. It is said that Chatsworth, when complete, will house 150,000 Indians.

The net result, as we see it, is that all Indians will be driven out of Durban proper. They will be some ten and more miles from the City, in their own locations running their own so-called local authorities or advisory boards.

This is the Group Areas master plan which we regard as a monstrous plan. . . .

In all this, of course, no one has thought fit to consult the Indian people or take Indian opinion. This we regard as one of the worst aspects of official planning.

If Indians are going to be thrown out eventually, let them not be thrown out willy-nilly. Let there be some method in the madness which is termed planning.

Or are Indians so much goat or sheep or cattle who may be moved about at the whim of authority?

OBJECTION TO INDIAN BUSES REJECTED (Natal Mercury, *Durban, English*) . . . *Sixty-nine angry ratepayers have urged Durban City Council to stop running Indian buses through Hillary, but their petition was rejected by the Council's Works Committee yesterday.*

The residents said that when they bought their homes 17 years ago "in this quiet residential area" there was not a single bus to disturb them.

After the meeting the chairman, Councillor Dave Panovka, said that the committee would press on with its policy of improving Freemantle and Chatsworth Roads for the use of Indian buses carrying Indians to the huge Chatsworth township. . . .

"It is essential that we go ahead with it; it has been on the cards for many years." The alternative of overloading the South Coast Road was not acceptable.

The ratepayers' petition was enclosed with a letter signed by Mr. G. G. Kemp, who said that residents were worried about the number of buses running along Stella, Freemantle and Chatsworth Roads on the way to Chatsworth.

Residents intended to submit the petition "to all authorities and representatives of the citizens," he added.

The petition makes it clear that residents will urge the State Community Development Department to order the Council not to construct access roads to non-White townships through White areas. . . .

BAD PLANNING OR BAD POLICY? (Editorial, The Leader, *Durban, Indian*) *. . . We have always believed that the main purpose of the Group Areas Act is to ruin the Indian economically. We must admit that this was no original thought on our part. Indeed, the advocates of group areas have on more than one occasion stated this to be the prime motivating factor behind the plans of the authorities.*

Now comes news that the Community Development Board (formerly known as the Group Areas Board) has flatly turned down a request by the Port Shepstone Town Council that Indian traders be allowed to stay on in a so-called open trade area in the town.

The whole of Port Shepstone has been declared a White group area and long-established Indian traders will be uprooted. . . .

What is most disturbing is the fact that the Government planners are quite unmoved by the views of the local people, those who are directly concerned.

It seems to us that anything that is contrary to Government policy is bad planning. Government policy demands Indians must go to their own group areas and live and die there. There is, therefore, no room for so-called open trade areas.

"OUR SUGARCANE INDUSTRY," my guide said when he drove me through the rustling green fields toward Tongaat on the Natal North Coast, "began in the 1860's, when the first Indians were brought into South Africa as indentured laborers. Most of the industry is right here in Natal and Zululand, extending about 160 miles north and ninety miles south of Durban, with an average width of about ten to fifteen miles. There is one other small area in the Eastern Transvaal. There are about 900,000 acres under cane, about half of which is reaped annually for a production which is getting close to 20,000,000 tons.

"We have more than 2,000 European farmers and some twenty-two large European estates. There are more than 3,500 African farmers and more than 1,800 Indian farmers. There are twenty-one sugar mills, of which the largest is owned by the Tongaat Sugar Company, where we're going now. Our people are very conscious of what your growers are doing in Hawaii, and they're always going over there to study your methods.

"Our industry is the seventh largest out of fifty-seven countries producing sugar. We are the thirteenth largest of ninety-seven countries having both cane and beet-sugar production. In the next ten years we expect South Africa to join the world's top five in cane production. . . .

"The Tongaat Company," he said, as we drove through the pleasant little company town with its neat, attractive brick houses and its open play and park areas, "has tried to make this a model community. The races live in separate housing, but there's never been any friction, everyone gets along well together. We have a municipal council on which the Indians, the Bantu, the Coloureds and the Whites sit down together and transact the community business, and it's worked beautifully.

"But," he said, and his tone became thoughtful and depressed, "the Government is moving in. They've notified the company that the council must be disbanded, and so I suppose before long our model experiment won't be working anymore. . . ."

PORTS AND HARBOURS

The ports of the Republic of South Africa and South-West Africa are owned by the Government and administered by the South African Railways—an arrangement which facilitates the correlation of rail traffic from and to the ports with the loading and discharge of ships.

The principal harbours are Durban, Table Bay (Cape Town), Algoa Bay (Port Elizabeth), Buffalo Harbour (East London) in the Republic, and Walvis Bay in South-West Africa.

Small harbours suitable for coastal shipping only, are Mossel Bay, Simonstown and Port Nolloth in the Republic and Lüderitz in South-West Africa. The harbour facilities at Port Nolloth are owned by the O'okiep Copper Company.

Although the Republic has five modern and well-equipped harbours, it has no natural harbours. The only river port is at Buffalo Harbour, the development of which required extensive dredging and the building of a turning-basin.

Volume of overseas cargo handled in calendar years (1,000 tons):

All ports, including South-West Africa, total cargo handled: 1960—18,586; 1961—19,489; 1962—20,046; 1963—21,707; 1964—30,117.

The following number of vessels, with their gross tonnage (tons million) in brackets, called at South and South-West African ports (year ended March 31):

1960—13,712 [58.1]; 1961—14,005 [59.6]; 1962—14,289 [61.7]; 1963—14,617 [64.6]; 1964—15,242 [72.3].

The Government is to spend R57 million, most of it in the next 10 years, on a big harbour expansion and development plan. The need for more dock space has become urgent because of South Africa's rapidly expanding economy. About R29 million is to be spent to provide 22 additional berths in Cape Town. Seven new berths and four cargo sheds are to be built in Durban at a cost of R10 million.

A new harbour for Table Bay's 300 fishing boats and deep-sea trawlers is to be built at Rietviel, near Cape Town, at a cost of R9 million. It will eventually also be used for shipbuilding. Another R9 million is being spent on Cape Town's new tanker basin.

The Minister of Transport, Mr. B. J. Schoeman, has stated that the Cape Town scheme would eventually increase the port's handling capacity by 75 per cent. The quay space would be increased from 18,500 ft. to 32,500 ft. A substantial amount of the work is expected to be completed by 1970.

—Official Sources

W E WERE SITTING in one of the official boxes at the Durban Turf Club—"the Durban Club outdoors," as a fellow-American remarked. Beyond the race track, on the edge of the sea, the city sparkled brightly in the sun. "They're off!" the announcer cried, and out of the stands there came the familiar surging roar. Persistently over it, as it mounted in volume and excitement, there came from in back of us the thoughtful ruminations of two heavy, well-fed English voices.

"Thought that was a marvelous speech you made," said the first, "by God, I did! Quite right, what you said about equal opportunity."

"Thank you," said the second modestly.

"Quite right. Everybody stand on his own two feet, everybody get ahead on his own merits, everybody on the same footing, equal chance, equal everything—by God, I thought that was great!"

"I thought it needed to be said," the second remarked quietly.

"It did," said the first, "it did! Equal opportunity for all, that's the only way we can possibly survive. Bring each of these bookmakers in here and let him make out the best case he can for being allowed to continue operations. Equal shake for all, what I say! I couldn't agree with you more."

GOVERNMENT PRESSES ON WITH PLANS FOR NEW TOWN-SHIP (Natal Mercury, *Durban, English*) . . . *The Government has started a tremendous drive to set in motion the giant scheme to build an African township of 60,000 units in the Ladysmith area.*

Government planners have already started on the land which, in addition to the Msgina Reserve, will create probably the biggest Bantu homeland in Natal, stretching to Mandini on the north coast.

It will bring the homeland within eight miles of the borders of Ladysmith.

Announcing this yesterday, Mr. D. J. Coughlan, Deputy Mayor of Ladysmith, said that already half the owners of the 30,000 acres of land required for the township had been paid out by the Government. The rest would go by the end of September.

Title deeds for the various farms had gone through to be finalised and prices which were being paid had satisfied the farmers.

"Most of them are happy to go. This is the impression I have got," said Mr. Coughlan.

He also announced that there would definitely be a buffer strip between the Bantu homeland and farms on its borders. "How wide that will be has not yet been disclosed."

Mr. Coughlan said that the present township in Ladysmith was absolutely full, with accommodation at a premium because building had been frozen in preparation for the new township in the Peter's Station area.

"It has created accommodation problems, but we are building temporary accommodations for our labour."

The township will be the main source of labour for the growing industrial complexes of Ladysmith and Colenso, and is expected to bring unprecedented economic boosts to both towns.

Mr. L. Stead, a farmer in the area who will soon be leaving his farm for another in Zululand, said yesterday that he was pleased with the Government offer for his property. He refused to disclose the figure.

He said farming in the area was difficult because of lack of water and the high rate of thefts. Many farmers were making very little progress and were actually quite glad to get rid of their farms for good prices.

Any hard feeling which farmers first harboured against the Government had disappeared with the realisation that the Government was paying good prices and was putting a definite policy into operation. . . .

T HE SMALL, round face was puffy, the eyes had a sleepy, half-glazed look, the short, stocky figure moved slowly across the room.

"Come over here by the window away from the telephone," the voice said in a gentle whisper. "The police may have it bugged, for all I know."

"How long have you been banned?"

The dark eyes blinked, the words came slowly.

"Eighteen months—nineteen—almost two years, it seems to me. Yes, two years." An apologetic little smile. "Time goes so quickly—it is hard to remember. One day becomes like another, to some extent . . . to some extent."

"You can still conduct your business?"

"Oh, yes. But they are going to take care of that, too. They are going to pass a bill denying the privilege of the bar to anyone who has been convicted of being a Communist, no matter how much he has paid for it. They are going to deny him a living, too." A wan little expression, ironic and hopeless. "The Government is very thorough. . . ."

There was a knock on the door, another Bantu entered with a glass of whisky, set it on the desk.

"Something to restore your energy," he said, gave him an encouraging smile and went out.

The sleepy eyes blinked again, he went over, picked up the glass, took a swallow, brought it back by the window, sat down.

"It's about the only pleasure I have left," he whispered with a sort of wistful, hopeless humor.

"Can you talk to your staff?"

"Oh, yes, I can talk to them. I can talk to them one at a time. I can't talk to them together. That would be violating the law. But they're not much company." He sighed and looked out into the night at the lighted windows of neighboring office buildings. "I don't have much company anymore, except"—he held the glass to the light and studied it for a moment. "I can't see my friends anymore. My family is not much consolation. My older children have fled the country and won't come back. My wife is terrified all the time. The younger children don't understand." He blinked again, slowly. "I used to finish work, go home and spend a nice evening with my family, see my friends. We'd have dinner, maybe, laugh, talk. I can't do these things anymore."

"Is there much underground activity going on now, do you think?"
His eyes tried to focus for a moment; he shook his head.

"I'm out of touch, I don't know. The Government makes sure the banned ones don't know things. It is my impression—my impression—that there is some. I think there is a little—some. I don't know how much, but I think a little. But how much good can it do, when the Government is on top? I don't know how much good it can do. . . . The bloody fools!" he said with a sudden but gentle, almost disinterested, anger, even then careful not to raise his voice above a whisper. "They actually think they can withstand the whole weight of the races. . . ." The life went out of the anger, the eyes blinked, the hand that held the glass began to tremble. He put the glass down. "Maybe they can," he whispered, "maybe they can. . . . Tell me. Do you think there is any chance I could go to America? I would like to go to America very much. Do you think there is any chance?"

So we talked about that for a bit before I left, trying to create some hope where no hope existed, while the eyes became increasingly difficult to focus and the gentle voice whispered on of a ruined life.

It is true that many of the banned were Communists, it is true that they wanted to destroy the Government, it is true that the Government, like any government, has the right to protect itself. But it is also true that when someone somewhere in Pretoria hit upon the idea of banning he came up with a fiendishly clever torture that is rather notable, even in the annals of civilized man.

34 NAMES ARE ADDED TO BANNING LIST (Cape Argus, English) . . . *Hard on the heels of controversy in Parliament over the explanation given by the Minister of Justice (Mr. Vorster) for the banning of Mr. Ian Robertson, former president of NUSAS, came the publication in Pretoria today of the biggest batch of banning notices ever gazetted in one week.*

Today's batch of 34 names—all of them non-European—brings the total of persons who are prohibited from gathering to 542, and is indicative of a greatly increased tempo in the issue of banning orders.

The new total reflects a considerable increase on the figure of 453 mentioned by the Minister in the Assembly as being subject to restriction as at the beginning of July.

TERMS OF BANNING ORDERS (Star, Johannesburg, English) . . . *Among the terms of the banning orders imposed on a Trafalgar High School teacher and part-time student at the University of Cape Town,*

Mr. F. A. Slingers, is one saying that he may not be connected with any organization which defends or criticizes State policy.

His wife, Mrs. Slingers, said today that the banning orders, signed by the Minister of Justice on May 17, will remain in operation until May 31, 1971.

Mrs. Slingers said one order prohibited her husband from entering any education institution, and from giving instruction to anyone other than his own children.

This order comes into effect on Friday, when the present school term ends.

In terms of another order, Mr. Slingers has to report to the police at Athlone between 7 A.M. and 6 P.M. every Monday.

Mrs. Slingers said they had three children, a girl aged twelve and two boys aged nine and five.

She did not know what work her husband was going to do once he had to give up teaching. He will also have to give up his studies at the University of Cape Town.

"Until he finds something, I will simply have to work a lot harder to support the family," Mrs. Slingers said. She is a nurse.

STATE SILENCE ON 34 S. A. EXILES (Star, Johannesburg, English)
. . . A curtain of silence has dropped over the future of South Africa's "forgotten people"—the 34 men and women banished from their homes under the 1927 Native Administration Act.

An appeal to President Swart to grant an amnesty to those under banishment was sent by the national president of the Black Sash movement, Mrs. Jean Sinclair.

In her letter written shortly before the Republic Festival, Mrs. Sinclair urged that "to celebrate the fifth anniversary of our Republic the 34 people who have been banished far from their homes might be granted an amnesty and sent back to their families, happy in the knowledge that their banishment orders have been removed."

A reply from the President's office noted receipt of Mrs. Sinclair's letter and said her suggestion of an amnesty had been transmitted to Ministers for consideration and disposal. Since then no further news has been received.

Inquiries made during the past three weeks to the Department of Information and the Department of Bantu Administration have proved fruitless.

An Information Department spokesman referred The Star *to the Hansard report of a parliamentary debate in February.*

On examination it was found that while questions were asked by Mrs.

Helen Suzman about banished persons, no replies were given by the Minister. . . .

WHAT A BARGAIN WE ARE! (Sunday Tribune, *Durban, English*)
. . . *"Once you have drunk the waters of South Africa," says the old Zulu proverb, "you will always be thirsty for more," and Elmer's already parched!*

So says the American top super-salesman Elmer Wheeler, who visited South Africa in May this year, in an article to his home-town newspaper, the Dallas Morning News.

In outlining South Africa's "assets," Elmer Wheeler wrote:

Trains: Their famous Blue Train. All service, tablecloths, bedsheets are delightful blues.

Planes: Jets galore.

Swimming pools: I saw more in Johannesburg than in Dallas.

Hotels: More modern than in Florida. Seems as if Durban has twice as many as Miami Beach—three times cheaper, with meals.

Beaches: More on the Garden Route between gay Cape Town and East London than in all of California.

"The only difference is South Africans eat with their left hand, drive on the left-hand side of the street and have a slight dialect.

"They call street signals robots, swim on Christmas Day, and say 'thank you' to all elevator operators.

"Truly, South Africa is the last of the bargain countries," Mr. Wheeler adds.

THE SQUARE, pleasant face bore the kindly lines of many years of dealing with the young, the gray hair was pushed back by a square, firm hand. The smile was broad and generous, the eyes friendly and keen, as suited one who has fought many long battles for the liberal cause against odds that have become increasingly grim. But the thoughts were moody, and there was not much hope.

"It is not good to talk to me at this particular moment in our country's history," she said. "You find me very depressed, I'm afraid. Very uncertain of what is going to happen, not very hopeful that much good is going to come.

"I suppose this is the result of many things. Ever since the Nats first came to power in 1948, some of us have been working and hoping that we might be able to bring about some softening of policy—some humanization, if you will. I think perhaps that is the most that many of us have hoped to accomplish, since I suppose most of us in our hearts have known that there could really be no ultimate settlement upon the basis of one man, one vote. At least not for many, many years, possibly many generations. The skills and ability simply are not in the Natives. It is not their fault, but we all know it to be the fact."

She paused and her eyes scanned the teeming city spread out below us, sparkling white against the deep blue of the Indian Ocean.

"That is a sophisticated civilization, there. I suppose in the final analysis it is unthinkable, really, to contemplate letting it be destroyed by incompetents, even though they may be sanctified in some minds because their skins are black. It isn't enough. . . .

"Possibly some of us are too impatient, possibly in our way we have been as intolerant as the Government. We criticize border industries, but how long does it take to establish a going industrial complex? And how long has it been, three or four years, since the program was started? We want it done overnight. Perhaps we demand too much, perhaps we are the impractical ones.

"And the constant outcry to raise the Bantu to equality. Equality with whom? With us, whom equality would not really threaten in the area that counts the most to the average man in the street who has a living to make, a family to raise, expenses to meet—the economic area?"

She smiled, a little grimly.

"It is all very well for Harry Oppenheimer to call for equality for the Bantu: no Bantu can possibly threaten Harry's job. But it's different if you're the average middle- or lower-income employee in the Republic. Then you could conceivably be hurt very much, even if your political rights and independence weren't taken from you."

She sighed and shook her head. The smile became kindlier, more self-directed.

"I am sounding almost like the Government, and that is horrible indeed, is it not? But sometimes I think we on the liberal side have been too self-righteous, too demanding, too intolerant. . . . I don't think, actually, that there is much grace in any of us in any party, right now. I think perhaps you are finding us at our unloveliest. We are afraid, you see, afraid of the outside world, afraid of your country, not knowing what the future is going to bring. And while this is increasing our unity as we face the world, it is also, perhaps, making us sharper and more savage in our relations with one another.

"I also wonder"—and again she paused and stared out across the busy, beautiful city—"I wonder sometimes whether the Bantu are capable of carrying the burden some of us say we would like to put upon them. In the ultimate sense in which I was talking a moment ago, I am sure they are not; but even in the shorter term, I wonder. The African National Congress was formed, but the Whites and the Indians had to run it for them. There was no unity, no sense of organization, no sense of joint destiny or communal planning. The idea of choosing a goal and submerging individual differences in order to work toward it is quite foreign to them. They are like children: each wants his own way. They do not want to take direction, and they are not willing to learn. I sometimes wonder what we are dealing with, when we try so hard for these people. Are they capable of anything, if we could get it for them?

"But perhaps—perhaps you find me feeling old, right now, because I have been active for so long in the liberal cause and so little, apparently, has been accomplished. Some of my friends say to me, you know, 'Why don't you leave? You have done your share. Leave, now, forget South Africa and all its problems, enjoy the remaining years.' "

She looked again out over Durban to the sea and a gentleness came into her eyes and her voice.

"But," she said softly, "it is such a lovely country—such a lovely country. It has so much potential, its peoples are so fine, really, there is such great possibility here, if we can only achieve it—and it is my country. I couldn't leave. I want to stay and help South Africa if I can."

HAIRCUTS "STILL TOO CHEAP" IN DURBAN (Natal Mercury, *Durban, English*) . . . *Within a few weeks of the prices of men's haircuts being increased to 50 cents in Durban comes a statement by city hair stylist William Steenman that they are still too cheap.*

"Ordinary haircuts are too cheap here for proper care to be taken over them," he says after a nine-week tour of Europe combing the capital cities for the latest in men's hair-dos.

After spending two weeks in Paris at a post-graduate college for 1,000 hairdressers from all over the world and having plenty of time to swop news on prices, he says: "Our haircuts must be the cheapest in the world. . . ."

There were too few places in South Africa where men could get the proper attention in the "chair," said Mr. Steenman, who runs a men's exclusive hairdressing salon. . . .

South African men looked all right on their own but were "scruffy" compared with the men-about-town in Germany or France, he said.

"Our men are as style-conscious as their European counterparts—they just don't get the proper treatment."

FORESTRY

Owing to adverse climatic conditions, South Africa, rich as it is in other resources, is poorly endowed with indigenous forest growth. It has been said of South Africa, and justifiably so, that it is "scarcely more clothed than the natives who first inhabited it."

Only in the humid areas where the rainfall exceeds 30 inches a year does one find indigenous forest. These areas occur along the coastal belt, in the Drakensberg mountains and in the belt from East London northwards. The indigenous forests total some 630,000 acres, most of which is owned by the State.

With the addition of just over 2,400,000 acres of State and private exotic forests, or "plantations" as they are generally called in South Africa, the total area of "forest" in South Africa is thus some 3,000,000 acres or just under 1 per cent of the total land area. In comparison with the United States, where the commercial forest area is 25 per cent of the land area and Canada where it is 27 per cent, the paucity of forest resources in South Africa is brought into striking relief.

Privately owned plantation land holds the main key to South Africa's future timber supplies. Of the country's .79 per cent total land under plantations, .58 per cent represents private ownership, while .21 per cent represents the ownership by the State and the South African Bantu Trust collectively. Of the 2.425 million acres of plantations in the Republic and Swaziland, 1.78 million acres, or 73 per cent of all commercial plantations, are in private holdings. Taking only conifer species into account, 49.7 per cent of the area is privately owned, while 93 per cent of the total area under broad-leaved species is in private hands.

—Official Sources

A CROSS THE BAY from the main part of Durban, where the land curves out around in a great embracing arm, is the fashionable peninsula known as The Bluff.

An interesting situation is developing on The Bluff, because here along one section of it the Government has decreed an Indian area, and a number of obviously wealthy homes are either already built or under construction. But the area the Indians have been given is quite the choicest on The Bluff, high on a hogback with stunning views from almost every site, off over the immensities of the Indian Ocean on the one side, off over Durban Harbor and the green hills of Natal on the other.

How long, one wonders as one rides along listening to the estimates of how much the houses cost ($30,000 there, $50,000 there, $90,000 there

—two of the Brothers D. live up here now), is this delightful area going to remain in the hands of those to whom it has been given? How soon after their fine homes have been completed will it suddenly occur to someone in the Government that this ideal location should really be a White area, after all? And how cheaply, in forced sales, will the choice land and the handsome homes be taken away?

But perhaps it will never happen. It is, however, the sort of thought that comes easily enough in the context of the Group Areas Act and the way in which it has quite often been administered. It is sometimes a little hard for the Government's more idealistic supporters to defend Group Areas, because there have been times when it has not been administered with quite the lack of cupidity they like to imagine. There have been times when hard cash has meant raw injustice.

However, such thoughts were quickly banished when we arrived at our destination, a charming English-speaking home in the White section, because here were Government supporters who admitted no evils, acknowledged no wrongs, were waiting and eager to do battle with someone they were sure, just from his nationality, must be hostile to them.

"How do you like South Africa?" someone asked the moment we had given our requests for cocktails, and something about the tone said: Don't you dare say you don't like it. So what should it be, Answer A, Answer B, Answer C?

"I find it a very fascinating country. Very complex."

"You don't think it's going to be so easy to tell us what to do, then?"

"No"—mildly—"I haven't any intention of telling you what to do."

"Well"—a victorious smile around, as if to say, He's vanquished—"that makes you a very unusual American, I must say! They always know what we should do!"

"As if they don't have enough problems of their own," someone said with a knowing laugh.

"Oh, yes, we have problems of our own, nobody ever said we didn't. But I'm here to find out about your country, not to—"

"How about those riots in Chicago?"

"All right, how about them?"

"Pretty bad, aren't they? Sounds like the whole country's going up in flames—"

"That's your press. Ours does the same thing about you. I dare say we'll both survive."

"*You* may"—grimly—"but I'm not so sure we will"—general nods—"at least as long as America's pounding us all the time."

"Oh, are we? I thought on the whole we'd been pretty reasonable. We believe in certain ways of doing things, just as you do. We're both prisoners of our history. Yours has given you one approach, ours has given us the other. But I don't think we're pounding you all the time."

"You won't convince many South Africans of that. What's the proportion of Negroes to Whites in your country?"

"You know perfectly well what it is. I haven't met a South African yet who didn't have our statistics on the tip of his tongue. You tell me."

"It's about twenty million Blacks out of 190 million population, isn't it?"

"You know it."

"Well"—triumphantly—"compare that with our three and a half million Whites to twelve and a half million Bantu."

"Why should I want to compare? I'm just here to find out things."

"You must admit it gives us a special problem."

"Have I denied it?"

"Most Americans do."

"Well: I don't. Now tell me about bannings and 180 days. Justify them for me, will you?"

"Why do we have to justify them? We think they're necessary for our survival, that's all."

"And it never disturbs you to think that the Government could be here five minutes from now and haul you in without any protections for you at all?"

"Why should it disturb us? We're not Communists!"

"No, and the Government certainly can't claim you're not Nats, either."

"We thank God for the Nats. Thank God we have a strong Government to face the outside world and America."

"Well, bully for you. I see where everybody in the country is going to have to carry a pass starting August 1. Doesn't that concern you a little?"

"No, why should it? We have nothing to conceal."

"And the idea that the police can challenge you and make you produce it at any time doesn't seem like an encroachment on your individual liberty?"

"My dear chap"—pityingly—"we aren't worried about our individual liberty, in South Africa! Our individual liberty is quite safe, thank you."

"The police challenge the Bantu and take them to jail if they don't have their passes. Will they do the same to you?"

"Not bloody likely!"

"Why not? You don't mean to tell me the laws are administered one way for the Whites and another for the Blacks, do you?"

"We're not worried."

"That's good. What about the reclassification that's going on in connection with the new passes? Isn't it causing a lot of hardship among some of the Coloureds who may have been accepted as Whites?"

"If they're accepted as White they'll be classified as White."

"What's all this fuss down in the Cape, then, about reclassifying? Hardships, suicides—"

"My dear fellow! Don't believe all you read in the English-language press!"

"There isn't any hardship, then."

"What's so hard about carrying a pass, for heaven's sake? Don't you carry identification with you—"

"I don't let my passport out of my sight."

"Very well! And you carry a driver's license, too, probably, and all those credit cards Americans are supposed to carry and we're just beginning to get—"

"Sure."

"Well: do they cause hardship?"

"You honestly don't see that each of these steps gives the Government just that much more control over the individual citizen. You honestly don't see that laws as broad as these, which depend solely on the discretion of the administrator, could be used to gradually choke out all opposition—"

"I'd like to see anybody choke out Helen Suzman!"

"I know Helen can take care of herself. But I'm talking about the average citizen who isn't protected by Parliamentary immunity, who is really, literally, helpless in the hands of the Government if it wants to act against him."

"You Americans worry so. We have more important things to think about, such as what the outside world is going to do about South-West Africa, and whether America is going to support those bloody buggers up north if they want to try some assault on us. Those are the important things for us."

"And bannings and passes and 180 days—"

"You don't seem to understand. We're not Communists. They don't apply to us."

"And you trust the Government."

"We thank God for the Nats. They're a damned sight tougher than we English would be, and thank God for it."

But later, after the delicious meal served by the inevitable silent Bantu, the coffee, the brandy, there came, as always, the more candid moments:

"You know, these Afrikaans are really something. I'll never forget when I was studying medicine at university I had this Afrikaans professor. He was a Fellow of the Royal College of Surgeons in London and a Fellow of the Royal College of Surgeons in Edinburgh. I was the only English-speaking student in this particular class of his, and he kept failing me test after test—to the point where I finally decided it must be something personal—I mean, I wasn't that stupid. So finally I went to him and I said, 'Why do you hate me?' He gave me a cold look and said, 'I hate the English. They put ground glass in the tea and porridge of the Boer women and children in the concentration camps.' I said, 'Look, in the first place I'm too young to know anything about that, and in the second place you know damned well if ground glass was put in tea it would sink to the bottom, and if it were put in porridge, there isn't any better antidote than porridge itself. I'll put some on porridge and eat it for you to prove it.' But he just gave me another cold stare and flunked me in the course. F.R.C.S. in London"—wonderingly—"and F.R.C.S. in Edinburgh!"

And later, driving me back to the hotel, as we came to City Hall Square and saw high atop the old General Post Office Building the slogan of South African Airways:

"You see that sign, 'Vlieg Suid-Afrikaanse Lugdiens'? It used to say in English, 'Fly South African Airways.' One week after they came to power in 1948 it was changed to Afrikaans. They weren't wasting any time letting us English know who was in control now."

"But you like them because they're tough."

"They're tough as hell."

INDIAN YOGA GIRL BANNED FROM SHOW AT WITS (Rand Daily Mail, *English*) . . . *The Government has refused to allow a 15-year-old Indian girl to give a demonstration of yoga in the University of the Witwatersrand Great Hall—to either an Indian and White audience or an all-White audience.*

Shanta Das has been studying yoga since childhood and is one of South Africa's most advanced yogis.

Proceeds from the demonstration would have gone to a fund to enable her to study overseas before entering a British university.

Because the demonstration was to be open to the public, the organisers had to apply for a permit from the Department of Community Development—in terms of the Government's "no-mixed-gatherings" regulation, non-Whites may not perform before a White audience without a permit.

"We asked for a permit for Miss Das to give the demonstration and we also asked whether we could allow members of the Indian community to see the demonstration," said one of the organisers yesterday.

"We did say, however, that if the 'mixed' audience were not allowed, we would still like the demonstration to go ahead before a White audience.

"Both applications were turned down—we received the reply only today—and no reasons were given."

A T CLOSE RANGE the bulldog face, the upthrust jaw, the bitter look are softened a little by an occasional gleam of humor in the eyes. But not much.

"I wish I could write another novel," Alan Paton said as we stood in the yard of his rambling old house in Kloof, fifteen miles north of Durban. The bougainvillea rioted everywhere, the azaleas and poinsettias and camellias were out, the sky was absolutely cloudless, a soft little wind stirred the palms and eucalyptus. It was a gorgeous day.

"Yes," he said, frowning deeply, "I wish I could write again. But I find it very difficult to concentrate in this climate of oppression. The Government's policies I find very repressive to any talent one may possess. It is just so hard to think, with so many terrible things going on. Come along to the rondevaal and we'll talk."

In the rondevaal—one of those round, whitewashed, thatch-roofed huts, copied from the Bantu, that are so popular with so many well-to-do Whites—he sat behind an enormous semicircular desk cluttered from one end to the other with books, letters, papers, reports, and described the world of South Africa as he sees it.

"I'm the chairman of the Liberal Party, you know, but I'm about the only major party leader left. The Government has banned more than forty of our officials right out from under me." A grim little smile. "One way to reduce your political opposition. I suppose I'll be next."

"You don't really think they'd dare—"

"Why not? Nothing I could do to stop them."

"I think they'd hesitate. You're not so unknown around the world, you know."

"They don't care what the world thinks. Or rather, they do and they don't. They're a strange mixture. I supposed you've noticed that. Have you met many Afrikaners who weren't charming?"

"Not many."

"And ruthless?"

"They haven't been with me, but, then, I'm in a favored position."

"You are. There's another side, as you know. They have my passport, you know, I can't travel. That's one of their weapons. Either they kick you out, throw you in jail, ban you, or make it impossible for you to move. A multiplicity of means, an embarrassment of riches. So far they've only used one on me, but any day now . . . I do wish"—again the deep frown, the unhappy, tortured expression—"I do wish I could write another novel."

"What would it be—will it be—about, when you do?"

"I think I would like to write about the struggle that some of our people have made to bring about change. There are certain ones who have fought hard for what they believed right, and have suffered for it in one way or another. I would like to write about the battle."

"It would be a marvelous story in your hands."

The bulldog jaw came up, the unhappy eyes stared out across the glistening lawn to the vivid bougainvillea.

"Too close to it, probably. That may be another reason I can't acquire the necessary objectivity or concentration. I'm too much a part of it."

"The Liberal Party favors an outright one-man, one-vote policy, as I understand it."

"Yes, we feel that if a man is a human being, if he has the inherent rights a human being ought to have, then he should be allowed to participate in his own governing."

"Even though he may not have the sophistication or the skills necessary to run a booming country like this—"

"How does he acquire them if you never let him learn, if you never put the responsibility on him? God, I am so tired of my friends in the Progressive Party and our dear, dull United Party who say it has to be gradual, it has to be qualified. Either you have faith in human beings or you don't."

"You do?"

"Yes."

"I was at the NUSAS opening the other night and heard you speak."

"Oh?" A pleased smile. "They're a brave bunch of kids. Very brave. Their days may be numbered, but they aren't letting it intimidate them."

"Have you had any response from the Government to your remarks about the Minister of Justice?"

"Response?" A snort. "From Vorster?" Another snort. "He doesn't respond to criticism, it's one of his strengths. No, I'm just a gadfly. Just a gadfly. They brush me off."

"Not entirely, I suspect. Do you see any signs of any kind of change at all in the Nats' policies, any time in the foreseeable future?"

"Where would it come from? They're agreed on what they want to do."

"Are they? I thought there was a split between the Transvaal and the Orange Free State people, and the Cape Nationalists. I thought the latter were more relaxed, more liberal. Maybe a change could come from them."

"Oh, yes, you'll like the Cape Nationalists, the Cape Afrikaners. They are more relaxed and more liberal. But they aren't running the Government. About all they can do is agitate a little—and that's damned muted. Don't get led astray into any idea of any great liberalizing influence from the Cape. They might like it but they haven't got the power to put it over. When all's said and done, they go along. They're Afrikaans too, after all."

"Then you really don't see much hope anywhere."

Again the jaw outthrust, the eyes gazing off into the beautiful day, the deep-furrowed forehead, the harried, unhappy look.

"If I were to predict South Africa's future a decade or two decades from now, I could not tell you what it would be. I know what I fear it will be, but I could be wrong. I hope I'm wrong. After all, it's my country."

"The beloved country."

An impatient little expression, but a pleased light in the eyes.

"It is beloved. They love it too. We all do. That's what makes it so damned difficult. I only wish," he said with a sigh, rising to lead me from the rondevaal, "that I could write another novel about it."

If you want more of what a passport's for . . . discover SOUTH AFRICA

If your passport has become a rubber-stamp album of carbon-copy places, it's time you wrapped it around South Africa, the most Western country east of Greenwich. A peaceful, restful escape from crowds and the commonplace, where passports still spell excitement and discovery. With the zestful tempo of a vigorous, prosperous Republic where language and culture are mirrors of your own . . .

—South African Tourist Corporation

SOUTH AFRICAN RAILWAYS

The Constitution provides that the Railways, Ports and Harbours shall be administered on business principles, due regard being had to agricultural and industrial development within the country and to promotion, by means of cheap transport, of the settlement of an agricultural and industrial population in the inland portions of all provinces.

It further provides that, so far as may be, the total earnings shall not be more than are sufficient to meet the necessary outlay for working, maintenance, betterment, depreciation and the payment of interest due on capital.

Control of the Railways is exercised through the Minister of Transport who is advised by a Board composed of three commissioners appointed by the State President-in-Council, with the Minister as Chairman.

The Railway system of South-West Africa forms part of the Republic's system.

The total mileage of open lines on March 31, 1964, was as follows:

Cape 5,459, Natal 1,530, Transvaal 3,541, Orange Free State 1,669, South-West Africa 1,454. Total 13,653.

—Official Sources

IT WAS A LOVELY Sunday on Durban beach. The weather was warm, dry, motionless, perfect. Thousands of bathers were on the sands, jumping the waves, riding the surf. Several large tankers lay offshore, come from far places to rest a while in the Indian Ocean. Across the bay the beautiful homes of The Bluff looked down.

There were English-speakers on the beach, unmistakable if they were of the older generation: the plain, practical, tweedy clothes, the lady's flowered hat, the gentleman's visored cap, the camera slung over the shoulder, the pipe, the cane. Unmistakable if they were older Afrikaners, too: Meneer fat and portly and calmly confident, Mevrou fat and stolid, little eyes peering contentedly out of a rosy round face upon a world well-ordered for Die Volk.

If they were young English or young Afrikaans, the distinctions were not so clear. When they were not jumping the waves or surfboarding, they strode up and down the esplanade posing for one another, or lay in tangled groups upon the sand flirting or playing cards while transistor radios blared out the latest American jazz, courtesy of the S.A.B.C. One could notice here and there an obvious English aspect, an undeniable Afrikaner look; but for the most part they were simply the indistinguishable young, lean and beautiful, light and dark, luxuriating in their holiday, forgetting their ominous heritage, happy to be alive.

This is the July world of the white South African at play, and nobody need feel too concerned about their fellow-South Africans, for off down the beach a way there are, are there not, special sections marked "Swimming Area for Indians," "Swimming Area for Coloureds," "Swimming Area for Bantu." The Indian Ocean embraces them all, and the gentle currents that caress Afrikaner limbs at 1 P.M. are laving Bantu bones or—shocking thought—vice versa—at 1:15.

So everyone is happy, and no one feels slighted or hurt. The sun is bright, the water warm, the scenery lovely and life felicitous.

Occasionally a lifeguard helicopter flies slowly up and down the beaches, a benevolent protector keeping an eye upon them all. Like the helicopter in the opening scene of "La Dolce Vita," it should perhaps be carrying a statue of Christ. But it does not, and it is probably just as well. There would have to be one of Him for the Whites, one for the Indians, one for the Bantu and one for the Coloureds; and that is quite a lot of Christs.

APARTHEID GRAVES (Daily Dispatch, *East London, English*) . . .
*The Pretoria City Council has exhumed more than 60 Africans from
Mooiplaats Cemetery. The bodies are to be moved to Atteridgeville
Cemetery because Mooiplaats Cemetery is in an Indian township.*

GAIN THE VOICE was feminine, the face old and tired, the claim to
liberalism unchallengeable. And again the mood was hopeless and
embittered, not only against the Government but against those upon
whom a lifetime's energies had been spent.

"They tell me," she said, as she drove me through the blowing night to
our appointment with two more Indians, one under ban, the other on the
verge of it, "that we should act in such-and-such a way because of what
the Native thinks. But who knows what the Native thinks? You work and
work for them, you think you are doing your best to help them, you think
you are doing what they want—and suddenly you find they have completely lost interest, or they have decided that you are insulting them in
some way, or they have taken umbrage over some fancied failure on your
part. It makes one feel hopeless, it really does. One works so hard and
one never gets anywhere. If there were only some gratitude. If there were
only some cooperation. They make it easy for the Government: it thinks
we are working with quicksand. Perhaps we are. . . ."

She laughed without humor, a dry, unhappy sound.

"A good many of my friends who used to be active have voluntarily
left the country, and they're always writing to urge me to do so, too.
Possibly one of these days I will. We used to think people were traitors
to the cause when they left. We thought they should stay to carry on the
struggle. But there isn't any struggle. . . ."

In the modest Indian home with its multiple locks inside the front
door and the steel bars on the windows, we talked for an hour or two
about the Government's move to take over Indian education, the tighten-
ing of regulations, the inhibition not only of protest but of thought. They
were still struggling here, though at times it was not entirely clear
whether it was against the Government or against fellow-Indians such as
Let-Us-Be-Honest-About-It. They mentioned him and were scornful of
his fawning upon the Government; and were scornful even of the
Brothers D., though they felt that possibly they were a little less cooperative than the others.

"The D.'s are looking out for the D's," said our host, giving me a
knowing but rather hopeless smile. "It is the curse of the Indians. Every-

one is looking out for his own economic advantage, no one wants to work together for all the community."

"Everyone is making too much money," said his younger friend, darkly beautiful in her green and silver sari. "The Indians, the Bantu, everybody. The boom is doing more than the Government can to stop unrest."

"There is no struggle," my driver repeated bitterly, as though in struggle she had found some justification for life that struggle's absence did not provide. "It is all hopeless."

When we left, the lady in the sari walked out first into the windy night to go toward her car. Suddenly she uttered an exclamation and stepped quickly back. Just beyond the car a drunken Bantu stood swaying in the warm, misty rain, propping himself against the hood with one hand, a bottle in the other, muttering disconnectedly in Zulu.

"I will go out," our host said quickly. "No, not you—I do not think a white man"—he chuckled, though a little tensely—"is exactly what is needed at this moment. You all step inside. It will be all right. This chappie is just drunk. I will shoo him along. It will be all right."

"This is right on the edge of a Bantu area," my driver explained as we stood inside the door and waited, trying to hear above the hurrying wind.

"Is there frequent trouble?"

"Quite often," the lady in the sari said. "It is a bad neighborhood."

We strained again to hear, but could not. In a couple of minutes our host returned, a little flustered but outwardly amused.

"He went along all right," he said with a smile. "No trouble now, my dear, you may safely go."

But we all went out with her and watched her drive off; and then our host remained while my driver and I got in and started our car and began to move away; and then our host went quickly back inside, and we could hear the sound of his multiple locks being quickly shot home, and could see at the steel-barred windows the shades being quickly drawn.

MOST LOYAL CITIZENS (*Editorial,* The Leader, *Durban, Indian*)— *The South African industrialist, Mr. C. J. Saunders, said at the Conference of the Institute of Race Relations in Durban that there were no more loyal citizens to South Africa or to the continent of Africa than the Indian population.*

We thank Mr. Saunders for broadcasting this fact because, from time to time, the loyalty of South Africa's Indians is, surprisingly, called into question. We fail to understand why even some persons in high places should doubt the Indian community's loyalty to the Republic.

The Indian community has always been loyal to the country of its adoption and will remain so.

But—and we must emphasise this—this loyalty must not be confused with meek submission to an all-powerful authority which is determined to assign it a place as second class citizens.

For, although Indians are treated as untouchables under the laws of the country and denied their just place in the African sun by the powers that be, one should never have any reason to doubt their loyalty.

They can become first class citizens in every respect if only the numerous legal fetters are removed and they are allowed to develop and advance to the full as all citizens should be allowed to do, irrespective of their race or class or religion, or skin colour.

We have said the Indian community has always been loyal to this country and it will remain so. But this loyalty to the Republic must not be interpreted as loyalty to the Government or its policy of so-called separate development.

Not only are the Indians loyal to this country. Crime statistics would show that they are a law-abiding community, too. What is more—they are also a God-fearing people, and we believe it is this belief in God which has seen them through thick and thin during their darkest days.

But, as Jawaharlal Nehru has said, "Affection and loyalty are of the heart. They cannot be purchased in the market place. Much less can they be extorted at the point of the bayonet."

Even the most powerful Government on earth must remember these wise words of one of the greatest leaders the world has ever seen.

"I THINK the average Afrikaner," said the handsome churchman in his gorgeous robes, in his enormous house on the hill in Durban, "is basically a very decent chap. I think he closes his mind to what is going on; I think he would be quite horrified if he knew some of the things that I, for instance, hear about all the time.

"Yet I am not so sure he would not accept them if he did know, for he feels that his very survival is at stake. His government is very adept at creating crises of nerves that induce that state of mind in him. And also, of course, it is to a large measure true. . . .

"I think there is very little organized resistance left. The idea of any mass uprising, any violent overthrow of the Government, may be the rather naive wish of certain people elsewhere but it has little relation to realities here. The leadership doesn't exist, the organization doesn't exist; I really wonder whether the desire exists. After all, the economy is prosperous, the Bantu are making more money than they have ever made, they are gradually beginning to get a stake in a stable society—why should they jeopardize it by revolting? They may be unlettered but they are not fools. They are very shrewd. They know what would happen if the order imposed by the Whites was removed. They would not contemplate with equanimity, I think, the thought of other African tribes from up north descending on their land and trying to take it away from them. Nor would most of them relish the thought of the Zulus turned loose again."

TOP RED JAILED (Scope, Government) . . . *Former Johannesburg Senior Advocate Abram Fischer was sentenced to life imprisonment in the Pretoria Supreme Court on May 9, 1966, on the main charge of conspiring to commit sabotage. Fischer, who is 59, was also sentenced to eight years' imprisonment on other charges. These sentences are to run concurrently with the life sentence.*

In an 80-page summation of the case, which took more than two hours to read, the judge, Mr. Justice Boshoff, said the Court was satisfied that Fischer conspired with the African National Congress and Umkhonto we Sizwe (Spear of the Nation) to commit sabotage. It was abundantly clear that the "liberation movement," with Umkhonto as its military wing, was under the guidance of the Communist Party.

Communism, under the Suppression of Communism Act, is defined to mean the doctrine of Marxist Socialism as expounded by Lenin or Trotsky, the Third Communist International (Comintern), or the Communist Information Bureau (Cominform), or any related form of that doctrine expounded or advocated in the Republic of South Africa for the promotion of the fundamental principles of that doctrine.

In a three and a half hour address during the trial, Fischer told the Court he had joined the Communist Party and had been acting chairman of the Central Committee of the South African Communist Party.

Fischer said the formation of the Umkhonto we Sizwe (Spear of the Nation), the military wing of the "resistance group," had resulted from the Government's "violent reaction" to passive campaigns for the easing of legislation and he had known of its formation in July, 1961. He had not disapproved of it. It proclaimed the violent overthrow of the State.

Abram Fischer studied first at a South African university. In 1932 he left for Oxford where he continued his studies for five years. It was apparently during this time that Fischer became interested in Communism and started to defend the ideology in conversations with his friends. It was a changed man who returned to South Africa, according to a recently published book about his life. He joined the Communist Party

and soon became one of its senior members. He had in the past acted on
many occasions as defense lawyer for persons tried on sabotage and
other charges.

While appearing with thirteen others last year on charges under the
Suppression of Communism Act, Fischer absconded, forfeiting bail of
$14,000. He was recaptured, heavily disguised, in a Johannesburg sub-
urb on November 11, 1965, after being at large for ten months.

In listing the charges brought against him, Mr. Justice Boshoff de-
scribed how Fischer, being a member of the Communist Party, was a
party to a conspiracy with the African National Congress and Umkhonto
we Sizwe to aid or procure the commission of acts of sabotage which
would have endangered the health and safety of the public and caused
general disruption in the country. This would have been done by train-
ing cadres in guerrilla warfare and teaching them how to make arms.
Buildings and installations were in fact damaged, all with the purpose of
causing a violent revolution in the country.

O NCE AGAIN I was driven north from Durban through the green hills
of Natal, along the beautiful shoreline, through the rustling fields
of sugarcane. It was Sunday, the traffic was light; only a few cars coming
and going on the two-lane macadamized road. Presently we came to a
cleft in the hills. "Tugela River," the sign said: "Zululand." We were in
the home country of Dingaan and Chaka, entering the bloody land of the
great warrior-tyrants, about to meet the people they led to glory and
defeat less than a century ago—the people whom other Natives to this
day fear and distrust, the people who to this day hold themselves superior
to, and contemptuous of, all other Natives.

My guide was the child of missionaries, reared in Zululand, in love
with it as all who know it seem to be. As we drove along she pointed out
the careful planning of the early British in Natal: strips of sugar plantations interlayered with strips of native land, from one point of view a
means of providing contiguous labor for the plantations, from another
point of view a guarantee that the Zulus should be separated so that it
would be difficult for them to organize again against the white man. It
gives the countryside a placidly domesticated appearance, first a broad
band of cane, then an open, rolling section dotted wherever one looks
with scattered kraals containing a handful of the round, thatched huts
where the Zulus live.

We turned off the main road that leads on to the capital of Zululand,
Eshowe (spoken softly and lovingly, "Eh-*sho*-we," a name taken, they
say, from the sigh of the wind through the forests that surround it) and
onto a road leading into one of the native sections. We met a kaleido-

scope of Africa, half-in, half-out of the twentieth century: little children spic-and-span in European clothing, on their way to Sunday school; a grave, tall man carrying a Bible; several women in Mother Hubbards, baskets on their heads; a white-powdered ngoma, all alone; a couple of naked boys with spears, out for a Sunday's hunting of small game. All smiled and waved with the friendly independent courtesy of a people who may be factually under White rule but who in their own hearts and minds have obviously not the slightest doubt that the land they walk upon is theirs forever by right of conquest and long habitation.

We were at this moment even more of a white minority than Whites are in their own areas of the Republic, yet there was not the slightest hint of uneasiness or worry as we drove along. On this sunny morning we were among friends and there was no sign anywhere of the tensions one sometimes feels so vividly in the teeming urbanized areas of the Witwatersrand or the Cape.

For a few minutes the road, no longer macadamized but rutted and dusty, twisted and turned through the open countryside. Then we came to a kraal containing five or six huts, close to the road on the right. "Would you like to go in?" our hostess asked.

"Is it all right?"

"They will love to see us," she said; and so they did.

At first when we drove up and stopped there was no sign of life save a couple of chickens that cackled and ran, a dog that came out and barked; but in a couple of minutes two women, the younger tall and dignified, the older thin and a little bent, both with friendly, open faces, came toward us from among the huts. My hostess got out and stepped forward.

"Sakubhona!" she said to begin the Zulu greeting, as ritualized as any other tribal custom: "I see you!"

"Yebo," responded the younger woman with a tentative smile: "Yes."

"U sa phila?" asked our hostess: "Are you still well?"

"Yebo, ngise khona," the younger woman said, the smile broadening. "Ngi ngezwa wena?": "Yes, I am still here. How about you?"

And then the clincher, in which we could distinguish the name of my hostess' father, retired ten years and more ago and now far from Zululand; and at once the courteous listening faces broke into enormous smiles, there was an excited burst of recognition and chatter, they seized her hands in both of theirs, the three of them rattled on like long-lost chums. "Come in," she called to the rest of us, who included her cousin and two children from Jo'burg, and we got out and went forward to be received with the most cordial and gracious hospitality.

Again there was the sense of being in another land, welcome strangers meeting dignified and hospitable people who were proud of their own ways and delighted to have us visit them. Pretoria at its own decision could root them out, put them in townships, turn their civilization upside down; but somehow one understood that this was one nation to which Pretoria would not do that. Toughness, perhaps, calls to toughness: and the Zulus are tough.

They took us, then, into three or four spotless huts. ("Which of us," my hostess' cousin asked later, "could have complete strangers come into her home unannounced in midmorning and find it as neat and clean as these?") It is true that the Zulu custom is to sweep the mud floor and the yards with cow dung, and its pungent, musky smell was everywhere; it is true that the furnishings (aside from the inevitable transistor tuned to Radio Bantu and the inevitable framed pictures of Dingaan and Chaka) were of the simplest, a chest or two, a small table, possibly a wood stove, a couple of chairs; it is true that there were no closets, that clothing was hung neatly from a rope stretched between two rafters; it is true there were no beds, only straw sleeping pallets, neatly rolled against one wall. But it is also true that these were pleasant, practical and comfortable homes, perfectly designed for their purpose, perfectly suited to their occupants. And neat: absolutely immaculate and well-ordered.

So we stayed and chatted for a while, a little embarrassed to go poking about inside people's homes like a group of visiting social workers, but eagerly encouraged to do so by the ladies of the kraal. Two of their sons were away at the mines on the Rand, they told us; their mutual husband and another son were off in the hills tending the cattle. They talked of the weather and of tribal life, asked my hostess and her cousin about their homes, went off into roars of laughter at the thought that the cousin, tiny and slight, should have been able to produce two such large, strapping children; and made some friendly but ribald comment on this that our hostess, overcome with laughter, refused to translate. Then we asked them to pose for pictures, had them stand beside the kraal fence—and instantly the animation disappeared, solemnity descended, two blank, frozen faces confronted the cameras. We snapped the shutters, smiles burst forth again, the formal moment was over. "They don't think they look very pretty for you," our hostess translated. "Tell them they're absolutely beautiful," I said. The younger uttered a shriek of laughter and struck one palm against the other with an indescribably wry, dismissing gesture that said as plainly as words: Oh, you funny white man, who do you think you're kidding? And then amid great protestations of friendship and good wishes, we said good-bye ("Sala kahle," said my hostess: "Stay well." "Hamba kahle," they replied: "Go well.") and drove off to the next kraal. There the performance was repeated at the home of one of the sub-chieftains, a descendant of Dingaan's white adviser, John Dunn, and his Zulu wife.

The Dunn descendants, our hostess told me later, still control some seven thousand acres of the grant given their forebear by Dingaan. This particular chieftain, middle-aged, heavy, illiterate, dressed in tattered old

European shirt and dungarees (a gorgeous shield and ceremonial regalia hung in a special place inside his hut), has jurisdiction over some ten thousand Zulus, prescribing rules for their behavior, judging their minor crimes, dispensing a limited justice and control in the small areas of suzerainty permitted by Pretoria.

From there we went to the mission, where Sunday services were in progress: a progress, our hostess said, that can easily last as much as four or five hours. The white minister who had come out from Sweden to succeed her father was holding forth in Zulu with high drama, his voice rising to a shout, sinking to a whisper. His solemn audience, ranging from infant to ancient, murmured agreement from time to time, now and then chuckled at some telling point, rose occasionally at his request to launch into some rhythmic rendition of a hymn.

We drove on to a great, whispering eucalyptus forest, took out the picnic hamper, had lunch; went then to a leper hospital, saw the patient faces and ravaged bodies of the native men and women the Government cares for in the program that is rapidly eradicating the terrible disease from the Republic; and then went on to gentle Eshowe, set high in beautiful mountains covered with pine.

By the time we started the hundred-mile drive back to Durban it was growing dark, and along the road the natives we began to see were less friendly. Some had bottles, others obviously had already consumed their contents. We began to meet and overtake a sizable number of drunken Zulus; made a wrong turning at one point, had to back around in a deserted service-station yard, and during this slow process were accosted by several tipsy souls who advanced upon the car with intentions we did not stop to analyze. Our hostess stepped on the gas and we shot away. She grew increasingly nervous, and so did we. The sunny day was over and we no longer felt so safe in Zululand.

"The Government has been very generous with the natives on some things," I was told admiringly in Johannesburg. "Why, up to a couple of years ago, it was illegal for them to purchase hard liquor. At first we thought it was unwise of the Government to permit it, but it has worked out very well."

There are several ways to explain this generous decision of the Government, and one of them was inescapable that night.

Presently we recrossed the Tugela and before long the welcoming lights of Durban and the White world loomed ahead.

FOOD PRODUCTS

During the past decade the range of products in South Africa has widened considerably and in addition to staple foods, a great variety of jellies, spices, mustards, condensed and powdered milk, mayonnaise, chutneys, breakfast foods, frozen foods, corn flour, baking powders, baby foods, custard powder, cake and pudding mixes, candied peel, flavourings, macaroni, pickles, sauces, etc., are now being manufactured. Many internationally known brands are produced locally under licenses or by subsidiaries of the parent companies. Prices are highly competitive. . . .

Production of quick-frozen foods started on a small scale in Cape Town after World War II. There are now several factories producing hundreds of tons of frozen food. Most retailers have installed freezing cabinets.

South Africa is one of the leading fruit-producing countries in the world. The fruit and vegetable canning industry in the Republic employs more than 25,000 workers and is essentially an export industry. Of some 80 countries to which South African canned fruit and vegetables are exported, the United Kingdom is the most important market.

—Official Sources

"H E'S HERE IN Durban," my American friend said. "Would you like to talk to him?"

I said I would and without pausing a moment he picked up his phone and put through a call, on a line that must be monitored by the police. If it isn't, they are overlooking the obvious, and this they don't do. I was here, he told the party on the other end, and wanted to see him; could we meet?

"He'd love to," my friend reported. "Shall he come to your hotel?"

"I didn't know his banning order permitted it."

"Oh, sure," my friend said casually. "He'll come down to see you."

And so he did, waiting a little uneasily for me in the lobby of the hotel, conversing, when we withdrew to talk, in a low tone of voice that indicated he was perhaps not quite so unconcerned about it as my friend.

Like the silenced lion, he, too, did not have anything particularly startling to say; but he, too, is a symbol and necessary to talk to.

He denied, of course, that there were any grounds for his banning; made a few carefully phrased comments on the Minister of Justice; gave much the same estimate of continuing underground activity as do all the banned.

"I would say there is some," he said thoughtfully. "But the extent of it isn't very great, and the Government is rapidly wiping out what remains. The police are very efficient, you know. They have so many informers. They don't miss much."

Did he feel he had done anything subversive to the interests of South Africa?

He did not.

Had the Minister given him any reasons for his banning?

He had not.

Did he find the banning hurtful? He tried to sound jaunty but didn't quite make it.

"Oh, it restricts my social life somewhat, you know. I can't be with more than one person at a time. I like company, I like parties, I've always had a great many friends. Now I can't see them. But aside from that, it doesn't bother me much. . . ." His voice trailed off, then sounded defiant. "I read a good deal. It gives me a chance to study things I didn't have time for before. Mr. Vorster may have helped me, after all."

And if he should decide to go into exile abroad, an option the Government would give him if he so desired?

A little expression of pain came into his eyes, the defiance didn't sound so sure of itself.

"I expect it wouldn't be so bad, though I expect I should be a little homesick for South Africa, now and then. After all, I'm South African, I was born and grew up here. That might be a little difficult sometimes . . . but I expect I could manage it."

Did he find that many of his fellow-students were voluntarily leaving the country?

"Oh, yes, a lot of them, at least the English-speaking. My Afrikaans friends are mostly pretty well satisfied to stay, but there are a lot of English-speakers who are deliberately deciding to go. They just can't see much future for the country, as things are going now. They feel South Africa is doomed. They don't want to go, you understand—I wouldn't want you to think they're a lot of deserters—but they have to think about their careers, the kind of country they want their children to grow up in, and all. They don't like to go any more than I do, but they are afraid of what the future holds for us in South Africa."

Then he saw no hope anywhere?

"Only one thing. There is still an amazing amount of goodwill toward the Whites among the Bantu, the Indians and the Coloureds. If the Whites could only respond and make use of it, by treating them decently. . . . Maybe, someday, there will be a Government that will. I suppose, really, that's all that some of us have wanted them to do."

SETTLERS ARE STREAMING INTO S.A. (Star, *Johannesburg, English*) . . . *South Africa is gaining nearly as many White people through immigration as she is through her own natural increase.*

If the present rate of immigration this year continues, South Africa will have gained about 41,000 people by the end of it, 9,000 fewer than the 50,000 gained by natural increase.

The actual migrant inflow will be about 50,000, but about 9,000 people are expected to emigrate, giving a net gain of 41,000.

Figures released by the Bureau of Statistics in Pretoria yesterday show that South Africa gained nearly 22,000 immigrants in the first six months of this year. This is about 5,000 more than in the same period last year.

The largest number of immigrants from a single country for the first six months was nearly 6,000, from the United Kingdom. For Portugal the figure was about 3,800 and for Europe as a whole, including the United Kingdom, 15,600.

Nearly 2,000 came from Germany, 1,100 from Italy and 600 from the Netherlands.

An interesting aspect is that South Africa lost more people to Canada, the United States, Finland and Malaysia than she gained from these countries in the first six months of the year.

About 1,500 South Africans left to settle in Britain, 400 in Germany and 200 in Canada.

W E HAD BEEN to the American mission back of beyond, driving a dirt road through the tumbled hills behind Durban until we found it drowsing on its eucalyptus hill; and now, after one of those mixed meals that mix not only color but a number of emotions including patience, impatience, tolerance, intolerance, condescension, lack of condescension and a sort of exasperated sense of Doing Good, By God, we were driving back talking as countrymen about another country.

Two Christian Bantu had sat at table with us and together we had chatted, not very volubly but rather in little bursts of polite comment interspersed with long, industrious eating silences, about such topics as the weather, the late-flowering aloes, and the subjects taught in the missionary school. None of these seemed to form any great bridge between the races, and only little Miss Y's eager smiles and little Mr. Z's polite little chuckles indicated that communication was being sustained. Their spoken comments were very short, and noncommittal, and most of them were rounded out and given editorial content by the kindly, careworn missionary lady who was in charge.

After the meal ended there were a few moments of more intimate talk among the missionaries, and it became apparent that there was considerable tension underlying the sunny noontime. They were being bothersome again, and this time the They was the white They in Pretoria. There was some talk of curtailing privileges, of cutting down the number of natives who could be taken in the classes, of perhaps requesting that the staff be reduced and that certain missionaries, who had been a trifle too industrious in spreading faith, hope and charity, be sent home. None of these things had actually been done, and upon probing it developed that the hints that they might be had been quite vague and inexplicit. But the fear clearly existed. "In our circumstances," one of the young male missionaries explained tersely, "it doesn't take much to start one sniffing the wind."

The circumstances were those which seem to be common to most foreign missions in the Republic: an uneasy condition of living on the sufferance of a Government quick to see opposition in every outside gesture of friendliness toward the natives; being made to feel that you are the immediate targets should any serious breach develop between the Government and your government; not knowing at what moment an arbitrary order may come down from Pretoria saying: get out. It puts a foundation of uncertainty under most missions and makes even more remarkable the fact that so many staunch-hearted and decent people should still be willing to come out and do what they can to alleviate the Republic's unhappier side.

But it is not only the Government which makes the task difficult; and now, as we drove along, high above beautiful valleys sweeping down to the distant blue of the Indian Ocean, the expressions of frustration were candid, and not all were directed at Pretoria.

"I find the Natives most timid," one of my hosts said in an exasperated tone. "I mean even when they're left alone, when the Government doesn't bother them or interfere. It is so difficult to get them to take responsibility. They are so dependent upon us for everything."

"Don't you think, though," said his friend, who had been out a much shorter time than he, "that this is due to the Government? Aren't they afraid of what it might do if they tried to show any independence of thought? Isn't the control maintained largely by threat?"

"I know that's a popular thesis with my friends back home," the first said, "and, if you'll pardon the thought, with people who haven't been here very long. I felt that way myself when I first came out. But after you've been here a while, your ideas begin to change. You begin to sense something fundamentally weak in the Natives themselves; some lack of something that you simply can't put into them, no matter how hard you work and pray. It's a frustrating thing."

"In what way?" his friend demanded.

"All right," said the first, "as simple as lunch, if you like. I do my best to talk to them and bring them out, but you know how difficult it is."

"Perhaps it's shyness."

"Shyness, yes—"

"Perhaps they don't understand the white man."

"Anybody can understand lunch. I know they're shy, but the point is,

they shouldn't be, after all the encouragement we've given them to speak
out and express themselves without fear. No, it's deeper than that, I
think: I think they don't express much of an opinion *because they don't
want to be held responsible for it.* They don't want to take a position
they can't get away from."

"They want us to do it for them."

"That's it, exactly. They want to put the burden on the white man, and
that isn't right. They ought to be getting to the point where they can
carry some of it themselves. We shouldn't have to do everything for
them."

"I still think that's their conditioning under this Government. When
have they had a chance to accept responsibility and carry it out?"

"Oh, yes, you can blame it to some extent on the Government, but I've
been here four years, now, and I've about concluded it goes deeper than
that. It's almost instinctive with them, it's ingrained. You know what it's
like in the tribes, everybody fits in the pecking order, everybody has his
place, right on up to the chiefs. And nobody—but nobody—steps out of
it. There isn't any individual responsibility in the tribal areas, the responsibility is always collective and exercised through the chief. In a sense
that's what makes it so easy for the Government to prevent them from
taking responsibility when they come into the white areas. Their whole
background has been against it, long before the white man came
around."

"I still think they're afraid of the Government—as well as their chiefs,
as you say."

"Oh, they are. I think fear is one of the keys to Africa. Everybody is
afraid of somebody, that's why it's such a bloody continent. They're
afraid of their chiefs, they're afraid of the Government, they're afraid of
any white man, basically; and above all, they're afraid to get out of line.
They just don't want to step forward. You see it in our ministerial conferences all the time. The native ministers refuse to take positions,
they're afraid somebody from their own ranks will inform the Government—and for sure somebody will, all right. But even more than that,
they're afraid they might make fools of themselves, they're afraid somebody might criticize them, they're afraid they'll be held responsible. It
makes it awfully difficult to help them. If I weren't an ordained minister,
I might give up."

ATTACK ON INFLATION (Natal Mercury, *Durban, English*) . . .
*In a four-point attack on inflation the Minister of Finance, Dr. T. E.
Donges, yesterday announced an increase in the Bank Rate from 5 to 6
per cent.*

The three other measures are:

Restrictions on interest rates payable on deposits with financial institutions are to be lifted immediately.

The Reserve Bank's pattern of interest rates for long-term Government securities is to be progressively increased.

Import control is to be relaxed on certain types of goods on a selective basis.

Other measures are to be taken which cannot be disclosed before the August Budget is introduced.

The Government was determined to ensure the internal and external stability of the rand and to combat inflation effectively, the Minister said.

The decision was described as a "bolt from the blue" in Durban financial circles. . . .

JOHANNESBURG STOCK EXCHANGE

The Johannesburg Stock Exchange was established on November 8, 1887, and is thus one year younger than Johannesburg itself. It is the only stock exchange in South Africa and it operates on the basis of a two-way auction between broker and broker. There are no jobbers and no specialists. This absence of a middleman results in keen prices for the investor.

The Exchange, which has to apply annually to the Treasury for a licence, is controlled by the Stock Exchanges Control Act of 1947 (as amended), and by its own Rules and Regulations—based on those of the Stock Exchange, London, and adapted to South African requirements. These are frequently more stringent than the law itself. . . .

The growth of the Exchange has been parallel with the growth of Johannesburg itself. It has been rehoused four times in 75 years to keep pace with the volume of trading. Its present home, which was officially opened in 1961, is a 13-story building in Hollard Street. The site and the building are owned by the proprietary members of the Exchange. The Trading Hall—an area of 6,000 square feet—rises through three floors.

The Exchange was founded to provide an orderly market place for the transaction of shares in the gold mining and financial companies which followed the discovery and development of the Witwatersrand goldfields. In its early years it was essentially a gold mining market, retaining this character up until the outbreak of World War II, when very few industrial shares were listed. In the 1940's South Africa showed remarkable industrial growth and this activity was reflected in the companies listed:

	MINING COMPANIES	INDUSTRIAL COMPANIES
1932	102	32
1944	116	89
1954	146	404
1964	134	356
1965	131	362

—Official Sources

A GAIN TO A home high above Durban, this time a charming modern house with enormous picture windows giving onto a broad terrace overlooking the twinkling city. The dinner company this night consisted of English-speakers, who had, as they say in the Republic, no time for the Government. In notable contrast to my English-speaking friends on The Bluff, these were Progs and Liberals, and far from having to defend America and ask probing questions about the Nats, I was swamped with admiration for my country and their hopeless frustrations about theirs.

The mood was typical of a certain segment of liberal opinion in South Africa—always found in expensive surroundings, always expressed against a background of Bantu in what is obviously regarded as their proper place, silently and efficiently serving the Whites. It is a perfectly sincere segment of opinion, springing from the warmest of hearts and the best of intentions. It looks to the United States or some other outside miracle to revolutionize South Africa; and it believes that this can be done in a way that will preserve expensive surroundings and the Bantu in their proper place—ennobled by the franchise, possibly, but still in their proper place.

"What is it you want us to do?"—finally, after a wonderful meal, coffee, K.W.V. brandy, a long discussion of how desperate everything was—"Invade the country? Do you really think that would help much?"

"Sometimes we think *anything* would be better than this."

"But, seriously, now, what do you think it would accomplish? Should we put Matanzima in power in Pretoria, or something? Is that what you would like to see for South Africa?"

"W—ell . . . no, not exactly. But we honestly don't see any hope for any change as long as the present Government lasts. And it looks as though that's going to be forever. So there's got to be *something* from outside. If there could be some sort of economic squeeze, maybe—but then, your government needs our gold and your big businessmen have such heavy investments here that that probably couldn't be done, either."

"No, I don't imagine it could. And I really wonder if you'd be happy with it, if it did. What do you suppose would happen in an economic collapse?"

"They wouldn't be able to maintain their damned apartheid then—" with relish.

"And what would the Bantu do if all the Government services and assistance had to be curtailed? Would they be content to just sit around and do nothing, or would they run amok? What would happen to your nice homes and comfortable living then?"

"The Bantu know who their friends are. They know we want to help them. It would be difficult for a while, but I think we'd get along with them all right."

"You really think so. You don't think there would be a wholesale slaughter of the Whites."

"There might be, at first, but it would settle down."

"And then, if you were lucky enough to survive it, you'd still have your nice homes here and your obedient servants—"

"Things would settle down. After all, the country would have to keep on running. They'd need us. We'd still have our position, but it would be on a basis of mutual friendship and trust rather than on one of domination."

"You'd still be right here, living as you do now—"

"I don't see why not."

"You're just arguing to be arguing, surely. You're not serious?"

"W—ell. . . ." And suddenly, melodramatically—"God, what are we to do, then? Are we to suffer forever from this insufferable tyranny and oppression? Is there no hope for us and our children? Are we never to escape the abominations that pass for government in this country? Will there be no end to human indignities, injustice and pain? I ask you, as one who comes from a fat, fortunate land! Does the future hold nothing but further despair for us?"

"Well, now"—interrupted by the silent black presences, who entered, served more coffee, dispensed more brandy, performed their proper duties in their proper place—"it doesn't have to be quite as dreadful as that, does it? Things change, don't they? There can be a modification—"

"Under the Nats? Ho!"

"How many of the Whites feel the way you do, do you think?"

"Obviously"—with some bitterness—"not very many, otherwise the Government would not have been returned with such a majority."

"Isn't a lot of that due to fear of just the outside pressure you talk about—because people are afraid it might happen, so they get behind the Government? Aren't you defeating your own hopes by your position? You certainly aren't going to get many adherents by advocating destruction of the country, are you?"

"We're not advocating destruction of the country! We're advocating reform of the country!"

"But you want us—or somebody outside, anyway—to do it. Not yourselves."

"My God, don't you think we've tried?"

"Of course. Are you still?"

"Yes, we are still! But it's going to take more than efforts from inside. Now, maybe if the South-West Africa case at the World Court goes against us—"

"Do you want it to?"

A sudden somber silence, all around. Finally:

"I don't know . . . I honestly do not know."

"You really want South Africa defeated?"

And again, somberly and slowly:

"I . . . just . . . don't . . . know. . . ."

Later one of the party, small, quiet, pleasant but not particularly noticeable during the evening, drove me home. He had not said much, sitting back and listening carefully while his more flamboyant brethren had their say. Now he spoke with a startling, agonized intensity.

"I know it probably sounds foolish to you, to hear some of us so upset and intense about things here. But we *are* upset, and it doesn't do any good to pretend we're not. Some of my Nat friends, English-speakers, you know, like us, they say to me: 'Why do you take it so hard? What does it matter to the rest of the world what happens way down here on the tip of Africa? Who cares how we treat our Natives, really?'

"But, Mr. Drury, it *does* matter! It *is* important to the rest of the world! We *are* trustees of White civilization in Southern Africa, and the world *is* watching what we do! It *is* important that we do right! We *are* bearing witness for the Christian ethic! *It does matter.*

"I feel very badly about it, really, because I ask myself, what am I doing about it? I talk some, and I vote Prog, and I contribute a little money to charity for the Bantu, and I do what I can. But I don't really take a very strong stand, and I know why, and I'm ashamed of it. There was a period a while back, you know, when protest was very active and there was a group in the country that really wanted to upset the Government by sabotage and violent means. One of my good friends was in it, and it got to the point where he wanted me to get involved in underground activities and finally I had to say, 'Look, man, I've got a wife and three children. I've got a home and a business, I can't jeopardize all that.' And I *couldn't,* you know. But it made me ashamed of myself, that I wasn't brave enough and strong enough to go with him for a cause we both felt was right.

"That's the trouble with most of us," he said bitterly. "Our life is too good. We have it too soft here, we Whites, and when it comes right to the pinch, we aren't really going to give it up, in spite of what you've heard tonight. That dramatic speech about a future of despair—why, hell. Whose despair is it, anyway, the Whites' or the Blacks'? He means it, at the moment, but you ought to see the house he has and the servants he's got. He won't really sacrifice them. He doesn't really want America or anybody else to put pressure on us, any more than I do. He knows we couldn't last ten minutes if the Blacks took over. He's not about to let them. No more are any of us.

"But, Mr. Drury, that still doesn't make it right, does it? We still bear Christian witness, don't we? We still represent Western civilization down here. The world still is watching, and we still are failing."

To this there wasn't much answer save sympathetic sounds and the inadequate wish for good luck when we shook hands on parting. I turned and looked across to City Hall Square as he drove off: Victoria, Jan Smuts and George still stood serene on their pedestals, the flying Pegasus of Suid-Afrikaanse Lugdiens still rode the sky triumphant above the G.P.O.

Such a wonderful country—but so sad.

So sad.

FARM MARKETING

In 1937 the Marketing Act was passed by Parliament. This Act revitalized the co-operative movement.

The two main purposes of the Act are to secure a greater measure of stability in the prices of agricultural products and to reduce price spreads between producers and consumers. The Act provides for the establishment of a National Marketing Council, which acts as a co-ordinating body to advise the Minister of Agricultural Economics and Marketing on all matters pertaining to the Marketing Act system and to investigate and report on all proposed new schemes. Since the promulgation of the Act in 1937 the following Marketing Boards have been established:

Chicory Control Board, Alexandria; Dried Bean Control Board, Pretoria; Lucerne Seed Control Board, Oudtshoorn; Mealie Industry Control Board, Pretoria; Oilseed Control Board, Pretoria; Peach Control Board, Paarl; Potato Board, Pretoria; Rooibos Tea Control Board, Clanwilliam; Tobacco Industry Control Board, Pretoria; Wheat Industry Control Board, Pretoria; Banana Control Board, Pretoria; Citrus Board, Pretoria; Deciduous Fruit Board, Cape Town; Dried Fruit Board, Stellenbosch; Dairy Industry Control Board, Pretoria.

Also, Egg Control Board, Pretoria; Livestock and Meat Industry Control Board, Pretoria; S. A. Wool Board, Pretoria; The Milk Board, Pretoria; Mohair Board, Port Elizabeth.

Some of these Boards have price-fixing powers and full control over the marketing of their respective commodities, while others have only regulatory powers.

The Boards have relieved the co-operatives of the extremely difficult task of marketing their members' products at satisfactory prices, thereby enabling the co-operatives to give their full attention to other functions such as supplying farming requisites, preparing, grading, packaging or storing farm produce, etc.

Without the existence of a strong co-operative movement which provides ready machinery through which control can be exercised, the various Control Boards could hardly function satisfactorily. The future of agricultural co-operation in South Africa seems to be closely linked with the Control Board organization, which has become a permanent feature of the marketing of agricultural products.

—Official Sources

4.

The Transkei

THERE ARE the elaborate tour buses that South African Railways operates down the Natal South Coast, three hundred miles from Durban to the Transkei, filled with conveniences, lush, plush, comfortable, passing through all the nice, clean resorts along the lovely, clean coast. And there is the public bus, old, grubby, rickety-rackety, through the high mountains of the Drakensberg and the swarming, grubby little back-country towns that most tourists never see, and in most cases don't want to see.

On this particular morning, though the day would certainly burn off later into the usual Durban July beach weather, it was cold and smoky when the public bus left for Umtata, capital of the Transkei. The passengers were a mixed bag, a couple of elderly Afrikaans couples; an ample English-speaking grandmother and her blond little granddaughter; two obvious civil servants with briefcases and mimeographed reports that they studied ostentatiously as they rode along; an old-maid English schoolteacher, thin-faced and disapproving; a husky young Afrikaner going back to his farm after a visit to the big city. There were seats for perhaps twenty passengers in the first-class White section in the front of the bus; from behind a door at the back came a murmur of voices full of clicks and gutturals. "Third class," explained the driver, a hard-eyed young Afrikaner. Apparently there was no second.

The bus pulled away from the railroad station, which is over behind the G.P.O. a couple of blocks from the hotel (a barefoot Bantu porter had brought the heavy baggage over, trotting along the street beside the bumper-to-bumper inbound traffic), and we were on our way, skirting the edge of the Indian district where Let-Us-Be-Honest-About-It and the Brothers D. had held forth, past the ramshackle office of the earnest little Bantu editor, on into the fashionable outer White suburbs, climbing on past Kloof where unhappy Alan Paton lives, chugging steadily higher toward beautiful Pietermaritzburg, called "Maritzburg."

Every few miles the bus would halt, disgorge a passenger or two, take on one or two more. At one stop a wide-eyed Indian boy, perhaps seventeen, and his little sister, possibly six, dressed in their very best clothes, each carrying a battered but clean valise, approached the driver and asked an earnest, diffident question. "You want the next bus, to go there!" the driver barked, slammed the door in their faces, pulled away. As he did so the other bus roared up the hill behind us, hesitated a second and then roared on. As we drove off there was a memory to carry along of two absolutely stricken little Indian faces, eyes enormous and mournful, trembling with tears; and a sudden comprehension of the careful weeks of planning, the diligent hoarding of money, the arrangements made with distant welcoming relatives, the panicky thoughts of what now, how to let them know, what to do, disaster, calamity, uncertainty, desolation, the enormous weight of the world pressing down on seventeen and six with no one at all to help, as the imperious buses pulled away.

This was a memory for the visitor to carry along, that is. No one else gave the slightest sign of even having noticed. Such is the insulation between the races that it is entirely likely that no one did.

From Maritzburg we began to head into vast and sparsely grown country, climbing slowly up sensational passes, winding down again, seeing and passing through far reaches of valleys and plains and mountain ranges stretching so far along the horizon that presently there came again that feeling of the immensities of Africa, immensities that we know nothing of, a harsh and impersonal environment that tends to make many of its peoples, if only in self-defense, harsh and impersonal too.

Everywhere on the lower ranges were the round native huts, thousands upon thousands upon thousands. Along the roads were the standard sights of Africa: Natives walking, Natives on bicycles, Natives on horseback; tall Xhosa women in their ochre robes, carrying firewood or baskets or bundles on their heads; quite frequently a youth with a guitar, walking along dreamily all by himself, playing away and singing at the top of his lungs. Now and then we met or passed a car, mostly driven by a White, rarely by a Native. Once in a great while we would see a white farm, a power station, some small sign of white habitation. But mostly there were only the huts, uniform, unchanging, uncountable, endless.

So we passed on through Richmond, Ixopo, Umzimkulu, and at each stop the same scene was played over. The town itself would be sprawling, dirty, unkempt, unattractive; there would be a few white stores, some Bantu stores, an occasional Indian; along the dusty, frequently unpaved streets the Bantu and Indians would be swarming; there would be a big central square where the buses stopped, and in the square, some in tattered European costume, some in native dress, loaded down with bundles and baskets, there would be hundreds and hundreds of Bantu waiting.

Each time as we drove up there would be a surge toward the bus; each time as we prepared to leave, another surge; and all the time, it seemed, the angry shouts of the driver in Afrikaans, the violent, screaming exhortations in Xhosa of the scrawny Bantu, dressed in a dirty white robe, who served as his assistant in charge of third class. And each time there would be the same ugly sound in all the voices, each time the desperate, wavelike surge of the Natives to cram into the few places in the already crowded back of the bus; not only into the back of the bus but sometimes right into the front as well.

And each time, the inescapable thought: what if They can't be stopped —what if the driver and his assistant can't hold Them back—what if the assistant reverts—what if the flimsy, tenuous, patchwork, white man's control suddenly snaps, out here in the back country—what then? And with this, of course, the fear, too, that comes with the chilling realization that out here it really isn't the twentieth century at all, it's No Century— primitive, ignorant, aboriginal, lawless, mindless, merciless, where if you don't forget philosophic niceties and look to your life, you don't survive.

Twice the driver, after violent shouts and physical tussles that included kicking one drunken Native in the chest, had to slam the door, step on the gas and hurtle the bus forward a couple of hundred yards. Each time the screaming mob ran after. The first two or three who reached us were hauled aboard by the Bantu conductor, the doors were hastily slammed again, we roared off. Each time, we made it, and apparently almost always the buses do, for it is rarely or never (even in the English-language press, which is always alert for such things) that one reads of a bus actually being waylaid. But the margin of safety is so narrow, the veneer of sanity so thin, that it is a daily miracle. Drivers are hard-eyed for a reason, evidently; and the bus through the Drakensberg is rather more of an adventure than the comfortable tourists on the South Coast specials ever realize. Or, undoubtedly, ever want to.

We stopped at Kokstad, ate lunch in a dismal little country hotel that still has its six courses, its fish, its savories, its coffee in the lounge, in earnest, rather pathetic memory of Mother Britain so long ago and far away. Then on through the swooping ridges, endless valleys, interminable huts as the afternoon deepened and the distances became even greater as they began to fade into the misty blueness of twilight.

Presently night came, sudden darkness descended. Now the lights were few and far between indeed, an occasional fire in some distant hut on some distant hill; a very occasional car, racing through the blackness on the narrow two-lane highway toward who knows what haven (in the mind of the driver, if it be a white mind, the inevitable worries of all who drive these savage reaches at night: Suppose the engine fails—the gas runs out—a tire blows—); and once or twice, far off, the small glow of some tiny town upon which the Government has decided to confer the blessing of electricity.

Twelve hours after we left Durban we drove into a rambling town of many dark areas broken here and there by a few electric lights, a place of broad paved streets, a few stores, a number of ramshackle houses, a number more substantial; a misty, murky place with coal smoke swirling, bitterly cold in the night of the high plateau: Umtata, capital of the Transkei, South Africa's Noble Experiment—which is noble or not, depending upon whom you listen to, Nat or Native, U.P. or Prog or Liberal.

There are no taxis, and the bus driver, urged on by the old-maid English schoolteacher, kindly drove me to the Savoy Hotel—"The Best in the Country," as its stationery asserts, if by country you take it they mean the Transkei. As I entered the lobby I saw a large, cheerfully excited group of Whites. "I'm cold!" cried a voice that was unmistakably Middle West: "I want a martini!" Somebody's Tours had, of all things, brought more than one American into Umtata this night. But in the loudly good-humored chafing about the cold, the loudly good-humored shouts for drinks, the loudly good-humored griping about accommodations, it was apparent that no unseemly insights had disturbed their journey; nor would, as long as Somebody's Tours and the Government had them in charge. I registered and passed by. It had been a long day, and it was not touring Americans I had come to Umtata to see.

"WHO IS MR. MILLS?"—when the Department of Information officials announced that the first interview in the Transkei had been arranged with Mr. Mills. "I had hoped to see Chief Matanzima—"

"It is quite possible that you will be able to see the Chief Minister, but first you would undoubtedly find it informative to see Mr. Mills."

So here, perforce, was Mr. Mills, behind his desk in the "Bunga," the dignified, white-pillared building that used to house the European-Bantu Joint Council of the Transkeian Territories, and now houses the Legislative Assembly of the semi-independent Transkei.

Outside it was a cold but sunny morning, and here the sun's rays slanted down through half-opened venetian blinds upon Mr. Mills' enormous desk and upon Mr. Mills himself: hefty-bodied, black-haired, well-dressed, with a round face, a little black moustache and none of that easygoing amicability so characteristic of so many in the Republic. Mr. Mills, quite obviously, was a hatchet man: that type of slicked-down, hard-eyed, smooth-talking servant that Pretoria, with an infallible instinct, selects to do the Government's tougher jobs.

Mr. Mills is chief secretary to Chief Kaiser Matanzima, but the one thing he is most anxious to impress upon the visitor is how independent and uncontrolled the Transkei is. Mr. Mills is very positive about this, and it sounds a recurring note through his statistical discourse on the origins and development of this first, and so far only, Bantu government established within the Republic.

"The Transkei," he said briskly, "comprises some 16,500 square miles in extent and has a population of about one and a half million of the approximately three million Xhosa peoples. These are broken down into various dependent tribal groups such as Tembos, Fingoes, and Pondoes. There is a Commissioner-General, Mr. Abrahams, for the Xhosa-speaking peoples and he is the political liaison between the Government of the Republic and the Government of the Transkei. But a substantial area of independent decision and action has been vested by the Republic Government in the Government of the Transkei. This came about because of the past history of the Transkei, which history, I believe, had much influence on the Government's creation of the so-called apartheid, or separate development, policy. It was a logical outgrowth of conditions that had existed here for many years.

"There has been in this area north, or across—'trans,' if you remember your Latin—the Kei River—a long tradition of independence, or semi-independence, going back to the creation of the first Territorial Council in the Transkei proper in 1895. This was composed of chiefs as well as leading white settlers of the Transkei, and gradually over the years—working with the Government of South Africa, but still exercising quite a bit of independent control—this system was extended over an increasingly large area until 1929, when all the various territorial councils in and adjoining the Transkei were consolidated into the Transkeian Territories General Council, known to us as 'the Bunga,' which met here, just as the Transkeian Legislative Assembly does now. You will have seen some of the pictures of the Bunga as you came along the hall."

And so I had, fifty or sixty Bantu and Whites sitting together for their formal portraits down the years, the earnest faces looking out from fifty, sixty, thirty, twenty, even ten, years ago. At least they were trying to work together in harmony, the faces said; at least they did try, until the Government came along and said it could no longer be.

"So," Mr. Mills said. "So: Then the Government decided that the time had come for the Bantu in this area to exercise full independence—"

"Full?"

"Exclusive"—smoothly—"of such matters as police, of course, and foreign relations—full independence, and so in 1962 the Prime Minister, Dr. Verwoerd, announced that self-government would be given to the Transkei. Six departments were created, Finance, Justice, Education, Interior, Roads and Works, and Agriculture and Forestry. Chief Kaiser D. Matanzima was elected Chief Minister—we did not want there to be confusion with the Prime Minister of the Republic, so we chose that title rather than Prime Minister—and also holds the portfolio of Finance.

"The jurisdiction of the Transkei Government runs not only to the Xhosa-speaking Bantu within the borders, but also to another estimated million and a half who are away working in the mines or in industry. These people vote here—which," he interjected with a dry little smile, "seems to infuriate our liberal critics, but which nonetheless gives them a voice in the affairs of their homeland, which to us seems the proper place for them to have a voice, rather than in white areas where they are only temporary residents—and it levies upon these outside Xhosa, as well as the residents, a poll tax. This raises about 3,500,000 rand annually. In addition, the Republic Government, upon granting independence, decided that monies previously voted for the Transkei by the White Parliament should continue to be voted at the same rate, which accounts for about another 10,000,000 rand annually. Last year's budget was 16,000,000 rand, so you can see that the Transkei"—the dry smile returned—"like any modern government, is operating somewhat in the red. This possibly is proof of sophistication."

"How many Whites are still in the Transkeian Government?"

"There are about 2,800 civil servants here, of whom about 382 are still White. Such people as engineers, architects, surveyors, etc., are also White. We have between 5,000 and 6,000 teachers, of whom 64 are White, mostly Afrikaans."

"How about police?"

"There are between 600 and 700 police, 200 of them White. We have a total of ten police for each district of 100,000 Bantu. We have no riots or upheavals, you know, everything is very peaceful here except for what we call 'Bantu faction fights' which occur when one headman's people will try to slaughter another headman's people, and we have to step in and break it up. I believe your newspapers sometimes report 'Riot in South Africa' or 'Native Revolt Quelled,' or something like that. It's ten chappies from one kraal going after ten from another. But I suppose it makes dramatic reading for people who aren't given the full facts on what it's all about. There are rarely any cases of assaults by Blacks upon Whites. One reason for this is the strength of the tribal system, and the influence of the chiefs and headmen who are able to keep the peace."

"And also the white police, of course, and the hand of the Republic Government."

"Oh, yes, that of course is also a factor. . . ."

"Would you say the Transkei experiment is proceeding well?"

"I would say it is proceeding well. The standard of debates in the Assembly is getting better. There is quite a bit of ripeness in the Assembly."

"Isn't there some feeling that by making the Assembly top-heavy with chiefs, Pretoria is simply guaranteeing that there will never be any true independence here, since of course the chiefs are going to go along with the Government that keeps them in power?"

"The Transkei Assembly," he said patiently, "is based on the traditional tribal chiefs, because to take away the traditional leaders would cause great confusion and ill will. This would come, naturally, from the chiefs themselves—the Opposition Party felt the chiefs should sit by themselves in an upper house, but this was rejected because the chiefs disagreed; naturally they object to being taken out of the main stream of politics. And also, there would be great dissatisfaction and unrest in the tribes. They are used to their traditional authorities, you see; they need the reassurance of the old leaders and the old ways. It is the Government's purpose, through separate development, to preserve and strengthen what each race has developed throughout its history. The Bantu themselves would be the first to oppose removal of the chiefs from political influence, I assure you."

"The Government, then, isn't simply preserving feudalism on the backs of the people in order to maintain its own control of the Transkei?"

"Certainly not," he said firmly. "Such a thing would be exactly opposite to the Government's intention. Well, now!"—briskly, picking up the telephone—"you want to see the Chief Minister, and I think, if you are lucky, he may be in. . . . Hello, Chief?"—and he went into Xhosa for a couple of minutes, clicking away busily. "He has just come in," he said with a cordial smile. "Do follow me." And he jumped up and led the way down a short corridor and into a pleasantly decorated, though not elaborate, anteroom where three or four Bantu were standing about.

Another, neatly dressed, self-effacing, came from the inner room. "The Honorable Chief George Matanzima, the Chief Minister's brother," Mr. Mills explained, "Minister of Justice." In a moment the door opened and we were ushered in. Across a modest expanse of carpet, behind a desk that was ample but not quite as big as Mr. Mills', a fact not as significant of their relationship as Mr. Mills perhaps believed, a tall, stately, young-looking Bantu in an expensive dark suit stood up.

"The Right Honorable, the Chief Minister, Chief Kaiser Matanzima," said Mr. Mills with a flourish, and took a seat at the end of the Chief's desk, scarcely four feet from him, where he sat throughout our brief interview with eyes intent and fingers drumming.

Under such circumstances, which could not very well have been avoided, and in all probability would have produced no other result in any case, the Chief Minister and his visitor did not exchange any profound thoughts about the Transkei. Yet the interview was not wasted, for there remains a vivid impression of shrewdness, calculation, craft, complexity which could in the long run indicate an independence considerably greater than the Government would like.

Indeed, there have already been signs of it, for Matanzima has pursued what appears to be an outwardly erratic but perhaps carefully planned policy of alternating good behavior with naughty which has already produced a profound uneasiness in Pretoria. Every so often the pattern of his dutiful pro-Government speeches has been interrupted by some startling demand for complete independence or some uncomfortable assertion that all white men must speedily leave the Transkei. And quite abruptly a year ago he announced that thereafter education would not be conducted in Xhosa, as the Government wanted, but in English. And although there was much alarm and scurrying about in Pretoria, he made it stick.

So I was not quite so prepared as some of his fellow-Bantu and his liberal White critics to call him stooge; and after our interview, even less so.

He rose and smiled and shook hands with a rather remote but easy cordiality, asked me to sit down, turned upon me eyes that were deliberately blank but could not entirely hide a tiny amusement at the sound of Mr. Mills' fingers going tap-tap-tap. He asked what I was there for, I told him, he said it was nice to have me. He spoke in the heavily-accented, guttural English of his legal education. We talked a little about the physical aspects of the Transkei, he said it had reasonably good soil. "Not the best in the country, as I've heard in Pretoria?" "No, not the best, but in spots it is not too bad." Mr. Mills went tap-tap-tap.

"How do you feel the Transkei experiment is progressing, Chief? Do you think you are making real advances toward self-government here?"

He gave me a quick glance, the blank look became a little more animated. Mr. Mills made a tiny hunch forward, eyes intent, fingers at it.

"We are concentrating very much on development, agricultural, financial, industrial, all kinds," Matanzima said. "Basically, it is our financial development that will decide the success of independence."

"When you are completely independent—as you have said you want to be—will that mean that you will want to control your own foreign affairs and your own foreign policy?"

Tap-tap-tap went Mr. Mills.

Another quick glance, a pause. Then, rapidly:

"When we are independent, I cannot say what we may do at that time. I may not even be Prime Minister!"

Quick, deprecating, of-course-you're-joking laughter from Mr. Mills. A sudden quite genuine burst of laughter from the Chief Minister.

"I hope the Ciskei will join us," he said, suddenly serious. "You know, the area south of the Kei River. They have nine magisterial districts to our twenty-six. Actually," he said to Mr. Mills, "some of them are coming up tomorrow to discuss it with me; we seem to be making headway, did I tell you?"

"Oh?" said Mr. Mills. "No, you didn't." Tap-tap-tap went the fingers.

"I don't know yet what arrangements will be worked out on that," Matanzima said, "but we desire it very much."

"How are your relations with the Government of the Republic?"

"Oh, very good," he said. "Oh, very good. . . . Our problem, you see, is national development. The country was without a single industry when we took over [Mr. Mills' eyes flickered slightly, whether at the fact or the phrase was not clear], but since we took over we have begun developing industries. The Government is aiding us through a Xhosa Development Corporation similar to the Industrial Development Corporation in the Republic. We are getting into textiles, furniture, meat processing. We are starting a mealie-bags industry, rope, and all that. We are also considering a tea and coffee industry. We are moving forward. It is necessary if we are to have a sound financial basis for our independence."

"And you think your relations with the Government will continue to be good?"

"Oh, yes!" he said with emphasis, and behind the blank eyes as he stood up and held out his hand again, the tiny amusement flickered. "Very, very, *very* good!"

And he laughed and I laughed and Mr. Mills laughed and everybody parted with great cordiality. And I went away thinking that tall Chief Matanzima has the Government over a barrel, and that Mr. Mills knows it and doesn't know what is going to happen next; a hunch confirmed that very evening when the S.A.B.C. carried the news that the Chief, "in a surprise move apparently unexpected in Pretoria," had shifted his brother George from his rather innocuous post of Minister of Justice to the not so innocuous post of Minister of Education.

"EMERGENCY" IN TRANSKEI CONTINUES (Rand Daily Mail, English) . . . *No end to the Transkei's five-and-a-half-year-old "State of Emergency" is in sight.*

This became clear in the Transkei Legislative Assembly debate—which ended yesterday—on Proclamation 400 of 1960.

The Assembly adopted, by 48–34 votes, a proposal by a Government M.P., Mr. E. H. Sihele, calling for the retention of the measure to safeguard the internal security and peaceful administration of the Transkei.

It was a counter move to the Opposition plea for the Proclamation's repeal.

During the debate, the Minister of Justice, Chief G. M. M. Matanzima, revealed that the South African Police favoured its retention.

Mr. O. O. Mpondo, the Opposition member who proposed the suspension, replying to the debate yesterday, said it was obvious the South African Government wanted to maintain the Proclamation to stifle opposition to separate development "so that the outside world will be bamboozled into believing all is well in the Transkei."

SO, PROC. 400 SURVIVED YET AGAIN (Editorial, Umthunywa, Umtata, Bantu) . . . *Another session of the Transkei Legislative Assembly has come to an end. And for the Opposition Democratic Party members, this was one of three successive legislative sessions in which they have suffered defeat in their determined fight for the repeal of the so-called Transkei emergency regulations—Proclamation 400 of 1960.*

Once again, the ruling party has turned a deaf ear to Opposition charges that, in effect, the legislation has:

Suspended the rule of law; rendered the public defenceless against a "wide range of arbitrary powers" given the chiefs; subjected the people to constant fear of arrests and . . . periods of detention in the course of which the innocent are denied opportunity to seek recourse in the courts of law; restricted the Opposition party members from communicating freely with the electorate.

THE FURNITURE FACTORY and the weaving plant are out a little from Umtata, set in the pleasantly rolling hills of the high plateau, framed against gentle fields and the far backdrop of the hazy blue mountains. It is expansive country, similar in some respects to the American West, save that everywhere the eye falls, the little white dots of the native huts march the landscape. There is the problem, and here in these two small factories is the start of the Government's attempt at an answer—a start, and an attempt, that I was to hear condemned scornfully in many places in the Republic and elsewhere, but a beginning, nonetheless. And a genuine one, at least as far as the Whites directly in charge are concerned.

There were two of these to show the visitor around this day, the lanky, weather-beaten Afrikaner at the furniture factory, and the buxom German Brünhilde who has found her immigrant's niche directing the operations of the weaving plant. Both were hard-working, good-natured, patient, dedicated. Both were quite obviously convinced of the value of what they were doing, and both were genuinely friendly toward the people they worked with.

The Afrikaner looked thoughtfully about the big warehouse piled high with cabinets, chairs, chests, tables. There were three or four other white men on the floor, but most of the workers were Bantu, perhaps sixty sawing, cutting, hammering, finishing. They were shouting good-naturedly to one another above the din of the machinery: no one stood over them with whips, they were not chained to their benches, they didn't have to work if they didn't want to. But they were working, and they were enjoying it. They looked pleased and proud of themselves. The critics may sneer, but there are so many more serious things to worry about in the Republic that it seems picayune to yap at the integrity of this effort, tiny though it is. It is being honestly done, and it is moving forward.

"The Bantu are very pleasant to work with," the Afrikaner said. "We have no trouble here. They are very happy people, most of them. Quite anxious to learn, eager to be instructed. It does take them five or six times longer, on the average, than it does a European to learn a job, and then in most cases it must be kept quite simple for them. But, after all" —and he said it matter-of-factly, without the slightest air of condescension—"it is a different culture, theirs, and it is unusual for them. It is natural that they should not adapt to our ways rapidly: it takes time. Once they get into the routine of a job, they stick with it pretty well. They are pretty reliable people. I enjoy working with them. . . .

"Most of the furniture made here is designed for use in Government departments. But we hope in time, of course, that this will be expanded into a real industry, and that other factories will be established to supply not only the Government but private commercial outlets as well. That way, the Transkei will eventually have an economic foundation on which to exist. We hope to do the same thing with other trades, too, but it is a slow process, you understand."

He smiled patiently, an artisan not too much concerned with politics but, as always in the Republic, unable to escape them.

"We are trying, whatever the critics say. I think the human material we have to work with is good, and we know from our experience here that the Bantu can be trained in productive industry. It will be a long time before he has the administrative skills to go with it, but we can supply those for a while longer, until he is ready. At least we are providing opportunity and beginning to create a functioning economy for him. This small factory isn't much to look at, but it is a beginning."

So, too, is the linen mill, although there the enthusiasm on the part of the employees was not quite so apparent. Fifty or sixty sullen little Bantu girls were sitting at their looms and sewing machines, and most of them looked resentful and bored to death. But here, too, nobody was forcing them to work, and the end products of their labor, the rugs and blankets and shawls and yard goods, were colorful, attractive and well done; so perhaps appearances were deceptive. They, too, may have been getting some pride and satisfaction out of their work, but it was apparent that it was rather more of an uphill struggle with them than it was with the men. Traditionally their duty is in the fields and the huts, and the concept of regular work at a regular job is even more foreign to them than it is to their menfolk, whose traditional role is to lie about the kraals, drink Kaffir beer, and talk.

Brünhilde, buxom, exclamatory, disorganized, amiable, blond hair flying in every direction and keen blue eyes snapping, as big as a house and possessing the heart to go with it, opened the door with a challenge.

"What kind of visitor are you?" she demanded with a good-natured skepticism, leading the way to her cluttered little office. "We have visitors from America, you know, mostly they"—she wrinkled her nose, gestured ironically with her hands—"you know, they say bad things about South Africa, they make fun. But maybe you're nice—maybe. Anyway, come in, come in. I show you what we have, you judge, go write what you like. I don't care! The Government can worry about that, I just work, I just try to get these girls to work.

"They make 3.50 rand a week (about $5.00) up to 6 rand ($8.40) a week, which is a lot for them. But it is hard"—she pushed one of the wilder strands of hair back with a humorously exasperated gesture—"to get them to stay at the job. They don't want to work very long, you know, then they want to go back to the kraal and make babies. My main trouble is babies, babies! There are eight babies inside, out there. I let them come back with one baby, I let them come back with two babies, but three babies I say, no, they must stay home and take care of their babies. And the way they act here! I try to give them white bread to eat, and, Gott, you know? They reach inside and tear out the insides to eat and throw the crusts all over the floor. And the restroom—the restroom, my Gott, it's more trouble for me to keep the restroom clean than it is to keep this entire floor clean. What they do on the floor, everywhere— whoof! You can go to their huts and eat off the floor, absolutely clean, but here—my Gott, what a mess!

"But," she said, and shrugged, "if they're happy—what do I care? They're good girls, they work hard when they understand it, it's getting better all the time, they're learning. In a while it won't be so bad. We are beginning to find more markets for our goods, it will grow. I'm not worried. It takes time."

She hit me on the arm and grinned.

"You go away and write nice things," she ordered. "You say we try to help."

"I will. You are."

N OW AND AGAIN as we walked the streets of Umtata from appointment to appointment, a big black car would slowly pass, a little official flag on its fender, from its windows three or four solemn black faces peering. These cars never seemed to be going much of anywhere, and their occupants did not appear to have much of anything to do.

"Who is that?" I would ask my Department of Information guide, and he would say:

"Oh, that's Mr. Madikizela, Minister of Agriculture and Forestry. . . ." Or, "That's Mr. M. S. Mvusi, Minister of Roads and Works. . . ." Or, "That's Chief Moshesh, Minister of Interior. . . .

"They don't do much, you know. Only the two Matanzimas, Chief Kaiser and Chief George, actually do very much. Mostly the white deputy ministers do it all."

The Deputy Minister of Agriculture and Forestry was a blond young Afrikaner, slim and charming, with a lopsided smile and an amiable manner. His grasp of his department was extensive, his worries about what he called "political instigation" never far from the surface.

"There has been an agricultural rehabilitation scheme under way in the Transkei since the 1950's," he said, "concentrating mainly on establishing good conservation practices in the Bantu areas. The Government issued a proclamation to start it off which gives us the legal machinery to do whatever we think has to be done. But"—he smiled, patiently and with some irony—"there is quite a lot of opposition from the Bantu against what we regard as necessary betterment, you know, and there are some things we consider advisable that we have decided it was better not to enforce.

"This was particularly true, at first, with regard to cattle, and there we did enforce what we thought best, because we absolutely had to. We were confronted with a situation in which the Bantu had no concept of herd selection and improvement, no idea of conservation or good grazing practices. His entire economy, and his entire social structure, rested on how many cattle he owned. Cattle were the medium of exchange—still are, in fact, in many areas—and his whole life was devoted to acquiring more, and to finding forage for them. They simply went over these valleys and hills like locusts, as they have done for the better part of a hundred years. When one grazing area played out, they simply moved on to the next; they never made any attempt to cultivate or replant, and they never made any attempt to cull out unhealthy animals. They simply devoured the land and kept all the cattle, no matter how poor. It's a miracle they were able to keep going as long as they did. I suppose if they hadn't killed each other off in periodic battles, they never would have.

"We," he said, and again the smile became slightly ironic, "decided we must step in and correct all this. The first step was to enforce strictly provisions to control the health of herds, and the second was to limit the amount of grazing land a man might use, and try to induce him to care for it and improve it instead of moving on whenever he felt like it.

"At first there was quite a bit of opposition, quite a bit of political instigation, but the Bantu could grasp the logic in it after a while, so presently it became generally accepted that there should be a culling process for cattle each year, to improve the herds and to hold them down to a level the land could support. Our cattle population in the Transkei now is somewhat above a million and a half, plus around 100,000 horses and some 3,500,000 head of small stock, mainly wool sheep. This we can handle in the present state of development of land in the Transkei.

"We also had some political instigation and problems when we inaugurated a program to move many of the Bantu to more centrally grouped residential areas. We group them in villages because it is simply impossible to get health and educational services to them when they are scattered all over the countryside. Also, it enables us to establish a commonage for grazing for each newly constituted village, which helps the stock and reduces friction among their owners. The Zulus, of course, are very much against grouping, they've always been very independent, and the Tembos also, and we haven't made many attempts to enforce it, with them. But the Pondos and the Xhosa generally are more accustomed to it, and it isn't proving too difficult gradually to bring them together in this fashion.

"It's true all this has cost money, but the Government has always tried to compensate those who had to be moved, defrayed the costs of their former homes, except for the very oldest native huts. We have also been able to improve their water supplies, once we have got them grouped together."

He looked thoughtfully at the enormous map of the Transkei on his wall and nodded his head with some satisfaction.

"All the Bantu seem to agree eventually that these betterment schemes are good for them, although it has taken a little while to spread the idea. There was some little political instigation against that, too. Actually, you know"—he leaned forward with an earnestly friendly smile—"it is very difficult to get them to take an active part in the development of their own country. It's their land, so our attitude at one point was, 'It's yours, we'll provide machinery and materials, but you've got to help.' That didn't work so very, very well indeed. In fact, a great many of the able-bodied men promptly went away to the labor market, to the Rand and to Cape Town, and so on. This meant that only the old women and the children were left. At that point"—he smiled dryly—"as one very well expects they knew, 'self-help' in terms of old women and children could very easily be pictured as 'slave labor' by our friends up north. So we decided we couldn't get caught in that trap. So we then established Bantu authorities and said we would subsidize work up to 100 per cent in some cases, and that brought a lot of them home, and that is generally how improvements have been brought about in the Transkei.

"Some Bantu authorities have not been too efficient"—again the wry smile—"the White officials have done the work, the Bantu have signed the checks. But we've made fairly great progress, on the whole, in a good many areas. . . .

"Our main problem has been political instigation. Temboland is virtually untouched, the Paramount Chief won't allow it—he's very much leftist. One of his chief councillors was recently convicted of an attempt to murder Matanzima, you know. . . .

"We're experimenting with new crops all the time, cotton, castor bean, coffee, sugar. We're concentrating on tea at the moment. The Government hopes to establish a few thousand acres of tea, then put them in Bantu hands. We're starting a jute experiment and hope to have a big factory in the near future, which we hope will make us independent of India and Pakistan. Sanctions and boycotts have been very stimulating to us, you know. Sometimes it does a country good to be forced to get busy and look to its own sufficiency. . . .

"There has been no decline in the progress of development since establishment of the Transkei. Agriculture in general is very good, because we have a very good and reliable rainfall, a very wide range of climate, quite a lot of good soil. Great diversification is possible, a very great potential capable of feeding the present population and many more besides. It doesn't do it at present, but the potential is there.

"Our main problem right now," he said with a humorous frown, "is political. . . ."

ECONOMIC NEEDS OF TRANSKEI (Cape Argus, *English*) . . . *A rapid increase in population but a more or less stagnant productivity is the basic economic problem confronting the Transkei, according to a detailed report published in the August issue of the Africa Institute bulletin after a visit to the Transkei by a five-man team from the institute.*

The report says that given the prevailing pattern of land use, the territory is unable to sustain a much larger population than at present.

For this reason large numbers of males and females are leaving the Transkei to seek employment in the Republic.

Dr. G. M. E. Leistner, head of the institute's economics department, estimates that about 260,000 Transkeians are in employment in the Republic at any given time.

"NO SENSATIONS HERE, we're just the nuts and bolts of the Transkei," said the Deputy Minister of the Interior (square face, little moustache, pleasant smile, perfect representative of that civil-service type one sees so often in Pretoria—the littler lions of the north). "Afraid you won't find much here. We keep the population records, births, deaths, marriages, land transfers, voters' register, social benefits, old-age, blind and survivors' benefits. We have 60,000 on the rolls getting assistance. We have about 918,000 voters, all told, in and out of the Transkei; we see that they're notified, registered, get absentee ballots if they need them. We have twenty-seven land districts, only seven of which have been surveyed, and that fifty years ago. We're going to survey the whole lot in the next couple of years; then we'll have all the land in the Transkei registered.

"We do quite a bit in the labor field, have a labor bureau that keeps a register of migratory labor to and from the Republic: employers in the Republic notify us when jobs are available, we send out word through the headmen, we try to keep the flow going back and forth according to the jobs that are available.

"We have seven European officials here in headquarters, thirty-three Bantu, and the Bantu are working out pretty well. No sensations here, just the bits and pieces, just the bits and pieces."

CRITICISM IN TRANSKEI "FORBIDDEN" (Cape Argus, *English*)
. . . *According to Mr. W. Vause Raw, M.P. for Durban Point, before
any White person can obtain a permit to visit the Transkei territory he
must first agree to abide by a condition he will not criticise the Government or any of its officials.*

*Speaking in the censure debate in the Assembly today, Mr. Raw said
it proved the Government was moving towards forbidding legitimate criticism.*

*He said a White who had recently wished to visit the Transkei applied
for a permit from the magistrate's office at Bizana. The reply authorised
the person's entry provided he agreed to behave in a dignified manner in
dealings with all Bantu and did not criticise the Government or any of its
officials. . . .*

TRANSKEI CHIEF SLATES UN STATEMENT (Scope, *Government*)
. . . *Compared with the political and administrational chaos at present
reigning in most of the Afro-Asian states which attacked South Africa,
the Transkei was an Utopia, the Acting Chief Minister of the Transkei,
Chief George Matanzima, said last week.*

*"We implore our fellow-black men of Africa to leave us in peace, to
achieve our own salvation in the land of our heritage. We really do not
need their advice and cannot tolerate their interference in our domestic
affairs."*

*Chief George Matanzima, who is Minister of Education, said that the
statement issued by the United Nations' Special Committee on the Policies of Apartheid of the South African Government, as reported in the
Press, could not go unchallenged by the Transkei Government since it
gave an "entirely warped" impression of the political and administrational
setup in the territory.*

*Chief George said the UN statement said inter alia that the Transkei
experiment was under "strict control by the Republic's Government."*

*In the first instance there was no such thing as an "experiment." The
Transkei was "a self-governing state, developing to total stable and en-
during independence. It is in full control of the departments of state
handed over to it by the Republican Government.*

*"We govern our country and our people without interference from
the Republican Government, our parent government—who is assisting
us in every respect to become a well-organized country—bound to exploit its potential for the benefit of our own people.*

"The Afro-Asian bloc and other advisers are out of touch with the realities of political developments in the Transkei," he said.

B IG EARS, a thin, craggy face, a nice smile, a patient, kindly manner— the Deputy Minister of Roads and Works, whose department handles all roads, official buildings, schools, transport in the Transkei.

"Nine hundred and ninety miles of main paved roads," he said thoughtfully, "forty-eight hundred miles of secondary district roads, over one thousand miles of forestry roads, no one knows quite how many tribal trails—bridle paths, foot trails, and the like.

"For our roads we have five major construction units, four large graveling units and some small construction gangs. The major units are equipped with 33,000-pound bulldozers and are run entirely by Bantu, under the supervision of Bantu overseers, though our senior road foremen are still White. We have a very large workshop, where the Bantu do their own repair work under the supervision of white mechanics.

"We are doing our best," he said seriously, "to train a large number of Bantu mechanics, but it is proving somewhat difficult. The problem is to get the Bantu to do work using their hands. In the kraals, you know, it's women who do the manual labor, that's beneath the dignity of the men. So they come to us and they all want to get into white-collar jobs. We want to give them five-year mechanics' training on the same basis as white boys in the Republic, but those we find who are capable don't want that kind of training. Bantu education is generally good, but their technical education is not too good—the facilities are there, but the great difficulty is in getting these chappies to make use of them.

"I've had a lot of talks with them"—a patient smile—"and I've told them, Look, this is a mechanical age, you won't get anywhere unless you take training. I don't think they believe me. We're moving ahead a bit, but we're not getting the quality we want, or the quantity either.

"Public works are going better. We're developing bricklayers, carpenters, trying to build up a corps of people who are really well qualified. We have no Bantu architects, as yet, but we're training draftsmen, and they're doing very well, taking to it like ducks to water, so it won't be long before we develop some qualified architects. Every building we put up is a chance for job training, and we're getting more applicants all the time.

"As for our public transport, there we run into the mechanical problem again. Our transport drivers are thoroughly trained, but the Bantu are careless, reckless, they have absolutely no consideration for any piece of machinery. We try to say, Look, this is your equipment—owned by your Government—paid for by your taxes—you must look after it like your cows or your kraal or other personal property. But"—a shrug and again that patient smile—"it doesn't always work. I had one Bantu who took a 33,000-pound bulldozer down the road thirty miles, driving as fast as he could go, to see his girl friend—it was a complete write-off. Another decided recently to take his wife to Durban for the weekend in a Government truck. There was an accident—it was a write-off.

"But they'll learn, after a while. We must be patient. Most of them don't do things maliciously; they drink too much, or they don't think, and something happens. They'll learn. . . .

"As you know, we Whites are trying to work ourselves out of our jobs here, so in this department we have forty-seven Whites supervising some four thousand Bantu in all types of jobs from laborers to clerks. On the whole, we find the Bantu work reasonably well, except for occasional lapses. They work well for a time, then they suddenly lose interest— they'll work for a year at something and then apparently forget it for a couple of days, and then you have to train them all over again. It's as though they never knew it, they seem to black out. I can't understand it.

"One thing they do have," he said soberly, "is a disconcerting tendency to exploit their own people. You'll find job bosses collecting from their fellow-Bantu, charging them to get a job, charging them to keep it, taking a cut of their wages under threat of firing them—things you find in other societies, I grant you, but not exactly desirable. Until they learn more integrity, these things will occur, there'll be injustices and losses. But they'll learn, after a while." He smiled again that tolerant, kindly, perfectly genuine smile. "We must be patient."

"**P**RETORIA SENT ME down to organize the civil service," the commissioner said in a satisfied tone, "and I must say we are making good progress so far. We have our problems, what organization doesn't, particularly starting from scratch. But on the whole, it is moving well."

He was one of the dark Afrikaners, young, compact, small moustache, quick smile, quick humor; sounding genuinely dedicated to his job, fascinated and pleased with the way the Bantu were fitting into the civil-service pattern. He was responsible, he said, to a three-man Civil Service Commission, all Bantu.

"We are empowered to make recommendations, but only recommendations, to the Cabinet. However, if the Cabinet rejects our recommendations they must state their reasons in a formal report to Parliament— the Transkeian Parliament." He chuckled. "That inhibits too much interference with what we want to do. . . .

"With the exception of the technical and professional white personnel that I brought down with me, you see, we really did start from scratch when the Transkei was given independence in 1962. And in the main we have been very successful.

"The first thing we did was require that all our employees have at least their 'Matric'—matriculation from ten years of schooling; that would correspond, I believe, to your junior high. That means that now all of our approximately 2,800 permanent posts in the Transkei are filled with matriculants. In addition to these we have upward of 5,000 clerks, and we are constantly upgrading them, too. Originally we had 463 Whites on the staff. Our saying is that we are here to work ourselves out of our jobs, and already nearly a hundred have been sent back. Replacement of professional and technical Whites is not taking so long, but replacement of administrative personnel seems to take longer. We are still top-heavy with Whites on the administrative side.

"However"—he smiled like a pleased child with a toy—"we are working on that, too, and we are getting quite a response because the Transkeians seem to be fascinated with administration. I've established a school for the higher supervisory levels and it's very successful, partly, I think, because I don't handle it like a classroom, but rather like an informal conference around a table. That appeals to them right off, it is reminiscent of tribal councils, I suppose, and it seems to put them at ease.

"So what I do, basically, is guide the discussion rather than lecture, proceeding from a mimeographed syllabus which is given to all participants. For example"—he riffled through the many papers on his desk, pulled out a couple—"it starts off with some general rules, elemental to you and me, maybe, but especially helpful here, because to them many of these are new concepts:

" '1. Be on time. 2. Attend regularly. 3. Take an active part in the discussions from the start. 4. Discuss—don't argue. 5. Give the group the benefit of your experience and viewpoint. 6. Respect the opinions of others. 7. Avoid private conversation' "—he smiled—" '8. Express opinions briefly. 9. Do not get angry if others disagree with you. Try to understand the other person's point of view. 10. Be critical, analytical and constructive. 11. Study the lectures carefully.'

"As I say, these may sound elemental, but they are sound, and they are helpful. And I find the participants really try to follow them. They are eager to learn.

"We will have, for instance, a session on interviewing an applicant for a job. One Bantu will pretend to be the applicant, another will be the supervisor who is doing the interviewing. The rest will observe and make notes. Then we have a criticism period at the end, and I can tell you there are no holds barred! They tell me they find it very helpful, and you can tell that they do. We have classes in such things as how to give orders, how to deal with grievances. . . .

"The thing they enjoy most? I would say without a doubt it is the lecture on human emotions. I try to put over a few home-truths here"— he referred again to his syllabus—"it's a long syllabus, but it concludes like this:

" *'Give the other person an opportunity to save face.* Most people realize that they make mistakes and usually know what the mistakes are. To point out mistakes, therefore, only serves to make the other person feel small and unimportant, and, when this happens, we cannot expect to get along well with him. Rather give him an opportunity to save face by refraining from comment or by accepting his explanation.

" *'Cultivate the habit of tolerance.* Tolerance is the ability to appreciate the other person, whether or not his language, his religion or his political views are the same as one's own.

" *'Never try openly to reform others.* No one likes to feel that he needs to be reformed, or that someone else is trying to correct his imperfections. Never argue with people who are emotionally disturbed. They cannot see reason under such circumstances.

" *'Check first impressions.* First impressions are often highly inaccurate. It is possible to take a violent dislike to a person at the very first meeting, for no very good reason—perhaps merely because the shape of his face recalls vague memories of someone else whom we had cause to dislike. Rather look for and find in every person some good point that can form the basis for a liking.

" *'Think more of giving than of getting.* One is more successful in social relationships when one thinks of what one can contribute toward the satisfaction of the needs of others, rather than of what one can get from them. Lasting friendships are built on this foundation.

" *'The supervisor's role.* Human beings react with greater sensitivity to changes in psychological atmosphere, to intentions, implications and suggestions, than they do to anything in their physical environment. By always remembering this fact and by seriously trying out the suggestions given above, the supervisor can make his dealings and contacts with his subordinates and others both effective and satisfying.' "

He laid down the paper and stared out for a moment at the cold, bright morning of Umtata.

"Now, mind you, I'm not claiming that all the Bantu follow these rules—or all Whites, either, you know—not by a long shot. But a good many do and the number is increasing. They like this human-relations course particularly, because basically it tells them that they must respect others, they mustn't pick out a man for public condemnation, every man has his place in the sun, every man has his need for approval and self-respect, and they must respect him.

"It has been very successful, so far. Just the other day one of our Bantu decided he didn't want to stay in the civil service so he went to work for one of our banks here. After a week he complained that six or seven people were giving him orders, that the bank organization was no good and should be changed. The bank manager said to me, 'Man, what are you teaching these boys of yours, anyway?' I said, 'He's right, you'd better change your organization.' It made him mad at first, but after he'd thought it over he agreed, and they made some changes. . . .

"As for our overall operation, we're attempting to establish once and for all, right now in the beginning, an ethical standard for the civil service that will be strong enough to survive when the Whites leave. We are very strict with misconduct of any kind, because we believe we must nip it in the bud right now if we are to lay a permanent foundation. If a man misappropriates funds, for instance, we sack him at once, without appeal; that serves as a lesson to everyone. We are severe on purpose, because our commissioners feel the time for laying the foundation is now. . . .

"I tell you," he said, and he said it with a genuine enthusiasm, "this is a terrific challenge. Bit by bit, we're turning it over to them. My Bantu assistant, for instance, has been trained now to the point where he can take over some of these courses. He still finds moments and points at which he doesn't know the answers, and he comes to me. And then's when I have to give him the answers, too, because the Bantu must have complete confidence in your ability and knowledge, otherwise you lose him. If you hesitate or indicate that you don't know the answer, he's gone, he loses confidence at once. By the same token, you must never promise him something and then not act, because then it's weakness on your part. You must follow up immediately. But if you do that, he's with you and you can gradually lead him in the right direction. . . .

"Will the Transkei work? Man, I maintain it's got to work! We've spent a lot of time and money on this experiment. It's got to work. . . .

"But," he said, and for the first time his sunny enthusiasm flagged a little, he frowned and did not look quite so confident, "I'm worried, I'll tell you frankly I am. They're terrifically perturbed about the idea that you might leave them; they are terribly afraid to take responsibility. I submit a report to my commission members, I address them by their titles and give them full dignity, and they say, 'Yes, Baas, we agree, that's right, it should be done as you say.' I say, 'Now, look, you're the commission, you have the authority, you've got to decide.' But they're afraid to, you know? They want you to do it. They're afraid they'll do something wrong. They don't want you to leave them. . . ."

13 AFRICANS RUN STORES IN TRANSKEI (Rand Daily Mail, *English*) . . . *Umtata—Thirteen Transkeians had completed satisfactory training and were now employed as managers of trading stations, the*

Minister of the Interior, Chief J. Moshesh, told the Legislative Assembly yesterday.

Chief Moshesh said five more Africans were being trained at the Bantu Investment Corporation's only training centre. Four other centres were being built in the Transkei.

There were 16 approved applications on the waiting list and another 43 Africans were waiting to be interviewed.

Training would be stepped up to keep pace with the number of trading stations taken over. Trainees were generally drawn from Africans who had, or were now gaining, trading experience in privately owned stations.

The Minister said that of the 38 stations so far controlled by the Investment Corporation, 13 were being managed by Africans. All could purchase the stations as soon as they had proved themselves.

Firm recommendations in respect of four very satisfactory African managers were at present being considered.

Whites still managed 25 trading stations on a temporary basis. As soon as an African was available to take over any one of them, the White would be moved to a new station, where his services might be required.

"THE TRANSKEI!" exclaimed the angry old English-speaker, son of early settlers, resident of the territory all his life, banker, farmer, leading citizen facing the end of the white rule he has always helped so vigorously to maintain. "The Transkei! It's like putting a three-year-old child in to run the high school! These people are unable to do anything, they can't make decisions, they don't want to work, they never have wanted to work! I've lived with them all my life, I'm personal friends to them, I meet Kaiser Matanzima on the street now and we stop and talk and he tells me his troubles. Kaiser's a good boy, but he's no more a Prime Minister than the man in the moon. And as for that so-called Legislative Assembly Pretoria's set up! All it's doing is rivet the chiefs on the backs of the people so they'll never get up.

"I used to serve with them in the old Bunga, our old Territorial Council. We knew how to handle them in those days, we all got along together, Whites and Blacks together for the Transkei. We didn't call them 'bloody niggers' the way that Transvaal bunch does now! We knew the African's faults and his weaknesses, but we respected him as a human being. We knew how to handle him, we didn't put him in a compartment, give him a government to toy around with, and call it 'The Transkei!'

"This Pretoria gang," he said bitterly, "have compartmentalized the whole country. They've split Whites from Blacks, Afrikaans from English-speaking, next it will be Afrikaners and English from the Jews, then it will be Afrikaners from English from Jews from foreigners! Next thing they'll be wanting to put the Jews in a Jewistan and then it'll be the English in an Englishstan!

"They take the little children in the schools and set up separate Afrikaans and English schools for them, so that the children of this coming generation can't know each other and understand each other as children, when it counts the most for their future life together. When a man or a race makes little children hate each other, then I say they deserve to perish.

"We live on hatred! That's what they've done to the country, because they're a tribe themselves. Afrikaner tribalism is what we suffer from! It's destroying the country!"

TRY TO SELL TO AFRICANS FIRST, TRANSKEI WHITES TOLD
(Daily Dispatch, *East London, English*) . . . *Whites and Coloureds who own property and trading stores in Transkei areas which have been earmarked for African occupation must try and sell their property to Africans first, before asking the State to buy it, the Minister of Bantu Administration and Development, Mr. M. C. Botha, said in a statement issued in Pretoria last night.*

The Minister's statement read: "As a result of the recent reservation of areas in towns in the Transkei for occupation and ownership by Bantu, owners of immovable property in such areas are now approaching the Government of the Republic to take over their properties.

"In view of these requests, it is considered advisable to explain the position and procedure applying to Whites, as well as Coloureds, who own immovable property in reserved towns or portions of towns.

"It is clear from Section B of the 1964 White Paper, that when applications in respect of properties in reserved areas are considered, the same basis and principles will apply as those laid down for trading sections in the Bantu areas and set forth in Section A of the White Paper.

"An Adjustment Committee appointed by the Minister has been giving its attention for some time now to cases where trading stations in the Bantu areas of the Transkei are offered for sale to the State.

"There are so many offers, however, that priority can be given only to urgent cases. . . ."

"I'M GLAD THAT we set up an appointment with Mr. Guzana for you," the information officer said. "It is best that you get both sides, I think." But they hadn't, of course, until I asked for it.

Mr. Guzana, whose first name is Knowledge, is the leader of the Democratic Party of the Transkei, which is the opposition to Kaiser Matanzima. He is a very likable member of the Fingo tribe of the Ciskei, well dressed, pleasant, quiet, looking younger than his fifty years, possessed of a beautiful command of the English language. He received his bachelor's degree in 1939 at the Bantu college of Fort Hare, where his major subjects were English and history. He also took a number of courses in constitutional law and politics, psychology, the Xhosa language and geography. After teaching for fourteen years in Bantu schools he decided to become an attorney and notary, went back to school, got his degree, practiced law in the Cape Province until the establishment of the Transkei, when he came to Umtata to open a law office and enter politics.

With Knowledge Guzana, possibly because arrangements for the interview were placed in the hands of a junior Government official who hadn't been adequately briefed on foreign visitors, I was permitted to talk alone for some forty-five minutes. No Mr. Mills sat beside us with fingers tapping, there was no sense of tension and undercover sparring such as had marred the few moments with the Chief Minister. Knowledge Guzana was free to talk as he pleased.

"I would say," he began with a grave thoughtfulness, "that a very big percentage of the voters in the Transkei are very sympathetic to us. We have about forty-two members of the Assembly, as against sixty-six for Chief Matanzima's Transkei National Independence Party. The Assembly, you know, consists of sixty-four chiefs and forty-five elected members. Of these, about fifty-one chiefs support Matanzima, thirteen support us. Of the elected members, fifteen support him and about thirty support us.

"I say 'about,' because our exact representation at the moment is somewhat clouded. One of our members has recently died, and there is some question as to how soon we will have a by-election to replace him. And two of our members have just been convicted at Grahamstown in the Cape Province of trying to murder the Chief Minister." He smiled slightly, but basically he was quite serious, with much the same earnest dignity as the young editor in Durban.

"We are still building our party. We have to be quite certain who joins us, because quite a few who have sought membership have had associations in the past with persons or individuals who have been banned by the Government in the Republic. Some seem to feel that the Transkei is ripe ground for them to make trouble. We have to guard against this. New members must make a declaration that they support our party, and no other.

"Our main object as a party is to create a multiracial society in the Transkei. Here we make a clear distinction between multiracialism and segregation. We hold that to maintain multiracialism, the races must be distinct and must not be merged into an integrated society in which intermarriages could occur.

"One of our principal objects, also, is to retain the Transkei as a part and parcel of the Republic. We are opposed to an independent Transkei, which may surprise you. Nonetheless, we believe that the path of multi-racialism within the Republic is best for us. We think that the other races should have a share in the government of the Transkei, should have voting rights, property rights, all the full rights of citizens. The rights of the minority have to be protected if a country is to be a viable society worthy of the loyalty of its citizens. We believe that the European race is essential to the economy and cultural development of South Africa, both in the Republic and in the Transkei.

"You see," he said earnestly, "we want to cooperate with the Republic, not across a border, but as people living together. We believe the Government of the Republic cannot turn back the economic clock in South Africa. The African who has moved away from his tribal area to enter the economy of the Republic cannot turn back in his metamorphosis toward Western civilization. He is acquiring a constantly greater stake in Western civilization. He is no longer a spectator in its development, he is directly and materially contributing to the maintenance and growth of Western civilization. Many Africans have been in the urbanized areas now for as many as two and three generations. They have no tribal areas left, no real tribal ties, many of them. How can they be told that they still belong to a tribal area, when their families have been in Johannesburg or the Cape for several generations?"

"How do you get along with the Government of the Republic, as an opposition? Do they recognize you and respect you?"

"The Republic Government," he said gravely, "has tried to look at the situation objectively and has conceded us the right to exist as an opposition. The Leader of the Opposition is accorded all democratic rights and privileges—he can urge a motion of no-confidence, he has a right to criticize. We have not been in any way interfered with, although" —he frowned a little—"we have had some difficulty in securing permits to hold political meetings. But we think that is local officials misinterpreting their instructions, rather than an example of Government policy.

"When the Minister of Bantu Administration came here," he said, and a note of quiet pride came into his voice, "he saw to it that the Leader of the Opposition was presented to him. . . . Of course," he added with a quiet little smile, "the question is, whether the Government would continue its tolerance if the Opposition came to power. We think it would. One factor that gives us confidence is that respect for the Opposition is part of their propaganda to the outside world that democracy is being followed in the Transkei. . . .

"Matanzima? I would say that Matanzima is doing a fair job. I wouldn't say doing a good job. He is inexperienced himself, and there is probably a lack of men in his party who could come up to the status of

Cabinet member. He's got to make do with what he has at his disposal. Sometimes," he said gently, "this shows. . . .

"One of the main problems in the Transkei, which his government is not handling properly, in our estimation, is land rights for the Africans. You see, the Republic Government transferred to the Transkei upon its creation all the land formerly held by the native trust. Now the Transkei Government has to bring in legislation to deal with land rights in the Transkei. Up to now, the African has had a certificate of occupation to grazing land or his kraal site—not actual ownership confirmed by legal title. We would like to see outright ownership of land given to the African, just as it is to the White. Most are settled on the land, and many have had the same site for generations. Those who have a traditional site should have a title deed issued to them for that site. Those who do not should be permitted to buy sites at a settled market price.

"We consider land reform the basic essential of a genuine and successful democracy in the Transkei. The present Transkei Government under Chief Matanzima is seeking to reestablish the chiefs in their old positions of arbitrary authority. It wishes to distribute the land through the chiefs, which inevitably puts the chiefs in a position where they can reward their friends and harm their enemies. As it stands now, a man can decide that he wants a certain new piece of land, he goes to the chief and says, 'I offer you so many beasts to change my land.' The chief has the power to give or withhold. If the man had to pay in money, and if he received a legal title deed direct from a land authority of the Government, many evils would automatically be ended. The community as a whole would be more established—there would be a genuine sense of independence—a mental emancipation—that is a necessity if we are going to develop democratically."

Did he think the Government would ever accept the idea of multiracialism as long as it was directing its whole effort toward the creation of separate development? A pause, a thoughtful frown, then slowly:

"With separate development, the African at least has a platform from which he can indicate what he favors to the Government. And there is one thing I have noticed, here in the Bantustan, which is a gain no matter what circumstance produces it: Here you have forced cooperation between white ministers and black ministers. It gives the Whites an understanding of the Africans' attitudes, they work together and cooperate. We in the Opposition say, Here is a germ of growing multiracialism despite the policy of separate development."

Thinking back upon the interview as I left Umtata and was driven down through the Transkei, the countryside getting gentler and mistier and bluer as I went south toward a weekend at King William's Town, it seemed possible that it was not only Kaiser Matanzima who has the Government over a barrel, but Knowledge Guzana as well; and that the

Government, forced to keep a promise to create a Bantustan, may have neatly hoist itself upon its own petard and may in time, thereby, find itself moving willy-nilly toward a more democratic conclusion than it perhaps had in mind at the outset.

CAUSE FOR UNEASINESS (Editorial, World, *Johannesburg, Bantu)*
. . . We suspect that there must be some uneasiness in Government cir-
cles over the forthright statement by Chief Minister Kaiser Matanzima
criticising the Government's policy of removing Africans from the "White
areas" of South Africa back to the Transkei.

Addressing the national conference of the Transkei National Inde-
pendence Party in Umtata, Matanzima accused the Government of
wielding a big kierie and chasing away Transkei people from the White
urban areas. "We cannot allow this to go on unchecked," he declared.

Critics of Matanzima have accused him in the past of being a Govern-
ment stooge. Yet here he has come out strongly against that Govern-
ment's policy.

The Chief Minister's statement, if we interpret him correctly, is a
major closing of the ranks with the Transkei opposition on a policy
which the Government has pursued earnestly as the fundamental corner-
stone of "separate development."

The Deputy Minister of Bantu Development, Mr. Blaar Coetzee, only
recently stressed that the Government is determined to reduce the pro-
portion of Africans to Whites in South Africa's urban areas to less than
one to one.

The World has always believed that the Government's policy in this
regard is a pipe-dream. We look forward with interest to the Govern-
ment's reaction to this trenchant criticism by the Transkei's Chief Minis-
ter.

To us it makes sense.

A DOUBTFUL VENTURE (Editorial, World, *Johannesburg, Bantu)*
. . . Plans are complete for teachers, businessmen, ministers, 324 beard-
men and others to tour the "homelands"—at an estimated cost of R32,-
000.

Frankly, we have difficulty in understanding the purpose of this whole
operation.

We can only assume that the aim of the tour is to provide the Govern-
ment with the opportunity of proving to the visitors what show places
the Transkei and other "homelands" are, with a view to persuading the

African urban population that there are great opportunities for them in the "homelands."

This, of course, ties up with the Government's declared policy of moving Africans to the homelands, in the interests of their official policy of apartheid.

We venture to suggest that even if the homelands could be presented as a veritable Garden of Eden, the fact remains that many of our people, born and bred to city life, have not the slightest desire to be uprooted from here.

Even if the touring visitors returned full of praise for what is being done in the Transkei—and here we have doubts—we cannot foresee their visit having any material impact on the way our people feel on the principle of being shunted willy-nilly from the towns to the "homelands." . . .

5.

King William's Town
Port Elizabeth
The Garden Route

"**Y**OU MUST UNDERSTAND the historical background," said my charming host and hostess in King William's Town, and if they said it once they said it a hundred times during the weekend that had obviously been arranged by the South Africa Foundation for the purpose of Putting Me Straight On A Few Things.

Virtually every fact I had acquired in a month of reportage, virtually every impression I had gained from a steady stream of enlightening interviews, was challenged with a charming but determined persistence that first amused, then annoyed, then amused again, and finally, left me saddened even more: so intensely defensive were they, so anxiously protective, so dreadfully fearful that no visitor could be trusted to make up his own mind fairly about their lovely, troubled land.

A proposition as simple as: "South Africans love to talk politics" was immediately challenged:

"We do? Oh, I don't really think we do, anymore than anyone else. I really don't think politics is a preoccupation with us"—after interview upon interview, social function after social function, at which South Africa—South Africa—South Africa—South Africa—was almost the sole and only burden of conversation.

"There seem to be tensions between Afrikaans and English—"

"There are? Oh, I don't think so. Everything is *so* much better than it was, there is such a *genuinely good* feeling between the White sections—" after interview upon interview, social function after social function . . .

"I have sensed a lot of resentment on the part of the Natives regarding what you people call 'petty apartheid,' the personal indignities and slights—"

"You have? Why, look at these chappies here, walking down the streets of King William's Town, going into the shops as naturally as can be with you and me and all the other Whites. Resentment? Where do you see resentment?—" after interview upon interview, social function after social function . . .

And if I heard once, I heard a hundred times, about the sad history of the Afrikaans, their troubles in the Boer War, the economic depression after, the struggle back from disaster, the present triumphant control. At the end of forty-eight hours it began to seem that I could not even remark, "It's a nice day, today," without being instantly told, "Now, you have to understand the background of the Afrikaner over the past sixty years. You have to understand their defeat in the war, and what their history has meant to them."

I understood; anyone with an ounce of perception and compassion can understand. It was just that I had concluded that there were a few other things to understand about South Africa, too.

But the attitude, of course, was instructive in itself, for it was typical of a certain excessive defensiveness that is to be found in many South Africans. It does not always announce itself so frankly, but it is there; and to a large extent, of course, "the outside world," including very actively the United States, has done a great deal to create it. It began with history. But it has been compounded by the chaotic childlike politics of present-day Black Africa, and the naive belief in certain White capitals that should know better, that the loyalty of anything so erratic and fickle can actually be won by a policy of appeasement based upon harassing South Africa.

But the farm—a luxurious spread set in the gentle blue hills near King William's Town, the "border country" where the British met the Kaffirs in many a bloody battle in the last century—was beautiful; the company —even when most argumentative—was charming; the hospitality was delightful; and it was a thoroughly pleasant halfway point in the journey.

And for some, of course, it was as effective as those who had sug-

gested it had obviously hoped it would be for me: Jimmy Doolittle had
been there a week or so before, and every paper you picked up now
seemed to be full of Jimmy Doolittle telling the world how wonderful
everything in South Africa was.

From it all, five topics of discussion remain.

On separate development, my host:

"I believe the present Government is a bridge between South Africa's
past and her future. It's got to carry not only its Afrikaans supporters
forward, but the English-speakers as well. And maybe the biggest job lies
with the Afrikaans. Of course there are some people who say Afrikanerdom is the most obedient community in the world, that if the Prime
Minister says lie on the right side, it lies on the right side, if he says lie on
the left side, it lies on the left side.

"It isn't quite like that. Many older Afrikaners resent very much what
the present Government is doing for the Bantu and the Indians and the
Coloureds. They have a saying out on the platteland, you know, about
the Bantu and the Indians: 'The Kaffir in his place and the coolie out of
the country'—and many of these old Boer types still feel that very
deeply, as instinctively as some of your Southerners do about your Negroes. They say the Government is doing far too much. And this pushes
the Government sometimes, you know? You'll find the Prime Minister or
some Cabinet member saying something far more extreme than he really
means, just because he feels the platteland is pushing him. They're like
all politicians; they want to stay in power, and they have to appeal to the
heart of Afrikanerdom to do it. At the same time, they want to make
progress with this problem we've got. So they're trying to build a bridge."

"If the Bantustans are the bridge, do you yourself feel that they can
work?"

"Personally, I don't. I believe that economic influences are so strong
that they will inevitably break down any artificial borders. I think by the
year 2000 we will be about thirty millions all told, some sixteen millions,
maybe six million Whites and ten million Blacks, living in the cities. All
with the same economic rights. The rest, some fourteen million Blacks,
will be living in tribal areas and"—with a comfortable tolerance—"continuing the tribal development that was interrupted by the white man."

"But how do you keep them in tribal areas when there are good jobs
available in the cities?"

"That's why we have influx control, to keep unneeded workers out of
the cities and let in only those who can be absorbed and maintained
usefully in the white economy."

"By the time your black population gets as big as everybody thinks it's
going to be, you'll have to ring your cities with guns to keep them out,
won't you?"

"You may have a point; you may have a point. But I believe we can do it peaceably, since the great majority of the tribes will be eager to continue their development in their traditional way. That's all they want: they don't want the white man's civilization. They just want to be left alone to develop in their own way."

"But you say the ten million in the cities will have equal economic rights with everyone else. Won't they want political rights too?"

"I believe they will be happy and satisfied when they have economic equality, which, if it develops as I foresee, will include equal pay and property rights."

"Do you really see any signs in present Government policy of any such conclusion?"

"I believe they're thinking—constantly testing and moving, testing and moving. Apartheid is a constantly changing thing, you know, constantly changing."

"Some people seem to think it's constantly changing for the worse."

"I don't believe so. Look at the Government's problem for a moment. Let's just consider the Afrikaner, conditioned by his hard losing fight in the Boer War sixty years ago, rejected and suppressed—"

On the nature of the Native, my hostess:

"The Natives are very dependent. You become in a sense de facto head of the tribe when you live surrounded by them, as we do here, in an area of scattered white farms. Each farm has its own community. We have some sixty-three Natives ourselves." (Something to think about, twentieth century and all, when one goes to bed at night: three Whites, two amiable mastiffs who wouldn't bite a flea, and sixty-three Natives. Alone in the silent countryside with only the light of a distant neighboring farmhouse twinkling far off against the hills.)

"All the problems are put upon you, and you had better solve them, because that's your job. You also find"—a wry smile—"that, at the same time, you have a definite place, and they let you know it: they let you know where you stand. When they come in and announce, 'We're not going to do the laundry this morning, we're going to town,' you know you've been put in your place and you might just as well get the laundry ready some other day, because they're off. But what can you do about it? Nothing.

"Sometimes, also, you come up dead against them—you realize what an utterly different people they are. One of our girls had twins recently, which is against their beliefs. It's considered bad luck, and they usually let them die. Deliberately, you understand. But I thought I'd try to save these, so I saw to it that the babies were well fed, and that they were taken to the doctor regularly. I was determined to save them. Then the girl suddenly announced that she was going back to the kraal for a while. At that point the doctor—who was white, incidentally, we Whites are terrible to the Natives, you know, we just refuse to do anything for them

—the doctor said they were a couple of the healthiest babies he'd ever seen.

"About a month later I heard from her sister that one of the babies had died in the kraal. Next thing I knew, she was back with the other: it was skin and bones. She had been deliberately letting them starve.

"Well, I was still determined, so I got some supplies together and asked her to feed it, and she refused. About that time we were getting ready to leave for our trip to America, so I asked her sister to feed it while I was gone. She said, 'Why should I feed it, it isn't mine.' That's the way they think. So I could have let it die. But I couldn't do that. You can't just let a child starve—at least, we can't. They can. So we delayed our trip for a week and I made arrangements to get it into a missionary orphanage, where it is now, coming along fine.

"But that's part of the problem, you see. They just think differently than we do."

On Group Areas, my host:

"You raise some question about so-called District 6 in Cape Town, where they're making the Coloureds move out because it's been declared a White area. Now, let's just look at that for a moment; let's just look at it. I don't believe the Coloureds have any particular attachment to that area. It's a terrible slum, it's dirty, it's dangerous—you be sure and have somebody drive you through, when you get to the Cape. They're going to get better homes out in the townships on the Cape Flats than they've ever had before. I don't believe it means a thing to them. It's just a chance for a lot of agitators like Helen Suzman and the Progs to raise a fuss."

"I have the feeling that possibly there, as well as in some other areas, such as certain Indian areas in Durban, it's very good property and a lot of Whites are going to step in and make a killing with real estate developments. Some of them in the Government or close to it, I hear, such as perhaps Ministers' wives."

"Oh"—a dismissing, comfortable laugh—"you can hear these things all the time, of course. You hear all sorts of gossip about your politicians, too, don't you? It's possible that in one or two places there have been white developments that have turned out to be quite profitable, but that's the exception and it has nothing to do with Government policy. You don't want to oversentimentalize these Group Areas decisions the way some of our liberals do. Most of these people who are being moved are going to be far better off. Most of them don't have any real attachment to these places."

"Except as the places have been their traditional homes for years, that's all. It's been their particular place, their home, and now they won't have it anymore. Maybe that's oversentimentalizing, I wouldn't know. The question that keeps coming back to me is, why is the Government so rigid about it? Why isn't there any allowance for the individual case, the human factor, in applying these laws? Why don't they ever relax a little? Why do they have to be so heartless?"

"The Government seems to have an almost desperate logic about the way it goes about things."

"Yes, I'd say that's a good word for it, but why?"

"It's typical, I suppose, of a certain type of mind and character. The Transvalers and the Free Staters are much harder than the Cape Dutch. They were the ones who trekked, as we've already discussed, they suffered the hardships, they fought the Anglo-Boer War. Their attitude toward the Bantu is conditioned by the fact that they fought them on the frontiers in the day when the only good Kaffir, as you Americans might say, was a dead Kaffir. And they just don't understand the Indians and the Coloureds at all, they've never had any real experience with them. But even so, one mustn't sentimentalize too much over the people in District 6 or these other places affected by the Group Areas Act. They're going to be much better off—much better off."

"It's all very well to talk so casually about rearranging lives, I suppose, but it might be different if the Whites were involved. Have you ever had the experience of being moved out of your home?"

"No"—quickly; and a little smile at his wife; and later:

"The reason I smiled back there when you asked if I had ever had the experience of being moved was because we were on the verge of it last year—"

"Still are," she interjected.

"Still are," he conceded. "Last year the Government wanted to declare this a Black area and expropriate our farm and all the others in the valley here. We had to get together with the other White residents and fight it. We think we've got it stopped, but we don't know for how long. But, I suppose it wouldn't matter really."

"You know we'd miss the farm terribly," she said.

"Oh, yes, but we could find another, in a white area."

"We'd miss it terribly. We built it up, we love it, it's ours."

"My dear, if there is a policy, it has to be followed consistently if it's to be successful."

"But you are fighting it," I said.

Again the little smile.

"That's what you can do when you're organized—"

"And are White, and have the money."

An offended expression for a moment; and then honestly, "You may be right. You may be right."

On liberals, my hostess:

"Sometimes I feel a real envy for the liberals. It must be nice to have an absolutely clear conscience and know that everything you are doing is absolutely, morally right and correct. For us, who are tortured all the time with doubts about whether we're doing the right thing, it's not so easy."

(In Cape Town a week later, the liberal lady, bitterly fighting the removal of District 6, heartbroken by the obdurate refusal of Government officials to listen: "It must be wonderful to be a supporter of the Nats and know without any twinges of conscience whatsoever that you are absolutely right in everything you do. We liberals are always so divided and so uncertain about the ultimate wisdom of what we do.")

On relations with the United States, my hostess:

"You see, there is a particular sense of betrayal in South Africa, I think, when we find the United States opposing us and joining Black Africa in punitive attempts to hamper us and make the solution of our problems more difficult. There has always been a sense of identification with America in this country, because of our somewhat parallel history, your Western pioneers and our ox-wagon treks, your wars against the Indians, our Kaffir wars, your racial problem and ours, and because we too have a booming, growing, industrialized society. We have always admired America and looked up to her—for many of us, I think, you have been a sort of shining beacon, on a much greater scale, of what we might someday be able to achieve here in Africa in a smaller way if only we have the time and the chance to do it. So there is a real sense of personal disappointment and betrayal about some of the things your government does."

"Just exactly what is the basis for this fear of the United States? I've been hearing this from a lot of people practically since the day I got here, but not with many specifics. What do you complain of?"

"President Kennedy saying the white man in Africa is expendable, for instance. Do you think we're expendable?"

"I think there'd be absolute chaos without you."

"And State Department officials constantly making speeches attacking us. And America's bowing to the UN and refusing to sell us certain types of military equipment. And the State Department issuing statements trying to put pressure on the judges at the World Court to decide against us in the South-West Africa case which will be handed down day after tomorrow. And issuing a statement warning everybody to abide by the decision, which they obviously think is going to go against us. Those are some of the things."

"On the other hand, many of us think the Government here has been deliberately provocative about such things as not permitting our battleship to come here simply because it has Negroes in the crew. And denying us the right to have a Negro on the staff at the tracking station in the Transvaal. I think you lose the sympathy of a great many Americans, sympathy that might be with you and help to ameliorate some of our Government's policies."

"The way we see it is that your government is deliberately trying to provoke *us,* not the other way round. We feel there was a deliberate attempt to create an issue last year by sending a battleship with Negro crew members here—"

"But most of our ships have Negro crew members, that's the way our country is—"

"Many of us feel that perhaps a battleship was deliberately chosen that would have a Negro complement, or that possibly if the battleship that was to be sent did not have Negro crew members, then they were deliberately assigned in order to create an incident. We think it was deliberate provocation to send it here, knowing our laws and way of doing things. We also feel it was deliberate provocation to ask that we allow a Negro to be assigned to the American tracking station."

"But that battleship is our property, and so is the tracking station, at least diplomatically speaking, as long as we have it under lease. There could have been an understanding with our government that the Negroes on the battleship would abide by your laws and not go in certain areas, a head-on collision could have been avoided—"

"We don't think there was any desire to avoid a head-on collision."

"—and as for the tracking station, that *is* our property for the time being, and we have a right to do as we please there—I think, and I think diplomatic practice says. We don't like the Russians having a little police state on 16th Street in Washington, either, but that's their property, just as we can have democracy in our embassy in Moscow—just as you can have apartheid at your embassy on Massachusetts Avenue, though we may not approve of it. Why do you deny us the same rights here? Why couldn't there be a clear understanding between our government and yours that if the Negroes came they would abide by the rules of your country whenever they were outside our diplomatic property?"

"We are afraid that they wouldn't. We are afraid that if they were permitted in here they would deliberately go into places they were not supposed to be and would deliberately provoke incidents that would cause trouble between our two countries and heap more international opprobrium on us. We think there would be more trouble after they came than if they were prevented from coming in the first place. That's the Government's reasoning, and I think most South Africans support it."

(In February, 1967, the aircraft carrier Franklin D. Roosevelt *put into Cape Town to refuel en route home from Vietnam. The Government and people of South Africa, led by Prime Minister Vorster, had prepared a welcome of segregated but lavish entertainments for officers and*

*crew during a four-day visit. The Government of the United States
professed to be well pleased with all arrangements. At the last moment
all shore leaves were canceled on the ground that apartheid would make
"organized integrated activities impossible." More than 100,000 Capetonians of all races visited the ship, and before it pulled out, twelve hours
ahead of schedule, a racially mixed group of some eighty crew members
went ashore and gave blood at a nonsegregated blood bank as a gesture
of sympathy with South Africa. The Afrikaans Sunday newspaper* Die
Beeld *remarked of the episode that "South Africa's hand of friendship,
which was given to the United States this weekend after months of careful preparation, has been suddenly and rudely knocked aside.")*

On seeing the right people, my host:
"We wonder, really, if you are seeing enough people to give you the
feel of the country, enough South Africans of the right kind for your
purposes—"
"I'm seeing you, aren't I?"
"No, seriously, now, we mean—"
"Who, clerks, shopkeepers, housewives, the Man in the Street, the
Informed Taxicab Driver all good reporters interview? I've talked to a
lot of them, I'll talk to more. In one degree or another they all say the
same things you do. The main thing I'm interested in is what you might
call the 'operative people' of the country, the ones who run things, the
ones who make things happen in one way or another. On the whole, I'm
doing pretty well so far with them, I think."
"But we wonder if they are really talking to you? Are they really being
frank with you and telling you what they think?"
"All I can do is record them as I see them and let the reader judge.
You, for instance, might emerge as two very intelligent, very hard-
working, very industrious spokesmen for the Government—"
"Oh, really?"—a startled look, a charming smile. "Now, we'll have to
think about that for a moment. We'll have to think about that. I think
perhaps we had really better find something, then, that we can criticize
violently. Otherwise you'll think we approve of everything the Govern-
ment does!"
"Almost."
Again the smile, a humorously chiding shake of the head.
"I'm afraid you're beginning to sound a little prickly, now. Just a little
bit prickly."
So we bickered amicably to the end, even as we drove in from King
William's Town to the airport at East London—over coffee while we
waited for the plane—almost to the moment of farewell.

T WAS AN HOUR'S FLIGHT to Port Elizabeth, South Africa's Little
America, home of Ford, GM, GE and other big investors. The day
was clear, the coastline placidly beautiful. "There's a whale!" the pilot
announced midway and obligingly banked so we could see it. It rolled
lazily in the blue immensities of the Indian Ocean, spouting gently from
time to time as we flew over. Everyone crowded to look; excited comments and the busy clicking of cameras filled the cabin. It was a curiously
innocent, curiously happy moment snatched from the incessant, inescapable problems of South Africa. But not, of course, for long.

N PORT ELIZABETH—"P.E."—they have a campanile on the waterfront, modeled on the one in Florence, that honors the English
"1820 Settlers." In P.E. they also have a brand-new university whose
switchboard answers in Afrikaans. P.E. is the center of American investment in South Africa. P.E. is a pleasant place encircling a busy harbor,
filled with booming industry, charming homes, an attractive waterfront.
P.E. is the hub of what is known as "the Eastern Cape," that portion of
the Cape Province that stretches northeasterly from Cape Town to East
London. It is an area almost four hundred miles in length and almost
every mile has been fought over by English, Boers, Bantu. Latterly it has
been fought over, in the sense of determined opposition and outright
subversion, by the Government and those who oppose the Government's
policies. A good many have been banned, jailed or exiled, and the Government thinks, now, that the battle is almost over.

In P.E. one meets well-fed, complacent Americans from the industries who have never had it so good in terms of soft living, multitudinous
cheap servants, low prices, the good life; tense, worried, unhappy Americans who have let their sympathies with the Natives take them so close to
subversion that it is a wonder they are still there; liberal, disheartened
English-speakers who have done their best, under great hostility from the
Government, to aid the wives and families of the Natives who have been
banned or taken off to Robben Island; newspaper people, lawyers, teachers, professionals who have been active against the Government but have
now been frightened into silence; liberal Afrikaners who are uneasy
about the direction of things and say so with a private vehemence that
belies their outward acceptance; conservative Afrikaners who are also
uneasy but resolve all doubts, as loyal Afrikaners do, by voting for the
Nats and not thinking too much about tomorrow.

P.E. is a curious town.

"LAST WEEK," the liberal Afrikaner at Ford remarked thoughtfully, "I took the maid and her daughter to Dolphin Park, where they have dolphins and aquatic shows, you know, similar to your Marineland. But I hadn't realized that it wasn't the Natives' day. There is one a week, now, and this wasn't it. This is something quite new, the Government just issued a regulation a couple of weeks ago, and I hadn't been aware of it. So we couldn't go in. Natives used to be permitted all the time, right along with Whites, you'd see a few scattered here and there, those who could afford it and were interested. Which is as it should be. There was no bother, it worked all right. But now the Government has moved in and that's all changed. I suppose"—with a use of irony that is very rare in South Africa, most people feeling too openly the unhappiness that irony cloaks—"this makes us all better human beings. Though I found it a little hard to explain to my maid's little girl. My maid wasn't surprised, you know, but the little girl was a rather more difficult case. . . ."

NEW CAR SALES STATISTICS

Sales of new cars last month brought the total for the first nine months this year [1966] to 102,509—an increase of 6,405 (or 6.7 per cent) on the corresponding figure for last year.

Statistics released in Port Elizabeth by the National Association of Automobile Manufacturers show that 96,104 new cars were sold in South Africa during the first nine months of 1965, but the beat-the-budget sales boom experienced in August had ended.

September sales of 10,310 were 3,912 (or 27.5 per cent) down on the record August figure of 14,222.

—Official Sources

"OH, YES, I was raided a little while ago," the professional man said. "I wasn't surprised. It began when I arrived at my office one morning and found in the mail, entirely unsolicited by me, a magazine from the Communist Party in London. It is absolutely against the law to send such things through the mails, of course, or to have them in one's possession. I told my partner, 'You mark my word, in a little while the Security Police will be here.' He had his hat in his hand and was on the way out anyway, so he casually slipped it in his pocket, took it away and burned it. Sure enough in about an hour there they were, two earnest young Afrikaners, very polite and diligent. They searched my wastebasket, the bookcase, the top of the wardrobe, the pockets of my jacket, made me show my personal papers—the only thing they didn't do was open the drawers of my desk, for some reason known only to them. They spent about two and a half hours snuffling round, turned my office upside down, of course didn't find anything. I'm convinced it was a plant, of course. The timing was too neat."

ESCOM PLANS GIANT POWER STATIONS

The construction of three new giant power stations, with outputs four to five times those of power stations built only a few years ago, will be the central feature of Escom's $560 million expansion program for the late 60's and early 70's. The program, when completed, will give South Africa 25 Escom [*Electric Supply Commission*] power stations, against the present total of 20.

The new stations, it is estimated, will raise total power output to approximately 31,000 million kilowatt hours by 1970. The comparable figure for 1965 was 23,000 million kilowatt hours.

Electricity consumption in the Republic has been rising by about 7 per cent a year. Escom's planning is based on the assumption that power needs will continue to increase at about the same rate, or by approximately 40 per cent by 1970.

—Official Sources

"AT GENERAL MOTORS, among our more than six thousand employees," the Afrikaans official said, "we have had Whites and Coloureds and Indians and Bantu working side by side for several years and we have never had any trouble. On the contrary, they get along very well together. This has gone on quite openly, you know, even Cabinet ministers have visited and seen it and apparently been undamaged, psychologically or morally or otherwise. But now the Government is beginning to step in. We are under strong pressure to replace our Bantu, Coloureds and Indians with Italians, Germans, Brazilians."

"And are you?"

A shrug, as we walked along the humming assembly line in the enormous building.

PLASTICS—S.A.'S FASTEST GROWING INDUSTRY

South Africa's plastics industry was born 21 years ago and in these 21 years $98 million has been invested in more than 300 plastics factories in the country. The industry has maintained a growth rate of 25 per cent a year in the past ten years—a dramatic expansion when seen in the perspective of the growth rate of 4.5 to 5 per cent of the South African economy as a whole.

Plastics '66, one of a series of trade fairs being held in Johannesburg this year, is the coming-out party of the industry. Plastics, machinery, raw materials and manufactured products worth about $1.4 million are being displayed at the exhibition, which opened at Milner Park, Johannesburg, last week. Exhibitors from Germany, France, Italy and Switzerland are exhibiting their latest machinery. South Africa's manufacturers are exhibiting a wide range of manufactured products, ranging from small containers to a 21-ft. fibre-glass reinforced plastic boat.

Plastics machinery imports worth $4.2 million during 1966 proved the industry's measure of confidence in its own future, Major W. Geach, Director of Imports and Exports, said when officially opening the exhibition. These imports had occurred in spite of the fact that the industry was working at only 75 per cent of its capacity. In 1965, imports of machinery for the plastics industry had cost $7 million.

Statistics show that during the past six years, the consumption of polyethylene had increased fourfold, from 0.8 pounds per head in 1961, to 3.2 pounds per head in 1966. Consumption of polyvinyl-chloride had doubled from the 1961 figure of two pounds per head. It is estimated, he added, that South Africa's consumption of plastics would double again by 1970.

—Official Sources

"NO, WE AREN'T having any trouble with the Government!" the English-speaker at Ford declared stoutly. "It is true that some of our contracts for heavy equipment, such as trucks, have been held up because of the U.S. embargo on arms shipments to South Africa. The Government seems to be taking something of a quid pro quo attitude. It is making things a bit sticky at the moment. But"—hastily—"don't say our relations with the Government are poor! They're tip-top."

FOREIGN TRADE

Imports and exports (including S.W. Africa, Lesotho, Swaziland and Botswana, in R million):

YEAR	IMPORTS	EXPORTS (EXCL. GOLD)
1938	191.6	67.4
1958	1,111.2	782.8
1964	1,525.8	953.6

—Official Sources

"I CAN SEE the Afrikaans point of view," said the liberal English-speaking lady who had worked herself close to exhaustion for the now-banned Defence and Aid Fund established to help families of political prisoners. "They really do feel they don't dare to be flexible, they feel they can't give the African an inch or he will try to take everything. I think they're basically quite honest in their feelings about it, even though we may not agree with them. Don't you?"

"I do not!" snorted the English-speaking lady whose family has always owned a beautiful farm in the rich mountain fringe of the Orange Free State that the British took away from the Basuto in the early days. "I grew up with them and I think they're absolutely devious, absolutely untrustworthy in every way."

Yet later in the evening, after the World Court had handed down the South-West Africa decision, holding that Ethiopia and Liberia were not members of the League of Nations and hence had no competence to challenge South Africa's exercise of the League mandate, we sat silently before the radio and heard the light, reasonable voice of Dr. Verwoerd hailing South Africa's victory. And the first English-speaking lady said:

"How would you have felt if it had gone against us?"

And the other, frowning, reflected for a long moment and then said slowly:

"It would have been awful, either way."

2,000 GIVE THANKS FOR S.W.A. (Cape Times, *English*) . . . *Stellenbosch—A special thanksgiving service conducted by the Rev. J. F. Gericke, who gave evidence in the World Court at The Hague, was held here last night.*

About 2,000 people attended the service in the Central Church.

Members of the legal team at the service were Mr. D. P. de Villiers, Mr. G. van R. Muller, SC, Mr. E. M. Grosskopf and Mr. R. F. Botha. Mr. Botha arrived from Pretoria earlier in the day.

Prof. E. P. Groenewald, of Pretoria, who gave evidence attended the service. The Speaker of the House of Assembly, Mr. Klopper, was present.

Mr. Gericke said the verdict of the World Court should be seen in its right perspective and all the honour be given to God.

Mr. Gericke said, "We want to see the verdict at The Hague as the merciful intervention of God to prevent starvation and maybe even bloodshed in this country."

VICTORY AT THE HAGUE (*Editorial,* Eastern Province Herald, *Port Elizabeth, English*) . . . *The judgment of the International Court of Justice in the South-West Africa case has been handed down. South Africa has won the prolonged legal battle foisted on her by Liberia and Ethiopia on the grounds, advanced all along by her representatives, that her opponents had no standing in law. The judgment went in favour of South Africa by the narrowest of margins, by the casting vote of the President of the Court, but it effectively reverses the 1962 judgment in which the Court held that it did have jurisdiction to hear the case.*

The essence of yesterday's judgment is that member States—in this instance Liberia and Ethiopia—of an international body, be it the League of Nations or the United Nations, have no direct legal interest in mandates or trusteeships, this interest being confined to the international body as an entity.

Sir Percy Spender declared that their remedy therefore lay not in the sphere of international law but in the sphere of politics. The World Court exists to interpret international law, and not to make such law or to act as a legislative body or to adjudicate on moral desiderata. In the words of the judgment, "right cannot be held to exist merely because it is desirable." So far so good, and the greatest credit is due to the team of South African lawyers for a splendid performance that has met with such signal success. They earned for their country a verdict few people expected.

The world over it was demanded of South Africa that she should accept a judgment which it was thought would go against her. Has not South Africa now the same right to demand of her adversaries that they should accept their *legal defeat?*

SOUTH-WEST AFRICA

South-West Africa covers an area of 318,261 square miles, including the Walvis Bay area of 434 square miles. It lies between longitude 17° and 29° East and latitude 12° and 25° South. It stretches for nearly 1,000 miles from the Orange River in the south to the Kunene River in the north. The average depth from the coast is approximately 400 miles. On the east it adjoins the Kalahari Desert of Bechuanaland. The Kunene, Okavango and Orange are the only rivers having perennial water. From North to South the Territory measures 1,280 km. (800 miles) and from West to East an average distance of 720 km. (350 miles) which gives it an oblong shape with nearly 80 per cent of the population concentrated in the northern half of the Territory, that is, north of a line taken just north of Walvis Bay. The Territory is nearly four times the size of the United Kingdom. While the area of the Territory is virtually the same as that of Nigeria, the latter carries a population sixty times larger than that of the Territory. The Territory constitutes nearly 3 per cent of the total area of Africa, while its population of approximately half a million amounts to only about .2 per cent of the total population of Africa.

With the exception of Bechuanaland, which adjoins the Territory, it has the lowest population density in Africa south of the Sahara, and one of the lowest density figures in the world.

South-West Africa can today be regarded, with the Republic of South Africa, as one of the most highly developed of more than fifty countries in Africa. The gross domestic product rose from R31 per capita in 1940 to R269 per capita in 1962. This represents an average annual growth ranking among the highest in the world. If this growth can be maintained the real national income per capita could be doubled in nineteen years.

Over the years of its administration, the Government of South Africa has supplied not only entrepreneur capital but also aid in the form of hard cash to the amount of about R165 million. On a per capita basis South African aid amounts to R300 per head of the total population.

Without this aid and without the Whites, therefore, the other population groups would not have attained the level that they have in fact reached. In broad perspective, the Whites have harnessed their knowledge and skill to develop the country's resources, thereby providing employment and cash wages as well as community services such as schools, hospitals and roads for everybody. Other population groups, at different levels of development, have entered employment, supplemented their own traditional subsistence economy and have made good use of the community services. This has served as a field of experience for them to transform their traditional background.

—Official Sources

"NO, I WOULDN'T say that I'm being harassed too much by the police," the American said thoughtfully. "I don't think they're after me, exactly, it's just that they laid on so many extra police during the subversive hunt here that now they just sit around with nothing to do. So they sic them on me and some others in the American community, just to keep them busy.

"But," he added, and the eyes darkened and the gaunt face with its lines of tension and bitterness looked still more ravaged, "the whole situation here just makes you cry, sometimes. It's just no good, in this country. I expect my wife and I wake up in the morning four or five times a week and say to one another, Here we are in this beautiful country with all these charming, industrious people—what are we so unhappy about? But then we think, and we know. . . . We know."

T HE CORPORATE LUNCH in South Africa is held around a beautiful rectangular table inlaid with many polished woods, served by silent Blacks, accompanied by many hearty jokes.

"What do you really think of South Africa?" I asked my business countrymen: and was told much about socializing in the American community, how someone's wife had sung, "I Left My Heart in San Francisco" at last night's party, how someone else had drunk too many martinis, and how pleasant it is to swim and golf in Port Elizabeth.

" I REALLY USED TO scoff at Germans who said they didn't know what was going on under Hitler," the Afrikaans lawyer said, "but now I'm beginning to believe it could really happen. I think there are thousands of Whites in this country who haven't the slightest idea what the Government is doing to destroy their liberties. They think it's just the Bantu, the Coloureds and the Indians who are being affected. They shut their minds to it, they don't know how it's being done, don't want to know. They don't see that the door is now wide open for it to be done to them."

HOTEL INDUSTRY

There are over 1,500 licensed hotels in the Republic in which between R110,000,000 and R120,000,000 have been invested. They range from small country hotels to luxury establishments which compare favourably with the best in the world. Even the hotels in small country towns are of a high standard and their charges are moderate, compared with those in many other countries.

In 1965 a Hotel Board was established consisting of seven members appointed by the State President. The Board was established to foster the development and improvement of accommodation establishments. The Board began operations in September, 1965.

—Official Sources

"THE THING YOU HAVE to understand about the purges in the Eastern Cape," the almost-banned lawyer said in his comfortable home in P.E. (after turning up the radio—"the Security Branch, you know," with an apologetic smile), "is that this area has traditionally been the region in which the Africans enjoyed more privileges and opportunities than any other in the country. English missionaries began to establish schools here more than a hundred years ago, and down the years a substantial number of educated Africans were graduated from them. Lovedale, Healdtown, Fort Hare University in particular, provided a large share of well-educated leaders. It was only natural, I suppose, that the Government should have launched its most vigorous and malevolent purges here."

"Was that because there were educated Africans, or because the educated Africans were Communists?"

"The Government likes to claim they were Communists—"

"They weren't."

"Well," he said, a little testily, "some of them apparently were, but certainly not all. Certainly not!"

"What were they charged with?"

"Many of them with nothing more serious than attending a few meetings of the African National Congress—"

"Banned?"

"Banned—or the Pan Africanist Congress—"

"Banned?"

"Banned—or distributing a leaflet or two, or contributing a few pennies—"

"Banned?"

"Yes, I'm afraid so. But you must realize that while the Government charged that many of the leaders of these organizations were Communist —yes, many of them apparently were—well, actually were—still there were a great many innocents who got caught up in the movement simply because they wanted to bring about better conditions for the Africans. Not *all* who have been arrested were Communists, after all. There have been well over a thousand arrested since 1963, over five hundred have been sentenced to anything from one to twelve years, and almost that many more are still waiting trial. Obviously not *all* have been Communists. I mean, that would assume that the Communists were some sort of superhuman devils, wouldn't it, out to conquer the whole country!"

"What have they been out for, do you think?"

"As I say, many have been innocents who simply wanted to improve conditions. Possibly one or two of the leaders may have had more grandiose schemes—"

"The Government obviously feels that it has proved that it was considerably more than one or two."

"Well, perhaps I am exaggerating, or minimizing, rather. There have been some, yes."

"Enough to warrant the Government's feeling that it is being attacked and must defend itself with whatever weapons?"

"I don't know what they think! All I am saying to you is that great hardship has been inflicted on many people in the Eastern Cape as a result of these police-state purges."

"For instance?"

"For instance: to begin with, many of these arrests are made entirely without warning, without any legal warrant, save the unchecked powers of the Minister of Justice, without any legal protections whatsoever for the persons involved. People have been dragged from their beds in the middle of the night, stopped in the street in broad daylight, taken from their businesses—everything without any legal safeguards, absolutely uncontrolled police-state methods. These things have been done, you know, this is how South Africa is run by the present Government."

"Yes, this I do know and have argued about ever since I got here."

"And this you will admit is not very nice?"

"This I will admit is very bad. After being seized, then what?"

"Then under our pleasant system they can be kept incarcerated, and many of them have been, for anything from four or five months up to twenty-two months, without bail, frequently without visitors, very often without any legal counsel. Often they don't know why they were arrested, what the charges are against them, what their crime is. Quite often, I suspect, the Government doesn't know either. It just takes the gamble that if it holds them long enough something will turn up—or if it doesn't turn up, it can be fabricated.

"Curiously enough, too, you know—or horribly enough, if you like— the Government often doesn't know whether its prisoners will be accused or witnesses. Over a hundred have turned state witness after being kept in jail awhile; there are quite well-substantiated stories of threats, intimidation, physical violence or psychological pressures to make a man turn state witness. Then if his evidence doesn't satisfy the prosecution, charges can always be brought and he can be turned back into one of the accused. It's really a vicious system."

"Is this all done under the Suppression of Communism Act?"

"Yes, but its definitions and authorities are so vague and so broad that it can be used, and is, to charge not only Communists but anyone the Government considers too liberal."

"I understand a lot of the trials are held in remote places far from P.E."

"Oh, yes, that's another gimmick. Trials involving physical violence are held in the Supreme Court in Grahamstown and the law requires a minimum sentence of five years' imprisonment. But all other cases are sent to what we call the regional courts, at Somerset East, Graaff-Reinet, Humansdorp, Adoo, Cradock and Port Alfred. These are mostly small villages, so remote and so far from P.E. that defendants have difficulty getting counsel to come out, and the press also has great difficulty in covering them. Frequently also a case will start in one place, be postponed, be resumed in another, be postponed again, be resumed in still another and maybe decided in a fourth—and all this sometimes in the course of six or seven days."

"There isn't what you might call a great urge for publicity, is there?"

"Oh, but that isn't all. Nine times out of ten an open trial also goes by the board. Just before a state witness takes the stand the prosecutor gets up and states that the police fear for his safety if it becomes known that he is giving evidence, and therefore he asks the judge to close the trial to the public. The judge always grants the request, the police clear the court, and there you are—in spite of the fact that some of these witnesses are practically professionals who are known to have testified at previous trials. . . .

"Under the 180-day law, if a prisoner hasn't given the evidence the police want, he can be sentenced to another 180 days. If he should be brought into court and refuse to give evidence, he is liable to a year's imprisonment. A lot of these witnesses are also subjected to a great deal of psychological torture, quite aside from any physical violence that has been alleged. They may be offered bribes, they may be told wild stories about what other witnesses have said, or be told that their families are being threatened, or that their children are ill, or their wives dying, and that they will be released to go home if they will just give the evidence the Government wants."

"Commissioner Steyn in Pretoria told me that no sensible man would submit to some of the tortures that have been alleged by critics of the police. Commissioner Steyn says—"

"Commissioner Steyn is a smug, comfortable white man sitting in a smug, comfortable office. He isn't a terrified black man in solitary in a jail cell."

"Well, yes, that was my thought too, but I'm just reporting what Commissioner Steyn said. What was the basic case the Government had against the African National Congress, anyway?"

"That it was Communistic. That it wanted to overthrow the Government by violence."

"And—?"

"We had a long series of treason trials in 1957–61, involving what was known as the 'Congress Alliance,' which consisted of the African National Congress, the Coloured People's Congress, the South African

Indian Congress, the Congress of Democrats and the South African
Congress of Trade Unions. They adopted what they called a 'Freedom
Charter' for South Africa. In 1961 the presiding judge handed down an
opinion that while these organizations 'were working together to replace
the existing form of State with a radically different one—' "

"?"

"—'a radically different one,' still the Government had not proved
'that such a new state would be a Communist one,' and furthermore, that
the Government had failed to prove 'that the accused have personal
knowledge of the Communist doctrine of violent revolution or that they
have propagated this doctrine. It is impossible for the Court to come to
the conclusion that the African National Congress policy is to overthrow
the State by violence.' "

"Then why did the Government ban the African National Congress?"

"That happened in 1960 at the time of Sharpeville when Pretoria pan-
icked and began to see Communists under every bed. One consequence
was that the African National Congress was banned and its leaders were
imprisoned. They then worked out what they called the 'New Plan' to
preserve the Congress when it went underground."

"And this plan, too, was not Communistic or violent?"

"The Government is still trying to prove that it was, and its state witnesses are still testifying to that effect to this day. But defense counsel
and witnesses say that the New Plan was only an organizational device
for working underground, and that it was not violent. The defense says
the violence was confined to an elite multiracial corps in the 'Umkhonto
we Sizwe,' or 'Spear of the Nation' movement—"

"Which was formed as the successor to the African National Congress."

"Yes, but—"

"So where does that leave things?"

"With more of these ghastly trials going on all the time, with hundreds
of families left destitute, with Africans in the Eastern Cape and everywhere else in the country terrified to raise their voices against the Government—"

"Which was seeking to defend itself against a plan to replace it with
'a radically different' state."

"Yes. And—er—yes. And there is the final infamy of Robben Island,
you know. Almost all the African males sentenced for political crimes
are sent there to prison and are held virtually incommunicado for as long
as the Government pleases. They are only allowed one visit every six
months and can only write or receive one letter every six months. The
reason I say they may be held as long as the Government pleases is that
this, in effect, is what occurs. There are various ways of doing it.

"Just before a prison term ends, a prisoner may be suddenly charged with additional offences, which supposedly occurred before he was sent to jail. Or he can be charged again with a similar offence, or he can even be charged again with the same offence if legislation has been passed during his sentence which carries heavier penalties than the law under which he was convicted. With Parliament as busy as it is"—acidly—"passing punitive legislation, the opportunities of this kind are obviously limitless.

"As if these weren't enough, after release a prisoner can be immediately rearrested and recharged with a variation of the same offence for which he has just finished serving time. And for those rare ones who are acquitted, or against whom it is absolutely impossible to trump up some other charge, the Government can always impose banning orders or place them under house arrest for a period of five years, renewable by the Minister of Justice for as many additional periods as he wishes.

"It is really all quite monstrous, you know, quite monstrous."

"And their only crime, basically, is that all they want to do is overthrow the Government—"

"Not by violence, mind you!"

"—and replace it with something 'radically different.'"

SPECIAL BRANCH HAS A THANKLESS TASK (Natal Mercury, *Durban, English*) . . . (*This is the ninth in our series on South African Police personalities in Natal.*) *There isn't a country in the world where you will not find them—the Special Branch or Security Police. Some people admire them while others treat them with suspicion, for who hasn't heard of secret agents like 007 and Q018?*

It is a dangerous job being a Special Branch man, and also a thankless one. The hours are irregular, and as nobody really trusts you, you can never make permanent friends.

You can't afford to buy a house, because you are always on the move. You can never tell where you are going to be next month or next year, and if you are a married man with school-going kids it isn't exactly a comfortable life.

In charge of Security in the Port Natal Police Division is Major C. F. Zietsman. A Transvaler, Major Zietsman was born and educated in the Bethal-Ermelo areas.

He joined the SAP in 1944, and between then and now he has served for stretches in the CID and the Special Branch. He got his commission in 1959, while working as a detective in Durban.

Through discussions with him, his predecessor, Col. W. A. Willers, and other Security men, [this newspaper] *managed to piece together the following highlights of the Special Branch in South Africa.*

1947: The Special Branch is established by the SAP to combat subversive organisations and activities.

1950: The Communist Party of South Africa is banned by the Government.

1952: Communists, assisted by the African National Congress (ANC) and the South African Indian Congress (SAIC), launch their "defiance campaign." Countrywide racial disturbances occur and the Special Branch detain 60 leaders of the ANC and SAIC.

1955: The Congress Alliance (CA), consisting of the ANC (Africans), the SAIC (Indians), the South African Congress of Democrats (SACD—Whites), and the South African Coloured People's Congress (SAPPC—Coloureds), is formed.

The CA now served as the front organisation for subversion, and in June a "people's congress" is held at Kliptown to prepare the ground for a future "people's democracy."

1956: On December 5, Security men arrest 156 people on charges of high treason, but after a long trial they are all found not guilty.

1959: Sobukwe and some of his lieutenants break away from the ANC to form the Pan-Africanist Congress (PAC).

1960: The ANC and the PAC launch intensive campaigns against reference [pass] books. This results in riots and demonstrations on a large scale which reaches a disastrous climax on March 21 at Sharpeville and Langa. On March 30 a state of emergency is declared in some areas and the ANC and PAC are banned.

1961: Amid acts of sabotage in various parts of the country, South Africa becomes a republic on May 31. Another underground organisation—Umkhonto we Sizwe—is discovered by the Security Police, and the PAC becomes active again under the name "Poqo"—a terrorist movement.

1962–63: The General Law Amendment Act—the so-called Sabotage Bill, which provides for house arrest, 90 days' detention and the death penalty for sabotage, is passed.

With the Special Branch tracking them down, several ringleaders of the PAC flee the country.

In Basutoland they form the "Presidential Council," and the self-styled leader, Potlakko Leballo, announces in March, 1963, that the time for revolution in South Africa is ripe.

On April 5 the "Revolutionary Council" of the PAC in Maseru send telegrams to South African addresses. They all read: "Wild dancing on the 8th. Everybody must dance that night."

The Special Branch knows that the command had been given and all known PAC members are rounded up. The PAC crumbles and by June, Poqo has been smashed.

All the attention of Security Police is now focused on Umkhonto we Sizwe—a military organisation under a "National High Command," consisting of members of the banned Communist Party and the ANC.

Between 1961 and 1963, members of this organisation are responsible for 200 acts of sabotage.

Intensive investigations result in the location of the South African Communist Supreme Command on the farm Lilliesleaf at Rivonia near Johannesburg, and on July 11 many leaders are arrested in a Special Branch raid.

Valuable documents, and a radio transmitter used for broadcasts on Freedom Radio, are seized.

One of the documents, entitled "Operation Mayibuye," constitutes a detailed plan to bring the S. A. Government down through sabotage, guerrilla warfare, and, in the final stage, a large-scale revolution in which "freedom fighters" from outside would join those already in the country.

The Ye Chi Chan Club—a sabotage organisation among Coloureds aiming at guerrilla warfare as expounded by the Chinese Communist leader Mao Tse Tung, is uncovered by the Security Branch and its leaders rounded up in July, 1964. A month later 11 of them are sent to gaol for periods ranging from five to 10 years.

But still acts of sabotage occur and the Special Branch discover that another subversive organisation known as either the National Liberation Committee, the Socialist League, the African Freedom Movement or the African Resistance Movement, guided by Communists and "intellectuals," is endeavouring to destroy the Government.

On June 24, one of its members, John Harris, places a bomb at the Johannesburg station which killed an elderly woman, Mrs. Ethyl Rhys, and injured many others. He pays the supreme penalty on April 1, 1965.

The organisation is soon cracked wide open.

In July, 1964, the Security Branch gives the propagandists of violence another shock when 14 members of the "Central Committee" are arrested and the evidence by Secret Agent G. Ludi—Q018, results in 12 being sent to gaol and one being discharged.

The 14th man, Bram Fischer, jumps bail and goes underground. In June the "180 days" Clause is passed and on November 11 Bram Fischer is arrested.

On May 4, Fischer is found guilty on 15 counts and is given a sentence of life imprisonment.

"But," in the words of a senior officer, "we in the Special Branch are not relaxing our vigil, and the last word has definitely not yet been written."

"LEEUWKOP," said the low, thoughtful voice, "is the halfway house for most of us on the way to Robben Island. . . . They didn't introduce you to the soft-spoken young warder who orders the prisoners to come close to him and then kicks them in the genitals, did they? And I suppose the chief warder, for all his charm, didn't tell you what he said to me when I showed him the blood on our tunics and complained about assaults: 'Evidence? Blood on a tunic is not evidence!' And they didn't show you the 'exercise groups' when the warders stand around and beat the prisoners as they run by? Well, perhaps you saw Leeuwkop on one of its better days. . . .

"It's a pity you won't be allowed to go to Robben Island, too: perhaps they would have a good day there for you. Sometimes they have really jolly days. I remember a number of occasions when they had what they call 'carry-ons.' The lieutenant in charge says, 'Carry on,' and all the warders join in with a will, using baton staves and pick handles while the prisoners scramble frantically in all directions trying to escape. Those are happy days. . . .

"And there is the business of forcing the prisoners to carry rocks from the sea, over jagged boulders made slimy by seaweed, so that you slide and slip and get terribly cut, all the time being beaten or kicked or thwacked with batons. Teachers and those who apply for permission to study always get it worst on occasions like that. Sometimes the warders do it, sometimes fellow-Africans whom they set over us and call 'boss-boys.' There is a gang known as the 'Big Five' that rules the prisoners with the encouragement of the warders. Sometimes there are vicious gang-fights, sometimes they beat younger boys into submission for a series of sexual assaults, sometimes they beat or even kill their fellow-prisoners. The warders know all this, they encourage the Big Five.

"Then there are things such as the 'three meals,' which means you are deprived of three meals for a day for some offence such as talking to another prisoner, or having a newspaper clipping on a political subject. Sometimes the warders give cigarette butts or even marijuana to prisoners who will inform on other prisoners, and then turn on the informer too, when they have what they want from him. If you get informed about, sometimes your diet is reduced to near-starvation level, based on rice water, for as long as eighteen days. Sometimes they will strip you, tie you to a frame and lash you with a cane. Sometimes a warder will urinate in a prisoner's face. . . .

"And there is the psychological pressure, too. The physical may be no worse, outwardly, than making you stay awake until you are so exhausted that you can't fight back. But the aim is the destruction of all control over your own individuality, and it succeeds with all but the strongest.

"Now, all of these," the grave voice said, "are common to prisons everywhere, no doubt, and for many of us in South Africa the tortures during interrogation are worse than those after sentence. But at Robben Island there is a special viciousness reserved for political prisoners, for all who dare to challenge the Government.

"Some"—the dark eyes were candid and impassive—"of course are Communists, there is no denying it. But for many others the crime is simply that they are genuine idealists, that they are brave men risking their lives, their fortunes"—a slight smile came and went—"and their sacred honor, for what they believe to be best for South Africa. After all, you know, *we* are South Africans, too. This is *our* country, too. You have seen it"—and again, as often before and since, I heard that special note of loving come into a voice—"it is, after all, a wonderful country. It is worth fighting for, and dying for."

"They think so too."

"Oh, yes."

"And your side has not had all clean hands, nor have some against the Government hesitated to be as vicious as the Government, isn't that right?"

A sigh, and one of those shrugs that says all that can be said about the human condition down all the corridors and convolutions of time.

"I BELIEVE IN EXERCISING my rights," the staunch little Afrikaner said, "yes, sir, I believe in using my franchise and doing my duty as a citizen. Why, at this last election the Nat candidate here was no good, absolutely, and I said so. My friend was shocked. He said, 'Say, man, you're a traitor to the Government.' I said, 'I'm no traitor, Jack. About all the democracy I've got left is that little cross of mine and I'm going to put it where I please.' But I tell you, man, I just couldn't vote for that Nat candidate. So"—triumphantly—"I stayed home and didn't cast my vote! They can't make me support a man I don't believe in. I know my democratic rights."

Later he discussed the Bantu.

"This Government is doing more for them than any other Government has ever done. But maybe it's too late, you know, man? I'm almost afraid it's too late. I don't know whether we can hang on, or not. . . . Of course"—earnestly—"they're funny people. If I have one talent, maybe, it's knowing how to get along with them. I don't shout at them or abuse them like some do; it doesn't get you anywhere. A long time ago a friend of mine, a police officer, told me, 'Don't be sharp, don't be impatient, the moment you do they freeze up. You may ask a Bantu what happened, and he may start in Cape Town and go through Kimberley and Bloemfontein to get to P.E. when he tells you about it, but give him time, let him tell it his own way, don't nag him. If you do, you won't get anything.' And it's true, man, it's true. You have to know how to handle them."

GENEROUSLY GENERAL MOTORS lent me a car and driver to make the trip down what is known to South Africa as "The Garden Route," the beautiful coast road from P.E. south two hundred miles to George. On our left was the Indian Ocean, broken by rocky promontories, lovely inlets, sweeping bays, beaches, resorts; on our right the dramatic upthrust mountain ridge that marches the coastline to the Cape. It is a beautiful stretch of the country, which South Africans feel must be the most beautiful anywhere; the Italian and French Rivieras, New Zealand, California, Oregon, Washington, some others might argue. Suffice that it is gorgeous and attractive country and that the trip furnished a pleasant interval, within the South African context. "This is a resort area for Bantu," my driver would explain. "Over there on the left, that beach is reserved for Indians. . . . Coloureds have a beach about ten miles below this point."

We stayed overnight at an enormous, almost-empty hotel at Wilderness. It was windy and sharp, the air was cold, the season over: I was moving back into winter again as we went south toward the Cape. Next morning we drove over high, dramatic mountain passes (markers showing the tortuous, almost impossible route of ox-wagon trekkers long ago) inland to the ostrich capital, doudy little Oudtshoorn, sitting in its flat, high valley ringed by distant mountain ranges. The tall, stupid birds wandered erratically around the landscape peering at the passersby, their feathers and hides the basis of a thrifty industry.

My driver left me at the airport, turned back to P.E. A rattletrap old Suid-Afrikaanse Lugdiens Dakota limped in from East London, disgorged, received, prepared to depart, developed wing-flap trouble, disgorged again. We stood about the modest waiting room while the pilots and copilots shouted long-distance in Afrikaans to some far-off control point. At the counter two old Afrikaans women gossiped, slipping from their language to English and back again almost sentence by sentence, as naturally as you please. Suddenly one of the copilots looked out at the plane, shouted something. "The flaps have gone up by themselves, the mechanism is working again," an English-speaking passenger said. We trooped back aboard. The pilot came up the aisle. "It's only the flaps," he remarked in English with a big grin. "We don't use them except for landing." We were off, more than two hours late.

Somewhere in the next two hours, flying over tumbled mountains, high valleys, the tortured, monotonous country from Oudtshoorn to the Cape, the clouds began to thicken, the light to fade. The sun went down, evening came on, we flew through the last tattered remnants of light into a mild but persistent storm. Presently through the spattered windows we could see distant lights, sprawled out on either side of a squat mountain mass; and so came at last, through wind and rain and cold, wet weather, to gentle Cape Town, where such charming people live and such terrible things are done.

6.
The Cape

ONCE IN A WHILE, of course, it did rain in Cape Town, sometimes heavily, insistently, in great savage sheets attacking the ground, other times with a gentle, implacable mist that soaks—and soaks—and soaks—and soaks. But looking back now there is principally an impression of sunny days impatient for winter to end and spring to come; days that were clear and often in the 60's, once or twice as high as 75; days in which the city sparkled, and Table Mountain and the beautiful bay stood out sharp and clear, and over everything the soft wind blew, and sweetly, inescapably, filtering through and over every other sound, there came the hushed, persistent, English-Afrikaans call of the turtledoves, saying, "Coo, Coo—Karrrooo! . . . Coo, Coo—Karrrooo! . . . Coo, Coo—Karrrooo!"

Turtledoves and the soft sun shining, and the long walk down Government Avenue from the Mt. Nelson Hotel through the beautiful Gardens, ornamental now instead of practical as they were in the days when Jan van Riebeeck's men first planted them; past Cecil Rhodes, standing in stone, pointing north and admonishing, "Your hinterland lies there"; past General Smuts, brooding and looking far away, past the State President's rambling house and so to the pink Parliament buildings and then immediately on into broad, bustling Adderley Street, the Strand and all the other busy shopping areas with their hodgepodge of faces and races. And on beyond, "down at the bottom," as they say in every land where the British have been, the reclaimed acres of the Foreshore, where once the ships of the Dutch East Indies Company rode at anchor but now the great steel-and-glass monoliths of booming commerce front the sea. And over all the brooding presence of Table Mountain, always there even when hidden in its drifts of fog, always there even when you don't look at it, Cape Town's most famous resident, almost a living thing, so powerfully and magnetically does it dominate the town.

Lovely Cape Town, gentle and benign. It is no wonder the Pretorians love you with a passion surpassed only by that of your own children. What an irony of fate has made you the legislative seat of such a Government; how skillfully history has linked your beauty forever with the harsh decisions of beleaguered men; what a serene and gracious setting you provide for horror.

How sad, Cape Town.

How sad.

"I SUPPOSE IT'S WRONG to feel this way," the charming refugee from Central Africa said in her charming home in the charmingly wealthy suburb of Sea Point, "but personally, we love it. They're where They belong, They know Their place, They aren't allowed to make trouble, and we like it. It's all very well to talk about justice and human rights and the poor, downtrodden black man, but when you've been through it, you jolly well know They're not all Their sentimental sympathizers want you to believe They are. . . .

"Of course," she admitted with a sudden chuckle, "I wouldn't want the Government to hear me say this, but I must admit the Afrikaners are rather difficult, too. However, at least they're White and think the way we do. That excuses a lot."

"It does indeed," the roseate old English immigrant agreed. "I must say, thank God for them! They may be difficult, *but*—"

"They are, you know," his quiet, self-effacing wife said thoughtfully. "And you come across it in the most unexpected contexts. When we first came here, many years ago, we lived out in the country for a while. There wasn't any English school there so we had to send our son to the little Afrikaans school. One day he came home and said, 'We're going to have a rugby game next week. The Hertzogites are going to play the Botha-ites.' Now, what could a little boy make of that? He had never heard of either of these two men, yet here were the adult Afrikaners, fighting out their political battles through little children in school.

"They are so intolerant, you know," she said with a worried air. "So determined to run everything, so determined to impose everything they believe on the country without any room for any dissenting opinion. And I feel it's getting worse all the time."

"So do I," the native English-speaking lawyer said slowly. "One example, just recently: we have a very close and friendly, relaxed relationship with the Coloureds here in the Cape, you know; we've lived together for three hundred years, we know and like each other, there's more of them" —a humorous little smile—"in a lot of families than the Government wants to admit. Our relations have always been easy here, and when I say 'our' I don't just mean the English-speakers, but the Cape Afrikaans, too, who are generally more relaxed and liberal right down the line than their brethren up north. We all like the Coloureds, we genuinely do. Many of us in both white sections of the Cape, in fact, have always hoped that before too many years the Coloureds could be integrated wholly into the white community.

"So we have always had Coloured members of the Cape bar, we have been good friends, they have used the same chambers, the same robing rooms and all. Now suddenly a little while back the Government issued a regulation that from now on our Coloured colleagues can't use the same rooms with us. This means that while they're still permitted to practice with us, they have to go out to the Coloured township and back again to change for their appearances in court. It's a petty, nasty business. And the next step, of course, will be to ban them from joining the same bar, restrict them to practicing only in Coloured townships, get them out of Cape Town and other White areas of the Cape altogether—and then one more link will have been severed, one more gulf created between the races. The old Cape tradition of equality is being scientifically destroyed by these fellows from the Transvaal. They just don't understand us. The tragedy of the Transvaal is that they can't relax. They're attempting to impose an iron rigidity on the whole country. It's a great pity . . . great pity."

"We're hoping, you know," the quiet wife said with a certain nervous wistfulness, "that now that they have the power they *will* relax a little and not be so *determined*. We all keep hoping."

"I don't want anything to do with them," our charming hostess said. "They've absolutely no sense of humor, they're very touchy—you have to treat them just like you do an African. I don't want to associate with them anymore than I do with their Blacks. You have to avoid offending them just like you do a Native. I want no part of them."

"Yet I will say," the quiet wife replied with a growing firmness in her voice, "thank God they have a strong government to stand up and preserve our white supremacy for us. I do say that."

"Hear, hear," her husband said. "Hear, hear. These fellows don't fool around. When they see something starting among the Natives"—an expression of great satisfaction, a sudden ruthless chopping motion with the hand—"*zap!* They root it out! That's good! We like that!"

"Well, of course, when you come right down to it," said our hostess with a smile as the silent black presence came in with tea, "I, too, say thank God for the Government."

NANNY BRINGS WHITE CHILDREN TO THE COURT (Cape Argus, *English*) . . . *Because there was no one at home to look after them, a Native domestic servant brought three White children, two girls and a boy between the ages of three and seven years, to court yesterday.*

A court official found the woman sitting with the children in the corridor among non-European accused and witnesses during the lunch hour and saw her feeding the children from a packet of fish and chips.

It transpired that the Native woman brought the children to court at Wynberg from Steurhof when she was told that she had to attend court today.

She said that the children's parents were both working and she did not know what to do with them. She therefore brought them to court with her.

The woman told an official that she was a witness in a case in which it is alleged she was stabbed by a man at Langa.

Nzimani Nkomane was charged yesterday before Mr. J. J. Vermeulen with assault with intent to do grievous harm.

Florence Falatsi, the domestic servant who brought the children to court, said that on May 17 at Langa she had an argument with Nkomane and when she turned away from him he stabbed her in the back with a pocket knife.

Mr. J. J. Lapping, the prosecutor, then said he required no further evidence from the woman.

He said: "It has been brought to my notice that this woman is here with the three White children of her employer. They were brought to court because the parents are apparently working and there is no one else to look after them. I would like her to be excused as soon as possible."

He asked that the case be adjourned to July 29 to enable a further witness to be called.

The magistrate said: "I regard it as wrong that these children should have been brought here."

He ordered Falatsi to take the children back to their home immediately.

H E IS OLD AND tired from battling for the Coloureds, whom he regards with that deep affection to be found in so many Capetonians. But he is not beaten yet, and on this day he was in fighting form.

"Sometimes I think the Government wants to repeal the Coloured problem altogether," he said, rumpling his shock of white hair with an angry hand, "but damn it to bloody hell, they can't do it. Jannie van Riebeeck landed down there on the shore with thirty white men and one white woman, his own wife, and nine months after Jannie got here his men had created the Coloured problem.

"And it isn't something the Transvaal can push off on the Cape, either," he added with an indignant snort. "There's plenty of black Afrikaners up there on the farms in the Northern and Eastern Transvaal. Plenty of families here in the Cape have a touch of the tarbrush, but you can find plenty up there, too, all piously White and looking down on everybody else. Plenty of black eyes, curly hair and round faces in this country qualifying for White identification cards; you don't have to look far to see that! It makes me sick, the hypocrisy of it.

"As of August 1, you know, everybody in the country has to carry an identity card, Whites along with everybody else. It's raising hell with our Coloureds here in the Cape. Many of them who have passed for White up to now are being reclassified back to Coloured and it's creating terrible hardship for them, terrible! But does the Government listen? Can you appeal to it and get a fair judgment? Does anybody show any compassion? Ha!

"You know what it means to be reclassified from White to Coloured in this country? It means loss of jobs, forced changes of residence, poorer education, breaking up of families, complete disruption of lives—even suicides. Heretofore, it hasn't been so hard to be classified White, you see; the law up to now has been reasonably generous, it said that if you were accepted as White, if a certain number of White people would vouch for you, if you were accustomed to living as a White, then it was all right, you were a White. So a lot of our Coloureds have naturally gone over into the White category over the years—'try for White,' they call it, and a good many of them have made it and nobody has objected. Now they come before the Race Classification Board and apply for their new identity cards, and some ham-handed little Afrikaner with a kink in his curly black hair stamps 'Coloured' on their application and genuine tragedy results.

"Damn it," he said bitterly, "these are human lives they're playing with here! They're not statistics. It's all so damned unfair. For instance, you know, members of the Dutch Reformed Church are divided on racial lines in their separate congregations, but few if any D.R.C. members are having any trouble being classified White. If there's the slightest question, the Classification Board makes them White. But members of other faiths, your Anglicans, Methodists, Roman Catholics, Presbyterians and so on, aren't so fortunate, even if their ministers go before the board and certify that they accept them as Whites. Oh, no, it's the D.R.C.s who get the breaks, you can be sure of that!

"We had a census in 1951, you know, and a lot of the trouble stems from that. The country was told that all the information given on parents, grandparents, family background and so on, was 'for statistical purposes only' and would never be divulged to any other authority. But now all that is being dragged out and used against people who have appealed in the courts against being classified as Coloured.

"I have one case here"—he shuffled among his papers—"and it's typical, just typical. Here's a woman in her fifties, supporting a mother of eighty on a very small income; owns a tiny little house in a white area; once was an alcoholic—so many of the Coloureds are, you know, but can you blame them, halfway between the races as they are?—but has come out of it, hasn't had any trouble for five or six years. Now the board says she and her mother must be classified Coloured. This means she will lose her job, which she has to have to support herself and her mother; will lose her house, since she will now have to move to a Coloured area, and God knows what she'll find for the two of them there; and under the strain of it she's started drinking again, so that means you can probably scratch off two human lives, as her mother's helpless without her. Sure, maybe they aren't worth much to the great glorious state of the Transvalers, but they're worth something to themselves. And you know what the board said when I interceded to try to get some compassion for them"—he tossed it across the desk.

"We have reviewed the classification in this case," said the cold little sentence, *"and we see no reason to change it.*

"And that, by God, is your justice and human decency!" he exploded. "That, by God, is your fine, decent, upstanding, Christian Government! They—make—me—sick.

"It isn't as though they have any definite formula in classifying people, you know. Unless one appeals to the courts, and that's a bloody poor business since nine times out of ten they support the board anyway, the classifying is entirely in the hands of officials who don't even have any pretense of sociological or cultural education to back up their decisions. They do it behind closed doors in their own way. They don't go by pigmentation only, if they did they'd catch some of their own people, so they go into all sorts of extraneous background excuses. There are a few officials who take the time to be compassionate, but as you can see from that letter they're bloody few, bloody few. Most are youngsters still wet behind the ears who are entrusted with the power to completely change and control the destinies of individual lives. And that isn't right. It just isn't right."

He took a deep breath and a gulp of tea and was off again.

"Now, they talk," he said scornfully, "of establishing 'border industries' on the edge of Coloured locations just as they plan with the Bantu. But what does that mean? The danger of that is that these industries will be established largely by Afrikaners who, under the pretense of uplifting the Coloureds, want to maintain a differential wage scale for them. We have one wage level for Whites in this country, you know, and a lower one for Coloureds, lower again for Indians and lower still for Bantu. And this often in the selfsame industry where they're all doing the selfsame work. That's what they want to maintain with their blessed 'border industries.'

"And they're getting at them through politics, too. The Coloureds used to be on the general voting roll in the Cape, that was traditional Cape practice. Then the Nats took them off and put them on a separate roll and gave them four members of the House of Assembly and four Senators to represent them. Now the Government is going to bring in this 'political interference' bill to provide that no racial group can 'interfere' in the politics of another racial group. And they plan to establish a 'Coloured Council,' and the final step then will be to abolish their representation in the white Parliament, using the excuse that the 'Coloured Council' can represent them in their dealings with the Government, instead.

"In the past the Coloured man looked to the White man as his leader and his friend. Now the Government through this proposed 'Coloured Council' is going to appoint their leaders—because in effect that's how it'll be, they talk about 'stopping political interference by one racial group in the affairs of another' but you know damned well Pretoria's hand will be in it every time—and right away that will cause unhappiness, jealousy, mistrust. The majority of the Coloureds won't trust the council members because they'll regard them as stooges of the Government, and so they'll be. The council won't have any real political weight at all.

"And of course there's District 6. I grant you District 6 is a mess and a menace, overcrowded, dirty, diseased, dangerous. But, damn it, it's home to these people and has been for hundreds of years. Why can't the Government clean it up, build new housing developments and let the Coloureds stay there? That's all it needs, and with a little compassion it's what could be done. But they've got to be moved out, clear out of Cape Town, and as for District 6—well, wait a bit, my boy, some smart white developer will be in there with a big real estate deal going before long.

"Oh, I tell you," he declared, "it's vicious—vicious. But the symbol of it all, for the Coloureds, is the reclassification and the identity card. ["You carry credit cards, don't you?" they had demanded scornfully on The Bluff in Durban. "What's so difficult about that?"] Any policeman or peace officer can demand your card, for no reason at all, any place—at a meeting, on the street, in a theater, at a dance, a public function, a private party, bus, train, any place at all.

"There's a definite compartmentalization into racial camps going on. Everybody is gradually being cornered. They're doing nothing but create bloody hate and fear everywhere in this country."

DOOLITTLE SAYS APARTHEID IS WORTHY OF TRIAL (Sunday Express, *Johannesburg, English*) . . . *South Africa's race policies are a worthwhile experiment and deserve the approbation and support of the world, former American flying ace, General James Doolittle, said in Johannesburg this week.*

General Doolittle, 70, who led the first Allied bombing raid on Tokyo in the Second World War, has spent three weeks in South Africa as guest of the South African Foundation with his wife, Jo. He left for Britain and America on Thursday.

Apartheid was something completely new in the field of race relations. Nobody knew how it would work, or what changes to the system would have to be made, but it should be given a chance.

General Doolittle spent two days in South-West Africa. "On the whole, South-West Africans are satisfied with their relationship with South Africa, and they hope it will continue. Some people believe it would be best for South-West Africa to be administered by the United Nations. These people are in a decided minority."

In the Transkei, too, he said, he found most of the people he met happy and contented with their lot. "The Transkei is quiet, very interesting and going along smoothly. Although, of course, you will never find any group of people who agree entirely."

Nowhere on his trip had he been subjected to propaganda. "I have not been sold on this system. I have sold myself. As a result of careful investigation, I have come up with the conclusion that the system is worthy of trial."

EXODUS (Editorial, Cape Herald, *English)* . . . *This week we must once again publish the tragic story of the exodus of Coloured people from the shores of South Africa.*

Whatever way you look at it, whatever name you wish to call it, the stark fact remains: People are getting out.

They are getting out in large numbers, numbers too high for us to afford. But it is not only numbers. The really important factor is quality. These people are in the main people of high qualifications, and good skill. They are people who would be an asset to any civilised country in the world today. That is why other countries, which place their future development before colour, are keen to get them.

But South Africa lets them go.

In the midst of her need for skill and manpower, whilst she spends a fortune looking for immigrants overseas, South Africa lets this most excellent human material slip through its fingers.

Why do they go?

With monotonous regularity they repeat the same story: We see no future here for ourselves or our children.

We, Cape Herald, do not believe this.

We say that South Africa offers a glorious future for all of her peoples. We plead with these people: Stick it out, stay here with us, help us row the boat to the shore, and we'll all reach the blessed land.

But it is no use. . . .

THE UNIVERSITY COLLEGE of the Western Cape sits out on the Cape Flats some twenty miles from Cape Town, its newly built, spic-and-span, completely modern buildings placed tastefully amid pleasant lawns and open esplanades. It is in every way a fine, modern, up-to-date, attractive school, and the Government can rightfully point to it and say to critics, "You see this fine university we have built with our own hard-earned rand? Try to deny its excellence, if you can." And no honest critic can, of course, for it is a model school.

The only things that distinguish it from similar newly created universities in California or Manchester or anywhere else are that its students are all some shade of brown or black; and that, being Coloureds, they are cut off from their white countrymen of the same college generation and are unable, now, to find their higher education anywhere else.

To head this expensive and modern experiment there was, when I came through, another of the big, old, rangy, craggy Boer types, Dr. Meiering, and this time there was a real, oily, unctuous, deliberately nasty attempt to provoke an argument about the United States and South Africa. It is worth noting because it was the only time in the entire journey that I met a South African of any prominence, English-speaker, Afrikaner, Indian, Coloured or Bantu, who was anything other than kind, courteous, hospitable and friendly. Many disagreed with America, many were sharply critical in the many arguments we had, but all were decent about it. The head of the University College of the Western Cape could not resist putting on a tricky, pious-pompous, nasty-nice performance, and after it had gone on for fifteen minutes, raking back and forth over everything from Soapy Williams to Watts, his visitor finally blew up and snapped that he wasn't there to argue about the United States, he was there to learn about the university. My two official companions, one Afrikaans and the other English-speaking, looked absolutely stricken; but Dr. Meiering of course was equal to it.

"Oh, my dear friend," he said in his heavily accented English, "my dear friend, I'm not passing judgments on anyone, not at all, my dear friend, not at all. We are just talking, my dear friend, just talking."

From that point, however, we talked about the university, and the official philosophy was very smoothly and competently stated:

"Our purpose here, you see, my dear friend, is to develop Coloured leaders who will take an interest in their own group, just as the purpose of the Indian universities is to do the same for them, the Bantu universities the same for them.

"Now, there is a parallel to be drawn here, Mr. Drroooreee, with the Afrikaner people, of whom, as you are doubtless aware, I am one. Sixty years ago the Afrikaner people were on the verge of bankruptcy, morally, politically, emotionally. We had a regeneration because we had leaders who were dedicated to their own people, to Afrikanerdom. And now, Mr. Drroooreee, now the Afrikaner is running the country—with the cooperation," he added smoothly, with a kindly look at my English-speaking companion, "with the cooperation, of course, of our English-speaking compatriots, for which we are very grateful. Of course. We have national unity, we have dedication, we have a purpose, Mr. Drroooreee.

"Now, the Coloured people"—and he spoke with a gentle, fatherly regret—"the Coloured people haven't got that unity, that dedication, that purpose. And the reason for that is that they don't have the leaders. That is what this university aims to do: provide them with leaders who will be proud of serving their own group, proud of their own group, happy to be in it, and stay in it.

"Many of the Coloured leaders in the past were agitators who tried to develop in our Coloured people a feeling of dissatisfaction and frustration —a kind of antagonistic feeling against the Whites *which will get them no place, Mr. Drroooreee, no place!* So the Government decided to start this university to remove that frustration, that pointless striving for things in the white man's world that they just can't have, Mr. Drroooreee; they just can't have, as South Africa is organized, and as the best interests of all our South African peoples dictate . . . they just can't have.

"I had some hesitations about it myself, my dear friend, I can tell you that, I did. When the Prime Minister first called me in and asked me if I would head this university, I said to the Prime Minister, on one condition only. I said to the Prime Minister that I would take this job if it would provide leaders for the Coloured people who would serve the Coloured people genuinely, exclusively—then I would give my whole heart to it, and gladly, gladly! The Prime Minister assured me that it would, and so I accepted.

"Now, you may ask why Coloured students can't go to mixed or 'open' universities, as we used to call them, mixed with Whites, as they were up to four years ago. Well, the answer to that, my dear friend, is very simple. Coloured people who go to mixed universities have a new ideal—to forget their own people and 'try for White.' They begin to despise their own people. The coloured people have lost many potential leaders because of this, many are now agitators.

"It is just not true, Mr. Drroooreee, that Coloured students don't want to remain with the Coloured people when they are educated. There is a great conservatism among the Coloured people, they have an appreciation for their own group. Healthy-minded, well-balanced Coloured people welcome the opportunity we are giving them to achieve separate development. We are doing our level best to get our students to realize that their best happiness lies in serving their own people. I think I may say that the great majority are responding.

"The education we are giving them here—and ultimately, Mr. Drroooreee, sometime before too long, all of us Whites will be gone and not only students but staff will all be Coloured—is the same as they received in the past at the University of Cape Town. They can get all the higher degrees that they could get at Cape Town. It is true, of course, that we must study the needs of the Coloured community and educate them in the skills that future leaders must have. Accordingly, we are giving them theological training—yes"—with some surprise—"D.R.C.— and we have a course to train high school teachers; and we teach social sciences, welfare—librarianship, there is a great need for librarians. For instance, Mr. Drroooreee, librarians: I can give you a fine example there.

"We had a young Coloured man who went to the University of Cape Town in 1959, and there he took a librarian's course and failed. He was also, I regret to say, under the influence of a leftist organization. In fact, he became secretary of a cell. Then he came to us, when this university was opened in 1960, and he found here a staff dedicated to helping. He gave up his leftist ideas. He resumed his library course, he became campus correspondent for one of our Coloured newspapers, he graduated as a librarian.

"I clapped him on the back and I said, 'Now you have an opportunity to serve your own people as a librarian! Now you can help them to find the type of books they should read!' And, my, you should have seen that young man's eyes light up, my dear friend, knowing he could now serve his own people as a librarian!

"We have courses in commerce, too, and I can tell you about another young man. The Coloured Development Fund had heard that a certain Coloured bank needed a manager, so they came to us for a recommendation. We talked to one of our graduates. He was overjoyed, Mr. Drrooo-reee. I clapped him on the back and I said, 'Just think, you have an opportunity to serve your own people and help them with their funds!' What joy on the face of that young man, Mr. Drroooreee! Just compare that with the dissatisfied young man at an open university! Restless and frustrated and becoming an agitator against the white man! What a difference, Mr. Drroooreee, what a difference!

"So you see, my dear friend, we are working, we are striving, we are achieving our purpose, to provide leaders for the coloured people *who are satisfied to be Coloured!* Why should they try for White, Mr. Drrooo-reee? There is so much more satisfaction and reward for them in remaining with their own Coloured group!"

And so we parted, more amicably, amid his self-congratulations, than we had met. He is now retired, someone else is carrying on the cause he so nobly represented. But it is certain it has not changed much, nor will.

After we left him we inspected some of the buildings, visited a spotless residence hall, two boys to a room, everything fresh, shining, attractive. The kids made us welcome, smiling shyly, explaining things with an obvious pride; elsewhere on campus, boys and girls alike gave us shy but friendly smiles as they went about their courses. It was just like any university anywhere. Only it wasn't.

NON-WHITE TO STAND IN SRC ELECTION (Cape Times, *English*)
. . . *Mr. Kemal Casoojee, a 24-year-old University of Cape Town law student, may be the last non-White to serve on the students' representative council of a "White" university.*

He is the only non-White standing in next week's UCT council elections. As chairman of the influential Day Students' Council, Mr. Casoojee stands a good chance.

But if Senator De Klerk's Extension of University Education Amendment Bill becomes law, Mr. Casoojee will have to relinquish all representative offices on the campus.

"At the moment it is quite legitimate for me to stand," he said yesterday.

The Government was "trying to reduce UCT and Wits to the same

level of the tribal colleges, like Turfloop, Stellenbosch, Fort Hare, Pre-
toria, and the University College of the Western Cape."

Mr. *Casoojee said the Bill, which would make it impossible for a non-*
White to belong to any society on the campus except one connected with
his field of study, hit at the very idea of a university education.

"Your education does not start or finish in the lecture room—it is a
question of discussing, debating, exchanging ideas."

LETTER (Cape Town, Die Burger, *Afrikaans) . . . One must expect*
that certain Whites support the apartheid policy because they cannot tol-
erate non-Whites. But if our existence as a separate White nation has to
be based on intolerance, then we are doomed.

"THERE ISN'T A single board in Cape Town that I haven't been on,"
the frisky little gentleman of seventy-six said proudly, and out of
his brown Cape Malay face the dark eyes blinked and twinkled and
rolled about like two busy little marbles. "City council, school board,
hospital board and all. That's the Cape tradition."

"I know it is, Councillor, that's why I'm a little puzzled to find you
supporting the Government's moves to isolate all the Cape Coloureds
and make it impossible for you to associate with the Whites any longer."

"Puzzling? Puzzling? Puzzling?" The little eyes snapped and corus-
cated. "Well, now: puzzling. Let me see. No, I wouldn't say it is so
puzzling. First of all, mind you, there are three groups, not just one, and
I assure you, we are all independent! Yes, sir, we are all very independent! There are the Cape Malays, of which I am one, and then there are
the Cape Griquas, and then there are the Cape Coloureds, close to
2,000,000 peoples, all told. You may lump us all together for easy
reference, the Government may do so, but I assure you we are all independent. V—ery independent.

"Now, then, why is it puzzling? You see, you have to understand that
heretofore we have been under the Cape Provincial Council, and when
we had a grievance, we had to appeal to them. Maybe they would do
something about it"—a pause, the little eyes debating which way to dart
next—"and maybe they wouldn't! Now we will be away from them,
with a vote entirely our own.

"Now, let us take the proposed Coloured Council, what will be the
situation? It will have thirty elected members, drawn from Coloured
areas throughout the Republic, and it will have sixteen nominated by the
Government."

"Why will it have sixteen nominated by the Government? Doesn't that give the Government an awfully big stick—"

"Why, to have an even balance, you know!"

"Even?"

"Yes, between moderates and extremists. The Government will name sixteen so that it can be sure we have some moderates on the Council. If you have all extremists, you never get anything done, isn't that right?"

"Some people might say that with a solid bloc of sixteen for the Government, you might not get anything done, either—at least anything except what the Government approves."

"Oh, some people, some people! Some people are always saying things. Some people, you know, say that we Coloureds should continue to have representatives in the White Parliament—keep the four we have now, you know, even after the Council is established. But why? Now the Progressives are trying to get control of all four of those seats, saying they will take care of the Coloured people. But what good would it do to have four Progressives in Parliament?" The bright little eyes twinkled mischievously. "We already have one in there, Mrs. Suzman. She shouts and what does she get? Eh? What does she get?

"Now, mind you, some people say that this proposed Coloured Council is discrimination. Well, we say, all right, it's discrimination, but it's something, it's better than nothing. When you belong to this new Council, you need not necessarily accept all the Government does. If all the thirty elected members vote together against the Government"—a twinkle and a knowing nod—"then they will carry the day over the sixteen nominated by the Government, will they not?"

"You expect this."

Another twinkle.

"It is possible, it is possible. Also, you know, the Government will appropriate specific sums just for us, in the budget of the Minister for Coloured Affairs. All the Coloured schools will be controlled by us and shall be maintained by us. Our businesses will be protected. We will be able to say to the Government, we didn't ask for separation, you gave us separation—now protect us. We can do this whenever we see in a Coloured business area, or some other aspect affecting Coloured life, a White, an Indian, a Bantu.

"They want us to retain our own identity, the Government says this. We want it too, mind you! We have our own mode of life and we would like to retain that. We want to be able to choose our own friends and business associates from within our own group."

"And you don't think the Coloureds will regret that they no longer have the opportunity to become White, to be really integrated in the white community?"

For a split second the perky little eyes lost their sparkle; but Councillor Dollie has not been on every board in Cape Town, dealing with the white Government all his life, for nothing. The sparkle surged back.

"White, White, White! What does it require, to be a white person under the laws of the Government? It does not take so very much, not so very much indeed! The law says that a White is 'a person who obviously is . . . or is accepted by the community as such.' Mind you, now, if I want to be White, it is not so difficult. I only have to entertain Whites in my home, be entertained in theirs, for three months or so, then I go to them and I say, 'Will you testify for me that I'm accepted as White?' And they say, 'Sure,' and so I become White. It is not so difficult!"

"Not, perhaps, if you're Councillor Dollie. But what about a lot of Coloureds who don't have your position, or your financial standing, maybe, who aren't known and can't afford to get Whites to testify for them?"

The eyes were thoughtful again for a second, and the rationale, for a brief moment, faltered a little.

"It is true, what about my brother, who perhaps is a shade darker than I am? I dare not associate with him then, after I am reclassified White. Once you are reclassified White, then you must be very cautious. This breaks up families, you know, it does cause hardship. And witnesses can be bought to testify that you are White, they can be bought if one has the money. It happens all the time.

"But"—and the bright birdlike gleam came back, the shrewd little face became quickly animated again—"under the new plan, the Government will stand behind us, it will protect the Coloureds. We are a people that need the support of the Government, you know; where would we be without it? In separation, we got nowhere, we have not achieved much, one must be frank. We fear the Bantu in competition for work, as things are now, there are so many of them. We also fear the Indians, although with them you might say, There are only half a million to our million and a half, why fear them? But the Indian is a born shopkeeper, he either had it from birth or he has learned it. The Coloured is afraid the Indian will come in and take business from him. He has patience, he is more thrifty, we can't compete with him. He is also more communal, the Indian is always helping other Indians. I probably wouldn't help another Malay, now; I would probably say, You'd better get on and help yourself. The Indian has many organizations to help Indians that we don't have.

"No, no!"—for the last time the bright little eyes clouded with thought, then sparkled back to life again.

"The Bantu—the Indians—we need the Government, we Coloureds. We will take what the Government proposes, we will make the best of it! We insist on having the law apply as the law is made, so that each has his own place and no one race can take advantage of the other. That is what we insist. That is what the Government tells us they will do for us. We will make the best of it!"

SEGREGATION AT STATION IS A "SUCCESS" (Cape Argus, English) . . . *The segregation of White and non-White suburban passengers at Cape Town Station, brought into operation yesterday, has proved a great success in the alleviation of congestion at entrances and exits previously used by all passengers, a Railway official said today.*

Segregation of the races was brought into force at noon yesterday with the opening of the new non-White concourse, which straddles the Woodstock end of the suburban platforms, and the two main entrances and exits for these passengers.

The official said the real proof of the new scheme came at yesterday's evening peak-hour rush. "Things went extremely well—in fact, better than we had hoped," he said.

By this morning non-White passengers were already becoming used to the scheme, and Railway police and officials who were again on duty to direct non-White passengers to their exits found their task very much easier than at noon yesterday.

BEAUTIFUL STATION—BUT OH THE STAIRS (Cape Times, English) . . . *It's a beautiful station but it's rather tiring getting there,"* seemed to be the general opinion of non-White train-users interviewed yesterday about their new suburban concourse at Cape Town railway station.

The concourse, which will cost R2m. when completed, is a large building supported on steel box girders above the main suburban lines and is about 400 yards down the platform from the White concourse.

There is no ground-level approach to it. Both entrances, from the Foreshore and Castle Street, lead up a long flight of stairs, as do the approaches from the concourse to the platforms.

Mr. Merriman Goduka, of Langa [Bantu township], a regular train passenger, said: "It's a very smart station and much nicer than the old one, but there are too many stairs. If there were automatic stairs it would be fine."

Said Mr. Devilliers Nxola, of Guguletu [Bantu township]: "The only trouble is that it takes much longer to catch a train because there is much farther to walk to get to the station, and then there are so many stairs to climb."

The younger people do not seem to mind the stairs and distance. . . .

COLOURED PASSENGERS' UNSHELTERED ROUTE (Cape Times, *English*) . . . *From Miss Mildred Dow* (*St. Elmo, Bell Road, Kenilworth*): *Coloured passengers seem delighted with the new facilities, Mr. J. M. Vlok, System Manager, Cape Western, is reported to have said* (Cape Times, *July 21*).

While not doubting that many may be pleased with the new station concourse once they arrive there, I make bold to say all Coloured passengers would be more gratified if they could approach their new concourse from the old station by a covered route instead of by a disused and for the most part roofless platform, at the end of which they have to cross along an exposed path to the entrance to their part of the new station.

Certainly all White passengers who have any conscience would be happier if their fellow-travellers of other races were offered the protection we enjoy on our daily journeys to and from the train.

Coloured skins feel the elements in the same way as White ones do, and age, frailness and childhood are common to the entire human family and not the prerogative of those with White skins.

I was deeply ashamed as I walked, protected from the rain, to my train the other evening, and saw the long line of Coloured and other races making their sad way through the elements to their part of the station to join the same train.

Will the Cape Times *and all right-thinking Capetonians join me in asking the Railways to give coverage to the Coloured route immediately, in the name of our common humanity.*

LETTERS TO THE CAPE TIMES . . . From Mr. Basil Davis (*Woodside, Fifth Avenue, Grassy Park*)—

Mr. Vlok says the Coloured people seemed delighted with the new station. I can assure him the only people delighted with it are the Whites, who don't have to walk halfway to Woodstock station and back, up and down staircases, to board a train, and on top of it run a gauntlet of armed policemen waiting.

There were no incidents. Of course not. Not with the entire SAR and H police force standing by, which, of course, was unnecessary, as was proved.

From "Michael"—

Now we have the non-European station ready for use. Did nobody think of the old folks who also use the station?

How do they expect these old-timers to climb up and down those steps?
Surely they would have thought of something if Whites had to use the
steps. I hope something will be done.

LETTERS TO THE CAPE ARGUS . . . Sir: The new apartheid ar-
rangements at Cape Town station are very heartbreaking and degrading
for our people.
   Why are we tortured like this?
   If millions are to be wasted on apartheid why not give us our own
Cape Town station?
LANSDOWNE   L

SIR: This latest piece of utter humiliation means that I personally have
to walk almost to the Castle, then towards the sea and then back again
towards Sea Point in order to get to my train seat.
   By the way, we are the Railways' best supporters.
LANSDOWNE   NON-WHITE

H E IS IN HIS mid-forties, graying, earnest, intelligent; the dark face
quick to show emotion, the words with a sharper bite than those
of some of his elders. He is a leader of his people, insofar as a group so
easygoing and amicable as the Coloureds in the midst of their buffeting
by the white man can be said to have a leader. They are not a group that
takes kindly to unified purpose ("We want to give them unity, my dear
friend, we want to give them pride in themselves"), there are almost as
many factions as there are Coloureds, but if anyone can be said to be a
leader, he probably is. On this day in the cluttered office of the newspaper he edits (owned and published, inevitably, by a White), he too was
pragmatic if restive.

"We want full citizenship for the Coloured people," he said slowly.
"We reject apartheid as a solution for our problems. At the same time,
however, we realize that there isn't any sort of easy solution such as full
citizenship for all South Africa's peoples, because many of them are not
capable as yet of exercising it. We are not prepared to work out a blue-
print for South Africa, the way some outsiders are. We know our own
difficulties and our own situation. But we do believe the Coloureds are in
a special relationship with the Whites, particularly here in the Cape. We
always have been, and despite what they may do in Pretoria, we always

will be. We are essentially part of the same stream of life and civilization, even of the same blood, in many cases. We are dealing here with 1,500,-000 people, who are in a special category.

"I don't favor the Coloured Council, but if one is going into politics at all, one can't avoid it. The Government is going along inexorably, step by step, on its policies. Therefore it becomes a matter of using the means we have at hand. The Council is going to be established, so our problem is, do we stay on the sidelines and stay out of it, with only an occasional protest which is here today, and tomorrow you forget all about it—or do we go in and try to exercise our influence?

"We think we should go in and use the Council for our own purposes. We feel we owe it to our people to urge that they go in. You see, if you only give a negative lead, then a new leadership is going to be built up and it may be a destructive one that could do great damage to the Coloured people. Also, in a situation in which the Government has so much power, it could also be a futile leadership. So *we* say, Get into this mechanism they're creating, and let's hope to make it reasonably effective.

"You see," he said, and his tone became that of a rather tired but patient man who has argued the point many times with disputatious colleagues, "if we go into this thing with the attitude, 'Smash the Council!' then the Government would simply create something we couldn't smash. Now, in the Council the Government may be creating something it can't control. We might be able to get somewhere with it, without getting where the Government wants to go—and not in any revolutionary or radical sense, either, but just in the direction of a more common-sense, compassionate, human solution for the Coloureds' problems. . . .

"And, too, you know, the climate of the outside world may also change. Once the Black question is settled, then I believe the Nats will go much farther than they are now prepared to say, to take in the Coloured people."

"The liberal Cape Nats I've talked to keep talking about 'five or six years' from now; that seems to be their magic deadline for some liberalizing change in policy, not only with regard to the Coloureds but to everything."

"Yes," he said tartly, "what they mean is, When Dr. Verwoerd retires. But they were saying 'five or six years'—five or six years ago. Whenever anything happens in the way of more restrictions, the liberal Cape Nats always say, in five or six years. There is a certain social level where it's very easy for these people to tell each other that in five or six years things will change, but when it comes to the point where they should act—they don't act. You take some of the liberal Afrikaners out at the University of Stellenbosch, which is sort of the Mother Church of Afrikanerdom, all their major leaders down the years have gone there or taught there, it's really the fount of their philosophy and mystique. The number of people at Stellenbosch who will speak out for what their consciences tell them is right is much less than it was three years ago. The number of voices raised against the Government in the Cape are fewer. They seem content to subside, and teach. After all, there was one leading one out there who was two years away from his pension. He spoke up, and somebody from the Government said to him, Look, you want your pension, you keep quiet or you'll be cut off and ostracized, you won't get it and you'll cut yourself off from your own roots in Afrikanerdom. Now he's quiet. . . .

"The illiberal North," he said quietly, "always wins over the liberal Cape. . . .

"If there's to be a relaxing of legislation, a change of tendency, a change of direction, if there is to be someone to say, Let us stop crushing them—I wonder if the only man who can do it is not Verwoerd himself? If someone is to have the guts to say, Let's go easier on the Coloured people, I think only Verwoerd can do it. All it needs is one powerful speech from him and the country will fall in line. I am quite convinced that if Hendrik Verwoerd takes it on himself to say that the survival of the Afrikaner people requires a Coloured presence in Parliament, it will be done. . . .

"As it is now," he remarked with a rueful smile, "people go along saying the Afrikaner will change toward the Coloured, but by golly, he doesn't. The Cape Town City Council, for instance, has balked at enforcing beach apartheid, which is something we've never had here. So the Government has arbitrarily taken over the power to do it and is forcing the Cape to go along."

"What about Coloureds who become reclassified and move over into the White world?"

He frowned and spoke without hesitation.

"The bulk of the Coloured people have very little sympathy with those who want to cross the line. We feel, Look, if you want to leave us, go ahead—but you're deserting us. We have so many cases of our better qualified people leaving us. If I were asked whether the Coloureds as a group should try to join the Whites, I would say no. We would lose all our best people. The Government wants us to, you know"—a dry little smile—"the Government has reclassified over five hundred recently from Coloured to White—it can reclassify, you know, even without a request from the individual, and sometimes it does. The Government skims off all our best people when they reach a certain level. The Government is cool to the idea of complete integration of the Coloureds"—again the dry smile—"but there is quite a noticeable willingness to swell the ranks of the Whites by taking our best people in. And then, of course, they become the greatest apologists and supporters of the Government. The man who is made White is going to be ultra-White—he's going to do so much for Government policy that it just isn't true. The

Government will sometimes say to the people in an area that has been declared White under the Group Areas Act, Look, have yourself declared White, stay here, we'll do it if you ask. And many, of course, take that way out. . . .

"We need leaders," he said with a worried frown. "We need all we can get. . . ."

ONE NATION (Editorial, Cape Herald, Coloured) . . . It used to be the fashion (and still is in many circles) to speak of South Africa as a multi-racial country. Probably this can be defended, as there is no doubt that there are many racial types in our total population.

But there is a new fashion now taking root, and one which we believe to be not only misleading, but also dangerous. It is the fashion of speaking of South Africa as a multi-national country. People who lean this way say: There are many nations within the one South Africa.

We cannot agree with this.

The multi-nation people would have us believe that there is a White South African nation, a Coloured South African nation, an African (or Bantu) South African nation, an Indian South African nation. We would probably have to add a Chinese South African nation and—yes—an Honorary White (Japanese) South African nation. What a business! . . .

There is great danger for the country, as well as for the peoples within it, unless we keep firmly to the idea of South African nationhood for all, and South African unity. Even party politics, the world over known for its divisive quality, should never be used to divide the nation. Where will such division end? Will it not end in the warring of the separate nations within our borders? To whom will the separate nations owe loyalty? . . .

AGAIN THE TALL, old, rangy Boer type, born on the platteland, Afrikaner of the Afrikaners, but this time a liberal, one of the Progressive candidates for the four Coloured seats in Parliament; fast-spoken, quick-humored, charming as the Afrikaans can be and so frequently are; tough.

After a pleasant lunch at the Mt. Nelson Hotel, a discussion of his candidacy—"The Government"—cheerfully—"will probably prevent us from running, they're using the Coloured Council as an excuse," there came the saving grace that so often characterizes all races in the strange society:

"I'm an optimist. I feel it will work out, here in South Africa, though I think we'll have a hell of a hard time of it. But this is a practical people, a pragmatic people. We Afrikaners have faced great hardships in our history and we've adapted to them and come through. When we realize we must face up to living in a multiracial society, we will, but we'll have a hell of a bloody time. Not any Russian Revolution, or any great bloodbath, mind you, but there'll be a lot of trouble before it settles down. Maybe I'm too optimistic, but I still think it will."

POLITICAL CYNICISM, SAYS PROG (Cape Times, *English*) . . .
The Progressive Party MP, Mrs. Helen Suzman, yesterday accused the Nationalist Government of "the height of political cynicism in proposing a bill to 'prohibit interference of one population group in the political affairs or institutions of another group.' "

Mention of this proposed bill was made yesterday in the State President's speech opening Parliament.

Mrs. Suzman said: "For a Government that has done nothing but 'meddle' in the politics of the non-Whites, to contemplate legislation to prevent such meddling is the height of political cynicism.

"Nobody yet knows what the contemplated measure will contain, but few will have any doubt that it is intended to prevent the Progressive Party from winning the four Parliamentary Coloured seats.

"The Government clearly realizes that the Coloured people do not support its policy of racial discrimination and will opt for candidates representing a party that does not use race as a yardstick.

"In fact the Progressive Party makes no distinction between the Coloured seats and the White seats.

"The Government's previous history regarding the Coloured franchise is shameful. Any further measures to reduce the value of the Coloured vote can only result in a worsening of relations between Whites and non-Whites. . . ."

SECOND CLASS CITIZENS (*Editorial*, Cape Herald, *Coloured*) . . .
Are there second-class citizens in South Africa? Yes, there are. And we need look no further than ourselves, the Coloured people, as examples. Ever since Union, in 1910, when the Coloured people were deprived of the right to be Members of Parliament, we have lost first-class status. Since 1956 we have not even the right to vote on the same roll as White voters, and our vote counts for so little one has to go into decimals to calculate it.

We ask ourselves, and the White voters of the country to tell us plainly and simply why, just why we should not be allowed to take part in discussions in Parliament and in the Provincial councils, on an equal basis with them.

We ask whether the White people in this country believe that their safety, security and welfare will be endangered if Coloured people are allowed to play a part in the legislation of this country.

We believe that the interests of Coloured and White cannot be separated in this country. We believe, too, that if an attempt is made, as is being made now, to separate them, to preach continually the idea of what is "in ons eie belange," then the White people are creating differences of interest which will divide these two population groups with bad results.

We make bold to say that if the Coloured people are given the vote, we will not use it on a colour basis. We will not use it to return Coloured men to Parliament simply because they are Coloured. We will return those people whom we consider to be the best for the position. Surely this is all that can be asked of the voter? . . .

IT CAME TIME FOR the Diplomatic Party, inevitable for the visiting American, generous and kind of his hosts. "You didn't bring a tuxedo?"—mild dismay at the other end of the line. "No, I decided I wouldn't use it more than twice and I wasn't about to lug it half around the world for that." "Oh, good," the quick recovery, "then we'll have an excuse to be informal. I really hate these Washington-type parties, don't you?"

But Washington-type party of course it was: limousines at eight—cocktails until eight-thirty—dinner with all its courses and all its wines until nine-thirty—the gentlemen withdrawing to talk politics until ten thirty, the ladies gossiping meanwhile—the gentlemen back for half an hour, the conversation turning to mutual jolly nothings—at 11 P.M. the Ambassador departing—and all the dutiful covey, up, up and awaaaaay.

Harsh comments on the Government from the lower ranks, not too diplomatic at times, but at higher levels, some patience and understanding:

"If you could only do away with this petty apartheid"—earnestly—"if we could only see some signs of a more human approach—then I don't think Washington would be so disturbed, we could argue with these northern Africans when they come to us and complain—"

The sad acknowledgment, the rueful agreement, the quiet despair. These, after all, were not Government people. Government people don't get invited to official American affairs very often, and it has created in them a state of mind in which they don't want to come.

This is too bad, because the way to soften the separators is not by separating them. . . .

Another night, another dinner, big and brassy, high in a gorgeous penthouse apartment overlooking Sea Point. The clever, charming banker of French-Huguenot descent, Jan Marais ("Mah-ray-yah"), his delightful wife Peggy. Soft lights, good food, many drinks; the white waves curling out beyond the beach highway, just at the edge of light. A buffet dinner, companions shifting, changing, coming, going. Again the second-level American diplomats, drunken and depressed, the smiling Afrikaners, the jovial English-speakers, the black presences serving silently. The host, head of the Trust Bank, proudly: "My bank is run on American methods. I visit the States all the time, I send our people there to study your methods. We're growing fantastically. We boom as South Africa booms." And on the Government, cautiously, "It's changing. Job classification is breaking down every day, the economic factor is working its inevitable changes. Give us time!" And then, afraid of becoming too serious—as who would want to, on such a balmy, gentle night in Cape Town, in such good, rich company, in such a beautiful home—"How about another drink, everyone? Is everybody getting enough of everything?" Hugs and kisses, greetings and exclamations, old friends and new. Money, money, money. When they have it, in the Republic, they have it big. . . .

And one other night, one other dinner, very small: the old Afrikaans family, steady and hard-working, risen very high in the industry and the publishing of South Africa. "We thought you might like just a plain Afrikaner family night, a chance to relax from all your activities, and talk." I did, and they couldn't have been nicer, conversing sometimes in English for my benefit, as happened in so many of the Afrikaans homes to which I was made welcome; slipping into Afrikaans frequently among themselves, but always stopping to translate and share the joke, for joke it usually was. The Afrikaner in his home is one of the friendliest, most good-natured, and kindliest persons on earth.

"We grew up in the country, you know," one cousin said. "We had hard times. Both our fathers were predicants, ministers you would say; life was very strict. That's why we always start with grace before meals, we always have; most Afrikaans families do, even now. We had simple food, such as we've served you tonight—we thought you would like a typical Afrikaner meal. It's always heavy on beef, venison, meats of all kinds; squash, potatoes, mealies—" He smiled. "Simple things for simple people."

"Delicious"—and it was.

"Thank you, we think so. We still like it best. My wife and I have traveled a lot in connection with business, eaten in many fine restaurants of the world, but it's always good to get home again and eat the food we grew up on. It's still the best.

"South Africa is changing, but basically the Afrikaner is still a very simple person. We went through a long depression, you know, after the Anglo-Boer War, on into the twenties. It's only lately that we've begun to have enough to afford luxuries. Many of us still like the simple ways best—"

"Except the young ones," his cousin interjected wryly.

"Yes, the young ones like fancier things. They are getting away from us a little, some of them. They don't seem to care as much about our history and our struggle as we do, who grew up with it. My cousin here wasn't able to afford an automobile until he was forty-five. Now the kids are after you for one the minute they get old enough to drive. Afrikanerdom is changing some. . . . No"—a charming smile—"not soft. I wouldn't say any Afrikaner is soft. But changing some. Changing. . . .

"Yes, I suppose you might say we are 'liberal Cape Nats.' We believe the 'Cape Dutch' modify the Transvalers some. At least"—again the smile—"we hope we do."

"We support the Government, though," his cousin said. "Make no mistake of that. Against the outside world, we naturally do. Though we hope we exercise some influence to soften things a little . . . if the outside world"—a sudden sad expression, out of place in the comfortable home, all of us snug before the crackling fire while outside in torrential rain and howling wind the Cape was being as nasty as the Cape can be—"will only let us alone."

Later they sent me, at my request, several packets of protea seeds. When our fall came, their spring, I planted them. They are growing rapidly now, thrifty and undaunted, sturdy little South Africans twelve thousand miles from home.

NATS., STUDENTS DIVIDED OVER RIGHTIST PAPER (Sunday Express, *Johannesburg, English*) . . . *Afrikaans universities and newspapers are sharply divided by the row in the Nationalist Party which has followed attacks on prominent Afrikaner businessmen by the editor of the* South African Observer, *Mr. S. E. D. Brown.*

Mr. Brown's attacks, linking the businessmen with "far Left" organisations and "a secret revolutionary purpose" aimed against South Africa, have provoked a sharp counter-attack from moderate Nationalists.

Supporting the moderates are the student bodies at Stellenbosch and Pretoria, the two biggest Afrikaans universities. And, on the side of Mr. Brown and his S.A. *Observer are students at the University of the Free State and, Transvaal Nationalists claim, at Potchefstroom University.*

At mass meetings this week, Stellenbosch and Pretoria students divorced themselves from a motion supporting Mr. Brown which was passed at the recent Afrikaanse Studentebond congress at Stellenbosch. They issued statements condemning his attacks on Afrikaans businessmen.

But the Students' Representative Council at the University of the Free State has decided to stand by the Afrikaanse Studentebond motion supporting Mr. Brown and has demanded to know why the Nationalist Party has withdrawn its support from the S.A. Observer.

Potchefstroom students have taken no decision in the matter but, according to Nationalist spokesmen, most students at the university are either indifferent to the controversy or favour Mr. Brown and his journal. Nationalist Press comment on the struggle has shown general condemnation of the S.A. Observer, *with* Die Burger *and* Die Beeld *most outspoken.*

B EFORE THE lunch my charming English-speaking host defended the Government stoutly: doing more for the Blacks than ever before—relations between English and Afrikaans better than ever before—South Africa better than ever before. But after drinks, food, wine, K.W.V. brandy, a less jolly prospect:

"Of course one has to admit"—unhappily—"that the Afrikaner is a very spiteful animal—very spiteful. They're a spiteful people. They don't want us to make any mistake about who's on top. . . . Every regulation has a hammer in it. If only they weren't so ham-handed!"

And at the door a little later when we met two of his Afrikaans friends, genuine liking and genuine friendliness: relations really were very good, right then. But then the first Afrikaner said to the second, "Have you heard the Van der Merwe joke about the gorilla?" Its convolutions were a little obscure but its purport was clear, and the punch line was something about, "But I thought that bloody gorilla was a bloody Englishman!" And great roars of laughter from the Afrikaners and from my English friend a hurried little laugh, a quick changing of subject: that tightly laughing discomfort one sees on similar occasions on the faces of Jews in America—the pained look, hastily concealed, the forced amusement, the quick diversion—that same ugly, instantaneous little insight into the heart of things that all too often leers out from beneath the happy, enforced joviality.

And other episodes of the same general tone, particularly in Cape Town; and the growing conviction that the English-speakers are afraid; the more perceptive and intelligent, for all that they thank God for the Government and whistle in the wind, are uneasy and afraid.

DOMINEE EXPLAINS HIS "BUY AFRIKAANS" PLEA (Sunday Express, *Johannesburg, English*) . . . *The Rev. P.S. Du Plessis, P.O. Box 53, Steynsrus, writes:*

As I am the person under fire, I would like to comment on the report from your Bloemfontein correspondent headlined "Buy Afrikaans is plea of Free State Dominee," which appeared in the Express *of July 3.*

The correspondent telephoned me and it was difficult to give over the telephone an exact version of my views which I expressed in a letter to Die Volksblad. *The line was by no means clear, and I could not make out who was speaking at the time.*

In fairness to your correspondent, I must admit that he has given a fairly good report of the trend of our conversation.

I have not expressed my views from any political motives. I have merely attempted to convey to the Afrikaans-speaking people that they have a moral duty towards their own Afrikaans-speaking traders.

I never wrote "that it is highly immoral for any Afrikaner to buy anything from a non-Afrikaans business." I stated quite clearly that as a basic principle it would be highly immoral only if an Afrikaner bought an article elsewhere if he could have bought it from one of his own people.

In other words, charity begins at home—even in business. Although an article may be cheaper elsewhere, the principle still stands. . . .

It was not my intention to disparage any other race or creed, or even to propound a policy of seclusion. It was a serious and honest opinion expressed in an Afrikaans paper for Afrikaans-speaking people only.

A T THE MT. NELSON, the hard-eyed young Afrikaner, the jolly, rotund old English-speaker, officials of the Fisheries Development Corporation:

One million three hundred thousand tons of fish annually, half a million of it from South-West Africa, the rest from the Republic . . . annual gross 61 million rand, 34 million South Africa, 27 million South-West . . . lobster, sardines, horse mackerel, anchovy, U.S. taking the bulk of the lobsters, 63 countries all told taking fish, fish meal and fish oil . . . 7,500 men on the boats, 70,000 in the canneries . . . the FDC an Investment Development Corporation offspring, loans for fishing equipment, boats, housing for workers . . . third largest fish-exporting country in the world, planning to be larger . . . two bottles of wine, U.S.-South Africa, World Court, Bobby Kennedy . . . cordial farewell, the Republic humming right along in yet another economic sector.

THE CRIME OF COLOUR (Editorial, Cape Herald, *English)* . . .
*Time and again the courts are required to settle the question: Is this
person White or Coloured? Have we ever stopped to ask what lies behind this seemingly straightforward, even innocent question?*

*If we do stop to think, we shall be horrified at the pain, the misery,
the very agony which must accompany every such inquiry. Here is a
human drama of the greatest magnitude. It is something which reaches
down to the depths of the soul of those concerned.*

*The inquiries come at a time when people have formed all sorts of
human associations. They have gone to school, to cinemas, to beaches.
They have made friends, found sweethearts, they have married, cele-
brated weddings with circles of friends, bought or occupied homes. They
have had and reared children. And they have jobs.*

*All of these are not only human, but normal, natural and to a large
extent private affairs. They should be matters in which the individuals
concerned should have the say. But, due to our race-laws, this is not so.*

*Because of race (which is natural) and race-discrimination (which
South African law decrees) these normal and intimate aspects of the
lives of people get examined, they are investigated by officials, they are
bared and exposed to the glare of the public courtroom and (save for
the names) to the press.*

*What happens to one's soul in a case such as this? Children look on
their parents as near-criminals, for their behaviour has brought the scorn
of their play-mates on them. Men or women look at their sweethearts
with changed feelings, thinking that they have betrayed them. Parents
regard their own families with shame, as though something terrible happened.*

*But what is the crime which lies at the root of all this humiliation? It
is the crime of having been born with a coloured skin. It is the crime of
having been created as God has seen fit to create.* . . .

AUDIENCE BAN BLIGHTS CULTURE (Cape Herald, *English)* . . .
*For the culture-loving Coloured person Cape Town has become a desert.
In the past few years, one after another of the leading theatres have
closed their doors to the Coloured theatre-goer.*

*For live theatre, Coloured people now have to rely mainly on church
halls and the Luxurama at Wynberg—where the Coloured Eoan Group
recently presented "Oklahoma."*

*Most of the present legislation on separate audiences dates from the
publicity-starred visits of British pop stars Adam Faith and Dusty Spring-
field.*

Following the rumpus over separate audiences the Government crystallised the law in Proclamation 26 in February, 1965, which required a permit for mixed and Coloured shows in White areas.

This week a "Herald" reporter rang some of the leading theatres to find out the audience position. At two of the theatres the position is still confusing—the Labia, now showing an American musical, "Once Upon A Mattress," and the Little Theatre sponsored by Cape Town University.

A spokesman at the Little Theatre said she had orders from the Director, Prof. Inskip, not to comment on the race position. She did say, however, that the theatre had been used to give mixed shows.

Then the Government had stepped in with orders for separate audiences. "The next show opens on March 1 and quite honestly I don't know what the position is at the moment or will be when we open."

At the Labia, Manager Mr. R. Hill said that the Government had stepped in with separate audience orders. "At the moment we are giving no performances for Coloured people although if a production warranted it we could try for a permit."

However, it is believed that the Labia often invites Coloured people to rehearsals.

"WE INSIST ON THEIR studying the whole continent," the Afrikaans professor at Stellenbosch said with satisfaction. "We've made Africa one of the compulsive continents, they can't get away from it. After all"—he laughed cheerfully—"they *can't* get away from it, can they? So we train them in African history, geography, geology, economics, the whole of it. . . .

"We tell our students that when they are abroad, they must attack, right? Whenever someone starts criticizing South Africa, they must attack. Now, I know from my own experience, when I was lecturing in America recently, I got along fine with American students, but I always remembered to attack. If you meet a heckler, the best way is to hit him down. I've found that works with students from other African countries, too, when they are overseas. They become very aggressive about South Africa, you know—the only way to get the aggressiveness stopped is to hit them down. I remember in America I had a question from a student from Malawi—so I asked right back about whether their government hadn't thrown its opposition into jail. It stopped him," he said with satisfaction. "I hit him right down."

At the City Hall Coloured people are allowed to watch the bi-weekly concerts but have separate seats and a separate entrance.

The Director of Capab, Mr. A. P. Theron, said that his group often gave shows for Coloured audiences. "We have given successful performances at Kimberley, Elsies River and other places.

"Really it depends on where we can get a hall or a stage. And when we do put on a show we get terrific support from the Coloured people. Also the prices are reduced from the White showings."

At the Alhambra where the Coloured Eaon group have shown "Oklahoma," Coloured audiences are never seen. Said the manager:

"I cannot remember if we ever gave shows here for Coloured people."

"A T THE TIME we left the Commonwealth and formed the Republic in 1961," the young English-speaking lawyer said, "opinion was very divided. The Nats try to give you the impression now that the referendum was one-sided and overwhelming, and as peoples' memories grow hazy, they may make the impression stick. The fact is that the vote for a Republic was 849,958 to 779,878 against, and that's a majority of only 74,080 out of an all-White electorate. Which isn't all that smashing.

"This was largely attributable, of course, to loyalty to England on the part of the English-speakers." His eyes narrowed and he stared thoughtfully out at the busy harbor from his office high above the Foreshore. "You won't find that loyalty now.

"Something has snapped, inside the English-descended here, and I think Rhodesia has been the principal cause of it. Rhodesia and Britain's equivocations on South-West Africa. But Rhodesia has been the main thing. Always before, my parents and their generation, even a good many of us younger ones, felt that we could rely upon England—that England was always there, no matter what, an anchor to the wind for us, a sort of protective force—distant, and getting rapidly weaker, though she might be.

"The Nats argued that this was a divided loyalty, that it was bad for South Africa, that once the English-speakers cut the last sentimental tie and made up our minds that South Africa is the only country we have, it would be better for everybody.

"In this," he conceded quietly, "time has proved them to be substantially right. It has been better for South Africa in many ways, it has contributed quite a bit to a greater unity in the face of outside pressures, it has forced many of us to reexamine the bases of our citizenship and our patriotism, and come to terms with the fact that we are South Africans, first and above all.

"But still there was this sentimental feeling lingering on despite the Republic—how could there help but be, given the same blood, and after so many years?

"Furthermore, there is our trade with Britain, which is very advantageous to both of us, and which is the main reason Britain doesn't dare get too tough with us. There were dire predictions that when we left the Commonwealth we would be economically ostracized, our trade would drop off drastically. But economic facts are more hardheaded than some politicians. In 1962 our exports to Britain were approximately 242,-000,000 rand. In 1963 they were up to 279 million, in 1964, 301, and last year 360. Approximately one-third of our exports go to Britain, and she in turn has steadily increased investments here that are now somewhere above 2,000,000,000 rand. New overseas investments are being curtailed somewhat by the Labour Government, but that is a matter of internal economic policy and not a political move.

"Nonetheless, there is Rhodesia, and there it has all broken down at last, at least in a sentimental sense. You'll find that the great majority of English-speakers are thoroughly fed up with Britain. The Afrikaners were anyway, and now Rhodesia has forced the great majority of us to join them. Even though Rhodesia has gone a lot further than we have toward a multiracial society—they have some twelve Bantu sitting in their Parliament, you know, which could never happen here under present circumstances—still the basic similarities between two White minority governments create a profound fellow-feeling. Britain's attempt to appease the other African states by attempting to knock down the Ian Smith regime has created great bitterness against her. We know the other African states and we know how much their loyalties are worth. Above all, many of us can't stomach the idea of Whites attempting to overthrow Whites for the benefit of Blacks. It goes beyond thinking, it becomes visceral.

"So you'll find that England has lost, probably forever, the great reservoir of sentimental goodwill she had here among the English-speaking. Financial goodwill remains, that's a practical, pragmatic matter the English themselves can understand. But 'Good old England—Hurrah for the Queen?' Not anymore. . . .

"And, too, you know, we are all concerned about what England will do on the South-West Africa issue now that it has moved out of the legal area of the World Court into the strictly political area of the United Nations. We see America trying to appease the Africans and Asians by going along with a strictly illegal, emotional attack upon South Africa, and we expect England to do the same. We can't for the life of us see what either of you hope to gain by it, but there it is.

"It turns us toward the Afrikaans, naturally enough." He smiled a knowing and rather weary smile, for one so young and prosperous. "By

England's own choice, there is no looking back to England anymore. Like Van der Merwe or don't like him, trust or mistrust, love or fear, here we are together. . . ."

"And yet, you know," the Afrikaans politician, as young as he, said thoughtfully a couple of days later, "there is one thing you can say for England, I really believe. Whatever her faults, and God knows there have been many, I think that during the heyday of the British Empire the world was probably better run, with more fairness and justice and basic human decency to a greater portion of mankind, over a wider area of the earth, than it ever was before, has been since, or probably ever will be again. And I say that, who am Afrikaner born and bred and had two grandmothers and an aunt in the concentration camps. I wouldn't want the Empire back, I'm glad we're free from England forever, but this I do believe. I think history will record it to be true, after all our present passions die away."

THE INEVITABLE Taxicab Driver, taking me to Parliament on a day when it was too wet to walk down the Avenue:

"Maybe all this debating will get us somewhere, I don't know. The Government says we're all happy here, but you talk to the Natives and the Coloureds privately and you'll find there's great unhappiness. Yet I'm amazed at how they accept their lot, I really am, but they do, there's really a genuine good feeling toward the Whites. Amazes me, but there it is. Politics is an awful game, isn't it? Awful things they do in that place to the Natives and Coloureds, it would drive you around the bend sometimes, wouldn't it? Still, we get along here, it's a wonderful country, isn't it?"

He deposited me near the Press Gate and drove off, as confused as a lot of other people in this somewhat confusing land.

"WHEN I WAS STUDYING in the States a couple of years ago," the charming young Afrikaner said, "one of the town's leading society ladies called me up one day to say she had heard I was in town and would I speak to her club. I said I would. 'You *will* be sure to wear your native costume, won't you?' she said anxiously. So I put on my best suit and tie and went along."

"They do have a funny conception, some of them," an equally charming English-speaker agreed from down the table. "I was over there on business for a month several years ago and was asked to speak at some club, Lions or Rotary or something. When I said I lived on the outskirts of Cape Town one of the chaps asked very seriously, 'Can you hear the wild animals roaring at night?' Well, we live right off the freeway, you know, De Waal Drive, near Groote Schuur, the Prime Minister's residence, Cecil Rhodes' old home. Rhodes had a small zoo, which is still maintained. So I was able to say, yes, I could actually hear the lions roaring at night where I lived, and a fearful sound it was." He chuckled. "Almost as fearful as the traffic on De Waal Drive, though I didn't tell him that. He seemed delighted with this confirmation of his picture of primitive South Africa."

INDUSTRIAL ACT CHANGES: WIDE IMPLICATIONS (Cape Argus, *English*) . . . *The introduction by the Minister of Labour (Mr. Marais Viljoen) of an amendment to the Industrial Conciliation Act— published in Parliament today—brings to the Assembly a controversy which has been raging among trade unions in the out-of-session period.*

Simply stated, the measure will provide for employers to be compelled to deduct trade union dues from the wages of workers who are members of certain trade unions. These trade unions will be specified by the Minister in notices in the "Government Gazette."

It is clear, however, from the dispute that has been going on in the trade unions that the measure has far wider implications.

The multi-racial Trade Union Council of South Africa is strongly opposed to the measure. TUCSA officials have said it is aimed at eliminating multi-racialism in the trade union movement.

They add that the strength of trade unionism lies in multi-racialism, claiming that the principle of equal pay for equal work is the best protection for workers of all races.

The all-White South African Confederation of Labour supports the measure as strongly as TUCSA opposes it, believing that it will strengthen the all-White body.

Its officials say that the system of equal pay for equal work no longer offers protection to the living standards of the White worker.

"I T IS VERY UNUSUAL for the average South African to think of government in terms of commercial self-interest or graft"—the businessman, out from England on a two-year study mission for his company—"because the top Afrikaners have succeeded so well in selling themselves to their own people as highly moral, religious men with a divine mission to run the country. Also, it's part of the pattern to look down on other countries and call them corrupt, as a means of building up the South African ego.

"But, there are cases.

"For instance, there was something here called the Parity Insurance Company, which carried third-party insurance for some 400,000 motorists. The company went into liquidation in 1964 and a great clamor went up. So last year the Government brought in a 'Motor Vehicle Insurance Amendment Bill'—they do love long titles that give a pious aspect to things—and it proposed that only eleven named companies should be permitted to deal in third-party insurance. Charges were made in Parliament and elsewhere that the Government had handpicked its pals and given them 2,000,000 rand of the public money. But the Government rode right over the protests, as it always does, and the bill became law. Now, I don't know that the Government's pals were singled out for preferential treatment, but those eleven companies are doing very well, thank you very much.

"Also, there's been a fight here similar to the one you had in the States a while back, between margarine and butter. Here, the dairy lobby won. The Dairy Control Board issued a regulation that margarine could not be artificially colored but must be sold white. Certain big dairy farmers, Afrikaans, are continuing to do very well as a result.

"Diamonds, sugar, wool, alcohol—all the major economic groups seek favors from the Government, and a lot of favors have been given, too. Often when some area is declared White under Group Areas, the next thing you know some Minister's company or Minister's wife has moved in before it became public knowledge, bought up property cutrate and started a charming real estate development. And there are cases in which certain favored farmers have been given unusually handsome recompense when their land has been taken for Bantu homelands.

"There is big money to be made here, and while the Afrikaner still doesn't dominate industry, he's making great strides. A lot of the wealth is beginning to come to him, and in a semisocialistic state such as they have here, with the Government really underwriting a great deal of the business enterprise, the opportunities for governmental favoritism, big deals and big profits for the Afrikaners are increasing all the time. It's probably only human that they should want to sup at the table who have so long had to sup on the stoop, but it is beginning to erode the selfless image of the Government. Too many people are making too much money with Government help. It's probably no different from other countries, no different from what the big English-speaking interests have always done here, but the difference is that the others have never pretended a pious approach to business. A lot of Afrikaners have, and now the juxtaposition of piety and greed is beginning to produce some rather startling contrasts between profession and practice."

HOUSEWIFE HELPED REBUILD NEWLANDS COTTAGE (Cape Times, *English*) . . . *Buying a cottage with a view to restoring it is one thing. Supervising the operation is quite another. This was the experience of Mrs. J. H. Selfe, whose role of housewife and mother was changed overnight into that of "OC Housebuilding."*

It all happened in April this year when the builder in charge of renovating the two semi-detached cottages which Mrs. Selfe and her husband, Minister Counsellor to South Africa's permanent delegation to the United Nations in Geneva, had bought in Wheelan Street, Newlands, told them he was unable to finish the job. When the shock of disappointment had worn off, Mrs. Selfe decided to carry on herself.

"There's very little she doesn't know about labourers' wages, working hours, or the Workmen's Compensation Act as a result," Mr. Selfe [said].

Living in the only two completed rooms, Mrs. Selfe supervised work, paid the workmen at the end of each week; and time after time loaded up her little car with bags of cement, pipes for the plumber, locks and other building materials.

"The existing building consisted of two four-roomed cottages with an extra three rooms tacked onto the back. Those we knocked down," she told me.

The only sign of them now is a built-in barbeque on the patio which was originally an outside toilet.

"We turned the house back to front so that the most important rooms, living room and two bedrooms, now face north while the study, dining room and bathroom look out onto Wheelan Street.

"You should have seen the lawn when we moved in. We sent away eight loads of rubble—corrugated iron, bicycle wheels and tin cans—before we could prepare it. . . ."

GROUP AREA APPEAL TO MAREE (Cape Times, *English*) . . . *The Cape Town City Council is to ask the Minister of Community Development, Mr. Maree, not to declare any more areas in the City for White occupation till disqualified people living in areas already declared have been rehoused.*

It will also ask him to receive a deputation consisting of the chairman of the Health and Housing Committee, Mrs. M. A. Hopkins, and officials concerned to discuss a number of housing problems.

In a memorandum to be sent to Mr. Maree the Council says that a slowing down of the resettlement of disqualified families in areas already declared for White occupation is essential as efforts to provide more housing are being impeded by staffing difficulties in the City Engineer's Department.

One of the conditions set by the National Housing Commission for a loan to build Heideveld Extension No. 1 was that all the houses be allocated to the Department of Community Development for resettling non-White families living in areas declared for Whites.

The Council will say that it has a waiting list of more than 11,000 for its houses and that it will have to close the list if it has to give the State all the houses in the Heideveld extension scheme.

It will suggest that 40 per cent of the houses be allocated to the State for resettling displaced families, 40 per cent to applicants on the waiting list, and 20 per cent for slum clearance—including the removal of pondoks but not slums in areas declared for Whites.

F AST-TALKING, bright-eyed, keen, decisive, having his ample share of the family intelligence and charm—Dr. Leonard Verwoerd, younger brother of the Prime Minister.

"We're changing, you know. We're changing. Separate development isn't static, it's moving all the time. But we're doing things at the right time, we're not letting ourselves be stampeded by the Opposition, or"—a chuckle—"by Mrs. Suzman, either. We're doing it in the right way, when the proper time comes. After all, a government can't do things just because the opposition says it must—the Opposition would say, Look, you're stealing our ideas, that would give them a political advantage. We can't move too fast, we have to do things gradually.

"After all, a lot of politics is timing, isn't it? Suppose a government rides roughshod over the feelings of its supporters and says bluntly, To-morrow morning we will do so-and-so for the Bantu. What happens? It's too rapid and too blunt. There has to be timing and a regard for feelings. When things change gradually, people don't realize they're changing. If things are done quietly—step-by-step—then change comes and people accept it.

"Enormous advances have been brought about by my brother for the Bantu, the Coloureds and the Indians in the past ten years. Housing, education, job improvement, medical and welfare—many things. Just one small example: we used to have a corps of Coloureds restricted to unarmed work-duty with the Army. It was unthinkable they'd be allowed to bear arms or work closely with the Whites. But we had a parade down the street here not so long ago and we had that Corps of Coloureds armed and marching down the streets with the Whites, carrying drawn bayonets—and everybody applauded and accepted. It was done gradually, you see, gradually. Now it's accepted. . . .

"Our basic purpose has to be one of morality, honesty and justice for all people. If we proceed on that basis, the future will take care of itself. We can't see into South Africa's future: all we can do is provide the foundation on which it will be built."

"It is changing," agreed our fellow-luncheon guest, the old Afrikaans industrialist, also bright-eyed, keen and charming (after he had explained several times how sorry he was about the latest race riots in America).

"We've got a think coming—oh, yes, we've got a think coming! Apartheid is changing, as Len says. Economic factors are bringing great changes. Job classification is changing, there are innumerable exemptions every day—it's all changing.

"But, as he says, it's being done quietly and gradually, because we want to do things that will genuinely help the Bantu and the Coloureds and the Indians. They are part of us, you see. Tell me, now! Did you ever meet a South African who didn't love the black man?"

POLICE HOLD AFRICAN WHO HELD WHITE (Rand Daily Mail, *English*) . . . *A young African who took a Free State farmer to the nearest magistrate's office on Wednesday after the farmer had shot the African's dog was yesterday arrested by the police on a charge of assault.*

This was confirmed in Pretoria by a Police Headquarters spokesman.

He said the farmer, a Mr. Taljaard, who farmed near Bultfontein, had shot the African's dog, claiming it had been killing his sheep.

The African allegedly attacked the farmer and grabbed hold of the farmer's 0.22 rifle. He beat the farmer with the butt of the gun, then forced him to drive to the local magistrate's office, where he turned him over to the police.

The spokesman said police investigated complaints by both parties and later arrested the African on a charge of assault.

5 YEARS FOR BEATING BOY TO DEATH (Cape Times, *English*) . . . *Bernard Lempert, 35-year-old father of three young children, was yesterday convicted in Louis Trichardt Circuit Court of culpable homicide and sentenced to five years for what Mr. Justice Cillie described as a "brutal and inhuman assault on a child."*

Lempert, a farmer, had been charged with the murder of 12-year-old

Wilson Konyane, who had at one time worked for Lempert on his Levubu farm and who died during a thrashing given by Lempert.

In his judgment Mr. Justice Cillie said that before an accused could be convicted of murder the State had to prove beyond reasonable doubt that there was an intention to kill.

The State had proved, and indeed it was admitted by Lempert, that he beat a boy with a number of sticks, all about an inch in diameter, till he died.

It was impossible to determine for how long the thrashing lasted, but Lempert himself suggested that it lasted for about 15 minutes—and the court accepted that this was the minimum time it would have taken to inflict the number of strokes which the doctor had described as "innumerable."

In all probability the thrashing lasted for considerably longer.

What saved Lempert from being convicted of murder was his evidence that he intended to beat the boy on the buttocks, which was the appropriate place for a thrashing.

On examining the photographs of the boy's body it seemed that the greatest injury was inflicted on or about the buttocks.

Lempert's motive in administering the thrashing was, apparently, to give the boy more severe punishment than that which the court imposed when Wilson was convicted of setting fire to Lempert's barn.

"But it was a brutal and inhuman assault on this child and out of all proportion to the punishment which would be imposed by a legally constituted court for a comparable offence," the judge said.

To a large extent Lempert was reckless, and all the facts showed that he knew what he was doing and realized what the consequences could be.

He had made himself guilty of culpable homicide of a serious nature.

Mrs. M. A. Wilken, a neighbour of Lempert, said that they farmed on the Levubu River, which was the boundary between White and African territory.

Theft and wire-cutting by marauding Africans, plus the drought, had embittered Lempert. When Wilson set fire to his barn, it was the last straw.

Mr. Justice Cillie said it was no easy task to pass an appropriate sentence.

The crime involved a child on the one hand and a fully grown man on the other. And the child remained a child, regardless of his race.

The court would be failing in its duty if it did not pass a severe sentence.

HOW TO TREAT SERVANTS (Star, *Johannesburg, English*) . . .
*All members of a farmer's household should treat their African servants
with respect and with recognition of their dignity as human beings.*

No farmer should ever give vent to annoyance in an undignified manner.

*An African should always be addressed by the name originally given
to him.*

*Use a language the African understands, or preferably, learn to speak
his own language.*

*All these instructions are taken from a new booklet for farmers which
has been introduced by the Department of Information in Pretoria.*

*African labour, subject as it is to so many restrictions and regulations,
has become a major problem to every South African farmer.*

*There are, for example, eight categories of Africans who may live on
farms. But there are another six categories governing Africans who may
be employed on farms.*

*The new booklet lists all these, tells farmers how to register service
contracts, how labour is to be obtained, how the State demands farm
labourers to be housed and so on.*

The booklet is obtainable from the Department of Information, Private Bag 152, Pretoria.

T HERE ARE IN South Africa, as there are in all societies with a basic
humanitarian tradition (however much it may have been eroded by
time and events), a group of gallant ladies who really do go out of their
way, sometimes at real risk to themselves, to help the Bantu. Some are
Afrikaans, busy with their charitable groups and donations, and to them
full credit. Others are English-speaking, and on them there seems to fall
the often grubby task of meeting the immediate evils, trying to ease the
direct pressures, doing what they can to alleviate the day-by-day suffer-
ings imposed by the strange society upon its darker children. Their men
talk: they do the dirty work. To them more credit, for their activities
constantly approach the line at which a jealous and defensive Government says: Go no further or you will be harassed, banned, jailed or
exiled.

What they do is humanitarian, but the mere fact of being humanitarian can sometimes be construed as a declaration of war upon policy. In
the context of South Africa today, they need to be brave to do this, and
they are.

On this particular morning in the Athlone Advice Bureau they were
doing just what they do every day and will continue to do every day as

long as the Government permits: trying to help bewildered Bantu find their way through the thousand-and-one petty regulations administered by a thousand-and-one petty officials whose end purpose seems to be to defeat and discourage the Natives in every possible way. No one in the Government of course will ever admit that this is the purpose, but it is the result. Therefore earnest, hard-working, patient and somehow good-humored housewives leave their comfortable homes, suppress their indignant emotions and offer their services, without pay and frequently without thanks from their dismayed and usually frightened clients, never knowing at what moment the Security Police may appear and close them down. It is an impressive and moving sight; and it, too, is South Africa.

To the visitor who asks how they stand it, there is the simplest of explanations: because it has to be done.

"You have to harden yourself, you see. You just can't afford to sentimentalize or you go mad. We are members of the Black Sash, the anti-Government women's organization. The newspapers"—a wry smile—"always photograph us picketing the Prime Minister or something, so you've probably seen our pictures in the States—and we run the bureau in cooperation with the Institute of Race Relations. Since many areas of giving political assistance to the Bantu are now denied us by the Government, this helps us feel that at least we're doing a little something. We pick up the pieces, you might say. We probably don't accomplish much —nine times out of ten about all we can do is pass these poor people along to the proper official, explain to him details of cases he hasn't had time to notice, and hope for the best. But at least you don't feel as though you're standing aside and letting injustice occur without a challenge." Again the wry smile and a gesture around the small, cluttered, threadbare office with its four or five white women, its two Bantu interpreters, and its dozen or so scared black supplicants. "Not a very large challenge, possibly, but—a challenge.

"At first we began by helping mostly women who were in trouble because of the pass laws. Pass-books were made compulsory for Bantu women for the first time in 1957; up to then it had only been men. The result was that many were arrested. Often they had to stay overnight in jail, frequently with babies. At first we began raising money for a bail fund, but it very soon got to be so many that we just couldn't handle it without some office to work from. So the Black Sash opened this and ran it alone until 1962. Since then the Institute of Race Relations has been contributing to the cost. We have two interpreters, one of them"—a woman in her fifties, rattling away in Xhosa to an elderly man who kept shaking his head uncertainly—"is very active politically, she is the wife of a man who has been banned. The other"—a bright-faced, shrewd-looking little hunchbacked man—"is very intelligent, very good with these people. We have an average of four or five white women who come in every day to help out.

"At first, as I say, we tried to raise bail; then that was prohibited, so now we just do what we can. Initially it was only women who were helped, now it's both; primarily it's trouble with passes, but we also get involved with jobs, housing, medical care—any area where they need help.

"All of our work here grows out of the Government's attempt to force them out of the Cape. The Government has always maintained that it must get the Natives out of the Western Cape because they aren't indigenous here; and this despite the obvious fact that the Cape is becoming more and more industrialized and more and more are needed here economically. A man can only be in the Cape temporarily on a seventy-two-hour pass. He can be here permanently only if he was born here, has been a resident fifteen years or has worked ten years for the same employer. If he is here on a work contract, it can only be renewed once. Most of these workers are from the Transkei, and no woman from the Transkei is permitted in permanently—no single women are supposed to come in at all, and married women are only allowed in to visit their husbands, and then only on permit from the Administrator of Bantu Affairs in their local area, and only for three months. A lot come down to conceive, or they have a sick child and want to be with the husband, or they lose track of their husband or hear he's living with another woman, so they come down and try to find him. More often than not they don't bother to get a permit—many don't even know it's required—they just come down. Then the police challenge them for their passes, and they get jailed or sent back because they don't have any.

"Supposing they do have proper papers, however, there are some other methods. If the husband is qualified to stay in the area, and his wife qualifies to stay with him, they must 'normally reside together' and 'suitable accommodation' must be available. Otherwise she can be declared 'idle' or 'undesirable.' Well, you know, of course building in the townships is simply not keeping up with the growth in population, so frequently housing just isn't available. Given the chronic shortage, the officials can almost always say that suitable housing isn't available. And the man, who may be living in bachelors' barracks when his wife comes down, can't change his residential area, because that would disqualify him and he too would be 'endorsed out,' back to the Transkei.

"Another way they get the men is that a man who is in the Cape on a work contract may receive word from home that his wife or family needs him there for some emergency—a death in the family, say, or a legal matter or something. But the catch here is that if he leaves the Cape to go home, he must return to the same employer, or be endorsed out. And if the emergency has required him to stay beyond a certain point, his employer naturally is going to fill the job with someone else, because usually the jobs are manual labor of some sort that has to go on, and that any unskilled worker can fill.

"Another aspect of the labor picture is that an employer here may send an appeal to the Transkei authorities for fifty laborers, the authorities will publish the appeal and fifty men will apply—but out of the fifty, maybe ten are useless and just want to get down to the Cape at the employer's expense. The law says the employer must take them all. But he can't be expected to keep them on if they're no good, so he has to sack them and set them adrift. And then, of course, they run afoul of the regulations, and there we go again.

"I will say," she remarked, "that many employers are very cooperative, many of them don't like the way the regulations work, and a great many of them will make a genuine and honest attempt to help us work things out. Quite frequently they will take a man back just to protect him from being endorsed out, and keep him until something else can be arranged."

She smiled.

"People aren't all bad. Frequently, it's just stupidity and thoughtlessness—compounded, of course, by these damnable regulations and the fact that some people *are* bad. Quite often, though, the administering officials themselves can't keep up with the law, it's changing so fast. And of course when you have thousands upon thousands of Bantu involved, it gets to be such a nightmare of crossed purposes, lack of understanding, incompetence, carelessness, malice, stupidity or simple inadvertence that it just about defies solution. . . .

"Why don't you go over there," she suggested, "and sit in with Mrs. Smith on the case she's handling now. It involves still another regulation, which says that if a woman who is qualified to live in the Cape marries a man who isn't qualified, she loses her qualification and can be endorsed out unless she gets special permission to stay. That girl was born in the Cape, her husband wasn't. You might find it interesting."

The little round face was solemn, the enormous brown eyes stared at us like those of a helpless puppy; there was a tiny baby, wrapped in a tattered blanket, which she nursed absentmindedly when it cried. She was perhaps eighteen.

"Agnes," Mrs. Smith said, "do I understand you correctly that your husband does not want to help you stay here in the Cape?"

"Yes, madam," very softly.

"What does he want you to do, Agnes?"

"He want me to go to the Transkei with his parents, madam."

"But the Transkei isn't your home, you've never met his parents, you don't understand the language there, is that it?"

"Yes, madam."

"Why doesn't he want you to stay with him, Agnes?"

"He fight with me all the time, madam, won't give me money for"—a nod down at the baby, little fists happily kneading away.

"Then you understand, Agnes, unless he wants you here and will help you, you must go to the Transkei. If you stay married to him, perhaps the Bantu affairs office can make him give you some money for the baby."

"Yes, madam." The big eyes, if anything, bigger.

"That is, unless you wish to divorce him, Agnes. You can do that and remain here, and we can try to help you get some support for the child. Do you understand me, Agnes?"

"Yes, madam." Two enormous tears welled up, spilled over and ran slowly down, unnoticed.

"You must decide, Agnes, whether to try to get permission to stay here with him, or to get a divorce. Now, if you decide to get the divorce, we will try to help you get the proper papers. Otherwise, you must go to the Transkei. You understand, Agnes?"

"Yes, madam."

"All right, you go now, Agnes, and think it over, and then come back and let us know what we can do to help you. All right, Agnes?"

"Yes, madam"—getting up, still enormous-eyed, solemn, giving the baby a hike to a more secure position, two more tears rolling. "All right, madam."

"They are so helpless," Mrs. Smith said as we watched her go slowly out the door. "So helpless." She sounded helpless herself. "Why don't you see what Mrs. Martin has?"

Mrs. Martin, aided by the clever hunchback, had three sisters.

"The oldest girl," she explained, while they stared at her with the same solemn bewilderment as Agnes, "has been a resident of the Cape for fifteen years, she is all right. Her two sisters, one sixteen and the other eighteen, have been living with their mother in one of the townships up north. The mother died about two weeks ago, and the minute she died the local Bantu affairs administrator ruled that her house was now vacant and these girls would have to go. No provision where they should go, you understand—just go. So naturally their instinct was to turn to their sister, so here they are, without passes, without permission to be in the Cape. The sister doesn't have room for them, and if they aren't permitted to find housing somewhere and stay near her, inevitably they're going to be forced into drifting about illegally and will probably wind up as prostitutes just to keep alive. . . .

"Now, girls," she said, addressing the three intent listeners, "you go and sit over there on the bench and I will call the Bantu affairs office and see if we can't help you to stay here. You just wait quietly, all right, and I will call. . . . They simply must do something for them," she said fiercely to me as the girls obediently trailed away and she picked up the phone and began to dial. "They simply *must*."

Mrs. Gibson had the last case I saw that morning, that of a man who had been sacked for incompetence and faced endorsement out if his employer would not take him back. The little hunchback rattled away emphatically to him in Xhosa as we talked.

"I called the employer," Mrs. Gibson said, "and he's agreed to take him back. He was somewhat reluctant, but a lot of employers do what they can to ease the burden of the law. Lord knows," she said with a wry laugh, "the law is so complicated that the Whites can't understand it, let alone the Bantu. This man has only been in the Cape since 1954, he doesn't have permanent rights. The employer is going to give him a note to take to the Bantu affairs office, which I've also called, and I think maybe we've taken care of it. Providing he gets to work on time and stays on the job. The employer is being good-natured about it, but reasonably enough, he does demand that. Our interpreter"—waving his hands, slapping the table and repeating several phrases over and over with a rising emphasis—"is doing his best to indicate that he must be on time and must do his work. Whether he will," she remarked as we watched the man give a final, obedient nod and shuffle out with that peculiar trot of so many Africans, just fast enough to make the white man think you're hurrying, not fast enough to really inconvenience you—"Lord only knows."

"One score for you today," the hunchback said with a cheerful grin. She laughed and agreed and then added in a genuinely tolerant tone:

"I honestly think the people who make these administrative decisions are just little clerks who don't have the slightest idea what the law really does to these people. How can you ever catch up with it?"

The Athlone Advice Bureau, one of several such activities around the country, averages about fifteen cases a day, three to four hundred a month, four to five thousand a year. The endless morass that cripples South Africa, and drags her down. . . .

LETTER TO THE Cape Argus . . . SIR:—*This morning I took my children for a walk and passed a dustman with a rosebud tucked in his hatband.*

I came home and the postman rang the bell to hand me an airmail letter, instead of just putting it in the box.

I got on a bus and the driver entertained the passengers by whistling a classical song.

After all this I couldn't help thinking what a warm, wonderful world we live in.

*The only part I can't understand is why I've never noticed these things
before!*

(MRS.) B. E. NAKAN

MUIZENBERG

"**M**Y COMMENT TO YOU," the liberal English-speaking lawyer said,
"would be that I really see no hope for this country. Possibly
in ten or twenty years there might be a change, but I am very pessimistic.
I really see no hope. Certainly there won't be any revolution. There may
possibly be flare-ups from time to time, a train wreck could suddenly
send ten thousand Bantu screaming out of the townships, but if it did,
the Government would only take harsher measures.

"Nor am I very optimistic about any liberalizing movement from
within the Nationalist Party. The Afrikaner who protests Government
policy is automatically a renegade, out of the tribe. If this occurs when
he's at university, he graduates and can't find a job with his own people.
He's marked for life. He must go to English-speaking firms, most of
whom are very willing to hire him, but he is definitely finished with his
own people. . . .

"This is a country sui generis, you know—the Afrikaners are sui
generis. They are a unique people, charming and stubborn and hyper-
sensitive and great and impossible, all at one and the same time. They
are a unique people. And of course in dealing with the Bantu, they are
dealing with a unique people, too."

His expression became wry.

"I don't know who's to blame, really, though it's fashionable for me
and my political colleagues to blame the Nats. I've been involved in a
good deal of legal work with the Bantu, you know, and time and again
you run into the same thing, a complete difference from the white man.
For example:

"About two months ago I got called in to help a fellow who had gone
back to his home location, caught a woman who lived near him doing her
washing at a stream, and chopped her to death. There was no apparent
reason for the crime as far as anyone could determine from a preliminary
examination, so before I agreed to take the case I decided to talk to him.
I said, 'Now, John, suppose you tell me what really happened, I have to
know if I am to defend you properly. Were you and this woman lovers,
had she stolen something from you, what was it?'

"He said, 'No, Baas, it wasn't like that. I was away working in the
mines and about six months ago I had a dream one night that this
woman was threatening to kill me. Next morning I hurt my finger. So
when I went home the next time, I went to her and I said, "Stay out of

my dream." But, Baas, about two weeks later she was in my dream again threatening to kill me. And two days after that I hurt my arm. So next time I went home I killed her, because, Baas, I knew that if I didn't kill her, she was going to kill me.' "

The lawyer shook his head.

"Now, really, despite what we like to say from the political platform at election-time, that really isn't one man, one vote material, now, you know, it really just isn't."

EDITORIAL (Die Vaderland, *Johannesburg, Afrikaans*) . . . *It is surprising when the Rand English-language afternoon newspaper, which is so convinced that the Bantu on the Rand are completely urbanized . . . reports that, now the Bechuanaland independence celebrations are nearing, many Bantu in the Republic want to go back there. Strange that such "tribeless" Bantu still yearn for their fatherland. If Bantu want to return to an impoverished Bechuanaland, why then should our own Bantu not want to go back to their much faster developing homelands?*

"IT BOTH SADDENS AND terrifies us," the English-speaking lawyer said, "to see the United States joining in the attack upon us as a result of our victory at The Hague in the South-West Africa case. We expected an illegal, emotional, irrational vendetta by half-formed, half-intelligent African tribal states, but we did not think America would join in—especially since the State Department issued a statement prior to the verdict declaring that everyone should abide by it. We would not want to describe Washington's actions now, in view of that statement, as being two-faced and hypocritical, but at any rate, we find you in rather strange company. But I suppose the State Department must think there is some advantage to be gained in international politics by siding with the Black mob. The hope seems to us to be a slender one.

"Now, I was not on the South African legal team at the World Court" —he smiled—"English-speakers were not exactly welcome, that was almost entirely an Afrikaans show, which perhaps was not such sound judgment when appearing before a world body." The smile became ironic. "The English accent, you know, still impresses a good many people, and it might have been helpful. Nonetheless, it was an excellent team and we think it made an excellent case. The country is quite united, I think, in the belief that in law and in fact we made a case that no honest person—and no honest government—can seek, with integrity, to overturn.

"We took South-West Africa from the Germans in 1915, you will recall, and instead of adding it to our territory by conquest, which we wish now we had done, as it would have settled all this at the source, we were law-abiding enough to ask the League of Nations for a mandate. It was a 'C' mandate, so-called, about as close to outright annexation as the League could come. The key phrases read"—he took a paper from the top of a neatly prepared pile of documents—" 'The mandatory shall have full power of administration and legislation over the territory . . . as an integral part of the Union of South Africa, (which is why we have members of the House of Assembly and the Senate from South-West) and may apply (its) laws . . . The mandatory shall promote to the utmost the material and moral well-being and the social progress of the inhabitants of the territory.'

"The general terms of the League mandatory system also provided that the 'well-being and development' of the peoples of the defeated powers' former colonies should be 'a sacred trust of civilization' and called for such safeguards as freedom of conscience and religion, prohibition of the slave trade, arms and liquor traffic, fortifications or military bases.

"So we went along until the end of the Second World War, and the creation of the UN, at which time Prime Minister Smuts asked the UN to grant full annexation of South-West. This was rejected. South Africa thereupon refused to convert South-West into a trusteeship territory under the UN and stated its belief that since the League was dead, the mandate was too. The UN appealed to the World Court for an advisory and in 1950 the Court ruled that the mandate was still in existence, that the UN had a right to receive regular reports on administration of the territory, that South Africa had no unilateral right to change the status of South-West, and at the same time was under no legal requirement to put South-West under the UN trustee system.

"Which," he remarked, "was a nice try at seeing how many angels you could get to dance on the head of a pin.

"Anyway, so the ruling came down, and since it was only advisory, the UN rejected it. This opened the floodgates for a long-continuing series of attacks upon South Africa, featuring a parade of so-called spokesmen for the Bantu of South-West Africa who gave the UN Trusteeship Council quite a packet of tales about genocide, atomic threats to the black population, and a lot of other horrible things—even though, meanwhile, South Africa went right along building up education, housing, medical care and better conditions for the Blacks in the territory, which the record shows and which anyone who cares to can come and see for himself.

"One of the things," he interjected acidly, "that rather clouds the good faith of some of our enemies in our minds is that when we invited the

World Court to come to South-West Africa and see for itself, it refused
to do so. And when South Africa invited the American Ernest Gross,
who was heading the legal team for our attackers, Ethiopia and Liberia,
to bring some of the witnesses who had appeared before the UN to The
Hague at our expense, he refused to do so.

"The suspicion sometimes arises in our minds—unjust though it doubtless is—that our critics in the United States, as well as our critics in
Africa, would much prefer to argue from emotional charges than meet
an honest case honestly with honest facts. Obtuse and hostile of us to
feel this, no doubt, but there it is. . . .

"Anyway," he went on, more amicably, "the UN charges continued
until 1960, when Sharpeville came along and a so-called native uprising
in the Sharpeville township caused the deaths of some sixty Bantu. Many
of us felt them to be the cream of the Communist crop, but as you know
they speedily became the world's great heroes. In that climate Ethiopia
and Liberia filed their suit in the World Court against our mandate, apparently expecting a lie-down on our part and an easy case. They fig-
ured," he smiled, "without South Africa. We filed briefs objecting that the
Court had no jurisdiction. In 1962 the Court ruled that it had, in an 8–7
vote.

"The next two years were occupied with the preparation and filing of
written briefs. When our chief counsel, Advocate David de Villiers of
Cape Town, opened his oral argument in March, 1965, he invited the
Court to come to South-West Africa and also, for the sake of an honest
comparison, to visit Ethiopia and Liberia. But such a direct challenge to
hypocrisy is very shocking in international affairs, you know, and of
course it just couldn't be done; the Court delayed a decision until the end
of the case and then voted against it. The Court never did see what is
being done in South-West—or in Ethiopia and Liberia, either.

"These two, through Gross, alleged that we were failing to promote
the well-being and social progress of the inhabitants of South-West, and
were indeed applying laws that were 'by their terms and in application
arbitrary, unreasonable, unjust, detrimental to human dignity.' There
were also allegations of 'oppression' and 'militarization' in the territory.

"The South African case was, first, that if the mandate does still exist,
it doesn't require accountability to the UN, but rather to the Council of
the League, and since the League was dissolved after World War Two
and since nobody really claims that there is a direct legal descent to the
UN, then that argument fails.

"As for the charge that we have violated the terms of the mandate, we
admitted that there was differentiation between the races, but argued that
this was to permit development of each in its own way and its own area,
and to bring each along as fast as possible in light of its own abilities.

"At this point your Mr. Gross—very well, then, *not* your Mr. Gross, but the American who was doing the dirty work for the Africans—began to shift ground. Even though the Court wouldn't go to South-West, plenty of other people had, and there was a great deal of documentation and proof that the general living conditions, health, education and so on, of the Bantu in the territory had been very dramatically improved by South Africa. So presently Ethiopia and Liberia, through Mr. Gross, withdrew their charges of oppression and began to talk about a world 'norm of non-differentiation' which they claimed applied throughout the world, but especially, of course, to South-West Africa. Not necessarily to Ethiopia or Liberia, you understand, or India or Russia or China or even, let us say the word in whispers, America, but just in some great, glorious, vague way to the whole wide world without embarrassing anybody by naming names—except us. *We* had to be named.

"To support this argument, which was all he had left, your Mr. Gross —I'm sorry, but you have found, I'm sure, haven't you, that a great many South Africans regard Mr. Gross and the United States as the prime movers in this World Court case? Very well, then—Mr. Gross stated that it was generally applicable, but then when the embarrassments of that position became obvious, backed away a bit and said that the norm was something that 'the organized international community' had established through the UN—when, he didn't say, just by thinking nobly about it, apparently—and that the UN meant it to apply to South-West Africa.

"In our opinion," he said shortly, "this was nonsense. But"—a quizzical expression came into his eyes—"as you know, the Court's 8–7 decision left everything in limbo and nothing was decided on its merits, and that, I suppose, is why America is trying to make time in Africa by going along with the African vendetta right now. Sir Percy Spender, the presiding Australian who cast the deciding vote and delivered the majority opinion, was scathing about the idea of the 'norm' but the Court didn't really rule on it. Nor did it rule on whether or not South-West's conditions are better, nor did it rule even on the general principle of separate development. It just said Ethiopia and Liberia were not members of the League and so weren't competent to bring the case, so out went the baby with the bath water and here we are.

"Of course basically, you know, what we think here"—and he put the tips of his fingers together and stared out at Table Mountain, half-lost in mist above us—"is that nobody in Africa really gives a damn about whether we oppress anybody or not. Who are *they* to talk about 'norms' and not oppressing people, for God's sake! South-West Africa has gold and diamonds and who knows what-all; South Africa has gold and diamonds and who knows what-all. That's what they want, that's what's at the bottom of all these attacks on us, whether about South-West or apartheid or what you will. They want what we've got and that's the real truth of it.

"Greed, plain and simple, underlies the campaign against South Africa."

COMING DOWN TO EARTH (*Editorial,* World, *Johannesburg, Bantu*) . . . *There is wide division in the ranks of the United Nations on the South West Africa problem.*

The committee appointed to make recommendations to the U.N. General Assembly on the territory has failed to produce concrete proposals. Its chairman, Mr. Max Jakobson of Finland, only this week reported that the outlook for reconciling different attitudes on this matter was "bleak."

In the circumstances, the resolution just proposed by a group of Afro-Asian States that South West Africa become an independent state by June, 1968, is ridiculous.

As several speakers at the U.N. have pointed out, the U.N. only makes itself a laughing stock if it continues to promote measures which are not realistic. . . .

After all, politics is the art of the possible and the sooner the Afro-Asians appreciate this the better.

Nobody is asking them to abandon the principle they hold so dearly. But South West Africa is not in a state of revolution, demanding emergency measures. The South African Government is actually ploughing money into the country for development.

American Ambassador A. Goldberg's warning that the U.N. should seek a peaceful, negotiated solution related to the historical complexity of the problem is the right approach.

Afro-Asian spokesmen must stop crying for the moon and come down to earth.

H E IS FIFTY, THIN, rangy, tall, with a rather stooping posture, a dark dramatic face, a big mobile mouth, keen eyes, eyebrows that constantly punctuate conversation, a positive, emphatic voice: Dr. Anton Rupert, head of the Rembrandt Corporation, cigarette king of the continent; with Harry Oppenheimer, probably one of the two prime politico-economic forces in the Republic; the man who has almost single-handedly brought about an upward revolution in the economic status of the Bantu by deciding a couple of years ago that he would establish in all his many enterprises a basic wage of two rand a day. Other industries have had to follow suit, and the effects are spreading through the country: one of those economic earthquakes whose shock-waves continue and grow and probably cannot be stopped even by the most determined of governments.

For it is one thing to deny the vote to people who don't care much one way or the other whether they have it; but it is quite another to reduce the pay of a man who has no other foundation upon which to build his security and self-esteem.

So the revolution begun by Anton Rupert is spreading, and from it other changes are inevitably coming. How extensive, no one can predict, but contributing to that condition of flux pictured by such as Leonard Verwoerd, and forcing the admission by even the most conservative Afrikaners that economic change is gradually bringing social change.

We met for lunch at beautiful old Lanzerac in charming Stellenbosch, home of wonderful wines and spiritual seat of Afrikanerdom, some thirty miles out from Cape Town. Lanzerac is an historic Cape Dutch farmhouse, stark white against the green fields of Stellenbosch, part of it converted now into a pleasant restaurant. My host, who began his commercial life selling tobacco over the counter in a shop in the Eastern Cape and now controls some thirty companies in as many countries, was in a philosophic mood.

"We in Africa, in spite of being very vocal so that the world must pay attention to everything we do, are basically a minority of two hundred millions in the world's population. White and Black, we are each other's shadows, particularly here in South Africa where we must share the land together. If the African doesn't eat, we don't sleep, and vice versa; even if we are 'apart,' if he doesn't succeed, we don't succeed, and if we don't succeed, he won't.

"We in this country have done more than any other area in Africa to better the African's well-being. More education, more housing, more welfare, more medical care—in all of Nigeria, with approximately the same population, there are five doctors. Our achievement has not been equalled, and we are so far ahead of any other African country that it is probably impossible for them ever to catch up—unless they tear us down, which some of them wish, but which we are determined they shall not do.

"And why should they wish to, in their own self-interest? The potentials of this continent are beyond belief. What we could all do together in partnership staggers the imagination. We can do it and we will, when they have decided that it is to the advantage of all to work together, as many of us are trying to do here.

"Africa needs stability, first of all. Communism attempts to make trouble in the continent, but Communism is outmoded because it is based on outdated economic theories. Politically it is simply another form of imperialism and colonialism, masquerading behind the guise of humanitarianism. Some African states have already learned this for themselves. It offers no answer for the problems of Africa. It is a foreign ideology for the benefit of foreign powers; it is no part of Africa.

"Nor is democracy in the Anglo-American sense—in that sense it is impossible in Africa, at least in this generation and maybe several more. I am for the African, I am for any group having control of its own destiny *when it can rule itself*. But the other African states must come to grips with reality, they must grow up. Independence is only the beginning, it is not the end. They have enormous problems, and they must be practical about it. . . .

"I suppose I am what you could call a 'liberal Cape Afrikaner,' yes. I have raised wages in my companies because I think the economic condition of the Bantu must be improved for the benefit of all of us. We must create economic partnership and a better life for all in South Africa, African and European. Economic opportunity is the key to all our problems, I believe. With it will come an amelioration of many things to which the outside world objects. I believe the Bantu's condition will greatly improve in the next few years, the Indian's also; I predict that before long we are going to have complete integration of the Coloureds in the White community.

"The tragedy here could come from someone striving for political advantage who would use the racial issue for his own purposes. Internationally, our basic problem right now is the confrontation with the United States, but the bitterness many South Africans feel at the moment will not be lasting, I think. For, again, the economic interest of the whole continent will, I believe, persuade your country that the way to achieve stability in Africa is not by weakening us, who are far and away the most stable force for leadership, but by helping all of Africa to work together in harmony for the benefit of all. . . .

"Men in the mass are nothing," he said thoughtfully. "The individual is everything. I think that is why I love the Karoo"—South Africa's great desert that runs north from the Cape into the southern edges of the Orange Free State. "It is stark—it is challenging—there a man is a man, standing or falling by his own efforts. . . . Individuals can do everything—but they must cooperate. They must work together for the benefit of all."

"THERE'S A HARSHNESS on top," said the liberal young Afrikaner, sensationally successful, whose business enterprises put him in touch with many influential people in all races, "but there is a great charity underneath. In time, I believe, the charity will well up and destroy the harshness.

"Because I'm Afrikaans, I suppose, I like to find a parallel in our experience for the other races of South Africa. In the great poverty that we suffered after the war and well into the twenties and thirties, there was a great movement on the part of Afrikaners to help one another. In 1932 I suppose we as a people were about at our lowest ebb. But because of this unity of purpose and helpfulness—plus, of course, many other factors, the boom that began with the Second World War, and so on—but basically, still, because of the Afrikaners' loyalty to one another and desire to lend a helping hand—we have made enormous strides to the present wealth and power of today.

"I think the same thing is going to happen to the rest. I think first will come the Coloured. The Coloured revolution in this country is already fantastic, and I think the next ten years will be even more fantastic. Very powerful forces are moving to give the Coloureds a much bigger stake in the country. All this bubbling up of their economic force is going to force a new era for them.

"The same applies to the Indians. And then will come the Bantu. One people inspires another, and they are already beginning to make economic strides. All of them are on the move. . . .

"We're at the end of an era. Verwoerd will go in the next five or six years, then there will be some sort of transition government, then finally there will appear the real leader to succeed Verwoerd. There are moderating influences. A liberalization will come. There are powerful elements in Afrikanerdom, powerful elements in the Nationalist Party, pressing for change. The main thing we need is time. . . .

"Do I think your country will permit us time? Well, I can tell you there is great concern here about some of your diplomats. Some of them are meddling in dangerous things, and of course it's all known to the Special Branch. For instance, the wife of one diplomat has said three times that the United States will attack South Africa. Of course she was drunk and it's stupid, but she said it at a party and it's traveled all over town. Many people when they hear something like that don't realize the circumstances, they just remember the words.

"Another one of your people here took some whisky to a group of Coloureds and said, 'Why don't you revolt?' They came to me very worried and said, 'What should we do?' I said, 'Tell the Special Branch.' So they did, and now the Special Branch is keeping a close watch all the time on this fellow.

"Another took his car out to Stellenbosch at midnight and picked up a group of students to bring them in here to a secret illegal meeting. And of course it was known all the time to the Special Branch.

"It's so stupid—it's so naive. It's creating great concern here, because it's simply inviting trouble, and if it keeps up sooner or later the Government is going to have to do something open about it, and that means another international fuss with the United States. Maybe that's what some of your diplomats want," he said with a rather grim little smile, "but it certainly isn't very diplomatic. And it makes it just that much harder for liberal Afrikaners to accomplish anything."

T ALL, SCHOLARLY, praying-mantis thin, bald, a very pleasant face, a charming manner, descendant of one of the oldest families of the Cape—"As a people we have, I think, two tragedies. One is that the relationship between Black and White has always been a master-servant relationship, and the other is that we came much too late to a realization and understanding of the educated non-White. When I went to Oxford and joined the debating society, its president was an Indian. Well, to my parents' generation, and indeed to mine when we were children, an Indian was a coolie, one of those difficult and unfortunate people that had been brought into Natal many years ago to work the sugarcane. He was scarcely to be considered a human being. You can imagine, therefore, what a shock I got at my first introduction to the debating society. I thought, What's this? What's happened to Britain, to let such a chap be head of the debating society? My reaction, which was quite instinctive, went deeper than that: What's wrong with Britain to let such a chap attend Oxford at all? That was how we thought, in those days.

"Well, you know, I soon found him to be one of the most charming people I had ever met, and we became, I am thankful and proud to say, very good friends. Then I came home and started teaching, and time went on, and one Government succeeded another, and now you know what we have. I can invite Coloureds and Indians and Bantu to my home, but nowhere else, and even that is running something of a risk. I can still take my Indian friends to the Mt. Nelson Hotel, but there is practically nowhere else that we can go in public together. Yet these are educated people, highly trained, intelligent, the sort one naturally associates with in an academic way. It is not as though I would propose to bring in a street sweeper. . . .

"And then there are all these other suppressions of liberty and restrictions upon the individual—these I cannot stand. The Government is afraid, it feels itself under fire from outside and inside, it reacts by moving in repressive ways. But some of these fears and pressures are created by the Government's own laws and policies. It is always raising bugaboos, it is adept at inflaming the country with one fear or another. . . .

"Now in the field of education with which I am familiar, we are criticized, I think, unjustly by the outside world, and there I do agree with the Government's insistence that we are doing a great deal for the other races. You know our history, defeat, a brief period of recovery, a setback with World War One, then a period of depression in the twenties and early thirties when we had a poor-white problem and thousands left the farms for the cities.

"It took us a while to work our way out of that and start educating our own children, you know. It was only after prosperity began to appear that we could really spend the time and money on our own, let alone eight or nine million illiterate Blacks that we had literally never had time to pay any attention to. The Blacks were the least of our worries, in those days, they were out in the kraals taking care of themselves. We didn't have time for them, and we didn't have then what some of us have now, a genuine concept and feeling that we have a responsibility to help them.

"Now the world comes along and says, Why haven't you got them all educated this minute! But it's only yesterday that we could educate ourselves."

He smiled, a kindly expression that lighted up his face.

"You know, we are not so long away from our frontier in this country; perhaps even a shorter time than you are. I remember only about fifty years ago, when we wanted to go from our farm over here at the foot of the Tygerburg to the beach, we went in two ox-carts and our milk supply went on ahead. A boy started out the day before and drove a cow the fifteen miles to where we stayed at the shore. And that wasn't much over fifty years ago. In some degree, the electorate that supports the Nationalist Government is still in the ox-cart stage in its attitude toward the non-Whites. It still can't realize what I learned in the debating society at Oxford, that a man whatever his color can be alert, intelligent, pleasant, charming, highly skilled, perhaps even brilliant. . . .

"Of course," he said, and the smile was a little ironic now, "world pressures are not very helpful to us in all this. We need time, and the world doesn't want to give us time."

"It's a very complex situation," I remarked a little lamely, that cliché about the Republic which is so true and so implacable in its refusal to be conquered by easy slogans.

"I tell you what you do," he said. The smile turned kindly again. "If you decide what the solution is, you let us know. We would really appreciate it. We're all trying to find it."

THE TWO YOUNG couples were Afrikaans and we ate dinner at a pleasant restaurant somewhere on the waterfront. We talked about children in grammar school, the rising prices of food and clothing, bridge clubs, mortgages, and the fight to save the lovely Constantia Valley, last unspoiled remnant of the old Cape Town area, from the threat of a freeway and the rapacious onslaughts of greedy real estate developers. It sounded just like home, and nobody mentioned politics once. "In many ways, we feel a great affinity for America," someone said. In many ways, they should.

OPEN NAT. WAR ON NAT. EXTREMISTS (Sunday Times, *Johannesburg, English*) . . . *True meaning of attacks on S. E. D. Brown: Dr. V. also seen behind move. Hertzog, Piet Meyer, Benson, Jaap Marais among Right-wingers—By J. H. P. Serfontein—Sunday Times Political Reporter.*

The Nationalist Party has declared open war on the group of extreme Right-wing Nationalist's who have tried to infiltrate the Afrikaanse Studentebond and other youth organisations. This is the real reason behind the full-scale attacks launched by the Nationalist Press on Mr. S. E. D. Brown, an obscure editor of an obscure publication, the South African Observer.

Nationalist attacks on Mr. Brown have specifically referred to the "little circle of Afrikaners" around him.

This "little circle of Afrikaners" is a clearly identifiable group of Right-wing extremists, associated with attacks on leading Afrikaners, and linked with extremist organisations overseas.

I can disclose that its "unofficial" leader and driving force is Dr. Albert Hertzog, Minister of Posts and Telegraphs. He has kept in the background.

Well-known political, church and cultural figures have close political affiliations with this "Hertzog Group." Die Transvaler calls it the "Brown Group" but "Hertzog Group" is the more accurate label.

The leading members include:

Dr. Piet Meyer, chairman of the S.A.B.C.,

Mr. Ivor Benson, former associate of Sir Oswald Mosley and S.A.B.C. broadcaster,

*Mr. Jaap Marais, M.P., Mr. S. P. Botha, M.P., Dr. C. P. Mulder, M.P.,
and Mr. Daan van der Merwe, M.P.,*

Professor A. D. Pont and Professor A. B. du Preez of Pretoria University,

The Rev. D. F. deBeer, the Rev. J. D. Vorster [brother of now Prime
Minister, John Vorster], *and the Rev. P. W. Jordaan. . . .*

*There are strong indications that the Nationalist attacks have the tacit
support of Dr. Verwoerd himself. He is known to be increasingly embarrassed
by the activities of the Hertzog Group; and his own paper,* Die
Transvaler, *has joined the onslaught.*

The only support for the Hertzog Group has come from Die Vaderland
*(with which Dr. Hertzog is connected and of which Mr. A. D. van Schoor
is editor).*

Die Vaderland *accuses* Die Burger *of trying "to drive a wedge" between
northern and southern Nationalists—a claim obviously incorrect
since* Die Transvaler *has also attacked the Hertzog Group.*

*Responsible Nationalists have become worried in recent years about
the growing influence of this Right-wing group, but until now have found
it difficult to expose the group's extremism and irresponsibility.*

*This is because the group have always been quick to take the lead in
exploiting "popular, emotional and patriotic issues."*

*The final straw, however, was the discovery that this "dangerous little
group" had succeeded in infiltrating the ASB leadership and other Afrikaans
youth organisations.*

*It is this event which set the spark to smouldering Nationalist resentment
against the Group. . . .*

AGAIN LANZERAC, a private dining room, pink and white and a little
garish, not quite in keeping with the rest of the old farm's quiet
Cape Dutch atmosphere. But a quiet company of good friends and ready
wits, all Afrikaans; and a long, long discussion that ran through a delicious
dinner and on through coffee and K.W.V. and more drinks and
well on toward midnight. These were liberal Cape Nats of the most influential
sort, writers, businessmen, professors. The magic phrase "five
or six years" recurred.

"There's going to be a change"—very earnestly—"in five or six years,
if you will just leave us alone—if the world will just leave us alone.
Many of us in the Cape don't agree entirely with present policies, we're
doing everything we can to change them. The Transvalers are much too
harsh and rigid"—sounds of agreement from all around the table—
"much too harsh."

"Yet we're South Africans first of all," someone interjected hastily, and the sounds of agreement were repeated. "If anything threatened this country, I don't believe there's a one of us, Afrikaans or English, who wouldn't take a gun and defend it."

"And the Natives and the Coloureds and the Indians would fight with us, too," someone else remarked with satisfaction, and again they all agreed.

"You see," the first speaker said, "you have to remember that we Afrikaners had a very hard time—"

And finally the visitor, emboldened perhaps by K.W.V. but also by the fact that these were highly intelligent and reasonable people:

"If I may say so, I think you Afrikaners cling too much to your old grievances. I think you all use what happened sixty years ago to excuse too many things. After all, it *was* sixty years ago, and what happened right after? Campbell-Bannerman gave you your independence, for all practical purposes, didn't he?—and for all practical purposes you've had your independence ever since—and Britain didn't really impede your progress much, because here you are after only sixty years, in undisputed control of the country. You've come right to the top, haven't you, you are on top—so what's your problem? Why can't you relax?"

And perhaps emboldened by K.W.V. also, the nephew of a former Prime Minister said quietly:

"Yes, that's right, we do cling too much to the past"—more sounds of agreement—"we *have* succeeded, we should let it go, you're right. Our problem"—soberly—"is that we've got to decide, we Afrikaners, which group is going to win out in the struggle—we have still another struggle in this country, with all our others, the struggle within Afrikanerdom itself—which is going to win out, the liberal Nats or the others?"

"*That* will determine what we can do in the whole of Africa," one of the businessmen said. "*That* will determine whether South Africa will really be free to provide the leadership our potential could give us."

"What exactly do the liberal Nats favor?"

"Integration of the Coloureds—"

"Better wages for the Bantu—"

"Less petty apartheid—"

"Representation in the White Parliament?"

"W——ell . . . Not in the White Parliament, perhaps, but—"

"Separate development in voting, probably—"

"Separate development in many things. But basically, better economic conditions all down the line, integration of the Coloureds, self-expression for all groups ultimately within some form of commonwealth such as Dr. Verwoerd proposes—

"Basically, an easing of pressures and tensions, more of a cooperative spirit of working together for all South Africans regardless of race."

"You think all White South Africans can be persuaded to go along with that?"

"Of course some African states won't ever be satisfied, they'll always hate us, but if we are strong enough and decent to our own, that will die down in time. We'll always have some of it, but the major part will die down."

"And you really think all the Whites here will support that liberal policy?"

"It's our only salvation!"—flatly.

A quiet little lady who hadn't said much spoke up: "Almiskie."

"What?" Everybody amused, her husband trying to shush her a little.

"Almiskie," she repeated firmly. "I always remember my old grand-mother, when she was in her nineties. Sometimes we would all get to arguing about something and she would just sit there folding her fingers together—like this—and finally, after we had all become very positive, she would speak up and say: 'Almiskie.' "

" 'Nevertheless,' " someone translated. She nodded.

"Almiskie. And that's how I feel about every statement about South Africa. You can say all the bad things—and then you say, Almiskie. And you can say all the good things—and then you say, Almiskie. And you can say what somebody will do or what he won't do—and then you say, Almiskie. So I say now: 'Almiskie.' "

Much laughter, a little embarrassed, and a writer, firmly—

"Well, just give us time. Just give us five or six years and there'll be a change. I'm convinced of it."

"And who will succeed Verwoerd—Vorster? What good will that do?"

"Well"—sobered silence, and then from somewhere down the table a mischievous chuckle and a masculine voice:

"Almiskie."

And after that, many toasts and the evening coming to a close, and finally our hostess proposing one last salute:

"To friendship between South Africa and America, and may it always be strong and may nothing come between us."

And on an emotional and perfectly sincere note of goodwill the party ended; and no one else thought to remark, as we left lovely Lanzerac and parted in genuine affection, Almiskie.

"HE GOES THROUGH his agonies once in a while," they had told me all along the line about the editor of the liberal Afrikaans news-paper at the Cape, "but he sticks with the Government when all is said and done."

And of course for Piet Cillié, editor of Die Burger, there really isn't much else to do. Yet he maintains a pleasant calmness about it, for the most part. Certainly he did on the day we went to lunch at Here Sewentien ("The Seventeen Gentlemen"—the directors of the Dutch East India Company), the club of Afrikanerdom in the Cape.

There, surrounded by the faces of Die Volk, round and rosy or lean and dark, we talked much of change, his pleasantly freckled face and sandy hair putting him somewhat outside the national physical stereotypes, as his ideas put him somewhat outside the mainstream of Nationalist thinking in the Government.

Yet, as always when the ultimate issues are faced, there was no real divergence from the basic position.

"The Government, you see, has a tactical problem to solve," he said, an amused expression crossing his rather puckish face. "The old-line Afrikaners—you know where they stand. With them it's still, 'The kaffir in his place and the coolie out of the country.' But the Government knows this is not quite the wicket for today's world, and even though it cannot accept the approach the outside world would like to have it accept—because we all believe that would be disaster—nonetheless it believes that it must gradually move toward a better accommodation with all the races here. . . .

"And not so gradually, either," he remarked thoughtfully after he had translated the menu and we had ordered. "Under Verwoerd we have made enormous strides in the direction of caring for the Bantu and the Coloureds and the Indians. It is really phenomenal, when you think back on their condition before he came to power. His psychology has been very clever—gradualism, but a rapid gradualism. You are aware of the rumblings against him in the more reactionary circles of the Transvaal, but his position is such, and his hold on the people is such, that he gets away with it.

"I expect that he is the only man who can lead the country with reasonable speed in the direction that logic and self-preservation, to say nothing"—he smiled—"of simple humanity and decency, indicate that it should go. One man, one vote is impossible here, but development of each race within its own context according to its own abilities is something else again. That is his vision, and so far he has made it work. As long as he stays in power, I think we will continue to move in that direction despite the complaints of some of his old-line supporters. . . .

"You ask how we differ, on *Die Burger?*" He laughed. "Now that, I suppose, is something that would be hard for a foreigner to understand. With us, too, maybe, it is a policy of gradualism—the gradual elimination of some of the features of apartheid which are so galling to the Bantu and the other races—what we call 'petty apartheid.' And then, too, sometimes there are aspects of foreign policy on which we disagree, where we think possibly the Government has moved too arbitrarily or

provocatively, perhaps . . . I don't know. I suppose it is hard to analyze in any pat, sloganistic way that could be easily understood abroad.
Suffice it that we seem to have acquired the reputation of being 'liberal'
—which is sometimes"—a dry little smile—"a bad word in South Africa
—in the eyes of our foreign friends.

"But you must not make the same mistake they do, and think that this
automatically means that we are leading a great flaming revolt against
the Government or its policies, or that we disagree in any fundamental
way with the Government's position. We, after all, are Afrikaans too,
you know, and we are Nationalists, and we have neither the capability
nor the desire to overturn or thwart major Government policies. Let us
say that perhaps we only wish to soften their application, make them a
little less arbitrary in some respects. But on the whole, we support the
Government, and we do it as a matter of conviction.

"One other thing our friends abroad mustn't conclude too eagerly,
also, is that we disagree in any way with the Government's basic positions in foreign affairs. The outside world is there for us, too, you know,
and we are just as conscious of its hostilities and its pressures, and just as
determined to withstand them. There is no question of our not supporting the Government, or of contributing in any way to any division in the
country in the face of foreign threats.

"In fact, of course, that applies to most of our English-speaking col-
leagues, too, even though they give us fits editorially about many things.
We are united enough when it comes to the question of outside pressure.
No one should make any mistake about that.

"There are changes coming, though, changes of method and application. This is not a static society, it is growing and changing every day.
There is a powerful group of Nats working for new approaches, businessmen principally, impelled by the realities of our booming economy.
Afrikanerdom is changing. Given reasonable time, we shall emerge in a
position much more acceptable to at least our intelligent and fair-minded
critics abroad. I'm sure of that. . . ."

"AFRIKANER MUST BROADEN CONTACTS" (Star, *Johannesburg,
English*) . . . *Increasing contact with the people of varying attitudes
is essential to the survival of the Afrikaner, the* Burger *says in an editorial today.*

*While acknowledging the need for vigilance, the editorial stresses the
danger that vigilance might degenerate into "sickly suspicion" and withdrawal into isolation which could prove fatal to the Afrikaners as a
whole.*

The paper points out that the number of Afrikaners involved in "situa-

tions of contact with other population groups inside South Africa or with overseas bodies and interests" will increase as national unity and the development of states on South Africa's borders progress.

"Such people do not deserve to be stabbed in the back by those of us who sit deep within the laager and allow our national vigilance to degenerate into suspicion and persecution."

AMERICAN PINPRICKS (Editorial, Die Burger, Cape Town, Afrikaans) . . . *South Africa is sometimes forced to the conclusion that a part of the American administration is positively exerting itself to worsen United States relations with our country as much as possible.*

How else are we to understand the official American interference in the question of an order for French aircraft for civil use in South Africa? These aeroplanes have to be equipped with American engines, but permission for their export to France has been refused. If the matter remains as it is, the French company cannot deliver the aircraft and South Africa will have to devise another plan, which it will most certainly do. What else is achieved but inconvenience and annoyance?

When UN took its decision in favour of an arms embargo against South Africa, the United States supported it with a proviso in connection with arms that might be necessary for external defence. In fact, whether some Americans want to know it or not, South Africa is a vitally important element in the Western grand strategy. In any case, this American proviso apparently revealed a realization that a certain flexibility in the application of the arms embargo by the United States would be in the American interest.

How much flexibility there has been since we do not know. But to put a spoke in the wheel of supply of purely civil aircraft to South Africa in the way mentioned shows that absolutely nothing remains of any earlier conciliatoriness. Indeed, it is not only a question of refusing arms to South Africa any more, but of a non-military product that is only partly American. . . . The full result of what has now happened to the order of French aircraft cannot be seen yet. Part of it will most likely be a further rise in South African indignation over American manners towards this country. It is becoming more and more difficult to laugh over the difference between what certain Americans have in view and what they really achieve in South Africa.

DILEMMA (Editorial, Die Burger, Cape Town, Afrikaans) . . . *It is clear that the American officials whose job it is to think about the relations of the United States with Africa expect an aggravation of their dilemma over action against Southern Africa.*

There exists an understandable unwillingness within the administration, and just about no significant national will, to be drawn or forced ever deeper into Southern African complications. On the other hand the American government sets store by her relations with the Black states. Her chief foreign preoccupation is the war in Vietnam which is becoming bitterly unpopular in the world and for which she must retain all possible diplomatic support.

The goodwill and the UN votes of the Black states could be decisive in this connection, and these can be obtained or retained most easily by means of strong views in the different Southern African questions which the Black states have raised.

What the Americans—according to their own acknowledgment—are doing now is to ask the Black states not to go so far in their proposals that the gulf between their demands and the American view of what is feasible becomes too deep. For then there develops between the United States and Black Africa the kind of position with which Britain had to cope in connection with Rhodesia: tensions and even breaches because the British Government will not or cannot do what the Black states desire against Rhodesia.

It is difficult at this stage to see how the United States can still avoid such a situation of increasing tension with the Black caucus at UN. The feeling of impotence and frustration in Black Africa over Southern Africa was heightened by the defeat in the World Court and has probably never been as strong as at present. What remains for the Black states, now that even Western fear of Communist takeovers in Africa has calmed down, is propagandist and diplomatic power which they would want to use to the utmost to make up for the lack of other weapons.

It points to demands for the most drastic action against South Africa at the address of the United States, with the hidden threat that otherwise the United States had better not rely on them over Vietnam and other matters.

Perhaps such a movement in the direction of a reckoning between the United States and the extravagant governments of Black Africa would not be a bad thing at all. Britain has so far survived it in connection with Rhodesia when she decided not to take fright at the Organization for African Unity's "ultimatum" on the breaking off of relations. Perhaps Washington has also discovered that everything does not collapse when a handful of Black governments recall their ambassadors and pretend to go over to Moscow or Peking.

The most dangerous thing in the long run, after all, is for the United States to be forced step by step into a position towards Southern Africa where they, as in Vietnam, cannot go backward or decisively forward.

It could happen if they, for the sake of preservation of a false unity front with Black Africa, should support measures against Southern Africa which the best policymakers know must lead to a morass.

I N THE RESIDENCE hall at the University of Stellenbosch where Hendrik Verwoerd once lived, three young Afrikaans, keepers of the flame: the first tall, blond, blue-eyed, good-looking in a rather heavy-jowled way; the second equally tall, raw-boned, blond, with a large forehead and that cavern-eyed Dutch-Germanic look; the third even taller, very dark, very handsome, child, as he told me later, of the Eastern Transvaal.

The first was "Boy" Geldenhuys ("Khrelldenhace"), president of the ASB—the Afrikaanse Studentebond—and the other two were his top lieutenants. The ASB is the Afrikaans opposite number to the English-speaking NUSAS, the National Union of South African Students whose convention I had attended in Durban. NUSAS' position was clear enough; I had come out to Stellenbosch to find out where the ASB stood. Liberal Cape Nats had been telling me for a couple of weeks how things were changing and only the day before Piet Cillié had assured me that, "These kids feel their oats now and then, but they'll steady down." I also knew that there was a sizable group on the Stellenbosch campus, sometimes several thousand in number, which did not favor many of the ASB policies and quite frequently said so.

Nonetheless, the ASB is the organized spokesman for Afrikaans youth and there is no doubt that it is regarded by the Government as its direct link with the younger generation. Every official encouragement is given to it, and whenever a Cabinet minister or other top leader of Afrikaans thought has nothing else to do he hurries out to Stellenbosch and makes a speech under the auspices of the ASB.

These, in short, are the chosen inheritors of the power that now runs the country. Did they, too, feel those intimations and impulses of change so earnestly described to me by Piet Cillié, by my friends at Lanzerac, and by many another liberal Nat I had met in my time at the Cape?

They greeted me with a cordial courtesy I did not entirely expect, made tea, and proceeded to talk. One of the most striking things about it was that Boy, head of the ASB and almost inevitably one of the future leaders of the Republic, literally did not know English very well. Frequently he would hesitate, search for such words as "speech," "acceptance," "variety." His dark friend would come to his assistance with a precise translation, usually after trying and rejecting several synonyms.

"The ASB," Boy said, "has existed since 1948 in its present state—"

"When the Nationalists came to power?"

"Ja—" quickly—"though that was not the cause of it—it was just a natural change, a natural development. The ASB was created in 1916, and is the oldest student organization in South Africa. NUSAS," he observed in a politely contemptuous tone, "did not begin until 1924. . . .

"Originally, the ASB was just a typical student organization, you know, concerned with campus government, and other student problems. Then in 1948, it was decided by the leaders of the ASB that it should put its stress upon language and culture—that it should play its part in the development of the Afrikaner people.

"Truly contribute to the future of Afrikanerdom," the cavern-eyed one agreed, "instead of wasting time on frivolous things."

"Ja," Boy said. "We have now about 25,000 members, at all the Afrikaans universities, Stellenbosch, Bloemfontein, Potchefstroom, Pretoria, and so on. The ASB was founded, and we try to continue it, on the Christian national principle. This idea was taken from the University of Amsterdam, which," he added with some pride, "was founded by a Caper."

"Does this mean a strongly nationalistic basis?"

"Nationalism—love for one's own—one's own language, own culture, own country. It does not mean disrespect for the culture of other groups" —murmurs of agreement from the other two—"we believe in doing to others as you want them to do to you. It is the Christian principle—the sovereignty of God in all aspects of life—"

"In the Calvinistic sense," said the dark one.

"Ja, in the Calvinistic sense."

"And you have no connection with the Nats."

"The ASB," he said firmly, "has no connection whatsoever with a political party. Its purpose is to unite all Afrikaans-speaking students in one organization—to encourage the common interest of all Afrikaans students. We believe in the upbuilding and preserving of White Christian civilization in its fight against Communism. We believe in preserving our White rule in all respects."

"I understand you've refused to debate national issues with NUSAS."

"We regard all of NUSAS," he said emphatically, "as very cunning. The Stellenbosch debating society suggested such a debate some time ago, and the spokesmen of NUSAS agreed. But it appeared that they wanted not merely debate but a conclusion—they wanted a decision, a final statement on whose ideas are better, who is right. We did not agree to that, so we do not debate NUSAS."

"What about the American Field Service, which I notice the ASB and some Afrikaans leaders are attacking right now?"

"We feel," he said slowly, "that the AFS represents a type of liberalism that is dangerous to our future in South Africa. We feel that the Christian national principle is threatened by liberalism—in the sense that liberalism would extinguish all differences."

"Even those the Bible tells us about," the cavern-eyed one remarked. Boy nodded.

"Ja. Our main objection, however, is not entirely to the AFS as such. It is that it takes South African students at fifteen or sixteen, when they are by no means able to be an ambassador for their country, when they are too young and very—?" "Susceptible." "Ja, susceptible to outside influences. These students have the potential to be leaders for South Africa but they come back from America with new ideas. We think it is unfair to them and to our country."

"It's their age you object to, then."

"We have no opposition to older students going abroad on an Abe Bailey scholarship, to England and the Continent. Or mature students, even, in their final year, going to America. But we believe the American Field Service now implants liberal ideas in them when they are too young to know what is best for them. That is our objection."

"Aside from NUSAS, how do you feel the two White groups are getting along these days?"

"The English and the Afrikaans are getting along very well at the moment," he said promptly, and his friends agreed, "but we are different peoples, you know, we have different cultural backgrounds and a different history. On a cultural basis"—firmly, and again his friends murmured agreement—"we will never be united on one basis in South Africa. But on a political basis, an economic basis, we are quite united, and it will continue as it is. We have united in spite of cultural differences. I think our unity is quite good.

"You see," he said very seriously, "we want to keep our cultural goals for ourselves, and also give the English-speaking their goals. We want to maintain our own language. We don't want to deprive the Englishman of his own language."

"Are you planning to go into politics later on?"

All three smiled.

"All of us," he said, "are going into the ministry, the Dutch Reformed Church."

"In fact you will find," the dark one said, "that most of the top leaders of the ASB throughout the country are going into the D.R.C."

Later we stood on the steps in the cool sunshine waiting for my ride to come along and take me back to Cape Town. Students passed, a beautiful little Afrikaans girl went swinging by. The dark one made a quick comment under his breath, they all laughed.

"I don't understand Afrikaans, but I think I got that."

"We were just discussing her statistics," he said with a cheerful grin.

"I'm surprised an old married man like you would be interested." The grin increased. "But I agree, they looked very good to me."

"Very good," he said happily, and we all laughed again, far for the moment from the problems of Die Volk. Then my ride came, we shook hands and parted cordially, I back to Cape Town and they, solemn again as they turned away, back to a dedication rather harsher, perhaps, than the earnest hopes of the liberal Cape Nats.

(When I got home I wrote Boy and asked if I might have a formal statement of ASB policy to print at length as I have the views of Margaret Mitchell of NUSAS. He never replied. Nor did the editors of *Dagbreek, Die Transvaler,* and *Die Vaderland,* when I asked for translations of some of their editorials to run with those of *Die Burger* and the English-language press. If they are not here, it is their own choice.)

ASB DELEGATE REPLIES: GOVERNED BY LOVE, NOT FEAR
(Cape Times, *English*) . . . *From Mr. H. O. Terblanche (Stellenbosch)—As a delegate to the Afrikaanse Studentebond congress, I cannot but comment on the negative and biased article headed "A week with the Studentebond"* (Cape Times, *July 16*).

As a cultural body the ASB has the right and duty to express itself on various aspects of human existence.

The one emotion we all have in common is not fear, as J. V. Scott says, but love. Love for our own national identity, love for our common fatherland, love for our own cultural heritage. For this reason alone did we attack "foreign elements polluting the Afrikaner way of life."

There is no reason why we should be governed by fear, since we are not underminers of our national security like that politically oriented body, NUSAS.

We want to strengthen national security by our anti-Communistic attitude, and by adopting this attitude do we wish to safeguard human freedom.

There is no difference between the reigning Government and the ASB about principles or purpose. The only difference is the fact that the Government is a political body and the ASB a cultural body.

The ASB, like the Government, believes true unity can only be achieved by safeguarding the cultural values held dear by the two White cultural groups and by maintaining our Christian National way of life.

The reason all motions and reports were accepted unanimously was because our conviction and principles are based on the Christian National way of life and because of our common purpose and our sole determination to defend, to hold, to love what is dear to us all. . . .

STELLENBOSCH STUDENT HIT AT ASB (Sunday Times, *Johannesburg, English*) . . . *More than 1,000 students at Stellenbosch University have signed a petition organised by the Stellenbosch Students' Union protesting against a recent Afrikaanse Studentebond (ASB) resolution praising Mr. S. E. D. Brown, editor of the extreme Right-wing monthly journal, the* South African Observer.

It is expected that by Monday, when the petition will be presented to Mr. "Boy" Geldenhuys, the ASB president, it will have several thousand signatures.

The resolution praising Mr. Brown was adopted at the recent ASB congress in Stellenbosch although Mr. Brown has violently criticised university authorities like the rector, Professor H. B. Thom, and leading Afrikaners like Dr. Anton Rupert.

Mr. Brown was a close associate of the British fascist leader, Sir Oswald Mosley and is a contributor to American Opinion, *mouthpiece of the politically discredited John Birch Society, in the United States.*

Mr. Geldenhuys [said] *he regarded the petition as "unofficial."*

"The students who have drawn up the petition have not discussed the matter with me, and I am ignoring it until official discussions are held. I have discussed other matters with the leaders of the Students' Union, but not the petition. . . ."

The petition calls on the campus to dissociate itself from the ASB resolution.

U. S. FIELD SERVICE URGED TO QUIT S.A. (Natal Witness) . . . *The Afrikaanse Studentebond yesterday condemned the activities of the American Field Service in South Africa and recommended that the organisation be denied access to schools. The ASB will also ask the Government to "bring an end to this drainage of South Africa's youth potential for the sake of American interests."*

A 23-page report, devoted entirely to an attack on the student exchange scheme, was read to the ASB congress in Stellenbosch by Mr. Sam de Beer, director of the Bond's Department of Foreign Student Affairs. . . .

Except for one abstention, the congress voted unanimously in favour of the report. The abstention was cast by Miss Anne-Marie Cronje, of

Pretoria University, who spent a year in America in 1962–63 as an AFS exchange student.

She told the congress she had gained insight through her visit. South Africa had so few friends among AFS countries as it was, that news of the ASB's action would come as a "severe blow. . . ."

LEADERS WARN OF FOREIGN INFLUENCES (Cape Argus, English) . . . *Three Afrikaans political and religious leaders, Mr. J. A. Marais, Dr. P. Koornhof and Dr. A. P. Treurnicht, yesterday warned Afrikaans students to be on their guard against internal and foreign influences aimed at the destruction of Afrikanerdom.*

Addressing about 100 students attending a leadership course arranged by the Afrikaanse Studentebond, Mr. Marais (M.P. for Innesdale) said: "Many people thought the realisation of the Republican ideal was the end of our struggle. But I want to warn you that our struggle has only started."

Mr. Marais said the American Field Service was a blatant indoctrination process by which the Afrikaans youth could be Americanised. "We have every right to fight it in every possible way," he said.

STUDENTEBOND PLANS A THREE YEAR OVERHAUL (Sunday Tribune, *Durban, English*) . . . *The Congress of the Afrikaanse Studentebond (ASB), which ended at Stellenbosch yesterday, decided that a thorough investigation should be held into the whole organisation and method of the ASB.*

A report to Congress said that the ASB was no longer receiving the attention it deserved and that it was getting a weak reception on the campus.

The proposal was submitted by the head of the ASB's Department of Study and Research, Mr. R. J. P. du Plessis.

It was unanimously accepted. . . .

The students expressed themselves strongly against such things as the Christian Institute and its organ, Pro Veritate, *the American Field Service, NUSAS and Afrikaans artists who allowed themselves to be influenced by the "humanism" of the outside world. . . .*

7.
Parliament

NAT MAJORITY IN ASSEMBLY SETS RECORD (Cape Argus, *English*) . . . *When Parliament assembles tomorrow for the second sitting of the year, the Nationalist Party will hold the biggest majority in the House of Assembly of any party in the political history of South Africa.*

The party will command 126 of the 170 seats, giving them an overall majority of three to one over the numbers held by the United Party (39), Progressive Party (one) and the four Coloured representatives.

The closest any party has previously approached this majority was in 1938 when, in the election of that year, the United Party won 111 of the 150 Assembly seats.

Compared with the sitting earlier this year, the number of seats has been increased by 10. This follows the delimitation prior to the General Elections in March this year, when the number of constituencies were increased by the same amount.

There is also a record number of 59 new faces in the Assembly, con-

sisting of 48 new Nationalist M.P.s and 11 new United Party M.P.s. Of these, 10 represent the new constituencies and the remainder replace former M.P.s defeated in nomination contests or in the general election, or they take the place of former M.P.s who resigned following the sitting earlier this year.

The Nationalist Party's big majority creates difficulties in debate procedure and it is doubtful if the past system of Government and Opposition members speaking alternately in debates will continue.

Party whips will reach agreement at discussions today and it is probable that there will be two Government speeches to one Opposition, with Government speakers probably curtailing their speaking time. . . .

I WAS THERE FOR a week, but it took no more than ten minutes to feel at home, for there is a universal familiarity about the parliamentary bodies descended from the British. A general informality is the keynote, and although there are guards and doorkeepers (mostly quite ancient, as in all legislatures where friends, relatives, retainers and less-bright party faithfuls are given this small reward), it is quite possible, with a busy manner and an air of knowing where one wants to go, to go almost anywhere. When there is added the extra authority of the Press Gallery, the floor itself would probably not be impossible if one cared to attempt it.

At least, it would not have been impossible then.

One month later, after someone did attempt it and killed Dr. Verwoerd, things changed.

The Parliament buildings—the most important is the House of Assembly, which does everything; there is also a Senate, but everyone dismisses it with a patronizing smile and a vague air of puzzlement as to exactly what it does do—stand in beautiful lawns and colorful gardens alongside the bottom end of the Avenue, just above Adderley Street. The original section was completed in 1884 and was added to in 1927, 1937, 1960, and 1964. The material is a soft pink brick interlaced with cream-colored columns, which gives a benign and peaceful appearance to the buildings amid the tall trees that surround them. The outward trappings of the Parliament of South Africa are gentle and pleasing to the eye.

Inside, the mood is maintained: wide, high-ceilinged, old-fashioned corridors; tall, dark, wooden doors; an air of leisurely bustle during sessions, an atmosphere of easygoing somnolence during periods of recess. The Assembly chamber is built on the British model with five banks of seats facing one another across a narrow aisle, Mr. Speaker's chair at the top (behind him on the wall two enormous spaces where portraits of royalty used to hang), Members' Lobby at the bottom; small, close, intimate, with steep, precipitous galleries above for visitors, diplomatic corps, press. The paneling is very dark, as are the desks; the benches are done in a deep green leather, and the carpet is a somewhat paler green, with a leaves-and-floral design in dusty pink and pale blue. It is a generally dark but not unpleasant room, with an aspect of quiet luxury; the quiet does not last long. Thirty-seven microphones hang down from the ceiling on long, thin wires, though the chamber is so small that amplification hardly seems necessary to carry the formal speeches by Government and Opposition or the informal and frequently nasty remarks with which individual members express their generally critical opinions of one another during debates. ("Awww—duh," says Mr. Speaker from time to time, as one would say "Shush!" absent-mindedly to schoolboys. "Awww—*duh*.")

Prior to the sessions, which usually open at two fifteen and run until five or six, the standard procedure for members is to invite their guests for the day to lunch with them in the dark-paneled, high-windowed room nearby which used to house the old Legislative Assembly of the independent Cape Province before the Act of Union in 1910. There beneath the portraits of five Prime Ministers and a painting of the National Convention which drew up the Act, the scene is pleasant and lively each noontime. Guests dine at square tables or at round; if it is a formal luncheon for a large number there are place cards, "Mr." and "Mrs." if the host is English-speaking, "Mnr." and "Mvr." if Afrikaans. Menus are in both languages, cocktails and wine are available and freely used. Sessions usually open with everyone in a slightly mellow glow which rapidly disappears as debate begins and the ugly bones of reality poke through the mildly alcoholic haze.

I had four lunches and one tea in the Parliamentary Dining Room. "My God," everybody said, "you're going to die of House of Assembly food!" But actually it is not all that bad, and after one has stood about in the Speaker's Lobby waiting for a host, listening to the deep, guttural Afrikaans greetings, the lighter, more hurried English, picking up the excitement as members gather and tension begins to build toward the session later on, the meal provides a congenial, enjoyable and sometimes enlightening interlude.

My first host and hostess were the Minister for Bantu Administration, M. C. Botha, and his lady, whom I had met in Pretoria. He is tall, dark, big-boned, quick-smiling; she is small, sharp-featured, slightly disapproving. I owe him a good deal for being the final catalyst in arranging my interview with Dr. Verwoerd.

There were some eight or ten other guests, all Afrikaans. The talk was informal, good-humored, moderately serious. It was impressed upon me again that, "If we were driven out, we would have nowhere else to go—this is the only country we have." I heard again about the Anglo-Boer

War. ("You should go to Bloemfontein and see the monument to the twenty thousand Boer women killed by the British in the concentration camps," said Mrs. Botha, perpetuating one of the favorite legends of Afrikanerdom. "That," she remarked thoughtfully, "is my favorite monument.") I was given one more impression of Afrikaners beleaguered but undaunted, determined and indomitable. And as almost always, I was inundated with charm, which is something they have plenty of when they are sitting relaxed in the seats of power—have plenty of, indeed, almost anytime, anywhere.

My second host was Sir de Villiers Graaff, Leader of the Opposition, head of the dwindling United Party, cast, apparently forever, in the unwelcome and uncomfortable role of the dutiful critic who can only carp, never construct. His carping is so well-mannered that its lack of bite causes a constant undertone of criticism throughout the country. "If we only had a really fighting Leader of the Opposition!" people say, many of them not really wanting one. It would just make them feel better if Div were more violent: it would ease their consciences about their basic, often covert, support of Nationalist policies.

He was accompanied by his two chief lieutenants, J. D. Du P. Basson ("Japie," pronounced "Yahppie"), small, compact, sandy-complexioned, keen-eyed; and Marais Steyn, lean, dark, saturnine, perceptive. Div Graaff, heavy-set, lumbering, with a round, dark face, curly black hair, a gleaming smile beneath a small black moustache, is a charming gentleman of the old school. (A few days later I was invited out to De Grendel, his ancestral home, to spend an afternoon and evening with him and his delightful family. "All that green area along the hills," his chauffeur said as he drove me out from Cape Town, "is De Grendel." It is more than seven thousand acres, the biggest private farm left at the Cape, and it appears to go on forever, except where the Government, some say with malice, has cut into it with power-line easements, freeways and Native townships.)

We talked for a while of the problems of the Opposition, which basically seem to be the problems that might be expected from 40 (one Coloured representative sitting with them) contending with 126. When I asked how the U.P. differed from the Nats, they spent some time earnestly trying to explain the rather hazy line that seems to separate the two parties on domestic policy. They do favor a multiracial nation, apparently, with eight White Bantu representatives sitting in Parliament, but with the Bantu otherwise firmly in their place; everybody working together for the economic good of all, but everybody carefully segregated otherwise; no Bantustans, because they might lead to foreign infiltration and become centers of subversion against the Whites; but no very definite substitute for them, either.

But it was all very charming and delightful, and later during the debate I was to perceive that Japie Basson and Marais Steyn are most skilled in-fighters for the cause expressed in more gracious and stately fashion by their likable leader. When I visited De Grendel, he took me all around in his Land Rover and showed me his prize sheep and prize cattle, with which he sweeps the field regularly at agricultural shows throughout the country, and of which he is rightly proud. We stood on a high hill and looked across miles of fields and towns and seascape to the beautiful bay and city, and Table Mountain draped in cloud. It all seemed far away. In a sense it seemed a little far away at lunch, too, even with Dr. Verwoerd and his Transvaal editors eating at the next table and ostentatiously ignoring the Opposition. "We rarely speak outside business hours," Graaff said with an ironic smile. "Our relations are very correct."

On the third day I lunched with Helen. ("I've just come from an interview with Balthazar J.," I said, meaning the Minister of Justice, Mr. Vorster. "I told him I thought I'd better let him know I was lunching with you so he wouldn't hold it against me if he saw us together. She laughed." "Balthazar J. hold it against you for lunching with *me?*" she demanded with a merry hoot. "What about *my* holding it against you for interviewing Balthazar J.?") Her other guests included the Rountrees, settling deeper and more comfortably into their ambassadorial niche, although with that certain walking-on-eggs good humor that goes with being on the spot when your government is taking a generally nagging line toward your host country. There were also colleagues from the Press Gallery, friendly and helpful. Again, charm: Parliament is awash with it, at least during lunchtime.

On the fourth day—"Good Lord, you really *must* love this food!"—I ate with three younger members of the United Party, Oswald Thompson from the Cape, W. V. Raw from Durban Point, and a newcomer, Dr. J. F. Jacobs from Hillbrow division in Johannesburg. Ollie Thompson and Vause Raw were undaunted by the steady erosions in the U.P., devoted to their leader, confident that in time the balance of seats in Parliament would be redressed to more accurately reflect the 40 per cent of the electorate which voted for the party in the last election. Dr. Jacobs, being new, was a little impatient for more direct action, a sharper bite in opposition, and a more clear-cut differentiation between the parties, but the other two were serenely confident that someday, somehow, the U.P. will rise again.

A day later, I was taken down to tea in midafternoon by two of the young Transvaal Nats, both doctors, one dark, one blond. The dark one was right up to the minute on the latest American troubles. Nobody had been pushed, slashed or murdered in the last twenty-four hours that he didn't know about. This provoked a certain asperity in return, I'm afraid.

"Why!" he said scornfully. "When I was in New York I had to ask three taxi drivers before I could find one brave enough to take me up to Harlem! What kind of business is that?"

"You wouldn't find a taxi driver to take you into Soweto at night either, would you?"

"It wasn't at night!"

"Well, you wouldn't go into Soweto any time and feel comfortable, would you? I wouldn't."

"I operate out there!"

"But you don't feel comfortable, do you? You're glad to get out, aren't you?"

"It's taking a chance," his colleague remarked thoughtfully. "It's taking a chance."

"Yes, it is," he admitted honestly. "It is. . . . But I suppose," he said, coming back strong, "that you're all in favor of mixed blood, aren't you? You won't care if America becomes like Brazil!"

"Two hundred years from now we may all be coffee-colored."

He shook his head as one dealing with a hopeless child.

"If it comes about peacefully in the natural passage of time, who cares?"

He shook his head as one dealing with a helpless child.

Two other things, and then some excerpts from the debate on the motion of the Leader of the Opposition to censure the Government, a debate which seemed to synthesize and sum up much of what I had seen and heard along the journey.

The first was a sudden unexpected meeting, as I was going down the back Press Gallery stairs one afternoon after an early adjournment, with my young Bantu editor friend from Durban. Without thinking twice I held out my hand. The building was almost deserted in the home-going rush, no one else was in sight, and for just a second it seemed that he might take it without thinking twice. He started to, then instinctively he stopped, glanced up and down the stairs, gave me a quick, rather shame-faced smile—and then shook hands.

We stood and chatted for several minutes—he was still squirreled away down in the basement somewhere, but he was enjoying the session—and then he walked with me out to the Press Gate that opens onto the Avenue, looking about a little, still, to see if anyone was watching, but increasingly easy as we talked. At the gate I almost—almost—invited him to come up to the Mt. Nelson for a drink. And then I remembered and stopped, for there would have been no point to it, in that country, only an embarrassment that neither of us had to underscore. But we did shake hands again, right out there in public in the soft springlike sunshine on the Avenue with the turtledoves softly going "Coo, Coo—Karrrooo!" in the trees above; and although several White passersby looked at us rather strangely, he seemed pleased, and I was glad that we had.

The second incident occurred somewhere around August 2 or 3, when a friend in the Press Gallery suggested we go back to the tiny typewriter-filled workroom for tea. A messenger brought it in and put it on the desk beside us. As he did so my host looked up and said in a kindly way, "You found it all right, did you?" There was a small, agreeing laugh, and the messenger said, "Yes, I did, the guard showed me where to go," in a peculiar accent, not English, not Afrikaans, something conglomerate and impossible to place. I remember now only a rather burly, rather large presence at my right elbow, whose features I cannot even recall, for I scarcely glanced up as we discussed Div Graaff, going full-tilt in his speech out on the floor. That is all that remains, that impression of somebody different, somebody leaning, a bulky presence, an odd accent, a new messenger in the gallery. It could have been Dmitrio Tsafendas, and I think now that it probably was, for he started work there on August 1; but if so, he was for me, as he apparently remained for so many, a faceless unknown until the afternoon a month later when Parliament's jolly lunchtime ended with an agitated messenger pushing his way through the gathering members to plunge a knife four times into the helpless body of Hendrik Verwoerd. His quarrel was not with me, or with anything, really, save his own sick mind, but it is hard not to experience an uncomfortable feeling, even now.

Before the debate on Graaff's censure motion—which he offered as the basis for the traditional debate on Government policy that starts each new session—there was the State Opening of Parliament, and here, as on so many occasions, I heard wry tribute to the shrewd psychology of the Prime Minister. "When he took us out of the Commonwealth, he didn't want the shock to be too great," they said admiringly at one of the Sea Point parties, "so although he got rid of the Governor-General as such, he simply devised a way to preserve the form of a Governor-General without having a Governor-General. He created the office of State President, which is strictly ceremonial and doesn't do anything, and gave it to 'Blacky' Swart, who was already Governor-General and who is pretty good at being ceremonial and not doing anything."

So in the bright noon sunshine the heir of the Governor-General rode to Parliament with his wife in an enormous open black limousine, coming along behind a company of mounted soldiers with flags flying, passing between two rows of soldiers with bayonets fixed who held back the crowds, four and five deep, on both sides of emptied Adderley Street. In the House as we awaited his arrival, the diplomats were there, the press and public galleries were jammed to overflowing, there was the same air of excitement and expectancy that surrounds an opening session in Congress or any other free, or semifree, legislative body.

Below on the floor we could see the dark-suited rows of the Nats, filling their own side and spilling over to take up almost half the side allotted to the Opposition. In a double row of chairs along the Government side of the aisle the ladies of the Cabinet, dressed in the finest taste that Afrikanerdom affords, preened and gossiped and busily studied one another. Officials of the House took up their stations. There came an extra stir and the Cabinet came in, sitting for this occasion to the left of the Speaker, across and scarcely fifty feet away, so that they were clearly in view: among them thin, white-bearded Albert Hertzog, Minister of Posts and Telegraphs, son of a Prime Minister, fanatic leader of the most reactionary elements of the Transvaal; round-faced, amiably tough-looking Ben Schoemann, Minister of Transport; heavy-jowled, dark-faced, dark-looking John Vorster, Minister of Justice, his upper lip protruding over his lower in that line, so beloved of the cartoonists of the Opposition press, which gives him a rather petulant, little-boy look; and the Prime Minister, clad in a dark suit that offset perfectly his rosy complexion and curling white hair.

At first he bowed and smiled and twinkled, and there could not have been a kindlier, more likable presence; his face in animation, I found when I talked to him later, was always like that. But now during the long ceremony there came moments when his face fell still, and in repose it was not a kindly face. The eyes were small and cold, the expression bleak and almost hagridden, the mouth bitter and curiously unhappy: strangely so, for was not everything in the Republic going exactly as he planned it, was he not in supreme and absolute command of the machinery he himself, above all others, had fashioned?

The State President spoke, a very tall, very thin, very upright old man, opening in Afrikaans, repeating his greeting in English (exempt, apparently, from the Parliamentary rule which says that a speech begun in one of the official languages must be continued in that language), going back to Afrikaans as he described the various new measures the Government proposed to bring in during the session, going back to English as he painted a glowing picture of a booming economy.

His speech ended with an invocation of God's blessings upon the Parliament's work, the Speaker banged his gavel, official parties and the members left, spectators, chattering loudly and cheerfully as the tension broke, hurried one another down the stairs to rush outside and watch the Presidential entourage depart. Hooves clopped, spurs jingled, soldiers sprang to attention and hands cracked sharply on bayonets as the big black limousine drove slowly back down Adderley Street. Behind "Blacky" Swart, Queen Victoria, still standing undisturbed on her pedestal in front of the Parliament that no longer honors her descendants, stared impassively after him, the clear sweep she once had down to the sea obscured now by the modern buildings of booming Cape Town.

Thus the session began, and after it the formal debate; and from that debate, in a chronological order that covered four days, here are some of the major spokesmen for Government and Opposition as they argued and contended for some clear vision of the ideals and purposes of the strange society.

Through it all, the Prime Minister spoke just once: when a United Party back-bencher asked a question. Crisply in English he stated that it would not be in the national interest to reply. He might enter the argument before it concluded, my press friends told me, but he never did; and it was not until the afternoon of September 6 that he was ready to make his first major speech to the First Session of the Third Parliament of the Republic of South Africa.

These, then, the voices of the Assembly, debating their beautiful, uneasy land:

FIRST SESSION, THIRD PARLIAMENT
OF THE REPUBLIC OF SOUTH AFRICA
July 29–August 5, 1966

ORAL QUESTION (prior to debate): Railway Accident between New Canada and Langlaagte . . .

SIR DE VILLIERS GRAAFF:

Mr. Speaker, with your leave, I wish to put the following question to the Minister of Transport: Whether he will make a statement in regard to the train disaster which occurred in Johannesburg on 1st August, 1966?

THE MINISTER OF TRANSPORT:

At this stage there is still considerable confusion, but according to available information a suburban passenger train conveying non-Whites to Johannesburg was delayed on the New Canada-Langlaagte section of the line yesterday morning owing to defective brakes. Instead of seven minutes it took this train nineteen minutes to traverse this section of the line. Three other passenger trains followed this train at short intervals.

The driver of one of this series of trains noticed a train on the section in front of him and brought his train to a halt. At approximately 7.07 A.M. another train collided with the rear of this train.

As a result of the collision one passenger coach was partially derailed, while a second was rammed in under another carriage. According to information, riotous Bantu wilfully set fire to some coaches on both trains and attempted to assault the train staff shortly after the collision. The riotous Bantu began throwing stones, and a railway policeman who had come from New Canada was forced to fire a shot in order to protect driver Van Tonder, who was being threatened by the Bantu. As a result one Bantu was killed.

After the incident and until approximately two hours later sporadic cases of riotousness occurred and both Railway and the South African Police who had been called to the scene were obliged to fire several shots. As a result, several Bantu received minor wounds.

The latest casualty figures are as follows:

6 killed (five in accident and one shot).

450 non-Whites have been treated for injuries in hospitals; 58 of these, of whom 30 sustained serious injuries, have been admitted to hospital. . . .

ON THE CENSURE MOTION OFFERED AGAINST THE GOVERNMENT BY THE LEADER OF THE OPPOSITION, SIR DE VILLIERS GRAAFF

SIR DE VILLIERS GRAAFF:

I want to take as my first example of Nationalist Government mismanagement one which I think goes to the root of certain of the differences between this Government and the Opposition. That is the lack of foresight which this Government has displayed in respect of its whole approach to the philosophy of government in South Africa. You see, Sir, it is so obsessed with party-political ambition and with authoritarian powers that it has adopted an attitude which does violence to the generally accepted respect for the freedom of the dignity of the individual which is generally accepted as one of the hallmarks of the Western states of the world and the countries which are regarded as being representative of Western standards of civilization. This disregard for the freedom and the dignity of the individual usually leads to certain results. Those are the tendencies to glorify the State and to identify a particular political party with the State, and the tendency to take up the attitude that the Government of the country has become something more than a mere political party representative of the views of a section of the population.

Because of this obsession we have seen this Government in the past, and we are seeing it now, being prepared to make tremendous inroads into the freedom and the dignity of the individual citizen in South Africa. There have been many examples in the past, and no doubt there will be many more in future if this Government remains in power. It is quite impossible to deal with them all. We find ourselves in the position here today that even though the State President speaking, I take it, on behalf of the Cabinet, in his opening speech to Parliament, speaks of the peace and good order required in South Africa and in the Bantu territories, nevertheless the first guinea pig Bantustan can apparently not be administered by this Government without Proclamation 400 remaining in force. I know, of course, that it has been asked for by the Legislative

Assembly there. I suppose the pupils have not been slow to follow their masters, but it is significant that they seem to think it necessary that it should still be retained.

We find the hon. the Minister of Justice still considering it absolutely necessary to restrict certain people in terms of the powers given him under various Statutes of this Parliament. I believe that there are possibly as many as 500 people so restricted at present. . . .

I want to pose the question this afternoon: For how long can we go on in this way? Because we have seen with the Government not only assaults upon the freedom and the dignity of individuals, but we have seen them using State institutions in a manner which is not consistent with that freedom and that dignity.

Here I want to take the easiest example, one that is well known to this House, and that is the example of the South Africa Broadcasting Corporation. We all know the story, Sir. We all know that it is a State-protected monopoly. We all know that we have to pay licences to Radio South Africa, and that it is presenting news and comments and points of view and that it is doing it almost to the exclusion of others. We know that the Prime Minister said that its function is to correct what he regards as misinformation from certain newspapers in South Africa. While he regards it as that, yet Radio South Africa regards itself as being above the Press Code. It can attack individuals or newspapers or institutions or societies or organizations. It is not called upon to give those individuals, societies or organizations the right to reply over the radio to the attacks upon them.

Sir, is that democratic? Is that in accordance with the best principles? Would any newspaper be allowed to do that? No, they would immediately be reported to the Press Board of Reference, and they would be reprimanded by that Board, and they might find themselves in trouble. Various individuals and organizations can testify to the manner in which the appeals to be heard in their own defence have been treated by Radio South Africa, the contempt with which they have been treated. There are various dignitaries of the Church and there are various individuals, newspapers and institutions of different kinds. When a State-protected institution virtually enjoying a State monopoly is entitled to act in this way, then it seems to me that it is taking or is being allowed to take totalitarian power. It is being allowed to deny the fundamental tenets of democracy. It is being allowed to make serious inroads into the rights and the freedoms of the individual.

Where is it all going to lead to, Sir? Today one can see with half an eye where things are going. It is going towards more dictatorial powers, more identification of a particular party with the State, more denials and restrictions on the individual. Is that really where we want to go in South Africa? We pride ourselves on being the bastion of Western civilization on the African Continent. Is that really Western civilization? It seems to me that this Government, in its attempts to combat certain foreign ideologies, is adopting so many of the weapons and so many of the worst features of those ideologies that we are in danger of lessening our own identity as a Western state and as a democratic country. What lack of foresight, Mr. Speaker! What a legacy!

There are other examples. I think this lack of foresight of this Government in dealing with the whole question of the philosophy of government is paralleled only by its lack of foresight in dealing with the question of the relationship between the two big groups of Whites in the Republic. Here it threatens to destroy the very core of the nation. I think there has always been a difference of opinion between members on that side of the House and members of this side on the question of national unity. It is an old argument which has gone on for many years.

I think that where we have sought to build a new nation based on the best in the culture and tradition and the history of both sections, an attempt by both to accept the language and the background of each as its own, hon. members opposite have sought to put one section, Afrikanerdom, first. In the past, when they spoke of national unity, what they meant was cooperation on terms, and nothing more than that. . . . I think this battle has gone on through the years, South Africanism on one side as opposed to those who stand for Afrikaner nationalism on the other side, the cooperation on terms being all take and no give and "you must vote Nationalist. . . ."

. . . There are also all the other problems which we have discussed so often and with which I do not propose to hold up the House. There is the question of controlling the timetable to [Bantu] independence. There is the question above all, Sir, of the urban Bantu. What is the position today with the urban Bantu? We have to look into this matter or we run the risk that they may become a threat to South Africa, and especially to the security of White South Africa. The hon. the Prime Minister is creating a new problem with his independent Bantustans. It is dramatic. It tends to draw people's attention. We devote our time to it. But we overlook what is perhaps the more pressing problem, and that is the Bantu outside the Reserves.

Can any man who really thinks about this problem think that the Government has got an answer in that respect? He knows the Reserves can never carry all the Bantu. He knows these people are going to be there permanently. He knows he is not allowed home ownership. He knows that family life is being disturbed. He knows they are not having political rights which will satisfy anybody.

Politically they are the most dangerous population element in South Africa at the present time. I believe the hon. the Minister of Justice believes that. They may cause us troubles here in comparison with which the troubles caused by the impoverished urbanized Negroes in the United States will fade into the background. The Government ignores their permanent existence here. It still tries to regard them as visitors.

There must be some cause for the sort of outburst we had in Johannesburg yesterday. The hon. the Minister has reported it this afternoon. Why is the natural reaction to attack the railway officials and burn the railway coaches?

We cannot let the Government get away with this pretence anymore, Mr. Speaker. They are creating dangers here to the White people owing to their lack of foresight which may undermine the whole of the civilization which has existed here. We as an Opposition cannot stand still and let them get away with this fantasy, this figment of the imagination, which is the manner in which they are dealing with this problem. . . .

THE MINISTER OF MINES AND PLANNING
(J. F. W. HAAK, Nationalist M.P. for Bellville, Cape Province):

[The leader of the Opposition] is trying to give this motion a sugar-coating by saying that it is a motion of censure and not a motion of no-confidence, but by doing so he is trying to do one thing only and that is to distract attention from the defeat suffered by him in the past election. That defeat suffered by the United Party was one of the most resounding that party had suffered, and it is probably the most resounding any party had ever suffered in the political history of South Africa. When Parliament was dissolved, there were 106 members on this side of the House. After the election there are 126 members here, an increase of 20. But on the other side they have shrunk; there has been a decrease in their numbers. On dissolution they numbered 49, and now there are only 39, and they are now 39 in number after there has been an addition of ten seats in Parliament.

But what is more significant about this victory is the fact that after this party has been in power for eighteen years, its popularity, the support which it enjoys outside is still increasing. Since 1910 there has never been a government which has been in power for such a long time. We find that the support of this party has gained, is stronger than ever before. Since 1933, when that party was at the peak of its power, it has only retrogressed; it has only become weaker all along, but for thirty-three years, since the regrouping of this party, it has gone from strength to strength all along. Surely there are reasons for that. One of those reasons is certainly the following. The hon. member accused us of abusing our powers, but certain duties rest on the Opposition too; they too have to use their powers properly, but what do we find? In the process of fighting this Nationalist Government, what have they not done?

They have tried their best to undermine our economy. They have tried their best to make the English-speaking section antagonistic towards the

National Party. They have had hopes of disturbing the labour peace; they have tried to bedevil good relations wherever they could. They have tried to incite bodies and persons against this Party, and when they were through doing that locally, they turned their backs on South Africa to see whether assistance for them was perhaps not forthcoming from abroad. . . .

. . . In 1961 our rate of growth was 4 per cent of the gross internal product. In 1962 it was 7 per cent, in 1963 7½ per cent, and in 1964 6½ per cent. That is a very high rate of growth. It shows that we do have the capacity, and the Government did not leave it at that but also started laying down an economic development programme, a five-year programme in which it put the rate of growth at 5½ per cent, and that rate of growth of 5½ per cent was higher than that of practically any country in Western Europe. I am giving the figure for 1965 which will give you an indication that where South Africa planned for a growth of 5½ per cent, the figure for the United Kingdom was only 2.8 per cent, for the United States of America 4.5 per cent, for Italy 6 per cent, for Western Germany 5 per cent, and for France 2.5 per cent. Not one of those countries maintained the rate of growth we want to maintain over a period. And South Africa's rate of growth is even higher than that. . . .

J. D. Du P. Basson, United Party M.P. for Bezuidenhout,
Transvaal:

The Government's Bantustan policy, as it is called, is anything but conservative. Seen from a South African point of view, it is radical, revolutionary and liberal. Here on this side we have the United Party which, in turn, is regarded as being a liberal party. But in terms of modern development its declared policy of "White control over the whole of South Africa for all time" is not only conservative but in fact ultra-conservative. I am not saying this because I want to dish out labels myself. That is a game I do not like. I am only mentioning it to demonstrate that our intrinsical quarrel with the Government does not concern the question whether it is "conservative" or "liberal" or whether we on this side are "left-wing" or "right-wing." The division in our politics is not that of being either left-wing or right-wing. Our intrinsic difference lies in our different approaches to the question of human relationships and of democratic government.

If one looks at the countries of the world the real division between them, too, is not that of being either left-wing or right-wing. In actual fact the division is one of those on the one hand who subscribe to the democratic philosophy and those on the other hand who have a state dogma, a national dogma which determines and dominates all their actions. Those countries having a national dogma all display the same traits, whether they are left-wing or right-wing. . . . All those countries adhering to a national dogma, whether it be Communism or Castroism on the left or Falangism or militarism on the right, they all display the same traits.

And that is where our danger lies under the Government which is in power today. We are already being classed among those countries having a national dogma, an "-ism," a national "-ism": namely the dogma of racialism or enforced racial apartheid. I do not believe its creators visualized or willed it thus. I do not believe they wanted to go much further than what has always been the general custom and convention in South Africa. But this thing has gradually got out of hand, it has gradually become more enveloping, more absolute and more merciless. As time went by reasonableness disappeared to an ever-increasing extent, and we approached ever closer to all that is characteristic of the "-ism" countries of the world.

Everywhere the pattern is the same. The first step usually taken by a country moving in that direction is that the government policy is elevated to a "state policy." The government party becomes identified with the state. Gradually those who speak and work against the so-called state policy—even though they do so within the framework of the law—are then classified as being unpatriotic and subversive. They can differ, but they must differ within the framework of the "state policy." The laws become stricter and more comprehensive. The courts are restricted to an ever-increasing extent. More and more powers pass into the arbitrary hands of ministers. The Security Police increase and their net is thrown further and further. The public radio is harnessed to the "state policy." The public Press are threatened and intimidated to an ever-increasing extent. Intolerance toward opposition increases in a hundred-and-one ways. . . .

Another feature—and we have arrived at that stage here too—is that sooner or later the machine turns on itself and then witch-hunting and ferreting out dissenters from amongst their own ranks begins. The more authoritarian the ruling faction becomes, the more ferreting out is done from amongst their own ranks. The question we should apply ourselves to is how far the present Government has already progressed along this road and where it is leading South Africa. . . .

DR. C. P. MULDER, Nationalist M.P. for Randfontein, Transvaal:

The hon. member for Bezuidenhout has devoted his entire argument to an attempt to prove that we are already, as he puts it, a dogma country, and in doing so he wants to establish an immediate connection between us and the totalitarian states and to dissociate us from the democracies of the world. His entire argument was along those lines, and that was in fact its only object, namely to brand this Government, in the eyes of the democracies of the world, as a government which is developing in the direction of the totalitarian states. I just want to tell the hon. member that in doing so he has certainly not done South Africa a service. . . . I maintain that by that speech of his the hon. member has done South Africa a very great disservice. . . .

At the moment we have an exceptional situation in South Africa, and every hon. member sitting here knows that attacks are being launched against South Africa in the most subtle way; that our country and our national security are being threatened; that attempts are being made to undermine us and to destroy law and order here, and that the Government, in view of those exceptional circumstances, needs exceptional powers to cope with that exceptional situation. That is the crux of the matter. All the Government's actions in respect of those so-called dogmatic and dictatorial powers have just been submitted to the tribunal of the people at the past election, and the people decided in a democratic way that under the circumstances it was perfectly in order, and that the Government needs all these powers and, in fact, even stronger powers. Democracy has fully endorsed the Government's actions. What right has the hon. member to come here and to claim that we are no longer democratic? . . .

In 1938 the United Party had 111 members here. In 1943 that number decreased to 89, in 1948 to 65, in 1953 to 57, in 1958 to 53; in 1961 it was 50, and now in 1966 they have 39 here. The Nationalist Party, on the other hand, showed the following graph over the same period. In 1938 there were 27 of us, in 1943 43, and in 1948 70, in 1954 94, in 1958 103, in 1961 105, and in 1966 126. That record is as clear as daylight. Since the struggle between the two parties began, one has consistently deteriorated and the other has made consistent progress.

And then the hon. member for Bezuidenhout maintains that this Government shows lack of foresight; it cannot govern the country; it does not know how to manage economic matters or agriculture, and the Government has made a great failure of things. Then the electorate of South Africa must surely be a bunch of nitwits if they return such a mistaken and foolish Government with larger majorities every time. On the contrary, the United Party has consistently proved one thing only, namely that they are the party which lacks foresight and which has no alternative policy.

Take the speech by the Leader of the Opposition today. I challenge him to name one single point in his speech, in his entire plan of attack, in which he presented the Government with an alternative possibility: what they would have done if they had been in power. Give us just one bit of positive criticism, which is after all the fundamental duty of the Opposition. But I repeat, as long as they fail in this fundamental duty the people

will reject them, so that we may eventually develop into a one-party
state, not because we are dictatorial, but because they are so hopeless. . . .

M. L. MITCHELL, United Party M.P. for Durban (North), Natal:
The hon. member for Randfontein [Dr. Mulder] is distressed because
it was suggested by the hon. member for Bezuidenhout [Mr. Basson]
that we should say that we are moving in the direction of a one-party
state, of a totalitarian state. But he must look at the facts. . . .

The history of this Nationalist Government should cause every South
African to listen twice when someone as responsible as the hon. members who have said these things say so. They should look back and consider in the light of the propaganda being put out by these people what
happened before.

Sir, consider the time when South Africa was in danger. The last time
we were at war, where was the hon. the Prime Minister [Dr. Verwoerd]?
He was the editor of a newspaper. He was described by someone as
being a tool of the Nazis and he sued that person for defamation, and in
the judgment of the court his case was dismissed on the basis that he was
in fact a tool of the Nazis; he had no cause for complaint. Sir, do not let
us talk about patriotism. Do not let us talk here about being South Africans, when the Prime Minister himself has set such an example.

And then there is the hon. the Minister of Justice [B. J. Vorster]. He
had to be locked up as well, for the same reason, when South Africa was
at war, and that Minister told this House a little while ago, when we
discussed the Official Secrets Bill, that in the same circumstances he
would do exactly the same things again. Now tell me, Sir, how does the
Minister distinguish himself from someone like Mandela, or from Sobukwe? [Bantu jailed by the Government for subversion.] (Interjections.) No, I am not ashamed of myself.

. . . What are we trying to maintain? What are the foundations of
our society, our democracy? What is the state we wish to maintain? Here
I want to say that I think that the time has come when every South
African must look at that State and at its foundations and ask himself
how far we can go along that road without damaging the foundations
themselves. This is a foundation: The individual is the kernel of Western
Christian democracy and if we call ourselves a Western Democracy and
Christians then that is what distinguishes us from the Godless Communist states and it is that which distinguishes us today in South Africa
from every totalitarian Black state to the north of us.

The responsibilities on us are very heavy. These responsibilities rest
on the shoulders of the hon. the Minister [Mr. Vorster] and on ours as
well. It rests on our shoulders because it has become evident that there is

not an hon. member anywhere on that side of the House who is going to be prepared to question the exercise of those powers. So those powers have to be questioned by us. . . .

One wonders, Sir, how far one has to go before we stop and think. I hope sincerely that the hon. the Minister will get up here and tell us what his attitude is, that is, whether he is prepared to allow the court to determine in terms of our Constitution what the rights of the individual are, e.g., whether he shall have liberty or whether he shall not have it.

The hon. the Minister has a magnificent Security Force at his disposal and he also has a magnificent Police Force at his disposal. Surely, if the Minister has evidence on which he acts, then he must also have evidence to get these people nailed in the courts. If he can do that, he will get the support of every single person in South Africa against any unlawful act that has been perpetrated.

But as I said, I think the time has arrived in South Africa where each one must ask himself the question how far the present position is going. Do we have to proceed to a stage where our people in looking back would have to say what they said in Germany in the time of Hitler? There they explained their attitude by saying that at one time it was only the Jews that were being taken and because they themselves were not Jews they did not worry; then, however, they took the Catholics and because they were not Catholics either they did not worry. But then all of a sudden it was their own turn.

Well, Mr. Speaker, we hope we in South Africa will not get to that stage. But the way the hon. the Minister is thinking and the way in which the Government is moving, the way in which they equate Communism with Liberalism and of closing any recourse to the courts—all these things do seem to have a similarity with things that happened in a country like Germany. The philosophy of this Government, Sir, where does it end? . . .

THE MINISTER OF JUSTICE (MR. B. J. VORSTER,
Nationalist M.P. for Nigel, Transvaal):

Surely it is not their [United Party] intention to convince anybody in South Africa that human rights are being suppressed in South Africa, because people in South Africa, whether they vote for my party or whether they vote for hon. members on the opposite side, know that South Africa is not a police state. They know that South Africa is not on the way to becoming a totalitarian state. They do know, however, that South Africa is a state in which all decent people can live together in peace and amity.

AN HON. MEMBER:

Who are the decent people?

THE MINISTER OF JUSTICE:

It is not necessary for me at this stage to say who are the decent people and who are not. But I do want to go so far as to say that I cannot regard any person as being decent if he does not hesitate to befoul his own nest as certain persons do sometimes do in South Africa. If there are any hon. members who want to wear this cap if it fits them, then I do not mind if they wear it. . . .

The hon. member asked me to give this House an explanation of my attitude in respect of the restriction of individuals. Restrictions are nothing new, neither is it I who introduced them. Restrictions were introduced under the Act of 1950 and both my predecessors acted in terms of that Act. The hon. member knows as well as I do that as far as dealing with Communists is concerned—and that is the premise adopted in the 1950 act—there are two basic principles embodied in that Act. The first is that Communism must be eradicated and that Communists must be punished for their deeds, but the second point of departure was that it is the Minister's duty—and that obligation has been placed upon him by law —to prevent as far as possible and by means of restriction orders the committing of actions which constitute a threat to the safety of the State.

That is why you impose restrictions on people; you restrict them not necessarily because they have done something in the past, but because their associations, their actions and their utterances are such that they might lead to the achievement of the aims of Communism. The hon. member for Bezuidenhout admitted that and so did the hon. member for Durban North. The hon. member for Bezuidenhout put it very clearly that Communism is of such a nature that one cannot always fight it with the ordinary democratic methods, and that other hon. member also conceded that. That is the spirit in which we have always acted.

At the present moment in South Africa—I am now furnishing the number as at 1st July—there are 453 people on whom restrictions have been imposed. Several dozen of these people are Poqos in whose case we deemed it advisable, after they had been released from prison, to keep them under observation for a period of two years and not five, as in the other cases, so that we could keep an eye on them in order to prevent any further acts of violence.

Is there any hon. member on the opposite side who wants to tell me I have not acted correctly? This is one of the motives for imposing restrictions on people; but we do not simply restrict people and then forget about them. Over the years I have in many cases amended the restriction orders imposed upon people and in many cases I have even lifted them. Only recently I lifted the restriction in respect of two lecturers at the Grahamstown University.

These people know that things are not the same today as they were in the days when hon. members on the opposite side were in power. They know that they have access to me at any time; they know that they can make representations to me and that I am prepared to consider those representations. But hon. members on that side, without having the facts at their disposal, come forward with a great display of verbosity and ascribe all kinds of motives to one. . . .

Mr. Speaker, I have a responsibility, not only to my side of the House but to the country as a whole, and if the evidence placed before me indicates that a man is toying with sabotage, or that he is not merely toying with it but that he is involved in such an organization, but the evidence is such that I cannot take him to court—and we have debated this point often in the past—what do hon. members expect me to do? Must I sit and wait until he has committed sabotage, or must I prevent it by imposing restrictions on him? . . .

MR. T. G. HUGHES, United Party M.P. for the Transkei:

. . . One thing I will say about this Minister is that he stands unrepentant. He said so. A few years ago he said he was not ashamed of what he had done and he would act in exactly the same way again. I refer to the time when the Government of the day thought it advisable to lock him up because he was a danger, as they thought, to the security of the State. Now the Minister chastises the hon. member for Durban (North) for referring to the country as being a police state, but this Minister accused the old United Party Government of having a police state. I would remind you, Sir, that the accusation was made when that Government was fighting not a cold war but a hot war.

Sir, sabotage is nothing new. Sabotage is a despicable offence. None of us approves of it; we all abhor it, but I would like to remind hon. members opposite that sabotage is not only now being committed for the first time and that homemade bombs were not made by Strachan for the first time. Did we hear any criticism of it when it was committed before from that side of the House? No, Sir. (Interjections.) Sir, nobody on this side has ever hesitated to denounce sabotage, and we must listen to this Nationalist propaganda put across over the radio all the time that we, the United Party, by insinuation, and the English Press, are the un-South African elements. Continually they ask: How do you stand with regard to South Africa? Why do they not ask how the Prime Minister stood when South Africa was fighting with her back to the wall against the greatest tyrant the world has ever known? (Interjections.)

MR. SPEAKER:

Order!

Mr. T. G. Hughes:

I should like to remind hon. members that they supported the Nazis when Hitler had a contract with Russia . . . (Interjections.) When they thought that the Communists would not fight for the democracies, the Communists were all right. Everybody is now so democratic. Why are they all democrats now? Because it pays them to be democrats. What was their attitude during the period 1939–45? . . . No, at that time it paid them not to be democratic because they thought Hitler was winning the war and they thought they would live in a totalitarian world. They thought the democracies would be defeated, but now the position has changed. Now they depend on the sympathy of the democracies, and now they are suddenly democrats. (Interjections.)

Mr. Speaker:

Order!

Mr. T. G. Hughes:

And when did they discover this sudden love for the English-speaking people and this sudden desire to work together? We remember that Constitution for the Republic which they published. Where were the rights of the English and their language then? . . . What was their attitude then? But now all of a sudden they want to work with the English. Why? Because they want the friendship of the English-speaking world. . . .

. . . The shortsightedness of the Nationalist Party as displayed during those years is being repeated today. The shortsighted policy of this Government is going to land this country in a terrible mess, in the same way that it would have done had they won their no-confidence motions during those war years and had they made a separate peace with Hitler. In the same way the policy of this Government is going to be rued. . . .

Mr. G. F. Van L. Froneman, Nationalist M.P. for Heilbron, Orange Free State:

I want to ask him [Mr. Hughes]: What National Party member committed sabotage at any stage or approved the making of bombs? He knows as well as anyone of us in this House that the then Leader of the National Party and the entire National Party disapproved of that. But let me remind him that under the regime of the United Party South Africa fought a war which was a henchman's war for Great Britain; it was not a war in the interest of South Africa; it was a war which was conducted in the interest of a foreign people. . . . Not only were they henchmen of Great Britain; they were also henchmen of Russia. We still remember the days of the "Friends of the Soviet Union," when United Party Ministers cooperated with Russia. I want to emphasize most strongly that the National Party has always been and will always be a democratic party. The predecessors of the National Party were democrats to the core. The old Republics (Transvaal and Orange Free State) were founded on democratic principles. . . .

. . . It will be a good thing if now, after the election, the United Party does some rethinking, if they take a look at the future of South Africa, and if they formulate a new policy for the party. . . . What is in fact needed in this House is that the United Party should formulate a policy that will make an impression on the people, a policy for which the people can vote; then there will be no need for them to juggle with figures. If they really have an alternative policy, the people will support that policy. . . .

The hon. the Leader of the Opposition brought a further charge against the Government in claiming that the Government is doing nothing to establish industries and factories in the [native] homelands to enable those homelands to become economically viable. . . .

It is clear . . . that economic considerations are not the basis for the development of an underdeveloped people, what is basic, is the human factor; the community should in itself be able to generate and produce the development. It should be able to absorb what is given to it, to appreciate and assimilate it. It is of no use merely to build factories and do other things which that underdeveloped people cannot appreciate, which it cannot absorb and from which it cannot benefit. . . .

It is on this basis that the Government's entire policy of separate development is founded. We do not develop our policy of separate development merely by establishing the outward symbols of development, such as factories and chimneystacks; we start with human development, and education is basic to human development. . . . The Department is also making arrangements to give the Bantu practical in-service training on the artisan and managerial level. This Government has also given serious attention to the matter by establishing vocational schools and other training centres. I want to emphasize this afternoon that the Transkei has taught us one thing in the past few years, something it has brought to our notice very pertinently, and that is that there is a shortage of trained Bantu who can serve their own people. The Department of Bantu Education is taking all the necessary steps in this regard and we have made a great deal of progress in that direction. Hon. members will be surprised to hear how rapid the progress in that direction has been. . . .

MR. J. O. N. THOMPSON, United Party M.P. for Pinelands, Cape:

Mr. Speaker, we are not impressed. We know that the Government's plans for the next five years require that approximately 80,000 Blacks shall be incorporated each year into our economy, and I do not doubt that the number will have risen at the end of that time, because we certainly look forward to greater prosperity in due course.

But there is another aspect of this. It is not only a question of these people coming from the Reserves to the White areas. There is the very birthrate in our big Native townships today. . . .

If one wants to think of any corner of South Africa which is not a Black man's land, one would think of the Western Province; and here the city is Cape Town. But what do we find here? We find that at present if the trend of 1964 and 1965 continues, there will be more Black births in the city of Cape Town than White births in this very year of grace. There were in the year 1964—and I have the official figures of the Medical Officer of Health of Cape Town on the subject—3,700 White births in the municipality of Cape Town, a rate of 18.7. In 1964 there were 3,054 Bantu births, a birthrate of 41.4. In 1965 there were 3,404 White births, a rate of 17.2 per 1,000, and there were 3,171 Bantu births, a rate of 40.3. That has merely got to continue into this year and we will have more Black births in Cape Town than White births.

So I say that not only these births but the influx is going on more strongly than ever. One knows of all the extra jobs into which Bantu are moving, not only in the Transvaal and Natal, but in Cape Town. More and more farming areas around Cape Town are demanding Native labour. We have recently had the case of the Durbanville-Philadelphia Farmers' Association, which was quite dissatisfied with the rate at which they were able to get contract labourers from the Transkei and elsewhere. They formed their own company, and they were so successful that they paid a 10 per cent dividend within the first year. That is what is happening. And the farmers' associations of Paarl and Constantia are considering doing the same thing. The very Government building which is rising across the road from here is being built by 80 per cent of Black men from somewhere.

Now, I am aware that the hon. member for Heilbron only just managed to restrain himself from saying that they are there on contract, and that they will go back, but I suggest that in this respect, too, the Government is showing a great lack of foresight. I say that we are doing immense harm to many of these people by insisting that this is the case. We are storing up trouble for ourselves as well as for them. There is a far greater denial of family life there, which is the foundation of our and the Bantu society, than is justified. (Interjection.) We have always said that there is a certain place for migrant labour, but equally we have always said that under our policy there would be more family life than under yours. But I ask the hon. member to take it from me that this is an evil which has to be watched. . . .

So hon. members opposite can have their choice. They can either try to keep the flood back in this way as I have indicated, and it makes so little difference to the numbers and the proportions that it is a waste of time or, if they wish to do that, they will fly in the face of what they know in their consciences is a state of affairs which they should not tolerate. . . .

MRS. HELEN SUZMAN, Progressive Party M.P. for Houghton,
Transvaal:

. . . I want to go further and challenge the hon. the Minister (Mr. Vorster) for his use of his very extensive powers. Other members here, especially the hon. member for Bezuidenhout, have most ably demonstrated how this country is gradually handing over more and more powers to the Minister in this regard. I say that if one reads the debates on the bills originally introduced in this House and the assurances which we had from the Minister at that time, one realizes how much further things have gone since the Minister introduced the bills and since he told us of the uses to which he was going to put the vast powers which he now possesses.

He told us that the General Law Amendment Bill of 1962 dealt with Communists and Communists only. He said: "I am not launching an attack on the freedom of the citizens. What I am doing is to restrain the liberty of the Communists to destroy the freedom of the citizens." In dealing with the same bill in the Other Place [the Senate] he said: "This bill is restricted to Communists and to Communists only." He went further and said: "It deals with Communists and only Communists; it will prevent only such people from attending meetings. . . ."

Over and over again he gave assurances that he intended to restrict his bill, his house-arrest bill, and his banning bills, to Communists and Communists only. But, Sir, the Minister has run out of Communists. There are no Communists left; he tells us every year that he has finished them off. His police officers tell us that they have completely destroyed the Communist movement, so they have to find other people and now they are using this weapon of intimidating people who are not Communists, who never were Communists and who do not even sympathize in any respect with Communist ideology.

I accuse the hon. the Minister of using his extensive powers to intimidate citizens who have no connection whatsoever with Communism or with any of the aims of the Communists. The hon. the Minister sits there secure in his power, knowing that he cannot be attacked in the courts of law and knowing, unfortunately, that his intimidatory tactics are succeeding; that people are becoming frightened to speak up outside this House, where there is a certain degree of protection. People are beginning to be afraid of being associated with certain organizations on which the Minister has cast his dark frown of disapproval. . . .

He no longer needs to tell anybody why he is doing anything; it is enough that he is doing it, and unfortunately a whole generation of our young people has now grown up under this Government and they know no other form of regime; they know no other form of "democracy." They only know what this Government has taught them and they accept these things as being perfectly legitimate. We have gone so far away from normal concepts of democratic practice that it is, indeed, no wonder that people today are intimidated and are nervous of taking part in ordinary organizations, and I believe that is the object and the purpose.

The hon. the Minister also said something extraordinary about the fact that he banned people in order to prevent them from committing certain actions. . . . My view is that if you really want to overcome Communism, if you really want to strip Communists of their ammunition and their weapons, then you must examine the genuine grievances and do your best to remove them.

AN. HON. MEMBER:

Must you join the Progressive Party?

MRS. H. SUZMAN:

No, you do not have to join the Progressive Party, but something you do not do is to join the Nationalist Party, because the Nationalist Party does not admit that there are genuine grievances in this country. It does not admit that any wrong is done to people by throwing them out of homes which they have occupied or that the generations before them have occupied for at least 100 years. The Nationalist Party does not think that it causes any grievance when it prevents Africans from living normal family lives, when it attempts to turn the whole system of labour in this country into a vast migratory labour system, which is the worst system sociologically and economically that one could imagine.

The Nationalist Party never admits that there are any grievances and that non-Whites suffer in South Africa, and until that party is able to realize that there are grievances and does something about those grievances, no matter how strong-armed the Minister is, no matter how large his Police Force is, one will always face the threat of further violence from dangerous people.

You have to give people hope. That is the only way in which you can develop a peaceful community of people of different races living together in South Africa; and whether we like it or not we are a people of different races living here. And by the year 2000, as one hon. member has told us, we will be a vast population of 70,000,000 I think he said. But whatever the size of the population he anticipates, we are already 18,000,000 people of different races, and banning people, putting them under restrictions, and the taking of vaster and vaster powers by the Minister will not, I fear, tend to allay the difficulties South Africa will have to face in the future. . . .

THE MINISTER OF BANTU ADMINISTRATION AND
DEVELOPMENT (M. C. BOTHA, Nationalist M.P. for
Roodeport, Transvaal):

. . . The Leader of the Opposition had a number of things to say but I want to return to only one of them. He said the Bantu in the White urban areas constituted a threat to the Whites, because they would always remain there, and he even dragged in the recent train disaster in Johannesburg, which occurred a few days ago, as an example of what threat they are to us. The hon. member for Transkei also mentioned this matter and said the Bantu in the towns kept our industries on the go, but they had no rights there, and that this situation was fraught with danger.

First of all I just want to deal with the random idea of the train disaster and tell the Leader of the Opposition that if there is one thing which reveals his ignorance of Bantu affairs, it is the fact that he has dragged the train disaster into this discussion. The actions of the Bantu after the train disaster have as little to do with politics in this country as with the man in the moon. The hon. Leader does not know the character and the nature of the Bantu. After any occurrence of that kind in an urban area their true natures appear and they throw stones, wield cudgels or commit arson. This is the instinctive reaction one finds in them, and it has nothing to do with politics. Even if they were to have eight representatives in this House under the race federation [proposed by the United Party], and such a train disaster were to occur, they would still do it, not because of the eight representatives but because of their nature. . . .

S. J. M. STEYN, United Party M.P. for Yeoville, Transvaal:

Let me show you, Sir, what is happening. The Government is now taking strong action to endorse certain Black people out of the White cities. Last year we were told by the then Minister, who is now unfortunately no longer with us, that in 1964 they endorsed 98,241 Natives out of the White areas and another 23,000 in the first three months of last year, a total of approximately 121,000. But in the same period they admitted into the White areas 175,099 new Black workers in 1964 and 49,540 in the first three months of last year. For every Black man endorsed out of the White cities of South Africa, two new ones were admitted! And this, Sir, is reducing South Africa's dependence upon Black labour! Have you ever heard greater nonsense in your life? . . .

Sir, in America they are having great difficulty with their American Negroes. There we find that they investigate; they do research, and what do they find? According to an article which I read recently by a former

Deputy Secretary for Labour in the United States Government, they found that one-quarter of the children born to the Negroes in the whole of the United States were illegitimate and that many families were headed by women; that 47 per cent of the family units in the urban areas of the United States were without a father, and the position in South Africa cannot be better. They found out that of every 1,000 Negro births, 263 were illegitimate.

It is infinitely worse in South Africa. What dragon's teeth are we sowing for ourselves in South Africa? The Minister will deny this but does this not lend significance to the reaction of the Black people in Johannesburg when their train was smashed? Was it not a deep-seated resentment that was coming to the fore, because there was an immediate stimulus that brought it to the fore? . . .

If you bring Native people with their families into the White areas to form a stable, law-abiding, stabilized labour force in our economy, then their families and their progeny will be needed by South Africa. The hon. the Deputy Minister of Bantu Administration will probably speak in this debate. I want to invite him to tell us, if they are sincere in their policy— and they must be sincere: they are my fellow-South Africans—how they are going to make South Africa's economy independent of Black labour. And, Sir, if we are not prepared to face that question and give an answer to it, then we must stop the cant.

S. L. MULLER, Nationalist M.P. for Ceres, Cape:

. . . You know, Sir, Dr. Skaife is at present giving a series of talks on "Uninvited guests in the House," and I think hon. members may safely tune in to these every morning. Last Monday he was talking about the flea and he said that a flea emerged from a chrysalis, and when it did so it could lie without food for weeks and months, in wait for its prey. That reminded me a great deal of the United Party. They do not look for their prey; they do not look for their food. In the field of politics or economics they have never planned ahead for South Africa. No, they act like the flea and lie in wait for their prey: if it comes, well and good, if it does not, it is immaterial.

What is more, Dr. Skaife said that the flea thrived on refuse. The dirtier the house, the better-off the flea. Before it becomes a chrysalis, it is a worm and it gets fat on any organic material it can obtain, and that is what the United Party has always tried to do. I can forgive them everything. I can forgive them for being stupid in the past, and for their lack of foresight, but I cannot forgive them for having thrived on dirt against South Africa. They can make as many excuses as they like, but they did thrive on dirt against South Africa. . . .

A. HOPEWELL, United Party M.P. for Pinetown, Natal:

. . . When we mention these problems and when we criticize the Government, we do it with a sense of responsibility and we repudiate suggestions made by the hon. member for Ceres than when we criticize the Government, its shortcomings and its lack of foresight, we are un-South African. We are entitled to criticize this Government and we criticize it as good South Africans. While we are criticizing the Government of the day, we are not criticizing South Africa. . . .

THE MINISTER OF FINANCE (T. E. DONGES, Nationalist
M.P. for Worcester, Cape):

. . . The problem which we have in South Africa, namely that our gross domestic expenditure in South Africa exceeds our gross domestic product, and the availability of too much money and quasi-money in relation to our domestic product, has been aggravated in South Africa, unlike the other countries to which I have referred, by the fact that we have had to incur considerable military and strategic expenditure on account of our particular position in the world today. The excessive expenditure in our country as a whole is to some extent attributable to the fact that we are living in a hostile world and are threatened, *inter alia,* with boycotts and sanctions and even open aggression. For that reason we have been compelled to spend much more money on defence in order to ensure our continued existence.

Now I want to ask hon. members opposite whether they have any objection to the necessary money being spent in order to ensure that we shall be able to resist any military or economic steps which may be taken against us? Let me mention at this stage that I have made a calculation of the additional military and strategic expenditure we have had to incur, and that I arrived at a figure of R300,000,000. I have also calculated what the estimates for defence would have been if we were not living in a hostile world and were not threatened as we are today. This calculation I based on the normal rate of growth up to 1960 and then projected it into the future. To that I added an extra R40,000,000. In that way I arrived at the conclusion that whereas at present an amount of approximately R270,000,000 is set aside for defence purposes in the estimates, the expenditure would have been R100,000,000 less under normal circumstances.

But apart from defence we also had to incur expenditure on other things. We had to develop more rapidly in certain directions in order to be able to survive and to be self-supporting in the event of being cut off. . . .

However, the steps taken by us would have checked the inflation, had it not been for a very unexpected factor which no one could have anticipated. I am referring to the tremendous inflow of capital from outside. During the period from 1st July 1965 to 30th June 1966, foreign capital to the value of R290,000,000 flowed into the country. That was a very good thing for our reserves, but as a result there was a tremendous increase in our supply of money, and because our rate of growth remained virtually unchanged, inflation simply continued on its merry way. . . .

MRS. C. D. TAYLOR, United Party M.P. for Wynberg, Cape:
. . . What has happened in South African politics is that our politics have become polarized into the two extremes, without the true answer lying in either of them. In dealing with any political alternatives in South Africa, let me say at once that I consider it to be absolutely essential that we should break the present dominant rhythm of totalities in our thinking. This has become a very dangerous habit, so much so that the electorate is persuaded year after year that we must, for example, have either total apartheid or total integration. The Bantu must either be given total independence or the Whites will suffer total submersion.

I regard these concepts as entirely false. Neither of the extremes presents a practical solution. We on this side of the House are accustomed to being howled down when we say that there are only two really sound bases on which any community, whether it is heterogeneous or homogeneous, can live and work together. The first of these principles is that we should maintain continuous communication between the various groups and the second one is that we should work on a basis of give-and-take. This means that we should be prepared to compromise, a word which has become a dirty word in South Africa today. Without these two bases we shall continue to live in South Africa in a state of unending tension. Do not let us make a mistake about it: We all live in watertight compartments. . . .

As hon. members know, we have pleaded in this party over the years for the two White groups to have at least the option—and I repeat the word "option"—of meeting in our schools, even if only in the secondary and the high schools. These children, who are our university students today, could have had seven long years in their primary schools of basic, exclusive mother-tongue education and later they could have rounded off the corners for one another—in an intellectual sense—before they crystallized into the rigid and inflexible patterns into which they both seem to have settled today. . . .

Could the history, the traditions, and the value of both population groups, which we all treasure in our own way in South Africa, not have been jointly instilled in a positive rather than a negative sense during those formative years? We believe most sincerely as a party that this could have been done and we still believe it, unless a large percentage of the present generation of students is irretrievably lost. Without this crazy separation by law in our education would South Africa ever have been faced, as it is faced today, with this tragic dichotomy of thought amongst our young people? . . .

. . . The sad thing about this is simply that these two groups of youngsters have been reared in isolation, thanks to the follies and the wickedness of this Government. (Interjections.)

English-speaking people—and I am one of them—will find it very hard indeed to forgive you for this. NUSAS is often accused by the ASB of no longer being a normal student organization. It is said that it is merely a political front for sinister international organizations. Well, that may or may not be the case, Sir. But the ASB, in its turn, can scarcely be designated a normal student body, since they also, judging by the resolutions adopted at their recent congress, back only the Government and its policies. They refuse to countenance any opposition, and they hand out political accolades to the hon. the Minister of Justice. The fact that all their resolutions were passed unanimously and apparently without discussion proves them to be no more, in their turn, than a political front for the Nationalist Government.

If the one attitude, namely that of NUSAS, is reprehensible when linked to universities, where open debates covering a wide field should be the order of the day, then the other attitude is equally reprehensible. It applies to both of them, Mr. Speaker.

But the Nationalist Party—and here I am going to be frank, very frank indeed—have used the English . . . yes, that is how they refer to us—an unspecified, ill-defined but a politically useful generalization . . . have used us as the whipping boy over the years. And now what has happened? This attitude has suddenly become a terrible disadvantage both to us and to them because South Africa is threatened by forces from overseas, and the need to stand together is the one thing that matters. . . .

THE MINISTER OF COMMUNITY DEVELOPMENT
(HON. W. A. MAREE, Nationalist M.P. for Newcastle, Natal):

Mr. Speaker, the hon. member was talking nonsense when she claimed that the National Party Government was to be blamed for the rift between English- and Afrikaans-speaking children in our schools, which has allegedly resulted in the rift between the ASB and NUSAS. The hon. member ought to know much better than that. The rift between those two organizations had already developed when I was at university years ago. That was round about 1938–40. The rift developed as a result of disputes on colour policy and not as a result of difference in language. The rift developed because NUSAS demanded implacably that it should be possible for all racial groups to belong to NUSAS and its organizations. That is what caused the rift. It was not caused by this Government, but in fact by the United Party, the party which seeks to lump together people of all races. . . .

DR. P. G. J. KOORNHOF, Nationalist M.P. for
Primrose, Transvaal:

. . . In what light did the United Party reveal itself in this debate, for example? It revealed itself as colourless, as spineless, as spiritless, as hopeless, as helpless, as discouraged and as a party without a policy. That is because it is so uninspired and so incompetent. In this debate the United Party has tried to run down the Government, but they have not succeeded in doing so, and they themselves have been slain on the political battlefield. . . .

MR. C. BENNETT, United Party M.P. for Albany, Cape:

I am going to waste very little time indeed on the speech which has just been delivered by the hon. member for Primrose. It has been a bitter and arrogant speech—in short, the speech of a demagogue. . . .

In the light of the likely population increase of this country, it is up to this Government—and so far they have shown few signs of realizing it—to devise a long-term plan to safeguard and increase the production capacity of the agricultural industry. Price fixing should be coordinated and there should be coordination in other fields amongst the various bodies governing the agricultural industry. The prime requisite is that we should ensure an adequate food supply, a food supply available to the consumer at prices which he can afford. . . .

There are many fields in which the Government can and should help the farmer to reduce his costs. They are, however, not doing so. First of all I should like to refer to the question of training. The Deputy Minister has recently made a statement about this and stated that we needed more trained farmers. With that I agree, but how can we expect that there should be more trained farmers if there remains one region at least where there is no college? Here I am referring to the Eastern Cape grassveld region. Training facilities are also required for farm managers. Here the same argument applies. There is still another aspect. In previous years we had a farm foreman class on the farm but they are there no longer. They have gone into the cities where they can draw higher wages in factories. . . .

This brings me to a subject which I have raised before in this House and it is unfortunate that it is necessary for me to raise it again but I am forced to do so because this Government has done absolutely nothing about it. This is the question of training Bantu labour on our farms. Wages paid out by a farmer to his workmen constitute a considerable proportion of his expenses. For the year 1961–62, for example, farmers in South Africa paid out in cash an amount of R96,000,000 as wages in

addition to R28,000,000 in kind. It is no exaggeration when I say that
our Bantu farm labour is untrained, inefficient and unreliable. Every
farmer knows this. The farmer is being burdened more and more with
paper work, and with filling in returns required by Government Departments. Because he has an inefficient and unreliable labour force it is
difficult for the farmer to get down to it and maintain his farm as an
economic unit. He is forced to spend too much of his time chasing
around supervising his labourers. . . .

But what is being done to train Bantu labourers on our farms? In this
field nothing at all is being done by this Government. Such training is,
however, being given by the Government to the Bantu in their own reserves. That is, for instance, being done at the agricultural college at Fort
Cox where peasant farmers and demonstrators are being trained. Training is also being given at Tsolo in the Transkei and at Taungs. The
farmers, however, have to see what can be done in this respect themselves. They do not get any assistance from the Government. . . . They
are neglecting to solve one of the biggest problems of high cost production in this country, namely, the inefficiency of farm labour. The reason
why they are neglecting it is not far to seek. . . .

AN HON. MEMBER:
Is it because they are "Boer-haters?" ["Farmer-haters"]

MR. C. BENNETT:
Yes, that may be one of the reasons. Another reason can be found in
what the economic adviser to the Prime Minister has had to say when he
talked about the training of non-White labour. He said that: It is an
integral part of Government policy to foster this development in the limits
set by its policy of separate development.

Here again we come to the problem of warping our economy by pursuing this particular political line of thinking. . . .

THE DEPUTY MINISTER OF BANTU ADMINISTRATION
(MR. BLAAR COETZEE, Nationalist M.P. for Vereeniging,
Transvaal):
[In the past eighteen years this Nationalist Government] had to solve
problems such as no other government has ever had to solve. I shall
mention a few of those problems. There has been the constitutional
struggle which dominated the debates in this House for many years. I
want to refer to the slum conditions which developed after the war, when
there were literally hundreds of thousands of squatters living all around
Johannesburg. The slum conditions which developed were of such a nature that the district surgeon of Johannesburg said that if those squatters

and slums were not removed the health of the entire population of Johannesburg would be endangered.

When one has such a problem on one's hands one cannot simply say that one was going to leave that problem as it was and was going to develop the homelands or the border industries. The most urgent problems have to be solved first. It has been this Government's task to clear up the worst and the most appalling slum conditions in South Africa. This Government has had to clear up the shanty towns surrounding Johannesburg in which hundreds of thousands of squatters lived under the most unhygienic conditions, and it has done so against the wishes of the Johannesburg City Council and of that party. They fought against us clearing up Sophiatown and establishing Meadowlands. They opposed us on every possible front.

Johannesburg placed so many obstacles in the way of the then Minister of Native Affairs that he had to establish his own local authority for the removal of Sophiatown. He was faced with resistance from the Opposition, the English Press, the Johannesburg City Council, and the Anglican Church, but he had to proceed. The most serious problems have to be solved first.

During those eighteen years we have been sitting on a volcano. We had a condition in which law and order were getting out of hand. We were dealing with something which was nothing else but a bare-faced attempt to achieve a Communistic revolution in South Africa. Need I remind the Opposition of Langa and Nyanga? Need I remind them of Sharpeville, Rivonia and the high treason case against Fischer?

If it appears that the country is on the verge of bloodshed, or a revolution is imminent, one cannot say that one is going to ignore that and develop homelands and border industries. That is childish talk. There are countries which have threatened to attack us. We were refused arms by our friends and arms were given to those who threatened to attack us. One is then compelled to deal with those problems first and to spend money for building up a strong defence force in South Africa. One then has to establish one's own arms factories. . . . The most serious problems have to be solved first.

We have succeeded in doing so. We have been threatened with boycotts and sanctions, even by our own friends. It has therefore been absolutely essential that we build up a strong White economy in the Republic. For that reason our position has become quite unassailable. Those, Sir, were the priorities which had to receive our attention first before we could give our undivided attention to the development of the homelands and the border areas and to decreasing Bantu labour in the metropolitan areas.

The Republic had to come and it did come. However, it was only after all these problems had been solved, after the slums had been cleared, the constitutional struggle had been terminated, law and order had been maintained, a strong defence force had been built up, that our economy is so strong today that it is virtually unassailable. Only after all those problems had been solved, could the Government give more attention to the development and the practical application of its policy of separate development.

I maintain that it is absolutely unrealistic to say that this Government has had eighteen years in which to have done so. It is much more realistic to say that this Government has had four or at the utmost five years' time for the practical application of that policy. What has the Government achieved in those four or five years? What is our task now? I repeat what I said previously. Our task is to stem the flow of Bantu labour to the metropolitan areas, to stop it and finally to turn it back, and nothing will prevent us from fulfilling that task. . . .

I read my Bible, in which is written, "The slothful man saith, 'There is a lion in the way.'" That is the trouble with that side [the United Party]. They are simply lazy. They are too lazy to think, they are too lazy to work, too lazy to make plans, too lazy to concentrate. For that reason, whenever we want to do something, they always see lions and snakes and crocodiles in the way and then they simply stay where they are. Let them be lazy. We are going to put our shoulders to the wheel. Let them doubt if they like. We shall have confidence in our policy and in ourselves. Let them be destructive. We shall be the builders of a future happy South Africa for White and non-White, for White and Bantu.

Sir De Villiers Graaff:

. . . It is very interesting to find how sensitive members on the other side are at the suggestion that South Africa is departing from democratic norms. They suggest that this side are trying to infer that this Government is creating a police state in South Africa. Mr. Speaker, I was at pains not to suggest that. I do not believe it is a police state. It never will be while this Opposition is here. . . .

Of course there are traditions of democracy in South Africa. As has been said in this debate, the Afrikaans-speaking people and the English-speaking people of this country come from other lands with tremendous democratic traditions. There is no doubt, Sir, that there was every effort to maintain and keep those democratic traditions here in South Africa, particularly in the formation of the early Boer republics. But somewhere it looks to me as though the Nationalist Party opposite has got off the road that was pointed out by its forefathers. That they ceased to be the upholders of the true traditions of South Africa, the true traditions of democracy, of which they pretend at the moment to be so proud. You see, Sir, they slipped badly. They slipped very badly during the war years when they thought Germany was going to win. . . .

They must forgive us, Sir, if we are a little suspicious of some of the things they are doing, because we are not a bit sure that their democratic tradition is so rooted in their ranks as they would like to have us believe. The fact of the matter is that they have given way to a rather extreme form of sectional nationalism, and in order to give vent to it they are prepared to take steps, many of which are not in accordance with democratic traditions either in this country or in the other countries of the world.

We have heard, of course, that we are in difficulties in this country and that steps must be taken to safeguard our position. We had been warned by the hon. the Minister of Justice that Liberalism is so often a forerunner of Communism. It may be, Sir, that the Liberal Party and liberals have been used as a front by Communists in South Africa. I agree. But do not run away with the idea that Liberalism is the forerunner of Communism, not true Liberalism.

What has tended to be the forerunner of Communism has been the very opposite of true Liberalism, it has tended to be extreme Nationalism exploited by the Communist, it has tended to be the breakdown of ordinary law and order exploited by the Communists. If one looks at the history of the states that have become Communist there is not a single one in which there was a decently functioning democratic government before the Communists took over. . . .

With that sort of background the danger we have here is that the sectional nationalism for which this Government is standing is setting an example to the Black nationalists which may be very dangerous indeed to the future of South Africa. That, Mr. Speaker, is the problem we are up against. You see, Sir, sectional nationalism is becoming more and more extreme. Instead of tending to be watered down as a result of years in power and years in office, it is tending to look for more and more victims, not only amongst its own ranks but amongst the ranks of the Opposition in South Africa.

The pattern tending to unfold is that one sees in so many countries that have strayed from the democratic path, namely attempts to victimize people and attempts to cast suspicion upon the ordinary legitimate objectives of others. . . .

A ND SO, *after a week of debate on the motion of the Leader of the Opposition to censure the Nationalist Government, the motion was put and a division was called. The House divided and on an "Aye" vote of 39 United Party and 1 Progressive to a "No" vote of 121 Nationalists, the motion of the Leader of the Opposition was defeated.*

O F THE INTERVIEWS I had with officials of the Government in Cape
     Town, those with the two Prime Ministers should be reported,
partly because they are interesting historical footnotes, more because in
them there spoke the past which is still the present and the present which
is still the past.

They occurred four days apart and in the opposite order to which they
are related here, but in view of the end result of Dmitrio Tsafendas'
intervention in the affairs of the Republic, I am taking the liberty of
presenting Dr. Verwoerd first and Mr. Vorster after.

I had written Dr. Verwoerd almost a year before, the first letter I wrote
to South Africa in preparation for my journey, telling him I hoped to
come, telling him I hoped that I might, in the fashion of writers in my
country, spend a day or two with him finding out what he was like, observing how he worked, trying to gain some understanding of his problems.

To this brash American effort there came, after two months, by surface mail (South African Prime Ministers, I know now, do not deign to
reply in haste) a letter from the Private Secretary, somewhat starchy but
not entirely so. The Prime Minister wanted him to inform me that he
appreciated my letter, but that in his country things weren't done like
that, and it would be quite impossible for me to have so extensive and
informal a meeting. But the letter was not entirely negative in tone, there
seemed to be a slight hope held out that if I were a good boy, something
might eventually be done. ("He wants to watch you going around the
country for a while," they told me in Pretoria. "He needs to make up his
mind that you aren't going to bite him.") The letter did say that I need
anticipate no difficulty in getting a visa, and many months later I learned
that Dr. Verwoerd had sent it along to the Department of Information
with a personal notation that I was to be given every assistance when I
arrived. So the effort was not wasted in the short range, nor was it wasted
in the long, though it took a while and the help of many good friends to
achieve the objective.

Almost from the moment I arrived, I began putting my request to
everyone I met who had the remotest influence with the Government.
Within three days I had met Minister M. C. Botha, the man who finally
arranged it; but he was the first to admit that it was only because many
generous people, including Dr. Leonard Verwoerd and many, many
others, kept my name before the Prime Minister that he finally agreed to
see me.

To questions why he was so remote and inaccessible, there were various answers. One had to do with the preservation of the image he had

established for himself: the kindly, all-knowing father, brooding over the nation and supervising every last detail of its forward progress—familiarity would spoil it. This I eventually came to discount, since his family life was well-publicized, he and his were frequently in the press in an informal and friendly fashion, and if he appeared to have a brooding, all-knowing father-image, it was because that was exactly what he was, not only for Afrikanerdom (curiously enough, for he was Holland-born) but for the country as a whole.

Another explanation seemed to me closer to the mark, and does still:

"He has had a bad time of it at the hands of foreign journalists. Some of them have interviewed him and then gone away to write the unfairest things. He has been hurt. He is suspicious. He is afraid to open up."

It was essentially the same explanation given me by others—not by him, when I inquired—when I wanted to know why he didn't travel more, why he didn't take his case abroad, to the United Nations or the World Court.

"Well, you know, he was almost assassinated once, in 1960 in Johannesburg. He doesn't like much to go out in crowds now. He prefers to stay close to Parliament, where he feels safe."

That this was the final irony of a controversial life does not change the fact that the statement, "He is afraid," was probably the key to it. In this he was Afrikaner through and through, Dutch-born though he was. There is a certain wounded-animal aspect of the Afrikaner, a certain huddling-away: it was present at his funeral, at which foreign journalists were excluded, English-speakers were given second place, and only members of Die Volk could truly draw near. It was present in his life, in which he held himself aloof because he had been hurt when he ventured out.

It made me appreciate his kindness even more when he finally agreed to see me, though as I had expected he did not say anything particularly newsworthy except for one thing: he flatly and instantaneously dashed any wistful hopes that the Coloureds might eventually be integrated. From this closed position there is no reason to suppose that his successor, or successors, will deviate.

Yet, both in the interview and in what I had heard and learned about him everywhere I went on my journey, I found him to be a remarkable man, extremely intelligent, extremely competent, much superior in brains and ability to most of his noisy critics around the world; in his own strange way, in his own strange context, a great man; in South African terms, a liberal; the only man who, because of his years in office and his almost mystical hold on Afrikanerdom, could possibly have continued to lead his people and his nation toward a gradually more reasonable, and ultimately more humane, accommodation with the other races.

The hope is gone now. It went with him. Tsafendas accomplished nothing but to turn back the clock, because Dr. Verwoerd's successor, for all his friendly image-building, is still old-line Transvaal at heart, and "the illiberal North always wins over the liberal Cape." It is one of the great tragedies of what in many ways is a very tragic country.

I arrived early, chatted for a few minutes with the Private Secretary, who proved to be much younger, more pleasant and less pompous than his letter had sounded so many months ago, and presently was told that the Prime Minister was ready to see me. I opened the door and walked in. He rose and came forward with hand outstretched, white-haired, blue-eyed, rosy-cheeked, twinkling, grandfatherly and benign. His voice was rather high but pleasant, his English virtually unaccented. He regretted he had not been able to see me earlier, thanked me for coming, settled back. I asked about the future of the Bantustans, and would the Transkei in time become fully independent.

"Bantustans," he said in his rapid fashion, leaning forward intently, "Bantustans. We do not like to use that term, it really means nothing. A better term would be 'Bantu homelands.' They aren't 'stans,' that is just a word we have used sometimes, as you would use Paki *stan,* say. We believe they are nations as distinct as France and Germany in Europe, with different languages, different heritages, different aspirations.

"People ask, 'Are you holding them back?' and that's a silly question. We are purchasing land from European farmers, we are encouraging the non-Whites to move forward as fast as possible, *but* we are not going to rush the process, because it doesn't make the land more arable just to turn it over to a Bantu. If you have a tendency to exploit the land rather than develop it, as they do, then it isn't going to do any good for the Government to give it to you—because the more you get, the more you spoil, unless you understand good conservation practices and good farming.

"We are trying to conserve the soil for them, trying to change the attitude of the Native toward the land, teach him good agricultural practices. We have promised him aid, we are conducting experiments to demonstrate to him how to farm successfully. At the same time we are trying to develop more markets for him to sell to. The Bantu have some of the best land in the country, a good quality of soil, good climate, et cetera, particularly in the Transkei.

"In the Transkei we are providing more and more help for the Bantu and, funnily enough, creating more and more discrimination against the White man. We are buying out White farms and trading stations, turning over more and more to the Bantu. We have a shortage of White civil servants in our society, you know, we want to get them back from the Transkei as fast as we can! We want the Bantu to take over from us as rapidly as possible, but the psychology of the Native makes it a slow process.

"The Transkei," he said thoughtfully, "has developed pretty far, but they tell us: Don't turn our hands loose, we still need the white father, we're not yet ready to be on our own.

"As for the future of the Bantu? It depends on themselves. We are prepared to let them develop to their full potentialities. The sky's the limit, but for their protection as well as ours we must exercise a continuing control until they have proved themselves able to handle independence. We are going to set them free, but only at a pace they can handle. We are trying to withdraw from their areas gradually, we are trying to help them by imparting knowledge, help them to learn how to handle funds, so that when they are ready to assume democratic control there will be no chance for them to fall back to military dictatorships such as have broken out elsewhere in Africa.

"We want to make sure that the masses whose guardians we are will be ready for independence when it comes.

"They are not ready yet."

I had found that many leading people, particularly in the Cape, were convinced that before long the Coloureds would be fully integrated with the Whites. Was this true?

His expression changed, lost some of its twinkling amiability, became somewhat stern.

"No," he said flatly, "they won't be integrated with the Whites. Many of the Coloureds have already mingled with the Blacks. How can you integrate such a group with the White people? And why should we? We say we are a community of nations here in the southern part of Africa, White, Bantu, Coloured, Indian. Differences are fundamental, not differences of nationalism only. We are fully prepared to admit the human dignity of each. The problem is, how can you find the best way of living together? In Europe, you have never really had integration between different nations and empires, they have all maintained their separate identities and developments but still have been able to cooperate together. That is the aim we have here.

"When the outside world attacks us for opposing the development of these people, it is quite wrong. In an integrated nation, everything would be in our hands, as the people having the greatest wealth, the strongest power, the best brains and the greatest experience. All the Blacks and Coloureds and Indians would be below, all the Whites would be on top. We reject that. We have always said, don't take away the traditional social things that each has.

"Now with the Bantu, who has his own homelands that either are being, or can be, developed, this is relatively easy for us to achieve, given time and patience. The case of the Coloureds and Indians is not so easy, as they do not have homelands.

"The question is, to what extent can we allow them independence when they have no homelands? They wouldn't want to go somewhere else, they are now South Africans, they belong here. What way, then, can we allow these minorities, the Coloureds and Indians, to rule themselves? Simple integration doesn't solve that problem.

"So under the Group Areas Act we are setting them up in townships and cities where they can rule themselves. In the past, in a situation that you could perhaps call 'semi-integration,' they have not been able to hold office, they have not had opportunities to advance in their own professions, they weren't able to develop their own governing bodies. But the moment we set aside an area for them—always at our own expense, the world should take notice—they can have city councils and mayors, they can have industries, they can have businesses, they can have their own universities and technical schools, they can begin to acquire their own individual identity and independence. Their area then doesn't become like a Harlem in New York City, it becomes a New York City of their own.

"Then comes the second stage. Once we have set them up in special areas, then they can cooperate with one another as municipalities do all over the world. They can discuss matters of interest to their own racial community with similar groups of their own people all over the country, in what you might call a parliament of their own. They can discuss roads, education, taxation for their own projects, in something that will be something more than a provincial council, something less than the central Government. They will have their own 'capital,' if they wish, that will exercise influence over all Coloured affairs throughout the country, with consultation with the national Parliament at those points where Coloured affairs touch White affairs.

"One must always remember," he said firmly, "that they will always be a minority that would be submerged in any other country, but we are going to provide self-government for them in their own affairs. . . .

"Will the four White representatives of the Coloureds remain in Parliament? Of course they will! But we want to be sure that they will not be used by other political parties to advance the ambitions of those parties. The Coloured representatives in Parliament must really reflect what the Coloured people are thinking."

"Some people fear you will abolish them altogether."

A quick smile, a dismissing expression—"Oh, well, that's just politics. When a problem arises in some area, such as roads or education, what you might call the Coloured 'Minister of Roads' or 'Minister of Education' can get in touch with the appropriate ministers here in Parliament. If they need the cooperation of the national Government in some project, then they will contact the appropriate minister and they can work it out together. . . .

"In the same way, the independent Bantu states here that will ultimately come, together with former British territories such as Basutoland, Bechuanaland, Swaziland, can work with us too if they want to. We are prepared to enter upon a common consultative body at which other nations can put forward their views. We are prepared for the development of such a consultative body in which all will meet as independent states, each having its own personality and dignity and standing. We don't want to interfere with their business, we don't want to be interfered with. We don't want to be interfered with, and we don't want to interfere.

"We would take it that in this consultative body, Coloureds and Indians along with Bantu states would also be taken in. The Indians will have the same countrywide type of consultative council as the Coloured, with ready access of their ministers to the sort of overall consultative body we contemplate. If others such as the Basutos or the Swazis do not want to come into such a body, then we are prepared to have a consultative body of only our own peoples. . . .

"It is not to our interest, after all, to have slummy, undeveloped areas in Southern Africa. We want them cleaned up, we have been trying for donkey's years to get the job done, and we have been spending our own money to do it, whether the rest of Africa or the outside world give us credit for it or not."

What did he think of the current state of U.S.-South African relations? He smiled in a somewhat quizzical way and stared out the window for a moment before swinging back to answer.

"I would say they are reasonably good—reasonably good. We want good relations and good friendship with the United States. We have always sought this. Our relations on the surface are always friendly and accommodating.

"We have hoped," he said, and the amicable air faded a little, his tone became tart and quite annoyed for a moment, "we have hoped that what has been happening elsewhere in Africa would open many eyes. We have always avoided saying, Look what's happening to you people! We have never said that. Our fundamental principle is the principle of noninterference—we do believe that. While South Africa has its own means of solving its problems, we do dislike very much being told constantly that we are oppressors and that our objectives are not good, but bad.

"We are being good Christians, in our view, we all want to see the best good for all the peoples of South Africa.

"It's a matter," he remarked more calmly, "of how you can do it in the circumstances in which you live. The U.S. may be right in seeking integration and absorption in their country, in which the non-Whites are only twenty millions out of two hundred millions. That's the U.S.' own business. I have my own opinion of how it will work ultimately, but that is the U.S.' business. In this country, I want to have happiness developed for all people in accordance with Christian civilization, so I can't put forward a policy of complete integration; our circumstances do not permit it.

"Yet despite the cries from the rest of Africa and the outside world, the black people have gathered around us like a magnet because we have created prosperity here and they want to share in it. We have got to find our own way out of our own problems, and quite clearly it is not by integration but by separation—give the Bantu his own separate land, help his development, make sure that he will not be just a little clique crying for independence, hand over to him a nation that can really function and be successful.

"We are quite as humane," he said, tartness returning, "quite as decent, as any of our critics in the United States. We have the same objective of being decent. We don't want to deny our peoples their human dignity, but we, in the interests of survival, we must do it in our own way, by letting each develop separately.

"Africa needs time. If only the metropolitan European nations had taken a reasonable time in freeing the nations of Africa, we wouldn't be in the mess we are in on this continent. . . ."

Did he consider that the laws of his Government restricted the liberties of the individual citizen? He frowned for a second, then smiled and shook his head.

"Individual liberties are not really restricted. When subversion takes place, you restrict those who are doing it, but only if a person is sinning against the state. The other person doesn't feel restricted, it doesn't affect other people."

"I've sometimes wondered why you don't take your case to the UN? They might walk out on you, but at least the newspapers couldn't ignore you, you'd be on all the front pages, you'd be on television, your case would get a full airing—"

"They wouldn't listen," he said, abruptly. "They wouldn't listen! I could go there, but they wouldn't listen. We've had people there to tell them, they either walk out or make a disturbance. If they did listen, they wouldn't believe it. They don't want to hear the facts.

"If we hadn't been handicapped by these incessant attacks over the years, you know, we would be much farther along than we are now. But even some of our own people attack us, they create a climate in which our own Bantu don't trust us. The climate isn't as easy to work in as we would like to have."

"What would you say is South Africa's greatest need, then? Time?"

He looked thoughtful for a moment and then spoke with a sudden indignation.

"What we need almost more than time is some sympathy from those who should be wise enough to see what a real problem we have, and that we are trying honestly to solve it in a decent and generous way.

"We are paying for this out of our pocket, you know, and in terms of real inconvenience to us in many ways. We are trying to sort out things for everyone in justice and decency. We not only want to hold what we have, but in doing so we want to see to it that it isn't going to stop. The only way we can assure this is by giving everyone development according to his abilities. That is what we are trying to do."

An hour had passed, he was obviously prepared to keep right on talking, but I felt I had taken enough of his time. I excused myself and rose to go. He got up too and came around the desk.

"Where do you go next?"

"Johannesburg again, and then the last four days in Kruger National Park."

His face lighted up with the pleased expression all South Africans get when you mention the Game Reserve, for they are proud of it and have a right to be.

"Oh, you'll find that fascinating, fascinating. Some friends of mine who came in here just yesterday were up there last week and they saw all the animals. You'll enjoy it very much, I know. In Kruger National Park, one can unwind. Everybody loves Kruger, there's nothing to do but get up early in the morning, spend all day looking for the animals, and then go to bed early at night. . . . Thank you very much for coming to see me. I wish you a good continuing trip and continued good luck."

"Good luck to you, too, sir."

We shook hands and he turned back to his desk, firm, confident, rosy and glowing, sincerely convinced of the justice of what he was doing, armored in righteousness, supreme in command. It was twenty-nine days to horror in the House, thirty-three to burial in Heroes' Acre.

I was not surprised that he did not meet me in Johannesburg, said Death, *for I had an appointment with him in Cape Town.*

"I wanted to see you," I said as we shook hands, "because I've been reading in the English-language press that you're the greatest villain who ever lived and I wanted to come and see for myself."

The square, heavy-jowled face, which had looked somber and serious when I came in, broke into a sudden grin and we were off and running.

"Sit down," John Vorster said, "and tell me what I can tell you about this awful police state of ours."

So began the interview with the present Prime Minister, then Minister of Justice. No lengthy persuasions had been needed here, no rather Byzantine sideways approaches to the then second most powerful man in the Government. Nor, friends write approvingly, is it necessary now. He

plays golf, he dines with the English-speakers, he even has the press to
lunch in the House. Balthazar Johannes Vorster knows the values of
publicity and a just-like-anybody image, and even in the days when few
or none could have foreseen that an act of murderous insanity would so
soon catapult him into the premiership, it did not take much more than a
routine request to the Department of Information to arrange an interview.

This was the man whom I had indeed seen portrayed in the English-
language press as the world's greatest villain. I had talked to ten or a
dozen people whose lives he had rearranged and quite probably ruined
by ban or jail. I had heard many denounce him with scorn and fear. I
had heard still others defend him, but with an approval tinged with a
deep and questioning uneasiness. And I could not forget, of course, any
more than I could during my interview with his legendary predecessor,
that this amiable, easygoing and charming Afrikaner could, entirely on
his own say-so—unhampered by legal protections, impervious to civil
liberties, courts or diplomatic protest—pick up a telephone and have me
thrown into jail, there to stay for a day, 90 days, 180, or whatever it
suited him.

With both of them, underneath all the welcoming warmth and cordiality, it was rather like having tea alone with a tiger: all right as long as
he was in a good mood, but there wasn't any keeper to restrain him if
he wasn't. For the time being, and indeed throughout the entire journey,
I simply had to acquire a little of that stout protection hugged to themselves so closely by supporters of the Government: *"I haven't done anything wrong, so it won't happen to me."*

It did not take a great deal of imagination, when in the presence of the
two men who actually had the power to do it, to realize how very easily,
in the Republic of South Africa, it can.

None of this, of course, was present in the interview, which got off to a
sailing start and proceeded on that basis throughout. I liked John Vorster, who is intelligent, blunt, pragmatic, practical, tough, direct and no-
nonsense. I do not think that because he has a charming side which he
showed to me, and which he has apparently shown to the country since
September 6, 1966, that he is any less tough, or that any of the underlying tensions, divisions and problems have been changed one iota by his
succession. I detect this hope in many of the letters I have received from
friends since he became Prime Minister, but I do not believe it is a valid
one; the problems are too enormous and the tensions too deep. But I am
not so sure, were I Afrikaner or English-speaker in a country which sees
my own and the rest of the world apparently beginning to close in on it,
that I should not be just as glad that John Vorster was there to step up
when Hendrik Verwoerd fell.

"I'm used to the English-language press," he said. "After five years as

Minister of Justice, I can't be bothered. I want to point out, however, that most of these laws they complain about were introduced before I became Minister. I have made it clear that as a lawyer I was sorry that I had to enforce such laws, and that I had to introduce such acts as I have subsequently introduced, and that I had to administer them in peacetime.

"But, we do not feel, and I do not feel, that our enemies have given us much choice. . . .

"The difficulty," he said thoughtfully, "springs from two opposing principles, the freedom of the individual and the security of the state. They don't stand opposed, as some like to maintain—it is a question of laying stress on one or the other as circumstances dictate.

"I feel we are now in control of the Communist situation, which is why I withdrew the ninety-day regulation. As a matter of fact, I have relaxed certain other restrictions as far as certain individuals are concerned. I'm going through the list right now, to see how they have behaved themselves, and if they are no longer a danger to the state, I will relax restrictions on them even further. This happened just the other day with two lecturers at Grahamstown University, and I think there will be others in future.

"We don't like to keep this dreadful police state," he said dryly, "in operation forever, you know. If our enemies will reform and behave we are quite ready to let them lead their lives in peace. But they have to let us lead ours in peace too. . . .

" 'Protections for the individual?' That is a phrase the critics like to use, of course, and I'm not surprised you've picked it up around the country. When they can't meet charges head-on with honest answers they begin to cry about 'protections for the individual.' I suppose they have you convinced the courts can't do a thing about it.

"The courts are not excluded from my administration of these laws. When I banned Defence and Aid, they took me to court, as they were entitled to do. The Cape Supreme Court said I had the right to ban them, and now it's gone to the Appellate Court. The processes of the courts are not excluded whatsoever.

"Of course, in all fairness I must say that it is difficult for any individual to prove his innocence if the burden of proof is on him, and being charged or banned is a difficult onus to bear, I concede that. But the courts are there, and he may appeal. . . .

"Further, there is the fact that out of a population of fifteen or sixteen million, only 450 have been restricted. And," he added with a certain contemptuous bluntness, "it's not any question of 'the political opponents of the Government' being banned, either. No action has ever been taken against any politician, or against anyone because he was a member of a particular political party. Action has been taken against him because of his acts as an individual. . . .

"Oh, yes, of course it is true that members of the Liberal Party have been banned, but no action has been taken against the party as such, nor is action contemplated agaist my party as such. . . .

"Students? Look," he said, leaning forward and speaking in an impatient tone, "I am a parent myself. What in hell satisfaction do I get out of keeping these kids in jail? I have a positive duty to their parents and the country to try to keep them out of trouble. It's not only my job to punish, it's my job to prevent. I have never refused to see the parents of banned persons. Hardly a week goes by without one or more interviews of that type. Good Lord, it's to my advantage to keep them out of trouble just as much as it's to their advantage to stay out of trouble. I can warn people, through a magistrate, to desist from acts which would aid the Communist cause, and I do. About 120 have been warned. Those that take heed and reform need have no fears. The others go into it with their eyes open. . . .

"No Minister of Justice can afford to allow his country to be threatened by Communist subversion. I would be false to my oath and my duty if I were to do that. I don't believe I have been false to either.

"Now, the critics say that there are about eight thousand political prisoners. I'll let you have the figures"—and he called a secretary and gave him instructions—"and you can print them if you like. If the weather were better and we had the time, I'd fly you out to Robben Island right now and let you see what's going on. . . . Now," he said when the secretary returned with a slip of paper, "we presently have a total of 1,439 political prisoners charged with subversion or other crimes against the state. We have 18 white males, 6 white females; 1,371 non-white males and 44 non-white females.

"Rather small for a 'police state,' it seems to me. . . .

"I know it's difficult for people not having our problems to understand them and understand what we are trying to do about them. But any unprejudiced person must concede that we are honest and sincere in what we are doing.

"There is very little friction between the races," he said. "We have our problems, but it's quite peaceful in spite of the fact that we are outnumbered four-to-one by the Blacks. The reason for that is that the Bantu, the Coloureds and the Indians realize that separate development doesn't only work to the benefit of the white man but to that of all racial groups.

"In the olden days, you see, we had horizontal segregation. Now it's vertical. Today the roof's been lifted off altogether. Each group is free to advance in its own area to the limit of its capabilities. . . .

"Yes, true enough, in the days of the so-called open universities all races could attend, but the best non-White student never had a chance to become a lecturer or professor. Certain doors were open, but others were firmly closed. Today there are no doors barred for the non-White student at his own university. We have created opportunities that never existed before, in education, housing, medical services, social services, every aspect of life. We have roughly a million illegal immigrants in the country now, and more are slipping over the border all the time, which certainly indicates something, wouldn't you say?" His expression became wry. "I always understood that people tried to get out of a police state, not come in. Apparently we must be doing some things correctly, our critics to the contrary.

"No," he said, more seriously, "no fair-minded person can deny that we have done and are doing a great deal for our non-White peoples. They are certainly appreciative of the opportunities we have created for them. That is one of the main reasons we have the domestic peace we have in spite of what the Communists and fellow-travelers say. We shall continue in our policies, no matter what the outside world says, because they are best for us.

"And now," he said, "are you sure you don't have any more questions about this terrible police state?"

But again, time had passed, it was close to session-time. I said no with thanks and left. Later I was to listen to him on the floor, slashing away with a quick, sarcastic skill at Helen and his opponents of the U.P., probably the most formidable debater on the Government side, as he is now in some ways the most formidable Prime Minister the Nats have selected.

8.
Johannesburg

So it came time to leave sweet Cape Town, which seems to take and hold forever some part of the heart of the stranger. There are many memories in addition to Parliament, interviews with Coloureds, Cape Nats and the dedicated young men of the ASB—many pleasant hours and pleasant friends . . . lunches at the Netherlands Club and Here Sewentien and other excellent restaurants whose names I no longer remember, hidden away unexpectedly on side streets . . . dinners on the waterfront, at Sea Point, in private homes both English and Afrikaans (many of them glued to the radio and the World Soccer Cup matches. England had plenty of supporters then) . . . a visit to the Castle of Good Hope, the grim historic old fort down at the bottom near the Foreshore where Simon van der Stel and his successor Governors for the Dutch East Indies Company held sway . . . a drive through swarming, dangerous, doomed District 6 . . . the inevitable shopping along Adderley Street for curios, all of which arrived safely . . . two delightful sight-seeing Sundays with G. L. Dickerson of the South Africa Foundation and his charming Dutch secretary, the invaluable Miss Fosson (who gave me more proteas which now grow beside the others), during which we visited Groote Constantia, the beautiful old Van der Stel home in the Constantia Valley; saw in the rain the enormous stone bust of Rhodes on the University of Cape Town campus ("His brooding presence still dominates the land," the inscription says, and so it does, at least that portion of it that looks down over his old home, Groote Schuur, now the Cape Town residence of the Prime Minister); went down the Indian Ocean side of the Cape Peninsula, visited the cottage where Rhodes died ("The English-speakers still feel a great admiration for him. The Afrikaners hate him."); went on down to the end, to Cape Point Lighthouse to see the Indian and Atlantic Oceans joining, and then back up the Atlantic side where surfers were out though the day had broken clear but cool; saw the great Atlantic breakers crashing in, much angrier than the gentle Indian Ocean just a few miles away on the other side of the Peninsula; stood on Table Mountain and looked down once more upon the delightful city. . . .

Many wonderful friends, much wonderful hospitality; and much work and many new insights into the strange society. One of these, on my last afternoon, a lovely day, soft and warm, full of the insistent invitations of spring:

The noon gun had been fired at the Castle, the turtledoves were uttering their sweet calls everywhere, a somnolent peace lay on the terrace of the Mt. Nelson Hotel when I decided to go out and sit in the sun for a while before going in to lunch. City and country and all their crushing problems seemed far away until I made ready to go; and then they came back and, as always in the Republic, I realized again that they were never more than an instant away.

There were several members of the hotel staff working about when I went out, a typical Cape Town mixture of the other races, busy at tasks on the grounds or in the lounge. I picked up a chair, took it into the sun, exchanged greetings with one or two near me, sat down. When one o'clock came I started to pick up the chair and take it back where I got it. Instantly, in a way that by now, even for the stranger, had become almost automatic, the thought:

But why bother? They'll do it. There are so many of Them. It's Their job, without jobs like that They couldn't survive. How could They live if the White man didn't disarrange things so that They could put them back in place? Who are you to upset the pattern, direct, uncomplicated American that you are? . . .

And so after a moment's hesitation, you find yourself leaving the chair where it is, thinking as you do that you probably should have asked one of Them to take it out for you in the first place. And then the final, completing thought that really makes you decide to leave it there: It wouldn't look right to Them for you to take it back. The White men they know don't do things like that. In fact, They probably thought it quite odd that you took it out there in the first place. . . . You really don't understand Them at all, do you?

So you leave it there. And later, returning to the lounge for coffee after lunch, you glance out and, sure enough, the chair is neatly back where it started: They haven't failed the White man.

And that state of mind, which is instinctive to the native-born, and which the visitor soon finds almost impossible to escape, is part of South Africa, too. . . .

Next morning good friends put me aboard the Trans-Karoo Express and I began the nine-hundred-mile train journey back to Johannesburg, thinking that this would at least give me some chance to see something of the countryside, since the timing of the interview with Dr. Verwoerd had canceled plans to stop in Bloemfontein. It would also give me time to meet and talk, as I did, with hearty, noisy Afrikaners in the club car; with an earnest young leader of NUSAS from the University of Cape Town, on his way to an interview with Harry Oppenheimer's people in Jo'burg; and with a kindly little old English-speaker who murmured quietly, as if fearful the solid Afrikaners across the aisle in the dining car would overhear and report him, as perhaps they might:

"These townships, now. They are so soul-destroying. Does that encourage a man to raise himself up by his bootstraps? It does seem that with all that money and all that planning, and architects and all, that they'd have come up with something better. . . . It's all part of this horrible regimentation they've placed on the country."

We passed up through the beautiful Hex River Valley, snow visible on the higher peaks that surround it; late in the afternoon moved into the great bare Karoo, looking like a piece of the American Desert transplanted; next morning were over the escarpment and back on the high plateau where the journey began.

Again, the platteland, again the heart of Afrikanerdom, flat, flat, flat as far as the eye could see; scattered farms, a few sheep, a few cattle; little dusty railroad towns that might be anywhere in Arizona, Colorado, Nebraska, Wyoming. This was what the Voortrekkers wanted when they hitched up their ox-wagons, and this is what they got. Once in a while, far, far off, dim misty mountains; but mostly flat, flat, flat.

And so once again, in bright, warm weather, the golden mine dumps and rushing traffic of booming Johannesburg, and the final stages of the journey.

"THE BROEDERBOND, or 'Brother Bond,' " said the tall old Afrikaner who knew, for he had been a member for many years before conscience took him out, "was established around 1920–21 as a cultural and social organization designed to foster the legitimate aspirations and ideals of the Afrikaner nation in all spheres of life, economic, social, political, religious. It did not begin, you understand, as anything sinister, nor can it honestly be considered so today, though it has gone far from its original idealism. Its creation must be seen against the background of the way the English-speaking people acted against the Afrikaners in those earlier days. It grew out of economic, social and cultural despair, you might say. There were attempts to suppress the Afrikaans language and force all children to be educated in English; there were attempts to hold us down economically. To many, Afrikanerdom seemed to be headed for extinction. There was a deep despair.

"So the leaders of the Afrikaner people formed this secret organization, the Broederbond, with the very sincere feeling that it was the only way to improve the future of the Afrikaans nation. Before long, almost every prominent Afrikaner became a member. It remained secret until 1948 when the Nationalists came into power. At that point, members of the Broederbond could see that their ideals were finally coming into realization, and with the establishment of the Republic in 1961, it seemed that most political objectives of the organization had been achieved.

"Political, and also to an ever-increasing degree, social and cultural and economic as well. But you know, funnily enough"—and he smiled as though he did not consider it really so very funny—"sometimes human organizations are not satisfied when they achieve the objectives for which they were founded. Sometimes they must go on and attempt much more. So it was with the Broederbond. The new objective became complete control of Afrikanerdom and complete control of South Africa. That objective, too, has now been almost completely achieved. . . .

"Those of us who part company from it do not do so lightly, and only because of a deep conviction. For me it came when the Broederbond began to become synonymous with the Nationalist Government—when it came out clearly for apartheid and worked to get the church to support it. I then felt that it was illegitimately using its position of honor and influence with the Afrikaner people to influence the church. So I resigned. . . .

"There are approximately 8,500 members now, about 500 of them in the top positions of the Dutch Reformed Church. All of the members are top people, in religion, in business, in politics, in the universities. Their common purpose is to see to it that everywhere, in all spheres, the Afrikaner position, which has now become synonymous with the Nationalist position, is maintained and strengthened.

"To forward this purpose, there is a smoothly operating organization which rules Afrikanerdom, almost like an invisible government, from a head office here in Johannesburg. It is run by an executive, referred to informally as 'The Twelve Apostles,' which is elected every two or three years at an annual conference of all the members of the Broederbond. The 'Twelve Apostles' decide on policy toward a given issue, or"—his expression became ironic—"in some cases, toward a given man—and this policy is then transmitted to all members of the Broederbond, who meet once a month in small groups all over the country to receive the directives from the head office, discuss them and decide how best to carry them forward in individual localities.

"Now, I would not want to make the mistake that so many foreigners do and assume that this is a sinister organization in the sense that the Ku Klux Klan, for instance, is sinister. The great majority of its members to this day are idealistic and sincere about their purpose to raise up the Afrikaner people. But where it is dangerous is that it not only has the ear of the Government, all of whose members from the Prime Minister on down are members—except for the two English-speaking Cabinet Ministers, of course—but that it is engaged upon a campaign of deliberate indoctrination of the Afrikaner people and the Afrikaner youth—a sort of stratified action of all its members following a unified plan.

"There it is dangerous, because it does control not only key members of the Government but key officials of the South African Broadcasting Corporation; leaders of the Afrikaans press; university presidents, heads of departments, leading professors; leaders of the church; leaders of business. There is a systematic indoctrination and control of thought that could eventually lead to an impossible situation.

"The Broederbond makes critical thought outside the rigid framework of conservative Afrikaner ideas almost impossible. If anyone attempts it, punitive results follow, either in his professional life or through a kind of ostracism in his social life, or both. This becomes even more punitive if someone resigns or breaks drastically with the Afrikaner pattern. . . .

"I must remind you again that the thing to do if you are to judge the Broederbond correctly without emotionalism or exaggeration is to keep in mind that it sprang originally from the legitimate aspirations of the Afrikaner people and that it still, today, believes itself sincerely at one with those aspirations. These are not cranks: they are the leaders of South Africa, top, key people who sincerely believe that this is the only way to serve Afrikanerdom and preserve the nation. One can't deny their sincerity or their honesty, if one is fair about it. But also, one cannot deny the danger of this great, organized, monolithic force of opinion which seeks to bind all Afrikanerdom to one rigid policy and punishes anyone who dares to raise a critical voice. . . ."

DETAILS OF VORSTER'S BILL TODAY (Rand Daily Mail, *English*)
. . . Full details of the new Bill to amend the Suppression of Communism Act—which will go further than prohibiting named Communists from practising law—will be published in Parliament this morning.

The Bill went through its first reading in the House of Assembly yesterday.

According to the notice of motion by the Minister of Justice, Mr. Vorster, the Bill will, apart from disqualifying "named" people from practising as advocates, attorneys, notaries or conveyancers—

Prohibit certain persons from making or receiving contributions for the benefit of certain organisations;

Prohibit certain specified people from participating in the activities of certain organisations;

Extend the provisions in respect of presumption and evidence; and

Extend grounds on which certain people may be removed from South Africa.

PROTEST RENEWED ON VORSTERS'S "RED LAWYER" MEASURE: ADVOCATES SLAM BILL (Rand Daily Mail, *English*) . . .
The Johannesburg Bar Council—the largest and most influential body of advocates in the country—yesterday denounced the Minister of Justice's Bill to control the admission of advocates and lawyers as "an unjustified reflection upon the adequacy of the Supreme Court to discharge its duties."

It also repeated an earlier condemnation that the Bill was "an unwarranted interference with the administration of justice."

When the Bill—an amendment to the Supression of Communism Act—was first introduced last session it was rejected by the Johannesburg, Natal and Cape Town Bars.

It was held over, but has now been reintroduced with the restrictive powers it grants the Minister considerably extended.

It takes away the right of the courts to decide who should be admitted to practise law and can compel the Supreme Court to remove certain practising advocates and lawyers from the Roll. . . .

THE YOUNG AMERICAN couple are quite delightful. He has a great deal of money and she has a great deal of charm. They are thinking very seriously about settling in Johannesburg because the business and investment opportunities are so good, what with low prices, available materials and abundant cheap labor.

But they want everyone to know that they are very liberal.

He will contribute heavily to the Progressives and she will do charitable work with the women and children in the Bantu townships.

They will live in a great big house in Houghton, supported by a small brigade of barely paid Blacks, and they will have a wonderfully soft and comfortable life. And they will make a great deal of money out of South Africa.

He will contribute to the Progs (with maybe an occasional rand sent home for Bobby Kennedy) and she will do charitable work in the Bantu townships.

And two finer little representatives of all that is most notable in certain sections of the United States of America in this rather odd century, you just won't be able to find anywhere in this great big world.

APARTHEID ON BEACHES: DRASTIC BILL (Cape Argus, *English*)
. . . A Bill empowering the Government to override local authorities and to impose apartheid at beaches, dams or "any public premise" was published in Parliament today.

It is entitled the Reservation of Separate Amenities Amendment Bill and has been introduced by the Minister of Planning (Mr. J. F. W. Haak).

The terms of the Bill are sweeping, authorising either the Minister of Bantu Administration and Development, the Minister of Community Development, or the Minister of Planning to order anybody, including local authorities, to implement apartheid at public places.

The Bill authorises one of the Ministers to order any person "to set apart or reserve any public premises or any portion thereof in such manner or by such means, and within the period specified in the direction, for the exclusive use of persons belonging to a particular race or class."

It provides for this ban on race mixing to be imposed "for a specified or unspecified period or for a special occasion."

Premises which have been made subject to restriction may be entered by members of another race only after special permits have been issued.

THERE WAS THE gorgeous home, probably the most lavish in the country; there were the servants in livery, the beautiful china, the gold utensils, the perfectly prepared and perfectly served meal; there were the breezy, attractive, cheerful wife and the small, shy host, very decent, very likable, very ingratiating, very quiet, as though perhaps still in the mental shadow of a dominant father, or possibly as though engaged upon some lifelong apology to the world for being the richest man in Africa.

And there was the dinner guest I had not met too often in the Republic, the overtight, overpositive fellow-American who flailed about him right and left through a sea of martinis, uttering alarming outcries and warnings of what America might do, hammering the table blearily and insisting, "You're not out of the woods yet, you know, you're not out of the woods yet!"

All down the enormous table as we sat in uneasy and inhibited silence while my compatriot continued to utter his wild, free-swinging prophecies of doom and retaliation, I could see the great financiers, the liberal doctors, the forward-seeing men of goodwill who are sufficiently powerful to be able to influence and moderate to some degree the course of Government policy, almost physically draw together and draw back . . . forced once more into the laager from which they would like to emerge, but never will as long as the well-meaning of the outside world attack and threaten and belabor their beloved land.

EMERGENCY BILL AGAIN INTRODUCED (Cape Argus, *English*)
. . . A Bill conferring wide powers on the Minister of Justice in times of emergency—including the calling up for compulsory training of every able-bodied man and woman from 17 to 65 who has not had military training or who does not fall under certain categories of public service— was published in Parliament today.

It is entitled the Emergency Planning Bill. It has now been introduced in Parliament three times.

It first appeared last year, but lapsed when it was not taken through all its stages.

It was again introduced by the Minister of Justice (Mr. B. J. Vorster) during the short session of Parliament earlier this year but again lapsed when the session ended early.

The Bill grants a higher status to the Division of Emergency Planning, which is at present a division of the Department of Justice. It confers upon it the status of a Directorate of Emergency Planning. It remains under the control of the Minister of Justice.

He will decide how people are to be called up for training and will formulate plans for coping with emergencies.

These would include a state of emergency declared in terms of the Public Safety Act, war and "any internal riots or any disaster, whether local or national in character" declared by the Minister by notice in the "Government Gazette" to be a state of emergency.

The Minister will have wide powers in any of these events of foraging and commandeering information, supplies, vehicles, industries and essential services.

T HE LIBERAL EDITOR is quiet, soft-spoken, haunted: skin taut, eyes sad, a deeply worried man obviously under great pressure.

"I've grown up here, I thought I knew the country, but the things the Government has done to intimidate and harass and hamper my staff and me are beyond all I could imagine. It's absolutely terrifying."

But for the most part we talked quietly of the relations between the Republic and my country, of the freedoms we enjoy, however imperfectly, in America, and of how nice it would probably be for me to return to my homeland, much as I had enjoyed my journey.

From time to time, as we did so, the Bantu houseboy would come in to help with the serving; and never, in any home, Afrikaans or English-speaking, in all of South Africa, did I hear such tones of boredom, sharpness, contempt and arrogant impatience with a servant as I heard in the liberal editor's home from the liberal editor's wife.

CAMPUS RACE BILLS CAUSE DISMAY (Cape Times, *English*)
. . . Shock and dismay were expressed in student circles yesterday when the terms of the Government's two bills dealing with university activities were published.

The Extension of University Education Amendment Bill will mean the end of NUSAS as a multi-racial organization. Mr. John Daniel, vice-president of NUSAS, promised yesterday that "the students of this country will fight this legislation as never before."

This bill will:
1. Prevent non-White students at "White" universities from becoming members of any student association, unless it is an academic association occupied exclusively with their course;
2. Make it necessary for non-Whites at "White" universities to form their own "ethnic" associations;
3. Give the Minister powers to expel a non-White student at a "White" university at any time if he considers it "in the public interest."

The second bill, the Universities Amendment Bill, will:
1. Prevent any person or society from being prejudiced "or subjected to any form of discrimination" on the grounds that they advocate racial separation on the campus;
2. The Minister's opinion as to whether there has been discrimination is final;
3. If a university does not comply with this clause, its State grant-in-aid may be partly or totally withheld. . . .

THE YOUNG EDITOR, vigorous, alert, intelligent, vital, has a habit of holding his smile and staring intently at you after he makes a point, waiting to see if you get it. He has taken an American idea for his publication, recast it in South African terms, and is making a mint. He is a bright and very knowledgeable fellow.

"What do we need? Well, for one thing there has to be a growth of English-speaking liberalism based on common sense, on what actually goes on in this country. Larry Gandar [editor of the *Rand Daily Mail*] and all his talk about the rights of man don't mean a damn to the white people in this country. They're too fat and too content. If you want them to move in a more progressive direction you've got to show them it's to their economic interest to back better programs. It's the only way they'll ever listen.

"You might say in a sense that Dr. Verwoerd is backing forward toward his program. In some ways he has led the Government to make enormous strides for the Bantu, but he's done it by timing and psychology and by not getting too far ahead of his popular support. The so-called liberal Nats can't compete. They aren't strong. When Verwoerd decides to retire, Vorster will succeed him. . . .

"The United Party?" He snorted. "The U.P. is a gentleman's club, passing out seats in Parliament as it pleases. If you're well-behaved and have the right family connections and mind your p's and q's, the U.P. will put you in Parliament. The U.P. doesn't want to rock the boat, it wants to preserve the status quo. Actually, it's far more reactionary than the Nats are under Verwoerd's peculiar backward-moving liberalism.

"The U.P. doesn't fight hard enough. It's all too comfy, you know. It's all too comfy. . . .

"The future of South Africa in Africa? I think that's where it is, myself; obviously it's where it's got to be. And I think there are two ways it can go. You haven't detected any signs of imperialism here, have you, any signs of wanting to interfere with anyone else?"

"Not the slightest."

"That's right. That's right. The South African doesn't want to go out and conquer anybody, he just wants to be left alone. But I think this: that it could go either way. In ten or twenty years, if the rest of Africa continues to fall apart, I think there could possibly be an imperialism growing out of a strong South Africa—unless the strength and energy of the country can be diverted to channels of partnership and cooperation.

"I think we could work out some sort of aid program with the rest of Africa—a partnership—something along the lines of Anton Rupert's share-partnership ventures that he's setting up in other African countries. It could be aid, but it wouldn't be foolish or unproductive aid—we wouldn't make the mistake the Americans made.

"You aided everybody and today everybody hates America. You're making the same mistake over again right now in Africa. You ought to be strong with the Africans, give them aid but be firm with them. It's the only way they respect you. If you aren't firm they take it as a sign of weakness and take advantage of you.

"We," he said flatly, "would be firm. They would know where they stood with us, they would know that we would be firm but fair, because that's how this country is. Together we could make this the greatest and most productive continent in history. They couldn't do it alone and neither could we. It would have to be partnership.

"In ten years we can lead this continent, if our race problems can be worked out. . . . We can lead this continent."

"SURE, I'm from the Transvaal!" cried the big, jolly, yellow-haired Afrikaner with the big, jolly, yellow-haired wife, on a bubbling roar of laughter. "A hundred and fifty years, my family, and always on the right side of it, too! Nobody strayed, you might say, nobody strayed! See these blue eyes, hey? See these blue eyes?" Our small, dark, dark-eyed, curly-haired host and hostess, also Afrikaans, also from the Transvaal, looked slightly pained for a second and changed the subject.

IN JOHANNESBURG the stores close at 1 P.M. on Saturday and the city immediately becomes almost deserted. On my last Saturday there I walked to the Post Office around three, noticed a crowd of Whites and Bantu gathered in the street beside one of the big department stores, heard the twang of a guitar and the rhythmic beat of a tin pan. A dozen solemn-faced Bantu men, single file, completely oblivious, were dancing their way along the sidewalk, moving forward in unison, jumping back, leaping, turning, moving forward . . . in the middle of modern Johannesburg, on a quiet, peaceful Saturday afternoon.

F IFTYISH, a round face, glasses, an earnest but humorous manner, quick-spoken, intelligent, fluent—one more charming Afrikaner, the Rev. Beyers Naudé, head of the breakaway Christian Institute whose drive for mixed congregations and a more human tolerance among the races has ranged against him the Dutch Reformed Church, the Security Police, the Government and undoubtedly the majority of his fellow Afrikaners. But he remains tough, charming and undaunted nonetheless.

"The Christian Institute is growing slowly in members," he said, "principally among the non-Whites because it is so difficult for the Whites, particularly the Afrikaans Whites, to do anything that places them against the will of the Government. I will say, however, that we are receiving more inquiries from interested Afrikaners than we've had in a very long time. However, we anticipate that as a result of steps being taken by the various branches of the Dutch Reformed Church, it will be very difficult for them to join.

"My status as a minister of religion, for instance, has been taken away. [He was formerly D.R.C. moderator for the Southern Transvaal.] Other ministers who are members of the Christian Institute have had serious difficulties with their congregations and local boards as a result of their association with the Christian Institute. A large number of younger ministers who are very, very sympathetic to us dare not show any support publicly because of reprisals. Lay members who wish to support us dare not do so because of social, economic and professional reprisals. For these reasons we do not anticipate a large increase in the near future.

"There is, however, not the least doubt that the activities of the Christian Institute cannot be bypassed or ignored, especially by the D.R.C. churches. This is proved by the fact of the recurrent attacks on the Institute in both Afrikaans churches and Afrikaans newspapers and publications.

"Some Afrikaners wish to ignore the Christian Institute's existence in the hope that if they do so it will die a natural death. It may die many kinds of deaths," he said with a grim little smile, "but that kind it will not die.

"The Christian Institute was never intended to be an opposition to the D.R.C., though that's how they view it. It was not our intention, but because of the D.R.C. reactions the Christian Institute has inevitably been built up in the minds of many as an opposing force.

"Will the Christian Institute ultimately have some effect on moderating Government policies? . . . It all depends on whether the Dutch Reformed churches accept the validity of our existence and our Christian witness. If so, then I am convinced it is going to have a strong influence eventually on the political policies of South Africa. Even as it is, the fact

that we are trying to give a clear witness and a voice of Christian conscience is a fact which nobody, least of all the Afrikaner, can ignore.

"In any case, though," he said in a matter-of-fact tone, "it is going to
be a long, hard struggle for us. The Security Police visited us last year,
searched our offices, put us under pressure of threats and warnings, but
up to now this year, at least so far, there have been no difficulties in this
respect. . . .

"Actually," and his tone became thoughtful, "I see no signs whatsoever of any major change in the outlook and attitude on racial matters
among our White population. Events in Nigeria, Ghana, Uganda, the
Sudan—unrest and trouble almost everywhere throughout Black Africa
—seem to have brought the majority of the Whites here to the opinion
that any increased participation by Africans in the political processes of
this country could only lead to chaos.

"By the same token, there are increased pressures from the Afro-
Asians and some Western powers against Rhodesia, Portugal and South
Africa in the United Nations and elsewhere, and as a result the White in
South Africa feels increasingly that he is more embattled and more
threatened. He 'goes into the laager,' as we say.

"All those forces that are trying to create a greater platform for an
open and realistic dialogue between Whites and non-Whites are automatically defeated, and all those organizations and individuals who favor
such a dialogue will find their task increasingly difficult if not altogether
impossible.

"If the pressures from outside could decrease, you will definitely have
a more liberal influence in Afrikanerdom and in the nation. There will be
more political rights to the Coloureds, some relaxing of the more stringent aspects of apartheid, the beginning of an encouraging dialogue between Whites and non-Whites.

"But mind you, if the pressures are not relaxed, then the disappear-
ance of Dr. Verwoerd in the next few years will not basically change the
situation in any way. He will be succeeded by someone equally if not
more harsh, and the laager will be strengthened and maintained. . . .

"Apart from the practical doubts aroused by apartheid in my mind,"
he said soberly, "it is my basic conviction that, with all the sincere intentions we may have in applying apartheid, if its success is to depend on
increasing discrimination and unjust laws being passed against the non-
Whites, then the Afrikaner is just preparing his own downfall and doom.
It is just this which I wish to avoid, with all my heart.

"But the world must give us time, Mr. Drury, *it must give us time!*"

NO RACE GROUPS IN POLITICS OF OTHERS (Cape Argus, *English*) . . . *A Bill to prohibit interference by one population group in the political affairs or institutions of another population group will be introduced this session. . . .*

The proposed Bill will itself constitute a far-reaching interference in normal political activities.

Though the draft legislation is not yet available the Minister of Justice (Mr. B. J. Vorster) has already indicated what the main provisions will be.

Unless the Government has modified its intentions since Mr. Vorster's earlier announcement the measure will, in addition to other more specific proposals, prohibit any campaign by members of one race group to influence members of a body representing another race group to adopt a policy which is in conflict with the purposes of an Act of Parliament, or which is designed to frustrate the objects of any Act of Parliament.

This would appear to mean that, for example, members of the future Coloured People's Representative Council would be committing an offence if they campaigned for Opposition pressures to amend existing legislation. If this were so they would be cut off from effective political action other than pleading with representatives of the Government for "concessions."

Under the draft Bill, as it was described by Mr. Vorster last year, Whites would be excluded from taking any part in the elections of the Coloured People's Representative Council, the Legislative Assembly of the Transkei, a Bantu authority, or the future Indian Council.

"Interference" in these elections would mean financial assistance, drafting propaganda, organising support for candidates, or providing transport for voters (except where employers transport their employees to polling booths).

"THIS PASSION for codification of everything!" said the labor expert at Wits. "It might be amusing if it were not so crushing upon everyone. . . .

"Our trade union movement is being fragmented—or compartmentalized, if you like—along with everything else. There was a time when the South African Trade and Labour Council purported to represent most of the unions in the country. But then came what the Government refers to as 'attempts to introduce politics'—which always means, essentially, that some person or organization has dared to sound a note of protest against the Government's racial policies—and the council was splintered into opposing factions; and then those factions in turn were splintered into further factions; and then inevitably we arrived at the situation we have now, in which the whole thing is based upon the race question and consequently no labour organization, with the possible exception of the Mine Workers' Union, is very strong. And the Mine Workers' Union sometimes seems to spend more time fending off what it regards as threats of competition from Bantu workers than it does in negotiating for its own people with employers. . . .

"But of course it is upon the Bantu that the law falls heaviest, and here the codification complex produced one of its most notable examples, in December of 1965, when the Government issued what it called 'Bantu Labour Regulations.' These regulations were not discussed in Parliament or given any kind of public airing prior to being put into effect, but were simply issued in the *Government Gazette.* Authority given was four priorly passed acts of Parliament. I suppose it was rather like what happens in America when Congress passes a law and an administrative agency issues regulations under it that go far beyond what Congress intended. Of course in our case"—he smiled with some irony —"Parliament would have intended exactly what the Government issued even if it had been given a chance to debate the matter, in all probability.

"At any rate, out they came, the Bantu Labour Regulations, and under them many hundreds of thousands of Bantu workers and their employers must conduct themselves now. The sum effect is to make both seeking work and hiring workers subject to a vast bureaucratic setup that gives neither employee nor employer any area of independent action. A Bantu, for instance, can't look for work until he first registers for a work permit in his magisterial district and secures the approval of his local Bantu Commissioner to go to town to find the work. When he reaches the work area, he can't negotiate directly with the employer; they both have to go through various Government and municipal offices to secure official approval. And when an employer wants a certain kind of labour, he can't go out and recruit it. He also has to go through official red tape and numerous civil servants who may or may not be cooperative. In almost all cases, also, he must take the workers who are sent to him whether they are good workers or not. This leads to all sorts of complications such as you were told about in Cape Town at the Advice Bureau. . . .

"But of course the burden lies heaviest on the worker himself. If, for instance, there is a shortage of farm labour in his home area, he will probably be refused a permit to seek work in town. This in effect gives him a choice between farm work or none. Again, if he is allowed to come into town, he can be sent to a particular type of work and if he doesn't want to take it, his work-permit can be canceled and he can be sent home.

"Further, if he is sent to an employer for whom, for some personal reason, he doesn't want to work, he can be sent back home. He might be given an option if he were lucky enough to be dealing with a compassionate official, but the number of those is not overly great. In effect, he has no choice either of work or of employer.

"You also know what happens when a worker goes back to visit his family and then wants to return to the same employer. It makes no difference whether or not his relations with his employer are friendly— he still must get clearance of his local Bantu Commissioner and the city officials to return to his employer.

"Similarly, if a Bantu has to leave his work area for health reasons, he has no guaranteed right that he can return to that area to work when he has recovered his health, even though he may have a medical certificate. The only way he can be readmitted is as a 'special case,' and special cases are becoming increasingly difficult to arrange.

"The whole thrust of the regulations, in fact, is to narrow the areas of discretion in which a well-disposed and compassionate official—and there are some, as they told you at the Advice Bureau—can make it easier on the worker who finds himself trapped in red tape. The whole aim seems to be depersonalization, with all its consequences of rigidity, inhumanity and possibly inadvertent but nonetheless crushing cruelty. . . ."

UNIONS

Formerly, the South African Trade and Labour Council was the central organization which represented all or nearly all trade unions in South Africa. Attempts to introduce politics into trade unionism, however, resulted in disunity and there is no longer any one organization which can claim to be representative of trade unionism as a whole. To restore peace and to stabilize trade unionism, the Industrial Conciliation Act, as amended in 1956, has prohibited the affiliation of trade unions with political parties or candidates.

	NUMBER OF TRADE UNIONS	MEMBERSHIP
1960	172	429,669
1961	166	440,473
1962	172	442,437
1963	170	448,165
1964	176	489,717

Of the 489,717 members of trade unions in 1964, 353,101 were white and 136,616 were coloured and Asiatic employees.

Before granting the Bantu workers an enhanced status the Government had to make the far-reaching decision whether to build up Bantu labour organizations on the lines of White trade unions, or to evolve some other form of representation.

Bantu labour organizations are not prohibited in South Africa, but they are not recognized by law. Though strenuous efforts have been made by certain Whites as well as by some Bantu to organize Bantu trade unions, they have never been a success. Their number and membership fluctuate continuously.

—Official Sources

TRADE UNION SPLITS "FOR PRACTICAL REASONS" (Sunday Express, *Johannesburg, English*) . . . *One of South Africa's oldest trade unions, the National Union of Distributive Workers, has separated into two units—one for Whites, the other for non-Whites.*

This racial division was made "purely for practical reasons flowing from pressures resulting from Government policy. . . ."

Miss B. Roberts, national president of the N.U.D.W., said it was utter nonsense to say that the setting up of the two bodies was another wedge driven into the Trade Union Council of South Africa, the non-racial trade-union coordinating body. It was purely a domestic decision.

The N.U.D.W. controls the affairs of 14,000 of the country's White shop assistants and is a member of TUCSA. TUCSA represents more than 75 trade unions with more than 200,000 members, and is the largest workers' coordinating body in the Republic. . . .

"Under the proposed Industrial Conciliation Act Amendment Bill, which is to receive the attention of Parliament this session, it is extremely difficult for mixed trade unions to enjoy the facilities of trade-union subscriptions. Racially pure unions would seem to be favoured by this Government measure," Miss Roberts said.

"Because of this, and in the interests of both White and non-White members of the N.U.D.W., the decision was taken. There was no pressure from White members for this move. . . ."

MID-FIFTIES, slim, quiet, keen-eyed, thoughtful—Dr. Tom Muller, brother of the Foreign Minister, Dr. Hilgard Muller; head of the General Mining Corporation, the first but obviously not the last mining combine to be controlled by the Afrikaans.

"About 12½ per cent of our annual national income comes from mining now, which represents a steady decline since 1911, when it was 27½ per cent. But this does not mean any decline in the importance or value of mining to our economy, it simply reflects the enormous growth in recent years of all the secondary industries that have come along as our industrial capacity has expanded.

"Mining is still tremendously important to us. The mines in 1911 were producing a gross income of 93 million rand, and in 1965 they produced a gross income of 1,153,000,000 rand. Gold of course is still our major product, accounting for about two-thirds of our mining income. The price of gold has never been higher than it is right now. We all keep thinking that it will decline, but this is the fourth or fifth time everyone has predicted a decline and still it keeps going higher. New discoveries are being made all the time; our earth is very kind to us. Our other main mineral products include diamonds, copper, asbestos, manganese, iron ore and quarry products, uranium. We have approximately fifty gold mines, very vast reserves of low-grade coal, a great many diamonds. There are signs that we are going to be one of the biggest producers of copper in the world. A lot of our ores are very low-grade, but we have been fortunate in developing new techniques to bring them along to production. Bantu mine labor is also becoming more expensive and harder to get, but at the same time advanced techniques are raising the output per man dramatically. The tonnage per man has about doubled in the past forty-five years.

"At the same time, capital structure and financing are moving away from dependence on foreign capital. Fifty per cent of our dividends used to go abroad—now it's dropped to less than 20 per cent. More than 80 per cent of our mining capital is now local, and this makes for considerably more stability because"—a slight smile—"the Afrikaner and the English-speaker understand the Native, they don't panic and shake the stock market every time there's a small riot reported on a location, the way the foreigners used to do. Further stability is lent by the fact that mining shares are becoming more and more widely spread among the general public. Very few individuals now hold major shares; the Oppenheimers are among the last and they are going steadily more public. . . .

"I would say that one of the most significant developments in recent years has been the advent of the Afrikaner entrepreneur. This company, General Mining, is the first house to come entirely under control of Afrikaner capital; it has control of about 15 per cent of all the mining in the Republic. That is quite a step," he said with a quiet pride, "from zero to 15 per cent in ten years.

"The Afrikaner, who now has about 60 per cent of the population, will probably control in due time about that much of the economy. The Afrikaner, you know, is much like the English-speaker, basically: they spring from basically the same North European stock, they have many of the same characteristics, they're both enterprising, hard-headed—"

"And stubborn."

He smiled.

"And stubborn. Therefore once the economic balance is adjusted, there is no reason why they should not work together in full harmony for South Africa. In effect, they do now and always have, but it will be on a more reasonable and comfortable basis before long, I think.

"There is a tendency, with rising costs of production and labor, for the mining companies to get together and form bigger combines. The small man can't continue alone, he asks the help of the bigger companies, they work out consolidated arrangements. There is also a tendency on the part of the combines to invest increasingly in secondary industries outside the mining field. All of this process is aided by the Government's increasing interest in mining, its policy of subsidizing through tax concessions, venture capital, and so on.

"I think the South African mining industry, with all its wealth and experience, is ideally suited to conditions in Africa and may very well be the key to the Republic's future economic cooperation with other African states. We can work with the other countries that have substantial gold supplies, such as the Congo, Zambia, Tanzania and the rest. Most of our sister states have mineral wealth; we can come to grips with it. We can say to them: Look, get yourselves stable governments, or we won't invest. At the same time, we may be able to work out some modifications of Government policy to suit our potential business partners in the rest of Africa.

"As for our own domestic situation, the world must sooner or later realize and accept the fact that we are giving our time and money to help the black man. When the Bantustans become prosperous, as we must help them to do, then our critics will be forced to realize that our policies can succeed.

"There must be men in these other African states," he said with a certain desperate humor, "who can finally realize that there is no point wasting time and energy fighting South Africa, and will let her come in and help them with their problems.They obviously can't go it alone, and they obviously would be foolish to try to topple us, who are the only really stable element in the entire continent of Africa."

MINE LABOUR PLEA IS WELCOMED (Star, *Johannesburg, English*) . . . *Spokesman for mine groups today welcomed the call by Mr. W. B. Coetzer, chairman of the Federale Mynbou—General Mining Group—for a new formula to solve the mine industry's most serious problem—the shortage of White workers.* . . .

The [previous] *mine labour experiment was abandoned in August, last year, after fifteen months' trial on eleven mines. Mr. Coetzer described it in his annual statement to shareholders as "successful."*

The purpose was to make more efficient use of scarce White labour by allowing trained Africans to do certain work reserved for Whites.

It was wrecked by a dissident group of mineworkers who feared for their jobs and who were able to bring pressure to bear on the Government by the threat of strikes and industrial unrest. . . .

ENGINEER FLOW TO MINES NOW A TRICKLE (Rand Daily Mail, English) . . . *The flow of university-trained engineers to South Africa's troubled mining industry, which is already short of 2,000 men and beset by a multitude of labour problems, has been reduced to a trickle.*

The Government's special Straszacker Commission, which has been studying the problem of engineers for nearly nine years, described the situation as "alarming."

The decline in the number of people studying for degrees in mining and metallurgy should be investigated. It was essential that the causes be eliminated.

"An alarming fact brought to light by this investigation is that the proportion graduating in mining and metallurgical engineering has decreased by half during the past 35 years," says the commission.

The findings have come on top of several other staff difficulties in the industry. The Minister of Mines, Mr. Haak, revealed in Parliament earlier this year that there was a shortage of 2,000 White miners. . . .

GIRLS NEEDED TO LIFT SUPPLY OF ENGINEERS (Rand Daily Mail, English) . . . *Far-sighted moves aimed at beating South Africa's crippling shortage of engineers have been recommended by the Straszacker Commission, which was appointed in 1957.*

In a bid to double the present output of qualified engineers, the commission has suggested that more women be drawn into the profession and that changes be made in the military training programme to aid prospective engineers.

As reported yesterday, the commission has also suggested that Africans, who received basic training in the tribal universities, be allowed to qualify in "open" universities.

South Africa, according to the report, produces the least number of engineers per head of any industrialised nation in the world. It estimates that there are 1,000 jobs waiting to be filled by qualified men.

It has found that the country needs more than double its present out-put of engineering graduates as soon as possible.

BIG DRIVE FOR SKILLED WORKERS (Sunday Express, *Johannes-burg, English*) . . . *The Department of Education, Arts and Science has started on the most ambitious* [white] *manpower training programme ever seen in South Africa.*

The Government hopes that this programme, which envisages among other projects the building of 61 new technical schools or additions to existing schools, will combine with the immigration drive to meet the manpower shortage.

At present there are 97 schools and colleges for vocational education. These accommodate about 31,000 full-time pupils up to Senior Certifi-cate standard, 20,000 apprentices up to the same standard and 3,000 advanced—post matriculation—students.

The new schools and additions to existing ones will mean that an additional 38,000 students and 4,850 apprentices can be accommodated.

3-POINT PLAN FOR MANPOWER SHORTAGE (Rand Daily Mail, *English*) . . . *A three-point solution to meet South Africa's manpower shortage was outlined last night by Dr. P. J. Riekert, Economic Adviser to the Prime Minister and chairman of the Economic Advisory Council.*

In a broadcast, Dr. Riekert said:

The first solution—of a long-term nature—was to increase the birth-rate of the Whites who had traditionally supplied the skilled labour.

The second long-term solution, but embracing all races, was to pro-vide training and retraining.

This meant increasing productivity by the better use of labour, better management, mechanisation and automation.

The third solution was to allow non-Whites more scope to perform skilled work, and in particular, to receive more vocational training.

"It is an integral part of Government policy to foster this develop-ment within the limits set by its policy of separate development, and the stage has now been reached where the non-Europeans, by serving their own communities, can play an important part in easing the pressure on the trained White manpower resources."

Dr. Riekert said "great progress" was being made in the economic development of the non-White labour supply.

While the number of economically active non-Whites increased by

*about 110,000 a year, their actual annual employment was some 186,-
000.*

"*Unemployment and under-employment are thus gradually being reduced as the non-Whites move from the subsistence to the market sector
of the economy, with a resulting increase in their earning power and
hence their standard of living. . . .*"

MINERS REJECT LABOUR EXPERIMENT (Rand Daily Mail, *English*) *. . . In a series of dramatic decisions, an emergency meeting of
the general council of the* [White] *Mine Workers' Union yesterday dashed
all hopes of agreement over a new labour experiment* [using more trained
Bantu] *on the mines. . . .*

[The Council said that] *the proposals by the Gold Producers' Committee of the Chamber of Mines for a new labour rationalisation scheme
should be rejected completely. The council felt that the present proposals
presented a greater danger to the White miner than did the original mines
experiment. . . .*

W E SAT ON THE balcony at Florian's café while rosy-cheeked Afrikaner families, romancing college boys and girls, and aging young
men in too-tight pants, pullover sweaters, dark glasses and tennis shoes
came and went; drank our tea, ate our delightfully fattening pastries, and
talked of subversion and the future. My companion was a tough and
likable young Afrikaans member of the Security Police, and he seemed
much less worried about subversion than he was about the future.

"I think we have the Commies pretty well licked," he said. "I'd say
there aren't more than one hundred Whites still left in the country and a
few—very few—members of the Pan African Congress. Thanks to the
non-Whites who come to us, tell us about them and ask for help and
protection, we have been able to spot and get rid of most of them.

"The Commies, you know, aren't really interested in apartheid at all.
Their own cells here are segregated because they are shrewd enough to
know that this is what works, in this country. They know they can't
really depend on the Bantu for organizational work, he just isn't made
that way. They regard him with contempt, and use him that way, too.

"It's always laughable to us—laughable when it isn't painful and
frightening—to hear the Commies fooling Western liberals with talk
about how concerned they are for the Natives. They want just one thing,
when they try to take South Africa: gold.

"They know that if they can deliver South Africa's gold to Russia,

then Communism can manipulate the world money market, destroy the
world economy and bring down the Western nations almost overnight.
There wouldn't be any way to stop it.

"Gold is what they want here, not any kind of social justice. It's an
absolutely cold-blooded campaign for the biggest stakes in history. . . .

"Most Afrikaners now are very suspicious of the United States," he
said thoughtfully. "They don't regard Britain as any threat—poor old
Britain! We don't believe Britain could fight her way out of a bloody
paper bag. America is the only power that could be a real threat to us.

"But, look, Mr. Drury, if America goes, the whole Western world
goes, we go, everyone goes and there's no one left to fight the Commies.
So we must stand with you, it's foolish to let ourselves turn against America even when your State Department does deliberate things to create
tension between us.

"Some of my Afrikaans friends say to me, 'Germany is our great
friend.' Germany," he said scornfully, "doesn't care bugger-all about us.
France, I will say, is very high with South Africa right now. Lots of
people think France isn't like the U.S., France won't let us down. France
is regarded maybe as our best friend of all, right now. . . .

"I believe our society is going to change. It's got to change, all human
things change. But as a policeman, and also as a father with a couple of
kids, my interest is in seeing it change peacefully and in an orderly way.
Maybe apartheid is not the answer in the long run, maybe it is transi-
tional. But nothing can work out if you have a revolutionary element
wanting to overturn everything.

"I think we owe a lot to the non-Whites," he said seriously. "I think
we should say to them honestly, Yes, we have done bad things to you in
the past, but now we are doing our best to make it up to you, we want
your nationalism, your strength for our country. We want all this as long
as the change is peaceful. But it must be orderly, otherwise everything is
destroyed for everybody and nothing is left.

"I feel, you know, that the Afrikaner is probably doomed if he doesn't
manage to give a better life to the non-Whites, if he doesn't raise them
up and try to work with them for the good of all the country. But you
can't say this," he remarked with a smile, "to Afrikaners of my parents'
generation, they'd kill you. They say they will never capitulate, that they
will never give up complete White domination.

"But this is foolish, Mr. Drury. It can't work in the long run, there will
have to be change, there must be a better future for all or we are
doomed.

"I'm thinking of my children and their future in this country," he said
soberly. "I want South Africa to grow and be strong, but we can't do it
unless improvements come. But they must be peaceful. They must
be. . . ."

9.
Kruger National Park
London
Edinburgh

"I N KRUGER NATIONAL PARK, one can unwind," Dr. Vervoerd had said. "Everybody loves Kruger, there's nothing to do but get up early in the morning, spend all day looking for the animals, and then go to bed early at night."

And that is what I did, for four relaxing days in which only once or twice did the Republic's problems come into the conversation. When they did my host, a most pleasant Afrikaner from the South African Tourist Corporation, made no attempt to propagandize. "I think you've been deluged with arguments enough," he remarked with a smile. The fact did not prevent him from stating the basic views that most Afrikaners have, but it was done briefly, dispassionately and without rancor toward anyone. It was hard to feel rancor, or indeed much of anything except the continuing excitement of seeing the great animals of Africa in their natural habitat, as we drove through the winter-stripped scrub of the

Game Reserve in the sort of primordial innocence that puts man in sometimes needed perspective.

Sleek, plump, busy little impala . . . shaggy, dirty, grumpy-looking wildebeeste . . . skeptical, inquisitive baboons . . . six lionesses floating through the bush like golden ghosts . . . zebras, uncertain and skittish . . . elephant, sometimes alone, sometimes in twos and threes, once, at one beautiful waterhole, fifty or sixty hobnobbing lazily in the sun . . . giraffe, gangling, awkward, lovable—"It seems ridiculous to keep calling a sixteen-foot animal 'cute,' but it's the word that seems to fit" . . . once, in the early dawn, a silky little jackal that ran ahead of the car for several hundred feet before skittering off the road . . . kudu, eland, the exquisite little red daiker, tiniest of deer . . . an eagle, some hawks, a giant stork, strange birds of all descriptions . . . hippos, bubbling blandly up out of the water and then bubbling blandly down again . . . crocodile, lying menacing and still along a sandy bank.

They were all there, mildly concerned about the human traffic but certainly not afraid of it.

The Park is approximately two hundred miles in length north-south, varying between thirty and sixty east-west. It lies in the northeastern corner of the Republic along the Mozambique border where the highveld of the central plateau drops abruptly over the northern Drakensberg massif into the flat, rolling, desertlike lowveld of the Eastern Transvaal. It is operated much like a U.S. national park, with some thirteen rest camps of varying degrees of luxury strung along its length. The three we stayed at, Skukuza, Olifants and Letaba, are equipped with as many as one hundred rondevals, most accommodating two to four people, ranged loosely around a central complex that includes a restaurant, telephones, post office, curio shop and service station. All camps are enclosed with high wire fences; gates are locked at 6 P.M. and not reopened until 6 A.M. Very frequently the animals prowl just outside, and at Olifants, set high on a cliff above the Olifants River, we sat on the porch of our rondeval, looked out across the endless miles of scraggly lowveld and listened to the lions coughing on the riverbank just below as twilight fell. Numerous signs warn that it is illegal to get out of your car while driving in the park and illegal to wander outside the camps during the hours of darkness, but they are really not necessary; self-preservation indicates as much.

On our way back we traveled the blue distances of the lowveld for a time, stayed overnight at the dramatic Sudwala Caverns which my host and his father are developing into a tourist attraction, came finally once again to the escarpment, drove up and onto the highveld, reached at last the main highway to Pretoria. There I spent my last afternoon in the Republic with my host, his delightful wife and their three little rosy-blonde-doll daughters in their charming Cape Dutch house overlooking the city. It was warmer in Pretoria now, we were much closer to spring. A slight haze of coal smoke was beginning to creep along the narrow valley as we started the drive to the airport, but the purple mists of jacaranda would not be far behind.

At the airport we were joined by one of the friends who had met me on arrival on a day which now seemed long ago. We joked and talked and discussed the journey; two earnest young men from *Die Transvaler* approached. As I had done throughout, I refused an interview, but my friend rattled away to them in Afrikaans so for all I knew they may have had a story in spite of me. Unless he took great liberties, though, it could not have contained anything very positive about South Africa, for I was much older in the country, now, and I knew that solutions were not so easily come by. At the beginning I had refused interviews because I did not want to offend prospective hosts by telling them what to do. Now I knew that I really did not know what to tell them to do.

And anyway, other Americans were traveling the country, and they were always popping into the newspapers with admonitions, approval or smug, superior advice.

So I let them do it: they were sure they had all the answers, and I no longer was.

And then almost before we knew it, genuinely affectionate good-byes were being said, the promises and hopes to see one another again, here, there, somewhere, were being exchanged; the handshakes, waves, farewells, were accomplished. And so into the plane, the seat belt fastened, the last look out at Jan Smuts Airport, and then Pretoria and Jo'burg racing into the distance, the highveld speeding away below; the lazy, dirty, gray-green Limpopo River once again, and so over Rhodesia, and so good-bye.

Good-bye, but not quite good-bye; never, probably, good-bye, for in some inescapable sense the Republic claims one, whether one hates it or loves it or, like myself, perhaps feels some baffling compound of both. Not good-bye in the writing of it, not good-bye in the many new friends one is fond of and hopes to see again sometime, not good-bye in a continuing interest and worry and concern; not good-bye, in all probability, forever.

TWO WEEKS LATER in London, the last of those endless, tortured, round-and-round discussions of what should be done, what shouldn't be done, what the right is, what the wrong, what-will-happen-where-will-it-all-end-good-God: this one with a group of exiled white South African Communists, in a drab little hotel, at tea-time on the after-

noon of September 5, 1966. . . . My theory that in five or six years,
after Dr. Verwoerd retired, there might be a transition period, some
chance for the liberal Nats to assume control; their bitter skepticism, possibly justified, possibly not, that no such thing would ever be possible.
. . . The inconclusive note on which such things always end, seeking
to put the social patch over fundamental differences—"Maybe you're
right," I to them; *"We* hope *you're* right," they to me. And nothing really
settled or decided or made any clearer, just one more confused discussion
of South Africa, swirling around the tenuous hope that maybe, somehow,
if things could just stay as they were for a little while and then change
peaceably, some advances and improvements, some modest hope for a
gallant, unhappy nation might ultimately come.

A ND SO on to Edinburgh, and next evening, coming down from the
Castle after *Tattoo,* the newsvendor shouting on the corner, the
enormous picture of the rosy-cheeked, blue-eyed, grandfatherly-twin-
kling face I had last seen across a desk in Cape Town a month ago, the
word ASSASSINATION leaping with a savage impact in the blowing,
gusty night.

And presently, through Helen's kindness, in the regular order of arrival of the copies of *Hansard, Record of Debates,* which she had arranged to have sent on to me for the duration of the session, the entries
for September 6 and 7, 1966:

TUESDAY, 6th SEPTEMBER, 1966

Prayers——2:40 P.M.
MOTION FOR ADJOURNMENT
The MINISTER OF TRANSPORT: Mr. Speaker, I have not yet heard
officially from the hospital whether the Prime Minister is still alive; I do
not think he is. At this stage I therefore wish to move as an unopposed
motion—

That the House do now adjourn.
Agreed to.
The House adjourned at 2:43 P.M.

WEDNESDAY, 7th SEPTEMBER, 1966

Prayers——2:20 P.M.
VACANCY

MR. SPEAKER: I deeply regret to have to announce that a vacancy has occurred in the representation in this House of the electoral division of Heidelberg owing to the death yesterday of Dr. The Honourable H. F. Verwoerd . . .

"I would dearly have loved to remind you," he said in a speech in London the night after he took South Africa out of the Commonwealth, "of the beauty of the South African scenery—its mountains, its blue sky, its white beaches and the surrounding sea, the open veld, the dry and healthy Karoo, the luxuriant lowveld, the vineyards and orchards of the north and south, the green maize lands, the great cultivated areas of yellow sunflower, the waving gold of the wheatlands, the tobacco plantations, the irrigation settlements—green borders stretching from horizon to horizon, beside miles of slowly flowing river, green even in the driest years. I would wish to guide you to the wild flowers of Namaqualand, the protea and the silver tree of the Cape and visit with you old homesteads, great national parks filled with wild animals from the smallest antelope to the lion, the rhinoceros, the giraffe and the elephant . . ."

Almiskie . . .

And so the journey finally ended, as much as it ever can.

III
JOURNEY'S END

READER:

It will not take long to summarize the lessons of the journey, for, aside from those interviews necessarily made confidential by fear of Government reprisal, you have been with me and have heard and seen it all.

If it has made you as confused and uncertain as the visitor about a most complex and difficult situation, then the effort has been well-spent: because with uncertainty may come humility, with humility understanding, with understanding compassion, and with compassion that patience indispensable if the Republic's problems are ever to be worked out in a way that will satisfy both her peoples and the conscience of her sincere and decent critics.

Not the little yappers and snappers in influential places around the globe who snarl and bite at the heels of serious matters. Those genuinely decent and responsible critics who would really like to see a constructive solution that would preserve the Republic as the great stabilizing force she is and at the same time permit her to work in harmony with her fellow-African states for the betterment of the entire continent.

With time and patience and compassion, this can be done. If it is, Africa will enter upon a fabulous era. If it is not, the continent will very likely be dragged down to destruction in the course of a bitter vendetta that may destroy South Africa but will also destroy her Black sister states. Because they should make no mistake about it: Pelindaba and an ever-growing military force do not exist for nothing. If they try to drive her from the world stage, she will take them with her.

It would seem advisable, therefore, for men of goodwill to seek some other answer.

What should it be, assuming South Africa to be as important to mankind as both her friends and enemies believe?

Certainly if one has any genuine interest in seeing matters solved in a constructive and peaceable way, the answer is not to clamor with an insensate rage for the scalps of South Africa's Whites.

That is the way of children, Black Africans, some (not all) State Department officials and some (not all) American politicians convinced that the way to bring home the bacon is through other people's back yards.

It is not the way of mature and responsible individuals who would like to see a sad situation solved in a fashion that will benefit all of Africa, not set all of Africa aflame.

Several basic truisms emerge from the journey. Some are in the Republic's favor, some are not.

Those that support the Republic's point of view are these:

1. The major Black ethnic groups, lumped together under the general term "Bantu," are as distinct from one another as Germany and France. They are largely illiterate, largely uncaring, mutually mistrustful, mutually antagonistic. They are not the great, single black mass yearning to be free that sentimentalists and self-servers in other lands try to portray them.

2. They are, as a race, distinctly different from the Whites, not only in traditions, practices, laws, but in the way they think, feel and react. When the traveler hears from liberals, conservatives, Afrikaners, English-speakers and American missionaries alike how different they are, how unpredictable, how baffling, how difficult to unify and work with, one must give credence to such comments. Sentimentalists and self-servers, again, to the contrary.

3. They are at this stage, and perhaps for generations to come, totally incapable of managing or leading the vigorous, booming, industrialized Western society that now exists from the Limpopo to the Cape. It may not be their fault, but it is the fact.

4. Nor are they native to Southern Africa, with some mystical claim

forever upon a land they came to late, and then only to slaughter, plunder and lay waste. The only native South Africans on the ground in 1652 were a scattered handful of Bushmen and Hottentots long since absorbed in the general population. South Africa was the White man's country before it was the Bantu's country.

5. When the Bantu eventually came down from the north, they had the same chance initially at the open veld. They destroyed it because they never learned the most elemental principles of grazing, farming or land management. Why did they not learn them? Why have they not learned them, anywhere in Africa? Why are conservation, good husbandry and the simplest principles of prudent living unknown to them? Who knows? But the fact is that they are not.

6. The Whites, given the same opportunity, applied themselves with skill, determination, intelligence and discipline and in time erected a major Western civilization that is today one of the world's most viable and sophisticated states; far and away the most viable and sophisticated from the Cape to Cairo and possibly beyond.

7. Confronted with the twin facts of White enterprise and Black sloth, and having created such a society from scratch, the Whites cannot understand why they must be expected to abdicate and give it up. They will not do so.

8. Confronted also by the fact that the Indians, Coloured and Bantu all hate and fear one another, they feel they must act as barriers between, and controllers of, the other races or see a dreadful and apocalyptic outbreak of racial war of all kinds, not only Black against White but all races against all races.

9. After a long period of uncertainty over what to do about the ever-expanding Black nations, which are the most numerous and therefore potentially the most explosive, the White nation of South Africa determined to spend many millions of rand giving them housing, education and medical care—imposing in return the condition that they stay in their own areas, in which, the theory runs, they are to be free to develop to their utmost capacities, whatever these capacities may be.

10. This plan has been in operation only a very few years, as nations go. It has many unhappy features. It is not perfect. It may never work. But at least it is an attempt, and for the most part—as hear these witnesses—an honest attempt, to solve a perhaps insoluble problem.

11. The Whites have made and are making great financial sacrifices to put this plan into operation. The majority are sincere about it and are doing their best to make it succeed.

12. The White nation, however, is not as unified in its approach to all phases of this program as some of its foreign critics, either truly ignorant or deliberately ingenuous, like to maintain. The great majority of English-speakers and Afrikaners are solidly behind it, but there are many sincere

and troubled people in both sections who do not agree with many aspects of separate development. They are saying so and trying to bring about modifications.

13. The efforts of these people are defeated every time, partly by what my friends in King William's Town call "the almost desperate logic" of the Government, but even more by the pressures of the outside world. Every time they show signs of making a little progress, someone in Washington or the UN decides it is time to jump on South Africa again, and back they all go into the laager, defeated once more by foreigners who profess to be their friends.

14. These outside pressures are about one-third sincere and two-thirds self-serving. Foreign politicians seek to ride to power on the back of South Africa's troubles. Foreign states, particularly the Black states of Africa, want South Africa's fantastic wealth and resources. "Greed, plain and simple, underlies the campaign against South Africa."

15. Nor is greed the only motive. The political leaders of Black Africa are also jealous. They don't like the contrast between their own chaotic incompetence and South Africa's trim efficiency. They don't like to be shown up. Since they are unable at this stage of their development to emulate or compete, many of them, like spiteful children, wish to destroy.

16. There has been, and to some extent still is, a definite internal Communist attempt to overturn the Government. Racial equality and human justice are the farthest things from the minds of these ruthless and cynical international operators who don't give two hoots in hell for the Poor Downtrodden Black Masses. Surrounded, as they are in all countries, by a group of idealistic innocents who provide the frosting for foreign consumption, the hard core aims at one thing: South Africa's gold and mineral wealth, with which they could bring down the world's currencies, throw the Western world into instant and complete economic collapse, and enrich themselves and their New Imperialism beyond imagining. "Greed, plain and simple, underlies the campaign against South Africa." And there is no infantile jealousy to complicate the issue for this crew: it is a strictly cold-blooded business.

17. A threatened Government has struck back and struck back hard, and much of the bitter outcry against South Africa springs from exactly this: the Government isn't equivocal or weak, it doesn't fool around, it is as tough and ruthless as they are. They have met their match and they just can't take it. So they go running to the UN and to the very West they wish to destroy to seek help in tackling an adversary who is too much for them.

18. The West, gullible and many-minded as always, is flirting with the disastrous idea of complying.

19. Therefore the Republic is convinced it can justify every move it makes to strengthen, toughen, beat down and suppress.

20. And the liberal elements within the Republic, who could gradu-

ally moderate things if left alone and given time—and the Government itself, which could gradually moderate things if left alone and given time —are forced together into a solid, immovable mass, facing outward with guns at the ready.

These are the truisms that support the Republic's point of view.

There are fewer truisms that support the Republic's honestly concerned, constructive critics, who are the only ones who have any place in a responsible discussion—those who do not serve the purposes of Communist imperialism, who are honestly disturbed and genuinely desirous of seeing better conditions in South Africa.

But though these truisms may be fewer, they lie with an equal if not greater weight in the scales in which South Africa must be judged. For they go to the fundamentals of human decency and human justice in nations which call themselves Christian; and they lay South Africa, justifiably, open to concerned and responsible criticism; and upon sympathetic and compassionate friends who would like to be able to defend her wholeheartedly, they impose inhibitions that are not easily overlooked nor lightly borne.

1. No amount of fear can justify, to the truly civilized Christian mind, the 180-day law, or the lack of jury trial, or what is far too often a one-sided, one-colored administration of justice, or laws infringing personal liberties which are so broad that the Government can incarcerate any citizen of any race at any time on any pretext, without genuine protections or genuine appeal.

2. Nothing can justify the "petty apartheid" of separate facilities, inferior categories imposed by law, harsh and deliberate slaps and snubs at helpless human beings, or the deliberately cruel and heartless withholding of adequate arrangements at such places as the new Cape Town railroad station, for instance. (Which may be corrected in time, and what difference does that make? It shouldn't have been done in the first place.)

3. Nothing can justify the heartless application of the Group Areas Act, the cruel uprooting of members of other races from areas that have been theirs for decades or even hundreds of years, the completely ruthless ignoring of human emotions, human decencies, human kindness. It may be possible to argue in many instances that they are better off in townships, but it can be done with patience and tolerance, and with compensating arrangements and rewards that would make it tolerable and give them a genuinely better life. It can also be done, and perhaps better, with new housing developments in the same place. Above all, it can be done by giving responsible Bantu the right of freehold, the indispensable foundation of homes, a settled existence, and stability. It does not need to be done like a cold-blooded machine. The individual Afrikaner is not a cruel person. What evil genius forces him to be so cruel as a government?

4. Nothing can justify the routine harshness displayed in the enforce-

ment of the pass laws. It may be possible here, also, to argue that in urban areas some control of influx and egress is needed, because there is a limit to the number that can be housed, supported and taken care of in a given metropolitan area; but here, also, the petty, deliberate annoyances and harassments create a terrible resentment. It is not yet, and perhaps never will be, a revolutionary resentment, but it is a resentment that makes impossible any truly solid foundation for the nation. Not even the Nats can live forever on a foundation of hatred, mistrust, resentment and fear. It will take its toll in one way or another, if not in the terrible way South Africa's enemies desire, then in something deeper, more subtle, more devastating, withering and destroying the very soul and fiber of the country.

5. Nothing can justify the deliberate dismantling of all bridges between the races, all common ground upon which the decent of all colors might meet and work out their joint destiny, such as the universities, the legal and medical professions, business and artistic associations, the churches. It is all very well to defend this with theories of separate development, but it is rapidly destroying the last few remaining areas where understanding might be created. The Government cries "unity!" and destroys it with the deliberate compartmentalization of the races. True, there is a unity of fear imposed upon the threatened, and in it Bantu, Indians and Coloureds join the Whites, for none wants their country overrun by outsiders. But it is a false unity and it means nothing in terms of the true blending-together of the nation. The Nats can't have it both ways: they can't cry for unity out of one side of their mouths and give the orders that destroy it out of the other.

6. Nor can the Nats achieve true unity on a basis of Afrikanerdom supreme and devil take everybody else. The English tried it for a while and it didn't work, and it won't work for the Afrikaners, either. They did have a tough time, they did have a struggle, they did make a remarkable comeback, they are indisputably on top—but somehow they have got to get over their feelings of vindictive triumph about it and stop being as arrogant and brutal as they can be in their worst moments. In their best moments there are no nicer or more charming or more remarkable or worthwhile people. But they have got to relax. Nobody can make them do it, it will have to come from within. It might pay the Broederbond to issue a directive, because it is time for them to begin to show a little maturity about it now. That, too, is one of the few genuine ways to create national unity. They can't get it with the basic attitude too many of them still cling to.

7. By the same token, they gain nothing by not permitting a freer flow of visitors to come and see for themselves what South Africa is like. It is true that some would come to cause trouble, as some have; but it is also true that there is a far greater group of influential people whose

minds are not yet closed on South Africa, who could contribute greatly to an ultimate solution of tensions if they were allowed to know of their own experience and witnessing what is going on there. At present the picture they get is largely one-sided, the creation of South Africa's enemies who haven't the slightest intention of being honest or fair. Some direct personal involvement of those who are still reasonably objective, some direct personal knowledge that No, it is not simple—No, it isn't a thing for easy slogans—Yes, there is a middle ground that can and must be found—would help enormously in creating a more constructive world climate in which a just conclusion might be reached. In this instance, Afrikaner and English-speaker alike huddle away too much. Let the world come and see. Keeping it out only inflames suspicion and exaggerates myth.

8. If the Bantustans are to be the final flower of separate development, then the Government had best get on with it. The Zulus are already convinced that the Government is too afraid of them to create a Bantustan for them, and the lively suspicion is abroad in the land that the Transkei and possibly one or two more may be the only such experiments. The Transkei may be a quite genuine experiment or a quite spurious one, but whatever it is, it is the standard the Government itself has set up to be judged by. Therefore it is too late to back down now without a loss of confidence in the Government's word that could only result in a great and perhaps fatal weakening at home and abroad.

9. If the Bantustans are not going to be tried sincerely, then the Government had best have the honest guts to abandon the pretense and move in the direction of some form of the Progressives' controlled franchise or the United Party's multiracial society, because the problem is not standing still. Ironically, all the assistance to the Bantu in the form of housing, medicine and welfare is making them healthier and healthier. Consequently they are breeding faster and faster and living longer and longer. And while "an amazing amount of goodwill," to quote one of the banned in Durban, still does exist among the Bantu toward the Whites, it may not last forever if the Bantu feel the White government is not being fair and honest with them. And then Bantustans and all could become quite academic, in some holocaust that not even Pelindaba and the Defence Forces could put down.

10. Finally, John Vorster may mock the term "police state," but the fact remains that a pervasive uneasiness and fear underlie South African life in all sectors of the community, even triumphant Afrikanerdom. The uneasiness and fear are a direct result of the rigidly harsh policies of the Government. Not all those policies can be excused by blaming somebody or something else, the English, the past, the Bantu, the UN, the Communists, or what have you. Many of them are attributable to sheer, direct, personal stupidity, intolerance and lack of imagination on the part of

those who make the laws and those who enforce them. It is time for them
to face up to the fact that if you want a nation to live, you cannot destroy
its decencies and wither its hopes forever. You have got to grow up and
be worthy of your trust. You have got to be brave enough to be human.
You have got to stop creating more fear because you yourself are afraid.
You have got to acquire the self-confidence to relax and be decent.

So much for the case for and against the Republic.

There is one other factor: that collection of genuine idealists, self-
serving adventurers, covetous Communists, responsible men of goodwill
and irresponsible fools of evil or unthinking intention, whom South Africans lump together under the term "the outside world."

If South Africa has obligations to the outside world, so, too, does the
outside world have obligations to South Africa.

If the outside world is to make South Africa an issue, keep her inces-
santly on the front pages, and hound and harry her around the clock,
then the outside world had better be honest about its own imperfections
and decent enough to be patient with those of others.

It is time for the outside world to grow up, too; and not the least of
those out there who need maturing are the United States of America and
the Black African states she is attempting to appease by aiding their
vendetta against the Republic.

This is no fun-and-games, look-at-me-Johnny-I-really-let-'em-have-it-
today piece of business: this is a serious matter, involving the fate of a
major nation and an entire continent. It is too important to be left to
children, in the State Department or elsewhere, who think it is fun to
attack people who, whatever one thinks of their prickly, awkward, difficult ways, are at least sincerely trying to solve as best they can the terrible difficulty history has handed them.

The way to help them is not with a child's smart-aleck vindictiveness
transferred to the arena of world diplomacy. It is to be patient and tolerant, offer them genuine understanding and friendship and then, having
secured their reliance and trust, seek to persuade them respectfully and
honorably toward the better course.

Nor is the way to help them, and guarantee the safe future of the
continent, to be found in appeasing Black African states who are one
inch from savagery and as guilty of apartheid of tribes, ruthless suppression of dissent, and harsh application of racially based laws as South
Africa ever was, and who don't even have the saving graces of intelligence, industry and common, ordinary, good sense and stability to excuse
them.

Where in that hagridden continent exists the nation—"nation?"—who
comes with clean hands to judge the Republic? Nowhere. Ghana, Nigeria, Guinea, Liberia, Ethiopia, Malawi, Kenya, Egypt—you name it, if
you can. It is not on any map that truthful people know.

"Give us time," they said, from Hendrik Verwoerd to Helen Suzman and back again, and time is what they need. Not completely forgiving time, for there is much that is impossible to forgive. Not completely approving time, for there is much that cannot be approved. But patient, understanding, helpful, encouraging, persuading, thoughtful, enlightened, responsible time, in which to make the changes that must be made if the Republic is to survive and Africa is to have the natural leader that she must have to emerge from the half-formed darkness that has succeeded the hasty abandonment of Western responsibilities.

The White South African, English-speaker and Afrikaner, is no fool. He knows he has a fearful, terrifying problem. He knows he must solve it somehow or be destroyed by it. He is as anxious as any of his responsible critics to find a solution for it. He welcomes their suggestions and advice *if they are sincere and constructive and as fair to him and his right to his hard-won society as they are to the sentimental myths of a pseudo and phony liberalism.*

But if they come with continued hostility and anger and the crude spitefulness of little boys, he will turn away and go back to the laager and the only way to get him out will be to blast him out. And he will die first, and he will take as much of Africa as he can manage with him. And he will feel justified in doing so. And so, perhaps, he will be.

This is no flimsy "nation," no inconsequential state. This is an important country that agitates the world. It has accomplished great things and has far greater in it. Something irreparable will be lost if South Africa is lost. And lost she will be, in one way or another, unless the responsible elements of the West understand her and give her genuine help, not the captious, self-serving hostility of greedy and inconsequential men.

There is in this land great good—

Almiskie.

And there is in this land great evil—

Almiskie.

And which will win out, no man from the Cape to the Limpopo, or anywhere else, can say with certitude. Time and tolerance, patience and compassion, understanding and encouragement to do the humanly decent thing—these and these alone can supply the answer, if answer there be.

O NLY ONE *thing is certain.*
    In the gently rolling Transvaal the Monument stands on the hill, the Old Man stands in the square. He faces north. His back is turned against the hated outlanders from the Cape.

He can turn around, now.

His charming heirs have captured their beloved country, and only the schemes of the greedy, the conscience of the decent, and the slow, inexorable judgments of time stand against them.

Appendix

Banning Orders

ORDER #1

TO: IAN ALEXANDER ROBERTSON,
132A, HATFIELD STREET,
CAPE TOWN.

NOTICE IN TERMS OF PARAGRAPH (a) OF SUB-SECTION
(1) OF SECTION *TEN* OF THE SUPPRESSION OF COM-
MUNISM ACT, 1950 (ACT NO. 44 of 1950).

WHEREAS, I, BALTHAZAR JOHANNES VORSTER, [then] Minister of Justice,
am satisfied that you engage in activities which are furthering or may further the achievement of the objects of communism, I hereby, in terms of
paragraph (a) of sub-section (1) of section *ten* of the Suppression of Communism Act, 1950 (Act No. 44 of 1950), prohibit you for a period commencing on the date on which this notice is delivered or tendered to you and
expiring on the 31st day of May, 1971, from—
   (1) absenting yourself from the area comprising the magisterial dis-
       tricts of Wynberg and the Cape;
   (2) being within—
       (a) any Bantu area, that is to say—
           (i) any location, Bantu hostel or Bantu village defined and
               set apart under the Bantu (Urban Areas) Consolida-
               tion Act, 1945 (Act No. 25 of 1945);
           (ii) any area approved for the residence of Bantu in terms
               of section 9(2h) of the Bantu (Urban Areas) Con-
               solidation Act, 1945 (Act No. 25 of 1945);
           (iii) any Scheduled Bantu Area as defined in the Bantu
               Land Act, 1913 (Act No. 27 of 1913);
           (iv) any Bantu Township established under the Regulations
               for the Administration and Control of Townships in
               Bantu Areas, promulgated in Proclamation No. R. 293
               of the 16th November, 1962;
           (v) any land of which the South African Bantu Trust, re-
               ferred to in section 4 of the Bantu Trust and Land
               Act, 1936 (Act No. 18 of 1936), is the registered
               owner of any land held in trust for a Bantu Tribal
               Community in terms of the said Bantu Trust and Land
               Act, 1936;
       (b) any Bantu Compound;
       (c) the premises of any factory as defined in the Factories, Ma-
           chinery and Building Work Act, 1941 (Act No. 22 of
           1941);
       (d) any place which constitutes the premises on which any pub-
           lication as defined in the Suppression of Communism Act,
           1950, is prepared, compiled, printed or published;
       (e) any place which constitutes the premises of any organiza-

tion contemplated in Government Notice No. R. 2130 of the 28th December, 1962, as amended by Government Notice No. R. 1947 of the 27th November, 1964, and any place which constitutes premises on which the premises of any such organization are situate;

(f) any place or area which constitutes the premises on which any public or private university, university college, college, school or other educational institution is situate, except the premises of the University of Cape Town for the sole purpose of attending *bona fide* lectures for the LL.B. degree:

(g) any area set apart under any law for the occupation of Coloured or Asiatic persons;

(h) any place or area which constitutes the premises of any superior or inferior court as defined in the Criminal Procedure Act, 1955 (Act No. 56 of 1955), except for the purpose of—

   (i) applying to a magistrate for an exception to any prohibition in force against you under the Suppression of Communism Act, 1950;

   (ii) attending any criminal proceedings in which you are required to appear as an accused or a witness;

   (iii) attending any civil proceedings in which you are a plaintiff, petitioner, applicant, defendant, respondent or other party or in which you are required to appear as a witness;

(i) any harbour as defined in section *one* of the Railways and Harbours Control and Management (Consolidation) Act, 1957 (Act No. 70 of 1957);

(j) any place which constitutes the premises of the National Union of South African Students or the World University Service;

(3) communicating in any manner whatsoever with any person whose name appears on any list in the custody of the officer referred to in section *eight* of the Suppression of Communism Act, 1950, or in respect of whom any prohibition under the Suppression of Communism Act, 1950, or the Riotous Assemblies Act, 1956 (Act No. 17 of 1956), is in force:

(4) performing any of the following acts, that is to say—

(a) preparing, compiling, printing, publishing, disseminating or transmitting in any manner whatsoever any publication as defined in the Suppression of Communism Act, 1950;

(b) participating or assisting in any manner whatsoever in the preparation, compilation, printing, publication, dissemination or transmission of any publication as so defined;

(c) contributing, preparing, compiling or transmitting in any manner whatsoever any matter for publication in any publication as so defined;

(d) assisting in any manner whatsoever in the preparation, compilation or transmission of any matter for publication in any publication as so defined;

(e) (i) preparing, compiling, printing, publishing, disseminating or transmitting in any manner whatsoever any document (which shall include any book, pamphlet, record, list, placard, poster, drawing, photograph or picture which is not a publication within the meaning of paragraph (4)(a) above); or

(ii) participating or assisting in any manner whatsoever in the preparation, compilation, printing, publication, dissemination or transmission of any such document, in which, *inter alia*—

(aa) any form of State or any principle or policy of the Government of a State is propagated, defended, attacked, criticised, discussed or referred to;

(bb) any matter is contained concerning any body, organization, group or association of persons, institution, society or movement which has been declared an unlawful organization by or under the Suppression of Communism Act, 1950, or the Unlawful Organizations Act, 1960;

(cc) any matter is contained concerning any organization contemplated in Government Notice No. R. 2130 of the 28th December, 1962, as amended by Government Notice No. R. 1947 of the 27th of November, 1964; or

(dd) any matter is contained which is likely to engender feelings of hostility between the White and the non-White inhabitants of the Republic of South Africa;

(f) giving any educational instruction in any manner or form to any person other than a person of whom you are a parent;

(g) taking part in any manner whatsoever in the activities or affairs of any organization contemplated in Government Notice No. R. 2130 of the 28th December, 1962, as amended by Government Notice No. R. 1947 of the 27th November, 1964;

(h) taking part in any manner whatsoever in the activities or affairs of the National Union of South African Students or the World University Service.

Given under my hand at Pretoria on this 3rd day of May, 1966.

/s/ **B. J. VORSTER**
MINISTER OF JUSTICE.

NOTE:

The Magistrate, Cape Town, has in terms of section 10 (1a) of Act No. 44 of 1950 been empowered to authorise exceptions to the prohibitions contained in this notice.

ORDER #2

TO: IAN ALEXANDER ROBERTSON,
132A, HATFIELD STREET,
CAPE TOWN.

NOTICE IN TERMS OF SUB-SECTION (1) OF SECTION *NINE*
OF THE SUPPRESSION OF COMMUNISM ACT, 1950 (ACT
NO. 44 of 1950).

WHEREAS, I, BALTHAZAR JOHANNES VORSTER, [then] Minister of Justice,
am satisfied that you engage in activities which are furthering or are calculated to further the achievement of any of the objects of communism, I
hereby, in terms of sub-section (1) of section *nine* of the Suppression of
Communism Act, 1950 (Act No. 44 of 1950), prohibit you for a period
commencing on the date on which this notice is delivered or tendered to you
and expiring on the 31st day of May, 1971, from attending within the Republic of South Africa or the territory of South-West Africa—
(1) any gathering contemplated in paragraph (a) of said sub-section;
or
(2) any gathering contemplated in paragraph (b) of the said sub-
section, of the nature, class or kind set out below:
(a) Any social gathering, that is to say, any gathering at which
the persons present also have social intercourse with one
another;
(b) any political gathering, that is to say any gathering at which
any form of State or any principle or policy of the Government of a State is propagated, defended, attacked, criticised
or discussed;
(c) any gathering of pupils or students assembled for the purpose of being instructed, trained or addressed by you.
Provided that this notice shall not debar you from attending *bona fide* gatherings of students of the University of Cape Town, assembled for the sole
purpose of attending lectures for the LL.B. degree.
Given under my hand at Pretoria on this 3rd day of May, 1966.
/s/ **B. J. VORSTER**
MINISTER OF JUSTICE.
NOTE:
The Magistrate, Cape Town, has in terms of section 9 (1) of the above-
mentioned Act been empowered to authorise exceptions to the prohibitions
contained in this notice.

ORDER #3

TO: IAN ALEXANDER ROBERTSON,
132A, HATFIELD STREET,
CAPE TOWN.

NOTICE IN TERMS OF SUB-SECTION (1) OF SECTION *TEN QUAT* OF THE SUPPRESSION OF COMMUNISM ACT, 1950 (ACT NO. 44 of 1950).

WHEREAS there is in force against you a prohibition under sub-section (1) of section *nine* of the Suppression of Communism Act, 1950 (Act No. 44 of 1950), by way of a notice addressed and delivered or tendered to you, I, BALTHAZAR JOHANNES VORSTER, Minister of Justice, hereby, in terms of sub-section (1) of section *ten quat* of the said Act, order you for a period commencing on the date on which this notice is delivered or tendered to you and expiring on the 31st day of May, 1971, to report to the officer in charge of the Caledon Square Police Station, Cape Town, on every Monday between the hours of seven in the forenoon and six in the afternoon.

Given under my hand at Pretoria on this 3rd day of May, 1966.

/s/ **B. J. VORSTER**
MINISTER OF JUSTICE.

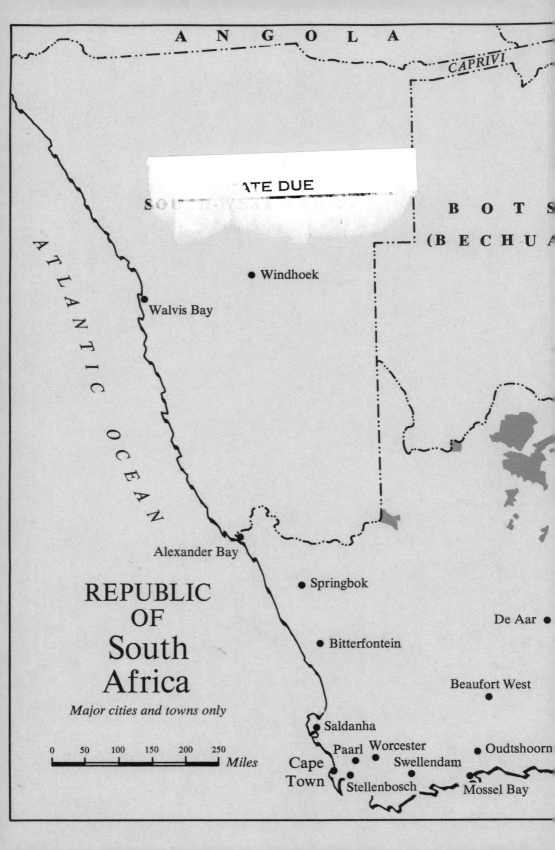